D0116239

Core Reference

Microsoft

MICROSOFT®
ADO.NET

Microsoft®
.net™

David Sceppa

PUBLISHED BY
Microsoft Press
A Division of Microsoft Corporation
One Microsoft Way
Redmond, Washington 98052-6399

Copyright © 2002 by Microsoft Corporation

All rights reserved. No part of the contents of this book may be reproduced or transmitted in any form or by any means without the written permission of the publisher.

Library of Congress Cataloging-in-Publication Data
Sceppa, David, 1972-
   Microsoft ADO.NET : core reference / David Sceppa.
      p. cm.
   ISBN 0-7356-1423-7
   1. Database design.   2. Object oriented programming (Computer science)   3. ActiveX.   I. Title.

TK5105.8885.A26 S24   2002
005.74--dc21   2001059195

Printed and bound in the United States of America.

1 2 3 4 5 6 7 8 9   QWT   7 6 5 4 3 2

Distributed in Canada by Penguin Books Canada Limited.

A CIP catalogue record for this book is available from the British Library.

Microsoft Press books are available through booksellers and distributors worldwide. For further information about international editions, contact your local Microsoft Corporation office or contact Microsoft Press International directly at fax (425) 936-7329. Visit our Web site at www.microsoft.com/mspress. Send comments to *mspinput@microsoft.com*.

IntelliSense, Microsoft, Microsoft Press, MSDN, Visual Basic, Visual C#, Visual InterDev, Visual Studio, Windows, and Windows NT are either registered trademarks or trademarks of Microsoft Corporation in the United States and/or other countries. Other product and company names mentioned herein may be the trademarks of their respective owners.

The example companies, organizations, products, domain names, e-mail addresses, logos, people, places, and events depicted herein are fictitious. No association with any real company, organization, product, domain name, e-mail address, logo, person, place, or event is intended or should be inferred.

Acquisitions Editor: Anne Hamilton
Project Editor: Lynn Finnel
Technical Editor: Dail Magee Jr.

Body Part No. X08-22452

Contents at a Glance

Table of Contents

Part IV   Building Effective Applications with ADO.NET

13   **Building Effective Windows-Based Applications**   **561**

Acknowledgments

First and foremost, I'd like to thank my mother and father for their constant support and patience, through this project as well as through my life in general.

I'd like to thank Jackie Richards for her encouragement, feedback, and inquisitiveness regarding ADO.NET's feature set.

Thanks to Sam Carpenter for dragging me out for a beer, a few laughs, and some well-needed perspective throughout this process.

I'd like to thank Steve DuMosch for putting up with my occasional rants and for convincing me to get some use out of my indoor soccer shoes again.

Thanks to Steve Ellis for helping me to complete this project the right way.

Thanks to Dr. Jonathan and Stephanie Braman for that trip to the Met earlier this year and for giving my Xbox a good home for the past few months.

I'd like to thank and congratulate the Microsoft WebData and Visual Studio .NET teams for developing the most powerful set of data access technologies that we've released to date.

Finally, thanks to everyone at Microsoft Press who has played a role in getting this book onto the shelves.

Introduction

Microsoft ADO.NET represents a major step forward for Microsoft data access technologies. It gives developers an unprecedented level of control over how their code interacts with their data—a welcome advance for developers who have been frustrated by the lack of control offered by previous "black box" technologies such as the ADO cursor engine, the Microsoft Visual Studio 6 Data Environment, and the MSDataShape OLE DB Provider.

ADO.NET is not only the most powerful and robust data access technology that Microsoft has produced to date, but it also requires arguably the steepest learning curve. I've watched a number of experienced Visual Studio 6 developers struggle with the ADO.NET object model in usability studies, trying to figure out where to get started. Developers who grasp the basic object model still wind up asking questions about some of the nuances in ADO.NET's feature set, such as "How do I control the table names that the *DataAdapter* uses to map the results of my batch query to my *DataSet*?" or "Why do I get duplicate rows in a *DataSet* that I build by hand if I fill it twice, when the same code doesn't create duplicate rows if I use a *DataSet* generated by Visual Studio .NET?"

Who Is This Book For?

I wrote this book as a thorough guide to ADO.NET for all developers, even those who have no experience with the technology. I do not assume that you know a *DataReader* from a *DataSet*. I've organized the book so that you can either read the chapters sequentially to learn the technology from scratch or, if you're more seasoned, you can find the information you need quickly and easily.

What's in the Book?

Each chapter that focuses on an object or a set of objects opens with a discussion of the object or objects followed by descriptions of how to use the major features of that object. Most chapters also show how you can save development time by building the object using Visual Studio .NET. The chapter includes reference information for the objects covered, followed by a section titled "Questions That Should Be Asked More Frequently," which addresses questions that are generally all too often overlooked. Some information in the reference section might repeat information from earlier in the chapter. I felt that this repetition was necessary in order to prevent the reader from having to jump back and forth within each chapter.

The book is divided into four parts. Part I provides an overview of the ADO.NET object model, followed by a guide to the Data Form Wizard. Part II shows how to use the various objects available in a .NET data provider—the *Connection, Command, DataReader,* and *DataAdapter* objects. Part III includes a discussion of the "disconnected" objects in the ADO.NET object model—the *DataSet, DataTable, DataColumn, DataRow, DataRelation,* and *DataView* objects. This part also covers basic and advanced scenarios that use the *Data-Adapter* to submit changes to your database, and it includes a discussion of ADO.NET's XML features. Part IV covers techniques for building effective Windows-based and Web applications using ADO.NET.

Code Samples, Tools, and Other Fun Stuff

Most of the code snippets in the book use the OLE DB .NET Data Provider. I chose to focus on this data provider because it's the more "generic" of the two .NET Data Providers included in the Microsoft .NET Framework. The code snippets are designed to communicate with the Microsoft Desktop Engine (MSDE) and Microsoft SQL Server, but they can be changed to communicate with any database that has an OLE DB provider. Appendix A includes code snippets that use the SQL Client, ODBC, and Oracle Client .NET Data Providers.

The book closes with Appendix B, which covers the three tools included on the book's companion CD: a Windows forms navigation control, an ad hoc query tool, and a tool that builds code for *DataAdapter* updating logic. Each tool is designed to work with any .NET data provider, not just the SQL Client and OLE DB .NET Data Providers, and the source code for each tool is also included on the companion CD. I've included the source code for developers who want to modify the tools' functionality, but please do not redistribute the tools or code in any way, shape, or form. The tools are not supported and are not intended for distribution.

Each of these tools represents a work in progress. I plan to add functionality to each tool as well as to fix bugs and make the tools available at *http://www.ininety.com* for everyone who has purchased a copy of the book.

The companion CD includes the book's sample code, the three tools described above, and a fully searchable eBook. The book's sample code can also be found on the Web at *http://www.microsoft.com/mspress/books/5354.asp.* To load the companion content page, which includes links for downloading the sample files, click on the "Companion Content" link in the menu to the right of the screen.

I hope you find this information helpful.

System Requirements

You'll need the following software to run the companion content:

■ Microsoft .NET Framework SDK (can be downloaded from *http://msdn.microsoft.com/net*)

■ Microsoft Visual Studio .NET (optional, but recommended)

■ Microsoft Internet Explorer 5.01 or later

Support

Every effort has been made to ensure the accuracy of this book and the contents of the companion CD. Microsoft Press provides corrections for books through the World Wide Web at the following address:

http://www.microsoft.com/mspress/support

To connect directly to the Microsoft Press Knowledge Base and enter a query regarding a question or an issue that you may have, go to:

http://www.microsoft.com/mspress/support/search.asp

If you have comments, questions, or ideas regarding this book or the companion content, please send them to Microsoft Press using either of the following methods:

Postal Mail:
Microsoft Press
Attn: *Microsoft ADO.NET (Core Reference)* Editor
One Microsoft Way
Redmond, WA 98052-6399
E-mail:
MSPINPUT@MICROSOFT.COM

Please note that product support is not offered through the above mail address. For support information regarding ADO.NET, Visual Basic .NET, Visual C# .NET, Visual Studio .NET, or the .NET Framework, please visit the Microsoft Support Web site at

http://support.microsoft.com

Part I

Getting Started with Microsoft ADO.NET

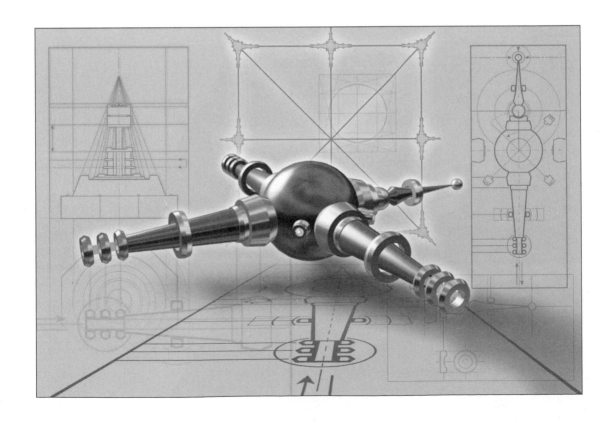

1

Overview of ADO.NET

ADO.NET is a set of libraries included with the Microsoft .NET Framework that help you communicate with various data stores from .NET applications. The ADO.NET libraries include classes for connecting to a data source, submitting queries, and processing results. You can also use ADO.NET as a robust, hierarchical, disconnected data cache to work with data off line. The central disconnected object, the *DataSet*, allows you to sort, search, filter, store pending changes, and navigate through hierarchical data. The *DataSet* also includes a number of features that bridge the gap between traditional data access and XML development. Developers can now work with XML data through traditional data access interfaces and vice-versa.

In short, if you're building an application that accesses data, you should be using ADO.NET.

Microsoft Visual Studio .NET includes a number of data access features you can use to build data access applications. Many of these features can save you time during the development process by generating large amounts of tedious code for you. Other features improve the performance of the applications you build by storing metadata and updating logic in your code rather than fetching this information at run time. Believe it or not, many of Visual Studio .NET's data access features accomplish both tasks.

As we examine ADO.NET throughout this book, we'll also look at features in Visual Studio .NET that you can use to save time and effort.

Why a New Object Model?

Developers who have experience with Microsoft's previous data access technology, ActiveX Data Objects (ADO), might ask, "Isn't that what ADO is for? Why has Microsoft built a new data access technology?"

It seems as if each successive version of Visual Basic has introduced users to a new data access model. Visual Basic 3 included Data Access Objects (DAO). Visual Basic 4 introduced developers to Remote Data Objects (RDO). Visual Basic 5 and Visual Studio 97 included ODBCDirect. The previous suite of developer tools, Visual Basic 6 and Visual Studio 6, featured ADO.

Some developers see this constant change as a thinly veiled attempt to sell technical books. Actually, Microsoft has introduced new data access technologies in an ongoing attempt to address developers' data access needs.

DAO was initially designed to communicate with local file-based databases. Soon Visual Basic developers wanted to talk to server-based databases such as Microsoft SQL Server and Oracle. DAO allows developers to communicate with such databases, but developers craved more control and better performance. So the Visual Basic development team created RDO to give developers a fast, lightweight data access layer designed to talk to larger server-based databases. Some developers wanted the power of RDO but did not want to give up the ease of use that DAO provides. Microsoft created ODBCDirect to give them the best of both worlds. Then came the Internet, and developers craved a data access model they could use more easily in server-side scripts, that would require fewer lines of code, and that would allow them to pass data structures from server to client and back. Thus ADO was born.

ADO has served many developers well for the past few years, but it lacks key features that developers need to build more powerful applications. For example, more and more developers want to work with XML data. While recent versions of ADO have added XML features, ADO was not *built* to work with XML data. For example, ADO does not allow you to separate the schema information from the actual data. Microsoft might add more XML features to future releases of ADO, but ADO will never handle XML data as efficiently as ADO.NET does because ADO.NET was designed with XML in mind and ADO was not. The ADO cursor engine makes it possible to pass disconnected ADO *Recordset* objects between different tiers in your application, but you cannot combine the contents of multiple *Recordset* objects. ADO allows you to submit cached changes to databases, but it does not give you control over the logic used to submit updates. Also, the ADO cursor engine does not, for example, provide a way to submit pending changes to your database via stored procedures. Because many database administrators allow users to modify the contents of the database only through stored procedures, many developers cannot submit updates through the ADO *Recordset* object.

Microsoft built ADO.NET to address these key scenarios, along with others that I'll cover throughout this book.

Like its predecessors, ADO was built for COM-based application development. With the advent of the common language runtime and the .NET Framework, Microsoft has completely overhauled Visual Studio. We now have

Microsoft Windows and Web-based forms packages designed to run in the common language runtime. Similarly, Microsoft has designed a new data access object model for the .NET Framework, ADO.NET.

ADO.NET is designed to combine the best features of its predecessors while adding features requested most frequently by developers—greater XML support, easier disconnected data access, more control over updates, and greater update flexibility.

The ADO.NET Object Model

Now that you understand the purpose of ADO.NET and where it fits into the overall Visual Studio .NET architecture, it's time to take a closer look at the technology. In this chapter, we'll take a brief look at the ADO.NET object model and see how it differs from past Microsoft data access technologies.

ADO.NET is designed to help developers build efficient multi-tiered database applications across intranets and the Internet, and the ADO.NET object model provides the means. Figure 1-1 shows the classes that comprise the ADO.NET object model. A dotted line separates the object model into two halves. The objects to the left of the line are "connected" objects. These objects communicate directly with your database to manage the connection and transactions as well as to retrieve data from and submit changes to your database. The objects to the right of the line are "disconnected" objects that allow a user to work with data offline.

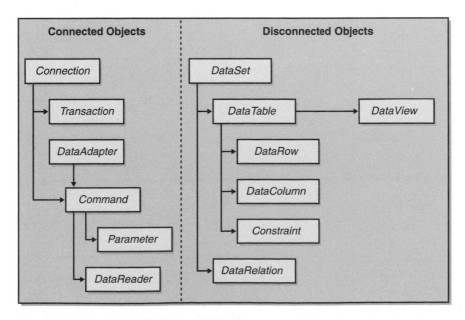

Figure 1-1   The ADO.NET object hierarchy

The objects that comprise the disconnected half of the ADO.NET object model do not communicate directly with the connected objects. This is a major change from previous Microsoft data access object models. In ADO, the *Recordset* object stores the results of your queries. You can call its *Open* method to fetch the results of a query and call its *Update* (or *UpdateBatch*) method to submit changes stored within the *Recordset* to your database.

The ADO.NET *DataSet*, which we'll discuss shortly, is comparable in functionality to the ADO *Recordset*. However, the *DataSet* does not communicate with your database. In order to fetch data from your database into a *DataSet*, you pass the *DataSet* into the *Fill* method of a connected ADO.NET object—the *DataAdapter*. Similarly, to submit the pending changes stored in your *DataSet* to your database, you pass the *DataSet* to the *DataAdapter* object's *Update* method.

.NET Data Providers

A .NET data provider is a collection of classes designed to allow you to communicate with a particular type of data store. The .NET Framework includes two such providers, the SQL Client .NET Data Provider and the OLE DB .NET Data Provider. The OLE DB .NET Data Provider lets you communicate with various data stores through OLE DB providers. The SQL Client .NET Data Provider is designed solely to communicate with SQL Server databases, version 7 and later.

Each .NET data provider implements the same base classes—*Connection*, *Command*, *DataReader*, *Parameter*, and *Transaction*—although their actual names depend on the provider. For example, the SQL Client .NET Data Provider has a *SqlConnection* object, and the OLE DB .NET Data Provider includes an *OleDbConnection* object. Regardless of which .NET data provider you use, the provider's *Connection* object implements the same basic features through the same base interfaces. To open a connection to your data store, you create an instance of the provider's connection object, set the object's *ConnectionString* property, and then call its *Open* method.

Each .NET data provider has its own namespace. The two providers included in the .NET Framework are subsets of the *System.Data* namespace, where the disconnected objects reside. The OLE DB .NET Data Provider resides in the *System.Data.OleDb* namespace, and the SQL Client .NET Data Provider resides in *System.Data.SqlClient*.

Namespaces

A namespace is a logical grouping of objects. The .NET Framework is large, so to make developing applications with the .NET Framework a little easier, Microsoft has divided the objects into different namespaces. Figure 1-2 shows a portion of the hierarchy of namespaces in the .NET Framework.

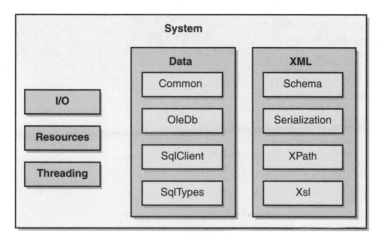

Figure 1-2   Namespaces in the .NET Framework

The most important reason for using namespaces is to prevent name collisions in assemblies. With different namespaces, programmers working on different components combined into a single solution can use the same names for different items. Since these names are separated, they don't interfere with each other at compile time. A more practical reason for namespaces is that grouping objects can make them easier to locate. Sometimes I forget the exact name of the object I'm looking for. If the objects in the .NET Framework were not broken out into smaller namespaces, I would have to find the desired object in an alphabetical list of all of the objects in the framework. Thankfully, I can usually remember the namespace of the desired object. Finding the object within its namespace is simpler because there are fewer objects to examine.

For more information on using namespaces in the Microsoft .NET Framework or Visual Studio .NET, see the documentation in MSDN.

Because each .NET data provider implements the same basic features, the code you write will look fairly similar regardless of the provider you use. As you can see in the following code snippets, all you need to do to switch from using the OLE DB .NET Data Provider to the SQL Client .NET Data Provider is to change the class you instantiate and the contents of the connection string to conform to the provider's standards.

Visual Basic .NET

```
'Open and close a connection using the SQL Client .NET Data Provider.
Dim cnOleDb As New OleDbConnection
cnOleDb.ConnectionString = "Provider=SQLOLEDB;
                           "Data Source=(local);InitialCatalog=Northwind;..."
cnOleDb.Open()
...
cnOleDb.Close()


'Open and close a connection using the SQL Client .NET Data Provider.
Dim cnSql As New SqlConnection
cnSql.ConnectionString = "Data Source=(local);" & _
                         "Initial Catalog=Northwind;..."
cnSql.Open()
...
cnSql.Close()
```

Visual C#

```
//Open and close a connection using the OLE DB .NET Data Provider.
OleDbConnection cnOleDb = new OleDbConnection();
cnOleDb.ConnectionString = "Provider=Provider=SQLOLEDB;
                           "Data Source=(local);InitialCatalog=Northwind;...";
cnOleDb.Open();
...
cnOleDb.Close();


//Open and close a connection using the SQL Client .NET Data Provider.
SqlConnection cnSql = new SqlConnection();
cnSql.ConnectionString = "Data Source=(local);" +
                         "Initial Catalog=Northwind;...";
cnSql.Open();
...
cnSql.Close();
```

Why Use Separate Classes and Libraries?

No previous Microsoft data access technology has used separate libraries and classes for different data stores. Many developers have asked why Microsoft has made such a major change. There are three main reasons: performance, extensibility, and proliferation.

Better Performance

How does moving to .NET data providers improve performance? When you write ADO code, you're essentially using the ADO interfaces as a "middleman" when communicating with your data store. You tell ADO which provider you want to use, and ADO forwards your calls to the appropriate provider. The provider performs the requested action and returns the result to you through the ADO library.

.NET data providers don't involve a middle layer. You communicate directly with the data provider, which communicates with your data store using the data store's low-level programming interfaces. Communicating with SQL Server using the SQL Client .NET Data Provider in ADO.NET is faster than using ADO and the SQL Server OLE DB provider because one less layer is involved.

Greater Extensibility

When SQL Server 2000 introduced XML features, the ADO development team faced an interesting challenge. In order to add features to ADO that would let developers retrieve XML data from SQL Server 2000, they had to add new interfaces to the OLE DB API and to the SQL Server OLE DB provider.

.NET data providers are more easily extensible. They need to support only the same basic interfaces and can provide additional provider-specific features when appropriate. The SQL Client .NET Data Provider's *Command* object (*SqlCommand*) exposes all of the same methods and properties that its OLE DB .NET Data Provider counterpart does, but it also adds a method to fetch the results of a query as XML.

Proliferation

Microsoft first shipped OLE DB providers for SQL Server, Microsoft Access, and Oracle with the release of the Microsoft Data Access Components (MDAC) version 2.0 in July 1998. Microsoft and other development teams have created native OLE DB providers to communicate with other data stores, but not a whole lot of OLE DB providers are available. If you're using ADO but aren't using a Microsoft-built OLE DB provider, there's a high probability that you're using an ODBC (OLE DB's predecessor) driver instead. Many more ODBC drivers are available, primarily because they were easier to develop. Many developers simply found it too difficult to build their own OLE DB providers.

By comparison, a .NET data provider is simple to write. There are far fewer interfaces to implement. Microsoft simplified the process of building providers for ADO.NET so that developers can build .NET data providers more easily. The more .NET data providers there are, the more different data sources you can access via ADO.NET.

Coverage of .NET Data Providers in This Book

Because each .NET data provider implements the same base interfaces, there's no need for me to cover using these interfaces for every .NET data provider. Instead, I'll mostly focus on one provider: the OLE DB .NET Data Provider. I've chosen to focus on this provider because it's included with the .NET Framework, provides basic provider-independent features, and is extremely flexible because it can be used against any database that has a native OLE DB provider. The features of the OLE DB .NET Data Provider covered here are also available through other providers and work the same way unless otherwise noted.

Appendix B will cover the features of the other .NET data providers. Chapter 12 will use the SQL Client Data Provider and the SQL XML .NET Data Provider to demonstrate the use of some of ADO.NET's XML features.

Until then, if I'm discussing an object that's common to all managed providers, I'll generally refer to it by its provider-independent name—for example, *DataAdapter* rather than *OleDbDataAdapter* or *SqlDataAdapter*.

Connected Objects

The ADO.NET object model includes classes designed to help you communicate directly with your data source. I'll refer to such objects, which appear to the left of the dotted line in Figure 1-1 (shown earlier), as ADO.NET's "connected" objects. Most of these objects represent basic data access concepts such as the physical connection to the database, a query, and the query's results.

Connection Object

A *Connection* object represents a connection to your data source. You can specify the type of data source, its location, and other attributes through the various properties of the *Connection* object. A *Connection* object is roughly equivalent to an ADO *Connection* object or a DAO *Database* object; you use it to connect to and disconnect from your database. A *Connection* object acts as a conduit through which other objects, such as *DataAdapter* and *Command* objects, communicate with your database to submit queries and retrieve results.

Command Object

Command objects are similar in structure to ADO *Command* or DAO *QueryDef* objects. They can represent a query against your database, a call to a stored procedure, or a direct request to return the contents of a specific table.

Databases support many different types of queries. Some queries retrieve rows of data by referencing one or more tables or views or by calling a stored procedure. Other queries modify rows of data, and still others manipulate the structure of the database by creating or modifying objects such as tables, views, or stored procedures. You can use a *Command* object to execute any of these types of queries against your database.

Using a *Command* object to query your database is rather straightforward. You set the *Connection* property to a *Connection* object that connects to your database and then specify the text for your query in the *CommandText* property. You can supply a standard SQL query such as this one:

```
SELECT CustomerID, CompanyName, ContactName, Phone FROM Customers
```

You can also supply just the name of a table, view, or stored procedure and use the *Command* object's *CommandType* property for the type of query you want to execute. The *Command* object offers different ways to execute your query. If the query does not return rows, simply call the *ExecuteNonQuery* method. The *Command* object also has an *ExecuteReader* method, which returns a *DataReader* object that you can use to examine the rows returned by your query. The *SqlCommand* includes a third execution method, *ExecuteXmlReader*, that is similar to *ExecuteReader* but is designed to handle queries that return results in XML format.

DataReader Object

The *DataReader* is designed to help you retrieve and examine the rows returned by your query as quickly as possible. You can use the *DataReader* object to examine the results of a query one row at a time. When you move forward to the next row, the contents of the previous row are discarded. The *DataReader* doesn't support updating. The data returned by the *DataReader* is read-only. Because the *DataReader* object supports such a minimal set of features, it's extremely fast and lightweight.

Transaction Object

At times, you might want to group a number of changes to your database and treat them as a single unit of work. In database programming, that unit of work is called a *transaction*. Let's say your database contains banking information and has tables for checking and savings accounts and a user wants to transfer money from a savings account to a checking account. In your code, you'll want to make sure that the withdrawal from savings and the deposit to checking complete successfully as a single unit or that neither change occurs. You use a transaction to accomplish this.

The *Connection* object has a *BeginTransaction* method that you can use to create *Transaction* objects. You use a *Transaction* object to either commit or cancel the changes you make to your database during the lifetime of the *Transaction* object. In our banking example, the changes to both the savings and checking accounts would be included in a single transaction and, therefore, would be either committed or cancelled as a single unit of work.

Parameter Object

Say you want to query your Orders table for all the orders for a particular customer. Your query will look something like this:

```
SELECT CustomerID, CompanyName, CompanyName, Phone FROM Customers
    WHERE CustomerID = 'ALFKI'
```

The value you use for the CustomerID column in the query's *WHERE* clause depends on the customer whose orders you want to examine. But if you use this type of query, you have to modify the text for the query each time you want to examine the orders for a different customer.

To simplify the process of executing such queries, you can replace the value for the CustomerID column with a parameter marker, as shown in the following query:

```
SELECT CustomerID, CompanyName, CompanyName, Phone FROM Customers
    WHERE CustomerID = ?
```

Then, prior to executing the query, you supply a value for the parameter. Many developers rely heavily on parameterized queries because they can help simplify your programming and make for more efficient code.

To use a parameterized *Command* object, you create *Parameter* objects for each of the parameters in your query and append them to the *Command* object's *Parameters* collection. The ADO.NET *Parameter* object exposes properties and methods that let you define the data type and value for your parameters. To work with a stored procedure that returns data through output parameters, you set the *Parameter* object's *Direction* property to the appropriate value from the *ParameterDirection* enumeration.

DataAdapter Object

The *DataAdapter* object represents a new concept for Microsoft data access models; it has no true equivalent in ADO or DAO, although you can consider the ADO *Command* and DAO *QueryDef* objects to be its second cousins, once removed.

DataAdapter objects act as a bridge between your database and the disconnected objects in the ADO.NET object model. The *DataAdapter* object's *Fill* method provides an efficient mechanism to fetch the results of a query into a *DataSet* or a *DataTable* so you can work with your data off line. You can also use *DataAdapter* objects to submit the pending changes stored in your *DataSet* objects to your database.

The ADO.NET *DataAdapter* object exposes a number of properties that are actually *Command* objects. For instance, the *SelectCommand* property contains a *Command* object that represents the query you'll use to populate your *DataSet* object. The *DataAdapter* object also has *UpdateCommand*, *InsertCommand*, and *DeleteCommand* properties that correspond to *Command* objects you use when you submit modified, new, or deleted rows to your database, respectively.

These *Command* objects provide updating functionality that was automatic (or "automagic," depending on your perspective) in the ADO and DAO *Recordset* objects. For example, when you run a query in ADO to generate a *Recordset* object, the ADO cursor engine asks the databases for metadata about the query to determine where the results came from. ADO then uses that metadata to build the updating logic to translate changes in your *Recordset* object into changes in your database.

So why does the ADO.NET *DataAdapter* object have separate *UpdateCommand*, *InsertCommand*, and *DeleteCommand* properties? To allow you to define your own updating logic. The updating functionality in ADO and DAO is fairly limited in the sense that both object models translate changes in *Recordset* objects into action queries that directly reference tables in your database. To maintain the security and integrity of the data, many database administrators restrict access to the tables in their databases so that the only way to change the contents of a table is to call a stored procedure. ADO and DAO don't know how to submit changes using a stored procedure, neither provides mechanisms that let you specify your own updating logic. The ADO.NET *DataAdapter* does.

With a *DataAdapter* object, you can set the *UpdateCommand*, *InsertCommand*, and *DeleteCommand* properties to call the stored procedures that will modify, add, or delete rows in the appropriate table in your database. Then you can simply call the *Update* method on the *DataAdapter* object and ADO.NET will use the *Command* objects you've created to submit the cached changes in your *DataSet* to your database.

As I stated earlier, the *DataAdapter* object populates tables in the *DataSet* object and also reads cached changes and submits them to your database. To keep track of what goes where, a *DataAdapter* has some supporting properties. The *TableMappings* collection is a property used to track which table in your database corresponds to which table in your *DataSet* object. Each table mapping has a similar property for mapping columns, appropriately called a *ColumnMappings* collection.

Disconnected Objects

You've seen that you can use objects in a .NET data provider to connect to a data source, submit queries, and examine their results. However, these connected classes let you examine data only as a forward-only, read-only stream of data. What if you want to sort, search, filter, or modify the results of your queries?

The ADO.NET object model includes classes to provide such functionality. These classes act as an offline data cache. Once you've fetched the results of your query into a *DataTable* (which we'll discuss shortly), you can close the connection to your data source and continue to work with the data. As mentioned earlier, because these objects do not require a live connection to your data source we call them "disconnected" objects.

Let's take a look at the disconnected objects in the ADO.NET object model.

DataTable Object

The ADO.NET *DataTable* object is similar to the ADO and DAO *Recordset* objects. A *DataTable* object allows you to examine data through collections of rows and columns. You can store the results of a query in a *DataTable* through the *DataAdapter* object's *Fill* method, as shown in the following code snippet:

Visual Basic .NET

```
Dim strSQL As String = "SELECT CustomerID, CompanyName FROM Customers"
Dim strConn As String = "Provider=SQLOLEDB;Data Source=(local);..."
Dim daCustomers As New OleDbDataAdapter(strSQL, strConn)
Dim tblCustomers As New DataTable()
daCustomers.Fill(tblCustomers)
```

Visual C#

```
string strSQL = "SELECT CustomerID, CompanyName FROM Customers";
string strConn = "Provider=SQLOLEDB;Data Source=(local);..."
OleDbDataAdapter daCustomers = new OleDbDataAdapter(strSQL, strConn);
DataTable tblCustomers = new DataTable();
daCustomers.Fill(tblCustomers);
```

Once you've fetched the data from your database and stored it in a *Data-Table* object, that data is disconnected from the server. You can then examine the contents of the *DataTable* object without creating any network traffic between ADO.NET and your database. By working with the data off line, you no longer require a live connection to your database, but remember that you also won't see any changes made by other users after you've run your query.

The *DataTable* class contains collections of other disconnected objects, which I'll cover shortly. You access the contents of a *DataTable* through its *Rows* property, which returns a collection of *DataRow* objects. If you want to examine the structure of a *DataTable*, you use its *Columns* property to retrieve a collection of *DataColumn* objects. The *DataTable* class also lets you define constraints, such as a primary key, on the data stored within the class. You can access these constraints through the *DataTable* object's *Constraints* property.

DataColumn Object

Each *DataTable* has a *Columns* collection, which is a container for *DataColumn* objects. As its name implies, a *DataColumn* object corresponds to a column in your table. However, a *DataColumn* object doesn't actually contain the data stored in your *DataTable*. Instead, it stores information about the structure of the column. This type of information, data about data, is called *metadata*. For example, *DataColumn* exposes a *Type* property that describes the data type (such as string or integer) that the column stores. *DataColumn* has other properties such as *ReadOnly*, *AllowDBNull*, *Unique*, *Default*, and *AutoIncrement* that allow you to control whether the data in the column can be updated, restrict what can be stored in the column, or dictate how values should be generated for new rows of data.

The *DataColumn* class also exposes an *Expression* property, which you can use to define how the data in the column is calculated. A common practice is to base a column in a query on an expression rather than on the contents of a column in a table in your database. For example, in the sample Northwind database that accompanies most Microsoft database-related products, each row in the Order Details table contains UnitPrice and Quantity columns. Traditionally, if you wanted to examine the total cost for the order item in your data structure, you would add a calculated column to the query. The following SQL example defines a calculated column called *ItemTotal*:

```
SELECT OrderID, ProductID, Quantity, UnitPrice,
     Quantity * UnitPrice AS ItemTotal
  FROM [Order Details]
```

The drawback to this technique is that the database engine performs the calculation only at the time of the query. If you modify the contents of the UnitPrice or Quantity columns in your *DataTable* object, the ItemTotal column doesn't change.

The ADO.NET *DataColumn* class defines an *Expression* property to handle this scenario more elegantly. When you check the value of a *DataColumn* object based on an expression, ADO.NET evaluates the expression and returns a newly calculated value. In this way, if you update the value of any column in the expression, the value stored in the calculated column is accurate. Here are two code snippets illustrating the use of the *Expression* property:

Visual Basic .NET

```
Dim col As New DataColumn()
...
With col
   .ColumnName = "ItemTotal"
   .DataType = GetType(Decimal)
   .Expression = "UnitPrice * Quantity"
End With
```

Visual C#

```
DataColumn col = new DataColumn();
col.ColumnName = "ItemTotal";
col.DataType = typeof(Decimal);
col.Expression = "UnitPrice * Quantity";
```

The *Columns* collection and *DataColumn* objects can be roughly compared to the *Fields* collection and *Field* objects in ADO and DAO.

Constraint Object

The *DataTable* class also provides a way for you to place constraints on the data stored locally within a *DataTable* object. For example, you can build a *Constraint* object that ensures that the values in a column, or multiple columns, are unique within the *DataTable*. *Constraint* objects are maintained in a *DataTable* object's *Constraints* collection.

DataRow Object

To access the actual values stored in a *DataTable* object, you use the object's *Rows* collection, which contains a series of *DataRow* objects. To examine the data stored in a specific column of a particular row, you use the *Item* property of the appropriate *DataRow* object to read the value for any column in that row. The *DataRow* class provides several overloaded definitions of its *Item* property. You can specify which column to view by passing the column name, index value, or associated *DataColumn* object to a *DataRow* object's *Item* property. Because *Item* is the default property of the *DataRow* object, you can use it implicitly, as shown in the following code snippets:

Visual Basic .NET

```
Dim row As DataRow
row = MyTable.Rows(0)
Console.WriteLine(row(0))
Console.WriteLine(row("CustomerID"))
Console.WriteLine(row(MyTable.Columns("CustomerID")))
```

Visual C#

```
DataRow row;
row = MyTable.Rows[0];
Console.WriteLine(row[0]);
Console.WriteLine(row["CustomerID"]);
Console.WriteLine(row[MyTable.Columns["CustomerID"]]);
```

Rather than returning the data for just the current row, the *DataTable* makes all rows of data available through a collection of *DataRow*s. This is a marked change in behavior from the ADO and DAO *Recordset* objects, which expose only a single row of data at a time, requiring you to navigate through its contents using methods such as *MoveNext*. The following code snippet is an example of looping through the contents of an ADO *Recordset*:

Visual Basic "Classic"

```
Dim strConn As String, strSQL As String
Dim rs As ADODB.Recordset
strConn = "Provider=SQLOLEDB;Data Source=(local);..."
strSQL = "SELECT CustomerID, CompanyName FROM Customers"
Set rs = New ADODB.Recordset
rs.CursorLocation = adUseClient
rs.Open strSQL, strConn, adOpenStatic, adLockReadOnly, adCmdText
Do While Not rs.EOF
    MsgBox rs("CustomerID")
    rs.MoveNext
Loop
```

To examine the contents of an ADO.NET *DataTable*, you loop through the *DataRow* objects contained in the *DataTable* object's *Rows* property, as shown in the following code snippet:

Visual Basic .NET

```
Dim strSQL, strConn As String
...
Dim da As New OleDbDataAdapter(strSQL, strConn)
Dim tbl As New DataTable()
da.Fill(tbl)
Dim row As DataRow
For Each row In tbl.Rows
    Console.WriteLine(row(0))
Next row
```

Visual C#

```
string strSQL, strConn;
...
OleDbDataAdapter da = new OleDbDataAdapter(strSQL, strConn);
DataTable tbl = new DataTable();
da.Fill(tbl);
foreach (DataRow row in tbl.Rows)
    Console.WriteLine(row[0]);
```

The *DataRow* object is also the starting point for your updates. For example, you can call the *BeginEdit* method of a *DataRow* object, change the value of some columns in that row through the *Item* property, and then call the *EndEdit* method to save the changes to that row. A *DataRow* object's *CancelEdit* method lets you cancel the changes made in the current editing session. A *DataRow* object also exposes methods to delete or remove an item from the *DataTable* object's collection of *DataRow*s.

When you change the contents of a row, the *DataRow* object caches those changes so that you can submit them to your database at a later time. Thus, when you change the value of a column in a row, the *DataRow* object maintains that column's original value as well as its current value in order to successfully update the database. The *Item* property of a *DataRow* object also allows you to examine the original value of a column when the row has a pending change.

DataSet Object

A *DataSet* object, as its name indicates, contains a set of data. You can think of a *DataSet* object as the container for a number of *DataTable* objects (stored in the *DataSet* object's *Tables* collection). Remember that ADO.NET was created to help developers build large multi-tiered database applications. At times, you might want to access a component running on a middle-tier server to retrieve the contents of many tables. Rather than having to repeatedly call the server in order to fetch that data one table at a time, you can package all the data into a *DataSet* object and return it in a single call. But a *DataSet* object does a great deal more than act as a container for multiple *DataTable* objects.

The data stored in a *DataSet* object is disconnected from your database. Any changes you make to the data are simply cached in each *DataRow*. When it's time to send these changes to your database, it might not be efficient to send the entire *DataSet* back to your middle-tier server. You can use the *GetChanges* method to extract just the modified rows from your *DataSet*. In this way, you pass less data between the different processes or servers.

The *DataSet* also exposes a *Merge* method, which can act as a complement to the *GetChanges* method. The middle-tier server you use to submit changes to your database, using the smaller *DataSet* returned by the *Merge* method, might return a *DataSet* that contains newly retrieved data. You can use the *DataSet* class's *Merge* method to combine the contents of two *DataSet* objects into a single *DataSet*. This is another example that shows how ADO.NET was developed with multi-tiered applications in mind. Previous Microsoft data access models have no comparable feature.

You can create a *DataSet* object and populate its *Tables* collection with information without having to communicate with a database. In previous data access models, you generally need to query a database before adding new rows locally, and then later submit them to the database. With ADO.NET, you don't need to communicate with your database until you're ready to submit the new rows.

The *DataSet* object also has features that allow you to write it to and read it from a file or an area of memory. You can save just the contents of the *DataSet* object, just the structure of the *DataSet* object, or both. ADO.NET stores this data as an XML document. Because ADO.NET and XML are so tightly coupled, moving data back and forth between ADO.NET *DataSet* objects and XML documents is a snap. You can thus take advantage of one of the most powerful features of XML: its ability to easily transform the structure of your data. For example, you can use an Extensible Stylesheet Language Transformation (XSLT) template to convert data exported to an XML document into HTML.

DataRelation Object

The tables in your database are usually related in some fashion. For example, in the Northwind database, each entry in the Orders table relates to an entry in the Customers table, so you can determine which customer placed which orders. You'll probably want to use related data from multiple tables in your application. The ADO.NET *DataSet* object is designed to handle this through the *DataRelation* object.

The *DataSet* class defines a *Relations* property, which is a collection of *DataRelation* objects. You can use a *DataRelation* object to indicate a relationship between different *DataTable* objects in your *DataSet*. Once you've created your *DataRelation* object, you can use code such as the following to retrieve an array of *DataRow* objects for the orders that correspond to a particular customer:

Visual Basic .NET

```
Dim dsNorthwind As DataSet
Dim rowCustomer, rowOrder As DataRow

'The code for creating the DataSet goes here.

dsNorthwind.Relations.Add("CustomersOrders", _
                    dsNorthwind.Tables("Customers").Columns("CustomerID"), _
                    dsNorthwind.Tables("Orders").Columns("CustomerID"))

For Each rowCustomer In dsNorthwind.Tables("Customers").Rows
    Console.WriteLine("Orders for customer " & rowCustomer("CompanyName"))
    For Each rowOrder In rowCustomer.GetChildRows("CustomersOrders")
        Console.WriteLine(vbTab & rowOrder("OrderID"))
    Next rowOrder
Next rowCustomer
```

Visual C#

```
DataSet dsNorthwind;

//Create and initialize DataSet.

dsNorthwind.Relations.Add("CustomersOrders",
                    dsNorthwind.Tables["Customers"].Columns["CustomerID"],
                    dsNorthwind.Tables["Orders"].Columns["CustomerID"]);

foreach (DataRow rowCustomer in dsNorthwind.Tables["Customers"].Rows)
```

(continued)

```
{
    Console.WriteLine("Orders for customer " +
                    rowCustomer["CompanyName"].ToString());
    foreach (DataRow rowOrder in rowCustomer.GetChildRows("CustomersOrders"))
        Console.WriteLine('\t' + rowOrder["OrderID"].ToString());
}
```

DataRelation objects also expose properties that allow you to enforce referential integrity. For example, you can set a *DataRelation* object so that if you modify the value of the primary key field in the parent row, the change cascades down to the child rows automatically. You can also set your *DataRelation* object so that if you delete a row in one *DataTable*, the corresponding rows in any child *DataTable* objects, as defined by the relation, are automatically deleted as well.

DataView Object

Once you've retrieved the results of a query into a *DataTable* object, you can use a *DataView* object to view the data in different ways. If you want to sort the contents of a *DataTable* object based on a column, simply set the *DataView* object's *Sort* property to the name of that column. You can also use the *Filter* property on *DataView* so that only the rows that match certain criteria are visible.

You can use multiple *DataView* objects to examine the same *DataTable* at the same time. For example, you can have two grids on a form, one showing all customers in alphabetical order, and the other showing the rows ordered by a different field, such as state or region. To show each view, you bind each grid to a different *DataView* object, but both *DataView* objects reference the same *DataTable*. This feature prevents you from having to maintain two copies of your data in separate structures. We'll discuss this in more detail in Chapter 8.

Metadata

ADO and DAO allow you to create a *Recordset* based on the results returned by your query. The data access engine examines the columns of data in the result set and populates the *Recordset* object's *Fields* collection based on this information, setting the name, data type, and so forth.

ADO.NET offers you a choice. You can use just a couple lines of code and let ADO.NET determine the structure of the results automatically, or you can use more code that includes metadata about the structure of the results of your query.

Why would you choose the option that involves writing more code? The main benefits are increased functionality and better performance. But how could having more code make your application run faster? That seems counterintuitive, doesn't it?

Unless you're writing an ad-hoc query tool, you'll generally know what the structure of your query results will look like. For example, most ADO code looks something like the following:

```
Dim rs as Recordset
'Declare other variables here.
  ⋮
'Initialize variables and establish connection to database.
  ⋮
rs.Open strSQL, cnDatabase, adOpenStatic, adLockOptimistic, adCmdText
Do While Not rs.EOF
    List1.AddItem rs.Fields("UserName").Value
    rs.MoveNext
Loop
```

In this code snippet, the programmer knows that the query contains a column named UserName. The point is that as a developer, you generally know what columns your query will return and what data types those columns use. But ADO doesn't know what the results of the query will look like ahead of time. As a result, ADO has to query the OLE DB provider to ask questions such as "How many columns are there in the results of this query?," "What are the data types for each of those columns?," "Where did this data come from?," and "What are the primary key fields for each table referenced in this query?" The OLE DB provider can answer some of these questions, but in many cases it must call back to the database.

To retrieve the results of your query and store this data in a *DataSet* object, ADO.NET needs to know the answers to such questions. You can supply this information yourself or force ADO.NET to ask the provider for this information. Your code will run faster using the former option because ADO.NET won't have to ask the provider for this information at run time.

Writing code to prepare the structure for your *DataSet* can become tedious, even if it improves the performance of your application. Thankfully, Visual Studio .NET includes design-time data-access features that offer the best of both worlds. For example, you can create a *DataSet* object based on a query, a table name, or a stored procedure, and then a configuration wizard will generate ADO.NET code to run the query and support submitting updates back to your database. We'll take a close look at many of these Visual Studio features in upcoming chapters.

Strongly Typed *DataSet* Objects

Visual Studio .NET also helps you simplify the process of building data-access applications by generating strongly typed *DataSet*. Let's say we have a simple table named Orders that contains two columns, CustomerID and CompanyName. You don't have to write code such as shown on the next page.

Visual Basic .NET

```
Dim ds As DataSet
'Create and fill DataSet.
Console.WriteLine(ds.Tables("Customers").Rows(0)("CustomerID"))
```

Visual C#

```
DataSet ds;
//Create and fill DataSet.
Console.WriteLine(ds.Tables["Customers"].Rows[0]["CustomerID"]);
```

Instead, we can write code like this:

Visual Basic .NET

```
Dim ds As CustomersDataSet
'Create and fill DataSet.
Console.WriteLine(ds.Customers(0).CustomerID)
```

Visual C#

```
CustomersDataSet ds;
//Create and fill DataSet.
Console.WriteLine(ds.Customers[0].CustomerID);
```

The strongly typed *DataSet* is simply a class that Visual Studio builds with all the table and column information available through properties. Strongly typed *DataSet* objects also expose custom methods for such features as creating new rows. So instead of code that looks like the following:

Visual Basic .NET

```
Dim ds as DataSet
'Code to create DataSet and customers DataTable
Dim rowNewCustomer As DataRow
rowNewCustomer = ds.Tables("Customers").NewRow()
rowNewCustomer("CustomerID") = "ALFKI"
rowNewCustomer("CompanyName") = "Alfreds Futterkiste"
ds.Tables("Customers").Rows.Add(rowNewCustomer)
```

Visual C#

```
DataSet ds;
//Code to create DataSet and customers DataTable
DataRow rowNewCustomer;
rowNewCustomer = ds.Tables["Customers"].NewRow();
rowNewCustomer["CustomerID"] = "ALFKI";
rowNewCustomer["CompanyName"] = "Alfreds Futterkiste";
ds.Tables["Customers"].Rows.Add(rowNewCustomer);
```

We can create and add a new row to our table in a single line of code, such as this:

```
ds.Customers.AddCustomersRow("ALFKI", "Alfreds Futterkiste")
```

We'll take a closer look at strongly typed *DataSet* objects in Chapter 9.

Questions That Should Be Asked More Frequently

Despite what its name implies, ADO.NET bears little resemblance to ADO. Although ADO.NET has classes that allow you to connect to your database, submit queries, and retrieve the results, the object model as a whole is very different from that of ADO. By now, you've probably picked up on many of those differences. In the coming chapters, we'll take a closer look at the main objects in the ADO.NET hierarchy. But before we do, it's worth addressing some of the questions that developers who are new to ADO.NET are likely to ask.

Q. Why didn't you mention cursors?

A. The initial release of ADO.NET doesn't support server-side cursors. Future releases might include such functionality. Currently, no object in the ADO.NET hierarchy acts as an interface to a server-side cursor. The *DataSet* and *DataTable* objects most closely resemble a client-side ADO *Recordset* object. The *DataReader* object most closely resembles a server-side ADO *Recordset* object that uses a forward-only, read-only cursor.

Q. How do I set the current position in a DataTable using ADO.NET? Previous object models exposed methods like *MoveFirst*, *MoveNext*, etc. Where are the positional properties and move methods?

A. The *DataTable* object exposes a *Rows* collection (of *DataRow* objects) that you can use to reference any row in the table at any given time; therefore, the *DataTable* object has no concept of a current row. Because any row can be addressed directly, there is no need for positional properties or navigation methods such as *Move-First*, *MoveLast*, *MoveNext*, and *MovePrevious*.

These positional properties and move methods were used in ADO most often when displaying data on a form.

2

Building ADO.NET Applications with the DataForm Wizard

Many books for developers focus on snippets of code in several chapters before piecing together those snippets to construct a simple working application. Instead of following this standard approach, I'll use this chapter to show you how to build a quick and simple application that will illustrate some of the major features of Microsoft ADO.NET.

Everyone Loves a Demo

I've learned from the developer conferences I've attended and spoken at, especially those geared toward Microsoft Visual Basic, that everyone loves a good demo. It's so much easier to discuss features and look at code once you've seen that code in action. So I'll start this discussion with a demo.

The Visual Studio .NET Data Form Wizard helps you build a data-bound form in a few simple steps. In this chapter, we'll use the wizard to build a data-bound form that allows you to retrieve data from a database, view and modify that data, and send the changes back to the database. We'll then look at the code that the wizard generated as a preview of the coming chapters. This simple application will serve as a working example of many of the objects, features, and concepts covered in later chapters.

> **Note**   Many developers hate wizards. Well, maybe *hate* is too strong a word, but developers often don't trust wizards, especially ones that use "black-box technology." Fortunately, the Visual Studio .NET Data Form Wizard generates code that you can examine and modify.

This chapter is designed to help you create a simple application using the sample Northwind database. Products such as Microsoft SQL Server, Microsoft Access, and Microsoft Data Engine (MSDE) include this database. The structure of the Northwind database might vary slightly from one product or version to the next, but it always contains tables such as Customers, Orders, Products, and Employees. This chapter assumes that you have access to a Northwind database.

Using the Data Form Wizard to Build a Data-Bound Form

You can add a number of different types of objects to a Visual Studio .NET project, such as forms, class modules, and code modules. With Visual Basic .NET and C#, you can add a data-bound form. When you add a data-bound form to your project, Visual Studio automatically launches the Data Form Wizard.

To help you build your data-bound form, the wizard prompts you for information about the database, tables in the database, columns in the table, and so forth, in a series of pages. We'll step through the wizard to build a sample data-bound form.

First in Visual Studio .NET, choose New, Project from the File menu or click the New Project toolbar button to open the New Project dialog box. Select your language of choice in the Project Types pane—Visual Basic or Visual C#—and then select the Windows Application icon, as shown in Figure 2-1. In the text box below the icons, change the name of the project you're about to create to **Chapter2**, and then click OK.

> **Note**   Building a data-bound Web form involves more complex concepts, which we'll cover in Chapter 14. For simplicity, we'll focus on building a data-bound Windows form in this chapter.

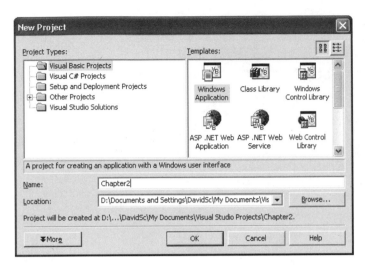

Figure 2-1   Creating a new Windows application

Now that you have your new project set up, you can use the Data Form Wizard to create a new data-bound form. Because using the wizard results in a new form in your project, the wizard is available through the Add New Item dialog box, which you open by choosing Add New Item from the File menu or clicking the Add New Item toolbar button in Visual Studio .NET. Select the Data Form Wizard icon, shown in Figure 2-2, and then click OK.

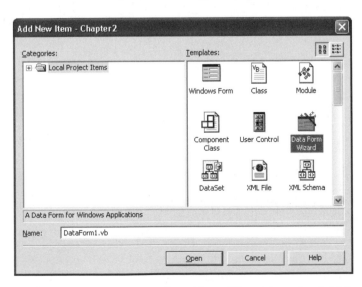

Figure 2-2   Launching the Data Form Wizard from the Add New Item dialog box

The wizard will launch and display a welcome page, shown in Figure 2-3.

Figure 2-3 The Data Form Wizard's welcome page

Click Next to go to the next page, which offers you a choice of using an existing *DataSet* object or a new one. You haven't created a *DataSet* yet, so you'll create a new one, as shown in Figure 2-4.

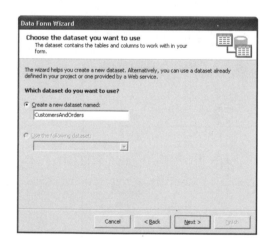

Figure 2-4 Creating a new *DataSet* object for your new form

Your *DataSet* object's name should indicate the type of data contained in your *DataSet*. In this example, the *DataSet* will store customer information and orders tables in the Northwind database. To name the new *DataSet*, type **CustomersAndOrders** in the text box and then click Next.

> **Note**   The Data Form Wizard builds strongly typed *DataSet* objects,
> which are new class files in your project. Always be sure that the name
> you type for your new *DataSet* is a valid class name—that is, one that
> begins with a letter and includes only letters, numbers, and under-
> score characters.

Choosing a Connection

Now it's time to connect the Data Form Wizard to your database. The Choose A
Data Connection page, shown in Figure 2-5, allows you to add new connections
or select a connection that's available in the Server Explorer window. If you
haven't already created a connection to your database, click the New Connection
button and the OLE DB Data Link Properties dialog box will appear.

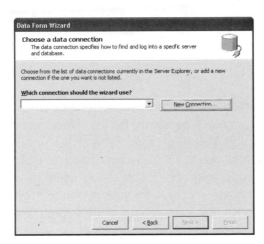

Figure 2-5   The wizard's Choose A Data Connection page

On the Connection tab of the Data Link Properties dialog box, you can
specify your connection. By default, it is set to connect to Microsoft SQL Server. To
connect to your database, specify a server name (or type **(local)** to communicate
with an instance of SQL Server running on your machine), a username, password, and a database name, as shown in Figure 2-6.

Figure 2-6 The Connection tab of the Data Link Properties dialog box

If multiple instances of SQL Server 2000 are installed on a machine, you can indicate which instance you want to use by specifying the server name, a back slash, and then the instance name—for example, *MyServerName\MyInstance*.

> **Note** The default password for the SQL Server administrator account is blank. Having a blank password for the master account is, generally speaking, a bad idea. For security reasons, you should change this password. Also, when you develop database applications for SQL Server, don't code your application to log users in with the administrator account. Create accounts for your users, or maybe one generic user account, with the appropriate permissions. You don't want your users to accidentally or intentionally make catastrophic changes to your database.

Notice that the Allow Saving Password check box is selected in the figure. By default, this check box is deselected. If you enter a password using the default settings, Visual Studio .NET will receive the entire connection string except for the password. As a result, you'll be prompted for the password at various times while you access the database at design time. I prefer to select this check box to remove the password from the connection string in my code. Select the check box for now. You'll learn more about this feature in Chapter 3.

If you want to connect to a database other than SQL Server, click on the Provider tab to select a different OLE DB provider. As shown in Figure 2-7, this tab lists all the OLE DB providers installed on your machine. I'll discuss using other providers with the Data Link Properties dialog box in more depth in the next chapter.

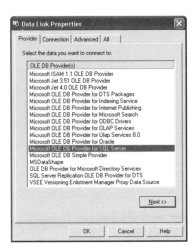

Figure 2-7   The Provider tab of the Data Link Properties dialog box

If you don't have access to a SQL Server or MSDE database but do have an Access version of the Northwind database, select the Microsoft Jet 4.0 OLE DB provider.

Click Next to move to the Connection tab of the dialog box, as shown in Figure 2-8.

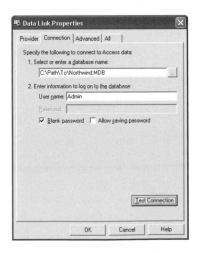

Figure 2-8   Specifying an Access database on the Connection tab of the Data Link Properties dialog box

Type the path to your Access database in the first text box, or click the ellipsis button to the right of the text box to open a dialog box in which you can select the database from your hard drive or network. Type a username and a password in the appropriate text boxes, and select the password check boxes (if desired) for the connection. Click OK.

Selecting Tables from Your Database

The next Data Form Wizard page, shown in Figure 2-9, lists the tables, views, and stored procedures that are available in your database's schema. Although tables and views are treated as different structures in different database systems, the output from either type of object is mapped to an ADO.NET *DataTable*. Thus, the wizard refers to all the objects as tables.

Select the tables you want to include in your *DataSet* in the Available Items list and move them to the Selected Items list by clicking the right arrow button. If you make a mistake and need to remove a table from the Selected Items list, select the table to remove and click the left arrow button. You can also select and deselect tables by double-clicking them.

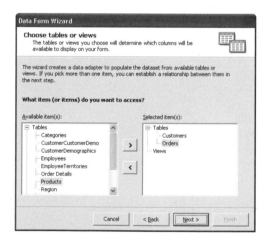

Figure 2-9   Selecting tables in the Data Form Wizard

For the purposes of our sample application, select the Customers and Orders tables from the Northwind database. Then click Next.

Creating Relationships in Your *DataSet*

If you've selected more than one table, the Data Form Wizard will display a page in which you can create relationships between the tables you selected. As you learned in Chapter 1, you can use relationships to easily locate data in related tables. Relationships also help enforce referential integrity rules by cascading changes from one table to another.

Adding a relationship to your *DataSet* using the wizard is simple. The most challenging part of the process might be naming the relationship. As a general guideline, combine the name of the parent and child tables (in that order) to create the name.

Here we'll relate the Customers and Orders tables you selected on the previous page. Name the relationship **CustomersOrders**.

The data in the two tables are related. Each entry in the Orders table relates to an entry in the Customers table. In other words, each order belongs to a particular customer. Because each customer row has order rows associated with it, the Customers table is the parent table in the relationship.

Select the Customers table as the Parent Table in the relationship and the Orders table as the Child Table in the relationship. The *CustomerID* defines the relationship between the two tables. Select *CustomerID* as the key field for each table, as shown in Figure 2-10. Click the right arrow button to add the relationship to the *Relations list*, and then click Next.

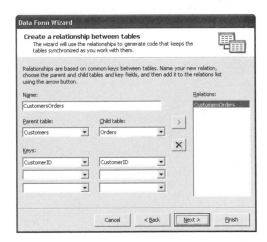

Figure 2-10   Creating relationships between tables

Selecting Columns to Display

On the next wizard page (shown in Figure 2-11), you can select the columns to display on the data-bound form. When you selected the tables to include in your *DataSet*, you didn't have the option to specify which columns to include. The Data Form Wizard retrieved all rows and all columns in the selected tables.

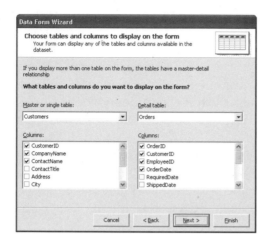

Figure 2-11 Choosing the tables and columns to display on your data-bound form

You can display a single table or two tables in a master/detail relationship. Once you select the table or tables to display, you'll see all the available columns for the selected tables. By default, all the columns are selected, but you can deselect any columns you don't want to have appear on the data-bound form.

When this page of the wizard appears, you'll see that the Customers table is already selected as the parent table and the Orders table is selected as the child table. This behavior is a pleasant result of the wizard's defaults. The wizard automatically selects the first table by alphabetical order as the parent table. Because "Customers" comes before "Orders," the Customers table is selected by default. The Customers table has only one related table, Orders, so Orders is selected by default as the child table.

To simplify the display of your form, select just the *CustomerID*, *CompanyName*, *ContactTitle*, and *Phone* fields from the Customers table and the *OrderID*, *CustomerID*, *EmployeeID*, and *OrderDate* fields from the Orders table. Then click Next.

Choosing a Display Style

The next wizard page provides a couple of options for showing the contents of the main table on data-bound Windows forms. You can display contents of the main table in a grid, which will allow the user to see multiple rows at the same time, or you can display the rows one at a time in a series of bound controls such as text boxes.

You'll have more options if you choose to display the contents of the main table one row at a time. The wizard lets you decide whether you want to include buttons that allow the user to navigate back and forth through the contents of the table, cancel pending changes on a row, or add and remove rows. For the purpose of this exercise, select the Single Record In Individual Controls option and all the check boxes that follow as shown in Figure 2-12.

Figure 2-12   Selecting the Single Record In Individual Controls display style

> **Note**   If you were building a Web application, the wizard would create *DataGrid* objects, which would convert the data in your tables to HTML tables to display in the browser on your Web form.

That's it. Click Finish to build your new data-bound form.

Using the New Data-Bound Form

Figure 2-13 shows the data-bound form that the Data Form Wizard created.

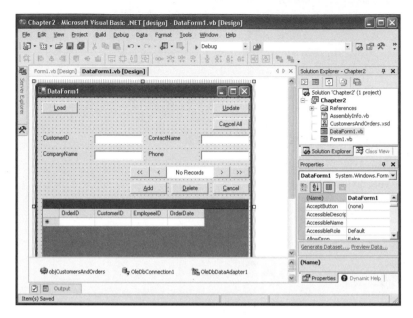

Figure 2-13   Your new data-bound form

If you build and run the project right now, you won't see the new data-bound form. Unless you've changed the properties for the project, the form that you'll see when you run the project is the form that was initially included with the project. To change the setting so the project starts with the new form, choose Properties from the Project menu in Visual Studio .NET or right-click on the project in Solution Explorer and choose Properties from the shortcut menu. You'll see the project's Property Pages dialog box. Change the project's *Startup Object* property to the new data-bound form, *DataForm1* as shown in Figure 2-14. Click OK to save your changes.

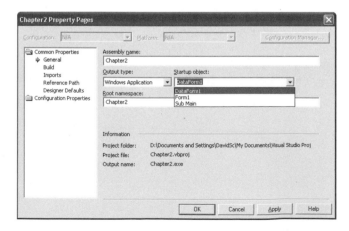

Figure 2-14   The Property Pages dialog box for the Chapter2 project

Showing Data in Your New Data-Bound Form

To run the project and see your new data-bound form, press F5, click the Debug menu and then click Start, or click the Start button on the toolbar. You'll see that the form has labels and text boxes for each field in the Customers table as well as a data-bound grid to display the contents of the Orders table. However, the form does not show any data. All the controls are empty. The form has created a *DataSet* object with the tables and relationship you defined in the pages of the Data Form Wizard, but that *DataSet* does not yet contain data. Click the Load button in the upper-left corner of the form to see the data in your controls, as shown in Figure 2-15.

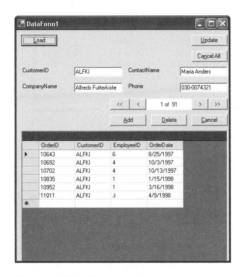

Figure 2-15   Viewing the data on the new data-bound form

A Behind-the-Scenes Look at the Wizard-Generated Code

To look at the code that your project runs when you click the Load button, close the form and return to the Visual Studio .NET development environment. Double-click the Load button, and you'll see that the code in the button's *Click* event calls the *LoadDataSet* procedure. Scroll down to the definition of this procedure and you'll see that it calls another procedure, *FillDataSet*. If you examine the code in this procedure, you'll find that it calls the *Fill* method on two *OleDbDataAdapter* objects, as shown in Figure 2-16.

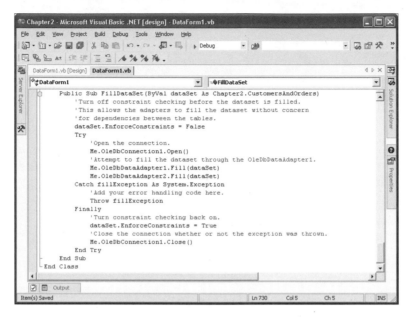

Figure 2-16   Wizard-generated code for filling your *DataSet*

Calling the *Fill* method of the *OleDbDataAdapter* object executes the query stored in the *SelectCommand* property in the *DataAdapter* and stores the results in the *DataSet* or *DataTable* objects specified. The Data Form Wizard created these *DataAdapter* objects to fetch the contents of each table that you chose to display. The *SelectCommand* for each *DataAdapter* contains a query in the following format:

```
SELECT Field1, Field2, ... , FieldN FROM MyTable
```

Most of the buttons on the form are self-explanatory—for example, clicking the Add button adds a new customer row and clicking the Delete button deletes the current customer row. The buttons with the arrows are navigation controls that take you to the first, last, previous, and next records.

Cascading Changes with the *DataRelation* Object

Click the right arrow button to move to the next customer. The text boxes on the data-bound form will display information about the next customer. Because of the *DataRelation* you built, the grid will show just the orders for this particular customer. This relation has other features that you can use on the form.

Using the navigation buttons, move to the first customer that has child orders. Unless you've modified the contents of the tables in the sample database, the first customer, whose *CustomerID* setting is ALFKI, will have several orders. Change the value in the text box for the *CustomerID* field to **Chap2**. Don't worry, this won't affect the contents of the database. Next, move to the next record and then back to this record. Look at the contents of the grid. The *CustomerID* field for all the orders will be set to *Chap2*, the value you just entered. The *DataRelation* object we built instructed the *DataSet* object to cascade the change to the *CustomerID* column in the customer row to all the related order rows. If you were to delete the current customer from the *DataSet*, the *DataSet* would delete all the related orders as well.

Submitting Changes to Your Database

I mentioned earlier that the change to the data in the *DataSet* object would not affect the contents of the database. To verify this claim, close the form and rerun the project. Load the data, and then use the navigation buttons to move to the customer that you previously modified. You'll see that the *CustomerID* field is still set to its original value rather than to *Chap3*. As I mentioned in Chapter 1, the data in the *DataSet* object is disconnected from the database. Changes you make to the *DataSet* object do not directly affect the data in your database. ADO.NET does provide features that allow you to submit changes to your database, but how do you use them? In order to submit the changes back to the database, you have to use some additional functionality from the ADO.NET *DataAdapter* class. We'll explore that next.

Let's make another change to a customer. Move to the first customer by clicking on the double left arrow button. Add **X** to the end of the company name. Click the right arrow button to move to the next row. Then click the left arrow button to move back to the modified row. You'll see that the change is still stored in the *DataSet* object. If you were to close the form and rerun the project, you'd lose this modification.

To submit the name change, click the Update button. You might see the mouse cursor momentarily change from an arrow to an hourglass and back while the form runs the code to send the change to your database. After the cursor returns to its normal arrow, close the form and rerun the project. When you click on the Load button, you'll see the modified company name.

What code did the Update button use to submit the change to the database? To see it, close the form and return to the Visual Studio .NET development environment. Double-click the Update button to see the code contained in its *Click* event. The wizard-generated code creates two procedures to update your database—*UpdateDataSet* and *UpdateDataSource*. The Update button's click event calls the *UpdateDataSet* procedure, which, in turn, calls *UpdateDataSource*. Look at the definition for these procedures of the form, and you'll see the code shown in Figures 2-17 and 2-18.

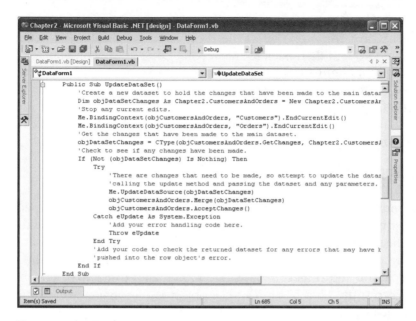

Figure 2-17   The *UpdateDataSet* procedure generated by the Data Form Wizard

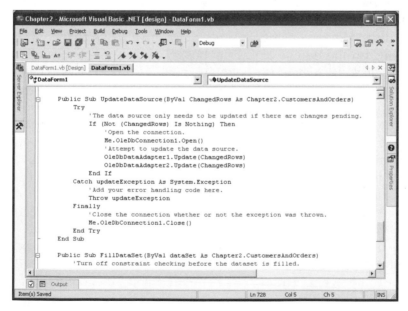

Figure 2-18   The *UpdateDataSource* procedure generated by the Data Form Wizard

This might look like complex code, but it's really very straightforward. For now, we'll focus on the general process and look at a couple lines of code at a time. In Chapter 10 and Chapter 11, we'll take a closer look at the process of sending updates to your database. Remember that the wizard generated this code in order to handle whatever changes you make to the data on the form. This code handles modified rows, newly created rows, and deleted rows in each table. The three methods that the wizard uses to control the update process are *GetChanges*, *Update*, and *Merge*.

Calling the *DataAdapter* Object's *Update* Method

Rather than discuss these methods in the order in which they appear in the code, I'd like to focus first on the *Update* method—the most critical part of the process.

In Chapter 1, you learned that the *DataAdapter* object acts as a bridge between the *DataSet* object and the database. The *DataAdapter* object's *Update* method submits changes stored in the *DataSet* to the database. Each *DataAdapter* object corresponds to one of the *DataTable* objects in our *DataSet*. In order to submit changes stored in both *DataTable* objects, you have to call the *Update* method on both *DataAdapter* objects.

When you call the *Update* method on a *DataAdapter* object, you must specify what data you want to submit to the database. The *DataAdapter* object is flexible and can accept a number of different structures in its *Update* method. The code generated by the Data Form Wizard uses a *DataSet* object, but you can also submit a *DataTable* object or an array of *DataRow* objects to the *Update* method.

The *DataAdapter* object examines the contents of the data structure to determine which rows it can handle. For example, the *DataAdapter* that the Data Form Wizard built based on the Customers table will look only at the *DataTable* that corresponds to the Customers table. The *DataAdapter* object knows which table to examine because of its *TableMappings* collection, which I described briefly in Chapter 1.

When the DataAdapter object detects a modified row, it determines the type of change—insert, update, or delete—and submits it to the database based on this type. If the row has been modified, the *DataAdapter* object executes the *DataCommand* stored in its *UpdateCommand* property, using the current contents of the row. Similarly, the *DataAdapter* object uses its *InsertCommand* to submit new rows and its *DeleteCommand* to delete rows.

Isolating Modified Rows

The code in the form's *UpdateRowSource* function calls the *GetChanges* method on the *DataSet*. The *GetChanges* method generates a new *DataSet* object named *objDataSetChanges* that contains only modified rows. The *GetChanges* method accepts an optional parameter that you can use to indicate whether you want all changes or just a specific type of change—inserts, updates, or deletes.

There's actually no need for the Data Form Wizard to use the *GetChanges* method to create a new *DataSet* object that contains only modified rows. If you call a *DataAdapter* object's *Update* method and the *DataSet* you supply as a parameter contains unmodified rows, those rows are simply ignored. So when would you use *GetChanges*?

The Data Form Wizard generates two-tier applications. The client application communicates directly with your database. If you build a multi-tiered application that uses Web services or COM+ components that run on a middle-tier server, you'll want to limit the amount of data that you pass back and forth between machines. The less data you have to pass across the wire, the faster your application will run.

If the client application has a *DataSet* that contains modified rows to submit to the database in such a multi-tiered application, the client sends data to the middle. There's no need to send unmodified rows back to the middle tier. Intelligent use of the *GetChanges* method can dramatically improve the performance of multi-tiered ADO.NET applications.

The Data Form Wizard builds two-tier applications, but the code that it generates is appropriate for multi-tiered applications.

Reintegrating Changes

When the *DataAdapter* object examines a modified row and successfully submits the pending change to the database, it marks the row as no longer containing a pending change. This way, the *DataAdapter* object doesn't send the same change to the database over and over again on subsequent calls to its *Update* method.

Earlier we discussed the *DataSet* class's *GetChanges* method. The code uses the *DataSet* object returned by the *GetChanges* method in the call to the *DataAdapter* object's *Update* method.

When the updates succeed, the *DataAdapter* objects mark the appropriate rows in the *objDataSetChanges* as having successfully updated the database. But the *objDataSetChanges* is separate from the main *DataSet* for the form. Somehow, we need to merge the changes that the *DataAdapter* objects made to the *objDataSetChanges* back into our main *DataSet*.

The *DataSet* class has a *Merge* method that you can use to merge data from two *DataSet* objects. If the rows in the *DataSet* objects represent different rows, ADO.NET simply places all the rows into the *DataSet* whose *Merge* method you called. In this case, the rows in the *objDataSetChanges* reference the same data in our main *DataSet*. We want the rows in the *objDataSetChanges* to overwrite the corresponding rows in the main *DataSet*. ADO.NET compares the primary key values stored in the rows to determine which rows represent the same row of data. By default, ADO.NET overwrites the row in the *DataSet* whose *Merge* method you've called. Thus, the changes that the *DataAdapter* objects make to the *dsDelta DataSets* are passed along to our main *DataSet*, and we can handle subsequent updates successfully.

The Component Tray

Before moving on, I want to draw your attention to another feature of the Visual Studio .NET development environment. Developers who've used earlier versions of Visual Studio products might be a little surprised when they look at the designer for the data-bound form in the development environment. One of the first questions that Visual Basic 6 developers ask is, "What is that section below my form?"

If you look below the form in Figure 2-19, you'll see the component tray. Visual Studio .NET allows you to drag items from the Toolbox onto designers. Many developers use the Toolbox to draw buttons on forms. But not all components are visible at run time.

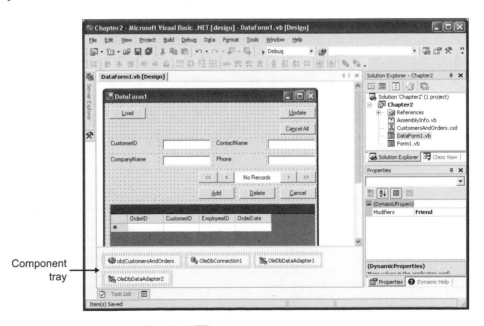

Figure 2-19   The Visual Studio .NET component tray

In Visual Basic 6, for example, you can place timer controls and common dialog box controls on a form. These controls aren't really visible at run time, however. They are components whose properties you can set at design time using the Properties window, but they don't have a visual user interface element. When you place such a control on a form in Visual Basic 6, you see an icon on the form, but when you run the form you don't actually see the control.

Visual Studio .NET places such nonvisual components in the component tray, which is located under the form. To access their properties from the Properties window, you can click items in the component tray. In the new form's components tray, you'll see the items for our *DataConnection*, *DataAdapter*, and *DataSet* objects.

You can drag components from the Data tab of the Toolbox onto the form or the component tray. Some components, such as the *DataAdapter*, are associated with configuration wizards. Drag an *OleDbDataAdapter* onto the form, and you'll see a wizard that helps you set properties on your new *DataAdapter* that allow you to communicate with your database. The wizard generates code based on your input in a similar fashion as the Data Form Wizard. The object variables in your component tray are initialized in a hidden area of the form's code. Open the section of the code marked "Windows Form Designer generated code," shown in Figure 2-20. This section contains all designer-generated code. Scroll down past the object declarations in this region, and you'll see the *InitializeComponent* procedure that contains the code that the DataAdapter Configuration Wizard generates. Creating components using these rapid application development (RAD) features can save you a great deal of development time.

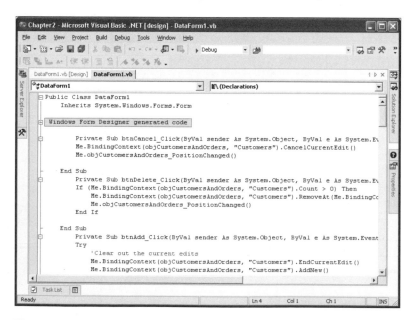

Figure 2-20   The region of the class that contains "hidden" designer-generated code

The Data Form Wizard as a Starting Point

Congratulations! You've just built a working database application.

Of course, if building database applications were this easy, this would be the final chapter of the book. This application is very simplistic. You probably would not want to deploy it on a network with a large number of users. Imagine every user selecting every row and every column in your database. Yikes! That's *a lot* of network traffic.

The Data Form Wizard is more valuable as a tool for creating a starting point than as a tool for creating finished solutions. It's a great tool for learning about ADO.NET because you can look at the code it generates, as you've done in this chapter.

Before moving to the next chapter to learn more about the *DataSet* object, take a few minutes to review the code the Data Form Wizard generated in our simple application. Don't worry about understanding what all that code does right now. Simply look at the amount of code that's there.

Although the wizards in Visual Studio .NET might not generate an entire application that you can deploy as-is, they can help shorten development time by generating a lot of code that you can use in your application. In subsequent chapters, I'll cover many of these tools and look at the code they generate, pointing out why the code might or might not be suitable for your applications.

Questions That Should Be Asked More Frequently

You've now built a relatively simple application that uses ADO.NET, and you've seen some of the power available in the technology. We've discussed how some of the major features work by looking at code snippets generated by the Data Form Wizard. This chapter is a starting point, but it's also a teaser. So instead of posing questions that developers might ask and then offering answers, as I do in the "Questions..." section of other chapters, here I will simply offer a few questions for you to consider. Some of the answers can be found in the code that the Data Form Wizard generates. For other answers, read on.

Q. I played with the form that the Data Form Wizard generated, and I noticed that I could add new orders. When I added a new order, the *OrderID* field contained data before I submitted the new order to the database. How did the *DataSet* generate this number?

Q. What happens if another user modifies the contents of a row between the time I retrieve it and submit the update?

Q. After I deleted a customer and clicked the Update button, I received an error saying that the *DELETE* statement conflicted with a column reference constraint. What does that mean? How can I change the code to better handle this situation?

Part II

Getting Connected: Using a .NET Data Provider

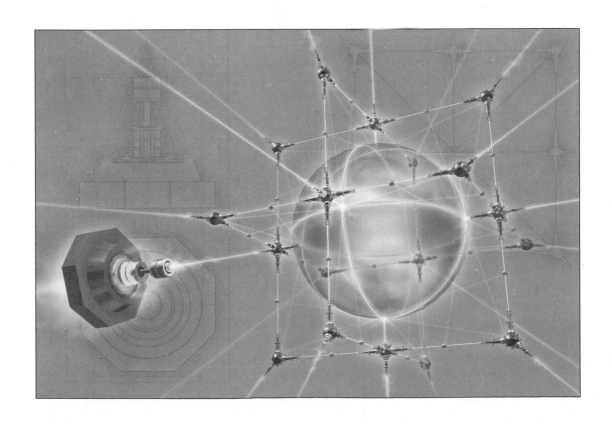

3

Connecting to
Your Database

Part of building a database application requires that you connect to your data source and manage that connection. In the ADO.NET object model, the *Connection* object represents a connection to your data source.

This chapter will serve as your guide to the ADO.NET *Connection* object by covering the major features of the object. In the process, we'll learn how to create and use *Connection* objects both in code and through the Visual Studio .NET development environment.

Throughout the chapter, we'll focus on the more generic of the two *Connection* objects that reside in the Microsoft .NET Framework, the *OleDbConnection* object. Unless otherwise noted, the features of the object are generic and apply to all *Connection* objects regardless of their .NET Data Provider.

Code snippets assume that you have used the appropriate construct to reference the *System.Data*, *System.Data.OleDb*, and *System.Data.SqlClient* namespaces. The following lines of code (Visual Basic .NET and Visual C#. NET, respectively) must appear at the beginning of your code modules. For more information on these constructs, please see the documentation of your language of choice.

In Visual Basic .NET, the code would look like this:

```
Imports System.Data
Imports System.Data.OleDb
Imports System.Data.SqlClient
```

In Visual C#. NET, the code would look like this:

```
using System.Data;
using System.Data.OleDb;
using System.Data.SqlClient;
```

Using *Connection* Objects

You can use the properties of the *Connection* object to specify user credentials and the location of your data source. The *Connection* object's methods allow you to control when you connect to and disconnect from your data source. You can also use the *Connection* object as a starting point for creating *Command* and *Transaction* objects. Let's look at how you can create and use connections in your application by working with the *Connection* object in code.

SQL Server for the masses!

The Microsoft .NET Framework SDK includes files that let you install Microsoft Desktop Engine 2000 (MSDE).

Like Access databases, MSDE is a royalty-free, redistributable database package. However, unlike Access databases and the Jet database engine, MSDE is a true client/server database system, just like SQL Server. You can create tables, views, and stored procedures in an MSDE database that will also run on SQL Server databases. Also, like SQL Server, MSDE supports both standard and integrated security. MSDE offers many of the same features of SQL Server because it's built on the same code base as SQL Server. As a result, you can take an application built to work with an MSDE database and port it to SQL Server with minimal effort.

There are some important differences between MSDE and SQL Server to keep in mind. MSDE does not provide many of the same "high end" features that SQL Server does. For example, the MSDE engine is geared to handle work on up to five simultaneous connections. Beyond that, you'll encounter performance degradation. SQL Server is designed to handle more simultaneous users. MSDE can handle databases up to 2 GB in size, whereas SQL Server can handle larger databases. Also, MSDE does not include the developer tools that ship with SQL Server, such as Enterprise Manager, Query Analyzer, and SQL Profiler.

For more information on the differences between SQL Server and MSDE, see the MSDN and SQL Server Web sites.

MSDE 2000 is designed to run on Windows 9*x* operating systems (Windows 98 or later), as well as all versions of Windows NT 4.0, Windows 2000, and Windows XP.

The connection and query strings used throughout this book are written to communicate with the local instance of MSDE included with the .NET Framework SDK. This way, you can copy code from the digital version of the book and run the code without having to change the connection string in order to make the code connect to your database.

To install MSDE, locate the Microsoft .NET Framework SDK program group on the Start menu and select the sub-item Samples And QuickStart Tutorials. This will call up the SDK's QuickStarts, Tutorials, And Samples page in your browser. If you have not already installed MSDE from this page, you'll see the screen shown in Figure 3-1 in your browser.

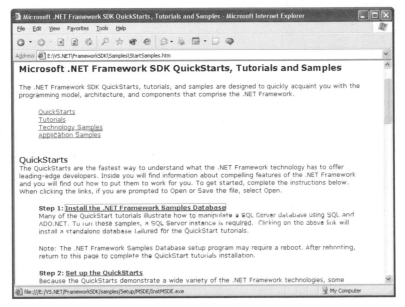

Figure 3-1   Installing MSDE from the Microsoft.NET Framework SDK

If you click on Install The .NET Framework Samples Database, you'll install MSDE on your machine. Clicking on Set Up The QuickStarts will install the sample databases (the standard SQL Server pubs and Northwind sample databases, along with the databases that the .NET Frameworks Samples use) as well as set up virtual roots in Internet Information Services (IIS) and the QuickStart Tutorial Web pages.

The following sample code connects to the .NET Framework install of MSDE using the SQL DMO library. You'll need to add a reference to the SQL DMO library in order to run the code. The SQL DMO library is a COM library rather than a .NET library, so remember to switch to the COM tab of the Add References dialog box when trying to locate the library.

The code demonstrates how to execute the contents of a script file, as well as how to examine information about logins and the structure of

(continued)

SQL Server for the masses!   *(continued)*

your databases. For more information on using the SQL DMO object library, see the help file (SQLDMO.chm).

Visual Basic .NET

```vbnet
Dim dmoServer As New SQLDMO.SQLServer()
dmoServer.LoginSecure = True
dmoServer.Connect("(local)\NetSDK")

Dim filSqlScript As IO.StreamReader
Dim strPathToFile As String
Console.WriteLine("Installing the sample Northwind database")
strPathToFile = "C:\VS.NET\FrameworkSDK\Samples\Setup\instnwnd.sql"
filSqlScript = IO.File.OpenText(strPathToFile)
dmoServer.ExecuteImmediate(filSqlScript.ReadToEnd)
filSqlScript.Close()

Console.WriteLine("Installing the sample pubs database")
strPathToFile = "C:\VS.NET\FrameworkSDK\Samples\Setup\instpubs.sql"
filSqlScript = IO.File.OpenText(strPathToFile)
dmoServer.ExecuteImmediate(filSqlScript.ReadToEnd)
filSqlScript.Close()

Dim dmoDatabase As SQLDMO.Database
Dim dmoTable As SQLDMO.Table
Console.WriteLine("Databases:")
For Each dmoDatabase In dmoServer.Databases
    If Not dmoDatabase.SystemObject Then
        Console.WriteLine(vbTab & dmoDatabase.Name)
        For Each dmoTable In dmoDatabase.Tables
            If Not dmoTable.SystemObject Then
                Console.WriteLine(vbTab & vbTab & dmoTable.Name)
            End If
        Next dmoTable
        Console.WriteLine()
    End If
Next dmoDatabase

Dim dmoLogin As SQLDMO.Login
Console.WriteLine("Logins:")
For Each dmoLogin In dmoServer.Logins
    Console.WriteLine(vbTab & dmoLogin.Name)
Next dmoLogin
Console.WriteLine()

dmoServer.DisConnect()
```

Visual C# .NET

```csharp
SQLDMO.SQLServer dmoServer = new SQLDMO.SQLServer();
dmoServer.LoginSecure = true;
dmoServer.Connect("(local)\\NetSDK", null, null);

System.IO.StreamReader filSqlScript;
string strPathToFile;
Console.WriteLine("Installing the sample Northwind database");
strPathToFile = "C:\\VS.NET\\FrameworkSDK\\Samples\\Setup\\instnwnd.sql";
filSqlScript = System.IO.File.OpenText(strPathToFile);
dmoServer.ExecuteImmediate(filSqlScript.ReadToEnd(),
                           SQLDMO.SQLDMO_EXEC_TYPE.SQLDMOExec_Default,
                           null);
filSqlScript.Close();

Console.WriteLine("Installing the sample pubs database");
strPathToFile = "C:\\VS.NET\\FrameworkSDK\\Samples\\Setup\\instpubs.sql";
filSqlScript = System.IO.File.OpenText(strPathToFile);
dmoServer.ExecuteImmediate(filSqlScript.ReadToEnd(),
                           SQLDMO.SQLDMO_EXEC_TYPE.SQLDMOExec_Default,
                           null);
filSqlScript.Close();

Console.WriteLine("Databases:");
foreach (SQLDMO.Database dmoDatabase in dmoServer.Databases)
    if (!dmoDatabase.SystemObject)
    {
        Console.WriteLine("\t" + dmoDatabase.Name);
        foreach (SQLDMO.Table dmoTable in dmoDatabase.Tables)
            if (!dmoTable.SystemObject)
                Console.WriteLine("\t\t" + dmoTable.Name);
        Console.WriteLine();
    }

Console.WriteLine("Logins:");
foreach (SQLDMO.Login dmoLogin in dmoServer.Logins)
    Console.WriteLine("\t" + dmoLogin.Name);
Console.WriteLine();

dmoServer.DisConnect();
```

Creating *Connection* Objects

There are two ways to create connections using *OleDbConnection* at runtime. You can simply create a new uninitialized *OleDbConnection* object, as shown here:

Visual Basic .NET

```
Dim cn As OleDbConnection
cn = New OleDbConnection()
```

Visual C# .NET

```
OleDbConnection cn;
cn = new OleDbConnection();
```

Or, you can initialize an *OleDbConnection* object using the class's constructor.

Constructors

The Microsoft .NET Framework supports constructors, a feature not available in classic Component Object Model (COM) programming. You can think of a constructor as a class method that you call when you initialize an object. The constructor generally accepts parameters that correspond to the most commonly used property or properties on the class. For example, the *OleDbConnection* class defines a constructor that accepts a value for the *ConnectionString* property of the *OleDbConnection* object that it creates.

The following code snippets are equivalent. For each language example, there are two code segments. The first instantiates an *OleDbConnection* and then initializes it, the second initializes the object as it's created by passing a parameter to its constructor:

Visual Basic .NET

```
Dim strConn As String
strConn = "Provider=SQLOLEDB;Data Source=(local)\NetSDK;" & _
          "Initial Catalog=Northwind;Trusted_Connection=Yes;"
Dim cn As OleDbConnection
cn = New OleDbConnection()
cn.ConnectionString = strConn
```

is equivalent to

```
Dim strConn As String
strConn = "Provider=SQLOLEDB;Data Source=(local)\NetSDK;" & _
          "Initial Catalog=Northwind;Trusted_Connection=Yes;"
Dim cn As OleDbConnection
cn = New OleDbConnection(strConn)
```

Visual C# .NET

```
string strConn;
strConn = "Provider=SQLOLEDB;Data Source=(local)\\NetSDK;" +
        "Initial Catalog=Northwind;Trusted_Connection=Yes;";
OleDbConnection cn;
cn = new OleDbConnection();
cn.ConnectionString = strConn;
```

is equivalent to

```
string strConn;
strConn = "Provider=SQLOLEDB;Data Source=(local)\\NetSDK;" +
        "Initial Catalog=Northwind;Trusted_Connection=Yes;";
OleDbConnection cn;
cn = new OleDbConnection(strConn);
```

Visual Basic .NET and C# also let you initialize variables as you declare them. We can combine this feature with the constructor to simplify the code snippets above to declare, instantiate, and initialize our objects in a single line of code, as shown here:

Visual Basic .NET

```
Dim strConn As String = "Provider=SQLOLEDB;Data Source=(local)\NetSDK;" & _
                    "Initial Catalog=Northwind;Trusted_Connection=Yes;"
Dim cn As New OleDbConnection(strConn)
```

Visual C# .NET

```
string strConn = "Provider=SQLOLEDB;Data Source=(local)\\NetSDK;" +
                "Initial Catalog=Northwind;Trusted_Connection=Yes;";
OleDbConnection cn = new OleDbConnection(strConn);
```

Connection Strings

In the code snippets above, we supplied a connection string for our new *Ole-DbConnection* objects. A connection string consists of a series of name-value pairs delimited by semicolons:

```
strConn = "Setting1=Value1;Setting2=Value2;..."
```

The settings and values depend on the data source you want to connect to, as well as on the technology you're using to connect to your data source.

The OLE DB .NET data provider is extremely flexible when it comes to connecting to databases, and it provides a variety of ways to build a connection string. Let's take a quick look at building connection strings for the three most commonly used OLE DB providers: the Microsoft OLE DB providers for Microsoft Access, Microsoft SQL Server, and Oracle databases.

OLE DB Provider for SQL Server Databases

If you're connecting to a SQL Server database, you can specify the native OLE DB provider, the location of your SQL Server, and the database you want to use, as well as a username and password:

```
Provider=SQLOLEDB;Data Source=MyServer;Initial Catalog=MyDatabase;
    User ID=MyUID;Password=MyPassword;
```

Starting with SQL Server 2000, you can have multiple instances of SQL Server installed on the same machine. You can specify the instance you want to connect to by using the following syntax in the *Data Source* attribute:

```
Provider=SQLOLEDB;Data Source=MyServer\MyInstance;
    Initial Catalog=MyDatabase;User ID=MyUID;Password=MyPassword;
```

If you want to connect to SQL Server using your network credentials, use the *Integrated Security* attribute and omit the username and password:

```
Provider=SQLOLEDB;Data Source=MyServer;Initial Catalog=MyDatabase;
    Integrated Security=SSPI;
```

Some old habits are hard to break. When connecting to SQL Server using the previous technology (ODBC), you can use your network credentials by using the *Trusted_Connection* attribute. The SQL Server OLE DB provider accepts this same attribute as an alias for *Integrated Security*. I continue to use this slightly older syntax primarily because the value *Yes* is easier to remember than *SSPI*:

```
Provider=SQLOLEDB;Data Source=MyServer;
    Initial Catalog=MyDatabase;Trusted_Connection=Yes;
```

See the *Microsoft Data Access SDK* for the full list of options available through this provider.

OLE DB Provider for Oracle Databases

Developers who want to use ADO.NET with Oracle databases need to do a little more than just install ADO.NET and build a connection string. Both the Microsoft OLE DB Provider for Oracle and the Microsoft ODBC Driver for Oracle communicate with Oracle's client components rather than directly with the

Oracle database. In order to use ADO.NET with Oracle, you have to install the appropriate version of the Oracle client utilities (SQL*Net) and create a database alias. Then you can use a connection string such as this:

```
Provider=MSDAORA;Data Source=MyDatabaseAlias;
    User ID=MyUID;Password=MyPassword;
```

If you're looking to learn more about any of the above database provider options, see the documentation for these OLE DB providers in the Microsoft Data Access SDK.

OLE DB Provider for Access Databases

If you're connecting to an Access database, you can use the OLE DB provider for Access databases, Microsoft Jet 4.0 OLE DB Provider. To use this provider, you specify the provider name and version and the location of your database in the connection string, as follows:

```
Provider=Microsoft.Jet.OLEDB.4.0;Data Source=C:\Path\To\MyDatabase.MDB;
```

If you don't specify the entire path to your database, ADO will look for the database in your application's working path. You can also use relative paths. For example, if your database is in the Data subdirectory of your application, you can use the following connection string:

```
Provider=Microsoft.Jet.OLEDB.4.0;
    Data Source=Data\MyDatabase.MDB;
```

A number of other options are available when you connect using the Jet OLE DB provider. See the Microsoft Data Access SDK for the exhaustive list. I'll show you examples of the two most commonly used options here. One option is connecting to an Access database that uses Jet security:

```
Provider=Microsoft.Jet.OLEDB.4.0;
    Data Source=C:\...\MySecure.MDB;
    Jet OLEDB:System database=C:\...\MySystem.MDW;
    User ID=MyUserName;Password=MyPassword;
```

Another option is connecting to an Access database that has a database password:

```
Provider=Microsoft.Jet.OLEDB.4.0;
    Data Source=C:\...\MyPasswordProtected.MDB;
    Jet OLEDB:Database Password=MyPassword;
```

OLE DB Provider for ODBC Drivers

Developers who have used ADO might be familiar with the OLE DB Provider for ODBC Drivers, which is often referred to by its code name, Kagera. Until version 2, this was the only provider included with the Microsoft Data Access Components. Kagera acts as a bridge from OLE DB to the earlier data access technology, ODBC, by translating OLE DB API calls to ODBC API calls. This provider enabled developers to use ADO to talk to ODBC drivers.

Using the OLE DB .NET data provider to talk to this OLE DB provider to then talk to ODBC drivers might sound overly complex. It is. This is why the Microsoft development team developed the ODBC .NET data provider, which I'll cover in Appendix A.

If you want to communicate with your data source through an ODBC driver, use the ODBC .NET data provider. Attempts to use Kagera with the OLE DB .NET data provider will generate an exception.

Using Data Links to Build Connection Strings in Code

If you want to build connection strings in code, you can use the same user interface that Visual Studio 6 and Visual Studio .NET use—the Data Links dialog box. This tabbed dialog box lets you select an OLE DB provider and then enter values for a data source, user name, password, and other provider-specific attributes. You might remember this dialog box from when we created a new Connection using the Data Form Wizard in Chapter 2.

To use the Data Links dialog box in your Visual Studio .NET application, you must first add a reference to the Data Link's library. From your project, right-click on your project in Solution Explorer and choose Add Reference. Click on the COM tab of the Add Reference dialog box and add references to Microsoft ActiveX Data Objects 2.7 Library (commonly referred to as ADO) and the Microsoft OLE DB Service Component 1.0 Type Library. See Figure 3-2.

> **Note** These libraries contain COM components. When you add a reference to them, Visual Studio .NET will ask whether you want a wrapper generated for the libraries. For the purposes of this sample, click Yes. For more information on COM interoperability, see the MSDN documentation.

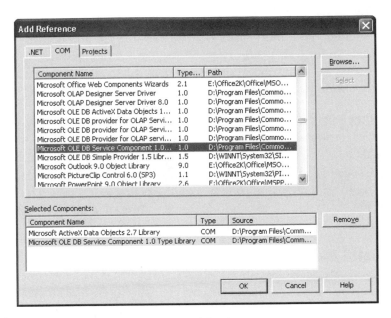

Figure 3-2   The Add Reference dialog box

You can then use the following code to launch the Data Links dialog box and retrieve the connection string that it returns based on the user's input:

Visual Basic .NET

```
Dim objDataLink As New MSDASC.DataLinks()
Dim cn As New ADODB.Connection()

objDataLink.PromptEdit(cn)
Console.WriteLine(cn.ConnectionString)
```

Visual C# .NET

```
MSDASC.DataLinks objDataLink = new MSDASC.DataLinksClass();
ADODB.Connection cn = new ADODB.ConnectionClass();
object objCn = (object) cn;
objDataLink.PromptEdit(ref objCn);
Console.WriteLine(cn.ConnectionString);
```

If, like me, you have trouble remembering the different connection string attributes, the Data Links dialog box will simplify your work by letting you quickly set options and then examine the resulting connection string. This approach lets me worry about more important things, like what Peter Gammons has to say about my beloved Red Sox in his columns on ESPN's Web site.

Using Data Links to Build Connection Strings Manually

You don't have to write code to examine the connection strings that the Data Links dialog box builds. You simply create a file with a .udl extension, and it will be associated with the Data Links dialog box. You then double-click on the file and set the appropriate properties on the dialog box's tabs. The file is a simple text file that you can examine in a text editor such as Notepad. *Voila!* You have your new connection string.

Using Data Link Files in a Connection String

Rather than hard-code a connection string in your application or build one dynamically, you can reference a Data Link file in your connection string. In this way, you can let the installation program (or the user, if you're trusting by nature) build the appropriate connection string and store it in the Data Link file.

To use a Data Link file in a connection string, you can use a name-value pair in the string, such as the following:

```
File Name=MyDataLink.udl;
```

If you don't specify a full path to the data link file, the OLE DB .NET data provider will look in the current working directory for your application. You can also use relative paths in your connection string:

```
File Name=SettingsSubDir\MyDataLink.udl;
```

Opening and Closing Connections

Once you have a *OleDbConnection* object with a valid connection string, you should open the connection so you can communicate with your data store. To open the connection, you simply call its *Open* method:

Visual Basic .NET

```
Dim strConn As String = "Provider=SQLOLEDB;Data Source=(local)\NetSDK;" & _
                        "Initial Catalog=Northwind;Trusted_Connection=Yes;"
Dim cn As New OleDbConnection(strConn)
cn.Open()
```

Visual C# .NET

```
string strConn = "Provider=SQLOLEDB;Data Source=(local)\\NetSDK;" +
                 "Initial Catalog=Northwind;Trusted_Connection=Yes;";
OleDbConnection cn = new OleDbConnection(strConn);
cn.Open();
```

To close a Connection object, you simply call its Close method:

Visual Basic .NET

```
Dim strConn As String = "Provider=SQLOLEDB;Data Source=(local)\NetSDK;" & _
                 "Initial Catalog=Northwind;Trusted_Connection=Yes;"
Dim cn As New OleDbConnection(strConn)
cn.Open()
...
cn.Close()
```

Visual C# .NET

```
string strConn = "Provider=SQLOLEDB;Data Source=(local)\\NetSDK;" +
                 "Initial Catalog=Northwind;Trusted_Connection=Yes;";
OleDbConnection cn = new OleDbConnection(strConn);
cn.Open();
...
cn.Close();
```

Closing the Connection object will not close the actual connection to your data source if you're using connection pooling.

Connection Pooling

Opening and closing database connections is expensive. If you're developing a multi-tiered application, connection pooling will probably improve your application's performance.

What Is Connection Pooling?

Connection pooling is a fairly simple concept. Imagine a multi-tiered application, such as the one shown in Figure 3-3.

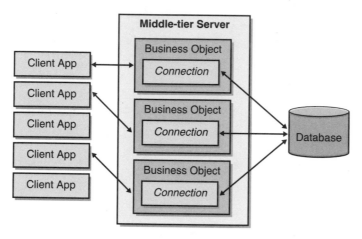

Figure 3-3   A simple multi-tiered application

Whenever a client application actively communicates with the middle-tier server, that server creates a business object that connects to and queries a database. Each business object maintains its own connection. When the middle tier creates a new business object, the business object creates a new *Connection* object. When the middle tier releases an existing business object, the business object closes and releases its connection.

Generally, the business object will close its connection in its clean-up code. As I mentioned earlier, database connections are expensive. Rather than close the database connection, what if we stored it in a pool? Then, when a new business object starts up, it will check the pool for an existing connection. If the pool contains an open connection, the business object can use it. Otherwise, the business object can create a new connection. Figure 3-4 shows an example of such an application.

Connection pooling in ADO.NET is that simple. In fact, in some ways it's even simpler. The .NET data providers included with ADO.NET each implement connection pooling. When you request a new connection, the .NET data provider examines the credentials you've supplied (database location, user name, and so forth) and searches the pool for an open connection with matching credentials. If it locates such a connection, it hands you that connection. Otherwise, it creates and returns a new connection.

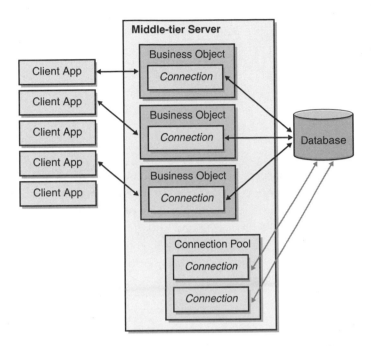

Figure 3-4   A multi-tiered application with connection pooling

When you close a connection object, the .NET data provider doesn't really close the actual database connection. It marks the connection object as closed but stores the database connection in a pool. If the database connection is not reused within a specified amount of time (60 seconds by default), the .NET data provider closes the connection.

How Do I Turn On Connection Pooling?

This is the simplest part. Connection pooling is turned on by default. The following code snippet opens and closes the same *Connection* object five times. Because connection pooling is turned on by default, the actual connection to the database isn't actually closed when you call the *Close* method. Instead, the database connection is sent to the pool where it is later reused.

Visual Basic .NET

```
Dim strConn As String = "Provider=SQLOLEDB;Data Source=(local)\NetSDK;" & _
                        "Initial Catalog=Northwind;Trusted_Connection=Yes;"
Dim cn As New OleDbConnection(strConn)
Dim intCounter As Integer
For intCounter = 1 To 5
    cn.Open()
    cn.Close()
Next
```

Visual C# .NET

```
string strConn = "Provider=SQLOLEDB;Data Source=(local)\\NetSDK;" +
                 "Initial Catalog=Northwind;Trusted_Connection=Yes;";
OleDbConnection cn = new OleDbConnection(strConn);
for (int intCounter = 1; intCounter <= 5; intCounter++)
{
    cn.Open();
    cn.Close();
}
```

Connection pooling is handled on a separate thread. As a result, the code might create a second connection to your database. When the code reaches the call to the *Open* method in the second iteration of the *For* loop, the connection pooling routine might not have finished storing the initial database connection to the pool. You can add the following line of code between the call to the *Connection* object's *Close* method and the end of the *For* loop to suspend the current thread and allow other threads to execute. The code will then use only a single connection:

```
System.Threading.Thread.Sleep(0)
```

What if I Don't Want to Pool My Connections?

OK, here's the not-quite-so-simple part. Sometimes you won't want to use connection pooling. For example, if you're working with a classic two-tiered application in which the client application communicates directly with the database, you probably won't want to use connection pooling. Connection pooling is turned on by default, so how do you turn it off?

The *OleDbConnection* class implements a *ReleaseConnectionPool* method. You could try to use this method in conjunction with the *Collect* method on the global garbage collection object to truly close the physical connection to your database. However, there's a more elegant way. You can add the following attribute to your OLE DB connection string:

```
OLE DB Services=-4;
```

When you use this connection string attribute, the OLE DB .NET data provider will mark your connection so that it doesn't participate in connection pooling. When you call the *Close* method on your *OleDbConnection* object, you'll close the actual connection to your database.

If you're using the *SqlConnection* object, you can add the following connection string attribute to tell the .NET data provider that you don't want to pool the connection:

```
Pooling=False;
```

How Do I Know Whether I've Truly
Closed My Connection or Have Simply Pooled It?

There are many ways to check the number of connections to SQL Server, but some are more elegant than others. I prefer using SQL Profiler or Performance Monitor to watch the number of connections to my databases. You can also use Enterprise Manager or you can check the results of repeated calls to a system stored procedure.

Destroying Connections

Many of the classes in the ADO.NET object model, such as the *Connection* class, expose a *Dispose* method. Calling this method on an object allows the object to free its resources prior to garbage collection. If you don't call the *Dispose* method explicitly, the object will release its resources when the common language runtime's garbage collection routine instructs the object to release its resources.

Releasing an open Connection by letting the object go out of scope or by setting the object variable to Nothing or null (depending on your language of choice) won't close the connection to your data source until the object is cleaned up by garbage collection. Calling *Dispose* on a Connection marked as open will implicitly call its *Close* method.

As a general rule, if an object exposes a *Dispose* method, you should call it when you want to release the object's resources.

Using Connections to Create Other Objects

You can use *Connection* objects to create other objects—*Command* objects and *Transaction* objects. Creating objects in this fashion might save you a couple lines of code.

Creating Commands

The *Command* object, which I'll cover in Chapter 4, is the object you use to query your data source. In order to execute a query, you must set the *Command* object's *Connection* property to a *Connection* object. The *Connection* object provides a *CreateCommand* method that you can use to simplify the process. This method returns a new *Command* object that's already initialized to use your *Connection* object.

The following code snippets are equivalent:

Visual Basic .NET

```
Dim strConn As String = "Provider=SQLOLEDB;Data Source=(local)\NetSDK;" & _
                        "Initial Catalog=Northwind;Trusted_Connection=Yes;"
Dim cn As New OleDbConnection(strConn)
cn.Open()
Dim cmd As New OleDbCommand()
cmd.Connection = cn
```

   is equivalent to

```
Dim strConn As String = "Provider=SQLOLEDB;Data Source=(local)\NetSDK;" & _
                        "Initial Catalog=Northwind;Trusted_Connection=Yes;"
Dim cn As New OleDbConnection(strConn)
cn.Open()
Dim cmd As OleDbCommand = cn.CreateCommand()
```

Visual C# .NET

```
string strConn = "Provider=SQLOLEDB;Data Source=(local)\\NetSDK;" +
                 "Initial Catalog=Northwind;Trusted_Connection=Yes;";
OleDbConnection cn = new OleDbConnection(strConn);
cn.Open();
OleDbCommand cmd = new OleDbCommand();
cmd.Connection = cn;
```

   is equivalent to

```
string strConn = "Provider=SQLOLEDB;Data Source=(local)\\NetSDK;" +
                 "Initial Catalog=Northwind;Trusted_Connection=Yes;";
OleDbConnection cn = new OleDbConnection(strConn);
cn.Open();
OleDbCommand cmd = cn.CreateCommand();
```

I occasionally use the *CreateCommand* method in my Visual Basic .NET code when I want to create and use a *Command* object that I'll use once. Using *CreateCommand* along with a *With* block allows you to create and use a *Command* object without explicitly using a variable name:

Visual Basic .NET

```
With cn.CreateCommand()
    .CommandText = "CREATE TABLE MyTable ..."
    .ExecuteNonQuery()
    .Dispose()
End With
```

C# offers somewhat similar functionality through the *using* statement. One major difference between the two languages is that the C# code implicitly calls the *Dispose* method on the *OleDbCommand* object at the end of the block, while the Visual Basic .NET *With* block does not. Thus, I've added the call to the *OleDbCommand* object's *Dispose* method in the Visual Basic .NET code:

Visual C# .NET

```
using (OleDbCommand cmd = cn.CreateCommand() {
    cmd.CommandText = "CREATE TABLE MyTable ...";
    cmd.ExecuteNonQuery();
}
```

Whether it's wise to use such programming constructs is debatable. Some might say that the preceding code snippet is simple and elegant. Others might argue that it lends itself to sloppy code that might be difficult to maintain. Personally, I think it's pretty slick. In the course of writing this book, I've written countless code snippets in Visual Studio .NET against the OLE DB, SQL, and ODBC .NET data providers. If I change the definition of the *Connection* object from an *OleDbConnection* to a *SqlConnection* (along with the connection string, of course), the code to create and execute the *Command* does not need to be changed. Sometimes there's something to be said for stupid coding tricks.

Starting Transactions

You can also use the *Connection* object to start transactions. The *Connection* object's *BeginTransaction* method returns a new open *Transaction* object on your connection. We'll discuss the *Transaction* object in detail in Chapter 10.

The following code snippets are equivalent:

Visual Basic .NET

```
Dim strConn As String = "Provider=SQLOLEDB;Data Source=(local)\NetSDK;" & _
                        "Initial Catalog=Northwind;Trusted_Connection=Yes;"
Dim cn As New OleDbConnection(strConn)
cn.Open()
Dim txn As New OleDbTransaction()
txn.Connection = cn
txn.Begin()
```

is equivalent to

```
Dim strConn As String = "Provider=SQLOLEDB;Data Source=(local)\NetSDK;" & _
                        "Initial Catalog=Northwind;Trusted_Connection=Yes;"
Dim cn As New OleDbConnection(strConn)
cn.Open()
Dim txn As OleDbTransaction = cn.BeginTransaction()
```

Visual C# .NET

```
string strConn = "Provider=SQLOLEDB;Data Source=(local)\\NetSDK;" +
                 "Initial Catalog=Northwind;Trusted_Connection=Yes;";
OleDbConnection cn = new OleDbConnection(strConn);
cn.Open();
OleDbTransaction txn = new OleDbTransaction();
txn.Connection = cn;
txn.Begin();
```

is equivalent to

```
string strConn = "Provider=SQLOLEDB;Data Source=(local)\\NetSDK;" +
                 "Initial Catalog=Northwind;Trusted_Connection=Yes;";
OleDbConnection cn = new OleDbConnection(strConn);
cn.Open();
OleDbTransaction txn = cn.BeginTransaction();
```

Retrieving Database Schema Information

The *OleDbConnection* lets you retrieve schema information about your database through the *GetOleDbSchemaTable* method. You supply a value from the *OleDbSchemaGuid* enumeration to specify the type of schema information you want, such as tables, columns, and procedures.

The *GetOleDbSchemaTable* method also requires a parameter called Restrictions, which acts as a filter on the schema information that the method returns. For example, rather than retrieving information for all columns in your database, you can retrieve information for just the columns in a particular table. The *Restrictions* parameter contains an array of values. Each schema type allows a different set of restrictions.

If you want to retrieve information about all of the columns in all of the tables in your database, you should omit the *Restrictions* parameter, as shown in the following code:

Visual Basic .NET

```
Dim strConn As String = "Provider=SQLOLEDB;Data Source=(local)\NetSDK;" & _
                        "Initial Catalog=Northwind;Trusted_Connection=Yes;"
Dim cn As New OleDbConnection(strConn)
cn.Open()
Dim tbl As DataTable
tbl = cn.GetOleDbSchemaTable(OleDbSchemaGuid.Tables, Nothing)
```

Visual C# .NET

```
string strConn = "Provider=SQLOLEDB;Data Source=(local)\\NetSDK;" +
                 "Initial Catalog=Northwind;Trusted_Connection=Yes;";
OleDbConnection cn = new OleDbConnection(strConn);
cn.Open();
DataTable tbl;
tbl = cn.GetOleDbSchemaTable(OleDbSchemaGuid.Tables, null);
```

However, if you want to retrieve the columns from just a specific table, you should use the *Restrictions* parameter and supply the name of the table whose columns you want to examine. The MSDN documentation for the *Tables* member of the *OleDbSchemaGuid* enumeration states that the *Restrictions* array for the member should have the following structure:

```
{"TABLE_CATALOG", "TABLE_SCHEMA", "TABLE_NAME", "COLUMN_NAME"}
```

Therefore, you can use the following code to retrieve just the columns from the Customers table:

Visual Basic .NET

```
Dim strConn As String = "Provider=SQLOLEDB;Data Source=(local)\NetSDK" & _
                        "Initial Catalog=Northwind;Trusted_Connection=Yes;"
Dim cn As New OleDbConnection(strConn)
cn.Open()
Dim objRestrictions As Object()
objRestrictions = New Object() {Nothing, Nothing, "Customers", Nothing}
Dim tbl As DataTable
tbl = cn.GetOleDbSchemaTable(OleDbSchemaGuid.Columns, objRestrictions)
```

Visual C# .NET

```
string strConn = "Provider=SQLOLEDB;Data Source=(local)\\NetSDK;" +
                 "Initial Catalog=Northwind;Trusted_Connection=Yes;";
OleDbConnection cn = new OleDbConnection(strConn);
cn.Open();
string strRestrictions;
object[] objRestrictions;
objRestrictions = new object[] {null, null, "Customers", null};
DataTable tbl;
tbl = cn.GetOleDbSchemaTable(OleDbSchemaGuid.Columns, objRestrictions);
```

For information on the *Restrictions* parameter for a particular *OleDbSchema-Guid* value, see the MSDN documentation for that value.

The *GetOleDbSchemaTable* method returns a DataTable (a structure we'll examine in detail in Chapter 6) that contains the schema information you requested. The structure of the DataTable that the method returns depends on the type of schema you requested. We can use the following code to loop through the rows in the schema table of column information that we just retrieved:

Visual Basic .NET

```
...
tbl = cn.GetOleDbSchemaTable(OleDbSchemaGuid.Columns, strRestrictions)
Console.WriteLine("Columns in Customers table:")
For Each row In tbl.Rows
    Console.WriteLine(vbTab & row("COLUMN_NAME").ToString())
Next row
```

Visual C# .NET

```
...
tbl = cn.GetOleDbSchemaTable(OleDbSchemaGuid.Columns, strRestrictions);
Console.WriteLine("Columns in Customers table:");
foreach(DataRow row in tbl.Rows)
    Console.WriteLine("\t" + row["COLUMN_NAME"].ToString());
```

You can build a fairly simple application that uses the *GetOleDbSchema-Table* method to display schema information about your database (tables, views, stored procedures, and so forth), much like Server Explorer does.

The *GetOleDbSchemaTable* method relies on functionality in the OLE DB provider that your *OleDbConnection* is using. Not all OLE DB providers support all schema methods. If you request a schema that your OLE DB provider doesn't support, you'll throw a trappable exception.

Visual Studio .NET Design-Time Features

The Visual Studio .NET development environment includes features that make it easy to create Connections at design time and use those Connections at run time.

Working with Connections in Server Explorer

The ADO.NET development team built ADO.NET to help you build fast, scalable database applications. The Visual Studio .NET development team built a number of features into Visual Studio .NET to help you build those database applications faster. One such feature is Server Explorer.

Server Explorer lets you examine various operating system services and integrate them into your applications. As you can see in Figure 3-5, Server Explorer lists many of the common operating system services such as event logs, message queues, and performance counters. You can also drag items from Server Explorer onto design surfaces such as forms and components in Visual Studio .NET to easily create components at design time that you can access at run time.

Figure 3-5   Visual Studio .NET Server Explorer

For example, if you want to access or add items to the machine's event log from your application, you can drag and drop an item from the Event Logs portion of Server Explorer onto a designer and then add code to your application to call that item.

Server Explorer also lets you interact with your database from within the Visual Studio development environment. SQL Server is one of the services that Server Explorer makes available through its server-based interface. There's also a separate category toward the top of Server Explorer called Data Connections.

In Chapter 2, we looked at the user interface that the Data Form Wizard displayed to request connection information. When we entered that connection information, Visual Studio added an item to the Data Connections area in Server Explorer. You can see this in Figure 3-6 on the next page.

The items available beneath a connection depend on the type of database you've specified. Most databases support tables, views, and stored procedures. Some databases, such as recent versions of Oracle and SQL Server, support database diagrams and functions. Oracle also supports synonyms and packages. All of this information is available in Server Explorer.

You can expand a table to see the list of columns in the table. Click on a column, and you can see properties of the column in the Properties window. If you want to view the contents of a table or view, you can right-click on the item and choose Retrieve Data From Table. Server Explorer will display the contents of the table or view in a grid. The data might be updateable if you have permission to modify the data, and Server Explorer can retrieve the key information necessary to submit changes.

Figure 3-6   Data Connections in Server Explorer

If you're using the Enterprise Edition of Visual Studio .NET, you can also manage your SQL Server and Oracle databases. You can modify, create, and delete SQL Server and Oracle tables, views, stored procedures, database diagrams, and functions.

Adding a Data Connection to Server Explorer

You can add a data connection to Server Explorer by clicking the button at the top of Server Explorer that shows a yellow cylinder with an electrical cord attached. You can see in Figure 3-7 the same Data Link dialog box that you saw when we added a connection using the Data Form Wizard.

> **Note**   In diagrams, databases are represented almost universally by cylinders. I'm not entirely sure why, but my technical editor, Dail, informed me that this is "likely because a cylinder is the old flowchart symbol for mass storage—chosen because long, long ago random-access mass-storage devices used drums rather than disks." He also claimed not to be old enough to remember such drives before saying "Now go away and let me drink my Geritol in peace." He gets a little cranky when he hasn't had his afternoon nap.

Figure 3-7   Adding a new data connection to Server Explorer using the
Data Link Properties dialog box

OLE DB, ODBC, and .NET Data Providers

Adding connections to Server Explorer is straightforward in most, but not all, cases. To understand why things aren't always so simple, we'll need to discuss some low-level data access technologies, both past and present. The next couple of pages might look like condensed alphabet soup as a result. This information is geared toward developers who want to use ODBC drivers or .NET data providers other than those built for OLE DB or SQL Server.

The Data Link dialog box was originally designed as an interface for building connection strings in Visual Studio 6. The central data access technology in version 6 is ADO, which is based on a lower-level data access technology called OLE DB.

The Providers tab of the Data Link dialog box displays a list of OLE DB providers built to help you connect to a particular type of database such as SQL Server, Oracle, or Microsoft Access.

Before Microsoft developed OLE DB, the most prevalent data access technology was ODBC, OLE DB's predecessor. Developers communicated with their databases through ODBC drivers. In fact, many developers still build applications that rely on ODBC drivers because some databases have ODBC drivers but not an OLE DB provider.

The first OLE DB provider that Microsoft developed acted as a bridge between the two technologies by translating OLE DB calls to ODBC calls. This allows developers to use ADO, which uses OLE DB providers, with ODBC drivers. You'll see this provider listed on the Providers tab of the Data Link dialog box as Microsoft OLE DB Provider For ODBC Drivers. If you select this provider and then click on the Connection tab, you can select an ODBC data source or enter an ODBC connection string.

So far, we've discussed how to use the Data Link dialog box to connect to a data source using OLE DB and ODBC. But what about .NET data providers? As I mentioned earlier, the Data Link dialog box was built for Visual Studio 6. As of the release of Visual Studio .NET, there is no user interface for building connection strings for .NET data providers in general. Thus, you can add Data Connections to Server Explorer only if the desired data source has an OLE DB provider or ODBC driver.

Saving Password Information

You can enter a password in the Data Link dialog box and click the Test button to verify that you can connect successfully. For security reasons, the Data Link dialog box will not save the password that you entered into the new connection string unless you select the Allow Saving Password check box. If you select this check box, you'll see the warning shown in Figure 3-8.

Figure 3-8   The warning that appears if you try to save a password into a connection string

If you choose to save the password into the connection string, the password information will be used both at design time by Server Explorer and at run time by the applications you build. Thus, you won't have to enter the password again when Server Explorer connects to your database. However, this also means that if you use this connection string in your application, the password will be built into the application.

Microsoft doesn't recommend storing the password in your application in this fashion because it is not secure. Visual Studio .NET builds managed code, which can be decompiled. This means that users can decompile your application and find the connection string. If this possibility makes you uncomfortable, you should omit the password from the connection string, and prompt the user for the password—or use integrated security, which we'll discuss next.

Integrated Security

Who says you need a password to connect to your database? Some database systems, such as SQL Server, allow you to connect using your network identity. This feature is known by a number of different names—network authentication,

Windows authentication, Windows NT authentication, or integrated security. It's a fairly simple concept. Rather than relying on the user to specify a username and password, the database asks the network to identify the user. The database then checks its user list to determine whether that user has permission to connect.

For more information on using SQL Server with integrated security, look under Administering SQL Server\ Managing Security\ Security Levels\ Authentication Modes in SQL Server Books Online.

Adding Connections to Your Application

Now that you've seen how to add data connections to Server Explorer, let's talk about how you can use Server Explorer to add a *Connection* to your application. It's as simple as dragging and dropping. Just select the desired connection in Server Explorer, and drag-and-drop it onto the designer in your project. You'll see a new *Connection* in the component tray for the designer.

The Component Tray

Many Visual Studio .NET project items—such as Windows forms, component classes, Web forms, and ASP.NET Web services—allow you to interact with controls and components in a visual fashion. If you're working with a simple Windows form, you can place visual controls such as buttons and text boxes on the form. You can set the properties of these controls in the Properties window. This feature is old hat to developers who've used development tools such as Visual Basic or Microsoft Visual InterDev.

But what if you want to add a component that, unlike a control on a form, has no user interface? Previous versions of Visual Basic treated such components as controls, and those components appeared as icons on your forms, but only at design time. Visual Studio .NET takes a slightly different approach. Components that have no user interface appear in a tray below the designer—the component tray. The component tray lets you interact with these components and set their properties at design time in the Properties window.

Using Your New Connection

When you drag-and-drop a data connection from Server Explorer onto a designer, you create a *Connection* object in the designer's component tray. The type of *Connection* will depend on the type of data connection you selected in Server Explorer. Dragging and dropping a SQL Server connection creates a *Sql-Connection*, while dragging and dropping a connection in Server Explorer that uses any other data source creates an *OleDbConnection*.

> **Note**   As of this writing, you cannot drag-and-drop connections from Server Explorer that use ODBC drivers. You'll receive an error stating that the OLE DB provider for ODBC drivers cannot be used. Look for the ability to create an *OdbcConnection* object, the *Connection* object for the ODBC .NET Data Provider, in this fashion in a future release.

Figure 3-9 shows what you'll see if you drag-and-drop a SQL Server data connection from Server Explorer onto a designer such as a Windows form:

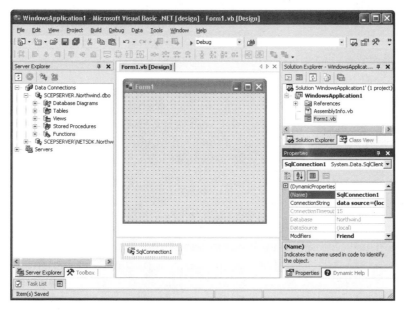

Figure 3-9   The new *SqlConnection1* object appears in the Visual Studio .NET components tray.

Because we dragged a SQL Server connection onto the designer, we received a *SqlConnection*. Visual Studio .NET automatically names new components based on the class name. This new *SqlConnection* is already initialized. Its *ConnectionString* property is set to the connection string for the corresponding data connection in Server Explorer.

Creating Connections Using the Toolbox

You can also create Connections by dragging and dropping items from the Data tab in the Visual Studio .NET Toolbox. This lets you specify which .NET data provider's *Connection* you want to use. Figure 3-10 shows a new *OleDbConnection* created by dragging and dropping the *OleDbConnection* from the Toolbox.

Figure 3-10   Setting the connection string using the Properties window

Note that none of the properties are set...yet. The main property for a *Connection* object, regardless of the .NET data provider you're using, is the *ConnectionString* property. You can select the *ConnectionString* property in the Properties window and type a value for the property by hand. Or, you can ask Visual Studio .NET for a little help.

You can select the *ConnectionString* property in the Properties window and view a drop-down list of available connections from Server Explorer. (Figure 3-9 shows an example.) At the end of the list, you'll see a <New Connection...> entry. Select this entry, and you'll launch the Data Link dialog box.

Using the New Connection at Run Time

Now that we've created a new connection at design time, let's use it at run time. Drag a button object onto your Windows form, and double-click the button to launch the code editor. You'll see that Visual Studio .NET creates a procedure to handle the button's click event. Add the following code to that event:

Visual Basic .NET

```
SqlConnection1.Open()
MessageBox.Show("Connection opened successfully!")

SqlConnection1.Close()
MessageBox.Show("Connection closed successfully!")
```

Visual C# .NET

```
sqlConnection1.Open();
MessageBox.Show("Connection opened successfully!");

sqlConnection1.Close();
MessageBox.Show("Connection closed successfully!");
```

> **Note** If you used an *OleDbConnection* instead of a *SqlConnection* in your project, change *SqlConnection*1 in the preceding code to *OleDbConnection1*.

Now launch your project and click the button. You'll see dialog boxes that tell you that you successfully opened and closed the connection to your database.

Where's the Code?

So far, we've built a fairly simplistic application. We created a *SqlConnection* at design time and added a button and some code to use it at run time. Figure 3-11 shows the code we added. But how did the *SqlConnection* get in the application?

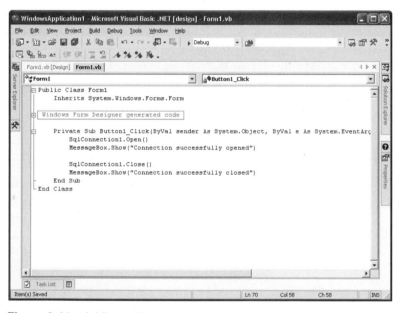

Figure 3-11 Adding code

Visual Studio .NET translates the objects that you create at design time, such as the *SqlConnection* in the component tray and the button on the form, into code. It then stores this code in the component's *InitializeComponent* procedure. This procedure is hidden by default in the region marked Windows Form Designer Generated Code, as shown earlier in Figure 3-11.

There are two main reasons why this code is hidden by default. First, developers generally want to focus on the code they've written rather than the code the designers have generated. You can click on the plus sign to the left to expand the region if you choose. Second, and more important, Microsoft strongly cautions against changing code in this region.

Most of the Visual Studio .NET designers that generate the code in this region are reentrant. The button we drew on the form is a simple example of this reentrancy. As you can see in Figure 3-12, the Windows Forms Designer translated the button we drew at design time into run-time code.

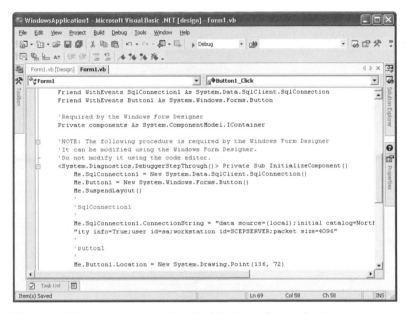

Figure 3-12   Code generated by the Windows Forms Designer

If you close and reopen the project and display the form in the Windows Forms Designer, the designer will use this code to draw the button on your form. Microsoft strongly cautions against changing code in this region because the designers that read the code might not be able to interpret the changes you make, so you might not be able to edit your component within the designer.

Will you get a warning ahead of time? Probably not. Will you know ahead of time whether the designer will successfully interpret the changes you've made in this region? Probably not. If you're going to make changes in this fashion, you should definitely create a backup of your project ahead of time.

OleDbConnection Object Reference

While writing this book I've wrestled with the structure of the reference-based Chapters, 3 through 8. I wanted to provide developers with a complete guide to ADO.NET but also wanted the text to flow smoothly. At this point I expect that you understand the role of the *Connection* object in database applications and are comfortable using its major features. The following section is intended to fill in some of the blanks and cover the less-frequently-used but still important features of the object.

Read it now or save it for later. This reference material does not introduce new characters, nor does it contain any unexpected plot twists that will affect your ability to understand subsequent chapters.

Without further ado, let's take a closer look at the properties and methods of the *OleDbConnection* object.

Properties of the *OleDbConnection* Object

The only property on the *OleDbConnection* class that's not read-only is the *ConnectionString* property. This property accepts a connection string that the *OleDbConnection* will use to try to connect to your data source when you call the Open method. Table 3-1 contains the properties you'll use most often when working with an *OleDbConnection* object.

Table 3-1   Commonly Used Properties of the *OleDbConnection* Object

Property	Data Type	Description
ConnectionString	*String*	Controls how the *OleDbConnection* object will connect to your data source
ConnectionTimeout	*Int32*	Specifies how long, in seconds, the *OleDbConnection* will try to connect to your data source (read-only)
Database	*String*	Returns the name of the database you are, or will be, connected to (read-only)
DataSource	*String*	Returns the location of the database you are, or will be, connected to (read-only)
Provider	*String*	Returns the name of the OLE DB provider the *OleDbConnection* will use to connect to your data source (read-only)
ServerVersion	*String*	Returns the version of your data source (read-only)
State	*Connection-State*	Indicates the current state of the *OleDbConnection* (open or closed) (read-only)

ConnectionString Property

The *ConnectionString* property controls how the *Connection* object will attempt to connect to your data source. You can set this property only when your *Connection* is not connected to your data source. When it's connected to your data source, the property is read-only.

ConnectionTimeout Property

The *ConnectionTimeout* property indicates the amount of time, in seconds, that the OLE DB provider will wait on an attempt to connect to your data source before timing out.

This property is read-only because not all OLE DB providers support this feature. For example, the Microsoft OLE DB provider for SQL Server supports this feature, while the Microsoft OLE DB providers for Jet and Oracle databases do not.

So how do you tell the OLE DB provider how you long you want to wait before timing out? By using the connection string attribute *Connect Timeout*. Here's an example of a connection string that uses the Microsoft OLE DB Provider for SQL Server and the *Connect Timeout* attribute:

```
"Provider=SQLOLEDB;Data Source=(local)\NetSDK;Initial Catalog=Northwind;
    Trusted_Connection=Yes;Connect Timeout=11;"
```

If you set a value for the *Connect Timeout* attribute in your connection string and the OLE DB provider you're using doesn't support this feature, you'll throw an exception when you call the *Open* method on the *OleDbConnection*.

Database and *DataSource* Properties

The terms *database* and *data source* are often used interchangeably, as they are in this book. But the *Connection* object exposes each as a separate property. So how do they differ?

In our discussion of connection strings, you might have noticed that each connection string used the *Data Source* attribute followed by the location of the data source we wanted to connect to. Similarly, the *Connection* object's *DataSource* property contains the location of the data source referenced in our connection string. If you're working with a server-based data store, such as SQL Server or Oracle, the *DataSource* property will return the name of the machine acting as the server. For file-based databases, such as Access, the *DataSource* property will return the location of the data file.

When we discussed connection strings that use the SQL Server OLE DB provider, you learned how to specify an instance of SQL Server in a connection string as part of the *Data Source* attribute. If you use a connection string that includes information specifying the desired instance of SQL Server, that information will be returned in the *DataSource* property, just as it appears in the connection string.

So, what information does the *Database* property return? This property is designed for data sources that support multiple databases, such as SQL Server. When we examined SQL Server connection strings, we specified the database on the server we wanted to connect to in the *Initial Catalog* attribute of the connection string.

> **Note**   The SQL Server ODBC driver supports the same functionality in the *Database* attribute. For the SQL Server OLE DB provider, the two attributes are interchangeable.

Provider Property

The *OleDbConnection* class exposes the *Provider* property to let you determine the OLE DB provider specified in the connection string. The *OdbcConnection* property exposes a similar property, *Driver*, which returns the name of the ODBC driver specified in the connection string. Because the *SqlConnection* class supports connecting only to SQL Server databases, there is no need for such a property.

ServerVersion Property

Most database systems introduce new features with each successive version. SQL Server 2000, for example, supports returning the results of a query as XML. For this reason, you can check the *ServerVersion* property to ensure you don't make unsupported calls to a server. The *SourceVersion* property returns a string containing the version of the database to which you're connected. Developers with a SQL Server background might be familiar with the SELECT @@Version query. The *SourceVersion* property returns a subset of the information returned by SELECT @@Version—the database's version number.

Let's say your application communicates with different SQL Server databases, using the OLE DB, ODBC or SQL .NET data provider, and there are certain queries that you can run only against servers running SQL Server 2000 or later. In such a situation, you can use the following code to determine whether to run your query:

Visual Basic .NET

```
Dim strConn As String = "Provider=SQLOLEDB;Data Source=(local)\NetSDK;" & _
                        "Initial Catalog=Northwind;Trusted_Connection=Yes;"
Dim cn As New OleDbConnection(strConn)
cn.Open()
If cn.ServerVersion >= "08" Then
    'Run your query here.
End If
```

Visual C# .NET

```
string strConn = "Provider=SQLOLEDB;Data Source=(local)\\NetSDK;" +
                 "Initial Catalog=Northwind;Trusted_Connection=Yes;";
OleDbConnection cn = new OleDbConnection(strConn);
cn.Open();
if (cn.ServerVersion >= "08") {
    //Run your query here.
}
```

State Property

The *Connection* object's State property returns the current state of the connection as a member of the *ConnectionState* enumeration in the *System.Data* namespace. Table 3-2 contains the constants, values, and descriptions of possible connection states.

Table 3-2 Connection State Constants

Constant	Value	Description
Broken	16	The connection is broken. A connection is considered broken if it has been opened but is then unable to communicate with the data store for whatever reason (such as network problems or the server being reset). Not used in initial release of ADO.NET.
Closed	0	The connection is closed.
Connecting	2	The connection is in the process of connecting. Not used in initial release of ADO.NET.
Executing	4	The connection is executing a query. Not used in initial release of ADO.NET.
Fetching	8	The connection is busy fetching data. Not used in initial release of ADO.NET.
Open	1	The connection is open.

The *ConnectionState* enumeration contains a number of values that aren't used in the initial release of ADO.NET. Currently, the *Connection* object's *State* property will return either *Open* or *Closed*. Future releases might support combinations of these values to indicate that a connection is open but is currently executing a query.

You can use the *Connection* object's *StateChange* event to determine when the value of the *State* property changes.

Methods of the *OleDbConnection* Object

Table 3-3 lists the *OleDbConnection* object's methods. Methods such as *GetType* and *ToString* that are common to most objects in the .NET Framework are omitted. Take a look at the table to familiarize yourself with these methods. I discuss each one following the table.

Table 3-3   Commonly Used Methods of the *OleDbConnection* Object

Method	Description
BeginTransaction	Begins a transaction on the connection
ChangeDatabase	Changes the current database on an open connection
Close	Closes the connection
CreateCommand	Creates an *OleDbCommand* for the current connection
GetOleDbSchemaTable	Retrieves schema information from the data source
Open	Opens the connection
ReleaseObjectPool	Releases the connection from the OLE DB connection pool

BeginTransaction Method

If you want to start a transaction on your connection—to lock data or to ensure that you can commit or roll back a series of changes to your data store—call the *BeginTransaction* method on the *Connection* object. This method returns a new *Transaction* object, a class we'll discuss in depth in Chapter 10 when we discuss updating your database.

> **Note**   Developers who've used the connection objects in ADO, RDO, or DAO might expect methods of the *Connection* object to commit or roll back a transaction. In the ADO.NET object model, the *BeginTransaction* method generates a new *Transaction* object. When you want to commit or roll back a transaction, call *Commit* or *Rollback* on the *Transaction* object.

Because *BeginTransaction* creates a new transaction, associates it with the connection that created it, and initializes the transaction, using this method of the *Connection* object can simplify your code slightly. The following code snippets are functionally equivalent:

Visual Basic .NET

```
Dim txn As OleDb.OleDbTransaction = cn.BeginTransaction()
```

is equivalent to

```
Dim txn As New OleDb.OleDbTransaction()
txn.Connection = cn
txn.Begin()
```

Visual C# .NET

```
OleDbTransaction txn = cn.BeginTransaction();
```

is equivalent to

```
OleDbTransaction txn = new OleDbTransaction();
txn.Connection = cn;
txn.Begin();
```

ChangeDatabase Method

Earlier in the chapter, we talked about SQL Server's ability to support multiple databases on a single server. If you're working with SQL Server, you can change the database you're communicating with by executing a query such as this one:

```
USE Northwind
```

ADO.NET also offers a simpler method for changing the database. The *Connection* object has a *ChangeDatabase* method that simplifies the process. The following code snippets are equivalent:

Visual Basic .NET

```
Dim cn As New OleDbConnection(strConn)
cn.Open()
...
cn.ChangeDatabase("Northwind")
```

is equivalent to

```
Dim cn As New OleDbConnection(strConn)
cn.Open()
...
Dim cmd As OleDbCommand = cn.CreateCommand()
cmd.CommandText = "USE Northwind"
cmd.ExecuteNonQuery()
```

Visual C# .NET

```
OleDbConnection cn = new OleDbConnection(strConn);
cn.Open();
...
cn.ChangeDatabase("Northwind");
```

> is equivalent to

```
OleDbConnection cn = new OleDbConnection(strConn);
cn.Open();
...
OleDbCommand cmd = cn.CreateCommand();
cmd.CommandText = "USE Northwind";
cmd.ExecuteNonQuery();
```

Close Method

To close a *Connection*, you call the object's *Close* method. Remember that if you're using connection pooling, you're simply sending the physical connection to your data source to the pool.

Calling the *Close* method on a *Connection* object that's already marked as closed will not generate an exception.

CreateCommand Method

You can also create new *Command* objects by using the *Connection* class's *CreateCommand* method. This method accepts no arguments and returns a new *Command* object whose *Connection* property is set to the *Connection* object that created it.

The following code snippets are functionally equivalent:

Visual Basic .NET

```
Dim strConn As String = "Provider=SQLOLEDB;Data Source=(local)\NetSDK;" & _
                        "Initial Catalog=Northwind;Trusted_Connection=Yes;"
Dim cn As New OleDbConnection(strConn)
Dim cmd As OleDb.OleDbCommand = cn.CreateCommand()
```

> is equivalent to

```
Dim strConn As String = "Provider=SQLOLEDB;Data Source=(local)\NetSDK;" & _
                        "Initial Catalog=Northwind;Trusted_Connection=Yes;"
Dim cn As New OleDbConnection(strConn)
Dim cmd As New OleDb.OleDbCommand()
cmd.Connection = cn
```

Visual C# .NET

```
string strConn = "Provider=SQLOLEDB;Data Source=(local)\\NetSDK;" +
                 "Initial Catalog=Northwind;Trusted_Connection=Yes;";
OleDbConnection cn = new OleDbConnection(strConn);
OleDbCommand cmd = cn.CreateCommand();
```

is equivalent to

```
string strConn = "Provider=SQLOLEDB;Data Source=(local)\\NetSDK;" +
                 "Initial Catalog=Northwind;Trusted_Connection=Yes;";
OleDbConnection cn = new OleDbConnection(strConn);
OleDbCommand cmd = new OleDbCommand();
cmd.Connection = cn;
```

GetOleDbSchemaTable Method

The *OleDbConnection* lets you retrieve schema information about your database through the *GetOleDbSchemaTable* method. You supply a value from the *OleDbSchemaGuid* enumeration to specify the type of schema information you want, such as tables, columns, and procedures.

The *GetOleDbSchemaTable* method also requires a parameter called *Restrictions*, which acts as a filter on the schema information returned by the method. For example, rather than retrieving information for all columns in your database, you can retrieve information for just the columns in a particular table. The *Restrictions* parameter contains an array of values. Each schema type allows a different set of restrictions.

If you want to retrieve information about all of the columns in all of the tables in your database, you should omit the *Restrictions* parameter, as shown in the following code:

Visual Basic .NET

```
Dim strConn As String = "Provider=SQLOLEDB;Data Source=(local)\NetSDK;" & _
                        "Initial Catalog=Northwind;Trusted_Connection=Yes;"
Dim cn As New OleDbConnection(strConn)
cn.Open()
Dim tbl As DataTable
tbl = cn.GetOleDbSchemaTable(OleDbSchemaGuid.Tables, Nothing)
```

Visual C# .NET

```
string strConn = "Provider=SQLOLEDB;Data Source=(local)\\NetSDK;" +
                 "Initial Catalog=Northwind;Trusted_Connection=Yes;";
OleDbConnection cn = new OleDbConnection(strConn);
cn.Open();
DataTable tbl;
tbl = cn.GetOleDbSchemaTable(OleDbSchemaGuid.Tables, null);
```

However, if you want to retrieve the columns from just a specific table, use the *Restrictions* parameter and supply the name of the table whose columns you want to examine. The MSDN documentation for the *Tables* member of the *OleDbSchemaGuid* enumeration states that the *Restrictions* array for the member should have the following structure:

```
{"TABLE_CATALOG", "TABLE_SCHEMA", "TABLE_NAME", "COLUMN_NAME"}
```

You can use the following code to retrieve just the columns from the Customers table:

Visual Basic .NET

```
Dim strConn As String = "Provider=SQLOLEDB;Data Source=(local)\NetSDK;" & _
                        "Initial Catalog=Northwind;Trusted_Connection=Yes;"
Dim cn As New OleDbConnection(strConn)
cn.Open()
Dim objRestrictions As Object()
objRestrictions = New Object() {Nothing, Nothing, "Customers", Nothing}
Dim tbl As DataTable
tbl = cn.GetOleDbSchemaTable(OleDbSchemaGuid.Columns, objRestrictions)
```

Visual C# .NET

```
string strConn = "Provider=SQLOLEDB;Data Source=(local)\\NetSDK;" +
                 "Initial Catalog=Northwind;Trusted_Connection=Yes;";
OleDbConnection cn = new OleDbConnection(strConn);
cn.Open();
object[] objRestrictions;
objRestrictions = new object[] {null, null, "Customers", null};
DataTable tbl;
tbl = cn.GetOleDbSchemaTable(OleDbSchemaGuid.Columns, objRestrictions);
```

For information on the *Restrictions* parameter for a particular *OleDbSchemaGuid* value, see the MSDN documentation for that value.

The *GetOleDbSchemaTable* method returns a *DataTable* (a structure we'll examine in detail in Chapter 6), which contains the schema information you requested. The structure of the *DataTable* that the method returns will depend on the type of schema you requested. You can use the following code to loop through the rows in the schema table of column information that we just retrieved:

Visual Basic .NET

```
...
Dim row as DataRow
tbl = cn.GetOleDbSchemaTable(OleDbSchemaGuid.Columns, objRestrictions)
Console.WriteLine("Columns in Customers table:")
For Each row In tbl.Rows
    Console.WriteLine(vbTab & row("COLUMN_NAME").ToString())
Next row
```

Visual C# .NET

```
...
tbl = cn.GetOleDbSchemaTable(OleDbSchemaGuid.Columns, objRestrictions);
Console.WriteLine("Columns in Customers table:");
foreach(DataRow row in tbl.Rows)
    Console.WriteLine("\t" + row["COLUMN_NAME"].ToString());
```

You can build a fairly simple application that uses the *GetOleDbSchema-Table* method to display schema information about your database (such as tables, views, and stored procedures) similar to how Server Explorer displays that information.

The *GetOleDbSchemaTable* method relies on functionality in the OLE DB provider that your *OleDbConnection* is using. Not all OLE DB providers support all schema methods. If you request a schema that your OLE DB provider doesn't support, you'll throw a trappable exception.

Open Method

To open a connection to your data source, call the *Connection* object's *Open* method. The *Connection* object will attempt to connect to your data source based on the information provided in the object's *ConnectionString* property. If the attempt to connect fails, the *Connection* object will throw an exception.

Visual Basic .NET

```
Dim strConn As String = "Provider=SQLOLEDB;Data Source=(local)\NetSDK;" & _
                        "Initial Catalog=Northwind;Trusted_Connection=Yes;"
Dim cn As New OleDbConnection(strConn)
Try
    cn.Open()
Catch ex As Exception
    Console.WriteLine("Attempt to connect failed!" & vbCrLf & ex.Message)
End Try
```

Visual C# .NET

```
string strConn = "Provider=SQLOLEDB;Data Source=(local)\\NetSDK;" +
                 "Initial Catalog=Northwind;Trusted_Connection=Yes;";
OleDbConnection cn = new OleDbConnection(strConn);
try
{
    cn.Open();
}
catch (Exception ex)
{
    Console.WriteLine("Attempt to connect failed!\n" + ex.Message);
}
```

Calling the *Open* method on a *Connection* object that's already opened will close and then reopen the connection. If connection pooling is enabled, this scenario might generate an additional connection to your data source. When the initial connection is closed, it's sent to the pool. However, because pooling is handled on another thread, the initial connection might not be available when the *Connection* object requests a connection to the data source based on the connection string.

ReleaseObjectPool Method

The *ReleaseObjectPool* method can help you manage OLE DB connection pooling within your components. Calling *ReleaseObjectPool* on your connection, or on the *OleDbConnection* class itself, releases your reference to the pool.

In all honesty, you'll rarely need to use this method. With the Visual Studio .NET beta, most developers wanted to use this method to truly close a physical connection to the data store rather than to simply send the physical connection to the pool. In such cases, you're better off creating your connection so it won't be pooled in the first place. To do that, include the following snippet in the connection string:

```
OLE DB Services=-4;
```

If you use this attribute and value in your connection string, your connection to the data source will be closed rather than pooled when you call the *Close* method on the *OleDbConnection* class.

Events of the *OleDbConnection* Object

The *OleDbConnection* object exposes two events, *InfoMessage* and *StateChange*, as described in Table 3-4.

Table 3-4   Events of the *OleDbConnection* Object

Event	Description
InfoMessage	Fires when the connection receives an informational message from the data source
StateChange	Fires when the *State* property of the connection changes

InfoMessage Event

Some database systems, such as SQL Server, support informational messages. SQL Server lets you send messages to the client via the PRINT command. These messages are not returned as errors, nor are they included with the results of a query.

You can use the *Connection* object's *InfoMessage* event to trap for such messages. The following code snippet shows how you can log informational messages.

Visual Basic .NET

```
Dim strConn As String = "Provider=SQLOLEDB;Data Source=(local)\NetSDK;" & _
                        "Initial Catalog=Northwind;Trusted_Connection=Yes;"
Dim cn As New OleDbConnection(strConn)
AddHandler cn.InfoMessage, AddressOf cn_InfoMessage
cn.Open()
With cn.CreateCommand()
    .CommandText = "PRINT 'Hello ADO.NET!'"
    .ExecuteNonQuery()
End With

Public Sub cn_InfoMessage(ByVal sender As Object, _
        ByVal e As System.Data.OleDb.OleDbInfoMessageEventArgs)
    Console.WriteLine("InfoMessage event occurred")
    Console.WriteLine(vbTab & "Message received: " & e.Message)
End Sub
```

Visual C# .NET

```
string strConn = "Provider=SQLOLEDB;Data Source=(local)\\NetSDK;" +
                "Initial Catalog=Northwind;Trusted_Connection=Yes;";
OleDbConnection cn = new OleDbConnection(strConn);
cn.InfoMessage += new OleDbInfoMessageEventHandler(cn_InfoMessage);
cn.Open();
OleDbCommand cmd = cn.CreateCommand();
cmd.CommandText = "PRINT 'Hello ADO.NET'";
cmd.ExecuteNonQuery();
```

(continued)

```
static void cn_InfoMessage(object sender, OleDbInfoMessageEventArgs e)
{
    Console.WriteLine("InfoMessage event occurred");
    Console.WriteLine("\tMessage received: " + e.Message);
}
```

> **Note**   SQL Server also supports generating informational messages using the RAISERROR command. Errors created with this command are treated as informational messages if the error's severity level is 10 or below. For more information, see *SQL Server Books Online*.

Visual Basic .NET code snippets involving events

Visual Basic .NET provides two ways for you to add code to handle the events that an object exposes. The first way, which we'll use throughout this book, is by using the *AddHandler* statement. There's also a way to add code to handle events that involves less typing.

In Figure 3-13 you see the Visual Basic .NET code editor. There's a variable named *cn* with module-level scope. The *Dim* statement includes the *WithEvents* keyword. When you declare a variable using this keyword, you can use Visual Basic .NET to easily create the procedures to handle the object's events.

Just above the code are two drop-down list boxes. The list box on the left lists the code module and any object variables with module scope that expose events. You'll see that the *OleDbConnection* object has been selected in this list box. When you select an object variable that exposes events in the list box on the left, the list box on the right lists the events that the object exposes.

Once you select one of the available events, Visual Basic .NET creates a procedure with the appropriate signature that you can use to handle the event of that object.

While this is an extremely handy feature for developers, it poses a challenge to authors. Object variables declared with the *WithEvents* keyword must be at module-level scope, which means I need to denote that anytime I declare variables in code. The code snippets would need to look like this:

```
'At module level
Dim WithEvents cn As OleDbConnection

Dim strConn As String = "Provider=SQLOLEDB;Data Source=(local)\NetSDK;" & _
                        "Initial Catalog=Northwind;Trusted_Connection=Yes;"
cn = New OleDbConnection(strConn)
AddHandler cn.StateChange, AddressOf cn_StateChange
cn.Open()
cn.Close()

Public Sub cn_StateChange(ByVal sender As Object, _
                          ByVal e As System.Data.StateChangeEventArgs)
    Console.WriteLine("StateChange event occurred")
    Console.WriteLine(vbTab & "From " & e.OriginalState.ToString)
    Console.WriteLine(vbTab & "To " & e.CurrentState.ToString)
End Sub
```

Using *AddHandler* simplifies the code snippets slightly. More important, if you're working with the electronic version of the book, code snippets that use *AddHandler* are a little easier to cut and paste.

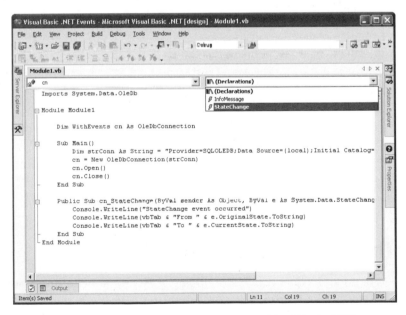

Figure 3-13   Adding code to handle events in Visual Basic .NET

StateChange Event

The *Connection* object's *StateChange* event fires whenever the value of its *State* property changes. This event can prove handy if you display the current state of your connection in, say, a status bar at the bottom your application's main form.

Visual Basic .NET

```
Dim strConn As String = "Provider=SQLOLEDB;Data Source=(local)\NetSDK;" & _
                        "Initial Catalog=Northwind;Trusted_Connection=Yes;"
Dim cn As New OleDbConnection(strConn)
AddHandler cn.StateChange, AddressOf cn_StateChange
cn.Open()
cn.Close()


Public Sub cn_StateChange(ByVal sender As Object, _
                          ByVal e As System.Data.StateChangeEventArgs)
    Console.WriteLine("StateChange event occurred")
    Console.WriteLine(vbTab & "From " & e.OriginalState.ToString)
    Console.WriteLine(vbTab & "To " & e.CurrentState.ToString)
End Sub
```

Visual C# .NET

```
string strConn = "Provider=SQLOLEDB;Data Source=(local)\\NetSDK;" +
                 "Initial Catalog=Northwind;Trusted_Connection=Yes;";
OleDbConnection cn = new OleDbConnection(strConn);
cn.StateChange += new StateChangeEventHandler(cn_StateChange);
cn.Open();
cn.Close();


static void cn_StateChange(object sender, StateChangeEventArgs e)
{
    Console.WriteLine("StateChange event occurred");
    Console.WriteLine("\tFrom " & e.OriginalState.ToString());
    Console.WriteLine("\tTo " & e.CurrentState.ToString());
}
```

Questions That Should Be Asked More Frequently

Q.   When I add a data connection to Server Explorer, I can shut down and restart, and Visual Studio .NET will remember my settings. Where does Server Explorer store those settings?

A.   Server Explorer stores its settings on a per-user basis. If multiple developers use Visual Studio .NET on the same machine, their Server

Explorer settings will be stored separately, in a file named (Default View).SEView. This file resides in a subfolder in that user's Settings folder. That means that unless you formatted your drive to use NTFS, passwords in Server Explorer data connections are readily available to anyone who can access that machine.

Q.   I'm building an application that will use SQL Server as the back-end database. Should I use standard or integrated security?

A.   This is a complex issue. The appropriate solution might depend on the architecture of your application and how you choose to manage security on your SQL Server database. I prefer using integrated security in two-tier applications and standard security in multi-tiered applications.

Using integrated security prevents you from having to prompt the user for credentials or hard-code them into the application. Using standard security in a multi-tiered application (where your data access code runs in a Web service or COM+ component) lets you take advantage of connection pooling. In this architecture, the component determines the user's credentials. That might sound like a cop-out, and in some ways it is. However, I think it's also a totally valid solution.

What if the only point at which your middle-tier component validates the user's credentials is in the data access code? If the database says that the user doesn't have access, that generally means you didn't want the user to access this feature of the middle-tier object in the first place. If that's the case, you're wasting time and might be compromising security by letting the user run the code in the component that precedes the call to connect to your database.

You're better off setting up security so that the user must have the proper credentials to access the component. You can then have the component use a standard connection string. Because all clients will use the same connection string, your component will be able to use all of their connections with a single pool. If all of your users connect to your database using different credentials, you're not taking advantage of pooling.

For more information on using SQL Server with standard and integrated security, see *SQL Server Books Online*.

Q.   For security purposes, the *Connection* that I'm using in my application has limited access to my database. However, I still want to take advantage of some of the database administration features in Server Explorer, such as creating or modifying the structure of my tables. How do I balance the security of the connection I'm using in my application at run time with the functionality I want to use at design time?

A.   Use multiple connections in Server Explorer. You can simply add a new connection to Server Explorer that uses an account with more database privileges. If you don't actually use the connection in your application, it won't be included in your application.

4

Querying Your Database

In Chapter 3, you learned how to connect to a database using the Microsoft ADO.NET *Connection* object. Now it's time to learn how to execute queries against your database. In the ADO.NET object model, you execute queries using the *Command* object.

In this chapter, I'll first focus on specific tasks you'll want to perform that involve the *Command* object. Along the way, I'll also introduce two other ADO.NET objects: the *DataReader* and *Parameter* objects. (*DataReader* objects allow you to examine the results of your queries, and *Parameter* objects allow you to execute parameterized queries.) Then I'll explain how you can create *Command* objects quickly and easily using features of the Microsoft Visual Studio .NET development environment. Finally, we'll examine the properties, methods, and events of the *Command*, *DataReader*, and *Parameter* objects.

Using *Command* Objects in Code

Command objects let you execute many different types of queries. Some *Command* objects retrieve data in the form of a result set, and others modify the content or structure of the data store. Let's look at how to create *Command* objects and use them to perform a variety of tasks.

Creating a *Command* Object

You can create a *Command* object in three ways. The first way is to simply create a new instance of an object using the new keyword and then set the appropriate properties. Or, you can use one of the available constructors to specify the query string and a *Connection* object. The third way is to call the *CreateCommand* method of the *Connection* object (which we examined in Chapter 3), as shown here:

Visual Basic .NET

```
Dim strConn, strSQL As String
strConn = "Provider=SQLOLEDB;Data Source=(local)\NetSDK;" & _
        "Initial Catalog=Northwind;Trusted_Connection=Yes;"
strSQL = "SELECT CustomerID, CompanyName FROM Customers"
Dim cn As New OleDbConnection(strConn)
cn.Open()
Dim cmd As OleDbCommand

cmd = cn.CreateCommand()
cmd.CommandText = strSQL

cmd = New OleDbCommand()
cmd.CommandText = strSQL
cmd.Connection = cn

cmd = New OleDbCommand(strSQL, cn)
```

Visual C# .NET

```
string strConn, strSQL;
strConn = "Provider=SQLOLEDB;Data Source=(local)\\NetSDK;" +
        "Initial Catalog=Northwind;Trusted_Connection=Yes;";
strSQL = "SELECT CustomerID, CompanyName FROM Customers";
OleDbConnection cn = new OleDbConnection(strConn);
cn.Open();
OleDbCommand cmd;

cmd = cn.CreateCommand();
cmd.CommandText = strSQL;

cmd = new OleDbCommand();
cmd.CommandText = strSQL;
cmd.Connection = cn;

cmd = new OleDbCommand(strSQL, cn);
```

Executing a Non-Row-Returning Query

Queries that don't return a result set are generally referred to as *action queries*—a term we'll use occasionally in this text. There are two main categories of action queries:

- **Data manipulation language (DML) queries** Also known as query-based updates (QBUs), these modify the contents of your database. Here are a few examples:

    ```
    UPDATE Customers SET CompanyName = 'NewCompanyName'
        WHERE CustomerID = 'ALFKI'
    ```

```
INSERT INTO Customers (CustomerID, CompanyName)
        VALUES ('NewID', 'NewCustomer')
```

```
DELETE FROM Customers WHERE CustomerID = 'ALFKI'
```

■ **Data definition language (DDL) queries**   These modify the structure of your database, as shown in the following examples:

```
CREATE TABLE Table1 (Field1 int NOT NULL
                        CONSTRAINT PK_Table1 PRIMARY KEY,
                        Field2 varchar(32))
```

```
ALTER VIEW View1 AS SELECT Field1, Field2 FROM Table1
```

```
DROP PROCEDURE StoredProcedure1
```

To execute an action query, you create a *Command* object, set its *Connection* property to an open connection, set its *CommandText* property to the query string you want to submit, and call the Command's *ExecuteNonQuery* method, as shown here:

Visual Basic .NET

```
Dim cn As New OleDbConnection()
cn.ConnectionString = "Provider=SQLOLEDB;Data Source=(local)\NetSDK:" & _
                    "Initial Catalog=Northwind;Trusted_Connection-Yes;"
cn.Open()
Dim cmd As OleDbCommand = cn.CreateCommand()
cmd.CommandText = "UPDATE Customers SET CompanyName = 'NewCompanyName'" & _
                " WHERE CustomerID = 'ALFKI'"
cmd.ExecuteNonQuery()
```

Visual C# .NET

```
OleDbConnection cn = new OleDbConnection();
cn.ConnectionString = "Provider=SQLOLEDB;Data Source=(local)\\NetSDK;" +
                    "Initial Catalog=Northwind;Trusted_Connection=Yes;";
cn.Open();
OleDbCommand cmd = cn.CreateCommand();
cmd.CommandText = "UPDATE Customers SET CompanyName = 'NewCompanyName' " +
                "WHERE CustomerID = 'ALFKI'";
cmd.ExecuteNonQuery();
```

> **Note**   Despite what the *ExecuteNonQuery* method's name implies, action queries are valid queries. They simply don't return rows. I'm not entirely sure why the method is called *ExecuteNonQuery*. (I just work here.)

Executing an action query is often only half the battle. When you execute the following query, there are two possible outcomes, success or failure:

```
CREATE TABLE NewTable (NewTableID int NOT NULL
                       CONSTRAINT PK_NewTable PRIMARY KEY,
                       OtherField varchar(32))
```

The query either successfully creates your new table or fails, perhaps because a table of the same name already exists, you didn't use the right syntax for the query, or you don't have an open connection to your database. The point here is that if you execute the query and it doesn't generate an error, you successfully created your new table.

With action queries that are designed to modify or delete an existing row, you need to do more than simply execute the query successfully. Let's take another look at the query we executed in a code snippet on the previous page (to change the company name for a specific customer):

```
UPDATE Customers SET CompanyName = 'NewCompanyName'
       WHERE CustomerID = 'ALFKI'
```

In some cases, executing this query might not modify that customer's company name—for example, if another user has deleted this row from your table. The database will execute the query, but because no rows satisfy the criteria in the WHERE clause, the query will not modify any rows. To the database, this outcome does not constitute failure.

So, how can you tell whether the query modified one row? If you submit this query in a tool such as Microsoft SQL Server Query Analyzer, you'll see a message like this one:

```
(1 row(s) affected)
```

Keep in mind that if the action query doesn't modify any rows because no rows satisfied the criteria in the WHERE clause, no error occurs.

The *Command* lets you retrieve this information by returning the number of rows affected by your query as the return value of the *ExecuteNonQuery* method, as shown here:

Visual Basic .NET

```
Dim strConn As String
strConn = "Provider=SQLOLEDB;Data Source=(local)\NetSDK;" & _
          "Initial Catalog=Northwind;Trusted_Connection=Yes;"
Dim cn As New OleDbConnection(strConn)
cn.Open()
Dim cmd As OleDbCommand = cn.CreateCommand()
cmd.CommandText = "UPDATE Customers SET CompanyName = 'NewCompanyName'" & _
                  " WHERE CustomerID = 'ALFKI'"
Dim intRecordsAffected As Integer = cmd.ExecuteNonQuery()
```

```
If intRecordsAffected = 1 Then
    Console.WriteLine("Update succeeded")
Else
    'Assume intRecordsAffected = 0
    Console.WriteLine("Update failed")
End If
```

Visual C# .NET

```
string strConn;
strConn = "Provider=SQLOLEDB;Data Source=(local)\\NetSDK;" +
          "Initial Catalog=Northwind;Trusted_Connection=Yes;";
OleDbConnection cn = new OleDbConnection(strConn);
cn.Open();
OleDbCommand cmd = cn.CreateCommand();
cmd.CommandText = "UPDATE Customers SET CompanyName = 'NewCompanyName' " +
                  "WHERE CustomerID = 'ALFKI'";
int intRecordsAffected = cmd.ExecuteNonQuery();
if (intRecordsAffected == 1)
    Console.WriteLine("Update succeeded");
else
    //Assume intRecordsAffected = 0
    Console.WriteLine("Update failed");
```

In the code, we assume that if the query didn't modify one row, it modified zero rows. But there are other possible return values from *ExecuteNonQuery*. If you execute anything other than a DML query, *ExecuteNonQuery* will return –1. There are also situations in which a DML query will modify more than one row.

However, in the code snippet, we used the table's primary key field in the WHERE clause. Because the Customer table uses the *CustomerID* field as its primary key, no two rows can have the same value for the *CustomerID* field. We therefore know that the query cannot modify more than one row.

Using a *DataReader* Object to Examine the Results of a Query

What if you want to execute a query that returns a result set? The *Command* object has an *ExecuteReader* method that returns a *DataReader* object that you can use to examine the results of your query.

The *DataReader* object is similar to other reader objects in the .NET Framework, such as the *XmlReader*, *TextReader*, and *StreamReader* objects. Each of these objects is an efficient, lightweight object that lets you examine (in a read-only fashion) the data that the object exposes. The *TextReader* object, for example, has methods that let you read the contents of a text file one line at a time. Similarly, the *DataReader* exposes properties and methods that let you loop through the results of your query.

Developers who've worked with RDO and ADO or the lower-level ODBC and OLE DB API might be familiar with the term *firehose cursor*. This is the mechanism that databases use to return the results of a query as quickly as possible. Firehose cursors forgo functionality in favor of performance. Once you've read one row from the result set and moved on to the next row, the previous row is no longer available. The results come at you fast and furious, like water from a fire hose—hence the name. The ADO.NET *DataReader* lets you access the firehose cursor directly. To create a *DataReader*, you simply call the *Execute-Reader* method on a *Command* object.

Fetching the Results

The following code snippet shows how to examine the results of a simple query using a *DataReader* object:

Visual Basic .NET

```
Dim strConn, strSQL As String
strConn = "Provider=SQLOLEDB;Data Source=(local)\NetSDK;" & _
          "Initial Catalog=Northwind;Trusted_Connection=Yes;"
Dim cn As New OleDbConnection(strConn)
cn.Open()
strSQL = "SELECT CustomerID, CompanyName FROM Customers"
Dim cmd As New OleDbCommand(strSQL, cn)
Dim rdr As OleDbDataReader = cmd.ExecuteReader()
While rdr.Read()
    Console.WriteLine(rdr("CustomerID") & " - " & rdr("CompanyName"))
End While
rdr.Close()
```

Visual C# .NET

```
string strConn, strSQL;
strConn = "Provider=SQLOLEDB;Data Source=(local)\\NetSDK;" +
          "Initial Catalog=Northwind;Trusted_Connection=Yes;";
OleDbConnection cn = new OleDbConnection(strConn);
cn.Open();
strSQL = "SELECT CustomerID, CompanyName FROM Customers";
OleDbCommand cmd = new OleDbCommand(strSQL, cn);
OleDbDataReader rdr = cmd.ExecuteReader();
while (rdr.Read())
    Console.WriteLine(rdr["CustomerID"] + " - " + rdr["CompanyName"]);
rdr.Close();
```

Note that the code calls the *Read* method before reading the first row of the result set because the first row is not available immediately after you call *ExecuteReader*. This represents a change from previous object models such as ADO. The *DataReader* that the *Command* object returns does not make the first row of data available until you call the *Read* method.

The first time you call the *Read* method, the *DataReader* moves to the first row in the result set. Subsequent calls to the *Read* method move to the next row.

The method also returns a Boolean value to indicate whether the *DataReader* had another row available. So, if *Read* returns *True*, the *DataReader* moved to the next available row. When the *Read* method returns *False*, you've reached the end of the results.

Fetching Faster

The *DataReader* has a default parameterized property named *Item*. The preceding code snippet implicitly used the *Item* property to access the values stored in the CustomerID and CompanyName columns in the result set. This code is inefficient, however. We can improve the performance of the code in two ways.

Using ordinal-based lookups   We supplied the name of the column in our code snippet. In order to return the value stored in that column, the *DataReader* has to locate the column in its internal structure based on the string we supplied. Remember that in our code snippet, we ask the *DataReader* to perform that string-based lookup for each row in the result set. Supplying the index, or ordinal, for the column will improve the performance of our code.

This coding technique can be applied to nearly all objects that expose collections. I've recommended this technique to many developers who were writing ADO code and looking for ways to improve performance. Most developers have agreed that this technique would improve performance, but some have hesitated for fear it might limit their flexibility.

The order of the columns in your result set won't change unless you change the query string or you make a change to the structure of your database object (table, view, or stored procedure) and you're retrieving all columns that your database object returns. In the vast majority of applications, you can hard-code the index values for each column into your application without encountering problems.

However, you might encounter situations where you'll know the column name but not its index. The *DataReader* offers an elegant way to determine a column's index based on its name. The *GetOrdinal* method accepts a string that represents the column name and returns an integer to denote that column's ordinal. This method is a welcome addition to the ADO.NET object model because it can help you improve performance without losing the flexibility that comes with string-based lookups.

The following code snippet improves on our original *DataReader* code snippet. It uses the *GetOrdinal* method to get the ordinal values for the two columns we want to examine and then uses those values to examine the contents of each row. This improves performance because we perform a string-based search of the collection only once per column. In our original code snippet, we performed the string-based search each time we fetched data from a column.

Visual Basic .NET

```
...
Dim rdr As OleDbDataReader = cmd.ExecuteReader()
Dim intCustomerIDOrdinal As Integer = rdr.GetOrdinal("CustomerID")
Dim intCompanyNameOrdinal As Integer = rdr.GetOrdinal("CompanyName")
While rdr.Read()
    Console.WriteLine(rdr(intCustomerIDOrdinal) & " - " & _
                        rdr(intCompanyNameOrdinal))
End While
rdr.Close()
```

Visual C# .NET

```
...
OleDbDataReader rdr = cmd.ExecuteReader();
int intCustomerIDOrdinal = rdr.GetOrdinal("CustomerID");
int intCompanyNameOrdinal = rdr.GetOrdinal("CompanyName");
while (rdr.Read())
    Console.WriteLine(rdr[intCustomerIDOrdinal] + " - " +
                        rdr[intCompanyNameOrdinal]);
rdr.Close();
```

But we're not done yet....

Using the appropriate type-specific *Get* method   The *DataReader* also exposes a series of methods that return data in the different .NET Framework data types (such as *string*, *32-bit integer*, *decimal*, and *double*). Currently, our code snippet implicitly uses the *Item* property, which returns the contents of the specified column in the generic *Object* data type. To display the value stored in the console window, the console has to convert the generic object to a string. Because the CustomerID and CompanyName columns contain string data, we can use the *GetString* method of the *DataReader* to return the contents of the columns as a string, as shown here:

Visual Basic .NET

```
...
Dim rdr As OleDbDataReader = cmd.ExecuteReader()
Dim intCustomerIDOrdinal As Integer = rdr.GetOrdinal("CustomerID")
Dim intCompanyNameOrdinal As Integer = rdr.GetOrdinal("CompanyName")
While rdr.Read()
    Console.WriteLine(rdr.GetString(intCustomerIDOrdinal) & " - " & _
                        rdr.GetString(intCompanyNameOrdinal))
End While
rdr.Close()
```

Visual C# .NET

```
...
OleDbDataReader rdr = cmd.ExecuteReader();
```

```
int intCustomerIDOrdinal = rdr.GetOrdinal("CustomerID");
int intCompanyNameOrdinal = rdr.GetOrdinal("CompanyName");
while (rdr.Read())
    Console.WriteLine(rdr.GetString(intCustomerIDOrdinal) + " - " +
                      rdr.GetString(intCompanyNameOrdinal));
rdr.Close();
```

You should always use the type-specific *Get* method that corresponds to the data returned by the column in the result set. Let's say we want to query the sample *Northwind* database for the OrderID and ProductID columns in the Order Details table and display the results in a list box. Even though the list box will display the data as strings, we need to use the *GetInt32* method to fetch the contents of each of the columns. After we retrieve the data into an integer, we can convert the data to a string and display it in the list box.

Fetching Multiple Results

Some databases, such as SQL Server, allow you to execute a batch of queries that return multiple results. Let's say we want to issue the following query against the sample *Northwind* database:

```
SELECT CustomerID, CompanyName, ContactName, Phone FROM Customers;
SELECT OrderID, CustomerID, EmployeeID, OrderDate FROM Orders;
SELECT OrderID, ProductID, Quantity, UnitPrice FROM [Order Details]
```

In our previous *DataReader* code snippets, we looped through the results of our query until the *Read* method returned *False*. Using that same code with a batch query will loop through the results of the only first query in the batch.

The *DataReader* exposes a *NextResult* method that lets you move to the results of the next row-returning query. The *NextResult* method is similar to the *Read* method in that it returns a Boolean value to indicate whether there are more results. However, unlike with the *Read* method, you should not call this method initially.

When the *Read* method returns *False*, you can check to see whether there are additional results to fetch by calling the *NextResult* method. When the *Next-Result* method returns *False*, there are no more result sets. The following code snippet shows how to use the *NextResult* method to fetch the results of a batch query:

Visual Basic .NET

```
...
cn.Open()
Dim strSQL As String
strSQL = "SELECT CustomerID, CompanyName FROM Customers;" & _
         "SELECT OrderID, CustomerID FROM Orders;" & _
         "SELECT OrderID, ProductID FROM [Order Details]"
```

(continued)

```
Dim cmd As New OleDbCommand(strSQL, cn)
Dim rdr As OleDbDataReader = cmd.ExecuteReader()
Do
    Do While rdr.Read()
        Console.WriteLine(rdr(0) & " - " & rdr(1))
    Loop
    Console.WriteLine()
Loop While rdr.NextResult()
```

Visual C# .NET

```
...
cn.Open();
string strSQL = "SELECT CustomerID, CompanyName FROM Customers;" +
                "SELECT OrderID, CustomerID FROM Orders;" +
                "SELECT OrderID, ProductID FROM [Order Details]";
OleDbCommand cmd = new OleDbCommand(strSQL, cn);
OleDbDataReader rdr = cmd.ExecuteReader();
do
{
    while (rdr.Read())
        Console.WriteLine(rdr[0] + " - " + rdr[1]);
    Console.WriteLine();
} while (rdr.NextResult());
```

Executing Batches of Action Queries

Developers often encountered a problem when they used ADO with SQL Server to retrieve the result set generated by a stored procedure. If you call a SQL Server stored procedure using the SQL Server OLE DB provider and the stored procedure executes an action query prior to the row returning query, your *Recordset* will be marked as closed instead of containing the results of the row-returning query.

This behavior is actually by design. The closed *Recordset* corresponds to the action query. More precisely, it corresponds to the informational message "*n* row(s) affected" that the query returns. You have to call *NextRecordset* to move to the results of the next query. Or you can add the statement *SET NOCOUNT ON* in your stored procedure to suppress these messages, which allows ADO to move immediately to the results of the first row-returning query.

This behavior is not restricted to stored procedures. You can create a similar situation by executing batch queries. Let's take a look at such a batch query with ADO 2.*x* and Visual Basic "Classic."

Visual Basic "Classic"

```
Dim cn As ADODB.Connection, rs As ADODB.Recordset
Dim strConn As String, strSQL As String
Dim intRecordsAffected As Integer
```

```
strConn = "Provider=SQLOLEDB;Data Source=(local)\NetSDK;" & _
          "Initial Catalog=Northwind;Trusted_Connection=Yes;"
Set cn = New ADODB.Connection
cn.Open strConn

strSQL = "INSERT INTO Customers ...;" & _
         "SELECT CustomerID, CompanyName FROM Customers WHERE ...;" & _
         "UPDATE Customers SET CompanyName = ... WHERE ...;" & _
         "SELECT CustomerID, CompanyName FROM Customers WHERE ..."

Set rs = cn.Execute(strSQL, intRecordsAffected, adCmdText)
Do Until rs Is Nothing
    Debug.Print "rs.State = " & rs.State & vbTab & _
                "intRecordsAffected = " & intRecordsAffected
    Set rs = rs.NextRecordset(intRecordsAffected)
Loop
```

Initially, the *Recordset* is closed and the *intRecordsAffected* variable contains 1. These results correspond to the INSERT query, which does not return rows and modifies one record in the database. Once we call *NextRecordset*, the *Recordset* is open and contains the results of the first SELECT query. Because the SELECT query doesn't modify any records in the database, the *intRecordsAffected* variable returns –1. The second call to *NextRecordset* returns a closed *Recordset*, and *intRecordsAffected* now contains the number of records affected by the UPDATE query. Calling *NextRecordset* again returns the results of the second SELECT query and sets *intRecordsAffected* to –1. The last call to *NextRecordset* returns a *Recordset* set to *Nothing*, indicating that there are no more results to process.

ADO.NET handles this same batch query differently. The ADO.NET development team saw this scenario as one of the top developer frustrations with ADO. To simplify the process of working with batch queries, the *DataReader* automatically moves you to the results of the first row-returning query. I think most developers will be pleased with this change in behavior. Unfortunately, it comes with a trade-off.

As a result of this change, the *DataReader* does not provide a way for you to determine the number of rows modified by each individual action query. The *RecordsAffected* property on the *DataReader* acts as a running total. Probably the best way to explain this behavior is by showing an example:

Visual Basic .NET

```
Dim strConn, strSQL As String
strConn = "Provider=SQLOLEDB;Data Source=(local)\NetSDK;" & _
          "Initial Catalog=Northwind;Trusted_Connection=Yes;"
Dim cn As New OleDbConnection(strConn)
```

(continued)

```
cn.Open()
strSQL = "INSERT INTO Customers ...;" & _
         "SELECT CustomerID, CompanyName FROM Customers WHERE ...;" & _
         "UPDATE Customers SET CompanyName = ... WHERE ...;" & _
         "SELECT CustomerID, CompanyName FROM Customers WHERE ..."
Dim cmd As New OleDbCommand(strSQL, cn)
Dim rdr As OleDbDataReader = cmd.ExecuteReader()
Do
    Console.WriteLine("RecordsAffected = " & rdr.RecordsAffected)
    Do While rdr.Read()
        Console.WriteLine(vbTab & rdr.GetName(0) & " - " & rdr.GetValue(0))
    Loop
    Console.WriteLine()
Loop While rdr.NextResult()
```

Visual C# .NET

```
string strConn, strSQL;
strConn = "Provider=SQLOLEDB;Data Source=(local)\\NetSDK;" +
          "Initial Catalog=Northwind;Trusted_Connection=Yes;";
OleDbConnection cn = new OleDbConnection(strConn);
cn.Open();
strSQL = "INSERT INTO Customers ...;" +
         "SELECT CustomerID, CompanyName FROM Customers WHERE ...;" +
         "UPDATE Customers SET CompanyName = ... WHERE ...;" +
         "SELECT CustomerID, CompanyName FROM Customers WHERE ...";
OleDbCommand cmd = new OleDbCommand(strSQL, cn);
OleDbDataReader rdr = cmd.ExecuteReader();
do
{
    Console.WriteLine("RecordsAffected = " + rdr.RecordsAffected);
    while (rdr.Read())
        Console.WriteLine("\t" + rdr.GetName[0].ToString() +
                          " - " + rdr.GetValue[0].ToString());
    Console.WriteLine();
}
while (rdr.NextResult());
```

You probably noticed that the ADO.NET code looks similar to the ADO code. The results, however, are slightly different. When we create the *Data-Reader* by calling the *ExecuteReader* method on the *Command*, the *DataReader* is ready to return the results of the first SELECT query immediately. When we call *NextResult*, we move to the results of the second SELECT query. The second call to *NextResult* returns *False* because there are no more row-returning queries to process, and we leave the loop.

The other major change in behavior from ADO is the behavior of the *RecordsAffected* property of the *DataReader*. Let's assume that the INSERT query and the UPDATE query each modify one record in the database. The *RecordsAffected* property will return the sum of the records affected by all action queries preceding the row-returning query that the *DataReader* is currently fetching.

So, when the *ExecuteReader* method returns the *DataReader*, its *Records-Affected* property will return 1. After we call the *NextResult* method, the *Records-Affected* property will return 2.

Keep in mind that non-DML action queries (such as CREATE PROCEDURE and DROP TABLE) return –1 for the number of records they affect because they're not designed to affect records.

If you need to determine the number of rows affected by individual queries using ADO.NET, split the batch into its individual queries and execute each query separately.

Closing a *DataReader*

In the ADO.NET object model, it's vitally important that you close your *Data-Reader* objects as quickly as possible. As of this writing, a *Connection* object that has an open *DataReader* is considered blocked. If you try to open a second *DataReader* before closing the first one, you'll receive an exception whose text indicates that the operation "requires an open and available connection."

Developers who have some experience with ADO might be surprised by this restriction, but those who've used RDO might not. Different Microsoft data access technologies have handled this scenario differently.

If you try to open two firehose cursors against a SQL Server database using ADO, everything will just work and you won't receive an error. This is because the OLE DB specification states that when the current connection is blocked, the OLE DB provider will perform the requested action on a new connection.

RDO developers might recognize the error message "Connection is busy with results from another hstmt." ODBC does not do any behind-the-scenes work to try to help you out. If you try to use a connection that's busy, you'll simply receive an error message.

Which of these approaches (raising an error or performing the desired action on a new connection) is better? Developers, both inside and outside of Microsoft, can't seem to agree. In fact, each successive Microsoft data access technology has handled the scenario differently than its predecessor: VBSQL raises an error, DAO/Jet creates a new connection, RDO raises an error, ADO creates a new connection, and ADO.NET raises an error. As they say in New England, "If you don't like the weather, just wait a while."

> **Note**   I believe VBSQL predates DAO/Jet, but carbon dating is diffi-
> cult and the results are not 100 percent accurate.

The *DataReader* is built for performance. Regardless of the restriction that an open *DataReader* blocks a *Connection*, you should pull the results of your query off the wire as quickly as possible after issuing the query. If you need to move back and forth between the results of separate queries, you should use a *DataSet* or consider storing the results of your queries in a business object of some sort.

Executing a Query That Returns a Single Value

What if you want to execute a query and retrieve a single cell (one row, one column) of data? Here are two examples of queries that return a single value:

```
SELECT COUNT(*) FROM Customers
```

```
SELECT CompanyName FROM Customers WHERE CustomerID = 'ALFKI'
```

Using a *DataReader* or a *DataSet* to retrieve this single value is probably over-kill. The *Command* object has a method specifically designed for such queries: *ExecuteScalar*. This method returns the value through the generic object data type, which you can then convert to the desired data type, as shown here:

Visual Basic .NET

```
Dim strConn As String = "Provider=SQLOLEDB;Data Source=(local)\NetSDK;" & _
                         "Initial Catalog=Northwind;Trusted_Connection=Yes;"
Dim cn As New OleDbConnection(strConn)
cn.Open()
Dim cmd As OleDbCommand = cn.CreateCommand()

cmd.CommandText = "SELECT COUNT(*) FROM Customers"
Dim intCustomers As Integer = CInt(cmd.ExecuteScalar())

cmd.CommandText = "SELECT CompanyName FROM Customers " & _
                  "WHERE CustomerID = 'ALFKI'"
Dim strCompanyName As String = Convert.ToString(cmd.ExecuteScalar)
```

Visual C# .NET

```
string strConn = "Provider=SQLOLEDB;Data Source=(local)\\NetSDK;" +
                 "Initial Catalog=Northwind;Trusted_Connection=Yes;";
OleDbConnection cn = new OleDbConnection(strConn);
cn.Open();
OleDbCommand cmd = cn.CreateCommand();
cmd.CommandText = "SELECT COUNT(*) FROM Customers";
int intCustomers = Convert.ToInt32(cmd.ExecuteScalar());

cmd.CommandText = "SELECT CompanyName FROM Customers " +
                  "WHERE CustomerID = 'ALFKI'";
string strCompanyName = Convert.ToString(cmd.ExecuteScalar());
```

The *ExecuteScalar* method is a great example of a feature that offers a better solution to a coding scenario that you might not have even realized was fairly inefficient.

Executing a Parameterized Query

Let's say you're building an application that lets a user examine the orders that your customers have placed. If you have 20 customers, you won't want to write 20 separate functions to return the orders for each specific customer. Instead, you should build a parameterized function that accepts information about the customer and returns the orders for that customer. Similarly, you can build queries that accept parameters. Let's look at the query that you'd use in the parameterized function to return the orders for a particular customer:

```
SELECT OrderID, CustomerID, EmployeeID, OrderDate
    FROM Orders WHERE CustomerID = ?
```

The question mark is a parameter marker—the standard way of denoting a parameter in a query.

Note   The SQL Server .NET data provider doesn't support the generic parameter marker *?*; it requires named parameters that use the *@* prefix instead. In the following query, *@CustomerID* is the named parameter:

```
SELECT OrderID, CustomerID, EmployeeID, OrderDate
    FROM Orders WHERE CustomerID = @CustomerID
```

We'll discuss executing parameterized queries with the SQL Server .NET data provider in more detail in Appendix A.

By simply changing the value of the parameter, we can use this query to retrieve the orders for any customer. The ADO.NET *Parameter* object is the structure you create to store the parameter information. The *Command* object also has a *Parameters* collection. The following code snippet creates a *Command*, adds a *Parameter* to its *Parameters* collection, supplies a value for the *Parameter*, and executes the *Command* to pull back information for the orders for a particular customer:

Visual Basic .NET

```
Dim strConn, strSQL As String
strConn = "Provider=SQLOLEDB;Data Source=(local)\NetSDK;" & _
        "Initial Catalog=Northwind;Trusted_Connection=Yes;"
Dim cn As New OleDbConnection(strConn)
cn.Open()
strSQL = "SELECT OrderID, CustomerID, EmployeeID, OrderDate " & _
        "FROM Orders WHERE CustomerID = ?"
Dim cmd As New OleDbCommand(strSQL, cn)
cmd.Parameters.Add("@CustomerID", OleDbType.WChar, 5)
cmd.Parameters(0).Value = "ALFKI"
Dim rdr As OleDbDataReader = cmd.ExecuteReader()
```

Visual C# .NET

```
string strConn, strSQL;
strConn = "Provider=SQLOLEDB;Data Source=(local)\\NetSDK;" +
        "Initial Catalog=Northwind;Trusted_Connection=Yes;";
OleDbConnection cn = new OleDbConnection(strConn);
cn.Open();
strSQL = "SELECT OrderID, CustomerID, EmployeeID, OrderDate " +
        "FROM Orders WHERE CustomerID = ?";
OleDbCommand cmd = new OleDbCommand(strSQL, cn);
cmd.Parameters.Add("@CustomerID", OleDbType.WChar, 5);
cmd.Parameters[0].Value = "ALFKI";
OleDbDataReader rdr = cmd.ExecuteReader();
```

Once you've executed the query using the *ExecuteReader* method, you can fetch the results of the query using the *DataReader* object, just as you do with standard queries that don't use parameters.

Using parameterized queries can greatly simplify your programming. Changing the value of a parameter is much easier than programmatically concatenating query strings, especially because when you supply values in a parameter you don't need to worry about delimiting them. For example, if you wanted to search for an employee whose last name is O'Leary without using parameters, you would need to build a query string that looks something like this:

```
SELECT EmployeeID, LastName, FirstName FROM Employees
    WHERE LastName = 'O''Leary'
```

Because you need to surround the literal value you're searching for with quotes, you have to replace the single quotes in the value with two consecutive single quotes. Developers who've tried to put double quotes into a string in their code can relate.

Calling a Stored Procedure

Let's say we have a stored procedure that can return a row of data. Here's an example of a SQL Server stored procedure designed to do just that:

```
CREATE PROCEDURE GetCustomer (@CustomerID nchar(5)) AS
    SELECT CustomerID, CompanyName, ContactName, ContactTitle
        FROM Customers WHERE CustomerID = @CustomerID
RETURN
```

> **Note**   Some databases, such as Oracle, cannot return a result set from a stored procedure call in this fashion. For more information on fetching a result set from an Oracle stored procedure using ADO.NET, please see the *Microsoft Knowledge Base*.

How do we call this stored procedure from a *Command?* One option is to use the *Command* object's *CommandType* property. You can set this property to any value in the *CommandType* enumeration: *Text, TableDirect,* or *Stored-Procedure.* The property is set to *Text* by default. Setting *CommandType* to *StoredProcedure* tells the *Command* that you're calling a stored procedure. The *Command* object will combine the value stored in its *CommandText* property with the information in its *Parameters* collection to generate the syntax to call your stored procedure, as shown here:

Visual Basic .NET

```
...
Dim cn As New OleDbConnection(strConn)
cn.Open()
```

(continued)

```
Dim cmd As OleDbCommand = cn.CreateCommand()
With cmd
    .CommandText = "GetCustomer"
    .CommandType = CommandType.StoredProcedure
    .Parameters.Add("@CustomerID", OleDbType.WChar, 5)
    .Parameters(0).Value = "ALFKI"
End With

Dim rdr As OleDbDataReader = cmd.ExecuteReader()
If rdr.Read() Then
    Console.WriteLine(rdr("CompanyName"))
Else
    Console.WriteLine("No customer found")
End If

rdr.Close()
cn.Close()
```

Visual C# .NET

```
...
OleDbConnection cn = new OleDbConnection(strConn);
cn.Open();

OleDbCommand cmd = cn.CreateCommand();
cmd.CommandText = "GetCustomer";
cmd.CommandType = CommandType.StoredProcedure;
cmd.Parameters.Add("@CustomerID", OleDbType.WChar, 5);
cmd.Parameters[0].Value = "ALFKI";

OleDbDataReader rdr = cmd.ExecuteReader();
if (rdr.Read())
    Console.WriteLine(rdr["CompanyName"]);
else
    Console.WriteLine("No customer found");

rdr.Close();
cn.Close();
```

The standard way to call the stored procedure is to use the following syntax:

```
{? = CALL MyStoredProc(?, ?, ?)}
```

The initial parameter marker represents the return value of the procedure call and can be omitted if you're not going to use the value returned. Leaving off the return parameter changes the query's syntax to this:

```
{CALL GetCustomer(?)}
```

I prefer using this syntax in my code rather than relying on the *CommandType* property. If you want to query a table, view, or stored procedure that contains odd characters such as spaces in its name, you must surround the object name with delimiters. With an *OleDbCommand* object, setting the *CommandType* property to *TableDirect* or *StoredProcedure* doesn't surround the object name with delimiters in such cases. You need to add the delimiters yourself. This behavior is not consistent for all *Command* objects. For example, the *SqlCommand* object will correctly delimit object names automatically. Of course, if you don't put spaces in your table and stored procedure names, this won't be an issue for you (nudge, nudge).

My advice is to avoid relying on the *CommandType* property and instead use the appropriate syntax for your query in the *CommandText* property, as shown here:

Visual Basic .NET

```
Dim cmd As New OleDbDataAdapter()
cmd.CommandText = "{CALL GetCustomer(?)}"
cmd.CommandType = CommandType.Text
```

Visual C# .NET

```
OleDbDataAdapter cmd = new OleDbDataAdapter();
cmd.CommandText = "{CALL GetCustomer(?)}";
cmd.CommandType = CommandType.Text;
```

Developers with some SQL Server experience might be used to using the EXEC syntax for calling stored procedures in tools such as Query Analyzer. You're welcome to use this syntax with your *Command* objects, but keep in mind that not all databases support this syntax. You might need to change your syntax slightly if you need to query a different type of database.

Retrieving Data from Output Parameters

Not all stored procedures return information through a result set. Many procedures return information through output parameters. Let's say our SQL Server *GetCustomer* stored procedure looks like the following instead:

```
CREATE PROCEDURE GetCustomer (@CustomerID nchar(5),
                             @CompanyName nvarchar(40) OUTPUT,
                             @ContactName nvarchar(30) OUTPUT,
                             @ContactTitle nvarchar(30) OUTPUT) AS
```

(continued)

```
SELECT @CompanyName = CompanyName, @ContactName = ContactName,
        @ContactTitle = ContactTitle
        FROM Customers WHERE CustomerID = @CustomerID
IF @@ROWCOUNT = 1
    RETURN 0
ELSE
    RETURN -1
```

How can we use a *Command* to retrieve data from the output parameters? The *Parameter* object has a *Direction* property that accepts values from the *ParameterDirection* enumeration: *ReturnValue*, *Input*, *InputOutput*, and *Output*. The default for the property is *Input*. In order to retrieve information from this stored procedure, we need to set the *Direction* property on the parameters that aren't input-only.

The stored procedure uses the return parameter to indicate success or failure. So, in our code snippet we'll examine the value of the return parameter to determine whether we successfully located the desired customer in the table:

Visual Basic .NET

```
...
Dim cn As New OleDbConnection(strConn)
cn.Open()

Dim cmd As OleDbCommand = cn.CreateCommand()
With cmd
    .CommandText = "{? = CALL GetCustomer(?, ?, ?, ?)}"

    .Parameters.Add("@RetVal", OleDbType.Integer)
    .Parameters.Add("@CustomerID", OleDbType.WChar, 5)
    .Parameters.Add("@CompanyName", OleDbType.VarWChar, 40)
    .Parameters.Add("@ContactName", OleDbType.VarWChar, 30)
    .Parameters.Add("@ContactTitle", OleDbType.VarWChar, 30)

    .Parameters("@ContactTitle").Direction = ParameterDirection.Output
    .Parameters("@RetVal").Direction = ParameterDirection.ReturnValue
    .Parameters("@CustomerID").Value = "ALFKI"
    .Parameters("@CompanyName").Direction = ParameterDirection.Output
    .Parameters("@ContactName").Direction = ParameterDirection.Output

    .ExecuteNonQuery()
    If Convert.ToInt32(.Parameters("@RetVal").Value) = 0 Then
        Console.WriteLine(.Parameters("@CompanyName").Value)
    Else
        Console.WriteLine("Customer not found")
    End If
End With
```

Visual C# .NET

```
...
OleDbConnection cn = new OleDbConnection(strConn);
cn.Open();

OleDbCommand cmd = cn.CreateCommand();
cmd.CommandText = "{? = CALL GetCustomer(?, ?, ?, ?)}";

cmd.Parameters.Add("@RetVal", OleDbType.Integer);
cmd.Parameters.Add("@CustomerID", OleDbType.WChar, 5);
cmd.Parameters.Add("@CompanyName", OleDbType.VarWChar, 40);
cmd.Parameters.Add("@ContactName", OleDbType.VarWChar, 30);
cmd.Parameters.Add("@ContactTitle", OleDbType.VarWChar, 30);

cmd.Parameters["@ContactTitle"].Direction = ParameterDirection.Output;
cmd.Parameters["@RetVal"].Direction = ParameterDirection.ReturnValue;
cmd.Parameters["@CustomerID"].Value = "ALFKI";
cmd.Parameters["@CompanyName"].Direction = ParameterDirection.Output;
cmd.Parameters["@ContactName"].Direction = ParameterDirection.Output;

cmd.ExecuteNonQuery();
if (Convert.ToInt32(cmd.Parameters["@RetVal"].Value) == 0)
    Console.WriteLine(cmd.Parameters["@CompanyName"].Value);
else
    Console.WriteLine("Customer not found");
```

Executing a Query Within a Transaction

The *Command* object has a *Transaction* property that you must set in order to execute your *Command* within a *Transaction*. In the previous chapter, you saw how to create a *Transaction* object using the *Command* object's *BeginTransaction* method. The following code snippet shows how you can execute a *Command* on that *Transaction*.

Visual Basic .NET

```
...
cn.Open()
Dim txn As OleDbTransaction = cn.BeginTransaction()
Dim strSQL As String = "INSERT INTO Customers (...) VALUES (...)"
Dim cmd As New OleDbCommand(strSQL, cn, txn)
Dim intRecordsAffected As Integer = cmd.ExecuteNonQuery()
If intRecordsAffected = 1 Then
    Console.WriteLine("Update succeeded")
    txn.Commit()
```

(continued)

```
Else
    'Assume intRecordsAffected = 0
    Console.WriteLine("Update failed")
    txn.Rollback()
End If
```

Visual C# .NET

```
...
cn.Open();
OleDbTransaction txn = cn.BeginTransaction();
string strSQL = "INSERT INTO Customers (...) VALUES (...)";
OleDbCommand cmd = new OleDbCommand(strSQL, cn, txn);
int intRecordsAffected = cmd.ExecuteNonQuery();
if (intRecordsAffected == 1)
{
    Console.WriteLine("Update succeeded");
    txn.Commit();
}
else
{
    //Assume intRecordsAffected = 0
    Console.WriteLine("Update failed");
    txn.Rollback();
}
```

Don't forget to call the *Commit* or *Rollback* method on the *Transaction* object (depending on whether you want to save or discard the actions performed within the transaction).

Creating Commands in Visual Studio .NET

Visual Studio .NET can save you time, effort, and quite a few headaches by helping you create and configure *Command* objects quickly and easily. Let's look at the Visual Studio .NET design-time features for working with *Command* objects.

Dragging and Dropping from the Toolbox

The primary starting point for creating *Command* objects in Visual Studio .NET is the Toolbox. On the Data tab, you'll find *Command* objects for each of the .NET data providers. To create an *OleDbCommand*, you simply drag-and-drop the OleDbCommand item from the Toolbox onto your design surface or to the design surface's components tray. You'll have a new *Command* object in your designer's components tray, as shown in Figure 4-1.

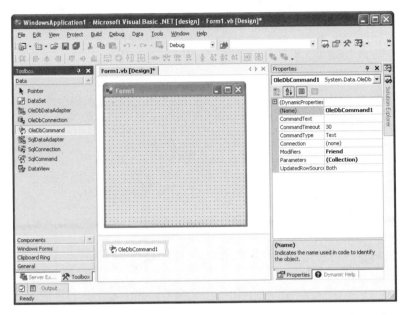

Figure 4-1   Dragging and dropping an *OleDbCommand* item from the Toolbox to create a new *Command*

As you learned earlier in this chapter, you must specify a *Connection* and a query string in order to create a useful *Command* object. Visual Studio .NET can help you set the *Connection* and *CommandText* properties of your new *Command* at design time.

Specifying a Connection

Once you've added a *Command* to your components tray, you'll want to set its *Connection* property to a *Connection* object. If you select the *Command* object's *Connection* property in the Properties window, you'll get a drop-down list of choices. You can opt to use an existing *Connection*, create a new *Connection*, or leave the *Connection* property blank (none). Figure 4-2 shows a Windows form with an *OleDbConnection* and an *OleDbCommand* in its components tray. The *OleDbCommand* is selected, and the Properties window shows how you can set the object's *Connection* property to the existing *OleDbConnection*.

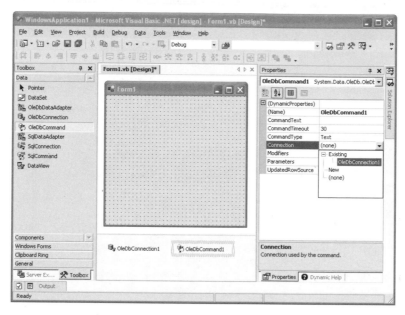

Figure 4-2 Setting a *Command* object's *Connection* property

If you select New from the drop-down list, Visual Studio .NET will open the Data Link Properties dialog box, where you can create a new connection string. Visual Studio .NET will add a new *Connection* object using the connection string you build and set your *Command* object's *Connection* property to this new *Connection* object.

Using Query Builder

Visual Studio .NET simplifies the process of building your query string through Query Builder. Select a *Command* object in your designer's components tray, and then select the object's *CommandText* property in the Properties window. You'll see a button that indicates that this property has its own property page. Click this button to invoke the Query Builder dialog box, shown in Figure 4-3.

Query Builder offers a simple graphical user interface to help you build queries. When it launches, Query Builder prompts you to select the tables, views, and functions you want to access in your query, as shown in Figure 4-3. As you select objects, you'll see them added to the design surface behind the Add Table dialog box.

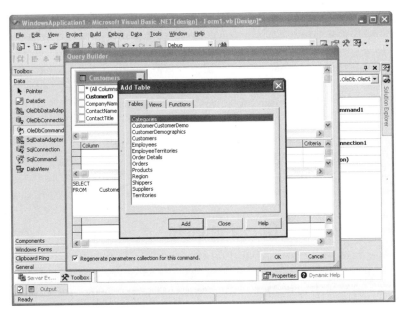

Figure 4-3   Selecting tables for your query

After you specify the tables you want to access in your query, Query Builder helps you graphically select the columns, apply filters and sorting order, and so forth. In Figure 4-4, we've selected the Customers table and specified the columns from the table that we want to fetch in the query. Notice that we've also specified a parameter for the CustomerID column.

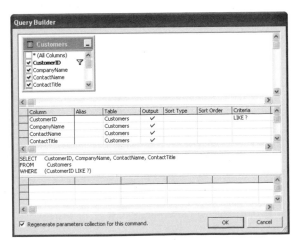

Figure 4-4.   Using Query Builder to select columns and criteria for a query

The Query Builder dialog box has three design panes. The top pane provides a simple way to select columns. The second pane simplifies the process of adding filters and sort orders to the result set. The third pane contains the text of the query you've built. Changes you make in one pane affect the other two. You can right-click in the text pane and choose Verify from the shortcut menu to find out whether the query you've built is valid.

Another handy command on the shortcut menu, Run, runs the query you've built and displays the results in the bottom pane. If you've created a parameterized query, Query Builder will display a dialog box to let you specify values for the parameters. Query Builder also contains logic that enables you to edit the data in the results pane to modify the contents of your database.

Using Your New *Command* Object in Code

We've successfully created and configured our *Command* object based on the following query:

```
SELECT CustomerID, CompanyName, ContactName, ContactTitle
    FROM Customers WHERE CustomerID LIKE ?
```

Before we add code to execute our *Command* and fetch its results, drag-and-drop a list box item from the Toolbox onto your form. Modify its size to take up most of the form. We'll use this list box to display the contents of the CompanyName column for the rows we retrieve.

Double-click on the form to enter the form's *Load* event. Now we want to execute the *Command*, fetch the results through a *DataReader*, and display the contents of the CompanyName column in our list box. Even though we specified a parameter for the CustomerID column, we can supply the wildcard character % so the query will return all customers.

Visual Basic .NET developers can add the code shown in Figure 4-5.

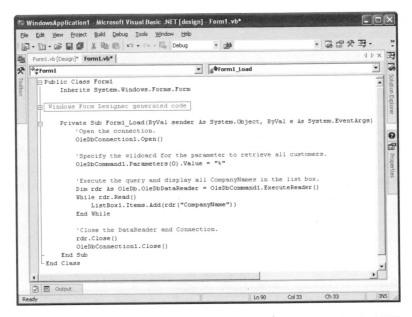

Figure 4-5   Using the *Command* object at run time in Visual Basic .NET

Visual C# .NET developers can add the following code:

```
//Open the connection.
oleDbConnection1.Open();

//Specify the wildcard for the parameter to retrieve all customers.
oleDbCommand1.Parameters[0].Value = "%";

//Execute the query and display all CompanyNames in the list box.
OleDbDataReader rdr = oleDbCommand1.ExecuteReader();
while (rdr.Read())
    listBox1.Items.Add(rdr["CompanyName"]);

//Close the DataReader and Connection.
rdr.Close();
oleDbConnection1.Close();
```

Visual C# .NET developers, don't forget to add *using System.Data.OleDb;* to the using block at the top of the form.

Run the project, and you'll see the list box filled with the names of the companies in the Customers table.

Dragging and Dropping from Server Explorer

If you're basing a *Command* on a stored procedure call, you can create and configure your *Command* object by dragging and dropping the stored procedure from Server Explorer onto your design surface. Dragging and dropping a SQL Server stored procedure creates a *SqlCommand*, and using a stored procedure from other data sources creates an *OleDbCommand*.

In Figure 4-6, we've dragged the SQL Server Northwind database's *CustOrderHist* stored procedure onto a Windows form. You can see in the Properties window that the *CommandText*, *CommandType*, and *Connection* properties are set so that you can call this stored procedure easily through code.

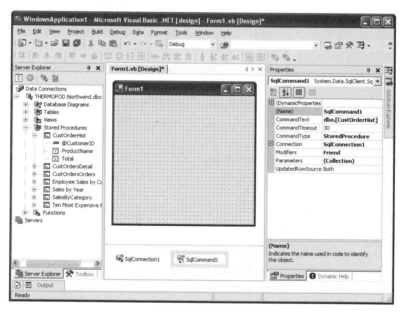

Figure 4-6   Creating *Command* objects based on stored procedures

> **Note**   Visual Studio .NET adds delimiters to the name of the stored procedure so that you don't run into problems calling stored procedures that have odd characters such as spaces in their names.

Visual Studio .NET has also populated the new *Command* object's *Parameters* collection. Select the *Parameters* collection in the Properties window, and then click the button to the right to launch its property page, as shown in Figure 4-7.

Figure 4-7   Viewing the *Parameters* collection for a stored procedure *Command*

Visual Studio .NET's data tools query your database for schema information about the stored procedure in order to populate the *Command* object's *Parameters* collection. However, many databases, such as SQL Server, don't differentiate between input/output and output-only parameters. As a result, if you want to call a stored procedure that uses output parameters, you might need to set the direction for those parameters by hand in the Properties window.

> **Note**   Dragging and dropping a table or view from Server Explorer creates a *DataAdapter* rather than a *Command*. We'll discuss *DataAdapter* objects in the next chapter.

Command, DataReader, and *Parameter* Object Reference

Now that we've examined the major features of the *Command, DataReader,* and *Parameter* objects, let's examine the properties and methods of each object.

Properties of the *OleDbCommand* Object

Table 4-1 lists the properties of the *OleDbCommand* object that you're most likely to use.

Table 4-1 **Commonly Used Properties of the *OleDbCommand* Object**

Property	Data Type	Description
CommandText	*String*	The text of the query that you want to execute.
CommandTimeout	*Int32*	Time (in seconds) that the adapter will wait for the query to execute before timing out. (Default = 30 seconds.)
CommandType	*CommandType*	Specifies the type of query to execute. (Default = Text.)
Connection	*OleDbConnection*	The connection to your data store that the *Command* will use to execute the query.
Parameters	*OleDbParameterCollection*	A collection of parameters for the query.
Transaction	*OleDbTransaction*	Specifies the transaction to use for the query.
UpdatedRowSource	*UpdateRowSource*	Controls how the results of the query will affect the current *DataRow* if the *Command* is used by calling the *Update* method of a *DataAdapter*. (Default = Both.) See Chapter 11 for more information on using this property when submitting pending changes to your database.

CommandTimeout Property

The *CommandTimeout* property determines how long, in seconds, the *Command* will wait for the results of your query before timing out. By default, this property is set to 30. If the query does not complete by the time specified in the *CommandTimeout* property, the *Command* will throw an exception.

Keep in mind that once the query starts returning results, the query won't time out. Let's say you want to use a *DataAdapter* to fetch the contents of a table into a *DataSet*. For the sake of argument, let's imagine that your table is so absurdly large that the process of fetching its contents takes more than 30 seconds, the default value for the *Command* object's *CommandTimeout* property. Because the *Command* that the *DataAdapter* uses retrieved the first row in less than the time specified in the *CommandTimeout* property, the query won't time out no matter how long it takes to retrieve the contents of the table—a minute, a day, or a year.

CommandType Property

ADO.NET can simplify the process of setting the text for your query through the *CommandType* property. You can set this property to any of the values in the *CommandType* enumeration (available in System.Data), which are described in Table 4-2.

Table 4-2   Members of the *CommandType* Enumeration

Constant	Value	Description
Text	1	The *Command* will not modify the contents of the *CommandText* property.
StoredProcedure	4	The *Command* will build a query to call a stored procedure using the value of the *CommandText* property as a stored procedure name.
TableDirect	512	The *Command* will prepend *"SELECT * FROM "* to the contents of the *CommandText* property.

By default, this property is set to *Text*. Using this default setting, the *Command* will use whatever text you've specified in the *CommandText* property to execute your query. In my opinion, you should leave the property set to the default. Here's why.

If you set the property to *TableDirect*, the *Command* will prepend *"SELECT * FROM "* to the contents of the *CommandText* property when you execute the query. This means that the *Command* will fetch all rows and all columns from the table—if the query succeeds.

If you query a table that has a space in its name, such as the sample Northwind database's Order Details table, the query will fail unless you surround the table name with a delimiter that the database can handle. I try to use square brackets rather than having to jump through hoops to embed double quote characters into my strings. Setting *CommandType* to *TableDirect* will not delimit your table name automatically. You still have to do that work yourself.

Of course, you can avoid such problems by not using spaces in the names of your tables, columns, views, and stored procedures. Seriously, how many times have database developers said, "Thank goodness I was able to put a space in that object name"?

> **Note**   The constant name *TableDirect* is a bit of a misnomer and might lead ADO developers to believe that it maps to *adCmdTableDirect* in ADO's *CommandTypeEnum*. That's a perfectly logical assumption, but the constant actually maps to *adCmdTable*. Despite what the constant's name implies, setting *CommandType* to *TableDirect* doesn't make the *Command* fetch the contents of your table through the low-level interfaces that the Jet and SQL Server OLE DB providers support.

The *StoredProcedure* constant simplifies the process of calling a stored procedure, as shown here:

Visual Basic .NET

```
Dim cmd As New OleDbCommand()
cmd.CommandType = CommandType.StoredProcedure
cmd.CommandText = "MyStoredProc"

cmd.CommandType = CommandType.CommandText
cmd.CommandText = "{CALL MyStoredProc}"
```

Visual C# .NET

```
OleDbCommand cmd = new OleDbCommand();
cmd.CommandType = CommandType.StoredProcedure;
cmd.CommandText = "MyStoredProc";

cmd.CommandType = CommandType.CommandText;
cmd.CommandText = "{CALL MyStoredProc}";
```

The code snippet shows the standard syntax for calling stored procedures: *{CALL MyStoredProc}*. SQL Server also supports the *EXEC MyStoredProc* syntax. In fact, the SQL Server OLE DB provider will translate calls that use the CALL syntax and actually use the EXEC syntax when communicating directly with the database. For this reason, you might want to use the EXEC syntax to try to get your code to run just a tiny bit faster. I avoid using this syntax because I often have to write code that's back-end independent. Later in the chapter, we'll look at how to call parameterized stored procedures, which can add a touch of complexity to the syntax.

Like the *TableDirect* constant, setting *CommandType* to *StoredProcedure* doesn't delimit the stored procedure name when you execute your query. For that reason, I prefer leaving *CommandType* as *Text* and using the CALL syntax in the *CommandText* property.

Parameters Property

The *Parameters* property returns an *OleDbParameterCollection*, which contains a collection of *OleDbParameter* objects. We'll examine the properties and methods of the *OleDbParameter* object later in the chapter.

Transaction Property

You use the *Command* object's *Transaction* property to execute your *Command* within a transaction. If you've opened a *Transaction* object on your *Connection* and try to execute your *Command* without associating it with that *Transaction* via this property, the *Command* object will generate an exception.

UpdatedRowSource Property

The *UpdatedRowSource* property is designed to help you refetch data for the row you're updating using a *DataAdapter* and *Command* objects that contain updating logic. Table 4-3 lists the values accepted by *UpdatedRowSource*. We'll discuss the use of this property in Chapter 11.

Table 4-3   Members of the *UpdateRowSource* Enumeration

Constant	Value	Description
Both	3	Command will fetch new data for the row through both the first returned record and output parameters.
FirstReturnedRecord	2	Command will fetch new data for the row through the first returned record
None	0	Command will not fetch new data for the row upon execution.
OutputParameters	1	Command will fetch new data for the row through output parameters

Methods of the *OleDbCommand* Object

Now let's take a look at the methods of the *OleDbCommand* object, which are listed in Table 4-4.

Table 4-4   Commonly Used Methods of the *OleDbCommand* Object

Method	Description
Cancel	Cancels the execution of the query
CreateParameter	Creates a new parameter for the query
ExecuteNonQuery	Executes the query (for queries that do not return rows)

(continued)

Table 4-4   Commonly Used Methods of the *OleDbCommand* Object   *(continued)*

Method	Description
ExecuteReader	Executes the query and retrieves the results in an *OleDbData-Reader*
ExecuteScalar	Executes the query and retrieves the first column of the first row, designed for singleton queries such as `"SELECT COUNT(*) FROM MyTable WHERE..."`
Prepare	Creates a prepared version of the query in the data store
ResetCommand-Timeout	Resets the *CommandTimeout* property to its default of 30 seconds

Cancel Method

You can use the *Cancel* method to cancel the execution of a query. If the *Command* object whose *Cancel* method you've called is not currently executing a query, the *Cancel* method does nothing.

The *Cancel* method also causes the *Command* object to discard any unread rows on a *DataReader* object. The following sample code fetches the results of a simple query. The code displays the results, followed by the number of rows retrieved. In the code, there's a call to the *Cancel* method that's commented out. Remove the comment character(s) and re-run the code to demonstrate that the *Cancel* method discards the results of the query.

Visual Basic .NET

```
Dim strConn As String = "Provider=SQLOLEDB;Data Source=(local)\NetSDK;" & _
                        "Initial Catalog=Northwind;Trusted_Connection=Yes;"
Dim strSQL As String = "SELECT CustomerID FROM Customers"
Dim cn As New OleDbConnection(strConn)
cn.Open()
Dim cmd As New OleDbCommand(strSQL, cn)
Dim rdr As OleDbDataReader = cmd.ExecuteReader()
Dim intRowsRetrieved As Integer
'cmd.Cancel()
Do While rdr.Read
    Console.WriteLine(rdr.GetString(0))
    intRowsRetrieved += 1
Loop
Console.WriteLine(intRowsRetrieved & " row(s) retrieved")
rdr.Close()
cn.Close()
```

Visual C# .NET

```
string strConn = "Provider=SQLOLEDB;Data Source=(local)\\NetSDK;" +
                 "Initial Catalog=Northwind;Trusted_Connection=Yes;";
string strSQL = "SELECT CustomerID FROM Customers";
OleDbConnection cn = new OleDbConnection(strConn);
cn.Open();
OleDbCommand cmd = new OleDbCommand(strSQL, cn);
OleDbDataReader rdr = cmd.ExecuteReader();
int intRowsRetrieved = 0;
//cmd.Cancel();
while (rdr.Read())
{
    Console.WriteLine(rdr.GetString(0));
    intRowsRetrieved++;
}
Console.WriteLine(intRowsRetrieved + " row(s) retrieved");
rdr.Close();
cn.Close();
```

ExecuteNonQuery Method

The *ExecuteNonQuery* method executes the query without creating a *Data-Reader* to fetch the rows returned by the query. Use *ExecuteNonQuery* if you want to issue an action query or don't want to examine the rows returned by the query. Values for return and output parameters are available upon completion of the call to *ExecuteNonQuery*.

ExecuteNonQuery returns an integer to indicate the number of rows modified by the query you've executed. If you're using batch queries, see the discussion of batch queries and the return value of *ExecuteNonQuery* earlier in this chapter.

ExecuteReader Method

If you want to examine the row(s) returned by a query, use the *Command* object's *ExecuteReader* method to return that data in a new *DataReader* object. We discussed the basic use of this method earlier in the chapter. However, there are some interesting options on the method.

The *Command* object's *ExecuteReader* method is overloaded and can accept a value from the *CommandBehavior* enumeration. Table 4-5 describes each of these options.

Table 4-5   Members of the *CommandBehavior* Enumeration

Constant	Value	Description
CloseConnection	32	Closing the *DataReader* will close the connection.
KeyInfo	4	Causes the *DataReader* to fetch primary key information for the columns in the result set.
SchemaOnly	2	The *DataReader* will contain only column information without actually running the query.
SequentialAccess	16	Values in the columns will be available only sequentially. For example, after you examine the contents of third column, you won't be able to examine the contents of the first two columns.
SingleResult	1	The *DataReader* will fetch the results of only the first row-returning query.
SingleRow	8	The *DataReader* will fetch only the first row of the first row-returning query.

CloseConnection   If you supply *CloseConnection* when calling the *Execute-Reader* method, when you call the *Close* method on the *DataReader*, the *Data-Reader* will call the *Close* method on the *Connection* with which it is associated.

This feature can be extremely handy if you're building business objects and passing data from one object to another. You might encounter situations in which you want a business object to return a *DataReader* to the calling object rather than returning the data in a *DataTable* or some other structure. In such cases, you might want the calling object to be able to close the *Connection* object after it's done reading the results of the query from the *DataReader*.

But what if you don't trust the calling object? You might not want to hand it a direct connection to the database. Using *CloseConnection* can simplify this scenario without compromising the security and architecture of your application.

KeyInfo* and *SchemaOnly   When we look at methods of the *DataReader* object, we'll discuss the *GetSchemaTable* method. This method returns metadata about the columns in the *DataReader*—column names, data types, and so on. Such information can be helpful if you're building code-generation tools. If you're going to use the *DataReader* object's *GetSchemaTable* method, you should also look at the *KeyInfo* and *SchemaOnly* options of the Command's *ExecuteReader* method.

If you call *ExecuteReader* and use the *SchemaOnly* value in the *Options* parameter, you'll retrieve schema information about the columns but you won't actually execute the query.

Using *KeyInfo* in the *Options* parameter forces the *DataReader* to fetch additional schema information from your data source to indicate whether the columns in the result set are part of the key columns in the tables in your data source.

If you use the *SchemaOnly* option, you don't need to include *KeyInfo* as well. The key information will be included in the schema automatically.

SequentialAccess   If you use the *SequentialAccess* option when calling *ExecuteReader*, the columns of data will be available only sequentially through the *DataReader*. For example, if you look at the contents of the second column, the contents of the first column will no longer be available.

Use of the *SequentialAccess* value might increase the performance of your *DataReader* slightly, depending on the data source you're using.

SingleRow and SingleResult   If you're interested in examining only the first row or first result set returned by your query, you might want to use *SingleRow* or *SingleResult* when calling *ExecuteReader*.

Supplying *SingleRow* in the *Options* parameter will create a *DataReader* that contains, at most, one row of data. If you issue a query that returns 10 rows of data but you use *SingleRow* in your call to *ExecuteReader*, only the first row of data will be available through the *DataReader*. All other rows will be discarded. Similarly, using *SingleResult* causes subsequent result sets to be discarded.

ExecuteScalar Method

The *ExecuteScalar* method is similar to *ExecuteReader* except that it returns the first column of the first row of the result set in a generic *Object* data type. If the query returns more than one cell of data, this data is discarded.

If your query returns a single cell of data, like the following query does, you can improve the performance of your code by using *ExecuteScalar*.

```
SELECT COUNT(*) FROM MyTable
```

Prepare Method

One of the major benefits of stored procedures is that they generally run faster than dynamic queries. This is because the database system can prepare an execution plan for them ahead of time. It's sort of like the difference between script code and compiled code. Script code is often more flexible because you can generate it at run time, but compiled code runs faster.

Most database systems support the notion of a "prepared" query. You can think of a prepared query as a temporary stored procedure. If you're going to execute the same query multiple times, you might get better performance by preparing the query.

To prepare a *Command*, you simply call its *Prepare* method.

If you're building multi-tiered applications, prepared queries aren't likely to improve the performance. In fact, I don't recommend using prepared queries in such situations. With multi-tiered applications, the code in your server components will likely connect, run a query or two, and then disconnect. Most multi-tiered applications take advantage of connection pooling at the middle-tier level.

Simply put, a connection pool will hold onto a connection for a brief amount of time. If your code requests a connection that matches one in a pool, your code will receive an open connection from the pool rather than opening a new one. This process can greatly improve the performance of your code at the middle tier.

However, if your connections are constantly recycled through connection pooling rather than being truly closed, your database won't have a chance to discard all of the temporary stored procedures that it created for your prepared queries. Recent versions of SQL Server have changed how these temporary stored procedures are stored in order to better handle this scenario, but you're better off not preparing your queries if you're building multi-tiered applications.

ResetCommandTimeout Method

Calling the *ResetCommandTimeout* method resets the *Command* object's *CommandTimeout* property to its default value of 30 seconds. If you find yourself wondering "Why would I need a property to do that?," you're not alone.

Properties of the *OleDbDataReader* Object

Now let's look at the properties of the *OleDbDataReader* (Table 4-6).

Table 4-6   Commonly Used Properties of the *OleDbDataReader* Object

Property	Data Type	Description
Depth	*Int32*	Indicates the depth of nesting for the current row (read-only).
FieldCount	*Int32*	Returns the number of fields contained by the *DataReader* (read-only).
IsClosed	*Boolean*	Indicates whether the *DataReader* is closed (read-only).
Item	*Object*	Returns the contents of a column for the current row (read-only).
RecordsAffected	*Int32*	Indicates the number of records affected by the queries submitted (read-only).

Depth Property and *GetData* Method

The *Depth* property and the *GetData* method are reserved for queries that return hierarchical data. These features are not supported in the current release of ADO.NET.

FieldCount Property

The *FieldCount* property returns an integer to indicate the number of columns of data in the result set.

IsClosed Property

The *IsClosed* property returns a Boolean value to indicate whether the *Data-Reader* object is closed.

Item Property

The *DataReader* object's *Item* property is similar, in form and function, to the *DataRow* object's *Item* property. You can supply the name of a column as a string or the integer position of a column, and the property will return the value stored in that column in the generic object data type.

If you know the data type of the column, you'll get better performance by calling the *Get<DataType>* method (such as *GetInteger* or *GetString*) instead.

RecordsAffected Property

You can use the *RecordsAffected* property to determine the number of rows that your action query (or queries) modified. If you want to execute a single action query, use the *ExecuteNonQuery* method of the *Command* object instead. The *ExecuteNonQuery* method returns the number of rows the action query affected.

If you're executing a batch of queries and you want to determine the number of rows affected, see the section on batch queries earlier in the chapter.

Methods of the *OleDbDataReader* Object

And now for your programming pleasure, Table 4-7 presents the methods of the *OleDbDataReader* that you're most likely to encounter.

Table 4-7   Commonly Used Methods of the *OleDbDataReader* Object

Method	Description
Close	Closes the *DataReader*.
Get<DataType>	Returns the contents of a column in the current row as the specified type based on its ordinal.

(continued)

**Table 4-7   Commonly Used Methods of the *OleDbDataReader*
Object**   *(continued)*

Method	Description
GetBytes	Retrieves an array of bytes from a column in the current row.
GetChars	Retrieves an array of characters from a column in the current row.
GetData	Returns a new *DataReader* from a column.
GetDataTypeName	Returns the name of the data type for a column based on its ordinal.
GetFieldType	Returns the data type for a column based on its ordinal.
GetName	Returns the name of a column based on its ordinal.
GetOrdinal	Returns the ordinal of a column based on its name.
GetSchemaTable	Returns the schema information (column names and data types) of the *DataReader* as a *DataTable*.
GetValue	Returns the value of a column based on its ordinal.
GetValues	Accepts an array that the *DataReader* will use to return the contents of the current column. This call returns a 32-bit integer that indicates the number of entries returned in the array.
IsDBNull	Indicates whether a column contains a *Null* value.
NextResult	Moves to the next result.
Read	Moves to the next row.

Read Method

The *Read* method accesses the next row of data. Remember that the first row in the result set will not be available through the *DataReader* until you call the *Read* method. The first time you call the *Read* method, the *DataReader* will move to the first row in the result set. Subsequent calls to *Read* will move to the next row of data.

   The *Read* method also returns a Boolean value to indicate whether there are any more results for the query. The sample code we examined earlier continually examines results until the *Read* method returns *False*.

GetValue Method

The *GetValue* method is similar to the *Item* property. Supply an integer, and the *GetValue* method will return the contents of that column in the generic object type. The *GetValue* method and the various *Get<DataType>* methods accept only integers for the column index and do not perform string-based lookups such as the *Item* property.

The *DataReader* is designed for speed; referencing an item in a collection by its ordinal value is faster than having the collection locate the item by its name.

Get<DataType> Methods

The *DataReader* also offers methods that return specific data types. If you know that a column contains string data, you can call the *GetValue* method of the *DataReader* and convert the data to a string or simply call the *GetString* method, as shown here:

Visual Basic .NET

```
Dim strCompanyName As String
Dim rdr As OleDbDataReader
...
strCompanyName = rdr.GetString(intCompanyNameIndex)
'or
strCompanyName = rdr.GetValue(intCompanyNameIndex).ToString
```

Visual C# .NET

```
string strCompanyName;
OleDbDataReader rdr;
...
strCompanyName = rdr.GetString(intCompanyNameIndex);
//or
strCompanyName = rdr.GetValue(intCompanyNameIndex).ToString();
```

The *DataReader* has methods to return each of the data types available in the .NET Framework—*GetByte, GetChar, GetDateTime*, and so on.

GetValues Method

The *GetValues* method lets you store the contents of a row in an array. If you want to retrieve the contents of each column as quickly as possible, using the *GetValues* method will provide better performance than checking the value of each column separately.

The *DataAdapter* uses a *DataReader* to fetch data from your database to store the results in *DataTables*. To provide the best performance possible, the *DataAdapter* objects in the .NET data providers included in Visual Studio .NET use the *DataReader* object's *GetValues* method. Here's a simple example of how to use *GetValues*:

Visual Basic .NET

```
Dim rdr As OleDbDataReader = cmd.ExecuteReader()
Dim aData(rdr.FieldCount - 1) As Object
While rdr.Read
    rdr.GetValues(aData)
    Console.WriteLine(aData(0).ToString)
End While
```

Visual C# .NET

```
OleDbDataReader rdr = cmd.ExecuteReader();
object[] aData = new object[rdr.FieldCount];
while (rdr.Read())
{
    rdr.GetValues(aData);
    Console.WriteLine(aData[0].ToString());
}
```

> **Note** Visual Basic .NET and Visual C# .NET create arrays differently. The preceding code snippets take this difference into account. For example, *Dim aData(4) As Object* creates an array of length 5 (0 to 4) in Visual Basic and Visual Basic .NET, but *object[] aData = new object[4];* creates an array of length 4 (0 to 3) in Visual C# .NET.

NextResult Method

If you're working with batch queries that return multiple result sets, use the *NextResult* method to move to the next set of results. Like the *Read* method, *NextResult* returns a Boolean value to indicate whether there are more results.

The sample code on page 145 shows how to use a *DataReader* to examine the contents of a batch query. It also shows how to use the *NextResult* method in a loop.

Close Method

When you're using *DataReader* objects, it's important that you loop through the results and close the *DataReader* as quickly as possible. Your *Connection* object is blocked from performing any other work while a live firehose cursor is open on the connection. If you try to use a *Connection* that has an open *DataReader* on it, you'll receive an exception that states that the operation "requires an open and available connection."

> **Note**   Some databases allow you to have multiple queries with pending results on the same connection. In the initial release of ADO.NET, having an open *DataReader* on a connection prevents you from performing any other operations on that connection until you've closed the *DataReader* object, regardless of whether the database supports having multiple queries with pending results on the same connection. This behavior might change in a future release of ADO.NET.

Developers who have some experience with ADO might be surprised by this restriction, but those who've used RDO might not. Various Microsoft data access technologies have handled this scenario differently.

If you try to open two firehose cursors against a SQL Server database using ADO, everything will work and you won't receive an error. This is because the OLE DB specification states that when the current connection is blocked, the OLE DB provider will perform the requested action on a new connection.

RDO developers might recognize the error message "Connection is busy with results from another hstmt." ODBC does not do any behind-the-scenes work to try to help you out. If you try to use a connection that's busy, you simply receive an error message.

Which of these approaches (raising an error or performing the desired action on a new connection) is better? Developers, both inside and outside of Microsoft, can't seem to agree. In fact, each successive Microsoft data access technology has handled the scenario differently than its predecessor. VBSQL raises an error, DAO/Jet creates a new connection, RDO raises an error, ADO creates a new connection, and ADO.NET raises an error.

GetName, *GetOrdinal*, and *GetDataTypeName* Methods

The *DataReader* has methods that you can use to learn more about the results returned by your query. If you want to determine the name of a particular column, you can call the *GetName* method. If you already know the column name you want to access but don't know its ordinal position within the result set, you can pass the column name into the *GetOrdinal* method to retrieve its ordinal position. The *GetDataTypeName* method accepts an integer denoting the ordinal position of the column and returns the data type for that column as a string.

GetSchemaTable Method

The *DataReader* object's *GetSchemaTable* method is similar to the *DataAdapter* object's *FillSchema* method. Each method lets you create a *DataTable* containing

DataColumn objects that correspond to the columns returned by your query. The *GetSchemaTable* method accepts no parameters and returns a new *Data-Table*. The *DataTable* contains a *DataColumn* for each column returned by your query, but the *Rows* collection of the *DataTable* is empty. *GetSchemaTable* populates the new *DataTable* with schema information only.

The data that *GetSchemaTable* returns might be a little difficult to grasp initially. The *GetSchemaTable* method returns a *DataTable* with a predefined structure. Each *DataRow* in the *DataTable* returned by this method corresponds to a different column in the query results, and the *DataColumn* objects represent properties or attributes for those columns.

The following code snippet prints the name and database data type for each column the query returns.

Visual Basic .NET

```
Dim strConn, strSQL As String
strConn = "Provider=SQLOLEDB;Data Source=(local)\NetSDK;" & _
          "Initial Catalog=Northwind;Trusted_Connection=Yes;"
strSQL = "SELECT OrderID, CustomerID, EmployeeID, OrderDate FROM Orders"
Dim cn As New OleDbConnection(strConn)
cn.Open()
Dim cmd As New OleDbCommand(strSQL, cn)
Dim rdr As OleDbDataReader = cmd.ExecuteReader
Dim tbl As DataTable = rdr.GetSchemaTable
Dim row As DataRow
For Each row In tbl.Rows
    Console.WriteLine(row("ColumnName").ToString & " - " & _
                      CType(row("ProviderType"), OleDbType).ToString)
Next row
```

Visual C# .NET

```
string strConn, strSQL;
strConn = "Provider=SQLOLEDB;Data Source=(local)\\NetSDK;" +
          "Initial Catalog=Northwind;Trusted_Connection=Yes;";
strSQL = "SELECT OrderID, CustomerID, EmployeeID, OrderDate FROM Orders";
OleDbConnection cn = new OleDbConnection(strConn);
cn.Open();
OleDbCommand cmd = new OleDbCommand(strSQL, cn);
OleDbDataReader rdr = cmd.ExecuteReader();
DataTable tbl = rdr.GetSchemaTable();
foreach (DataRow row in tbl.Rows)
    Console.WriteLine(row["ColumnName"] + " - " +
                      ((OleDbType) row["ProviderType"]).ToString());
```

> **Note** The code snippet for each language converts the integer
> stored in the ProviderType column to the *OleDbType* enumeration.

Various .NET data providers use different table schemas in the *DataTable* returned by *GetSchemaTable*. For example, the *DataTable* returned by the SQL Server .NET data provider *DataReader* object's *GetSchemaTable* method includes columns not available through the OLE DB .NET data provider.

GetData Method and *Depth* Property

The *Depth* property and the *GetData* method are reserved for queries that return hierarchical data. These features are not supported in the current release of ADO.NET.

Creating *Parameter* Objects

The *Parameter* has six constructors. The *ParameterCollection* has six over-loaded *Add* methods that you can use to create a *Parameter* and append it to the collection. You can also use the *CreateParameter* method on the *Command*. So many choices.

Which method of creating a *Parameter* is right for you? That depends on which properties on the *Parameter* you want to set. One of the constructors for *OleDbParameter* that lets you supply values for the *ParameterName*, *OleDb-Type*, *Size*, *Direction*, *IsNullable*, *Precision*, *Scale*, *SourceColumn*, *SourceVersion*, and *Value* properties. Think about the properties you want to set and then use the constructor that provides the functionality you need.

Properties of the *OleDbParameter* Object

Table 4-8 lists the commonly used properties of the *OleDbParameter* object.

Table 4-8   Commonly Used Properties of the *OleDbParameter* Object

Property Name	Data Type	Description
DataType	*Type*	Specifies the data type for the parameter object.
DbType	*OleDbType*	Specifies the database data type for the parameter.
Direction	*ParameterDirection*	Specifies the direction for the parameter—input, output, input/output, or return.

(continued)

Table 4-8   Commonly Used Properties of the *OleDbParameter* Object   *(continued)*

Property Name	Data Type	Description
IsNullable	*Boolean*	Indicates whether the parameter can accept *Null*.
OleDbType	*OleDbType*	Specifies the OLE DB data type for the parameter.
ParameterName	*String*	Specifies the name of the parameter.
Precision	*Byte*	Specifies the precision for the parameter.
Scale	*Byte*	Specifies the numeric scale for the parameter.
Size	*Int32*	Specifies the size of the parameter.
SourceColumn	*String*	Specifies the name of the column in the *DataSet* that this parameter references. See Chapter 10 for more information on binding query parameters to *DataSet* objects.
SourceVersion	*DataRowVersion*	Specifies version (current or original) of the column in the *DataSet* that this parameter references. See Chapter 10 for more information on binding query parameters to *DataSet* objects.
Value	*Object*	Specifies the value for the parameter.

ParameterName Property

Generally speaking, the *ParameterName* property of the *Parameter* is designed solely to let you locate the desired *Parameter* in a *Command* object's *Parameters* collection. If you're calling a stored procedure with the OLE DB .NET data provider, for example, you don't need to have the *ParameterName* property on your *Parameter* objects match the names of the parameters in your stored procedure. But setting the *ParameterName* property on your *Parameter* objects can make your code easier to read.

> **Note**   The SQL Server .NET data provider matches your *Parameter* objects to the parameter markers in your query based on the *ParameterName* property of the *Parameter* objects. So, if you use
>
> ```
> SELECT OrderID, CustomerID, EmployeeID, OrderDate
>     FROM Orders WHERE CustomerID = @CustomerID
> ```
>
> as your query, you need to set the *ParameterName* property of your *Parameter* to *@CustomerID*.

Direction Property

If you're calling a stored procedure and you want to use output or return parameters, you should set the *Direction* property of your *Parameter* to one of the values listed in Table 4-9.

Table 4-9   Members of the *ParameterDirection* Enumeration

Constant	Value	Description
Input	1	Default value. The parameter is input-only.
Output	2	The parameter is output-only.
InputOutput	3	The parameter is input/output.
ReturnValue	6	The parameter will contain the return value of a stored procedure.

Because the default value for *Direction* is *Input*, you need to explicitly set this property only on *Parameter* objects that are not input-only.

Most code generation tools will query your database for parameter information, including the direction of the parameters. Even if you're using a robust code generation tool, such as the ones included in Visual Studio .NET, you might still need to modify the *Direction value* of your *Parameter* objects in some cases.

Why, you ask? Most databases support the use of input, output, and input-output parameters on stored procedures, but not all databases have language constructs to let you explicitly specify the direction for your stored procedure parameters. SQL Server, for example, supports the OUTPUT keyword in stored procedure definitions to specify that the parameter can return a value. However, the definition of the parameter in the stored procedure is the same regardless of whether the parameter is input/output or output-only. As a result, code generation tools cannot determine whether the parameter is input/output or output-only. The Visual Studio .NET tools assume that the parameter is input/output. If you want an output-only parameter, you must set the direction explicitly in your code.

Value Property

Use the *Value* property to check or set the value of your *Parameter*. This property contains an *Object* data type. As a result, you might need to convert the data in order to store it in a data type such as a string or integer.

SourceColumn and *SourceVersion* Properties

The *SourceColumn* and *SourceVersion* properties control how the *Parameter* fetches data from a *DataRow* when you submit pending changes to your database by calling the *Update* method on the *DataAdapter*.

I'll cover this feature in much more depth in Chapter 10 when I cover updating your database.

DbType and *OleDbType* Properties

The *Parameter* is the only class in the ADO.NET object model that requires you to use the data types used by your database.

For example, when you retrieve the *CustomerID* field from the Customers table into a *DataSet* using a *DataAdapter*, you don't need to know whether the field in the database is a fixed length or a variable length, nor do you need to know whether the field in the database can handle Unicode data. The data type for the *DataColumn* object is simply a string.

The *DataColumn* object's *DataType* controls the data type that ADO.NET will use to store the contents of the column and accepts a .NET type as returned by the *GetType* or *typeof* function, depending on your language of choice. This data type has a loose connection to the data type that the database uses to store the data. String-based database data types (such as *char* and *varchar*) are mapped to the .NET data type *String*, noninteger numeric database data types (*money*, *decimal*, *numeric*) are mapped to the .NET data type *Decimal*, and so forth.

The data type for the *Parameter* must be more precise. In the earlier code snippet, we used the query

```
SELECT OrderID, CustomerID, EmployeeID, OrderDate
    FROM Orders WHERE CustomerID = ?
```

with a parameter whose data type is *wchar* (the *w* stands for *wide* to indicate that the string handles double-byte Unicode characters rather than single-byte ANSI characters) and whose length is 5. If we don't use the appropriate data type for the parameter, the database might not handle the information stored in the parameter the way we expect.

Each *Parameter* exposes a *DbType* property and a data type property that's specific to the .NET data provider. For example, the *OleDbParameter* has an *OleDbType* property and the *SqlParameter* has a *SqlDbType* property.

The *DbType* and *OleDbType* properties are closely related. Setting the value of one of these properties affects the value of the other. For example, if you set the *DbType* property of an *OleDbParameter* to *DbType.Int32*, you're implicitly setting the *OleDbType* to *OleDbType.Integer*. Similarly, if you set the *OleDbType* to *OleDbType.UnsignedTinyInt*, you're implicitly setting the *DbType* property to *DbType.Byte*.

Precision, *Scale*, and *Size* Properties

When you define the structure for a table in a database, some data types require that you specify additional information beyond simply the name of the data type. Binary and character-based columns often have a maximum size. If you're using a *Parameter* with such data, you must set the *Size* property to the desired size. Numeric data types often let you specify the scale (number of digits) and precision (number of digits to the right of the decimal point).

Questions That Should Be Asked More Frequently

Q.   I called a stored procedure that returns a set of rows. Everything seems to work except that the output and return parameters are empty. Why is that?

A.   You can think of a stored procedure as a function in your code. The function doesn't return a value until it has executed all of its code. If the stored procedure returns results and you haven't finished processing these results, the stored procedure hasn't really finished executing. Until you've closed the *DataReader*, the return and output parameters of your *Command* won't contain the values returned by your stored procedure.

Let's say we have the stored procedure

```
CREATE PROCEDURE RowsAndOutput (@OutputParam int OUTPUT) AS
    SELECT @OutputParam = COUNT(*) FROM Customers
    SELECT CustomerID, CompanyName, ContactName, Phone FROM Customers
```

and we call it with the following code:

Visual Basic .NET

```
Dim strConn, strSQL As String
strConn = "Provider=SQLOLEDB;Data Source=(local)\NetSDK;" & _
        "Initial Catalog=Northwind;Trusted_Connection=Yes;"
Dim cn As New OleDbConnection(strConn)
cn.Open()
strSQL = "{CALL RowsAndOutput(?)}"
Dim cmd As New OleDbCommand(strSQL, cn)
Dim param As OleDbParameter
param = cmd.Parameters.Add("@OutputParam", OleDbType.Integer)
param.Direction = ParameterDirection.Output
Dim rdrCustomers As OleDbDataReader = cmd.ExecuteReader
```

(continued)

```
Console.WriteLine("After execution - " & CStr(param.Value))
Do While rdrCustomers.Read
Loop
Console.WriteLine("After reading rows - " & CStr(param.Value))
Do While rdrCustomers.NextResult()
Loop
Console.WriteLine("After reading all results - " &
                    CStr(param.Value))
rdrCustomers.Close()
Console.WriteLine("After closing DataReader - " & CStr(param.Value))
```

Visual C# .NET

```
string strConn = "Provider=SQLOLEDB;Data Source=(local)\\NetSDK;" +
                    "Initial Catalog=Northwind;Trusted_Connection=Yes;";
OleDbConnection cn = new OleDbConnection(strConn);
cn.Open();

string strSQL = "{CALL RowsAndOutput(?)}";
OleDbCommand cmd = new OleDbCommand(strSQL, cn);
OleDbParameter param;
param = cmd.Parameters.Add("@OutputParam", OleDbType.Integer);
param.Direction = ParameterDirection.Output;
OleDbDataReader rdrCustomers = cmd.ExecuteReader();
Console.WriteLine("After execution - " + (string) param.Value);
while (rdrCustomers.Read())
{}
Console.WriteLine("After reading rows - " + (string) param.Value);
while (rdrCustomers.NextResult())
{}
Console.WriteLine("After reading all results - " +
                    (string) param.Value);
rdrCustomers.Close();
Console.WriteLine("After closing DataReader - " +
                    (string) param.Value);
```

Even though the stored procedure sets the value of the output parameter before running the query that returns rows from the Customers table, the value of the output parameter is not available until after the *DataReader* is closed.

Q. I saw a snippet of sample code in the MSDN documentation that set the value of parameters without setting the *DbType* or the .NET data provider-specific data type property. How does that work? Is using that type of code safe?

A. This is a rather impressive ADO.NET feature, but I've been hesitant to discuss it in much depth because, well, frankly, it scares me. That's probably just due to my background in technical support, but I'd rather explicitly set the data types for my parameters.

In the vast majority of applications, you know the data types of the parameters you're calling. Ad-hoc query tools are probably the only types of applications in which you might need to call a parameterized query or stored procedure without knowing the data types of the parameters involved.

Getting back to the feature, if you leave the data type properties of a *Parameter* uninitialized but set the *Value* property, the *Parameter* will automatically choose the appropriate data type to use. The following code successfully retrieves all customers whose CustomerID column begins with the letter *A*.

Visual Basic .NET

```
Dim strConn, strSQL As String
strConn = "Provider=SQLOLEDB;Data Source=(local)\NetSDK;" & _
        "Initial Catalog=Northwind;Trusted_Connection=Yes;"
Dim cn As New OleDbConnection(strConn)
cn.Open()
strSQL = "SELECT CustomerID, CompanyName FROM Customers " & _
        "WHERE CustomerID LIKE ?"
Dim cmd As New OleDbCommand(strSQL, cn)
cmd.Parameters.Add("@CustomerID", "A%")
Dim rdr As OleDbDataReader = cmd.ExecuteReader
Do While rdr.Read
    Console.WriteLine(rdr(0))
Loop
rdr.Close()
cn.Close()
```

Visual C# .NET

```
string strConn, strSQL;
strConn = "Provider=SQLOLEDB;Data Source=(local)\\NetSDK;" +
        "Initial Catalog=Northwind;Trusted_Connection=Yes;";
OleDbConnection cn = new OleDbConnection(strConn);
```

(continued)

```
cn.Open();
strSQL = "SELECT CustomerID FROM Customers WHERE CustomerID LIKE ?";
OleDbCommand cmd = new OleDbCommand(strSQL, cn);
cmd.Parameters.Add("@CustomerID", "A%");
OleDbDataReader rdr = cmd.ExecuteReader();
while (rdr.Read())
    Console.WriteLine(rdr[0]);
rdr.Close();
cn.Close();
```

This query retrieves the desired rows, but you won't see the *DbType*, *OleDbType*, or *Size* properties of the *OleDbParameter* set to the expected values. The *Parameter* determines the appropriate values for these properties when you execute the query and only sets these properties internally. If you use the SQL Profiler tracing tool in SQL Server 2000, you'll see that the Command executed the following query:

```
exec sp_executesql
    N'SELECT CustomerID FROM Customers WHERE CustomerID LIKE @P1',
    N'@P1 nvarchar(2)', N'A%'
```

The *Parameter* assumed that the parameter should be a variable-length Unicode string of length 2. I've successfully called parameterized queries against SQL Server, Oracle, and Access databases using string-based and numeric parameters (such as currency) without encountering a problem.

This fact that this feature works so well really impressed me. My technical support background still makes me uneasy when I see a feature like this, however. It's not that I don't have confidence in the feature, it's just that I'd rather see developers set the data type and size properties explicitly.

Q.   Why can't I call a stored procedure and successfully retrieve the value of the return parameter? I've been able to use output parameters successfully, but not a return parameter.

A.   First, if you used the *Command* to create a *DataReader*, make sure you've closed the *DataReader* before trying to examine the contents of the return parameter. (See the question on page 145 for more on this process.)

The other day, a co-worker stopped by my office and said he'd been trying to retrieve the value of the return parameter for his stored procedure. He knew to close the *DataReader* first, but that wasn't the problem. His stored procedure looked something like this:

```
CREATE PROCEDURE GetReturnParameter (@CustomerID nchar(5)) AS
SELECT OrderID, CustomerID, EmployeeID, OrderDate
      FROM Orders WHERE CustomerID = @CustomerID
RETURN @@ROWCOUNT
```

And his Visual Basic .NET code looked like this:

```
Dim cmd As New OleDbCommand("GetReturnParameter", cn)
cmd.CommandType = CommandType.StoredProcedure
cmd.Parameters.Add("@CustomerID", OleDbType.WChar, 5)
cmd.Parameters("@CustomerID").Value = "ALFKI"
cmd.Parameters.Add("@RetVal", OleDbType.Integer)
cmd.Parameters("@RetVal").Direction = ParameterDirection.ReturnValue
```

To make a long story short, his parameters were in the wrong order. It was a simple mistake that anyone could have made. The fact that he was setting the *CommandType* to *StoredProcedure* made the problem more difficult to discover, which is part of why I've never been a big fan of the *CommandType* property in ADO.NET or in ADO. The ADO.NET development team meant well by adding this feature, but I think developers are better off learning how to build the real query.

The appropriate *CommandText* in this case is

```
{? = CALL GetReturnParameter(?)}
```

The syntax is similar to calling a function in Visual Basic or C#. You want a parameter to store the value returned by the stored procedure. Here's the full code for calling the stored procedure:

Visual Basic .NET

```
Dim strConn, strSQL As String
strConn = "Provider=SQLOLEDB;Data Source=(local)\NetSDK;" & _
          "Initial Catalog=Northwind;Trusted_Connection=Yes;"
Dim cn As New OleDbConnection(strConn)
cn.Open()
strSQL = "{? = CALL GetReturnParameter(?)}"
Dim cmd As New OleDbCommand(strSQL, cn)
cmd.Parameters.Add("@RetVal", OleDbType.Integer)
cmd.Parameters("@RetVal").Direction = ParameterDirection.ReturnValue
cmd.Parameters.Add("@CustomerID", OleDbType.WChar, 5)
cmd.Parameters("@CustomerID").Value = "ALFKI"
Dim rdr As OleDbDataReader = cmd.ExecuteReader
Do While rdr.Read
    Console.WriteLine("OrderID = " & rdr(0).ToString)
Loop
rdr.Close()
Console.WriteLine(cmd.Parameters(0).Value.ToString & " orders")
```

Visual C# .NET

```csharp
string strConn, strSQL;
strConn = "Provider=SQLOLEDB;Data Source=(local)\\NetSDK;" +
          "Initial Catalog=Northwind;Trusted_Connection=Yes;";
OleDbConnection cn = new OleDbConnection(strConn);
cn.Open();
strSQL = "{? = CALL GetReturnParameter(?)}";
OleDbCommand cmd = new OleDbCommand(strSQL, cn);
cmd.Parameters.Add("@RetVal", OleDbType.Integer);
cmd.Parameters["@RetVal"].Direction = ParameterDirection.ReturnValue;
cmd.Parameters.Add("@CustomerID", OleDbType.WChar, 5);
cmd.Parameters["@CustomerID"].Value = "ALFKI";
OleDbDataReader rdr = cmd.ExecuteReader();
while (rdr.Read())
    Console.WriteLine("OrderID = " + rdr[0].ToString());
rdr.Close();
Console.WriteLine(cmd.Parameters[0].Value.ToString() + " orders");
cn.Close();
```

Q. I'm trying to migrate code from ADO to ADO.NET. My old program used the *Refresh* method on ADO *Parameters* collection. Doesn't the ADO.NET *ParameterCollection* object have a *Refresh* method?

A. There is no *Refresh* method on the ADO.NET *ParameterCollection* object, at least not yet. As of the initial release, there is no way to use the ADO.NET object model to "auto-magically" supply parameter information for a generic parameterized query.

However, if you're calling a stored procedure, there is a solution. The *CommandBuilder* object, which we'll discuss later in Chapter 10, exposes a *DeriveParameters* method that can populate a *Command* object's *Parameters* collection if the *Command* calls a stored procedure. The following code snippet demonstrates how to use this functionality.

Visual Basic .NET

```vb
Dim strConn As String = "Provider=SQLOLEDB;" & _
                        Data Source=(local)\NetSDK;" & _
                        "Initial Catalog=Northwind;" & _
                        Trusted_Connection=Yes;"
Dim cn As New OleDbConnection(strConn)
cn.Open()
Dim cmd As New OleDbCommand("SalesByCategory", cn)
cmd.CommandType = CommandType.StoredProcedure
OleDbCommandBuilder.DeriveParameters(cmd)
Dim param As OleDbParameter
```

```
For Each param In cmd.Parameters
    Console.WriteLine(param.ParameterName)
    Console.WriteLine(vbTab & param.Direction.ToString())
    Console.WriteLine(vbTab & param.OleDbType.ToString())
    Console.WriteLine()
Next param
cn.Close()
```

Visual C# .NET

```
string strConn = "Provider=SQLOLEDB;Data Source=(local)\\NetSDK;" +
                 "Initial Catalog=Northwind;Trusted_Connection=Yes;";
OleDbConnection cn = new OleDbConnection(strConn);
cn.Open();
OleDbCommand cmd = new OleDbCommand("SalesByCategory", cn);
cmd.CommandType = CommandType.StoredProcedure;
OleDbCommandBuilder.DeriveParameters(cmd);
foreach (OleDbParameter param in cmd.Parameters)
{
    Console.WriteLine(param.ParameterName);
    Console.WriteLine("\t" + param.Direction.ToString());
    Console.WriteLine("\t" + param.OleDbType.ToString());
    Console.WriteLine();
}
cn.Close();
```

Q.   The ADO object model supports asynchronous queries. How do I use the ADO.NET object model to execute a query asynchronously?

A.   As of the initial release of ADO.NET, the object model does not provide such functionality.

The ADO *Command* object does allow you to execute queries asynchronously, but the major reason that this feature was added to the ADO object model was that writing threading code in Visual Basic "classic" was next to impossible for the majority of Visual Basic developers.

The .NET Framework greatly simplifies the process of working with threads. That's not to say that writing threading code is simple. Writing solid multi-threaded code is still a challenge because multi-threaded code exposes you to an entirely new level of possible problems. It's very easy to write multi-threaded code that can create problems that you might not discover until long after you've deployed your application. If you want to write multi-threaded code in either Visual Basic .NET or Visual C# .NET, I strongly recommend picking up a book that thoroughly discusses all the ins and outs of writing solid multi-threaded code.

The following code snippet uses multi-threading strictly as an example of how you can execute a query on another thread. The code also includes an example of using the *Command* object's *Cancel* method to cancel the execution of the query. I do not claim to be a threading guru. This code is intended as a very simple example and should not be used in a production application.

To use this code, create a new Console application in your language of choice. Then add a new Class to the project whose class name is *clsSlowQuery*. Paste the code into the code files as described in the comments. The code calls the *CallSlowQuery* method of the class, which starts a new thread and starts a query on that thread. The query continues to run on the background thread, and the method returns immediately after starting the query. When and if the query completes, the results will appear in the Console window. The code waits 2.5 seconds and then calls the *CancelQuery* method on the class to cancel the execution of the query.

Visual Basic .NET

```
'Use this code in Module1.vb
Dim obj As New clsSlowQuery()
obj.CallSlowQuery()
Threading.Thread.Sleep(2500)

obj.CancelQuery()

'Use this code in clsSlowQuery.vb
Public Class clsSlowQuery
    Dim cn As OleDbConnection
    Dim cmd As OleDbCommand

    Dim ts As Threading.ThreadStart
    Dim th As Threading.Thread

    Dim blnRunningQuery, blnCancelledQuery As Boolean

    Public Sub CallSlowQuery()
        If Not blnRunningQuery Then
            SyncLock Me
                blnRunningQuery = True
                ts = New Threading.ThreadStart(AddressOf CallQueryAsync)
                th = New Threading.Thread(ts)
                th.Start()
                Console.WriteLine("Running query")
            End SyncLock
```

```vbnet
    Else
        Dim strMessage As String
        strMessage = "Can't execute CallSlowQuery method." & _
                    vbCrLf & _
                    vbTab & "I'm still waiting on the results " & _
                    "of a previous query."
        Throw New Exception(strMessage)
    End If
End Sub

Public Sub CancelQuery()
    If blnRunningQuery Then
        SyncLock Me
            Try
                blnCancelledQuery = True
                cmd.Cancel()
            Catch ex As Exception
                Console.WriteLine(ex.Message)
            End Try
        End SyncLock
    Else
        Dim strMessage As String
        strMessage = "Can't execute CancelQuery method." & vbCrLf & _
                    vbTab & "I'm not currently running a query."
        Throw New Exception(strMessage)
    End If
End Sub

Private Sub CallQueryAsync()
    Dim strConn As String
    strConn = "Provider=SQLOLEDB;Data Source=(local)\NetSDK;" & _
            "Initial Catalog=Northwind;Trusted_Connection=Yes;"
    Dim strSQL As String = "WAITFOR DELAY '00:00:10';" & _
                        "SELECT Count(*) FROM Customers"
    cn = New OleDbConnection(strConn)
    cn.Open()
    cmd = New OleDbCommand(strSQL, cn)

    Dim intNumCustomers As Integer
    Try
        intNumCustomers = CInt(cmd.ExecuteScalar)
        Console.WriteLine(intNumCustomers)
    Catch ex As Exception
        If blnCancelledQuery = True Then
            Console.WriteLine("Query cancelled")
        Else
            Console.WriteLine(ex.Message)
```

(continued)

```
            End If
        End Try

        cn.Close()
        blnRunningQuery = False
        blnCancelledQuery = False
    End Sub
End Class
```

Visual C# .NET

```csharp
//use this code in Class1.cs
clsSlowQuery obj = new clsSlowQuery();
obj.CallSlowQuery();
System.Threading.Thread.Sleep(2500);

obj.CancelQuery();

//use this code in clsSlowQuery.cs
public class clsSlowQuery
{
    OleDbConnection cn;
    OleDbCommand cmd;

    System.Threading.ThreadStart ts;
    System.Threading.Thread th;

    bool blnRunningQuery, blnCancelledQuery;

    public void CallSlowQuery()
    {
        if (!blnRunningQuery)
            lock (this)
            {
                blnRunningQuery = true;
                ts = new System.Threading.ThreadStart(this.CallQueryAsync);
                th = new System.Threading.Thread(ts);
                th.Start();
                Console.WriteLine("Running query");
            }
        else
        {
            string strMessage;
            strMessage = "Can't execute CallSlowQuery method.\n\t" +
                        "I'm still waiting on the results " +
                        "of a previous query.";
```

```
            throw new Exception(strMessage);
        }
    }

    public void CancelQuery()
    {
        if (blnRunningQuery)
            lock(this)
            {
                try
                {
                    blnCancelledQuery = true;
                    cmd.Cancel();
                }
                catch (Exception ex)
                {
                    Console.WriteLine(ex.Message);
                }
            }
        else
        {
            string strMessage;
            strMessage = "Can't execute CancelQuery method.\n\t" +
                        "I'm not currently running a query.";
            throw new Exception(strMessage);
        }
    }

    private void CallQueryAsync()
    {
        string strConn;
        strConn = "Provider=SQLOLEDB;Data Source=(local)\\NetSDK;" +
                    "Initial Catalog=Northwind;Trusted_Connection=Yes;";
        string strSQL = "WAITFOR DELAY '00:00:10';" +
                        "SELECT Count(*) FROM Customers";
        cn = new OleDbConnection(strConn);
        cn.Open();
        cmd = new OleDbCommand(strSQL, cn);

        int intNumCustomers;
        try
        {
            intNumCustomers = (int) cmd.ExecuteScalar();
            Console.WriteLine(intNumCustomers);
        }
        catch (Exception ex)
```

(continued)

```
        {
            if (blnCancelledQuery)
                Console.WriteLine("Query cancelled");
            else
                Console.WriteLine(ex.Message);
        }

        cn.Close();
        blnRunningQuery = false;
        blnCancelledQuery = false;
    }
}
```

5

Retrieving Data Using *DataAdapter* Objects

As you learned in the previous chapter, you can use *Command* objects and *DataReader* objects to execute queries and examine their results. But what if you want to store the results of a query in an ADO.NET *DataSet* object? You could write code to populate a *DataSet* with new rows by looping through the data available in a *DataReader*, like this.

Visual Basic .NET

```
Dim ds As New DataSet()
Dim tbl As DataTable = ds.Tables.Add("Customers")
'Prepare DataTable.
Dim cmd As New OleDbCommand()
'Prepare Command.
Dim rdr As OleDbDataReader = cmd.ExecuteReader()
Dim row As DataRow
Do While rdr.Read()
    row = tbl.NewRow()
    row("CustomerID") = rdr("CustomerID")
    'Fetch data from other columns.
    tbl.Rows.Add(row)
Loop
rdr.Close()
```

Visual C# .NET

```
DataSet ds = new DataSet();
DataTable tbl = ds.Tables.Add("Customers");
//Prepare DataTable
OleDbCommand cmd = new OleDbCommand();
```

(continued)

```
//Prepare Command.
OleDbDataReader rdr = cmd.ExecuteReader();
DataRow row;
while (rdr.Read())
{
    row = tbl.NewRow();
    row["CustomerID"] = rdr["CustomerID"];
    //Fetch data from other columns
    tbl.Rows.Add(row);
}
rdr.Close();
```

Yikes! Storing the results of your query in a *DataSet* should be simple. This code isn't simple, and it certainly isn't RAD. Who wants to write code like that?

Thankfully, you don't have to. The ADO.NET object model offers a more elegant solution: using the *DataAdapter* object. In this chapter, you'll learn how to use this object to store the results of queries into *DataSet* objects and *DataTable* objects.

What Is a *DataAdapter* Object?

The *DataAdapter* class acts as a bridge between the connected and disconnected halves of the ADO.NET object model. You can use a *DataAdapter* to pull data from your database into your *DataSet*. The *DataAdapter* can also take the cached updates stored in your *DataSet* and submit them to your database. Chapter 10 will cover updating your database with *DataAdapter* objects. In this chapter, we will focus on using *DataAdapter* objects to fetch data from your database.

How the *DataAdapter* Differs from Other Query Objects

When I describe the *DataAdapter* object to database programmers, most nod their heads and say that it sounds similar to the ADO *Command* object, the RDO *rdoQuery* object, and the DAO *QueryDef* object—all of which let you submit queries to your database and store the results in a separate object.

But there are some major differences between the *DataAdapter* and its predecessors, as I'll detail in the following sections.

The *DataAdapter* Is Designed to Work with Disconnected Data

ADO, RDO, and DAO all support disconnected data. Each object model can store the results of a query in a disconnected structure. For example, you can use an ADO *Command* object to fetch data into a *Recordset* that's disconnected from the *Connection* object. However, none of these object models provided disconnected functionality in their initial release. As a result, their query-based objects were never truly designed for disconnected data.

The *DataAdapter* is designed to work with disconnected data. Perhaps the best example of this design is the *Fill* method. You don't even need a live connection to your database to call the *Fill* method. If you call the *Fill* method on a *DataAdapter* whose connection to your database is not currently open, the *DataAdapter* opens that connection, queries the database, fetches and stores the results of the query into your *DataSet*, and then closes the connection to your database.

There Is No Direct Connection Between the *DataAdapter* and the *DataSet*

You fill a *DataTable* in your *DataSet* by passing your *DataSet* as a parameter to the *DataAdapter* object's *Fill* method, as shown here:

Visual Basic .NET

```
OleDbDataAdapter.Fill(DataSet)
```

Visual C# .NET

```
OleDbDataAdapter.Fill(DataSet);
```

Once this call completes, there is no connection between the two objects. The *DataSet* does not maintain a reference, internally or externally, to the *DataAdapter*, and the *DataAdapter* does not maintain a reference to the *DataSet*. Also, the *DataSet* contains no information indicating where the data originated—no connection string, no table name, and no column names. Thus, you can pass *DataSet* objects from your middle-tier server to your client applications without divulging any information about the location or structure of your database.

The *DataAdapter* Contains the Updating Logic to Submit Changes Stored in Your *DataSet* Back to Your Database

The *DataAdapter* acts as a two-way street. You can use a *DataAdapter* to submit a query and store its results in a *DataSet*, and you can use it to submit pending changes back to your database. This is a major change from previous data access models.

For example, in ADO, you use a *Command*, explicitly or implicitly, to fetch the results of your query into your *Recordset* object. When you want to update your database, you call the *Update* method of the *Recordset*. The *Command* object is not involved in the update process.

With ADO.NET, you use the *DataAdapter* object's *Update* method to submit the changes stored in your *DataSet* to your database. When you call the *Update* method, you supply the *DataSet* as a parameter. The *DataSet* can cache changes, but it's the *DataAdapter* object that contains your updating logic.

You Control the Updating Logic in the *DataAdapter*

That statement bears repeating: you control the updating logic in the *Data-Adapter*. As far as I'm concerned, this is the number-one reason to move from ADO, DAO, or RDO to ADO.NET. You can use your own custom INSERT, UPDATE, and DELETE queries or submit updates using stored procedures. The first time I noticed this feature while examining the structure for the *Data-Adapter*, three thoughts ran through my mind: "Wow!," "I can't wait to see developers' reactions to this feature!," and "Why didn't we think of this earlier?"

Because none of the previous data access models offer this level of control over updating logic, many developers have been unable to use many of the rapid application development (RAD) features offered by those object models. Many database administrators will permit users to modify data in the database only by calling a stored procedure. Users don't have permissions to modify data by running UPDATE, INSERT INTO, or DELETE queries. But these are the queries that DAO, RDO, and ADO generate to translate changes made to *Recordset* objects and *rdoResultset* objects into changes in your database. This means that developers building a database application with ADO cannot take advantage of the *Recordset* object's ability to submit changes to the database.

I spoke to one developer during the Visual Studio .NET beta who was skeptical about moving to ADO.NET. As if attempting to dismiss the new object model, he asked, "Can I use stored procedures to update my database?" He looked shocked when I smiled and responded, "Yes." I could almost hear the wheels in his brain turning for a moment or two before he asked, "How?"

Part of the reason he was so perplexed is that database administrators create separate stored procedures for updating, inserting, and deleting rows. So, in order for a data access object model to support submitting updates using stored procedures in a RAD way, the data access model must let you specify separate stored procedures for updates, inserts, and deletes.

And that's exactly what the *DataAdapter* does. The *DataAdapter* has four properties that contain *Command* objects—one for the query to fetch data, one for submitting pending updates, one for submitting pending insertions, and one for submitting pending deletions. You can specify your own action queries or stored procedures for each of these *Command* objects, as well as parameters that can move data from your *DataSet* to your stored procedure and back.

Developers can be a difficult bunch. (As a developer, I'm allowed to make that observation.) We like control and performance, but we also like ease of use. The *DataAdapter* offers all of the above. You can provide your own updating logic, or you can request that ADO.NET generate action queries similar to the ones that ADO and DAO automatically generate behind the scenes. You can even use some features in Visual Studio .NET to generate the updating logic at design time, an option that combines ease of use with control and performance.

We'll look at sample updating code and discuss the actual mechanics of updating your database using the *DataAdapter* in Chapter 10. In this chapter, we'll focus on the structure of the *DataAdapter* and how to use it to fetch the results of your queries.

Anatomy of the *DataAdapter*

Now that you understand a little more about what the *DataAdapter* does, let's look at the structure of the object to understand how it works.

The *DataAdapter* is designed to help you store the results of your query in *DataSet* objects and *DataTable* objects. As you learned in Chapter 4, the *Command* object lets you examine the results of your query through a *DataReader* object. The *DataAdapter* object consists of a series of *Command* objects and a collection of mapping properties that determines how the *DataAdapter* will communicate with your *DataSet*. Figure 5-1 shows the structure of the *DataAdapter*.

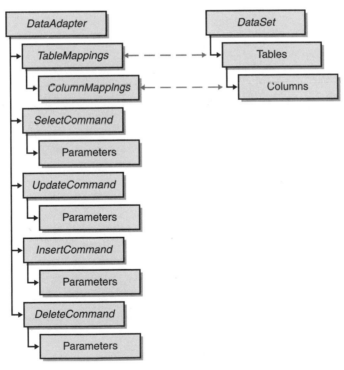

Figure 5-1   The structure of the *DataAdapter*

Child Commands

When you use a *DataAdapter* to store the results of a query in a *DataSet*, the *DataAdapter* uses a *Command* to communicate with your database. Internally, the *DataAdapter* uses a *DataReader* to fetch the results and then copies that information into new rows in your *DataSet*. This process is roughly similar to the snippet of code shown at the start of this chapter.

The *Command* object that the *DataAdapter* uses to fetch data from your database is stored in the *DataAdapter* object's *SelectCommand* property.

The *DataAdapter* object also has other properties that contain *Command* objects—*InsertCommand*, *UpdateCommand*, and *DeleteCommand*. The *DataAdapter* uses these *Command* objects to submit the changes stored within your *DataSet* to your database. We'll look closely at how the *DataAdapter* uses these *Command* objects to submit updates to your database in Chapter 10.

TableMappings Collection

By default, the *DataAdapter* assumes that the columns in the *DataReader* match up with columns in your *DataSet*. However, you might encounter situations in which you want the schema of your *DataSet* to differ from the schema in your database. You might want to use a different name for a particular column in your *DataSet*. Traditionally, developers have renamed columns in this fashion within the query by using an alias. For example, if your Employees table had columns named EmpID, LName, and FName, you could use aliases within the query to change the column names to EmployeeID, LastName, and FirstName within the results, as shown in the following query:

```
SELECT EmpID AS EmployeeID, LName AS LastName, FName AS FirstName
    FROM Employees
```

The *DataAdapter* offers a mechanism for mapping the results of your query to the structure of your *DataSet*: the *TableMappings* collection.

The query above describes a table with column names such as EmpID, LName, and FName. Let's take this example a step further and say that the database's table name is something obscure, like Table123. We want to map that data to a table in our *DataSet* named Employees that contains friendlier column names such as EmployeeID, LastName, and FirstName. The *DataAdapter* object's *TableMappings* collection allows you to create such a mapping layer between your database and the *DataSet*.

The *TableMappings* property returns a *DataTableMappingsCollection* object that contains a collection of *DataTableMapping* objects. Each object lets you create a mapping between a table (or view or stored procedure) in your database and the corresponding table name in your *DataSet*. The *Data-TableMapping* object also has a *ColumnMappings* property that returns a *Data-ColumnMappingsCollection* object, which consists of a collection of *DataColumnMapping* objects. Each *DataColumnMapping* object maps a column in your database to a column in your *DataSet*.

Note   The *DataColumnMappingCollection* class has the longest name I've encountered so far. Thanks to the wonders of IntelliSense and statement completion, I don't have to type the entire class name when I'm working in Visual Studio .NET.

Figure 5-2 shows how the *DataAdapter* object's *TableMappings* collection maps the employee data structure from our database table to the corresponding structure in our *DataSet*.

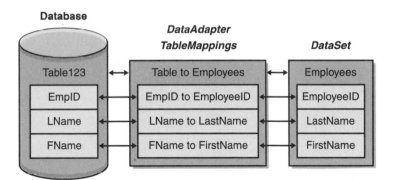

Figure 5-2   The *DataAdapter* object's *TableMappings* collection

In the figure, we're mapping the database's Table123 table to the *DataSet* object's Employees table, but the mapping information implies that it's mapping Table to Employees. This is because the *DataAdapter* really has no idea which table it's communicating with in the database. The *DataAdapter* can retrieve column names from the result of the query using the *DataReader* but has no way of determining the table name. As a result, the *DataAdapter* assumes that the table name is Table, and the entry in the *TableMappings* collection maps Table to Employees.

The following code snippet shows how you can populate the *Data-Adapter* object's *TableMappings* collection in our example.

Visual Basic .NET

```
Dim da As OleDbDataAdapter
'Initialize DataAdapter.
Dim TblMap As DataTableMapping
Dim ColMap As DataColumnMapping
TblMap = da.TableMappings.Add("Table", "Employees")
ColMap = TblMap.ColumnMappings.Add("EmpID", "EmployeeID")
ColMap = TblMap.ColumnMappings.Add("LName", "LastName")
ColMap = TblMap.ColumnMappings.Add("FName", "FirstName")
```

Visual C# .NET

```
OleDbDataAdapter da;
//Initialize DataAdapter.
DataTableMapping TblMap;
DataColumnMapping ColMap;
TblMap = da.TableMappings.Add("Table", "Employees");
ColMap = TblMap.ColumnMappings.Add("EmpID", "EmployeeID");
ColMap = TblMap.ColumnMappings.Add("LName", "LastName");
ColMap = TblMap.ColumnMappings.Add("FName", "FirstName");
```

Creating and Using *DataAdapter* Objects

You now know what a *DataAdapter* is and what it can do for you, so let's examine how to create and use one.

Creating a *DataAdapter*

When you create a *DataAdapter*, you generally want to set its *SelectCommand* property to a valid *Command* object. The following code snippet sets the *SelectCommand* for a new *DataAdapter*.

Visual Basic .NET

```
Dim strConn As String = "Provider=SQLOLEDB;Data Source=(local)\NetSDK;" & _
                        "Initial Catalog=Northwind;Trusted_Connection=Yes;"
Dim cn As New OleDbConnection(strConn)
Dim strSQL As String = "SELECT CustomerID, CompanyName FROM Customers"
Dim cmd As New OleDbCommand(strSQL, cn)
Dim da As New OleDbDataAdapter()
da.SelectCommand = cmd
```

Visual C# .NET

```
string strConn = "Provider=SQLOLEDB;Data Source=(local)\\NetSDK;" +
                 "Initial Catalog=Northwind;Trusted_Connection=Yes;";
OleDbConnection cn = new OleDbConnection(strConn);
string strSQL = "SELECT CustomerID, CompanyName FROM Customers";
OleDbCommand cmd = new OleDbCommand(strSQL, cn);
OleDbDataAdapter da = new OleDbDataAdapter();
da.SelectCommand = cmd;
```

DataAdapter Constructors

The *DataAdapter* class has three constructors that you can use to simplify the process of creating a *DataAdapter*, as shown in the following code. One constructor accepts a query string and a connection string.

Visual Basic .NET

```
Dim strConn As String = "Provider=SQLOLEDB;Data Source=(local)\NetSDK;" & _
                        "Initial Catalog=Northwind;Trusted_Connection=Yes;"
Dim strSQL As String = "SELECT CustomerID, CompanyName FROM Customers"
Dim da As New OleDbDataAdapter(strSQL, strConn)
```

Visual C# .NET

```
string strConn = "Provider=SQLOLEDB;Data Source=(local)\\NetSDK;" +
                 "Initial Catalog=Northwind;Trusted_Connection=Yes;";
string strSQL = "SELECT CustomerID, CompanyName FROM Customers";
OleDbDataAdapter da = new OleDbDataAdapter(strSQL, strConn);
```

There's a potential drawback to this approach. Say you're going to use a series of *DataAdapter* objects in your application. Creating your *DataAdapter* objects in this fashion will create a new *Connection* object for each *DataAdapter*. You can ensure that your *DataAdapter* objects use the same *Connection* object by using the *DataAdapter* constructor that accepts a query string and a *Connection* object. The following code snippet creates two *DataAdapter* objects, each using the same *Connection* object:

Visual Basic .NET

```
Dim strConn As String = "Provider=SQLOLEDB;Data Source=(local)\NetSDK;" & _
                        "Initial Catalog=Northwind;Trusted_Connection=Yes;"
Dim cn As New OleDbConnection(strConn)
Dim daCustomers, daOrders As OleDbDataAdapter
daCustomers = New OleDbDataAdapter("SELECT ... FROM Customers", cn)
daOrders = New OleDbDataAdapter("SELECT ... FROM Orders", cn)
```

Visual C# .NET

```
string strConn = "Provider=SQLOLEDB;Data Source=(local)\\NetSDK;" +
                 "Initial Catalog=Northwind;Trusted_Connection=Yes;";
OleDbConnection cn = new OleDbConnection(strConn);
OleDbDataAdapter daCustomers, daOrders;
daCustomers = new OleDbDataAdapter("SELECT ... FROM Customers", cn);
daOrders = new OleDbDataAdapter("SELECT ... FROM Orders", cn);
```

The *DataAdapter* also offers a third constructor that accepts a *Command* object. If you've already created a *Command* object and want to create a *Data-Adapter* that uses your *Command* object to populate a *DataSet*, you can use the following code:

Visual Basic .NET

```
Dim strConn As String = "Provider=SQLOLEDB;Data Source=(local)\NetSDK;" & _
                        "Initial Catalog=Northwind;Trusted_Connection=Yes;"
Dim cn As New OleDbConnection(strConn)
Dim strSQL As String = "SELECT CustomerID, CompanyName FROM Customers"
Dim cmd As New OleDbCommand(strSQL, cn)
Dim da As New OleDbDataAdapter(cmd)
```

Visual C# .NET

```
string strConn = "Provider=SQLOLEDB;Data Source=(local)\\NetSDK;"
                 "Initial Catalog=Northwind;Trusted_Connection;";
OleDbConnection cn = new OleDbConnection(strConn);
string strSQL = "SELECT CustomerID, CompanyName FROM Customers"
OleDbCommand cmd = new OleDbCommand(strSQL, cn);
OleDbDataAdapter da = new OleDbDataAdapter(cmd);
```

Retrieving Results from a Query

Now that we've looked at a few different ways to create a *DataAdapter* programmatically, let's look at how to use one to store the results of a query into a *DataSet*. First let's create a simple *DataAdapter* to fetch data from the Customers table in the Northwind database.

Using the *Fill* Method

Calling the *DataAdapter* object's *Fill* method executes the query stored in the *DataAdapter* object's *SelectCommand* property and stores the results in a *DataSet*. The following code calls the *Fill* method:

Visual Basic .NET

```
Dim strConn, strSQL As String
strConn = "Provider=SQLOLEDB;Data Source=(local)\NetSDK;" & _
          "Initial Catalog=Northwind;Trusted_Connection=Yes;"
strSQL = "SELECT CustomerID, CompanyName, ContactName, Phone " & _
          "FROM Customers"
Dim da As New OleDbDataAdapter(strSQL, strConn)
Dim ds As New DataSet()
da.Fill(ds)
```

Visual C# .NET

```
string strConn, strSQL;
strConn = "Provider=SQLOLEDB;Data Source=(local)\\NetSDK;" +
          "Initial Catalog=Northwind;Trusted_Connection=Yes;";
strSQL = "SELECT CustomerID, CompanyName, ContactName, Phone " +
          "FROM Customers";
OleDbDataAdapter da = new OleDbDataAdapter(strSQL, strConn);
DataSet ds = new DataSet();
da.Fill(ds);
```

In this code snippet, calling the *Fill* method creates a new *DataTable* in the *DataSet*. The new *DataTable* contains columns that correspond to the columns returned by the query—CustomerID, CompanyName, ContactName, and Phone.

Creating *DataTable* Objects and *DataColumn* Objects Using the *Fill* Method

Calling the *Fill* method in the previous example created a new *DataTable* in the *DataSet*. The new *DataTable* has columns named CustomerID, CompanyName, ContactName, and Phone, but the name of the *DataTable* object is Table, not Customers.

We already touched on this behavior when we discussed the *DataAdapter* object's *TableMappings* collection. We can add an item to this collection to inform the *DataAdapter* that we want to map the results of the query to a *DataTable* named Customers, as shown here:

Visual Basic .NET

```
'Same initialization of connection and query strings
'as in previous snippet
Dim da As New OleDbDataAdapter(strSQL, strConn)
da.TableMappings.Add("Table", "Customers")
Dim ds As New DataSet()
da.Fill(ds)
```

Visual C# .NET

```
//Same initialization of connection and query strings
//as in previous snippet
OleDbDataAdapter da = new OleDbDataAdapter(strSQL, strConn);
da.TableMappings.Add("Table", "Customers");
DataSet ds = new DataSet();
da.Fill(ds);
```

We'll cover the *TableMappings* collection in more detail shortly.

Using Overloaded *Fill* Methods

There's more than one way to use the *DataAdapter* object's *Fill* method to fill a *DataSet*. Let's look at the available *Fill* methods in groups.

Specifying the *DataTable*   The *DataAdapter* offers two *Fill* methods that allow you more control over the *DataTable* that it will use.

Rather than having to add an entry to the *DataAdapter* object's *Table-Mappings* collection, you can specify a table name in the *Fill* method:

```
DataAdapter.Fill(DataSet, "MyTableName")
```

I often use this *Fill* method to fill a table in my *DataSet* without having to use the *TableMappings* collection.

You can also specify a *DataTable* to the *Fill* method instead of a *DataSet*:

```
DataAdapter.Fill(DataTable)
```

This *Fill* method is useful when you've already created the *DataTable* you want to populate.

Paging with the *DataAdapter* object's *Fill* method   You've browsed through product catalogs on line that display items a page at a time. If the catalog has a hundred items, the Web site might display 20 of the items per page. The *Data-Adapter* has a *Fill* method that you can use to fetch only a portion of the results of your query, as shown here:

```
DataAdapter.Fill(DataSet, intStartRecord, intNumRecords, "TableName")
```

Remember that the parameter for the starting record is zero-based. So, the following code snippet fetches the first 20 rows:

```
DataAdapter.Fill(DataSet, 0, 20, "Products")
```

It's also important to keep in mind that using this *Fill* method affects only which rows are stored in your *DataSet*. Let's say you're querying a table that contains 1000 rows and you're fetching this data in pages of 20 records each. The following call

```
DataAdapter.Fill(DataSet, 980, 20, "Products")
```

stores the last 20 rows from the query in your *DataSet*. But the actual query still returns 1000 rows. The DataAdapter simply discards the first 49 pages of data.

So, while this Fill method can make it easy to break your query into pages, it's not terribly efficient. There are more efficient (but more complex) ways to achieve paging with *DataSet* objects and *DataReader* objects, which we'll discuss in Chapter 14 when I explain how to build efficient Web applications.

Using a *DataAdapter* to fill a *DataSet* with the contents of a *Recordset* The OLE DB .NET Data Provider has two *Fill* methods you can use to copy data from an ADO *Recordset* into an ADO.NET *DataSet*:

```
OleDbDataAdapter.Fill(DataSet, AdoRecordset, "TableName")
```

```
OleDbDataAdapter.Fill(DataTable, AdoRecordset)
```

These methods can be helpful if want to use existing code or components that return ADO *Recordset* objects in your .NET application.

Opening and Closing Connections

In the code snippets that showed how to use the *Fill* method, you might have noticed a major difference between how the *DataAdapter* and the *Command* handle *Connection* objects. In Chapter 4, before calling one of the *Command* object's execute methods, we opened the *Connection* object associated with the *Command*. Otherwise, the *Command* would throw an exception. The *DataAdapter* has no such requirement.

If you call a *DataAdapter* object's *Fill* method and the *SelectCommand* property's *Connection* is closed, the *DataAdapter* will open the connection, submit the query, fetch the results, and then close the *Connection*. You might say that the *DataAdapter* is very tidy. It always returns the *SelectCommand* property's *Connection* to its initial state. If you open the *Connection* before calling the *Fill* method, the *Connection* will still be open afterwards.

The way the *DataAdapter* handles *Connection* objects can come in handy because you're not required to open your *Connection*. However, there are times when you should write code to open your *Connection* explicitly.

Let's say that as your application starts up, you use multiple *DataAdapter* objects to populate your *DataSet* with the results of a few queries. You've already learned how to use one of the *DataAdapter* object's constructors to force each *DataAdapter* to use the same *Connection* object. So, your code looks something like this:

Visual Basic .NET

```
Dim strConn As String = "Provider=SQLOLEDB;Data Source=(local)\NetSDK;" & _
                        "Initial Catalog=Northwind;Trusted_Connection=Yes;"
Dim cn As New OleDbConnection(strConn)
Dim daCustomers, daOrders As OleDbDataAdapter
daCustomers = New OleDbDataAdapter("SELECT ... FROM Customers", cn)
daOrders = New OleDbDataAdapter("SELECT ... FROM Orders", cn)
Dim ds As New DataSet()
daCustomers.Fill(ds)
daOrders.Fill(ds)
```

Visual C# .NET

```
string strConn = "Provider=SQLOLEDB;Data Source=(local)\\NetSDK;" +
                 "Initial Catalog=Northwind;Trusted_Connection=Yes;";
OleDbConnection cn = new OleDbConnection(strConn);
OleDbDataAdapter daCustomers, daOrders;
daCustomers = new OleDbDataAdapter("SELECT ... FROM Customers", cn);
daOrders = new OleDbDataAdapter("SELECT ... FROM Orders", cn);
ds = new DataSet();
daCustomers.Fill(ds);
daOrders.Fill(ds);
```

You're actually opening and closing the *Connection* object twice, once each time you call a *DataAdapter* object's *Fill* method. To keep from opening and closing the *Connection* object, call the *Connection* object's *Open* method before you call the *Fill* method on the *DataAdapter* objects. If you want to close the *Connection* afterwards, you call the *Close* method as shown here:

```
cn.Open()
daCustomers.Fill(ds)
daOrders.Fill(ds)
cn.Close()
```

Making Multiple Calls to the *Fill* Method

What do you do if you want to refresh the data in your *DataSet*? Maybe your *DataAdapter* fetches the contents of a table when your application starts up and you want to add a feature so that the user can see more timely data. The simple solution is to clear your *DataSet* (or *DataTable*) and then call the *DataAdapter* object's *Fill* method again.

Hypothetically speaking, let's say that you didn't realize that this was the best way to go. Instead, you just called the *DataAdapter* object's *Fill* method a second time, as shown here:

Visual Basic .NET

```
Dim strConn, strSQL As String
strConn = "Provider=SQLOLEDB;Data Source=(local)\NetSDK;" & _
          "Initial Catalog=Northwind;Trusted_Connection=Yes;"
strSQL = "SELECT CustomerID, CompanyName, ContactName, Phone " & _
          "FROM Customers"
Dim da As New OleDbDataAdapter(strSQL, strConn)
Dim ds As New DataSet()
da.Fill(ds, "Customers")
...
da.Fill(ds, "Customers")
```

Visual C# .NET

```
string strConn, strSQL;
strConn = "Provider=SQLOLEDB;Data Source=(local)\\NetSDK;"
          "Initial Catalog=Northwind;Trusted_Connection=Yes;";
strSQL = "SELECT CustomerID, CompanyName, ContactName, Phone " +
          "FROM Customers";
OleDbDataAdapter da = new OleDbDataAdapter(strSQL, strConn);
DataSet ds = new DataSet();
da.Fill(ds, "Customers");
...
da.Fill(ds, "Customers");
```

By calling the *Fill* method twice, you're asking the *DataAdapter* to execute the specified query and to store the results in the *DataSet* twice. The first call to the *Fill* method creates a new table within the *DataSet* called Customers. The second call to the *Fill* method copies the results of the query into that same table in the *DataSet*. Thus, each customer will appear twice in the *DataSet*.

With only this snippet of code, the *DataAdapter* has no way to know which customers are duplicates. Database administrators generally define primary keys on tables in a database. One of the benefits of this practice is that it prevents users from creating duplicate rows. The *DataTable* object has a *Primary-Key* property. If the *DataTable* that the *DataAdapter* is filling has a primary key, the *DataAdapter* will use this key to determine which rows are duplicates.

For more information on setting the *PrimaryKey* property of a *DataTable*, see the section titled "Fetching Schema Information" later in the chapter, as well as the discussion of the *DataTable* object's *PrimaryKey* property in Chapter 6.

Getting back to the example at hand: if we define a primary key on the Customers *DataTable* in the *DataSet* before we call the *DataAdapter* object's *Fill* method the second time, the *DataAdapter* will locate the duplicate rows and discard the old values.

For example, say a customer's name and phone number have changed in the database. Calling the *Fill* method again will retrieve this new information.

The *DataAdapter* will use the *DataTable* object's primary key to determine whether the *DataTable* already has a row for this particular customer. If the customer already exists within the *DataTable*, that row will be discarded and the newly retrieved information will be added to the *DataTable*. However, rows deleted from the database will not be removed from your *DataTable*.

Say that a deadbeat customer was in the database the first time you called the *DataAdapter* object's *Fill* method and the *DataAdapter* added that customer to your *DataTable*. Afterwards, someone realized that the customer was a deadbeat and purged the customer from your database. If you call the *DataAdapter* a second time, the *DataAdapter* will not find information for that customer in the results of your query but will not remove the row from your *DataTable*.

And now we've come full circle. If you need to refresh all of the data, you should clear the *DataSet* or *DataTable* and call the *DataAdapter* object's *Fill* method again. Using this methodology ensures that you will not have duplicate rows (even if you haven't defined a primary key for your *DataTable*) and you will not see rows in your *DataSet* that no longer exist in your database.

Mapping the Results of Your Query to Your *DataSet*

Earlier in the chapter, I described the role of the *DataAdapter* object's *TableMappings* collection. Now it's time to take a closer look at how to use this collection in code.

The *DataAdapter* Object's *TableMappings* Collection

The *TableMappings* collection controls how the *DataAdapter* maps your *DataSet* to your database. If you leave a *DataAdapter* object's *TableMappings* collection empty, call the *Fill* method, and supply a *DataSet* as a parameter without specifying a table name, the *DataAdapter* will assume that you want to work with a *DataTable* called Table.

The *TableMappings* property returns a *DataTableMappingCollection* object. This object contains a collection of *DataTableMapping* objects. Adding the following line of code adds a *DataTableMapping* object to the *TableMappings* collection to tell the *DataAdapter* that it should communicate with a *DataTable* called Employees instead:

```
DataAdapter.TableMappings.Add("Table", "Employees")
```

Once you've created a *DataTableMapping* object, you can create column mappings for the table. In an example earlier in the chapter, we mapped columns in the database named EmpID, LName, and FName to columns in the *DataSet* named EmployeeID, LastName, and FirstName using the following code:

Visual Basic .NET

```
Dim da As OleDbDataAdapter
'Initialize DataAdapter.
Dim TblMap As DataTableMapping
Dim ColMap As DataColumnMapping
TblMap = da.TableMappings.Add("Table", "Employees")
ColMap = TblMap.ColumnMappings.Add("EmpID", "EmployeeID")
ColMap = TblMap.ColumnMappings.Add("LName", "LastName")
ColMap = TblMap.ColumnMappings.Add("FName", "FirstName")
```

Visual C# .NET

```
OleDbDataAdapter da;
//Initialize DataAdapter.
DataTableMapping TblMap;
DataColumnMapping ColMap;
TblMap = da.TableMappings.Add("Table", "Employees");
ColMap = TblMap.ColumnMappings.Add("EmpID", "EmployeeID");
ColMap = TblMap.ColumnMappings.Add("LName", "LastName");
ColMap = TblMap.ColumnMappings.Add("FName", "FirstName");
```

Both the *DataTableMappingCollection* and *DataColumnMappingCollection* objects have an *AddRange* method that you can use to add an array of mappings to the collection in a single call, as shown here:

Visual Basic .NET

```
Dim da As New OleDbDataAdapter()
'Initialize DataAdapter.
Dim TblMap As DataTableMapping
Dim ColMapArray As DataColumnMapping()
TblMap = da.TableMappings.Add("Table", "Employees")
ColMapArray = New DataColumnMapping() _
            {New DataColumnMapping("EmpID", "EmployeeID"), _
             New DataColumnMapping("LName", "LastName"), _
             New DataColumnMapping("FName", "FirstName")}
TblMap.ColumnMappings.AddRange(ColMapArray)
```

Visual C# .NET

```
OleDbDataAdapter da = new OleDbDataAdapter();
//Initialize DataAdapter.
DataTableMapping TblMap;
DataColumnMapping[] ColMapArray;
TblMap = da.TableMappings.Add("Table", "Employees");
ColMapArray = new DataColumnMapping[]
            {new DataColumnMapping("EmpID", "EmployeeID"),
             new DataColumnMapping("LName", "LastName"),
             new DataColumnMapping("FName", "FirstName")};
TblMap.ColumnMappings.AddRange(ColMapArray);
```

The *MissingMappingAction* Property

You now understand how to populate a *DataAdapter* object's *TableMappings* collection with table and column information. However, you might have noticed that you don't *have* to supply this information. Earlier in the chapter, you saw examples that used a *DataAdapter* object's *Fill* method to create and fill a new *DataTable* even though the *DataAdapter* had no column mapping information.

In the majority of cases, developers use the same column names in the *DataSet* as in the database. The ADO.NET development team wisely realized that developers would not appreciate having to populate the *DataAdapter* object's *TableMappings* collection with identical database and *DataSet* column names in order to fetch data into their *DataSet*. When the *DataAdapter* examines the results of your query, if it finds a column that does not exist in its mappings collection, it checks its *MissingMappingAction* property to determine what to do with those columns.

The *MissingMappingAction* property accepts values from the *MissingMappingAction* enumeration in the *System.Data* namespace. By default, this property is set to *Passthrough*. When the *MissingMappingAction* property is set to this value, the *DataAdapter* maps missing columns in your results to columns with the same name in your *DataSet*. Setting this property to *Ignore* tells the *DataAdapter* to ignore columns that don't appear in the mappings collection. You can also set the *MissingMappingAction* property to *Error*, which will cause the *DataAdapter* to throw an exception if it detects a column in the results of your query that does not exist in the mappings collection.

Working with Batch Queries

All of the queries in the chapter so far have retrieved a single set of results. Some databases, such as Microsoft SQL Server, let you submit a batch of queries that return multiple result sets, as shown here:

```
SELECT CustomerID, CompanyName, ContactName, Phone
    FROM Customers WHERE CustomerID = 'ALFKI';
SELECT OrderID, CustomerID, EmployeeID, OrderDate
    FROM Orders WHERE CustomerID = 'ALFKI'
```

If you build a *DataAdapter* with the query shown above and fetch the results into a *DataSet* using the code

```
DataAdapter.Fill(DataSet)
```

you'll fetch the results into two *DataTable* objects within the *DataSet*. The results of the first portion of the query, which references the Customers table, will be stored in a *DataTable* named Table. The results of the second portion, which references the Orders table, will be stored in a *DataTable* named Table1. Chances are, you'll want to choose more descriptive names for your *DataTable* objects.

The *DataAdapter* object's *TableMappings* collection can contain multiple *DataTableMapping* objects. You can add entries to the collection to control the table names that the *DataAdapter* will use to store the results of the batch query. The following code fetches the results of the batch queries into two *DataTable* objects, named Customers and Orders, within the *DataSet*.

Visual Basic .NET

```
Dim strConn, strSQL As String
strConn = "Provider=SQLOLEDB;Data Source=(local)\NetSDK;" & _
          "Initial Catalog=Northwind;Trusted_Connection=Yes;"
strSQL = "SELECT CustomerID, CompanyName, ContactName, Phone " & _
         "FROM Customers WHERE CustomerID = 'ALFKI'; " & _
         "SELECT OrderID, CustomerID, EmployeeID, OrderDate " & _
         "FROM Orders WHERE CustomerID = 'ALFKI'"
Dim da As New OleDbDataAdapter(strSQL, strConn)
da.TableMappings.Add("Table", "Customers")
da.TableMappings.Add("Table1", "Orders")
Dim ds As New DataSet()
da.Fill(ds)
```

Visual C# .NET

```
string strConn, strSQL;
strConn = "Provider=SQLOLEDB;Data Source=(local)\\NetSDK;" +
          "Initial Catalog=Northwind;Trusted_Connection=Yes;";
strSQL = "SELECT CustomerID, CompanyName, ContactName, Phone " +
         "FROM Customers WHERE CustomerID = 'ALFKI'; " +
         "SELECT OrderID, CustomerID, EmployeeID, OrderDate " +
         "FROM Orders WHERE CustomerID = 'ALFKI'";
OleDbDataAdapter da = new OleDbDataAdapter(strSQL, strConn);
da.TableMappings.Add("Table", "Customers");
da.TableMappings.Add("Table1", "Orders");
DataSet ds = new DataSet();
da.Fill(ds);
```

Retrieving Rows from a Stored Procedure

If you have stored procedures that return result sets, you can use a *Data-Adapter* to fetch those results into a *DataSet* or *DataTable*. Say you have the following stored procedure definition:

```
CREATE PROCEDURE GetAllCustomers AS
    SELECT CustomerID, CompanyName, ContactName, Phone FROM Customers
RETURN
```

You can fetch the results of the stored procedure call into a *DataSet* by using either of the following query strings:

```
{CALL GetAllCustomers}
```

or

```
EXEC GetAllCustomers
```

You can also base the *DataAdapter* on a *Command* with a *CommandType* of *StoredProcedure*. For more information on using *Command* objects with *CommandType* values other than the default, see the discussion of the *Command* object's *CommandType* property in Chapter 4.

Oracle Stored Procedures

Oracle stored procedures cannot return rows from a query in the way that SQL Server stored procedures can. Oracle stored procedures can return data only through output parameters. However, the Microsoft OLE DB Provider for Oracle and the Microsoft ODBC Driver for Oracle allow you to call Oracle stored procedures and fetch the results of a query through output parameters. This feature is documented in various articles in the Microsoft Knowledge Base. A query string would follow this syntax:

```
{CALL PackageName.ProcName (?, {resultset 20, OutParam1,
                            OutParam2, ... })}
```

Fetching Schema Information

The *DataTable* object, which we'll discuss in detail in the following chapter, is designed to enforce constraints on your data such as a primary key, maximum length of string fields, and nullability constraints. Fetching this information at run time can be costly, and in many cases developers have no need to retrieve this information. So, by default the *DataAdapter* does not fetch this information. However, if you encounter a situation in which you're willing to pay the performance penalty to retrieve schema information about your results, there are a couple key features of the *DataAdapter* that you can use: the *MissingSchema-Action* property and the *FillSchema* method. (Yes, I know that's an absolutely terrible pun.)

The *MissingSchemaAction* Property

You might have noticed that, so far, all of the examples that use the *Data-Adapter* object's *Fill* method use *DataSet* objects and *DataTable* objects that contain no schema information. By default, the *DataAdapter* will add columns to store the results of your query if those columns do not already exist in your

DataSet or *DataTable*. This behavior is governed by the *MissingSchemaAction* property.

This property accepts values from the *MissingSchemaAction* enumeration in the *System.Data* namespace. The default value for this property is *Add*. As with *MissingMappingAction*, you can ignore missing columns by setting the property to *Ignore* or throw an exception in such circumstances by setting the property to *Error*.

There's another value in the *MissingSchemaAction* enumeration: *AddWithKey*. The name of this value is slightly misleading. If you set the property to this value and the *DataAdapter* encounters a column that does not exist in your *DataSet* or *DataTable*, the *DataAdapter* adds the column and sets two additional schema attributes of the property: *MaxLength* and *AllowDBNull*. If the *DataTable* does not yet exist or does not contain any columns, this value also causes the *DataAdapter* to query the database for primary key information.

The *FillSchema* Method

The *DataAdapter* also has a *FillSchema* method that you can use to fetch only schema information into your *DataSet* or *DataTable*. The *FillSchema* method's signatures mirror the basic *Fill* signatures. You can supply a *DataSet*, a *DataTable*, or a *DataSet* and a table name in the *FillSchema* method.

Each *FillSchema* method also requires a value from the *SchemaType* attribute: *Mapped* or *Source*. The value you specify in this parameter determines whether the *DataAdapter* will apply the settings in its *TableMappings* collection to the results of the query. If you call the *FillSchema* method and use *Source* as the *SchemaType*, the *DataAdapter* will use the column names that the query returns. Using *Mapped* as the *SchemaType* will cause the *DataAdapter* to apply the settings in its *TableMappings* to the columns returned by the query.

FillSchema will set the *AutoIncrement*, *AllowDBNull*, and *MaxLength* properties on the columns returned and will also create a primary key on the resulting *DataTable* if the database indicates that a column or set of columns represents a primary or unique key.

Creating *DataAdapter* Objects in Visual Studio .NET

Now that you've learned about the key features of the *DataAdapter*, let's see how you can use Visual Studio .NET to create *DataAdapter* objects in your applications more quickly.

Dragging and Dropping a *DataAdapter* from the Toolbox

Both the *OleDbDataAdapter* and *SqlDataAdapter* are available on the Data tab of the Visual Studio .NET Toolbox. Dragging either *DataAdapter* from the Toolbox onto a designer, as shown in Figure 5-3, will create a new *DataAdapter* in the designer's Components Tray. This process also launches the Data Adapter Configuration Wizard.

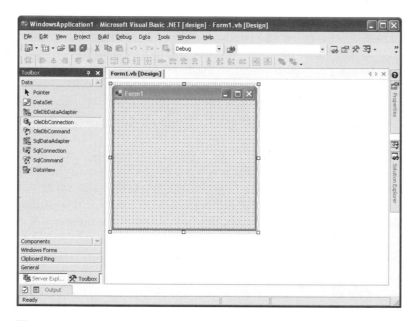

Figure 5-3   Dragging and dropping a *DataAdapter* onto a designer

Using the Data Adapter Configuration Wizard

The Visual Studio .NET Data Adapter Configuration Wizard allows you to configure your *DataAdapter* objects without having to write any code.

Once you've launched the wizard and acknowledged the standard welcome page, you'll see a page where you can specify a connection to your database. This page, shown in Figure 5-4, is similar to the Choose Connection page of the Data Form Wizard. It lists the connections available and lets you create new connections. If you've selected an *OleDbDataAdapter*, the wizard will list all of the data connections available in Server Explorer. If you've selected the *SqlDataAdapter*, only the connections that you've added through the SQL Server OLE DB provider will be available. Select the connection you want to use to communicate with your database and then click Next to move to the next page of the wizard.

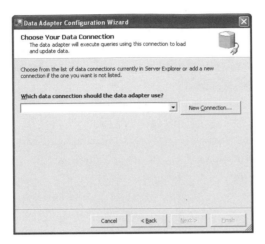

Figure 5-4   Selecting a connection for your *DataAdapter*

Next, the wizard will ask you to specify a query type for your *Data-Adapter*. You can either enter a SQL statement (such as *SELECT CustomerID, CompanyName FROM Customers*) or rely on stored procedures. The Data Adapter Configuration Wizard can even help you build stored procedures based on a query that you specify. For now, we'll focus on the simplest case—using a SQL statement. We'll look at using stored procedures in a *DataAdapter* in Chapter 10, when we discuss updating your database. Select Use SQL Statements, as shown in Figure 5-5, and then click Next.

Figure 5-5   Specifying a query type for your *DataAdapter*

The next wizard page will display a text box for your query, as shown in Figure 5-6. The page also lets you set some advanced options related to updating your database. We'll take a closer look at those options in Chapter 10.

Figure 5-6 Specifying a query string for your *DataAdapter*

This wizard page also has a button labeled Query Builder. Click this button to launch Query Builder, which provides a simple user interface for building queries, similar to the one used by Microsoft Access. Query Builder can be helpful if you're not completely sure of the query you want to use for your *DataAdapter*. When you launch Query Builder, you will see a dialog box (shown in Figure 5-7) that lists the tables, views, and functions available in your database.

Query Builder makes it simple to select the table(s) and field(s) to return, define the search criteria, and specify the sort order for your query. You can even execute your query and examine the results from within Query Builder by right-clicking in one of the panes and choosing Run from the shortcut menu. Figure 5-8 shows many of Query Builder's features. You can click on columns in the top pane to add them to the results of your query. You can specify sort orders or criteria in the second pane. If you're more comfortable typing in the SQL for your query, you can do so in the third pane. Changes in any one of the top three panes affect the other two.

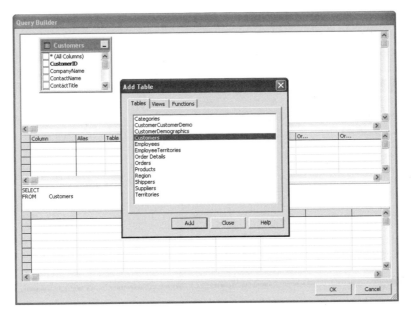

Figure 5-7   Query Builder's Add Table dialog box

Figure 5-8   Using Query Builder to construct your query

After you've constructed your query, click OK and Query Builder will return the query string that you built to the Data Adapter Configuration Wizard. When you click Next, the wizard will take your query and connection information and generate and configure your new *DataAdapter*. The wizard will display the results of this process on its next page, as shown in Figure 5-9.

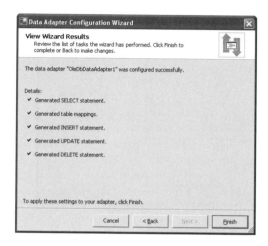

Figure 5-9   The Data Adapter Configuration Wizard's results

In order to configure your *DataAdapter*, the wizard must query your database for metadata such as table names, column names, and primary key information. If the wizard is unable to generate updating logic because your query references multiple tables or does not have a primary key or your database does not return this metadata, it will indicate on this page which attributes of your *DataAdapter* it was unable to set.

After you've built your *DataAdapter* using the wizard, you can select it in the designer's Components Tray and examine its settings in the Properties window. Figure 5-10 shows how you can drill down into the properties of your new *DataAdapter*. The query you entered in the wizard appears in the *CommandText* property of the *DataAdapter* object's *SelectCommand*.

The Data Adapter Configuration Wizard is reentrant. You can select a *DataAdapter* in your designer's Components Tray and click the Configure Data Adapter link in the lower half of the Properties window to reconfigure your *DataAdapter* by running through the wizard again.

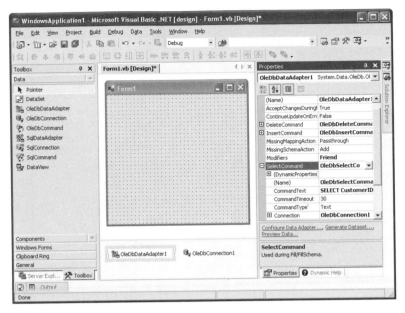

Figure 5-10   Examining properties of your new *DataAdapter*

Dragging and Dropping from Server Explorer

You can also create *DataAdapter* objects by dragging and dropping a table or view from Server Explorer onto your designer. This might sound like a good idea at design time, when your database might contain only a few sample rows per table, but you have to consider how much data your *DataAdapter* will fetch when you deploy your application, especially if the tables in your database will continually grow in size. But if you get a note from your mother that says you promise not to fetch thousands of rows from your database through your *DataAdapter*, I guess it's all right.

While you can't set a filter on the rows you retrieve by dragging and dropping from Server Explorer, you can indicate which columns you want to include in your *DataAdapter* object's query by selecting specific columns from your table or view in Server Explorer. Hold down the Ctrl key while clicking on the desired columns to select them. The result is shown in Figure 5-11.

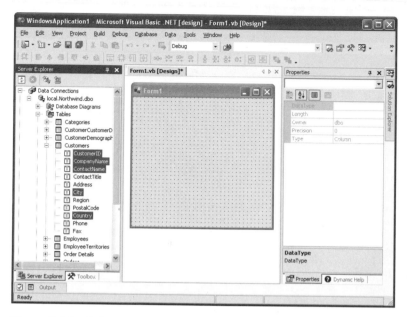

Figure 5-11   Selecting specific columns from your table for your *Data-Adapter*

Previewing the Results of Your *DataAdapter*

I usually enter my query by hand rather than launch Query Builder. Years of programming have helped me learn a lot of things about myself. Among them are: I'm stubborn, which explains why I occasionally scoff at wizards as well as why I continue to believe that *this* will be the Red Sox's year; also, I'm not the world's best typist. So, when I enter queries by hand, they don't always do what I expect them to do. When that happens, I run the query in an ad-hoc query tool and examine the results to try to figure out where I went wrong. Query Builder is helpful, but there's an easier way to examine the data returned by your *DataAdapter* at design time.

When you select a *DataAdapter* in a designer's Components Tray, you'll see a link in the lower half of the Properties window labeled Preview Data. Click this link to display the Data Adapter Preview dialog box, shown in Figure 5-12. To view the data your *DataAdapter* returns, click the Fill Dataset button.

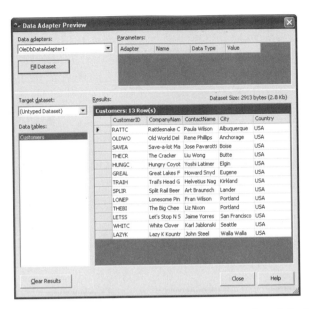

Figure 5-12   Previewing data returned by a *DataAdapter*

Examining the Code that the Wizard Generated

I strongly recommend looking at the code that the wizard generated. The code might not always be easy to read, and it might not be the most efficient or highly recommended approach, but it's a great way to learn how the different objects in the ADO.NET object model interact. As you read about the *Data-Adapter*, *Command*, and *Parameter* objects in this book, you can refer back to the code that the Data Adapter Configuration Wizard generated to reinforce the lessons in the text.

You can find the wizard-generated code in your component's *Initialize-Component* procedure, which resides in the hidden designer-generated code region.

DataAdapter Reference

The *DataAdapter* object offers properties, methods, and events to meet your every need. Let's meet them now.

Properties of the *DataAdapter* Object

You can divide the *DataAdapter* object's properties into two groups—those that control communication with the data store and those that control communication with the *DataSet*.

The properties that control communication with the data store are the ones that contain *Command* objects: the *SelectCommand*, *UpdateCommand*, *InsertCommand*, and *DeleteCommand* properties. These properties contain *Command* objects that the *DataAdapter* executes when you want to move information back and forth between a *DataSet* and your data store—to retrieve rows into your *DataSet* or to submit changes stored in a *DataSet* to your data store. Table 5-1 describes the properties.

Table 5-1   **Properties of the *OleDbDataAdapter* Object**

Property	Data Type	Description
AcceptChangesDuringFill	*Boolean*	Determines the *RowState* of the rows retrieved by the *Data-Adapter*. (Default = *True.*)
ContinueUpdateOnError	*Boolean*	Controls whether the *Data-Adapter* will continue to submit changes if it encounters an error. (Default = *False.*)
DeleteCommand	*OleDbCommand*	Command used to submit pending deletions.
InsertCommand	*OleDbCommand*	Command used to submit pending insertions.
MissingMappingAction	*MissingMappingAction*	Controls the *DataAdapter* object's behavior when fetching columns that do not appear in the *TableMappings* collection. (Default = *Passthrough.*)
MissingSchemaAction	*MissingSchemaAction*	Controls the *DataAdapter* object's behavior when fetching columns that do not appear in the *DataTable* object's *Columns* collection. (Default = *Add.*)
SelectCommand	*OleDbCommand*	Command used to query database and fetch results into a *DataSet* or *DataTable*.
TableMappings	*DataTableMapping-Collection*	Collection of information the *DataAdapter* uses to map the results of the query to the *DataSet*.
UpdateCommand	*OleDbCommand*	Command used to submit pending updates.

SelectCommand, *UpdateCommand*, *InsertCommand*, and *DeleteCommand*

Each of these properties of the *DataAdapter* stores a *Command* object. The specific object type will depend on the .NET Data Provider you're using. For example, an *OleDbDataAdapter* object's *SelectCommand* property contains an *OleDbCommand* object, and a *SqlDataAdapter* object's *SelectCommand* property contains a *SqlCommand* object. (The *Command* object is discussed in more detail in Chapter 4.)

If you supply a query string in the constructor for the *DataAdapter*, this query string will become the *CommandText* property for the *DataAdapter* object's *SelectCommand*. If you supply a *Command* rather than just a query string, that *Command* will be assigned to the *DataAdapter* object's *SelectCommand*.

If you supply a *Connection* in the *DataAdapter* object's constructor, that *Command* will be assigned to the *Connection* property for the *DataAdapter* object's *SelectCommand*. If you supply a connection string, the *DataAdapter* will create a new *Connection*, sets its *ConnectionString* property to the string you supplied, and then assign the new *Connection* to the *Connection* property of the *DataAdapter* object's *SelectCommand*.

TableMappings Property

Earlier in the chapter, you learned that the *DataAdapter* and the *DataSet* are completely disconnected from each other in the ADO.NET object model. So how does the *DataAdapter* know how to communicate with the *DataSet*? For example, the *OleDbDataAdapter* and *SqlDataAdapter* can each accept a *DataSet* as a parameter in their *Update* methods. What if the *DataSet* contains multiple *DataTable* objects? How will the *DataAdapter* know which *DataTable* to examine?

The *DataAdapter* class has a *TableMappings* property that contains a collection of *DataTableMapping* objects. Each *DataTableMapping* object has a *ColumnMappings* property that returns a collection of *DataColumnMapping* objects. This hierarchy of objects corresponds to the collection of *DataTable* objects and *DataColumn* objects in your *DataSet*.

When the *DataAdapter* retrieves data from your data store, it uses the information in the *TableMappings* collection to determine where in your *DataSet* to store the results of your query. Generally speaking, if you fetch the results of the query

```
SELECT CustomerID, CompanyName, ContactName, Phone FROM Customers
```

you'll want to create a *DataTable* named Customers that contains *DataColumn* objects whose names correspond to the columns in the results of the query. If you want to provide alternative names for the *DataTable* or any of its *DataColumn* objects, you'll want to populate the *DataAdapter* object's *TableMappings* collection with the desired mapping information.

The following code is an example of populating a *DataAdapter* object's *TableMappings* collection based on the query. With each *TableMapping* and *ColumnMapping*, the first string corresponds to the name of the item that the *DataAdapter* retrieves from the database, and the second string corresponds to the name of the item in the *DataSet*.

Visual Basic .NET

```
Dim strSQL, strConn As String
strSQL = "SELECT CustomerID, CompanyName, ContactName, Phone FROM Customers"
strConn = "Provider=SQLOLEDB;Data Source=(local)\NetSDK;" & _
          "Initial Catalog=Northwind;Trusted_Connection=Yes;"
Dim da As New OleDbDataAdapter(strSQL, strConn)
With da.TableMappings.Add("Table", "Customers").ColumnMappings
    .Add("CustomerID", "CustomerID")
    .Add("CompanyName", "CompanyName")
    .Add("ContactName", "ContactName")
    .Add("Phone", "Phone")
End With
```

Visual C# .NET

```
string strSQL, strConn;
strSQL = "SELECT CustomerID, CompanyName, ContactName, Phone FROM Customers";
strConn = "Provider=SQLOLEDB;Data Source=(local)\\NetSDK;" +
          "Initial Catalog=Northwind;Trusted_Connection=Yes;";
OleDbDataAdapter da = new OleDbDataAdapter(strSQL, strConn);
da.TableMappings.Add("Table", "Customers");
DataColumnMappingCollection cm = da.TableMappings[0].ColumnMappings;
cm.Add("CustomerID", "CustomerID");
cm.Add("CompanyName", "CompanyName");
cm.Add("ContactName", "ContactName");
cm.Add("Phone", "Phone");
```

You can also use the *AddRange* method of the *DataTableMappingCollection* or *DataColumnMappingCollection* object to add multiple items to the collection in a single call, as shown here:

Visual Basic .NET

```
Dim cm As CommonDataColumnMapping = da.TableMappings(0).ColumnMappings
cm.AddRange(New Common.DataColumnMapping() _
          {New Common.DataColumnMapping("CustomerID", "CustomerID"), _
           New Common.DataColumnMapping("CompanyName", "CompanyName"), _
           New Common.DataColumnMapping("ContactName", "ContactName"), _
           New Common.DataColumnMapping("Phone", "Phone")})
```

Visual C# .NET

```
DataColumnMappingCollection cm = da.TableMappings[0].ColumnMappings;
cm.AddRange(new DataColumnMapping[]
          {new DataColumnMapping("CustomerID", "CustomerID"),
           new DataColumnMapping("CompanyName", "CompanyName"),
           new DataColumnMapping("ContactName", "ContactName"),
           new DataColumnMapping("Phone", "Phone")});
```

What if the query the *DataAdapter* executes contains information that does not appear in the *DataAdapter* object's *TableMappings* collection for the *DataTable* in your *DataSet*? By default, the *DataAdapter* will assume that you want to retrieve this information and store it in your table. In fact, you could execute the following code:

Visual Basic .NET

```
Dim strSQL, strConn As String
strSQL = "SELECT CustomerID, CompanyName, ContactName, Phone FROM Customers"
strConn = "Provider=SQLOLEDB;Data Source=(local)\NetSDK;" & _
          "Initial Catalog=Northwind;Trusted_Connection=Yes;"
Dim da As New OleDbDataAdapter(strSQL, strConn)
Dim ds As New DataSet
da.Fill(ds)
Console.WriteLine(ds.Tables("Table").Rows(0)("CustomerID").ToString)
```

Visual C# .NET

```
string strSQL, strConn;
strSQL = "SELECT CustomerID, CompanyName, ContactName, Phone FROM Customers";
strConn = "Provider=SQLOLEDB;Data Source=(local)\\NetSDK;" +
          "Initial Catalog=Northwind;Trusted_Connection=Yes;";
OleDbDataAdapter da = new OleDbDataAdapter(strSQL, strConn);
DataSet ds = new DataSet;
da.Fill(ds);
Console.WriteLine(ds.Tables["Table"].Rows[0]["CustomerID"].ToString());
```

MissingMappingAction and *MissingSchemaAction* Properties

Notice that we did not populate the *DataAdapter* object's *TableMappings* collection. In fact, we did not even create a *DataTable* in our *DataSet*; the *DataAdapter* did that automatically.

When the *DataAdapter* fetches the results of your query, it looks for corresponding tables and columns in its *TableMappings* collection. The *MissingMappingAction* property of the *DataAdapter* controls its behavior in situations where the *DataAdapter* retrieves tables or columns that don't correspond to entries in the *TableMappingsCollection*. By default, this property is set to *Passthrough*, but you can set it to the other values in the *MissingMappingAction* enumeration, which is in the *System.Data* namespace. Setting *MissingMappingAction* to *Ignore* will cause the *DataAdapter* to ignore tables and columns that do not appear in the *TableMappings* collection. If you set *MissingMappingAction* to *Error*, you'll receive an exception if the query contains tables or columns that do not appear in the *DataAdapter* object's *TableMappings* collection.

The *DataAdapter* also has a *MissingSchemaAction* property that controls the behavior of the *DataAdapter* if the tables or columns in the results of the query do not appear in the destination *DataSet*. By default, *MissingSchemaAction* is set to *Add*, which forces the *DataAdapter* to add the expected tables and columns to the *DataSet*. You can set the property to other values in the *MissingSchemaAction* enumeration in *System.Data*—such as *AddWithKey*, *Ignore*, and *Error*. Setting *MissingSchemaAction* to *Ignore* causes the *DataAdapter* to ignore tables and columns that do not appear in the *DataSet*, and setting the property to *Error* will generate an exception in the same scenario, just as the *MissingMappingAction* property does.

Setting *MissingSchemaAction* to *AddWithKey* will add the missing tables and columns to the *DataSet* but will also add key information for the table. This behavior is similar to calling the *FillSchema* method of the *DataAdapter*, a feature I'll cover shortly.

AcceptChangesDuringFill Property

When I worked as a support engineer helping developers who were having problems using ADO, I was amazed at how many developers were trying to use ADO as some sort of data synchronization tool. They would query one database and then point their *Recordset* at a different database and call *Update*, expecting that ADO would synchronize the tables in the two databases. ADO could not do that. But ADO.NET can...sort of.

The *DataAdapter* object has an *AcceptChangesDuringFill* property that accepts a Boolean value. This property, which is set to *True* by default, controls the *RowState* of the rows retrieved by the *DataAdapter*. If the property is set to *True*, the new *DataRow* objects will each have a *RowState* of *Unchanged*. Setting *AcceptChangesDuringFill* to *False* causes the new *DataRow* objects to have a *RowState* of *New*.

This means that if you set *AcceptChangesDuringFill* to *False*, you can query a table in one database and then pass the *DataSet* to a *DataAdapter* that's set to communicate with another database and insert all of the newly retrieved rows into this other database.

ContinueUpdateOnError Property

If you use a *DataAdapter* to submit updates to your database, you're relying on optimistic updating. If you fetch the contents of a row, modify that row in your *DataSet*, and then submit the pending change to the database using a *DataAdapter*, your update attempt might fail if another user has already changed the contents of the same row in your database. Don't worry; we'll discuss this functionality in depth in Chapter 10 and Chapter 11. For now, just know that when you're an optimist, things don't always work out the way you'd like.

The *DataAdapter* object's *ContinueUpdateOnError* property controls how the *DataAdapter* reacts when it detects that an attempt to submit the pending changes stored in a *DataRow* fails. By default, this property is set to *False*, which means that the *DataAdapter* will stop when it encounters a failed update attempt. If you want the *DataAdapter* to continue under such circumstances and try to submit the changes stored in the remaining pending *DataRows*, set this property to *True*.

Why would you want the *DataAdapter* to stop when it encounters a failed update attempt? Maybe the pending changes in your *DataSet* represent an order and the customer does not want to submit a partial order. It's an all-or-nothing proposition. So, you start a transaction before submitting the changes and if one update fails, you roll back the transaction. Under these circumstances, there's no reason to attempt to submit the rest of the changes if an error occurs while submitting changes for a prior row.

Methods of the *DataAdapter* Object

The *DataAdapter* has many properties, but it has just four methods, as described in Table 5-2.

Table 5-2   **Methods of the *OleDbDataAdapter* Object**

Method	Description
Fill	Executes the query stored in the *SelectCommand* and stores the results in a *DataTable*
FillSchema	Retrieves schema information for the query stored in the *SelectCommand*
GetFillParameters	Returns an array containing the parameters for the *Select-Command*
Update	Submits changes stored in your *DataSet* (or *DataTable* or *DataRows*) to your database

Fill Method

Calling the *Fill* method on a *DataAdapter* executes the query stored in the *DataAdapter* object's *SelectCommand* property and stores the results in a *DataTable* in your *DataSet*. The *Fill* method also returns a 32-bit integer that indicates the number of rows the *DataAdapter* retrieved.

This quick snippet of sample code shows how to use the *Fill* method:

Visual Basic .NET

```
Dim da As New OleDbDataAdapter(strSQL, strConn)
Dim ds As New DataSet()
Dim intRowsRetrieved As Integer = da.Fill(ds)
```

Visual C# .NET

```
OleDbDataAdapter da = new OleDbDataAdapter(strSQL, strConn);
DataSet ds = new DataSet();
int intRowsRetrieved = da.Fill(ds);
```

The *DataAdapter* examines the contents of its *TableMappings* collection to determine which *DataTable* object(s) and *DataColumn* object(s) to use in the *DataSet* you supply. If the *DataAdapter* does not find the expected schema information in its *TableMappings* collection or within the *DataSet*, it checks its *MissingMappingAction* and *MissingSchemaAction* properties to determine how to react.

The *DataAdapter* object's *Fill* method is overloaded. You can supply a *DataTable* rather than a *DataSet*. Or, you can supply a *DataSet* and a string for the name of the *DataTable* you want to populate or create, as shown here:

Visual Basic .NET

```
Dim da As New OleDbDataAdapter(strSQL, strConn)
Dim ds As New DataSet()
Dim intRowsRetrieved As Integer

intRowsRetrieved = da.Fill(ds, "Customers")
intRowsRetrieved = da.Fill(ds.Tables("Customers"))
intRowsRetrieved = da.Fill(ds, 11, 10, "Customers")
```

Visual C# .NET

```
OleDbDataAdapter da = new OleDbDataAdapter(strSQL, strConn);
DataSet ds = new DataSet();
int intRowsRetrieved;

intRowsRetrieved = da.Fill(ds, "Customers");
intRowsRetrieved = da.Fill(ds.Tables["Customers"]);
intRowsRetrieved = da.Fill(ds, 11, 10, "Customers");
```

The *DataAdapter* also has a *Fill* method that can come in handy if you're building a Web application that has to support paging. Let's say you want to allow users to view the contents of your product catalog 10 items at a time. You can supply a starting row number and the number of rows to retrieve in the *DataAdapter* object's *Fill* method:

Visual Basic .NET

```
Dim da As New OleDbDataAdapter(strSQL, strConn)
Dim ds As New DataSet()
Dim intStartingRow As Integer = 10
Dim intRowsToRetrieve As Integer = 10
Dim intRowsRetrieved As Integer
intRowsRetrieved = da.Fill(ds, intStartingRow, _
                        intRowsToRetrieve, "Customers")
```

Visual C# .NET

```
OleDbDataAdapter da = new OleDbDataAdapter(strSQL, strConn);
DataSet ds = new DataSet();
int intStartingRow = 10;
int intRowsToRetrieve = 10;
int intRowsRetrieved = da.Fill(ds, intStartingRow,
                        intRowsToRetrieve, "Customers");
```

The *DataAdapter* submits the query, and if you say that you want to start fetching at row 10 (as shown in the example), the *DataAdapter* will simply discard the first 10 rows. The *DataAdapter* will then fetch the number of rows you've requested. If the query (ignoring the discarded rows) does not contain the number of rows you've requested, the *DataAdapter* will simply fetch all remaining rows without throwing an exception.

Is this the best way to break up the results of a query into pages? No. Let's say your query returns 100 rows and you break it up into 10 pages of 10 rows each. When you fetch the first page, you simply fetch the first 10 rows. When you fetch the second page, you discard the first 10 rows and fetch the second set of 10 rows. Keep in mind that the database returns 20 rows in order for you to fetch the second page. When you fetch the tenth page, the database has to return all 100 rows. The *DataAdapter* simply discards the first 90. If that sounds inefficient, that's because it is. So why does the *DataAdapter* support this feature? Because it's simple.

A more complex but much more efficient way to achieve the same functionality is to store the key value(s) for the last row from the previous page. Say you fetch the first set of 10 rows using the following query:

```
SELECT TOP 10 CustomerID, CompanyName, ContactName, Phone
    FROM Customers ORDER BY CustomerID
```

If the tenth customer has a CustomerID of "BSBEV", the following query retrieves the next 10 rows:

```
SELECT TOP 10 CustomerID, CompanyName, ContactName, Phone
    FROM Customers ORDER BY CustomerID
    WHERE CustomerID > "BSBEV"
```

Using this type of architecture will improve the performance of your database because it will fetch fewer rows. Your data access code will run faster because it won't need to discard an initial set of rows to get to the desired rows and because the database will perform better.

The *OleDbDataAdapter* has two more overloaded *Fill* methods, which can help you leverage your preexisting ADO code. You can fetch the contents of an ADO *Recordset* into your ADO.NET *DataSet*, and you can supply a *DataSet*, a *Recordset*, and a table name or a *DataTable* and a *Recordset*. Here are examples of both syntaxes:

Visual Basic .NET

```
Dim rs As New ADODB.Recordset()
rs.CursorLocation = ADODB.CursorLocationEnum.adUseClient
rs.Open(strSQL, strConn)
Dim da As New OleDbDataAdapter()
Dim ds As New DataSet()
Dim intRowsRetrieved As Integer

intRowsRetrieved = da.Fill(ds, rs, "Customers")
intRowsRetrieved = da.Fill(ds.Tables("Customers"), rs)
```

Visual C# .NET

```
Recordset rs = new RecordsetClass();
rs.CursorLocation = CursorLocationEnum.adUseClient;
rs.Open(strSQL, strConn, CursorTypeEnum.adOpenStatic,
        LockTypeEnum.adLockReadOnly, (int) CommandTypeEnum.adCmdText);
OleDbDataAdapter da = new OleDbDataAdapter();
DataSet ds = new DataSet();
int intRowsRetrieved;

intRowsRetrieved = da.Fill(ds, rs, "Customers");
intRowsRetrieved = da.Fill(ds.Tables["Customers"], rs);
```

The *DataAdapter* provides a way to move data from an ADO *Recordset* to an ADO.NET *DataSet*, but there is no feature to move data from a *DataSet* back to a *Recordset*.

FillSchema Method

The *FillSchema* method lets you retrieve schema information about your query before executing it. Like the *Fill* method, the *FillSchema* method retrieves names and data types for each of the columns in your query. *FillSchema* also retrieves information on whether a column can accept *Null* values and sets the *AllowDBNull* property of the *DataColumn* objects it creates accordingly.

To help you determine how to update your data store, the *FillSchema* method also attempts to generate a primary key on your *DataTable*. The logic for this operation is somewhat complex, but I'll try to simplify it.

When you call *FillSchema*, the *DataAdapter* first asks the data store whether the table referenced in the query contains a primary key. If the table does not contain a primary key, the *DataAdapter* checks for a unique index.

Once the *DataAdapter* finds that the table contains a primary key (or unique index if there is no primary key), it checks the results of the query to locate the column(s) specified in the primary key (or unique index). If the *DataAdapter* locates the column(s), it sets that column or columns as the primary key in the *DataTable*. Otherwise, the *DataAdapter* does not create a primary key on the *DataTable*.

Using the *FillSchema* method is rather straightforward and will remind you of the *Fill* method, with one slight difference. As with the *Fill* method, you can supply a *DataSet*, a *DataSet* and a table name, or a *DataTable*. The slight difference is that the *FillSchema* method adds a parameter to let you control whether to retrieve schema information straight from the data source or apply the *Data-Adapter* object's *TableMappings* to the schema information the *DataAdapter* retrieves.

You can specify either value from the *SchemaType* enumeration in *System.Data—Source* or *Mapped*. If you specify *Source*, the *DataAdapter* will generate schema information using just the column names retrieved from the data source. Specifying *Mapped* will force the *DataAdapter* to apply the contents of its *TableMappings* collection, the same way the *DataAdapter* maps the columns when you call the *Fill* method. Here are examples of all three ways to call *FillSchema*:

Visual Basic .NET

```
Dim da As New OleDbDataAdapter(strSQL, strConn)
Dim ds As New DataSet()

'Supply a DataSet and a SchemaType.
da.FillSchema(ds, SchemaType.Source)

'Supply a DataSet, a SchemaType, and a table name.
da.FillSchema(ds, SchemaType.Source, "Table")

Dim tbl As New DataTable()
'Supply a DataTable and a SchemaType.
da.FillSchema(tbl, SchemaType.Source)
```

Visual C# .NET

```
OleDbDataAdapter da = new OleDbDataAdapter(strSQL, strConn);
DataSet ds = new DataSet();

//Supply a DataSet and a SchemaType.
da.FillSchema(ds, SchemaType.Source);

//Supply a DataSet, a SchemaType, and a table name.
da.FillSchema(ds, SchemaType.Source, "TableName");

DataTable tbl = new DataTable();
//Supply a DataTable and a SchemaType.
da.FillSchema(tbl, SchemaType.Source);
```

The *FillSchema* method returns an array of *DataTable* objects that contain the *DataTable* objects that the *FillSchema* method populates.

You can call the *FillSchema* method and reference a *DataTable* that already exists. In this scenario, the *DataAdapter* will not overwrite the columns that already appear in the *DataTable* but will add new columns if the columns that the query returns do not already appear in the *DataTable*.

GetFillParameters Method

The *GetFillParameters* method acts as a shortcut to the *Parameters* collection of the *DataAdapter* object's *SelectCommand*, with one minor difference. *GetFill-Parameters* returns the parameter information as an array of *IParameter* objects rather than the *Parameter* type for the specific .NET Data Provider (such as *Ole-DbParameter* or *SqlParameter*). Unless you need to check or set the parameters' size, precision, or scale properties, you'll be able to access your parameters using the *GetFillParameters* method, as shown here:

Visual Basic .NET

```
Dim strSQL As String = "SELECT CustomerID, CompanyName " & _
                       "FROM Customers WHERE CustomerID LIKE ?"
da = New OleDbDataAdapter(strSQL, strConn)
da.SelectCommand.Parameters.Append("@CustomerID", _
                                   OleDbType.VarWChar, 5)
da.GetFillParameters(0).Value = "ALFKI"
```

Visual C# .NET

```
string strSQL = "SELECT CustomerID, CompanyName FROM Customers " +
                "WHERE CustomerID LIKE ?";
OleDbDataAdapter da = new OleDbDataAdapter(strSQL, strConn);
da.SelectCommand.Parameters.Append("@CustomerID", OleDbType.VarWChar, 5);
da.GetFillParameters[0].Value = "ALFKI";
```

We discussed *Command* objects and *Parameter* objects in further detail in Chapter 4.

Update Method

To submit the pending changes stored in a *DataTable* or *DataSet* to your data store, you use the *DataAdapter* object's *Update* method.

As with the *Fill* and *FillSchema* methods, you can pass a *DataSet*, a *DataSet* and a table name, or a *DataTable* to the *Update* method. The *Update* method offers another overloaded method—you can also pass an array of *DataRow* objects to the *Update* method. This option can come in handy if you want to pass a subset of rows in a table based on a filter or a relation.

The *Update* method returns an integer that contains the rows you successfully updated in your data store.

We'll discuss how the *Update* method submits changes to your data store in detail in Chapter 10.

Visual Basic .NET

```
Dim da As OleDbDataAdapter
Dim ds As DataSet
Dim intChangesSubmitted As Integer

intChangesSubmitted = da.Update(ds)
intChangesSubmitted = da.Update(ds, "TableName")
```

(continued)

```
intChangesSubmitted = da.Update(ds.Tables("TableName"))

Dim aRows() As DataRow
intChangesSubmitted = da.Update(aRows)
```

Visual C# .NET

```
OleDbDataAdapter da;
DataSet ds;
int intChangesSubmitted;

intChangesSubmitted = da.Update(ds);
intChangesSubmitted = da.Update(ds, "TableName");
intChangesSubmitted = da.Update(ds.Tables["TableName"]);

DataRow[] aRows;
intChangesSubmitted = da.Update(aRows);
```

Events of the *DataAdapter* Object

The *DataAdapter* object offers only three events, all of which are listed in Table 5-3.

Table 5-3 Events of the *OleDbDataAdapter* Object

Event	Description
FillError	Fires when the *DataAdapter* encounters an error filling your *DataSet* or *DataTable*
RowUpdating	Fires before submitting a modified row to your database
RowUpdated	Fires after submitting a modified row to your database

FillError Event

If the *DataAdapter* encounters an error when filling your *DataSet* or *DataTable*, you might be able to trap for that error using the *FillError* event, as shown in the following code snippet:

Visual Basic .NET

```
Dim strConn, strSQL As String
strConn = "Provider=SQLOLEDB;Data Source=(local)\NetSDK;" & _
          "Initial Catalog=Northwind;Trusted_Connection=Yes;"
strSQL = "SELECT TOP 1 OrderID, CustomerID, EmployeeID FROM Orders"
Dim da As New OleDbDataAdapter(strSQL, strConn)
da.MissingSchemaAction = MissingSchemaAction.Error
AddHandler da.FillError, AddressOf da_FillError
Dim tbl As New DataTable("Orders")
tbl.Columns.Add("OrderID", GetType(Integer))
```

```
tbl.Columns.Add("CustomerID", GetType(String))
da.Fill(tbl)

Public Sub da_FillError(ByVal sender As Object, _
                        ByVal e As FillErrorEventArgs)
    Console.WriteLine(e.Errors.Message)
    e.Continue = True
End Sub
```

Visual C# .NET

```
string strConn, strSQL;
strConn = "Provider=SQLOLEDB;Data Source=(local)\\NetSDK;" +
          "Initial Catalog=Northwind;Trusted_Connection=Yes;";
strSQL = "SELECT TOP 1 OrderID, CustomerID, EmployeeID FROM Orders";
OleDbDataAdapter da = new OleDbDataAdapter(strSQL, strConn);
da.MissingSchemaAction = MissingSchemaAction.Error;
da.FillError += new FillErrorEventHandler(da_FillError);
DataTable tbl = new DataTable("Orders");
tbl.Columns.Add("OrderID", typeof(int));
tbl.Columns.Add("CustomerID", typeof(string));
da.Fill(tbl);

static void da_FillError(object sender, FillErrorEventArgs e)
{
    Console.WriteLine(e.Errors.Message);
    e.Continue = true;
}
```

As far as I can tell, you cannot use the *FillError* event to trap for situations where the data retrieved by the *DataAdapter* violates a constraint in your *DataSet* or *DataTable*.

RowUpdating and *RowUpdated* Events

The *DataAdapter* also fires events when submitting pending changes to your database via the *DataAdapter.Update* method. If you want to examine the pending changes in your row prior to submitting the change, use the *Row-Updating* event. If you want to execute code immediately after submitting a change, use the *RowUpdated* event.

The following code snippet demonstrates how to use both of the events.

Visual Basic .NET

```
Dim strConn, strSQL As String
strConn = "Provider=SQLOLEDB;Data Source=(local)\NetSDK;" & _
          "Initial Catalog=Northwind;Trusted_Connection=Yes;"
strSQL = "SELECT TOP 1 OrderID, CustomerID, EmployeeID FROM Orders"
Dim da As New OleDbDataAdapter(strSQL, strConn)
AddHandler da.RowUpdated, AddressOf da_RowUpdated
AddHandler da.RowUpdating, AddressOf da_RowUpdating
```

(continued)

```vb
Dim tbl As New DataTable("Orders")
da.Fill(tbl)
tbl.Rows(0)("EmployeeID") = CInt(tbl.Rows(0)("EmployeeID")) + 1
Dim cb As New OleDbCommandBuilder(da)
da.Update(tbl)
tbl.Rows(0)("EmployeeID") = CInt(tbl.Rows(0)("EmployeeID")) - 1
da.Update(tbl)

Public Sub da_RowUpdating(ByVal sender As Object, _
                          ByVal e As OleDbRowUpdatingEventArgs)
    Console.WriteLine("RowUpdating Event: " & e.StatementType.ToString)
    Console.WriteLine(vbTab & "OrderID = " & e.Row("OrderID"))
    Console.WriteLine(vbTab & "EmployeeID from: " & _
                      e.Row("EmployeeID", DataRowVersion.Original))
    Console.WriteLine(vbTab & "EmployeeID to  : " & e.Row("EmployeeID"))
    Console.WriteLine()
End Sub

Public Sub da_RowUpdated(ByVal sender As Object, _
                         ByVal e As OleDbRowUpdatedEventArgs)
    Console.WriteLine("RowUpdated Event: " & e.StatementType.ToString)
    Console.WriteLine(vbTab & "OrderID = " & e.Row("OrderID"))
    If e.Status = UpdateStatus.ErrorsOccurred Then
        Console.WriteLine(vbTab & "Errors occurred")
    Else
        Console.WriteLine(vbTab & "Success!")
    End If
    Console.WriteLine()
End Sub
```

Visual C# .NET

```csharp
string strConn, strSQL;
strConn = "Provider=SQLOLEDB;Data Source=(local)\\NetSDK;" +
          "Initial Catalog=Northwind;Trusted_Connection=Yes;";
strSQL = "SELECT TOP 1 OrderID, CustomerID, EmployeeID FROM Orders";
OleDbDataAdapter da = new OleDbDataAdapter(strSQL, strConn);
da.RowUpdated += new OleDbRowUpdatedEventHandler(da_RowUpdated);
da.RowUpdating += new OleDbRowUpdatingEventHandler(da_RowUpdating);
DataTable tbl = new DataTable("Orders");
da.Fill(tbl);
tbl.Rows[0]["EmployeeID"] = (int) tbl.Rows[0]["EmployeeID"] + 1;
OleDbCommandBuilder cb = new OleDbCommandBuilder(da);
da.Update(tbl);
tbl.Rows[0]["EmployeeID"] = (int) tbl.Rows[0]["EmployeeID"] - 1;
da.Update(tbl);
```

```
static void da_RowUpdating(object sender, OleDbRowUpdatingEventArgs e)
{
    Console.WriteLine("RowUpdating Event: " + e.StatementType.ToString());
    Console.WriteLine("\tOrderID = " + e.Row["OrderID"]);
    Console.WriteLine("\tEmployeeID from: " +
                        e.Row["EmployeeID", DataRowVersion.Original]);
    Console.WriteLine("\tEmployeeID to  : " + e.Row["EmployeeID"]);
    Console.WriteLine();
}

static void da_RowUpdated(object sender, OleDbRowUpdatedEventArgs e)
{
    Console.WriteLine("RowUpdated Event: " + e.StatementType.ToString());
    Console.WriteLine("\tOrderID = " + e.Row["OrderID"]);
    if (e.Status == UpdateStatus.ErrorsOccurred)
        Console.WriteLine("\tErrors occurred");
    else
        Console.WriteLine("\tSuccess!");
    Console.WriteLine();
}
```

Questions That Should Be Asked More Frequently

Q.   Of my three options for creating *DataTable* objects, which should I use?

❑   Creating them using code before populating them using a *DataAdapter*

❑   Creating them implicitly by calling *DataAdapter.Fill*

❑   Creating them by calling *DataAdapter.FillSchema*

A.   I strongly recommend the first option. As of this writing, creating tables using code is about 20 times faster than calling the *FillSchema* method of the *DataAdapter*.

Q.   I created my *DataTable* objects in code, as you recommended, but now the code that fills my *DataTable* objects runs much more slowly. Why is that?

A.   I'm so glad you asked. You'll see this slowdown if your *DataTable* objects have constraints. As you retrieve data from your data store and add rows to your *DataTable* objects, ADO.NET will validate each new row based on these constraints. Also, constraints, such as primary keys and unique constraints, require ADO.NET to examine your *DataTable* to ensure that each new row you create does not violate these constraints. This means that you will pay a greater performance penalty as you add more rows to the *DataTable*.

Generally speaking, the constraints you create in your *Data-Table* objects also exist in your database. Assuming that's the case, your database has already validated the data that you're going to pull into your *DataTable* objects. There's no reason to validate the data again. Is there some sort of middle ground that lets you create constraints on your *DataTable* objects but not pay the performance penalty that comes with validating the data you retrieve using *Data-Adapter.Fill*?

You could build your *DataTable* objects without constraints and then populate them using *DataAdapter.Fill* and *then* add your constraints, but that's an inelegant solution at best.

Ah, but the ADO.NET development team anticipated this scenario and provided a more elegant solution. The *DataSet* class has an *EnforceConstraints* property. By default, it's set to *True*, which means that ADO.NET will enforce the constraints in the *DataSet*. However, you can set this property to *False* just before you call the *Fill* method on your *DataAdapter* objects and then set the property back to *True*, as shown here:

Visual Basic .NET

```
ds.EnforceConstraints = False
da1.Fill(ds.Tables("Table1"))
da2.Fill(ds.Tables("Table2"))
ds.EnforceConstraints = True
```

Visual C# .NET

```
ds.EnforceConstraints = false;
da1.Fill(ds.Tables["Table1"]);
da2.Fill(ds.Tables["Table2"]);
ds.EnforceConstraints = true;
```

Now the *Fill* method will retrieve data as quickly as if you had no constraints on your *DataTable* objects.

Part III

Working with Data Off Line—The ADO.NET *DataSet*

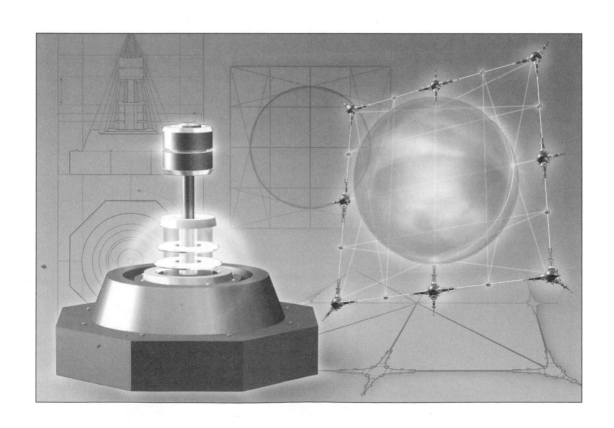

6

Working with *DataSet* Objects

In the previous three chapters, I covered the basic functionality of the connected classes in the ADO.NET object model, which compose a .NET data provider. Now it's time to discuss the disconnected half—the classes that ADO.NET uses to provide a feature-rich, relational, disconnected data cache. In this chapter, I'll cover the basics of storing data in the *DataSet* class and many of the classes that reside in a *DataSet* object.

Features of the *DataSet* Object

At its core, a *DataSet* object is a set of data. When developers picture the results returned by a query, they generally picture data in a grid, much like a Microsoft Excel spreadsheet. You can use a *DataSet* to store the results of a query, but a *DataSet* more closely resembles an Excel workbook because it can hold the results of multiple queries.

But the ADO.NET object model already lets you examine the results of a query through the *DataReader* object. Why would you need another object?

In Chapter 4, you learned about the *DataReader*, which is a fast and efficient structure that lets you retrieve the results of a query. The *DataReader* is built for speed because it supports very limited functionality. The data in the *DataReader* is read-only, and once you've moved on to read the next row, there's no going back to reexamine previous rows.

The *DataSet* object provides much more powerful functionality. Let's take a look at some of the features available through the *DataSet* object.

Working with Disconnected Data

The data in your *DataSet* is disconnected from your database. Once you fetch the results of a query into a *DataSet* using a *DataAdapter* object, there is no longer a connection between your *DataSet* and your database. Changes you make to the contents of the *DataSet* will not affect your database. If other users modify data in your database that corresponds to the data in your *DataSet*, you will not see those changes in your *DataSet*.

Working with disconnected data structures definitely has its benefits. The first major benefit of working with disconnected data is that it does not require a live connection to your database. Once you've fetched the results of your query into a *DataSet* object, you can close the connection to your database and continue to work with the data in your *DataSet*.

Disconnected data structures such as *DataSets* are also helpful when you build multi-tiered applications. If your application uses business objects running on a middle-tier server to access your database, your business object needs to pass disconnected data structures to your client application. The *DataSet* object is designed for use in such situations. You can pass the contents of a *DataSet* from one component to another. The component that receives the data can work with the information as a *DataSet* (if the component is built using the Microsoft .NET Framework) or as an XML document.

Scrolling, Sorting, Searching, and Filtering

The *DataSet* object lets you examine the contents of any row in your *DataSet* at any time. You can loop back and forth through the results of your query as often as you like. This makes the *DataSet* object ideal for scenarios in which your code needs to loop through data, such as in reporting routines. You can also easily build an application that allows a user to scroll back and forth through the results of a query.

DataSet objects also let you change the way you view the results of queries. You can sort the data in a *DataSet* based on a column or a series of columns. You can search for a row of data based on simple search criteria. You can also apply a filter to the data in your *DataSet* so that only rows that satisfy the desired criteria are visible. We'll examine these features in more depth in Chapter 8.

Working with Hierarchical Data

DataSet objects are designed to work with hierarchical data. In Chapter 2, we used the Data Form Wizard to build a simple Microsoft Windows application that let us retrieve information from two tables—customers and orders. When you ran the application, the form that the wizard built let you scroll through the customer data. As you moved from one customer to the next, the form displayed only the orders for the current customer.

The *DataSet* object lets you define relationships between the tables of data stored in the *DataSet*. The Data Form Wizard used the input you provided to build such a relationship. The wizard then bound a *DataGrid* to the relationship to show only the orders for the current customer. (We'll take a closer look at the *DataRelation* object in the next chapter.)

Caching Changes

Working with read-only data is easy. One of the biggest challenges in building a database application is to transform the user's input into changes to the contents of your database. Building such logic into a multi-tiered application can present an even greater challenge if your application needs to cache changes and submit them to your database all at once.

The *DataSet* object lets you cache changes to a row of data so that you can submit the changes to your database using a *DataAdapter*. You can also examine modified rows in your *DataSet* to determine how the row has changed (inserted, modified, or deleted) as well as to compare both the original and current values for each row.

In this chapter, you'll learn about modifying the contents of a *DataSet*. I'll discuss submitting pending changes to your database using the *DataAdapter* object in Chapter 10 and Chapter 11.

XML Integration

The ADO.NET *DataSet* was built from the ground up to work with XML. You can save and load the contents of a *DataSet* to and from files as XML documents. The *DataSet* also lets you separate the schema information (table, column, and constraint information) into an XML schema file.

In ADO.NET, *DataSet* objects and XML documents are almost interchangeable. It's easy to move from one data structure to the other. This duality allows developers to use the interfaces they're most comfortable with. XML programmers can work with *DataSet* objects as XML documents, and database programmers can work with XML documents as *DataSet* objects.

We'll take a closer look at the *DataSet* object's XML features in Chapter 12.

Uniform Functionality

Developers who have worked with ADO might be aware that the *Recordset* object has features similar to those of the *DataSet*. The ADO *Recordset* object supports features such as filtering, searching, sorting, and caching updates.

However, the manner in which you open a *Recordset* plays a large part in determining what functionality is available in the *Recordset*.

For example, if you use just the default settings for the ADO *Recordset* and *Connection* objects, you cannot get an accurate count of the number of rows in the *Recordset*. The *Recordset* object has a *Supports* method that developers often use to determine the functionality available: Can I modify the contents of the *Recordset*? If I update a row, will the *Recordset* send the change to the database immediately or will it be cached? Can I bind my *Recordset* to a grid? Can I move to the previous row?

The reason that not all *Recordset* objects support the same functionality is that the *Recordset* object tries to be everything to everyone. Whether you're working with a firehose cursor, a server-side cursor, or disconnected data in ADO, you're using a *Recordset* object.

The ADO.NET *DataSet* object does not require such integration because it's designed strictly for disconnected data. As a result, ADO.NET developers will never send mail to an e-mail alias asking such questions as "Why is the *RecordCount* for my *Recordset* –1?" or "What does 'The rowset is not bookmarkable' mean?"

Using *DataSet* Objects

In some ways, the *DataSet* and its child objects resemble *matryoshka*—those nested wooden Russian dolls. A *DataSet* contains *DataTable* objects and *DataRelation* objects. A *DataTable* contains *DataRow*, *DataColumn*, and *Constraint* objects.

Rather than try to explain how each object is used one at a time, I will cover the basic functionality of the *DataSet* in this chapter by working through simple examples. Along the way, you'll learn a little about each of the other objects I just mentioned.

Creating a *DataSet* Object

Instantiating a *DataSet* object in code is straightforward. You simply use the *New* keyword in your language of choice. The *DataSet* object has one optional constructor that you can use to set the *DataSetName* property of the *DataSet*:

Visual Basic .NET

```
Dim ds As New DataSet("DataSetName")
Console.WriteLine(ds.DataSetName)
```

Visual C# .NET

```
DataSet ds = new DataSet("DataSetName");
Console.WriteLine(ds.DataSetName);
```

The *DataSet* class and the classes contained in *DataSet* objects—*Data-Table*, *DataColumn*, *DataRow*, *Constraint*, and *DataRelation*—reside in the *System.Data* namespace.

Examining the Structure Created by Calling *DataAdapter.Fill*

In Chapter 5, you learned how to fetch the results of a query into a *DataSet* using the *DataAdapter* object's *Fill* method, as shown here:

Visual Basic .NET

```
Dim strConn, strSQL As String
strConn = "Provider=SQLOLEDB;Data Source=(local)\NetSDK;" & _
        "Initial Catalog=Northwind;Trusted_Connection=Yes;"
strSQL = "SELECT CustomerID, CompanyName, ContactName, Phone " & _
        "FROM Customers"
Dim da As New OleDbDataAdapter(strSQL, strConn)
Dim ds As New DataSet()
da.Fill(ds, "Customers")
```

Visual C# .NET

```
string strConn, strSQL;
strConn = "Provider=SQLOLEDB;Data Source=(local)\\NetSDK;" +
        "Initial Catalog=Northwind;Trusted_Connection=Yes;";
strSQL = "SELECT CustomerID, CompanyName, ContactName, Phone " +
        "FROM Customers";
OleDbDataAdapter da = new OleDbDataAdapter(strSQL, strConn);
DataSet ds = new DataSet();
da.Fill(ds, "Customers");
```

Before we examine the results of the query, let's take a quick look at the structure that the *DataAdapter* created to store those results.

DataTable Object

The *DataAdapter* stores the results of your query in a *DataTable*, an object similar to the *DataReader* object we discussed in Chapter 4. You can use either object to examine the results of a query. Each object exposes the results as a collection of rows and columns.

As you might recall, the *DataReader* is tuned for performance. It lets you tear through the results of your query quickly but offers little functionality beyond that. You already know that you can't modify the data in the *Data-Reader* and that you can't move back to a previous row. The *DataTable* is designed for more durable data and thus provides more robust functionality than the *DataAdapter*. You can modify, sort, and filter the data in a *Data-Table*—features not available through the *DataReader*.

In order to handle this more durable data, the *DataTable* exposes a more durable structure for the data it contains. The *DataTable* object has a *Columns* property that returns a collection of *DataColumn* objects. Each *DataColumn* corresponds to a column in the results of your query.

This structure will be familiar to programmers with DAO and ADO experience because the *Recordset* object in DAO and ADO has a *Fields* property that returns a collection of *Field* objects.

DataColumn Object

Simply put, *DataColumn* objects define the schema for your *DataTable*. When you use the *DataAdapter* object's *Fill* method to create a new *DataTable*, the *DataAdapter* also creates a *DataColumn* object for each column in the results of your query. The new *DataColumn* objects that the *DataAdapter* creates will have only their most basic properties set—*Name*, *Ordinal*, and *DataType*.

Here's a quick sample that displays basic information about the *Data-Column* objects created by calling *DataAdapter.Fill*:

Visual Basic .NET

```
Dim strConn, strSQL As String
strConn = "Provider=SQLOLEDB;Data Source=(local)\NetSDK;" & _
          "Initial Catalog=Northwind;Trusted_Connection=Yes;"
strSQL = "SELECT OrderID, CustomerID, EmployeeID, OrderDate " & _
         "FROM Orders"
Dim da As New OleDbDataAdapter(strSQL, strConn)
Dim ds As New DataSet()
da.Fill(ds, "Orders")

Dim tbl As DataTable = ds.Tables(0)
Console.WriteLine("Column information for " & tbl.TableName & _
                  " DataTable")
Dim col As DataColumn
For Each col In tbl.Columns
    Console.WriteLine(vbTab & col.ColumnName & " - " & _
                      col.DataType.ToString)
Next col
```

Visual C# .NET

```
string strConn, strSQL;
strConn = "Provider=SQLOLEDB;Data Source=(local)\\NetSDK;" +
          "Initial Catalog=Northwind;Trusted_Connection=Yes;";
```

```
strSQL = "SELECT OrderID, CustomerID, EmployeeID, OrderDate " +
        "FROM Orders";
OleDbDataAdapter da = new OleDbDataAdapter(strSQL, strConn);
DataSet ds = new DataSet();
da.Fill(ds, "Orders");

DataTable tbl = ds.Tables[0];
Console.WriteLine("Column information for " + tbl.TableName +
                " DataTable");
foreach (DataColumn col in tbl.Columns)
    Console.WriteLine("\t" + col.ColumnName + " - " +
                    col.DataType.ToString());
```

There's a lot more information available in the *DataColumn* object than name, position, and data type. But for now, we'll take a quick break from the *DataColumn* object and learn how to examine the data that the *DataAdapter* placed in our new *DataTable*.

Examining the Data Returned by a *DataAdapter*

At this point, the *DataTable* takes a sharp right turn from previous object data access models. The *Recordset* object in both ADO and DAO, RDO's *rdoResultset* object, and ADO.NET's *DataReader* all support the concept of a "current row" of data. Each object lets you examine the results of your query one row at a time. The *Recordset* and *rdoResultset* objects let you control the currently available row using methods such as *MoveFirst*, *MovePrevious*, *MoveNext*, and *MoveLast*.

The ADO.NET *DataTable* takes a different approach, which is more in line with XML documents in which you can access any node in the tree at any given time. With the *DataTable*, all rows are available all the time—24 hours a day, 7 days a week, 365 (and change) days a year, and...well, you get the general idea.

The *DataTable* class exposes a *Rows* property that returns the collection of *DataRow* objects available in your *DataTable*. Now let's look at how you can use *DataRow* objects to examine the results of your query.

DataRow Object

The *DataRow* object lets you examine and modify the contents of a row in your *DataTable*. To assign a *DataRow* object to a particular row in the *DataTable*, you use the *DataTable* object's *Rows* property. This property returns a *DataRowCollection* object that contains a collection of *DataRow* objects. Like most collection objects, the *DataRowCollection* object lets you specify an integer to indicate the item you want to access.

The following code snippet uses the *DataAdapter* object's *Fill* method to fetch the results of a query into a new *DataTable* object. The code then assigns the first row returned to a *DataRow* object and displays the contents of two of the columns in the row.

Visual Basic .NET

```
Dim strConn, strSQL As String
strConn = "Provider=SQLOLEDB;Data Source=(local)\NetSDK;" & _
          "Initial Catalog=Northwind;Trusted_Connection=Yes;"
strSQL = "SELECT OrderID, CustomerID, EmployeeID, OrderDate " & _
          "FROM Orders"
Dim da As New OleDbDataAdapter(strSQL, strConn)
Dim ds As New DataSet()
da.Fill(ds, "Orders")

Dim tbl As DataTable = ds.Tables(0)
Dim row As DataRow = tbl.Rows(0)
Console.WriteLine("OrderID = " & row("OrderID"))
Console.WriteLine("CustomerID = " & row("CustomerID"))
```

Visual C# .NET

```
string strConn, strSQL;
strConn = "Provider=SQLOLEDB;Data Source=(local)\\NetSDK;" +
          "Initial Catalog=Northwind;Trusted_Connection=Yes;";
strSQL = "SELECT OrderID, CustomerID, EmployeeID, OrderDate " +
          "FROM Orders";
OleDbDataAdapter da = new OleDbDataAdapter(strSQL, strConn);
DataSet ds = new DataSet();
da.Fill(ds, "Orders");

DataTable tbl = ds.Tables[0];
DataRow row = tbl.Rows[0];
Console.WriteLine("OrderID = " + row["OrderID"]);
Console.WriteLine("CustomerID = " + row["CustomerID"]);
```

As you can see, once you set the *DataRow* object to a row in the *Data-Table*, accessing the value of a particular column is similar to accessing data in a *DataReader*. The *DataRow* object has a parameterized *Item* property that returns the contents of the specified column. You can supply a column name, as shown in the preceding code snippet, or an integer that represents the column's ordinal position in the *DataTable*. As with the *DataReader*, using an index-based lookup will return data more quickly than a string-based lookup. I've used column names to make the code snippet easier to follow.

Examining the Data Stored in a *DataRow*

What if you want to write a more generic routine to display the contents of a *DataRow*? Let's say you want to write a procedure that accepts a *DataRow* object and displays the column names and values contained in that *DataRow*.

If you were writing code using the *DataReader* object, you could check its *FieldCount* property to determine the number of columns. You could then use the *GetName* and *Item* properties to retrieve the name and value for each column. However, the *DataRow* does not have a counterpart to the *DataReader* object's *FieldCount* property.

Instead, the *DataRow* object exposes a *Table* property. This property returns the *DataTable* that contains the *DataRow*. You can use this property to get back to the *DataTable* to retrieve the total number of columns as well as the name of each column. Here's a quick sample that uses this property of the *DataRow* object to display the contents of a *DataRow*, including column names:

Visual Basic .NET

```
Private Sub DisplayRow(ByVal row As DataRow)
    Dim tbl As DataTable = row.Table
    Dim col As DataColumn
    For Each col In tbl.Columns
        Console.WriteLine(vbTab & col.ColumnName & ": " & row(col))
    Next col
End Sub
```

Visual C# .NET

```
static void DisplayRow(DataRow row)
{
    DataTable tbl = row.Table;
    foreach (DataColumn col in tbl.Columns)
        Console.WriteLine("\t" + col.ColumnName + ": " + row[col]);
}
```

The preceding code snippet demonstrates a third way to examine the contents of a particular column. The *DataRow* object's *Item* method accepts a *DataColumn* object. As of this writing, fetching the contents of a row by supplying a *DataColumn* slightly outperforms (by about 6 percent) ordinal-based lookups.

Examining the *DataRow* Objects in a *DataTable*

You can loop through the *DataRow* objects in a *DataTable* as easily as with any other collection in the .NET Framework. You use a *For* loop or a *For Each* loop in your language of choice. The following code snippet loops through the contents of the *DataTable* created by calling *DataAdapter.Fill* and relies on the *DisplayRow* procedure developed in the previous snippet.

Visual Basic .NET

```
Dim strConn, strSQL As String
strConn = "Provider=SQLOLEDB;Data Source=(local)\NetSDK;" & _
          "Initial Catalog=Northwind;Trusted_Connection=Yes;"
strSQL = "SELECT OrderID, CustomerID, EmployeeID, OrderDate " & _
         "FROM Orders"
Dim da As New OleDbDataAdapter(strSQL, strConn)
Dim ds As New DataSet()
da.Fill(ds, "Orders")

Dim tbl As DataTable = ds.Tables(0)
Dim row As DataRow
Dim intCounter As Integer
For Each row In tbl.Rows
    intCounter += 1
    Console.WriteLine("Contents of row #" & intCounter)
    DisplayRow(row)
Next row
```

Visual C# .NET

```
string strConn, strSQL;
strConn = "Provider=SQLOLEDB;Data Source=(local)\\NetSDK;" +
          "Initial Catalog=Northwind;Trusted_Connection=Yes;";
strSQL = "SELECT OrderID, CustomerID, EmployeeID, OrderDate " +
         "FROM Orders";
OleDbDataAdapter da = new OleDbDataAdapter(strSQL, strConn);
DataSet ds = new DataSet();
da.Fill(ds, "Orders");

DataTable tbl = ds.Tables[0];
int intCounter;
foreach (DataRow row in tbl.Rows)
{
    intCounter++;
    Console.WriteLine("Contents of row #" + intCounter);
    DisplayRow(row);
}
```

Validating Data in Your *DataSet*

Databases offer different mechanisms that you can use to ensure that the data in your database is valid. The sample Northwind database has many rules and constraints defined. The CustomerID column in the Customers table must be populated with a string of up to five characters, and that value must be unique within the table. The Orders table generates a new OrderID value for each row and requires that the CustomerID value for each row refer to an existing entry in the Customers table.

Sometimes you'll want to apply similar rules to validate data in your application before submitting changes to your database. For example, let's say you're shopping on line and reach the page where you purchase the items in your basket. Most Web sites will make sure you've entered information into each of the required fields before they submit your order information to the appropriate database.

This type of logic might seem redundant because the database probably has similar validation rules defined. However, adding validation rules to your application can improve its performance. If a user fails to enter a credit card number, either by accident or in the hope that the system programmers were extremely lazy, the code for the Web page can easily determine that it can't successfully submit the order without having to contact the database. The other benefits of this approach are a slight reduction of network traffic and a lighter load on your database.

The ADO.NET *DataSet* offers many of the same data validation mechanisms available in database systems. You can separate these validation mechanisms, also called *constraints*, into two categories—column-level restrictions and table-level restrictions.

Validation Properties of the *DataColumn*

The *DataColumn* object exposes a number of properties that you can use to validate your data.

ReadOnly   The simplest way to ensure that your data is valid is to not let users modify it. If you want to make the data in a *DataColumn* read-only, set the *ReadOnly* property of the *DataColumn* to *True*.

AllowDBNull   Some database columns require values, while others accept empty, or null, values. The *DataColumn* object exposes an *AllowDBNull* property that you can set to control whether the column in your *DataSet* accepts null values.

MaxLength   Many databases place restrictions on the size of a string in a column. In the Customers table, for example, the CustomerID column accepts a string of up to 5 characters and the CompanyName column accepts up to 40 characters. You can place similar restrictions on a *DataColumn* using the *MaxLength* property.

Unique   The *DataColumn* lets you specify which values in a column are unique using the *Unique* property. When you set this property to *True* on a *DataColumn*, ADO.NET will examine the value stored in this column of each row in your *DataTable*. If you add or modify a row in your *DataTable* to create a duplicate value in a unique column, ADO.NET will throw a *ConstraintException*.

The *DataTable* Object's *Constraints* Collection

You can also validate data in your *DataSet* by setting properties of the *Data-Table* object. The ADO.NET object model includes two classes that you can use to define constraints in a *DataTable*. These classes, *UniqueConstraint* and *Foreign-KeyConstraint*, are derived from the *Constraint* class. The *DataTable* exposes a *Constraints* property that you can use to add to, modify, or examine the constraints on the *DataTable*.

UniqueConstraints   If you set the *Unique* property of a *DataColumn* to *True*, you've defined a unique constraint in the *DataTable* that contains that column. At the same time, you've also added a *UniqueConstraint* object to the *Data-Table* object's *Constraints* collection. Setting the *Unique* property of a *Data-Column* is simpler than creating a new *UniqueConstraint* in a *DataTable* object's *Constraints* collection. However, there are times when you'll want to explicitly create a *UniqueConstraint*, such as when you need to make sure that the combinations of values from multiple columns are unique.

PrimaryKey   A primary key is a special type of unique constraint. The ADO.NET *DataRowCollection* object has a *Find* method that you can use to locate a row in your *DataTable* by the value or values in its primary key column, as shown here. (I'll discuss the *Find* method in detail in Chapter 8.)

```
row = MyTable.Rows.Find("ALFKI")
```

A *DataTable* can have multiple unique constraints but can contain at most one primary key. You can set or examine a *DataTable* object's primary key using its *PrimaryKey* property.

ForeignKeyConstraint   You can also add foreign constraints to a *DataTable*. I described an example of a foreign key constraint just a couple pages back. Each order in the Northwind database's Orders table must have a value for its Custo-merID column that is used in the Customers table. You can place similar restrictions on the data in your *DataSet* by creating a *ForeignKeyConstraint* and adding it to the table whose rows you want to validate.

You generally won't need to explicitly create a *ForeignKeyConstraint*. Creating a *DataRelation* between two *DataTable* objects within your *DataSet* creates a *ForeignKeyConstraint* in the process. In the next chapter, I'll discuss the *DataRelation* object and how you can use it to work with relational data.

Note   ADO.NET does not know what data resides in your database. Constraints you define on columns and tables within your *DataSet* are valid only within that *DataSet*. This is an important point to keep in mind. Here's why.

Say you define a *UniqueConstraint* based on the CustomerID column in your *DataTable*. If you add a row with a CustomerID of ZZZZZ, ADO.NET will throw an exception only if another row in your *DataTable* has that same value for the CustomerID column.

Foreign key constraints are enforced in a similar fashion. If you define a foreign key on your orders *DataTable* object based on the CustomerID column in your orders and customers *DataTable* objects, ADO.NET will let you add only orders with a value for the CustomerID column that appears in your customers *DataTable*. ADO.NET will throw an exception if you add a new order with a CustomerID that is used in your database but that does not reside in your customers *DataTable*.

Retrieving Schema Information Using *DataAdapter.FillSchema*

Validating data takes time. In many scenarios, you don't want to set validation properties on your *DataSet*, so the *DataAdapter* does not set validation properties on *DataColumn* objects or add constraints to a *DataTable* object's *Constraints* collection when it creates the *DataTable* in the *DataAdapter* object's *Fill* method unless you make an explicit request.

There are two ways to tell the *DataAdapter* that you want to retrieve this schema information from your database when adding columns to your *DataTable*—by setting the *DataAdapter* object's *MissingSchemaAction* property to *AddWithKey* or by calling the *DataAdapter* object's *FillSchema* method. (I covered these features of the *DataAdapter* in Chapter 5.)

Try This at Home, But Only at Home....

ADO.NET has a few features that you should avoid using in your applications whenever possible. Fetching schema information for your *DataSet* through the *DataAdapter* is one of them.

Using the *DataAdapter* to gather schema information can save time during the design process. In fact, Visual Studio .NET uses the *DataAdapter* to generate your *DataSet* objects at design time (as you'll see later in this chapter). If you're building a small sample or a proof-of-concept application, you might find that using the *DataAdapter* to gather schema information reduces the amount of code you have to write.

But unless your application is an ad-hoc query tool, you should know which columns your queries return, so you should have no need to use features such as *DataAdapter.FillSchema* in your full-blown applications.

If you ask your *DataAdapter* to fetch additional schema information using these features, the *DataAdapter* will query your database for schema information beyond the name and data type for each new *DataColumn* it creates. Examine any of these *DataColumn* objects and you'll find that the *ReadOnly*, *AllowDBNull*, *MaxLength*, and *ReadOnly* properties are set correctly.

The *DataAdapter* will also attempt to generate a primary key for your *DataTable*. This is where you pay a significant performance penalty to fetch schema information. Here's why.

The *DataAdapter* has to query the database to determine which table your query references, and then it has to query the database again to gather information about the primary key for that table. If no primary key is defined for your table, the *DataAdapter* will request information about unique indexes for the table. Once the *DataAdapter* has gathered this information about your table, it will examine the columns returned by your query. This ensures that if your table contains a primary key comprising two columns but the query you're using does not include both of these columns, the *DataAdapter* will not use this primary key in your *DataTable*.

> **Note**   The *DataAdapter* will also set the *AutoIncrement* property of new *DataColumn* objects. I'll cover this property briefly later in this chapter. For more in-depth information on using this property, see Chapter 11.

Creating *DataTable* Objects in Code

You've learned how to create *DataTable* objects using the *Fill* and *FillSchema* methods of the *DataAdapter*. You've also learned that you should create your own *DataTable* objects, especially if you want to validate your data using column or table-level restrictions. Now it's time to learn how to build *DataTable* objects using code.

Creating a *DataTable* Object

You can create a *DataTable* object the same way that you create a *DataSet* object. The *DataTable* has an optional constructor that you can use to set the *TableName* property of the new *DataTable* object, as shown here:

Visual Basic .NET

```
Dim tbl As New DataTable("TableName")
Console.WriteLine(tbl.TableName)
```

Visual C# .NET

```
DataTable tbl = new DataTable("TableName");
Console.WriteLine(tbl.TableName);
```

Adding Your *DataTable* to a *DataSet* Object's *Tables* Collection

Once you've created a *DataTable*, you can add it to an existing *DataSet* object's *Tables* collection using the *DataTableCollection* object's *Add* method, as shown here:

Visual Basic .NET

```
Dim ds As New DataSet()
Dim tbl As New DataTable("Customers")
ds.Tables.Add(tbl)
```

Visual C# .NET

```
DataSet ds = new DataSet();
DataTable tbl = new DataTable("Customers");
ds.Tables.Add(tbl);
```

That's not much code, but the always-clever developers at Microsoft have actually provided a simpler way of adding a new *DataTable* to a *DataSet* object's *Tables* collection by overloading the *DataTableCollection* object's *Add* method. You can create a new *DataTable* and add it to an existing *DataSet* object's *Tables* collection in a single call, as shown in the following code snippet.

Visual Basic .NET

```
Dim ds As New DataSet()
Dim tbl As DataTable = ds.Tables.Add("Customers")
```

Visual C# .NET

```
DataSet ds = new DataSet();
DataTable tbl = ds.Tables.Add("Customers");
```

You can determine whether a *DataTable* resides within a *DataSet* by checking the *DataTable* object's *DataSet* property. If the *DataTable* resides in a *DataSet* object's *Tables* collection, the *DataSet* property returns that *DataSet*. Otherwise, the property returns *Nothing* or *null*, depending on your language of choice. The *DataSet* property of the *DataTable* object is read-only.

It is also worth noting that a *DataTable* can reside in at most one *DataSet*. If you want to add a *DataTable* to multiple *DataSet* objects, you must use either the *Copy* or *Clone* method. The *Copy* method creates a new *DataTable* with the same structure that contains the same set of rows as the original *DataTable*. The *Clone* method creates a new *DataTable* with the same structure, as the *Copy* method does, but it creates a *DataTable* that contains no rows.

Adding Columns to Your *DataTable*

It's time to add some meat to the structure of our new *DataTable*. In order to store the results of a query, the *DataTable* needs to have columns. Earlier in the chapter, you saw how the *DataAdapter* can create new *DataColumn* objects for you. Now let's create our own *DataColumn* objects. We can add *DataColumn* objects to a *Table* object's *Columns* collection using code that's nearly identical to the code we used to add a new *DataTable* to a *DataSet* object's *Tables* collection:

Visual Basic .NET

```
Dim ds As New DataSet()
Dim tbl As DataTable = ds.Tables.Add("Customers")
Dim col As DataColumn = tbl.Columns.Add("CustomerID")
```

Visual C# .NET

```
DataSet ds = new DataSet();
DataTable tbl = ds.Tables.Add("Customers");
DataColumn col = tbl.Columns.Add("CustomerID");
```

Specifying a Data Type for a *DataColumn*

When you create a new *DataColumn*, you'll also want to specify the data type that the *DataColumn* contains. You can use the *DataType* property of the *Data-*

Column to set or check the data type that the column will contain. The *Data-Column* object's *DataType* property is read-write until you add data to the *DataTable* object's *Rows* collection.

Although the data type you select for your *DataColumn* will depend on the data type for that column in your database, there isn't a one-to-one mapping between database data types and *DataColumn* data types.

For example, Microsoft SQL Server lets you choose from a number of data types for string-based data. When you define the structure of a table in a SQL Server database, you can specify whether you want to store your string-based data as a fixed-length or variable-length string. You can also control whether SQL Server stores that data as single-byte (ANSI) or double-byte (Unicode) characters.

However, as far as ADO.NET is concerned, a string is a string. Regardless of whether the database data type is fixed-length or variable-length, single-byte or double-byte, the data type for the *DataColumn* is simply *string*. The *DataType* property of the *DataColumn* object works with .NET data types rather than database data types.

By default, *DataColumn* objects have a *DataType* property of *string*. The *DataColumn* has a constructor that allows you to specify a data type, as well as a column name, for the new column you're creating. Similarly, the *DataColumnCollection* object's *Add* method is overloaded to let you specify values for the *ColumnName* and *DataType* properties for your new *DataTable* object's new *DataColumn*, as shown here:

Visual Basic .NET

```
Dim ds As New DataSet()
Dim tbl As DataTable = ds.Tables.Add("Orders")
Dim col As DataColumn = tbl.Columns.Add("OrderID", GetType(Integer))
```

Visual C# .NET

```
DataSet ds = new DataSet();
DataTable tbl = ds.Tables.Add("Orders");
DataColumn col = tbl.Columns.Add("OrderID", typeof(int));
```

The data type for the *DataType* property is *Type*. The preceding code snippet demonstrates how to get a *Type* value that corresponds to the integer data type in each language. Visual Basic .NET and Visual C# .NET use different functions to generate types for backward-compatibility reasons. Prior to .NET, both C++ and Visual Basic included a *typeof* function, although the function did not return the same information in each language. As a result, Visual Basic .NET includes a *GetType* function to return type information.

Adding a Primary Key

I gave a bit of a lecture earlier in the chapter extolling the virtues of setting validation features of the *DataColumn* and *DataTable* in your own code rather than relying on the *DataAdapter* to query your database for this information. That lecture would ring hollow without an explanation of how to set validation properties on your *DataColumn* objects and *DataTable* objects.

Just before that lecture, you learned about the *AllowDBNull*, *ReadOnly*, *MaxLength*, and *Unique* properties of the *DataColumn* object and how to use them to validate the data stored in your columns. Setting those properties in your code is simple.

Visual Basic .NET

```
Dim ds As New DataSet()
Dim tbl As DataTable = ds.Tables.Add("Customers")
Dim col As DataColumn = tbl.Columns.Add("CustomerID")
col.AllowDBNull = False
col.MaxLength = 5
col.Unique = True
```

Visual C# .NET

```
DataSet ds = new DataSet();
DataTable tbl = ds.Tables.Add("Customers");
DataColumn col = tbl.Columns.Add("CustomerID");
col.AllowDBNull = false;
col.MaxLength = 5;
col.Unique = true;
```

Setting the primary key for a *DataTable* is slightly more complicated. The *PrimaryKey* property contains an array of *DataColumn* objects. So you can't simply set the property to the name of the column or columns that you want to use for your primary key.

Some of the *DataTable* objects you create will rely on single columns as their primary keys; others will rely on combinations of columns. The following code snippet includes code for each scenario. The Customers table uses a single column, CustomerID, while the Order Details table uses a combination of two columns, OrderID and ProductID. In both cases, you need to create an array of *DataColumn* objects and assign that array to the *DataTable* object's *PrimaryKey* property:

Visual Basic .NET

```
Dim ds As New DataSet()
'Create the Customers DataTable.
With ds.Tables.Add("Customers")
```

```
    .Columns.Add("CustomerID", GetType(String))
    ⋮
    .PrimaryKey = New DataColumn() {.Columns("CustomerID")}
End With

'Create the Order Details DataTable.
With ds.Tables.Add("Order Details")
    .Columns.Add("OrderID", GetType(Integer))
    .Columns.Add("ProductID", GetType(Integer))
    ⋮
    .PrimaryKey = New DataColumn() {.Columns("OrderID"), _
                                    .Columns("ProductID")}
End With
```

Visual C# .NET

```
DataSet ds = new DataSet();
DataTable tbl;
//Create the Customers DataTable.
tbl = ds.Tables.Add("Customers");
tbl.Columns.Add("CustomerID", typeof(string));
⋮
tbl.PrimaryKey = new DataColumn[] {tbl.Columns["CustomerID"]};

//Create the Order Details DataTable.
tbl = ds.Tables.Add("Order Details");
tbl.Columns.Add("OrderID", typeof(int));
tbl.Columns.Add("ProductID", typeof(int));
⋮
tbl.PrimaryKey = new DataColumn[] {tbl.Columns["OrderID"],
                                   tbl.Columns["ProductID"]};
```

> **Note**   When you set the primary key for your *DataTable*, ADO.NET
> automatically sets the *AllowDBNull* property of the *DataColumn* object
> or objects referenced in your primary key to *False*.

Adding Other Constraints

Primary keys are the most widely used constraint, but you can also add unique
key and foreign key constraints to a *DataTable*. The *DataTable* object's *Constraints* collection has an overloaded *Add* method that you can use to add new
primary key, unique key, and foreign key constraints. The following code snippet demonstrates how to use the *Add* method to add single-column and multi-
ple-column unique keys as well as how to create a new foreign key constraint.

The code adds a unique key to the Customers *DataTable* based on the CustomerID column and adds a unique key to the Order Details *DataTable* based on the OrderID and ProductID columns. It also adds a foreign key constraint to the Order Details table to ensure that the value for the OrderID column matches a corresponding row in the Orders *DataTable*.

In each case, the code includes two ways to create the constraint. The first example explicitly creates a new constraint object and appends that item to the *DataTable* object's *Constraints* collection. It looks something like this:

```
tbl.Constraints.Add(New UniqueConstraint(...))
```

The *ConstraintCollection* object's *Add* method accepts any object that inherits from the *Constraint* object, so you can supply either a *UniqueConstraint* object or a *ForeignKeyConstraint* object.

The second example uses the *ConstraintCollection* object's *Add* method to create the new constraint and add it to the collection.

```
tbl.Constraints.Add("ConstraintName", ColumnInformation)
```

The *Add* method is overloaded so that you can create new unique, primary key, or foreign key constraints. However, I generally avoid using this syntax. I prefer to explicitly create constraints because I find the resulting code easier to read. I've included both syntaxes in the following code snippet because you might encounter situations in which you want to use the overloaded *Add* methods that create and append your new constraint all at once.

Visual Basic .NET

```
Dim ds As New DataSet()
'Create the Customers DataTable.
With ds.Tables.Add("Customers")
    .Columns.Add("CustomerID", GetType(String))
    :
    'Add a unique key based on the CustomerID column.
    .Constraints.Add(New UniqueConstraint(.Columns("CustomerID")))
    'or
    .Constraints.Add("UK_Customers", .Columns("CustomerID"), False)
End With

'Create the Order Details DataTable.
With ds.Tables.Add("Order Details")
    .Columns.Add("OrderID", GetType(Integer))
    .Columns.Add("ProductID", GetType(Integer))
    :
    'Add a unique key based on the OrderID and ProductID columns.
    Dim cols As New DataColumn() {.Columns("OrderID"), _
                                  .Columns("ProductID")}
```

```
    .Constraints.Add(New UniqueConstraint(cols))
    'or
    .Constraints.Add("UK_Order Details", cols, False)
    'Add a foreign key constraint based on the OrderID column that
    'requires a corresponding OrderID in the Orders table.
    .Constraints.Add(New ForeignKeyConstraint _
                  (ds.Tables("Orders").Columns("OrderID"), _
                   .Columns("OrderID")))
    'or
    .Constraints.Add("FK_Order Details_Orders", _
                  ds.Tables("Orders").Columns("OrderID"), _
                  .Columns("OrderID"))
End With
```

Visual C# .NET

```csharp
DataSet ds = new DataSet();
DataTable tbl;
//Create the Customers DataTable.
tbl = ds.Tables.Add("Customers");
tbl.Columns.Add("CustomerID", typeof(string));
    ⋮
//Add a unique key based on the CustomerID column.
tbl.Constraints.Add(new UniqueConstraint(tbl.Columns["CustomerID"]));
//or
tbl.Constraints.Add("UK_Customers", tbl.Columns["CustomerID"],
                    false);

//Create the Order Details DataTable.
tbl = ds.Tables.Add("Order Details");
tbl.Columns.Add("OrderID", typeof(int));
tbl.Columns.Add("ProductID", typeof(int));
    ⋮
//Add a unique key based on the OrderID and ProductID columns.
DataColumn[] cols = new DataColumn[] {tbl.Columns["OrderID"],
                                      tbl.Columns["ProductID"]};
tbl.Constraints.Add(new UniqueConstraint(cols));
//or
tbl.Constraints.Add("UK_Order Details", cols, false);

//Add a foreign key constraint based on the OrderID column that
//requires a corresponding OrderID in the Orders table.
tbl.Constraints.Add(new ForeignKeyConstraint
                  (ds.Tables["Orders"].Columns["OrderID"],
                   tbl.Columns["OrderID"]));
//or
tbl.Constraints.Add("FK_Order Details_Orders",
                  ds.Tables["Orders"].Columns["OrderID"],
                  tbl.Columns["OrderID"]);
```

Working with Autoincrement Columns

ADO.NET includes support for autoincrement columns through three properties of the *DataColumn*: *AutoIncrement*, *AutoIncrementSeed*, and *AutoIncrementStep*.

If you want ADO.NET to generate such autoincrement values for new rows in your *DataTable*, set the *AutoIncrement* property of your *DataColumn* to *True*, as shown here:

Visual Basic .NET

```
Dim ds As New DataSet()
Dim tbl As DataTable = ds.Tables.Add("Orders")
Dim col As DataColumn = tbl.Columns.Add("OrderID", GetType(Integer))
col.AutoIncrement = True
col.AutoIncrementSeed = -1
col.AutoIncrementStep = -1
col.ReadOnly = True
```

Visual C# .NET

```
DataSet ds = new DataSet();
DataTable tbl = ds.Tables.Add("Orders");
DataColumn col = tbl.Columns.Add("OrderID", typeof(int));
col.AutoIncrement = true;
col.AutoIncrementSeed = -1;
col.AutoIncrementStep = -1;
col.ReadOnly = true;
```

The preceding code snippet marked the OrderID column as autoincrement, but it also set the *AutoIncrementSeed* and *AutoIncrementStep* properties to –1. I strongly recommend setting these two properties to –1 whenever you set *Auto-Increment* to *True*. Allow me to explain why.

The *AutoIncrementSeed* and *AutoIncrementStep* properties control how ADO.NET generates new values. When you're working with an empty table, ADO.NET will assign the value stored in *AutoIncrementSeed* to the autoincrement column for your first row. ADO.NET will use the *AutoIncrementStep* property to generate subsequent autoincrement values.

For example, if you set *AutoIncrement* to *True* and set both *AutoIncrementSeed* and *AutoIncrementStep* to 2, ADO.NET will generate the following values for the autoincrement column of your first five rows: 2, 4, 6, 8, 10.

This behavior changes slightly if you add rows to your *DataTable* by calling *DataAdapter.Fill*. Say you're working with a *DataTable* whose structure matches the Orders table in the Northwind database and you've set the *AutoIncrementSeed* and *AutoIncrementStep* properties to 5 for the OrderID *DataColumn*. If you add new rows to this *DataTable* while it's empty, those new rows will have values of 5, 10, 15, 20, and so on for the OrderID column. However, if you add rows to the *DataTable* from your database using *DataAdapter.Fill* and then add new rows using *DataTable.Rows.Add*, the new values you generate for the OrderID column will depend on the data you fetched from your database. ADO.NET will generate subsequent autoincrement values based on the largest autoincrement value that appears in the *DataTable* and the value of the *AutoIncrementStep* properties.

Let's say that in this example, the largest current value for the OrderID column in your *DataTable* is 973. If you generate a new row at this point, ADO.NET will add the value stored in the *AutoIncrementStep* property (5) to the largest current value in the *DataTable* (973) for a new OrderID of 978.

It is extremely important to keep in mind that ADO.NET is aware only of data that exists in your *DataTable*. It does not know what your database will generate for the next autoincrement value. I said that the largest value for the OrderID column that appears in our *DataTable* based on the results of our query was 973. Maybe the query fetched orders only for a particular customer:

```
SELECT OrderID, CustomerID, OrderDate FROM Orders WHERE CustomerID = 'ALFKI'
```

The database might contain larger values for the OrderID column than the ones that appear in the *DataTable*. ADO.NET has no way to know, so it might generate autoincrement values for new rows in your *DataTable*, but those autoincrement values might already be in use in your database.

I've included this information to help you understand how the ADO.NET autoincrement features work. Armed with this information, you should be able to make intelligent decisions about when and how to generate new autoincrement values using ADO.NET.

During the development of ADO.NET and the .NET Framework as a whole, a developer asked me whether there was any way to achieve paging in a *DataTable* (that is, he wanted to return or display just a portion of the contents of a *DataTable*). Rather than try to count the rows and construct elaborate filters based on search criteria and row ordering, you can achieve paging in a much simpler way by letting ADO.NET count the rows as they're added to the *DataTable*, thanks to ADO.NET's autoincrement features.

Autoincrement Do's and Don'ts

Here's a quick list of autoincrement do's and don'ts:

Do: Use the ADO.NET autoincrement features.

Don't: Submit autoincrement values that ADO.NET generates to your database. The values that ADO.NET generates are merely placeholders. Let the database generate the real new values. Chapter 11 includes examples that show how to let the database generate values as well as how to fetch these new values into the corresponding rows in your *DataTable*.

Don't: Display autoincrement values for new rows that have not been submitted to the database. The database will probably generate different values from the ones ADO.NET generates. The user of your application might not be aware that the autoincrement value that ADO.NET generated for the new row is just a placeholder. If your application is an order-entry system, do you really want to take the chance that the user, who is taking orders over the phone from customers, might mistakenly assume that the value ADO.NET generated for the Order ID is accurate—and then read that value to the customer?

Do: Set the *AutoIncrementSeed* and *AutoIncrementStep* properties to –1. Doing so ensures that you're generating placeholder values that do not appear in your database. Even if you display this value in your application, it will prevent users from mistakenly assuming that the autoincrement values that ADO.NET generates will be the same as the ones the database will generate.

The following code snippet fills a *DataTable* based on the results of a simple query. Before filling the table, the code adds an autoincrement column to the table. Because the query does not return data for this autoincrement column, ADO.NET generates new values for the column for each row returned by the query.

The code snippet uses the *DataView* and *DataRowView* objects. We'll discuss these objects in Chapter 8, but in this sample their use should be self-explanatory. Once we've filled the *DataTable* based on the results of the query, we'll use the *DataView* to view just one "page" of the *DataTable* and write the contents of that page to the screen.

Yes, I know I used the *FillSchema* method to create the structure of my *DataTable*, but I used it only to compress the code snippet. I would not have used it in a real-world application. Scout's honor.

Visual Basic .NET

```
Dim ds As New DataSet()
Dim strConn, strSQL As String
strConn = "Provider=SQLOLEDB;Data Source=(local)\NetSDK;" & _
          "Initial Catalog=Northwind;Trusted_Connection=Yes;"
strSQL = "SELECT CustomerID, CompanyName, ContactName " & _
         "FROM Customers"
Dim da As New OleDbDataAdapter(strSQL, strConn)
da.FillSchema(ds, SchemaType.Source, "Customers")
Dim tbl As DataTable = ds.Tables("Customers")
Dim col As DataColumn = tbl.Columns.Add("RowID", GetType(Integer))
col.AutoIncrement = True
col.AutoIncrementSeed = 1
col.AutoIncrementStep = 1
da.Fill(ds, "Customers")
Dim vue As New DataView(tbl)
Dim intPageSize As Integer = 10
Dim intPageNum As Integer = 3
vue.RowFilter = "RowID > " & (intPageNum - 1) * intPageSize & _
                " AND RowID <= " & intPageNum * intPageSize
Dim row As DataRowView
Dim intCounter As Integer
For intCounter = 0 to vue.Count - 1
    row = vue(intCounter)
    Console.WriteLine(row("RowID") & vbTab & row("CustomerID") & _
                      vbTab &  row("CompanyName"))
Next intCounter
```

Visual C# .NET

```
DataSet ds = new DataSet();
string strConn, strSQL;
strConn = "Provider=SQLOLEDB;Data Source=(local)\\NetSDK;" +
          "Initial Catalog=Northwind;Trusted_Connection=Yes;";
strSQL = "SELECT CustomerID, CompanyName, ContactName " +
         "FROM Customers";
OleDbDataAdapter da = new OleDbDataAdapter(strSQL, strConn);
da.FillSchema(ds, SchemaType.Source, "Customers");
DataTable tbl = ds.Tables["Customers"];
DataColumn col = tbl.Columns.Add("RowID", typeof(int));
col.AutoIncrement = true;
col.AutoIncrementSeed = 1;
col.AutoIncrementStep = 1;
```

(continued)

```
da.Fill(ds, "Customers");
DataView vue = new DataView(tbl);
int intPageSize = 10;
int intPageNum = 3;
vue.RowFilter = "RowID > " + (intPageNum - 1) * intPageSize +
                " AND RowID <= " + intPageNum * intPageSize;
DataRowView row;
for (int intCounter = 0; intCounter < vue.Count; intCounter++) {
    row = vue[intCounter];
    Console.WriteLine(row["RowID"] + "\t" + row["CustomerID"] +
                    "\t" + row["CompanyName"]);
}
```

Should you use this code to achieve paging in your Web applications? Probably not. It's not very scalable. We'll discuss other ways to achieve paging in Chapter 14. I've included this sample strictly to demonstrate that you can solve some interesting problems using the ADO.NET autoincrement features.

Adding an Expression-Based Column

Database administrators generally avoid including data in their databases that can be derived from data that already exists within the database. For example, the Order Details table in the Northwind database contains columns that store the unit price and quantity for each line item in an order, but it does not contain a column for the total cost of the line item.

Users don't care whether the total cost of the line item is stored in the database or not, as long as they can see the total cost of the line item.

Most databases support expressions in their query language so that you can include calculated columns in the results of your query. If you want the database to calculate and return the total cost of a line item in the result set, you could use the following query:

```
SELECT OrderID, ProductID, UnitPrice, Quantity,
    UnitPrice * Quantity AS ItemTotal FROM [Order Details]
```

If you fill a *DataTable* with the results of this query, you'll have a column that contains the results of the desired expression. But if you change the contents of the UnitPrice or Quantity column in a row in your *DataTable*, the contents of the calculated column will remain unchanged. That's because the definition for the calculated column appears in the query itself. The database performs the actual calculation, and you simply retrieve the results of the query. Once you've retrieved the results of the query, the contents of the calculated column will not change.

ADO.NET lets you create expression-based *DataColumn* objects. Rather than including an expression such as the preceding one into your query, you can set the *Expression* property of a *DataColumn* to an expression. When you examine the contents of the column, ADO.NET will evaluate the expression and return the results. You can then modify an order item by changing the unit price or number of units in the order, and when you check the contents of the item total column, you'll see that the column value has been recalculated to include the change you've made.

The following code snippet adds a column to our order detail *DataTable* that will contain the total cost of the order item:

Visual Basic .NET

```
Dim ds As New DataSet()
Dim tbl As DataTable = ds.Tables.Add("Order Details")
⋮
tbl.Columns.Add("Quantity", GetType(Integer))
tbl.Columns.Add("UnitPrice", GetType(Decimal))
tbl.Columns.Add("ItemTotal", GetType(Decimal), _
            "Quantity * UnitPrice")
```

Visual C# .NET

```
DataSet ds = new DataSet();
DataTable tbl = ds.Tables.Add("Order Details");
⋮
tbl.Columns.Add("Quantity", typeof(int));
tbl.Columns.Add("UnitPrice", typeof(Decimal));
tbl.Columns.Add("ItemTotal", typeof(Decimal),
            "Quantity * UnitPrice");
```

> **Note**   This isn't actually the proper way to calculate the total cost of a line item for an order in the Northwind database. The Order Details table contains a Discount column that is used to compute discounts on line items. The column accepts values between 0 and 1. If a line item has a value of .25 in the discount column, there's a 25 percent discount on the total cost of the line item. Thus, the true way to calculate the total cost of a line item is as follows:
>
> ```
> Quantity * UnitPrice * (1 - Discount)
> ```
>
> I simplified the process in the earlier code snippets because I wanted to focus on creating calculated columns rather than have to digress about the structure of the Northwind database.

The *Expression* property supports a wide variety of functions, including aggregate functions that can reference data in other *DataTable* objects in the *DataSet*. We'll create expression-based columns that use aggregate functions in the next chapter when we discuss working with relational data. For more information on the list of functions that the *Expression* property supports, see the MSDN documentation on the *Expression* property.

Creating *DataTable* Objects for the Customers, Orders, and Order Details Tables

We've covered a lot of features of the *DataSet*, *DataTable*, and *DataColumn* objects. Now let's tie all of them together into a single *DataSet*. The following code snippet creates a new *DataSet* that contains three *DataTable* objects. (Smaller snippets shown earlier in the chapter demonstrated how to create pieces of each of these *DataTable* objects.) In the process, the code sets properties on the *DataColumn* objects (including *DataType*, *AllowDBNull*, and *AutoIncrement*) and creates both primary key and foreign key constraints.

The *DataSet* that this code snippet creates mirrors the one that we created in Chapter 2 when we used the Data Form Wizard, except for a few key differences. This code adds a couple more refined settings to our *DataSet* and sets the *AutoIncrementStep* and *AutoIncrementSeed* values on the OrderID column in the Orders *DataTable* to obtain more control over the autoincrement values that ADO.NET generates for new orders. It also sets the *MaxLength* property of the string-based columns.

The code creates foreign key constraints but does not populate the *DataSet* object's *Relations* collection. (I'll cover the *DataRelation* object in the next chapter.)

The Data Form Wizard creates a strongly typed *DataSet*. I'll cover strongly typed *DataSet* objects in Chapter 9. For now, think of a strongly typed *DataSet* as a class that has all the features of a *DataSet* but also exposes structures such as *DataTable* objects and *DataColumn* objects as well-defined properties rather than as simple collections. The following code creates a *DataSet* that's not strongly typed:

Visual Basic .NET

```
Dim ds As New DataSet()
Dim col As DataColumn
Dim fk As ForeignKeyConstraint

'Create the customers table.
With ds.Tables.Add("Customers")
    col = .Columns.Add("CustomerID", GetType(String))
    col.MaxLength = 5
    col = .Columns.Add("CompanyName", GetType(String))
```

```
        col.MaxLength = 40
        col = .Columns.Add("ContactName", GetType(String))
        col.MaxLength = 30
        col = .Columns.Add("Phone", GetType(String))
        col.MaxLength = 24
        .PrimaryKey = New DataColumn() {.Columns("CustomerID")}
End With

'Create the orders table.
With ds.Tables.Add("Orders")
        col = .Columns.Add("OrderID", GetType(Integer))
        col.AutoIncrement = True
        col.AutoIncrementSeed = -1
        col.AutoIncrementStep = -1
        col.ReadOnly = True
        col = .Columns.Add("CustomerID", GetType(String))
        col.AllowDBNull = False
        col.MaxLength = 5
        .Columns.Add("EmployeeID", GetType(Integer))
        .Columns.Add("OrderDate", GetType(DateTime))
        .PrimaryKey = New DataColumn() {.Columns("OrderID")}
End With

'Create the order details table.
With ds.Tables.Add("Order Details")
        .Columns.Add("OrderID", GetType(Integer))
        .Columns.Add("ProductID", GetType(Integer))
        .Columns.Add("UnitPrice", GetType(Decimal))
        col.AllowDBNull = False
        col = .Columns.Add("Quantity", GetType(Integer))
        col.AllowDBNull = False
        col.DefaultValue = "1"
        col = .Columns.Add("Discount", GetType(Decimal))
        col.DefaultValue = "0"
        .Columns.Add("ItemTotal", GetType(Decimal), _
                     "UnitPrice * Quantity * (1 - Discount)")
        .PrimaryKey = New DataColumn() {.Columns("OrderID"), _
                                        .Columns("ProductID")}
End With

'Create the foreign key constraints.
fk = New ForeignKeyConstraint(ds.Tables("Customers").Columns("CustomerID"), _
                              ds.Tables("Orders").Columns("CustomerID"))
ds.Tables("Orders").Constraints.Add(fk)
fk = New ForeignKeyConstraint(ds.Tables("Orders").Columns("OrderID"), _
                              ds.Tables("Order Details").Columns("OrderID"))
ds.Tables("Order Details").Constraints.Add(fk)
```

Visual C# .NET

```csharp
DataSet ds = new DataSet();
DataTable tbl;
DataColumn col;
ForeignKeyConstraint fk;

//Create the customers table.
tbl = ds.Tables.Add("Customers");
col = tbl.Columns.Add("CustomerID", typeof(string));
col.MaxLength = 5;
col = tbl.Columns.Add("CompanyName", typeof(string));
col.MaxLength = 40;
col = tbl.Columns.Add("ContactName", typeof(string));
col.MaxLength = 30;
col = tbl.Columns.Add("Phone", typeof(string));
col.MaxLength = 24;
tbl.PrimaryKey = new DataColumn[] {tbl.Columns["CustomerID"]};

//Create the orders table.
tbl = ds.Tables.Add("Orders");
col = tbl.Columns.Add("OrderID", typeof(int));
col.AutoIncrement = true;
col.AutoIncrementSeed = -1;
col.AutoIncrementStep = -1;
col.ReadOnly = true;
col = tbl.Columns.Add("CustomerID", typeof(string));
col.AllowDBNull = false;
col.MaxLength = 5;
tbl.Columns.Add("EmployeeID", typeof(int));
tbl.Columns.Add("OrderDate", typeof(DateTime));
tbl.PrimaryKey = new DataColumn[] {tbl.Columns["OrderID"]};

//Create the order details table.
tbl = ds.Tables.Add("Order Details");
tbl.Columns.Add("OrderID", typeof(int));
tbl.Columns.Add("ProductID", typeof(int));
col = tbl.Columns.Add("UnitPrice", typeof(Decimal));
col.AllowDBNull = false;
col = tbl.Columns.Add("Quantity", typeof(int));
col.AllowDBNull = false;
col.DefaultValue = 1;
col = tbl.Columns.Add("Discount", typeof(Decimal));
col.DefaultValue = 0;
tbl.Columns.Add("ItemTotal", typeof(Decimal),
                "UnitPrice * Quantity * (1 - Discount)");
tbl.PrimaryKey = new DataColumn[] {tbl.Columns["OrderID"],
                                   tbl.Columns["ProductID"]};
```

```
//Create the foreign key constraints.
fk = new ForeignKeyConstraint(ds.Tables["Customers"].Columns["CustomerID"],
                              ds.Tables["Orders"].Columns["CustomerID"]);
ds.Tables["Orders"].Constraints.Add(fk);
fk = new ForeignKeyConstraint(ds.Tables["Orders"].Columns["OrderID"],
                              ds.Tables["Order Details"].Columns["OrderID"]);
ds.Tables["Order Details"].Constraints.Add(fk);
```

Modifying the Contents of a *DataTable*

You now know how to create *DataSet*, *DataTable*, and *DataColumn* objects, and you know how to use a *DataAdapter* to store the results of a query into *DataTable* objects. You also know how to examine the contents of a *DataTable*. Now let's look at how to add, modify, and delete *DataRow* objects.

Adding a New *DataRow*

Now that we have a *DataSet*, let's add some data to it. In Chapter 5, you learned how to use *DataAdapter* objects to fill a *DataTable* with data from a database. You can also load data from an XML file, a feature we'll examine in Chapter 12. For now, we'll focus on loading data on a row-by-row basis.

Each *DataTable* object has a *Rows* property that returns a *DataRow-Collection* object, which contains a collection of *DataRow* objects. As with most collections, you can use the *DataRowCollection* object's *Add* method to add a new object to the collection. However, *DataRow* objects differ from other ADO.NET objects in how you create them.

Let's say you want to programmatically add 10 *DataRow* objects to a *DataTable* that contains 10 *DataColumn* objects. To add a row to the table, you assign values to each of the columns. But how does the *DataRow* determine its structure—which columns it contains? The *DataTable* object has a *NewRow* method that returns a new *DataRow* object that contains information about each of the columns in the table.

Visual Basic .NET

```
Dim row As DataRow = ds.Tables("Customers").NewRow
row("CustomerID") = "ALFKI"
```

Visual C# .NET

```
DataRow row = ds.Tables["Customers"].NewRow();
row["CustomerID"] = "ALFKI";
```

Once you've created your new *DataRow*, you can populate the various columns using its *Item* property. You can also use the *Item* property to examine the contents of a column in your row. The *Item* property is the default property of the *DataRow* object, so you don't even need to explicitly call *Item* in order to use it. To set the value of a column in a *DataRow*, you supply the name of the column (or its index or the *DataColumn* itself) and then assign the desired value.

The *NewRow* method of the *DataTable* creates a new row, but it does not add that row to the *DataTable*. Generally speaking, you don't want to add your new row as soon as you've created it because at that point it's empty. The values in the columns are set to the appropriate default values or to *Null* if they don't have defaults. By creating the new *DataRow* but not adding it to the *Rows* collection, you can assign values to your columns before making the new *DataRow* part of your *DataTable*. The CustomerID column of our Customers table does not accept *Null* values but does not have a default value. Say you have a Customers *DataTable* that has a primary key based on the CustomerID column. If you try to add a new *Customers* row to the table without assigning a value to the CustomerID column, you'll generate an exception.

Once you've supplied values for all the desired columns in your new row and you're ready to add it to the *DataTable*, you use the *Add* method of the *DataRowCollection* and supply your new row, as shown here:

Visual Basic .NET

```
Dim row As DataRow = ds.Tables("Customers").NewRow
row("CustomerID") = "ALFKI"
...
ds.Tables("Customers").Rows.Add(row)
```

Visual C# .NET

```
DataRow row = ds.Tables["Customers"].NewRow();
row["CustomerID"] = "ALFKI";
...
ds.Tables["Customers"].Rows.Add(row);
```

The *DataTable* object offers a second way to add a new row to the table: the *LoadDataRow* method. To use this method, you supply an array of values in the first parameter. The items in the array correspond to columns in the table. The second parameter of the *LoadDataRow* method, *AcceptChanges*, lets you control the value of the *RowState* property of the new *DataRow*. Passing a value of *False* into this parameter, as shown in the following code snippet, causes the new row to have a *RowState* of *Added*, just as if you'd added the row by using *DataTable.NewRow* and *Rows.Add*, as in the earlier examples.

Visual Basic .NET

```
Dim aValues As Object() = {"ALFKI", "Alfreds Futterkiste", _
                           "Maria Anders", "030-0074321"}
ds.Tables("Customers").LoadDataRow(aValues, False)
```

Visual C# .NET

```
object[] aValues = {"ALFKI", "Alfreds Futterkiste",
                    "Maria Anders", "030-0074321"};
ds.Tables["Customers"].LoadDataRow(aValues, false);
```

When you submit changes to your database by calling the *Update* method of the *DataAdapter* object, the *DataAdapter* examines the *RowState* of each *DataRow* to determine how to update the database—by modifying an existing row, adding a new row, or deleting an existing row. If you pass a value of *True* to the second parameter in *LoadDataRow*, the new *DataRow* will have a *RowState* of *Unmodified*, which means that the row does not contain a pending change that the *DataAdapter* would submit to the database. We'll discuss the *DataRow* object's *RowState* property and updating your database in more detail in Chapter 10.

Modifying an Existing Row

There are three ways to modify the contents of a row programmatically. Let's start with the simplest.

Once you have a *DataRow* object, you can set the value of a column using the *DataRow* object's *Item* property. Earlier in the chapter, you saw how to use this property to check the contents of a column. The property is read/write, so you can also use it to set the value of a column. The code snippets that follow use the *Rows* collection's *Find* method to locate a row in the Customers *DataTable* and then change the values in the CompanyName and ContactName columns. We'll discuss the *Find* method in more detail in Chapter 8. For now, consider this a preview.

Visual Basic .NET

```
Dim rowCustomer As DataRow
rowCustomer = ds.Tables("Customers").Rows.Find("ANTON")
If rowCustomer Is Nothing Then
    'Customer not found!
Else
    rowCustomer("CompanyName") = "NewCompanyName"
    rowCustomer("ContactName") = "NewContactName"
End If
```

Visual C# .NET

```
DataRow rowCustomer;
rowCustomer = ds.Tables["Customers"].Rows.Find("ANTON");
if (rowCustomer == null)
    //Customer not found!
else {
    rowCustomer["CompanyName"] = "NewCompanyName";
    rowCustomer["ContactName"] = "NewContactName";
}
```

The second way to update a row is similar to the first, except that you add calls to the *DataRow* object's *BeginEdit* and *EndEdit* methods.

Visual Basic .NET

```
Dim rowCustomer As DataRow
rowCustomer = ds.Tables("Customers").Rows.Find("ANTON").
If rowCustomer Is Nothing Then
    'Customer not found!
Else
    rowCustomer.BeginEdit
    rowCustomer("CompanyName") = "NewCompanyName"
    rowCustomer("ContactName") = "NewContactName"
    rowCustomer.EndEdit
End If
```

Visual C# .NET

```
DataRow rowCustomer;
rowCustomer = ds.Tables["Customers"].Rows.Find("ANTON");
if (rowCustomer == null)
    //Customer not found!
else {
    rowCustomer.BeginEdit();
    rowCustomer["CompanyName"] = "NewCompanyName";
    rowCustomer["ContactName"] = "NewContactName";
    rowCustomer.EndEdit();
}
```

Using *BeginEdit* and *EndEdit* lets you buffer the changes to the row. Calling *EndEdit* saves the changes to the row. If you decide that you don't want to keep the changes, you can call *CancelEdit* instead to undo the changes and the row will revert to its state at the time you called *BeginEdit*.

There's another difference between these two ways of modifying a row. The *DataTable* has events such as *RowChanging*, *RowChanged*, *ColumnChanging*, and *ColumnChanged* that you can use to examine the changes to a row or column. When, or if, these events fire depends on how you modify a row—with or without calling *BeginEdit* and *EndEdit*.

In the first example, the contents of the row changed each time we modified a column in the row. The *DataTable* object's events fire each time you modify the contents of a column. Using *BeginEdit* blocks the events from occurring until you call *EndEdit*. (If you call *CancelEdit* instead of *EndEdit*, the buffered changes will be discarded, and because the row is not updated, the events will not fire.)

The third way to modify the contents of a row is by using the *ItemArray* property. Like the *Item* property, this property can be used to retrieve or modify the contents of the row. The difference between the properties is that the *Item* property works with one column at a time and the *ItemArray* property returns and accepts an array in which each item corresponds to a column.

Visual Basic .NET

```
Dim aCustomer As Object() = {"ALFKI", "NewCompanyName", _
                             "NewContactName", "NewPhoneNo"}
Dim rowCustomer As DataRow
rowCustomer = ds.Tables("Customers").Rows.Find("ALFKI")
rowCustomer.ItemArray = aCustomer
```

Visual C# .NET

```
object[] aCustomer = {"ALFKI", "NewCompanyName",
                      "NewContactName", "NewPhoneNo"};
DataRow rowCustomer;
rowCustomer = ds.Tables["Customers"].Rows.Find("ALFKI");
rowCustomer.ItemArray = aCustomer;
```

If you want to use the *ItemArray* property but you don't want to change the value of every column in your row, you can use the *Nothing* keyword in Visual Basic .NET or *null* in Visual C# .NET. The following code snippets leave the first column in the *DataRow* untouched but modify the other three columns:

Visual Basic .NET

```
Dim aCustomer As Object() = {Nothing, "NewCompanyName", _
                             "NewContactName", "NewPhoneNo"}
Dim rowCustomer As DataRow
rowCustomer = ds.Tables("Customers").Rows.Find("ALFKI")
rowCustomer.ItemArray = aCustomer
```

Visual C# .NET

```
object[] aCustomer = {null, "NewCompanyName",
                      "NewContactName", "NewPhoneNo"};
DataRow rowCustomer;
rowCustomer = ds.Tables["Customers"].Rows.Find("ALFKI");
rowCustomer.ItemArray = aCustomer;
```

> **Note**   Modifying the contents of a row does not automatically modify the contents of the corresponding row in your database. The changes you make to the row are considered pending changes that you can later submit to your database using the *DataAdapter* object. We'll discuss this process in more detail in Chapter 10 and Chapter 11.

So which method should you use to modify rows in your *DataTable*? I prefer using *BeginEdit* and *EndEdit* because it forces me to write code that's better structured, easier to read, and easier to maintain. Plus, this approach allows me to cancel the entire set of updates to a row if an unexpected problem occurs.

In this book, however, I'll generally avoid using the *BeginEdit* and *EndEdit* methods in order to make the code snippets more concise.

Working with *Null* Values in a *DataRow*

During the .NET beta, developers asked a lot of questions about setting database values to *Null* or checking database values for *Null*. Determining whether a column in a row contains a *Null* value is actually very simple.

The *DataRow* object has an *IsNull* method that you can use to check whether a column contains a *Null* value. Like the *DataRow* object's *Item* method, the *IsNull* method accepts a column name, an integer that represents the index for the column, or a *DataColumn* object.

The following code snippet demonstrates the use of the *DataRow* object's *IsNull* method.

Visual Basic .NET

```
Dim rowCustomer As DataRow
rowCustomer = ds.Tables("Customers").Rows.Find("ALFKI")
If rowCustomer.IsNull("Phone") Then
    Console.WriteLine("It's Null")
Else
    Console.WriteLine("It's not Null")
End If
```

Visual C# .NET

```
DataRow rowCustomer;
rowCustomer = ds.Tables["Customers"].Rows.Find("ALFKI");
if (rowCustomer.IsNull("Phone"))
    Console.WriteLine("It's Null");
else
    Console.WriteLine("It's not Null");
```

When you want to set the value of a column to *Null*, don't use the *Null* keyword from your programming language of choice. The .NET Framework includes a class in the *System* namespace called *DBNull*. To set the value of a column in a *DataRow* to *Null*, use the *Value* property of the *DBNull* class, as shown here:

Visual Basic .NET

```
Dim rowCustomer As DataRow
rowCustomer = ds.Tables("Customers").Rows.Find("ALFKI")
rowCustomer("Phone") = DBNull.Value
```

Visual C# .NET

```
DataRow rowCustomer;
rowCustomer = ds.Tables["Customers"].Rows.Find("ALFKI");
rowCustomer["Phone"] = DBNull.Value;
```

Deleting a *DataRow*

Deleting a row is simpler than modifying one. You simply call the *Delete* method on the *DataRow*. However, deleting the row does not remove it from the *DataTable*. Instead, ADO.NET marks the row as a pending deletion. Why doesn't ADO.NET just remove the *DataRow* from the table?

Remember that the data storage objects in the ADO.NET object model act as a data cache so that you can retrieve data from your database, modify that data in a disconnected mode, and later submit the pending changes. When you call the *Delete* method on the *DataRow*, you're not deleting the corresponding row in your database. Instead, you're marking the row as a pending deletion so that you can later submit that pending change to the database. If you completely remove the row from your *DataTable*, you will not delete the corresponding row in your database when you submit the pending changes stored in your *DataSet* or *DataTable*.

We'll examine submitting pending changes to your database in Chapter 10.

Removing a *DataRow*

If you really want to remove a row from your *DataTable* rather than mark it as a pending deletion, you can use the *Remove* or *RemoveAt* method on the *DataRowCollection* class, as shown in the following code snippet. Use the *Remove* method if you have a reference to the *DataRow* you want to remove. If you have the index number for the *DataRow*, use the *RemoveAt* method instead.

Visual Basic .NET

```
Dim rowCustomer As DataRow
rowCustomer = ds.Tables("Customers").Rows.Find("ALFKI")
ds.Tables("Customers").Remove(rowCustomer)

'or

ds.Tables("Customers").RemoveAt(intIndex)
```

Visual C# .NET

```
DataRow rowCustomer = ds.Tables["Customers"].Rows.Find("ALFKI");
rowCustomer.ItemArray = aCustomer;
ds.Tables["Customers"].Remove(rowCustomer);

//or

ds.Tables["Customers"].RemoveAt(intIndex);
```

I generally prefer using the *Remove* method. The *RemoveAt* method requires that you determine the index of the *DataRow* you want to remove. The *DataRow* object does not expose a property to return this information.

In addition, the *DataSet* and *DataTable* classes each have a *Clear* method that you can use to remove all *DataRow* objects from the *DataSet* or *DataTable* while preserving its structure.

Using the *DataRow.RowState* Property

The *DataSet*, *DataTable*, and *DataRow* objects act as an offline data cache. You can query your database and store the results in these objects. As you've just learned, you can add, modify, and delete rows. Because these ADO.NET objects are not connected to your database, the changes you make will not affect the contents of your database. Of course, modifying data off line isn't very useful if you can't submit those changes to your database later.

ADO.NET supports submitting changes back to your database. In Chapter 10, I'll cover this functionality in depth. For now, I'll cover some of the basics of how the *DataSet* supports this functionality. In order to cache a change to a *DataRow* so that ADO.NET can later submit the change to your database, ADO.NET must remember what type of change you've made to the row. Why, you ask?

One way to update the data stored in your database is to issue action queries such as this:

```
UPDATE MyTable SET FieldToModify = NewValue
        WHERE PKField = PKValue AND FieldToModify = OriginalValue
```

or this:

```
INSERT INTO MyTable (Field1, Field2, ... FieldN)
          VALUES (Value1, Value2, ... ValueN)
```

or this:

```
DELETE FROM MyTable WHERE PKField = PKValue
```

You can also use stored procedures to perform updates in a similar fashion.

The point is that the logic used to modify a row is different from the logic used to insert a row and the logic used to delete a row. Therefore, ADO.NET must keep track of what kind of change you've made to your *DataRow* in order to successfully submit the change to your database later.

ADO.NET stores this information in a property of the *DataRow* called *RowState*, which uses the values in the *DataRowState* enumeration. (See Table 6-1.) By checking this property, you can determine whether the row has been changed, along with the type of change (modification, insertion, or deletion) the row contains.

Table 6-1   The *DataRowState* Enumeration

Constant	Value	Description
Unchanged	2	The row does not contain any pending changes.
Detached	1	The row is not a member of a *DataTable*.
Added	4	The row has been added to the *DataTable* but does not exist in the database.
Modified	16	The row contains pending changes.
Deleted	8	The row is a pending deletion.

The list of possible values might lead you to believe that the *RowState* property can return a combination of values from *DataRowState*, but the *RowState* property always returns a value from the enumeration. Table 6-2 provides a few scenarios and the resulting value.

Table 6-2   *RowState* Examples

Example	DataRowState

Newly created but detached row:
`row = tbl.NewRow`
`row("ColX") = "InitValue"`
	Detached

Adding the new row to a *DataTable*: `tbl.Rows.Add(row)`	*Added*
Newly retrieved row: `row = tbl.Rows(0)`	*Unchanged*

After an edit:
`row.BeginEdit()`
`row("ColX") = "NewValue1"`
`row.EndEdit()`
	Modified

After deleting a row: `row.Delete()`	*Deleted*

Examining the Pending Changes in a *DataRow*

Let's say that we've looped through the contents of your *DataTable* and, thanks to the *RowState* property, we've located a modified row. You've seen how to use the *Item* property of the *DataRow* to examine the contents of the columns in the row. You can also use the *Item* property to determine what the contents of the columns were *before* you modified the row.

The *Item* property accepts a second optional parameter from the *Data-RowVersion* enumeration, as described in Table 6-3.

Table 6-3   The *DataRowVersion* Enumeration

Constant	Value	Description
Current	512	The current value stored in the column
Original	256	The original value stored in the column
Proposed	1024	The proposed value for the column (valid only while editing a row using *BeginEdit*)
Default	1536	Default action

Generally speaking, the *DataRow* has two "versions"—what's currently stored in the row and what was originally stored in the row. You'll usually need both sets of information to locate the row. After you've updated a row, you can check the current contents of a column as well as the original contents of a column. The following code changes the contents of the CompanyName column in a *DataRow* and then retrieves both the current (new) value and the original value of the column.

Visual Basic .NET

```
Dim rowCustomer As DataRow
rowCustomer = ds.Tables("Customers").Rows.Find("ALFKI")
rowCustomer("CompanyName") = "NewCompanyName"
Dim strNewCompanyName, strOldCompanyName As String
Console.WriteLine(rowCustomer("CompanyName", _
                              DataRowVersion.Current))
Console.WriteLine(rowCustomer("CompanyName", _
                              DataRowVersion.Original))
```

Visual C# .NET

```
DataRow rowCustomer;
rowCustomer = ds.Tables["Customers"].Rows.Find("ALFKI");
rowCustomer["CompanyName"] = "NewCompanyName";
string strNewCompanyName, strOldCompanyName;
Console.WriteLine(rowCustomer["CompanyName",
                              DataRowVersion.Current]);
Console.WriteLine(rowCustomer["CompanyName",
                              DataRowVersion.Original]);
```

When you edit a row using *BeginEdit* and *EndEdit*, you might want to examine another version of the column: the "proposed" version. Once you call *EndEdit*, the changes will be stored in the current version of the row. Before then, however, the changes you make to the row will only be pending because you can still cancel the changes by calling *CancelEdit*.

While you're editing a row, you can check the proposed view of a column by checking its *Item* property and supplying the *Proposed* constant from the *DataRowVersion* enumeration. Using the *Current* constant will return the value of the column before *BeginEdit* is called—which is not necessarily the original version of the column.

Let's look at the various states of a *DataRow* and the different values the *Item* property returns based on the value of *DataRowVersion* you use. (This is sort of like how a bill becomes a law, but without the Saturday morning cartoon animation.)

Table 6-4 lists the values returned by the *Item* property, depending on the *DataRowVersion* enumeration specified and the current state of the row. Entries marked as *[Exception]* represent scenarios in which calling the *Item* property with the *DataRowVersion* enumeration specified will throw an exception.

Table 6-4   Values of Various Versions of a Column in a *DataRow*

Example	Current	Original	Proposed	Default

Newly created but detached row:
 	
`row = tbl.NewRow`
`row("ColumnX") = "InitValue"`
	InitialValue	[Exception]	[Exception]	*NewValue*

Adding the new row to a *DataTable*: `tbl.Rows.Add(row)`	*InitialValue*	[Exception]	[Exception]	*NewValue*
Newly retrieved row: `row = tbl.Rows(0)`	*Retrieved-Value*	*Retrieved-Value*	[Exception]	*Retrieved-Value*

During first edit:
 	
`row.BeginEdit()`
`row("ColX") = "NewValue1"`
	Retrieved-Value	*Retrieved-Value*	*NewValue1*	*NewValue1*

After first edit: `row.EndEdit()`	*NewValue1*	*Retrieved-Value*	[Exception]	*NewValue1*

(continued)

Table 6-4   **Values of Various Versions of a Column in a *DataRow***   *(continued)*

Example	Current	Original	Proposed	Default

During second edit:
 	
`row.BeginEdit()`
`row("ColX") = "NewValue2"`
	NewValue1	*Retrieved-Value*	*NewValue2*	*NewValue2*

After second edit: `row.EndEdit()`	*NewValue2*	*Retrieved-Value*	[Exception]	*NewValue2*

After canceled edit:
 	
`row.BeginEdit()`
`row("ColX") = "ValueToCancel"`
`row.CancelEdit()`
	NewValue2	*Retrieved-Value*	[Exception]	*NewValue2*

After deleting a row: `row.Delete()`	[Exception]	*Retrieved-Value*	[Exception]	[Exception]

> **Note**   Performing a successful edit changes the current value but does not affect the original value. Calling *CancelEdit* resets the current value to the value before *BeginEdit* is called, which is not necessarily the same as the original value.
>
> After you've deleted a row, you'll receive an exception if you try to examine its current values, but you can still access its original values.

We've discussed three of the four values in the *DataRowVersion* enumeration. Now let's talk about the *Default* value. Using this value in the *Item* property will not return the default value for the column. That's the *DefaultValue* property's job. This *Default* value in the enumeration represents the default value for the parameter on the *DataRow* object's *Item* property.

Earlier in the chapter, I said that the *Item* property returns the current value of a column in the row. The accuracy of that statement might depend on your definition of "current."

If you're not in the process of editing a row, calling *Item* and omitting the optional parameter is equivalent to supplying the *DataRowVersion.Current* constant for the optional parameter. However, if you're in the process of editing a row and you omit the optional parameter on the *Item* property, you'll receive the "proposed" version for the column.

Working with *DataSet* Objects in Visual Studio .NET

You now know a great deal about the structure of *DataSet* objects and how to create them in code. But, man, that's a lot of code to write! Let's look at some features of the Visual Studio .NET development environment that you can use to create *DataSet* objects with a lot less effort.

Generating a *DataSet* from *DataAdapter* Objects

Early in the chapter, I explained that the structure of your *DataSet* generally depends on the structure of the data your *DataAdapter* objects will return and that you can use *DataAdapter* objects to create the structure for your *DataSet*. Visual Studio .NET also lets you create *DataSet* objects based on *DataAdapter* objects.

When you're working with a designer—such as a Windows form or a Web form—that contains *DataAdapter* objects, you can choose to generate a *DataSet* based on the data returned by those *DataAdapter* objects. Choose Generate Dataset from the Data menu, click on the Generate Dataset link in the Properties window, or right-click on the designer and choose Generate Dataset from the shortcut menu to open the Generate Dataset dialog box. The latter approach is shown in Figure 6-1. Figure 6-2 shows the Generate Dataset dialog box.

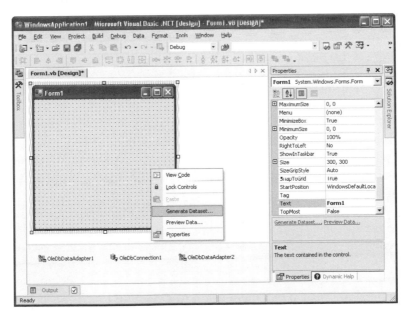

Figure 6-1   Launching the Generate Dataset dialog box

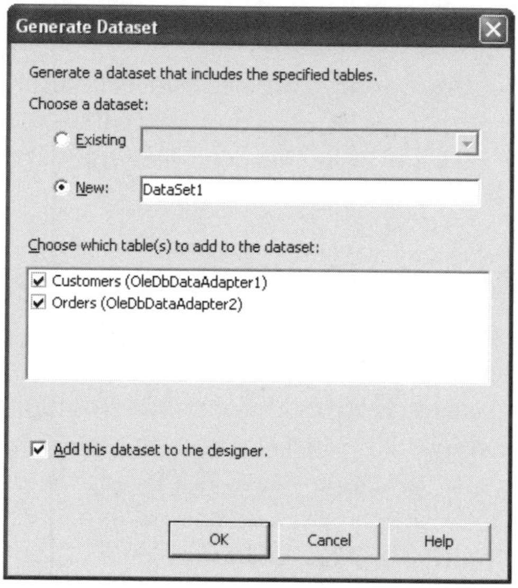

Figure 6-2   The Generate Dataset dialog box

In the dialog box, you can choose to create a new *DataSet* or modify the structure of an existing *DataSet*. The dialog box also allows you to select the *DataAdapter* objects to use in generating your new *DataSet*. As you can see in Figure 6-2, the dialog box shows both the *DataAdapter* name and the name of the table it references. Having both pieces of information can make it easier for you to determine which *DataAdapter* objects you want to use to build your *DataSet*. The dialog box also has a check box that you can select to add an instance of your new *DataSet* to the designer.

If you choose to add an instance of your new *DataSet*, it will appear in the designer's components tray. Figure 6-3 shows an example in which we've created a new *DataSet* and added an instance to the designer. When you select the instance of your *DataSet*, you'll see the *DataSet* object's properties listed in the Properties window.

You'll also see a new file in the Solution Explorer window. The new file will have the same name as the name you specified for your new *DataSet* and will have an .xsd extension. Where does that come from, you ask? Visual Studio .NET creates a new *DataSet* object, calls the *FillSchema* method on the *DataAdapter* objects you referenced in the Generate Dataset dialog box, and then calls the *WriteXmlSchema* method on that *DataSet* to save its schema information to a file.

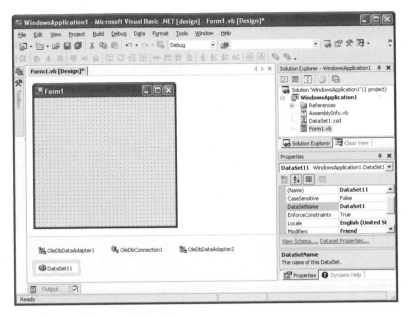

Figure 6-3   The new *DataSet*

> **Note**   This feature of the Visual Studio .NET development environ-
> ment highlights how useful a feature such as *DataAdapter.FillSchema*
> can be when used properly.

Let's take a look at the .xsd file we created using the Generate Dataset dialog box. Double-click on the file in the Solution Explorer window to invoke the
Visual Studio .NET XML schema designer, as shown in Figure 6-4. The .xsd file
simply contains an XML schema file with a few added *DataSet*-specific
attributes. The *DataTable* objects appear as elements within the *DataSet*. Similarly, *DataColumn* objects appear as elements within the *DataTable* objects.
You can select an object—a *DataColumn*, a *DataTable*, or the design surface
that represents the *DataSet*—and the Properties window will display properties
for that object.

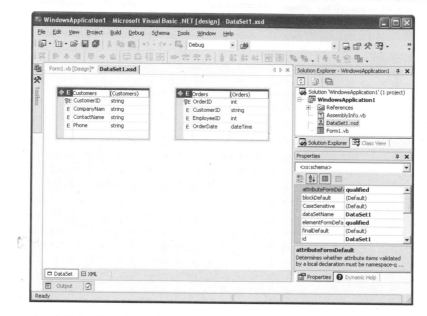

Figure 6-4   Examining the contents of the new *DataSet* schema file

Creating a New *DataSet* from Scratch

What if you want to create a new *DataSet* but you don't have *DataAdapter* objects to define its structure? You can add a new *DataSet* .xsd file to your project using the Add New Item dialog box. (See Figure 6-5.)

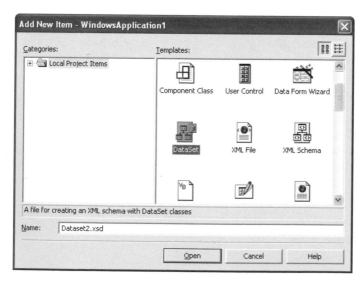

Figure 6-5   Adding a new *DataSet* to your project

Be sure to select the DataSet template in the dialog box rather than XML Schema. Selecting either item will add a new .xsd file to your project and launch the XML schema designer. However, *DataSet* schema files have an additional attribute set in their schema that Visual Studio .NET looks for to determine whether to treat the file as a standard XML schema or as a *DataSet*.

Once you've added a new *DataSet* to your project, you'll see the same designer that you saw when we generated a *DataSet* based on *DataAdapter* objects, except that your new *DataSet* will be empty. Let's add a new *DataTable* to the *DataSet*. Figure 6-6 shows the shortcut (context) menu that appears when you right-click on the designer. Choose Add and then New Element from the shortcut menu to add a new *DataTable* to the *DataSet*. You can also choose the same command from the Schema menu.

Figure 6-6   Adding a new *DataTable* to your new *DataSet*

> **Note**   ADO.NET can store *DataSet* schema information in XML schema format, so using an XML schema designer as a way to examine and modify the structure of your *DataSet* objects might seem like a natural fit. Unfortunately, this design choice has some shortcomings. XML-savvy developers will quickly pick up on concepts such as the fact that a *DataTable* in the *DataSet* corresponds to an element within the schema file, but developers with less XML experience might be confused by this interface. You might see a more data-specific *DataSet* designer in a future release of Visual Studio .NET. In the meantime, I'll cover the basic features of constructing a new *DataSet* using this interface.

Once you have a new *DataTable*, you'll want to add some *DataColumn* objects. Click on the leftmost cell in the first row in the box that represents your new *DataTable* in the XML schema designer. This should make an arrow appear just to the right of that cell. Click on the arrow and you'll see a list, similar to the one shown in Figure 6-7, of available items you can add to the *DataTable*. To add a new *DataColumn*, select Element from the list and then specify the name for your new *DataColumn*. The text you enter will be stored in the *DataColumn* object's *ColumnName* property.

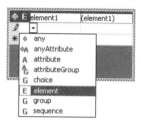

Figure 6-7   Adding a new *DataColumn* to a *DataTable*

To set other properties on a *DataColumn*, select the desired column in the XML schema designer. Figure 6-8 shows part of the list of available properties that appears in the Properties window when you select a column in the XML schema designer. You'll notice that some of the properties are specific to the *DataColumn* and others are more applicable to XML elements. Some properties that were added to the ADO.NET object model late in the development cycle, such as the *DataColumn* object's *MaxLength* property, are not available through this interface.

Once you've created your new *DataSet* with the appropriate structure, save your changes and close the XML schema designer. You've now created a *DataSet* schema file in your project. To add an instance of your *DataSet* to a designer, select DataSet on the Data tab of the Visual Studio .NET Toolbox just as you would if you wanted to add another component, such as a button, to a designer. Double-click on the Toolbox item, or drag-and-drop the item onto the designer or its components tray. Either of these actions will launch the Add Dataset dialog box, shown in Figure 6-9.

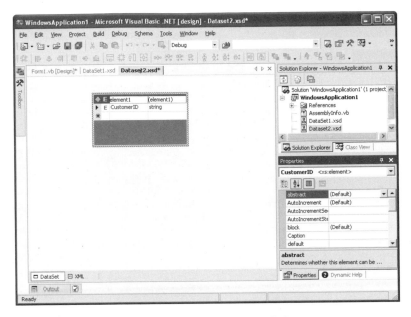

Figure 6-8   Setting properties on the new *DataColumn*

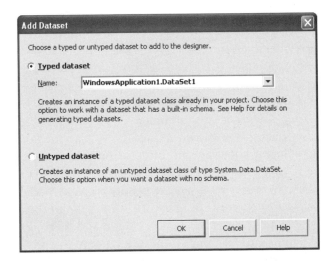

Figure 6-9   Adding an instance of the new *DataSet*

The Add Dataset dialog box lets you select any of the *DataSet* schema files in your project. Simply select a *DataSet* from the list and click OK, and you'll add a new instance of the *DataSet* to your component.

If you want to add an instance of the new *DataSet* in code, you'll find that the *DataSet* is available as a new class defined within your project. Figure 6-10 shows an example of adding an instance of the new *DataSet* in code in a Visual Basic .NET code module.

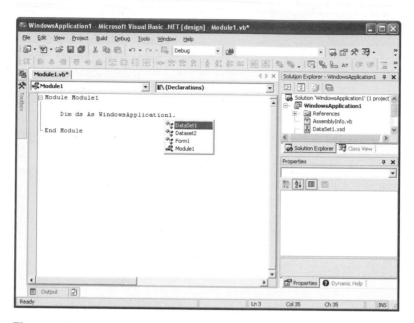

Figure 6-10   Adding an instance of the new *DataSet* in code

Creating an Untyped *DataSet*

I've mentioned that Visual Studio .NET builds strongly typed *DataSet* objects, a topic I'll cover in more depth in Chapter 9. But what if you don't want to use strongly typed *DataSet* objects? Or what if you want to use an instance of a simple untyped *DataSet* but you want to add *DataTable* objects and *DataColumn* objects to your untyped *DataSet* at design time?

The Add Dataset dialog box shown in Figure 6-9 also includes an option button that you can select if you want an untyped *DataSet*. Let's see how you can use that feature to create an untyped *DataSet*.

First, use the DataSet item on the Data tab of the Visual Studio .NET Toolbox to add another *DataSet* to your designer. This time, when the Add Dataset dialog box appears, select the Untyped Dataset option and then click OK. You'll see your new *DataSet* in your designer's components tray.

Select the *DataSet* in the components tray, and you'll see its properties listed in the Properties window. To add *DataTable* objects to the *DataSet*, select the *Tables* property in the Properties window and then click on the ellipsis button to the right. Doing so will launch the Visual Studio .NET Collection Editor. Many components within Visual Studio .NET use the Collection Editor. Figure 6-11 shows how the Collection Editor appears when it is used to modify the *Data-Table* objects within a *DataSet*.

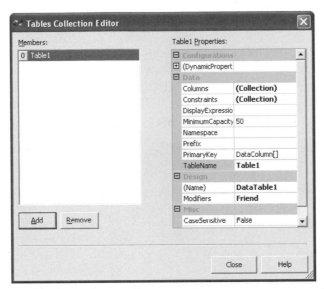

Figure 6-11   Adding a new *DataTable* to an untyped *DataSet*

You'll also see the same editor when you add *DataColumn* objects to your new *DataTable*. To add *DataColumn* objects, select the *DataTable* to which you want to add columns in the Collection Editor. Then select the *Columns* collection in the window on the right and click the ellipsis button. You'll launch a new Collection Editor, shown in Figure 6-12, which is used for building *Data-Column* objects.

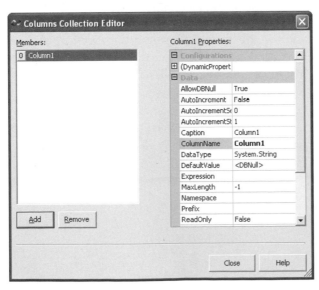

Figure 6-12   Adding a new *DataColumn* to a *DataTable*

Once you've added your *DataColumn* objects, you might want to specify a primary key for your *DataTable*. Select your *DataTable* in the Collection Editor, and you'll see *PrimaryKey* listed as a property in the window on the right. Select this property, and then click on the arrow to the right. You'll see the list of columns that appear in the *DataTable*, as shown in Figure 6-13. Select the *DataColumn* object you want to use for the *DataTable* object's primary key, and then dismiss the drop-down list by clicking elsewhere in the Collection Editor.

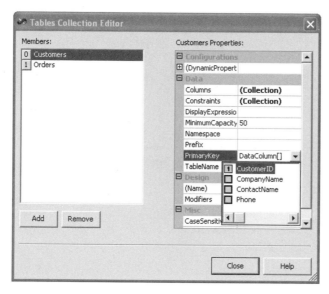

Figure 6-13 Specifying the primary key for a *DataTable*

You can also add items to the *Constraints* collection of your *DataTable* objects. Click on the *Constraints* property for your *DataTable* in the Collection Editor, and then click on the ellipsis button to launch another Collection Editor. This new Collection Editor, shown in Figure 6-14, lets you modify the contents of your *DataTable* object's *Constraints* collection. If you already have a primary key defined on your *DataTable*, you'll see that there's already an item in the *Constraints* collection.

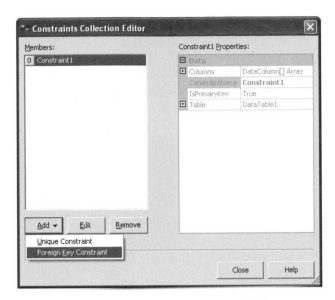

Figure 6-14   Adding constraints to a *DataTable*

You can use the Collection Editor to add unique or foreign key constraints. Click the Add button, and you'll see a shortcut menu asking which type of constraint you want to add. Figure 6-15 shows the user interface for adding new unique constraints. The interface is pretty straightforward. You simply select the *DataColumn* object you want to include in the new unique key. You can also specify a name for the key and indicate whether this unique key should also be the *DataTable* object's primary key.

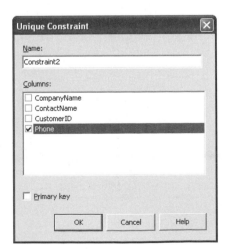

Figure 6-15   Adding a new *UniqueConstraint* to a *DataTable*

Figure 6-16 shows the user interface for adding new foreign key constraints. This interface should need no explanation because it's nearly identical to the one we used when we worked with the Data Form Wizard in Chapter 2 to build the relationship between the Customers and Orders tables in the *DataSet*.

Figure 6-16   Adding a new *ForeignKeyConstraint* to a *DataTable*

DataSet, *DataTable*, *DataColumn*, *DataRow*, *UniqueConstraint*, and *ForeignKeyConstraint* Object Reference

Now that you understand how to use the basic features of the *DataSet* and its related objects, let's look at each of the properties, events, and methods that those objects expose.

Properties of the *DataSet* Object

The commonly used properties of the *DataSet* object are shown in Table 6-5.

Table 6-5   Properties of the *DataSet* Object

Property	Data Type	Description
CaseSensitive	*Boolean*	Controls whether string comparisons are case sensitive
DataSetName	*String*	Indicates the name of the *DataSet*

(continued)

Table 6-5   Properties of the *DataSet* Object   *(continued)*

Property	Data Type	Description
DesignMode	*Boolean*	Indicates whether the *DataSet* is in design mode
EnforceConstraints	*Boolean*	Controls whether the *DataSet* will enforce the constraints that it contains
ExtendedProperties	*PropertyCollection*	Contains a collection of dynamic properties and values
HasErrors	*Boolean*	Indicates whether the *DataSet* contains errors
Locale	*CultureInfo*	Controls the locale that the *DataSet* will use to compare strings
Namespace	*String*	Contains the namespace that ADO.NET will use when writing the contents of your *DataSet* to XML or when loading XML data into your *DataSet*
Prefix	*String*	Contains the prefix for the namespace that ADO.NET will use when writing the contents of your *DataSet* to XML or when loading XML data into your *DataSet*
Relations	*DataRelation-Collection*	Contains the collection of *DataRelation* objects for your *DataSet*
Tables	*DataTableCollection*	Contains the collection of *DataTable* objects for your *DataSet*

CaseSensitive Property

The *CaseSensitive* property of the *DataSet* controls whether string comparisons within the *DataSet* are case sensitive. The default value for this property is False.

Changing the value of the *CaseSensitive* property of the *DataSet* will change the value of the *CaseSensitive* property of *DataTable* objects within the *DataSet* whose *CaseSensitive* property has not been set.

The *DataTable* object also exposes a *CaseSensitive* property.

DataSetName Property

The *DataSetName* property contains the name of the *DataSet*. You can specify a value for this property in the *DataSet* object's constructor. If you do not specify a value in the constructor, this property will be set to "NewDataSet".

If you write the contents of your *DataSet* to an XML document, the *DataSetName* property controls the name of the root node for the XML document. The *DataSetName* property also controls the name of the class you'll generate if you use the XSD.exe utility to generate a class file based on the contents of an XML schema file.

DesignMode Property

The *DesignMode* property of the *DataSet* object returns a Boolean value that indicates whether the *DataSet* is in design mode. This property can be useful when you write code in a user control. If the *DataSet* is being used at design time within a component, *DesignMode* will return *True*. Otherwise, it will return *False*.

The *DataTable* object also exposes a *DesignMode* property. This property is read-only.

EnforceConstraints Property

You can use the *EnforceConstraints* property to control whether the *DataSet* will enforce the constraints that it contains. By default, this property is set to *True*. If you want to temporarily turn off constraints, you can set *EnforceConstraints* to *False*.

Setting the property to *True* will throw a *ConstraintException* if the current contents of the *DataSet* violate any of its constraints.

ExtendedProperties Property

You can use the *DataSet* object's *ExtendedProperties* property to store miscellaneous information. The property returns a *PropertyCollection* object, which is designed to store various objects. Even though you can store objects within the *DataSet* object's *ExtendedProperties* collection, you should probably stick with simple strings.

When you save the contents of a *DataSet* object's schema to a file or a stream, ADO.NET will write the contents of the *ExtendedProperties* collection as strings.

The *DataTable*, *DataColumn*, *DataRelation*, and *Constraint* objects also expose an *ExtendedProperties* property.

The following code shows how to add entries to a *DataSet* object's *ExtendedProperties* collection, as well as how to access the contents of the collection:

Visual Basic .NET

```
Dim ds As New DataSet()

'Add extended properties.
ds.ExtendedProperties.Add("Prop1", "Value1")
```

```
ds.ExtendedProperties.Add("Prop2", "Value2")
ds.ExtendedProperties.Add("Prop3", "Value3")

'Retrieve the value of an extended property.
Console.WriteLine(ds.ExtendedProperties("Prop2"))

'Retrieve and enumerate all extended properties.
Dim objEnum As IDictionaryEnumerator
objEnum = ds.ExtendedProperties.GetEnumerator
Do While objEnum.MoveNext
    Console.WriteLine(objEnum.Key & " = " & objEnum.Value)
Loop
```

Visual C# .NET

```
//Requires "using System.Collections"
DataSet ds = new DataSet();

//Add extended properties.
ds.ExtendedProperties.Add("Prop1", "Value1");
ds.ExtendedProperties.Add("Prop2", "Value2");
ds.ExtendedProperties.Add("Prop3", "Value3");

//Retrieve the value of an extended property.
Console.WriteLine(ds.ExtendedProperties["Prop2"]);

//Retrieve and enumerate all extended properties.
IDictionaryEnumerator objEnum;
objEnum = ds.ExtendedProperties.GetEnumerator();
while (objEnum.MoveNext())
    Console.WriteLine(objEnum.Key + " = " + objEnum.Value);
```

HasErrors Property

The *HasErrors* property returns a Boolean value that indicates whether any *DataRow* objects within the *DataSet* contain errors. If you're submitting batches of changes to your database and you've set the *ContinueUpdateOnError* property of your *DataAdapter* objects to *True*, you should check the *HasErrors* property of your *DataSet* after submitting changes to determine whether any of the update attempts failed.

The *DataTable* and *DataRow* objects also expose a *HasErrors* property.

For more information on handling failed update attempts, see Chapter 11.

Locale Property

Different languages and cultures employ different rules when comparing the contents of strings. By default, the *DataSet* will use the current culture information for your system to compare strings. You can change this behavior by setting the *Locale* property of your *DataSet*.

This property accepts a *CultureInfo* object, which resides in the *System. Globalization* namespace. For more information on the *CultureInfo* object, see the MSDN documentation.

Like the *CaseSensitive* property, the *Locale* property also exists on the *DataTable* object. Setting the *Locale* property of a *DataSet* will change the *Locale* property of all *DataTable* objects in the *DataSet* whose *Locale* property has not been set.

The *DataTable* object also exposes a *Locale* property.

The following code snippet shows how to set the *Locale* property of the *DataSet* to *English (Australia)*:

Visual Basic .NET

```
Dim ds As New DataSet()
ds.Locale = New System.Globalization.CultureInfo("en-AU")
Console.WriteLine(ds.Locale.DisplayName)
```

Visual C# .NET

```
DataSet ds = new DataSet();
ds.Locale = new System.Globalization.CultureInfo("en-AU");
Console.WriteLine(ds.Locale.DisplayName);
```

Namespace and *Prefix* Properties

You can use the *DataSet* object's *Namespace* and *Prefix* properties to specify an XML namespace and prefix for your *DataSet*. ADO.NET will use these settings when it writes the contents of your *DataSet* to XML and when it loads data from an XML document into your *DataSet*.

The *DataTable* and *DataColumn* objects also expose *Namespace* and *Prefix* properties.

For more information on XML namespaces, see the MSDN documentation.

Relations Property

The *Relations* property returns a *DataRelationCollection* object, which contains the *DataRelation* objects that reside in the *DataSet*. You can use this property to examine existing *DataRelation* objects as well as to add, modify, or remove *DataRelation* objects.

Tables Property

You can use the *Tables* property to examine existing *DataTable* objects as well as to add, modify, or remove *DataTable* objects. This property returns a *Data-TableCollection* object, which contains the *DataTable* objects that reside in the *DataSet*.

You can access a *DataTable* using the *Tables* property by supplying either the desired *DataTable* object's *TableName* property or its index within the collection. Accessing a *DataTable* based on its index will yield better performance.

Methods of the *DataSet* Object

The commonly used methods of the *DataSet* object are shown in Table 6-6.

Table 6-6   Methods of the *DataSet* Object

Method	Description
AcceptChanges	Accepts all pending changes within the *DataSet*
BeginInit	Used by the Visual Studio .NET designers before adding schema information to the *DataSet*
Clear	Removes all *DataRow* objects from the *DataSet*
Clone	Creates a new *DataSet* object with the same schema but with no *DataRow* objects
Copy	Creates a new *DataSet* object with the same schema and the same *DataRow* objects
EndInit	Used by the Visual Studio .NET designers after adding schema information to the *DataSet*
GetChanges	Returns a new *DataSet* with the same structure that contains modified rows from the original *DataSet*
GetXml	Returns the contents of the *DataSet* as an XML string
GetXmlSchema	Returns the schema for the *DataSet* as an XML string
HasChanges	Returns a Boolean value that indicates whether any *DataRow* objects in the *DataSet* contain pending changes
InferXmlSchema	Loads schema information from an XML schema and allows you to supply a list of namespaces whose elements you want to exclude from the *DataSet* object's schema
Merge	Merges data from another *DataSet*, *DataTable*, or array of *DataRow* objects into the existing *DataSet*
ReadXml	Reads XML data into your *DataSet* from a file, a *Stream*, a *TextReader*, or an *XmlReader*
ReadXmlSchema	Reads XML schema information into your *DataSet* from a file, a *Stream*, a *TextReader*, or an *XmlReader*
RejectChanges	Rejects all pending changes within the *DataSet*
Reset	Resets your *DataSet* to its original, uninitialized state

(continued)

Table 6-6   **Methods of the *DataSet* Object**   *(continued)*

Method	Description
WriteXml	Writes the contents of your *DataSet* as XML to a file, a *Stream*, a *TextReader*, or an *XmlReader*
WriteXmlSchema	Writes the schema of your *DataSet* as XML to a file, a *Stream*, a *TextReader*, or an *XmlReader*

AcceptChanges and *RejectChanges* Methods

You can use the *AcceptChanges* and *RejectChanges* methods to accept or reject all pending changes within your *DataSet*.

When you modify the contents of a *DataRow* object, ADO.NET will mark the *DataRow* object as having a pending change and set the *RowState* property of the *DataRow* object to the appropriate value—*Added*, *Modified*, or *Deleted*. ADO.NET will also maintain both the original values and the current values for the contents of the *DataRow*.

If you call the *AcceptChanges* method on your *DataSet*, ADO.NET will accept all pending changes stored in the *DataRow* objects in your *DataSet*. Any rows whose *RowState* property is set to *Added* or *Modified* will have their *RowState* property set to *Unchanged*. Doing this will also reset the "original" values for the *DataRow* to the current contents of the *DataRow*. Any *DataRow* objects marked as *Deleted* will be removed from your *DataSet* when you call *AcceptChanges*.

When the *DataAdapter* object successfully submits pending changes stored in a *DataRow* object, it implicitly calls the *AcceptChanges* method on that *DataRow*.

Calling the *RejectChanges* method on your *DataSet* will cancel any pending changes within your *DataSet*. Any *DataRow* objects marked as *Added* will be removed from your *DataSet*. Other modified *DataRow* objects (*RowState* = *Modified* or *Deleted*) will return to their previous states.

The *DataTable* and *DataRow* objects also expose *AcceptChanges* and *RejectChanges* methods.

BeginInit and *EndInit* Methods

The *BeginInit* and *EndInit* methods are used by designers and aren't meant to be used directly in your code. If you create an untyped *DataSet* at design time using the Visual Studio .NET designers, you'll see that the designer generates code that uses these methods. The code calls the *BeginInit* method of the *DataSet* object, adds structure to the *DataSet*, and then calls the *EndInit* method.

I've tried using these methods in my code in the hope that I could offer some insight as to what they do. However, I was unable to envision any scenarios (such as adding an expression-based column before adding the column that it references) using these methods that weren't already possible.

The *DataTable* object also exposes *BeginInit* and *EndInit* methods.

Clear Method

You can use the *DataSet* object's *Clear* method to remove all *DataRow* objects from the *DataSet*. Using this method is faster than releasing a *DataSet* and then creating a new *DataSet* with the same structure.

The *DataTable* object also exposes a *Clear* method.

Clone and *Copy* Methods

You use the *Copy* method to create a new *DataSet* that contains the same structure and the same set of rows as the original *DataSet*. If you want to create a new *DataSet* object that contains the same structure but doesn't contain any rows, use the *Clone* method instead.

The *DataTable* object also exposes *Clone* and *Copy* methods.

GetChanges Method

The *DataSet* object's *GetChanges* method returns a new *DataSet* with the same structure as the original *DataSet* and also includes all rows from the original *DataSet* that contain pending changes. We'll discuss this feature in more depth in Chapter 11.

The *DataTable* object also exposes a *GetChanges* method.

> **Note**   The new *DataSet* object might also include some unmodified *DataRow* objects in order to conform to referential integrity constraints in the *DataSet*. If you have a modified child row but the parent row is unmodified, the parent row will be included in the new *DataSet*. If the new *DataSet* were to contain the child row but not the parent row, it would violate the referential integrity constraint.

GetXml and *GetXmlSchema* Methods

You can use the *GetXml* method to retrieve the contents of your *DataSet*, including its schema, into a string in XML format. If you want to retrieve just the schema information, use the *GetXmlSchema* method instead.

I'll discuss the ADO.NET XML features in more depth in Chapter 12.

HasChanges Method

The *HasChanges* method returns a Boolean value that indicates whether the *DataSet* has *DataRow* objects that contain pending changes.

If you're building an application that allows users to modify data in a *DataSet* and submit the changes to the database using a *DataAdapter*, you might want to check the *HasChanges* method. There's no reason to try to submit changes to your database if the *DataSet* does not contain any pending changes.

Merge Method

The *DataSet* object's *Merge* method allows you to load data from another *DataSet* or *DataTable* or an array of *DataRow* objects into your existing *DataSet*.

I'll discuss the *Merge* method in detail in Chapter 11.

ReadXml and *WriteXml* Methods

You can use the *ReadXml* method to load XML data into your *DataSet* from a file, a *TextReader*, a *Stream*, or an *XmlReader*. You can also control how the *DataSet* will read the XML using the mode parameter. This parameter accepts values from the *XmlReadMode* enumeration and allows you to specify options such as whether you want to read a full XML document or just an XML fragment and whether to read or ignore the XML schema.

The *DataSet* object also exposes a *WriteXml* method so that you can write the contents of your *DataSet* as XML. The *WriteXml* method offers all the same options as the *ReadXml* method.

I'll discuss the ADO.NET XML features in more depth in Chapter 12.

ReadXmlSchema, *WriteXmlSchema*, and *InferXmlSchema* Methods

The *ReadXmlSchema* and *WriteXmlSchema* methods are similar to their counterparts *ReadXml* and *WriteXml*, but they're designed to work with XML schemas. Like the *ReadXml* and *WriteXml* methods, these methods accept a *TextReader*, a *Stream*, an *XmlReader*, or a string that contains a filename for your XML data.

The *InferXmlSchema* method is similar to the *ReadXmlSchema* method, but it provides an added level of control. It lets you specify a list of namespaces whose elements you want to ignore. For more information on this difference between the features, see "Loading DataSet Schema Information from XML" in the MSDN documentation.

I'll discuss the ADO.NET XML features in more depth in Chapter 12.

Reset Method

The *DataSet* object's *Reset* method returns the *DataSet* to its original, uninitialized state. If you want to discard an existing *DataSet* and start working with a new *DataSet*, use the *Reset* method rather than create a new instance of a *DataSet*.

Events of the *DataSet* Object

The most commonly used event of the *DataSet* object is shown in Table 6-7.

Table 6-7   Event of the *DataSet* Object

Event	Description
MergeFailed	Fires if the *Merge* method of the *DataSet* generates an exception

MergeFailed Event

You can use the *MergeFailed* event to handle any failures that occur when you use the *DataSet* object's *Merge* method. Personally, I've been unable to cause the *MergeFailed* event to fire. You might have more success causing *MergeFailed* to fire.

Properties of the *DataTable* Object

The commonly used properties of the *DataTable* object are shown in Table 6-8.

Table 6-8   Properties of the *DataTable* Object

Property	Data Type	Description
CaseSensitive	*Boolean*	Controls whether string comparisons are case sensitive
ChildRelations	*DataRelationCollection*	Returns the *DataRelation* objects that contain child data for the *DataTable*
Columns	*DataColumnCollection*	Contains the collection of *DataColumn* objects for the *DataTable*
Constraints	*ConstraintCollection*	Contains the collection of *Constraint* objects for the *DataTable*
DataSet	*DataSet*	Returns the *DataSet* to which the *DataTable* belongs
DefaultView	*DataView*	Returns the *DataView* object that bound controls will receive for the *DataTable*
DesignMode	*Boolean*	Indicates whether the *DataTable* is in design mode
ExtendedProperties	*PropertyCollection*	Contains a collection of dynamic properties and values
HasErrors	*Boolean*	Indicates whether the *DataTable* contains errors

(continued)

Table 6-8 **Properties of the *DataTable* Object**   *(continued)*

Property	Data Type	Description
Locale	*CultureInfo*	Controls the locale that the *Data-Table* will use to compare strings
MinimumCapacity	*Integer*	Controls how much memory, in rows, that the *DataTable* will reserve initially
Namespace	*String*	Contains the namespace that ADO.NET will use when it writes the contents of your *DataTable* to XML or when it loads XML data into your *DataTable*
ParentRelations	*DataRelationCollection*	Returns the *DataRelation* objects that contain parent data for the *Data-Table*
Prefix	*String*	Contains the prefix for the namespace that ADO.NET will use when it writes the contents of your *DataTable* to XML or when it loads XML data into your *DataTable*
PrimaryKey	Array of *DataColumn* objects	Contains information about the primary key for the *DataTable*
Rows	*DataRowCollection*	Contains the collection of *DataColumn* objects for the *DataTable*
TableName	*String*	Contains the name of the *DataTable*

CaseSensitive Property

The *CaseSensitive* property of the *DataTable* controls whether string comparisons within the *DataTable* are case sensitive. The *DataSet* object also exposes a *CaseSensitive* property.

By default, the *DataTable* object's *CaseSensitive* property contains the same value as the *CaseSensitive* property of the parent *DataSet* object. If you set the *CaseSensitive* property of your *DataTable*, this value will override the setting for the parent *DataSet* object.

The default value of the *CaseSensitive* property for a *DataTable* that does not reside in a *DataSet* is *False*.

ChildRelations and *ParentRelations* Properties

The *ChildRelations* and *ParentRelations* properties let you examine the *DataRelation* objects that contain child or parent relations for the current *DataTable*.

Say you're working with a hierarchy of customers, orders, and order details data and you have a reference to the *DataTable* that contains order information. The *ParentRelations* collection will contain the *DataRelation* that relates the order *DataTable* to the customer *DataTable*. The *ChildRelations* collection will contain the *DataRelation* that relates the order *DataTable* to the order details *DataTable*.

Columns Property

You can use the *Columns* property to examine existing *DataColumn* objects as well as to add, modify, or remove *DataColumn* objects. This property returns a *DataColumnCollection* object, which contains the *DataColumn* objects that reside in the *DataTable*.

You can access a *DataColumn* using the *Columns* property by supplying the desired *DataColumn* object's *Ordinal* property or *ColumnName* property. As with most searches, accessing a *DataColumn* based on its *Ordinal* property will yield better performance.

Constraints Property

The *Constraints* property lets you examine the constraints defined for your *DataTable*. Like the *Columns* property, you can use the *Constraints* collection to add, modify, or remove constraints from the *DataTable*. This property returns a *ConstraintCollection* object.

You can access a *Constraint* using the *Columns* property by supplying either the desired *Constraint* object's *ConstraintName* property or its index within the collection. Performing the search using the desired *Constraint* object's index will yield better performance.

DataSet Property

The *DataSet* property returns the *DataSet* in which the *DataTable* resides. If the *DataTable* does not reside in a *DataSet*, the *DataSet* property returns an uninitialized object.

The *DataSet* property is read-only.

DefaultView Property

If you bind a control to your *DataTable*, the control will actually bind to the *DataView* object returned by the *DataTable* object's *DefaultView* property. For example, you can use the following code to apply a filter so that only the customers from Spain appear in the *DataGrid* bound to the *DataTable*. The *DataTable* will still contain all customers, regardless of the filter.

Visual Basic .NET

```
tblCustomers.DefaultView.RowFilter = "Country = 'Spain'"
gridCustomers.DataSource = tblCustomers
```

Visual C# .NET

```
tblCustomers.DefaultView.RowFilter = "Country = 'Spain'";
gridCustomers.DataSource = tblCustomers;
```

I'll discuss the *DataView* object in more detail in Chapter 8.

DesignMode Property

The *DesignMode* property of the *DataTable* object returns a Boolean value that indicates whether the *DataTable* is in design mode. This property can be useful when you write code in a user control. If the *DataTable* is being used at design time within a component, *DesignMode* will return *True*. Otherwise, it will return *False*.

The *DataSet* object also exposes a *DesignMode* property.

The *DesignMode* property is read-only.

ExtendedProperties Property

The *DataTable* object's *ExtendedProperties* property returns a *PropertyCollection* object, which is designed to store various objects.

The *DataSet*, *DataColumn*, *DataRelation*, and *Constraint* objects also expose an *ExtendedProperties* property.

For more information, including a code example, see the information on the *ExtendedProperties* property under the earlier section titled "Properties of the *DataSet* Object."

HasErrors Property

The *HasErrors* property returns a Boolean value that indicates whether any *DataRow* objects within the *DataTable* contain errors. If you're submitting batches of changes to your database and you've set the *ContinueUpdateOnError* property of your *DataAdapter* objects to *True*, you should check the *HasErrors* property of your *DataSet* after you submit changes to determine whether any of the update attempts failed.

The *DataSet* and *DataRow* objects also expose a *HasErrors* property.

For more information on handling failed update attempts, see Chapter 11.

Locale Property

The *Locale* property controls how ADO.NET will compare strings within your *DataTable*.

The *DataSet* object also exposes a *Locale* property.

For more information, including a code example, see the information on the *Locale* property under the earlier section titled "Properties of the *DataSet* Object."

MinimumCapacity Property

If you know approximately how many rows your *DataTable* will contain, you can improve the performance of your code by setting the *DataTable* object's *MinimumCapacity* property prior to filling your *DataTable* with the results of a query.

By default, the *MinimumCapacity* property is set to 50, which means that ADO.NET will reserve enough memory for your *DataTable* to hold 50 rows of data. If you know approximately how many rows your *DataTable* will contain, you might be able to improve the performance of your code by setting the *MinimumCapacity* property to a more appropriate value. Setting this property to a lower value when you work with *DataTable* objects will also reduce the memory footprint of your application.

If you add more rows to the *DataTable*, you won't receive an out-of-memory error. ADO.NET will simply request more memory.

Namespace and *Prefix* Properties

You can use the *DataTable* object's *Namespace* and *Prefix* properties to specify an XML namespace and prefix for your *DataTable*. ADO.NET will use these settings when it writes the contents of your *DataTable* to XML and when it loads data from an XML document into your *DataTable*.

The *DataSet* and *DataColumn* objects also expose *Namespace* and *Prefix* properties.

For more information on XML namespaces, see the MSDN documentation.

PrimaryKey Property

The *PrimaryKey* property contains an array of *DataColumn* objects that constitute the primary key for your *DataTable*.

This primary key serves two purposes. First, it acts as a unique constraint. No two *DataRow* objects can have the same values in the primary key columns. For example, say you have a *DataTable* of customer information and you define the primary key based on the CustomerID *DataColumn*. If you add a new *DataRow* to your *DataTable* object's *Rows* collection and the new *DataRow* has a value for the CustomerID *DataColumn* that already exists in your *Data-Table*, you'll receive an exception.

You can also locate a *DataRow* in a *DataTable* based on its primary key values using the *Find* method of the *DataTable* object's *Rows* collection. I'll discuss this feature in more detail when I discuss sorting, searching, and filtering in Chapter 8.

The following code snippet shows an example of setting the *PrimaryKey* property of a *DataTable*.

Visual Basic .NET

```
Dim tbl As New DataTable("Customers")
tbl.Columns.Add("CustomerID", GetType(String))
tbl.Columns.Add("CompanyName", GetType(String))
tbl.PrimaryKey = New DataColumn() {tbl.Columns("CustomerID")}
```

Visual C# .NET

```
DataTable tbl = new DataTable("Customers");
tbl.Columns.Add("CustomerID", typeof(string));
tbl.Columns.Add("CompanyName", typeof(string));
tbl.PrimaryKey = new DataColumn[] {tbl.Columns["CustomerID"]};
```

Rows Property

The *DataTable* object's *Rows* property returns a *DataRowCollection* object that contains the *DataRow* objects in the *DataTable*. You can use the *Rows* property to add a *DataRow* object to the *DataTable*, as well as to access any of the existing *DataRow* objects.

You can use only the *DataRowCollection* object to locate a *DataRow* based on its ordinal value within the *DataTable*. If you want to locate *DataRow* objects based on their primary key values or other search criteria, you can use the various methods described in Chapter 8.

TableName Property

The *TableName* property contains the name for the *DataTable* object. You can set this property in the *DataTable* object's constructor.

When you store the contents of your *DataSet* as XML, ADO.NET uses the *TableName* property of each *DataTable* as the element tag for each row of data in the *DataTable*.

Methods of the *DataTable* Object

The commonly used methods of the *DataTable* object are shown in Table 6-9.

Table 6-9   Methods of the *DataTable* Object

Method	Description
AcceptChanges	Accepts all pending changes within the *DataTable*
BeginInit	Used by the Visual Studio .NET designers before adding schema information to the *DataTable*
BeginLoadData	Turns off constraints while loading data
Clear	Removes all *DataRow* objects from the *DataTable*

(continued)

Table 6-9   Methods of the *DataTable* Object   *(continued)*

Method	Description
Clone	Creates a new *DataTable* object with the same schema but with no *DataRow* objects
Compute	Returns the value of an aggregate expression based on the contents of your *DataTable*
Copy	Creates a new *DataTable* object with the same schema and the same *DataRow* objects
EndInit	Used by the Visual Studio .NET designers after adding schema information to the *DataSet*
EndLoadData	Reenables constraints after you've loaded data
GetChanges	Returns a new *DataTable* with the same structure that contains modified rows from the original *DataTable*
GetErrors	Returns an array that contains the *DataRow* objects that contain errors
ImportRow	Imports an existing *DataRow* into your *DataTable*
LoadDataRow	Adds a new *DataRow* to your *DataTable* based on the contents of an array
NewRow	Returns a new *DataRow* object for your *DataTable*
RejectChanges	Rejects all pending changes within the *DataTable*
Reset	Resets your *DataTable* to its original, uninitialized state
Select	Returns an array of *DataRow* objects based on the specified search criteria

AcceptChanges and *RejectChanges* Methods

You can use the *AcceptChanges* and *RejectChanges* methods to accept or reject all pending changes within your *DataTable*, respectively.

The *DataSet* and *DataRow* objects also expose *AcceptChanges* and *RejectChanges* methods. For more information on these methods, see the earlier section titled "Methods of the *DataSet* Object."

BeginInit and *EndInit* Methods

These methods are used by designers and aren't meant to be used directly in your code.

The *DataSet* object also exposes *BeginInit* and *EndInit* methods. For more information on these methods, see the earlier section titled "Methods of the *DataSet* Object."

BeginLoadData and *EndLoadData* Methods

If you're adding a series of *DataRow* objects to your *DataTable* object, you might be able to improve the performance of your code by using the *BeginLoadData* and *EndLoadData* methods.

Calling the *BeginLoadData* method turns off constraints for the *DataTable*. You can reenable the constraints by calling *EndLoadData*. If the *DataTable* contains rows that violate the constraints, you'll receive a *ConstraintException* when you call *EndLoadData*. To determine which rows caused the exception, you can examine the rows returned by the *GetErrors* method.

Clear Method

You can use the *DataTable* object's *Clear* method to remove all *DataRow* objects from the *DataTable*. Using this method is faster than releasing a *Data-Table* and then creating a new *DataTable* with the same structure.

The *DataSet* object also exposes a *Clear* method.

Clone and *Copy* Methods

You can use the *Copy* method to create a new *DataTable* that contains the same structure and the same set of rows. If you want to create a new *DataTable* object that contains the same structure but doesn't contain any rows, use the *Clone* method instead.

The *DataSet* object also exposes *Clone* and *Copy* methods.

Compute Method

You can use the *Compute* method to perform an aggregate query on a single column in your *DataTable* based on the search criteria you specify.

The following code snippet demonstrates using the *Compute* method to count the number of orders that include chai. The code snippet also computes the total number of chai units ordered.

Visual Basic .NET

```
Dim strSQL, strConn As String
strConn = "Provider=SQLOLEDB;Data Source=(local)\NetSDK;" & _
          "Initial Catalog=Northwind;Trusted_Connection=Yes;"
strSQL = "SELECT OrderID, ProductID, Quantity FROM [Order Details]"
Dim da As New OleDb.OleDbDataAdapter(strSQL, strConn)
Dim tbl As New DataTable("Order Details")
da.Fill(tbl)
Dim intNumChaiOrders As Integer
Dim lngNumChaiUnits As Long
intNumChaiOrders = CInt(tbl.Compute("COUNT(OrderID)", _
                                    "ProductID = 1"))
lngNumChaiUnits = CLng(tbl.Compute("SUM(Quantity)", _
                                    "ProductID = 1"))
```

```
Console.WriteLine("# of orders that include chai: " & _
                 intNumChaiOrders)
Console.WriteLine("Total number of units ordered: " & _
                 lngNumChaiUnits)
```

Visual C# .NET

```
string strSQL, strConn;
strConn = "Provider=SQLOLEDB;Data Source=(local)\\NetSDK;" +
         "Initial Catalog=Northwind;Trusted_Connection=Yes;";
strSQL = "SELECT OrderID, ProductID, Quantity FROM [Order Details]";
OleDbDataAdapter da = new OleDbDataAdapter(strSQL, strConn);
DataTable tbl = new DataTable("Order Details");
da.Fill(tbl);
int intNumChaiOrders;
Int64 intNumChaiUnits;
intNumChaiOrders = (int) tbl.Compute("COUNT(OrderID)",
                                     "ProductID = 1");
intNumChaiUnits = (Int64) tbl.Compute("SUM(Quantity)",
                                     "ProductID = 1");
Console.WriteLine("# of orders that include chai: " +
                 intNumChaiOrders);
Console.WriteLine("Total number of units ordered: " +
                 intNumChaiUnits);
```

You cannot use the *Compute* method to compute an aggregate that involves multiple columns, such as *SUM(Quantity * UnitPrice)*. However, you can use an expression-based column to perform the calculation between the two columns and then use that expression-based column in the *Count* method: *SUM(ItemTotal)*.

The *Compute* method returns its results using the generic *Object* data type. When you perform a calculation using the *Compute* method, the data type that the *Compute* method uses to store the results might surprise you. For example, the *DataType* property for the *Quantity* column is a 16-bit integer, but the call to the *Compute* method returns a 64-bit integer.

If you're unsure what data type to use to store the results of the *Compute* method, you can use code such as the following:

Visual Basic .NET

```
Dim objRetVal As Object = tbl.Compute("SUM(Quantity)", _
                                      "ProductID = 1")
Console.WriteLine(objRetVal.GetType.ToString)
```

Visual C# .NET

```
object objRetVal = tbl.Compute("SUM(Quantity)",
                               "ProductID = 1");
Console.WriteLine(objRetVal.GetType().ToString());
```

GetChanges Method

The *DataSet* object's *GetChanges* method returns a new *DataTable* with the same structure and also includes all rows from the original *DataTable* that contain pending changes. I'll discuss this feature in more depth in Chapter 11.

The *DataSet* object also exposes a *GetChanges* method.

GetErrors Method

You can use the *GetErrors* method to access the *DataRow* objects that contain errors, whether those errors constitute constraint violations or failed update attempts. The *GetErrors* method returns an array of *DataRow* objects.

ImportRow, *LoadDataRow*, and *NewRow* Methods

The *ImportRow* method accepts a *DataRow* object and adds that row of data to the *DataTable*.

The *LoadDataRow* method accepts an array as its first argument. Each item in the array corresponds to an item in the *DataTable* object's *Columns* collection. The second argument in the *LoadDataRow* method takes a Boolean value to control the *RowState* of the new *DataRow* object. You can supply *False* for this parameter if you want the new *DataRow* to have a *RowState* of *Added*, and you can supply *True* if you want a *RowState* of *Unmodified*. The *LoadDataRow* method also returns the newly created *DataRow* object.

The *NewRow* method returns a new *DataRow* object for the *DataTable*. The new *DataRow* will not reside in the *DataTable* object's *Rows* collection at this point. You'll need to add the item to the *Rows* collection after you've populated the desired columns on the *DataRow*.

So which of these three methods should you use? Here are some guidelines:

- Use the *ImportRow* method if you want to import a row from a different *DataTable*.

- Use the *LoadDataRow* method if you want to add a number of new rows at a time, perhaps based on the contents of a file. Adding a row to a *DataTable* using *LoadDataRow* requires fewer lines of code than using the *NewRow* method.

- Otherwise, use the *NewRow* method.

Reset Method

The *DataTable* object's *Reset* method returns the *DataTable* object to its original, uninitialized state. If you want to discard an existing *DataTable* and start working with a new *DataTable*, use the *Reset* method rather than create a new instance of a *DataTable*.

Select Method

You can use the *Select* method to locate a row or multiple rows in a *DataTable* based on various search criteria. The *Select* method returns an array of *DataRow* objects that satisfy the specified criteria.

I'll take a closer look at the *Select* method in detail when I discuss sorting, searching, and filtering in Chapter 8.

Events of the *DataTable* Object

The commonly used events of the *DataTable* object are shown in Table 6-10.

Table 6-10   Events of the *DataTable* Object

Event	Description
ColumnChanged	Fires after the contents of a column have changed
ColumnChanging	Fires just before the contents of a column change
RowChanged	Fires after the contents of a row have changed
RowChanging	Fires just before the contents of a row change
RowDeleted	Fires after a row has been deleted
RowDeleting	Fires just before a row is deleted

ColumnChanged and *ColumnChanging* Events

The *ColumnChanged* and *ColumnChanging* events fire each time the contents of a column in a row change. You can use these events to validate your data, enable or disable controls, and so forth.

The events include an argument of type *DataColumnChangeEventArgs*, which has properties such as *Row* and *Column* that you can use to determine which row and column have been changed.

Remember that if you use the events to modify the contents of the row, you might cause an infinite loop.

RowChanged and *RowChanging* Events

The *RowChanged* and *RowChanging* events fire when a *DataRow* object's contents change or its *RowState* property changes.

You can determine why the event fired by checking the *Action* property of the *DataRowChangeEventArgs* argument of the event. You can also access the row that's being modified using the *Row* property of the same argument.

RowDeleted and *RowDeleting* Events

The *RowDeleted* and *RowDeleting* events expose the same arguments and properties as the *RowChanged* and *RowChanging* arguments do. The only difference is that these events fire when a row is deleted from the *DataTable*.

Properties of the *DataColumn* Object

The commonly used properties of the *DataColumn* object are shown in Table 6-11.

Table 6-11 Properties of the *DataColumn* Object

Property	Data Type	Description
AllowDBNull	Boolean	Controls whether the column will accept null values
AutoIncrement	Boolean	Controls whether ADO.NET will generate new autoincrement values for the column
AutoIncrementSeed	Integer	Controls what value ADO.NET will use for the first new autoincrement value
AutoIncrementStep	Integer	Controls the value ADO.NET will use to generate subsequent autoincrement values
Caption	String	Controls the caption of the column when displayed in a bound data grid
ColumnMapping	MappingType	Controls how ADO.NET will store the contents of the column in an XML document
ColumnName	String	Contains the name of the *DataColumn* object
DataType	Type	Controls the data type that ADO.NET will use to store the contents of the column
DefaultValue	Object	Controls the default value that ADO.NET will use to populate this column for new rows
Expression	String	Controls how ADO.NET will generate values for expression-based columns
ExtendedProperties	PropertyCollection	Contains a collection of dynamic properties and values
MaxLength	Integer	Specifies the maximum length of the string that the column can contain

(continued)

Table 6-11   **Properties of the *DataColumn* Object**   *(continued)*

Property	Data Type	Description
Namespace	*String*	Contains the namespace that ADO.NET will use when it writes the contents of the *DataSet* to XML or when it loads XML data into your *DataSet*
Ordinal	*Integer*	Returns the index of the *DataColumn* within the *DataTable* object's *Columns* collection
Prefix	*String*	Contains the prefix for the namespace that ADO.NET will use when it writes the contents of your *DataSet* to XML or when it loads XML data into your *DataSet*
ReadOnly	*Boolean*	Controls whether the contents of the column are read-only
Table	*DataTable*	Returns the *DataTable* to which the *DataColumn* belongs
Unique	*Boolean*	Controls whether ADO.NET requires that the values for the column be unique within the *DataTable*

AllowDBNull Property

You can use the *AllowDBNull* property to control whether the *DataColumn* will accept null values. By default, this property is set to *True* when you create new *DataColumn* objects.

Using a *DataAdapter* object's *Fill* method to create new *DataColumn* objects will not set the *AllowDBNull* property to *True* even if the corresponding column in the database does not accept null values. The *DataAdapter* will not fetch this schema information from your database when you call the *Fill* method. Calling the *FillSchema* method instead will fetch this information and apply it to new columns in your *DataTable*.

AutoIncrement, *AutoIncrementSeed*, and *AutoIncrementStep* Properties

You can use these properties to control how or whether ADO.NET will generate new autoincrement values for the column.

Setting the *AutoIncrement* property to *True* will force ADO.NET to generate new autoincrement values for your column. By default, this property is set to *False*. As with the *AllowDBNull* property, you must call the *DataAdapter* object's *FillSchema* method to set the *AutoIncrement* property to *True* for *Data-Column* objects that correspond to autoincrement columns in your database.

If you set the *AutoIncrement* property to *True*, ADO.NET will use the values in the *AutoIncrementSeed* and *AutoIncrementStep* properties to generate new autoincrement values. By default, *AutoIncrementSeed* is set to 0 and *AutoIncrementStep* is set to 1. For reasons stated earlier in the chapter, I prefer to set both of these properties to *-1* when I use ADO.NET to generate new autoincrement values. Using the *FillSchema* method of the *DataAdapter* will not set the *AutoIncrementSeed* or *AutoIncrementStep* properties on new auto-increment *DataColumn* objects.

Earlier in the chapter, I also explained that you should not use the ADO.NET autoincrement features to generate new values for your database. Let your database handle generating the actual values, and let ADO.NET generate autoincrement values as placeholders within your *DataSet*.

Caption Property

If you're showing the contents of your *DataTable* in a bound data grid, you can use the *Caption* property to control the caption for the column. By default, the *Caption* property will return the same value as the *ColumnName* property. However, once you set the *Caption* property to a value, it will return that value rather than the value stored in the *ColumnName* property.

ColumnMapping Property

You can use the *ColumnMapping* property to control how ADO.NET will write the contents of the column when returning the data in your *DataSet* as XML.

The *ColumnMapping* property accepts values from the *MappingType* enumeration in the *System.Data* namespace. By default, the *ColumnMapping* property is set to *Element*, which means that the value of each column within your *DataRow* will appear in an element tag. You can also set *ColumnMapping* to *Attribute*, *Hidden*, or *SimpleContent*.

The following examples show the difference between using elements and attributes for data within your *DataSet*.

Using *Column.ColumnMapping = MappingType.Element*

```
<MyDataSet>
  <Customers>
    <CustomerID>ABCDE</CustomerID>
    <CompanyName>New Customer</CompanyName>
    <ContactName>New Contact</ContactName>
    <Phone>425 555-1212</Phone>
  </Customers>
</MyDataSet>
```

Using *Column.ColumnMapping = MappingType.Attribute*

```
<MyDataSet>
  <Customers CustomerID="ABCDE" CompanyName="New Customer"
             ContactName="New Contact" Phone="425 555-1212" />
</MyDataSet>
```

For more information on using the ADO.NET XML features, see Chapter 12.

ColumnName Property

The *ColumnName* property contains the name of the *DataColumn*. You can set this property in the *DataColumn* object's constructors.

DataType Property

The *DataType* property controls the data type that ADO.NET will use to store the contents of the column. By default, this property is set to store a string.

ADO.NET stores the data using a .NET data type. Previous data access models such as ADO store the results of queries in a data type designed to mirror the one that the database uses.

For example, SQL Server has different data types for fixed-length strings and variable-length strings, and for strings that contain single-byte characters and those that contain double-byte characters. ADO treats all these data types differently. As far as the ADO.NET *DataColumn* is concerned, a string is a string is a string.

The *DataType* property accepts a value of type *Type*. The following code snippet shows how to set a *DataColumn* object's *DataType* property directly and use the *Add* method of the *DataColumnCollection* object:

Visual Basic .NET

```
Dim col As New DataColumn("NewColumn")
col.DataType = GetType(Decimal)

Dim tbl As New DataTable("Products")
tbl.Columns.Add("ProductID", GetType(Integer))
tbl.Columns.Add("ProductName", GetType(String))
tbl.Columns.Add("UnitPrice", GetType(Decimal))
```

Visual C# .NET

```
DataColumn col = new DataColumn("NewColumn");
col.DataType = typeof(Decimal);

DataTable tbl = new DataTable("Products");
tbl.Columns.Add("ProductID", typeof(int));
tbl.Columns.Add("ProductName", typeof(string));
tbl.Columns.Add("UnitPrice", typeof(Decimal));
```

DefaultValue Property

You can use the *DefaultValue* property to generate a default value for the column in each new *DataRow* object.

SQL Server lets you define default values for columns in your tables. However, the *DefaultValue* property of the *DataColumn* object doesn't work quite the same way as the SQL Server feature.

When you define a default value for a SQL Server column, you supply a string that contains an expression. SQL Server evaluates that expression each time it assigns a default value to a column.

The *DefaultValue* property accepts a static value via the generic *Object* data type. For example, say you're working with order dates. You can use the *DefaultValue* property to specify the default value for an OrderDate column. However, the default value is static. It will return the same value tomorrow as it does today.

The *DefaultValue* property is handy but not nearly as flexible as the corresponding SQL Server feature.

Expression Property

You can store an expression in the *Expression* property, and ADO.NET will evaluate that expression any time you request the contents of the column. Setting the *Expression* property of a *DataColumn* to anything other than the default empty string will automatically set the *ReadOnly* property of the *DataColumn* to *True*.

The following code snippet demonstrates how to set the *Expression* property of a *DataColumn* to return the product of two other columns in the *DataTable*—*Quantity* and *UnitPrice*. The code also adds a new *DataRow* to the *DataTable* and displays the contents of the expression-based column in the Console window.

Visual Basic .NET

```
Dim tbl As New DataTable("Order Details")
tbl.Columns.Add("OrderID", GetType(Integer))
tbl.Columns.Add("ProductID", GetType(Integer))
tbl.Columns.Add("Quantity", GetType(Integer))
tbl.Columns.Add("UnitPrice", GetType(Decimal))
Dim col As New DataColumn("ItemTotal", GetType(Decimal))
col.Expression = "Quantity * UnitPrice"
tbl.Columns.Add(col)
Dim row As DataRow = tbl.NewRow()
row("OrderID") = 1
row("ProductID") = 1
row("Quantity") = 6
row("UnitPrice") = 18
tbl.Rows.Add(row)
Console.WriteLine(row("ItemTotal"))
```

Visual C# .NET

```
DataTable tbl = new DataTable("Order Details");
tbl.Columns.Add("OrderID", typeof(int));
tbl.Columns.Add("ProductID", typeof(int));
tbl.Columns.Add("Quantity", typeof(int));
tbl.Columns.Add("UnitPrice", typeof(Decimal));
DataColumn col = new DataColumn("ItemTotal", typeof(Decimal));
col.Expression = "Quantity * UnitPrice"
tbl.Columns.Add(col);
DataRow row = tbl.NewRow();
row["OrderID"] = 1;
row["ProductID"] = 1;
row["Quantity"] = 6;
row["UnitPrice"] = 18;
tbl.Rows.Add(row);
Console.WriteLine(row["ItemTotal"]);
```

In Chapter 7, you'll learn how to reference the contents of other *Data-Table* objects in an expression-based column. For more information on the functions you can use in the *Expression* property, see the MSDN documentation.

ExtendedProperties Property

The *DataColumn* object's *ExtendedProperties* property returns a *PropertyCollection* object, which is designed to store various objects.

The *DataSet*, *DataTable*, *DataRelation*, and *Constraint* objects also expose an *ExtendedProperties* property.

For more information, including a code sample, see the information on the *ExtendedProperties* property in the earlier section titled "Properties of the *DataSet* Object."

MaxLength Property

You can use the *MaxLength* property to make sure that a user does not enter a longer string into your *DataColumn* than the database will allow.

By default, the *MaxLength* property is set to −1, which means that there is no maximum length for the column. As with the *AllowDBNull* and *AutoIncrement* properties, the *DataAdapter* will not set the *MaxLength* property of *DataColumn* objects that it creates via the *Fill* method. However, you can use the *DataAdapter* object's *FillSchema* method to set this property.

Namespace and *Prefix* Properties

You can use the *DataSet* object's *Namespace* and *Prefix* properties to specify an XML namespace and prefix for your *DataSet*. ADO.NET will use these settings when it writes the contents of your *DataSet* to XML and when it loads data from an XML document into your *DataSet*.

The *DataSet* and *DataTable* objects also expose *Namespace* and *Prefix* properties.

For more information on XML namespaces, see the MSDN documentation.

Ordinal Property

The *Ordinal* property returns the position of the *DataColumn* within the *DataTable* object's *Columns* collection. This property is read-only and will return *−1* if the *DataColumn* object is not part of a *DataTable* object's *Columns* collection.

ReadOnly Property

You can use the *ReadOnly* property to control whether the contents of the column are read-only. By default, this property is set to *False*.

If you set the *Expression* property of a *DataColumn*, the *ReadOnly* property will be automatically set to *True*. At that point, the *ReadOnly* property becomes read-only.

If you attempt to change the value of a column whose *ReadOnly* property is set to *True*, ADO.NET will throw a *ReadOnlyException*. But even though the *ReadOnly* property is set to *True*, you can still modify the contents of the column before adding it to a *DataTable* object's *Rows* collection.

Like the *AllowDBNull* and *AutoIncrement* properties, the *ReadOnly* property is one of the properties that the *DataAdapter* will set via the *FillSchema* method but not via the *Fill* method.

Table Property

The *Table* property returns the *DataTable* to which the *DataColumn* object belongs. This property is read-only and returns an uninitialized *DataTable* if the *DataColumn* does not reside in a *DataTable* object's *Columns* collection.

Unique Property

You can use the *Unique* property to ensure that all values for a column within a *DataTable* are unique. By default, the *Unique* property is set to *False*.

Setting the *Unique* property to *True* will implicitly create a *UniqueConstraint* object for the *DataTable* in which the column resides. Similarly, adding a *UniqueConstraint* based on a single column will set the *Unique* property of that *DataColumn* to *True*.

If you create a unique constraint or a primary key on a collection of columns, the *Unique* property of each *DataColumn* will not be set to *True* because the values within the column are not necessarily unique. For example, the Order Details table in the Northwind database has a primary key based on the combination of the OrderID and ProductID columns. Neither column on its own is unique because there can be multiple entries in the table for an order and multiple orders can include the same product.

Like the *AllowDBNull* and *AutoIncrement* properties, the *Unique* property is one of the properties that the *DataAdapter* will set via the *FillSchema* method but not via the *Fill* method.

Properties of the *DataRow* Object

The commonly used properties of the *DataRow* object are shown in Table 6-12.

Table 6-12   Properties of the *DataRow* Object

Property	Data Type	Description
HasErrors	*Boolean*	Indicates whether the current row contains errors
Item	*Object*	Returns or sets the contents of a column
ItemArray	Array of *Object*	Returns or sets the contents of the row
RowError	*String*	Returns or sets error information for the row
RowState	*DataRowState*	Returns the state of the row
Table	*DataTable*	Returns the *DataTable* to which the row belongs

HasErrors Property

You can use the *HasErrors* property to determine whether the row contains errors. The *HasErrors* property returns a Boolean value and is read-only.

Item Property

The *Item* property allows you to examine or modify the contents of a column of information in the row. You can access the contents of the column by specifying the ordinal for the column, its name, or the *DataColumn* object itself.

The *Item* property also lets you supply a value from the *DataRowVersion* enumeration so that you can choose which version of the column you want to see. For example, you might want to view the original contents of a column for a row that has changed.

ItemArray Property

You can retrieve or set values for all columns in your row by using the *Item-Array* property. This property returns or accepts an array of type *Object*, where each item in the array corresponds to a column in the *DataTable*.

When you use the *ItemArray* property to change the contents of a row, you can use the appropriate keyword for your language of choice to keep from modifying certain fields. For example, Visual Basic .NET programmers would use *Nothing* and Visual C# .NET programmers would use *null*.

The following line of code modifies the contents of the second, third, and fourth columns in the row but does not modify the contents of the first or last columns. Such code is necessary when you work with *DataTable* objects that contain read-only columns.

Visual Basic .NET

```
row.ItemArray = New Object() {Nothing, 2, 3, 4, Nothing}
```

Visual C# .NET

```
row.ItemArray = new object[] {null, 2, 3, 4, null};
```

RowError Property

The *RowError* property returns a string that contains error information for the row. You can set the *RowError* property to a string to indicate that the row has an error.

The *DataRow* object's *HasErrors* property might return *True* even if the *RowError* property is empty. See the documentation for *SetColumnError* for more information.

RowState Property

The *RowState* property returns a value from the *DataRowState* enumeration to indicate the current state of the row. This property is read-only.

I discussed the various values that the *RowState* property can return earlier in the chapter.

Table Property

The *Table* property returns the *DataTable* to which the *DataRow* object belongs. This property is read-only.

There are times when a *DataRow* object does not reside in a *DataTable* object's *Rows* collection—for example, after the *DataRow* is created using *DataTable.NewRow* but before it is added to the *DataTable* object's *Rows* collection. However, the *DataRow* object's *Table* property will always return the *DataTable* to which the *DataRow* belongs.

Methods of the *DataRow* Object

The commonly used methods of the *DataRow* object are shown in Table 6-13.

Table 6-13 Methods of the *DataRow* Object

Method	Description
AcceptChanges	Accepts the pending changes stored in the *DataRow*
BeginEdit	Starts the editing process for the *DataRow*
CancelEdit	Cancels the changes made since the *BeginEdit* method was called

(continued)

Table 6-13   Methods of the *DataRow* Object   *(continued)*

Method	Description
ClearErrors	Clears the errors for the *DataRow*
Delete	Marks the *DataRow* as deleted
EndEdit	Commits the changes made since the *BeginEdit* method was called
GetChildRows	Returns an array of child *DataRow* objects for the current *DataRow* based on a *DataRelation*
GetColumnError	Retrieves error information for a particular column
GetColumnsInError	Returns an array of *DataColumn* objects that contain errors for the current row
GetParentRow	Returns the parent *DataRow* for the current *DataRow* based on a *DataRelation*
GetParentRows	Returns an array of parent *DataRow* objects for the current *DataRow* based on a *DataRelation*
HasVersion	Returns a Boolean value to indicate whether the *DataRow* can return that version of data
IsNull	Indicates whether a particular column in the row contains a *Null* value
RejectChanges	Discards the pending changes stored in the *DataRow*
SetColumnError	Sets error information for a particular column in the row
SetParentRow	Changes the parent *DataRow* for the current *DataRow* based on a *DataRelation*

AcceptChanges and *RejectChanges* Methods

The *DataRow* object stores pending changes so that you can later submit those changes to the database. The *AcceptChanges* and *RejectChanges* methods let you accept or discard those changes, respectively.

By default, when you successfully submit pending changes to your database using a *DataAdapter*, the *DataAdapter* will implicitly call the *AcceptChanges* method on the *DataRow* object. The *DataRow* will then have a *RowState* of *Unmodified*.

You can discard the pending changes stored in a *DataRow* by calling its *RejectChanges* method. As with the *AcceptChanges* method, the *DataRow* object's *RowState* will then return *Unmodified*.

Say you have a row of customer data that contains a pending change. The CompanyName column originally contained *Initial CompanyName* but now contains *New CompanyName*.

If you call the *AcceptChanges* method, the *DataRow* will no longer maintain the old original value of *Initial CompanyName*. The *DataRow* will return

New CompanyName regardless of whether you request the current or original value using the *DataRow* object's *Item* method.

If, instead, you call the *RejectChanges* method, the *DataRow* will no longer maintain the *New CompanyName* value. The *DataRow* will return *Initial CompanyName* regardless of whether you request the current or original value using the *DataRow* object's *Item* method.

To gain a better understanding of how ADO.NET uses the original values for a *DataRow* to submit changes to your database, see Chapter 10 and Chapter 11.

BeginEdit, *CancelEdit*, and *EndEdit* Methods

The *BeginEdit*, *CancelEdit*, and *EndEdit* methods allow you to store or cancel a series of changes to the *DataRow*. For example, you might want to let the user modify the contents of a row and then display a dialog box that gives the user the chance to accept or cancel those changes.

CancelEdit and *EndEdit* behave differently than *AcceptChanges* and *RejectChanges* do. The best way to explain the difference between the sets of methods is to show some sample code. The following code snippet creates a new *DataRow* and modifies its contents. It then calls *BeginEdit*, modifies the contents of the row again, and displays the various versions of the row.

Visual Basic .NET

```
Dim tbl As New DataTable("Customers")
tbl.Columns.Add("CustomerID", GetType(String))
tbl.Columns.Add("CompanyName", GetType(String))
Dim row As DataRow

'Create a new row using the LoadDataRow method.
row = tbl.LoadDataRow(New Object() {"ABCDE", _
                                    "Initial CompanyName"}, True)

'Modify the contents of the DataRow.
'row.RowState will now return Modified.
'The 'Original' value for the column is "Initial CompanyName."
row("CompanyName") = "New CompanyName"

'Call BeginEdit and modify the CompanyName column again.
row.BeginEdit()
row("CompanyName") = "Even Newer CompanyName!"

'Display the different versions of the column.
Console.WriteLine("Proposed: " & _
                  row("CompanyName", DataRowVersion.Proposed))
Console.WriteLine("Current:  " & _
                  row("CompanyName", DataRowVersion.Current))
Console.WriteLine("Original: " & _
                  row("CompanyName", DataRowVersion.Original))
```

Visual C# .NET

```
DataTable tbl = new DataTable("Customers");
tbl.Columns.Add("CustomerID", typeof(string));
tbl.Columns.Add("CompanyName", typeof(string));
DataRow row;

//Create a new row using the LoadDataRow method.
row = tbl.LoadDataRow(new object[] {"ABCDE",
                                "Initial CompanyName"}, true);

//Modify the contents of the DataRow.
//row.RowState will now return Modified.
//The 'Original' value for the column is "Initial CompanyName."
row["CompanyName"] = "New CompanyName";

//Call BeginEnit and modify the CompanyName column again.
row.BeginEdit();
row["CompanyName"] - "Even Newer CompanyName!";

//Display the different versions of the column.
Console.WriteLine("Proposed: " +
                row["CompanyName", DataRowVersion.Proposed]);
Console.WriteLine("Current:  " +
                row["CompanyName", DataRowVersion.Current]);
Console.WriteLine("Original: " +
                row["CompanyName", DataRowVersion.Original]);
```

Run the code, and you'll see that the proposed value for the column is *Even Newer CompanyName!*, the current value is *New CompanyName*, and the original value is *Initial CompanyName*.

You can call the *EndEdit* method to accept the edit. The current value of the column will be set to the proposed value. The original value for the column will remain the same.

You can call the *CancelEdit* method to discard the edit. The current and original values of the column will remain the same.

Keep in mind that while you're editing the contents of a row after using the *BeginEdit* method, the *Item* method will return the proposed values for the columns by default. For more information on this behavior, see the section titled "Examining the Pending Changes in a *DataRow*" earlier in this chapter.

ClearErrors Method

To clear all errors in a *DataRow*, call the object's *ClearErrors* method. The method clears the error information for the *DataRow* object as a whole as well as for each column in the row.

Delete Method

The *Delete* method does not actually remove a *DataRow* from its table's *Rows* collection. When you call a *DataRow* object's *Delete* method, ADO.NET marks the row as deleted so that you can later remove the corresponding row in your database by calling the *DataAdapter* object's *Update* method.

If you want to completely remove the *DataRow*, you can call its *Delete* method and then call its *AcceptChanges* method. You can also use the *Remove* method of the *DataRowCollection* object to accomplish the same task in a single line of code.

GetChildRows Method

You can use the *GetChildRows* method to access the child rows for the current *DataRow*. In order to use the *GetChildRows* method, you must supply a *DataRelation* or the name of a *DataRelation*. You can also supply a value from the *DataRowVersion* enumeration to control the version of the child data that you retrieve.

The *GetChildRows* method returns child data in an array of *DataRow* objects.

GetColumnError and *SetColumnError* Methods

To set or examine error information for a particular column in a row, you can use the *GetColumnError* and *SetColumnError* methods. You can supply a column name, its ordinal position within the *DataTable*, or the *DataColumn* object itself with either method.

You can also use *SetColumnError* to clear the error information for a particular column by passing an empty string as the second parameter.

GetColumnsInError Method

If the *DataRow* object's *HasErrors* property returns *True*, you can use the *Get-ColumnsInError* method to determine which column (or columns) in the *DataRow* contains error information.

The following code snippet demonstrates how you can use the *GetColumns-InError* method in conjunction with the *GetColumnError* method to return error information for a particular *DataRow*:

Visual Basic .NET

```
Dim row As DataRow
    ⋮
If row.HasErrors Then
    Console.WriteLine("The row contains the following errors:")
    Console.WriteLine("RowError: " & row.RowError)
    Dim colError As DataColumn
```

```
      For Each colError In row.GetColumnsInError
        Console.WriteLine("Error in " & colError.ColumnName & ": " & _
                          row.GetColumnError(colError))
      Next colError
Else
    Console.WriteLine("The row does not contain errors")
End If
```

Visual C# .NET

```
DataRow row;
  :
if (row.HasErrors)
{
    Console.WriteLine("The row contains the following errors:");
    Console.WriteLine("RowError: " + row.RowError);
    foreach (DataColumn colError in row.GetColumnsInError())
    Console.WriteLine("Error in " + colError.ColumnName + ": " +
                      row.GetColumnError(colError));
}
else
    Console.WriteLine("The row does not contain errors");
```

GetParentRow, *GetParentRows*, and *SetParentRow* Methods

The *GetParentRow* and *SetParentRow* methods provide an easy way for you to examine or set the parent row of the current row in a *DataRelation* object, respectively.

Like the *GetChildRows* method, the *GetParentRow* method accepts relation information—either the name of the *DataRelation* or the object itself—as well as a value from the *DataRowVersion* enumeration to control the version of the row that the method returns. The *GetParentRow* method returns a *DataRow* object.

If the current *DataRow* can have multiple parent rows via a relation, you can use the *GetParentRows* method to access those rows. This method accepts the same parameters as the *GetParentRow* method, except that it returns an array of *DataRow* objects.

The *SetParentRow* method allows you to change a row's parent row in a relation. To use the method, you simply pass the row's new parent. If the current row's *DataTable* is the child table in multiple relations within the *DataSet*, you should use the overloaded method that allows you to pass the *DataRelation* object as the second parameter so the *SetParentRow* method will know which relation you want to reference.

HasVersion Method

We've discussed some of the versions of data that a *DataRow* object maintains—current, original, and proposed. The *DataRow* object does not maintain values for all these versions all the time.

For example, a *DataRow* whose *RowState* is *Added* will have a current version but not an original version. A *DataRow* whose *RowState* is *Deleted* will have an original version but not a current version.

You can use the *HasVersion* method to determine whether a *DataRow* has data for that particular version. The *HasVersion* method accepts a value from the *DataRowVersion* enumeration and returns a Boolean value that indicates whether the *DataRow* currently maintains that version of data.

IsNull Method

Say you're working with a *DataRow* that contains customer information and you want to retrieve the contents of the ContactName column into a string variable. If you use the following code, you might run into problems if the Contact-Name column contains a *null* value:

Visual Basic .NET

```
Dim row As DataRow
⋮
Dim strContactName As String
strContactName = CStr(row("ContactName"))
```

Visual C# .NET

```
DataRow row;
⋮
string strContactName;
strContactName = (string) row["ContactName"];
```

To avoid such problems, you can do one of two things: set up your database and *DataSet* so that the column does not support *null* values, or check the contents of the column for *null* values before accessing its contents.

The *IsNull* method can simplify the second of these options. This method accepts the name of a column, its ordinal position, or the *DataColumn* object itself and returns a Boolean value to indicate whether the column contains a *null* value.

We can change our previous code snippet to use the *IsNull* method, as shown here:

Visual Basic .NET

```
Dim row As DataRow
⋮
Dim strContactName As String
```

```
If row.IsNull("ContactName") Then
    strContactName = "<Null>"
Else
    strContactName = CStr(row("ContactName"))
End If
```

Visual C# .NET

```
DataRow row;
⋮
string strContactName;
if (row.IsNull("ContactName"))
    strContactName = "<Null>";
else
    strContactName = (string) row["ContactName"];
```

The *IsNull* method also supports a fourth overloaded method that accepts a *DataColumn* object and a value from the *DataRowVersion* enumeration. You can use this method to determine whether a particular version of a column contains a *null* value.

Properties of the *UniqueConstraint* Object

The commonly used properties of the *UniqueConstraint* object are shown in Table 6-14.

Table 6-14   Properties of the *UniqueConstraint* Object

Property	Data Type	Description
Columns	Array of *DataColumn* objects	Returns the columns that are part of the constraint
ConstraintName	*String*	Contains the name of the constraint
ExtendedProperties	*PropertyCollection*	Contains a collection of dynamic properties and values
IsPrimaryKey	*Boolean*	Indicates whether the constraint constitutes the primary key for the *DataTable*
Table	*DataTable*	Returns the *DataTable* to which the constraint belongs

Columns Property

The *Columns* property returns an array of *DataColumn* objects that contains the columns that make up the constraint. This property is read-only.

ConstraintName Property

You can use the *ConstraintName* property to examine or set the name of the *UniqueConstraint*.

ExtendedProperties Property

The *UniqueConstraint* object's *ExtendedProperties* property returns a *Property-Collection* object, which is designed to store various objects.

The *DataSet*, *DataColumn*, *DataRelation*, and *ForeignKeyConstraint* objects also expose an *ExtendedProperties* property.

For more information, including a code sample, see the information on the *ExtendedProperties* property under the earlier section titled "Properties of the *DataSet* Object."

IsPrimaryKey Property

The *IsPrimaryKey* property returns a Boolean value that indicates whether the *UniqueConstraint* object is the primary key for the *DataTable*.

The *IsPrimaryKey* property is read-only. The *UniqueConstraint* object lets you specify whether the constraint is a *DataTable* object's primary key only through its constructors.

You can also set a *DataTable* object's primary key through its *PrimaryKey* property.

Table Property

The *Table* property returns the *DataTable* to which the *UniqueConstraint* belongs. This property is read-only.

Properties of the *ForeignKeyConstraint* Object

The commonly used properties of the *ForeignKeyConstraint* object are shown in Table 6-15.

Table 6-15   Properties of the *ForeignKeyConstraint* Object

Property	Data Type	Description
AcceptRejectRule	*AcceptRejectRule*	Controls whether the effects of a call to a parent row's *AcceptChanges* or *RejectChanges* method cascade to the child rows
Columns	Array of *DataColumn* objects	Returns the columns in the child table that make up the constraint
ConstraintName	*String*	Contains the name of the constraint
DeleteRule	*Rule*	Controls how or whether a deletion of a parent row cascades to the child rows

(continued)

Table 6-15 **Properties of the *ForeignKeyConstraint* Object** *(continued)*

Property	Data Type	Description
ExtendedProperties	*PropertyCollection*	Contains a collection of dynamic properties and values
RelatedColumns	Array of *Data-Columns*	Returns the columns in the parent table that make up the constraint
RelatedTable	*DataTable*	Returns the parent table for the constraint
Table	*DataTable*	Returns the child table for the constraint
UpdateRule	*Rule*	Controls how or whether changes to the parent row cascade to the child rows

AcceptRejectRule, *DeleteRule*, and *UpdateRule* Properties

The *AcceptRejectRule*, *DeleteRule*, and *UpdateRule* properties control how or whether changes to a parent row cascade to the child rows.

The *AcceptRejectRule* property accepts values from the *AcceptRejectRule* enumeration. By default, the *AcceptRejectRule* property is set to *None*, which means that if you call the *AcceptChanges* or *RejectChanges* method on a row, its child rows will not be affected. If you set the *AcceptRejectRule* property to *Cascade*, the action will cascade down to the child rows defined by the *ForeignKeyConstraint* object.

The *DeleteRule* and *UpdateRule* properties behave in a similar fashion, but they accept values from the *Rule* enumeration. By default, both properties are set to *Cascade*, which means that the changes you make to a parent row will automatically cascade down to the child rows.

For example, if you call the *Delete* method on a *DataRow*, you're implicitly calling the *Delete* method on its child rows as well. Similarly, if you change the value of a key column in a *DataRow*, you'll implicitly change the contents of the corresponding column in the child rows.

You can set the *DeleteRule* and *UpdateRule* properties to *None* if you don't want to cascade changes. You can also set the properties to *SetDefault* or *SetNull*. Setting the properties to *SetNull* will assign *null* values to the related columns in child rows if the parent row is deleted or if the contents of its related columns change. The *SetDefault* value causes similar behavior, except that the contents of the related columns in child rows will be set to their default values.

Columns and *RelatedColumns* Properties

The *Columns* property returns an array of *DataColumn* objects that contain the columns in the child table that are part of the constraint. The *RelatedColumns* property returns the same information for the parent table.

Both properties are read-only.

ConstraintName Property

You can use the *ConstraintName* property to examine or set the name of the *ForeignKeyConstraint*.

ExtendedProperties Property

The *ForeignKeyConstraint* object's *ExtendedProperties* property returns a *Property-Collection* object, which is designed to store various objects.

The *DataSet*, *DataColumn*, *DataRelation*, and *UniqueConstraint* objects also expose an *ExtendedProperties* property.

For more information, including a code sample, see the information on the *ExtendedProperties* property under the earlier section titled "Properties of the *DataSet* Object."

RelatedTable and *Table* Properties

The *Table* property returns the child *DataTable* for the constraint. The *Related-Table* property returns the parent *DataTable* for the constraint. Both properties are read-only.

Questions That Should Be Asked More Frequently

Q.   Do I need to use a *DataSet* if I want to work with only a few rows of data?

A.   In this situation, you can use just a *DataTable* object without using a *DataSet*. The *DataSet* offers support for relations between tables, the ability to read and write data to files or streams, and support for XML features. If you don't need to use any of these features, you can use just a *DataTable*.

Q.   I added a row to my *DataTable*, and when I submitted the new row to my database, I received an error that said the new row violated the primary key constraint on the table. Why didn't I receive this error when I added the row to the *DataTable*?

A.   ADO.NET enforces the constraints you create based on the data in your *DataSet*. The new row that you created will not violate the primary key constraint on your *DataTable* unless the *DataTable* already contains a row with the same values in the primary key columns. ADO.NET does not have any inherent knowledge of what data exists in your database.

Q.   How do I examine the contents of a deleted row?

A.   Use *DataRowVersion.Original* for the optional parameter on the *Item* property.

Q.   Is there any way to undo the changes I've made to my rows?

A.   Yes. You can call the *RejectChanges* method on a *DataRow*, *Data-Table*, or *DataSet* to discard any pending changes in the affected rows.

Q.   How can I tell whether a *DataTable* has a primary key defined?

A.   You can use the following snippet of code:

Visual Basic .NET

```
If tbl.PrimaryKey.Length > 0 Then
    'DataTable has a primary key.
Else
    'DataTable has no primary key.
End If
```

Visual C# .NET

```
if (tbl.PrimaryKey.Length > 0)
    //DataTable has a primary key.
else
    //DataTable has no primary key.
```

Q.   What of *DataSet* objects and the *Dispose* method?

A.   The *DataSet*, *DataTable*, and *DataColumn* objects are each derived from the *MarshalByValueComponent* class, which exposes both a *Dispose* method and a *Disposed* event. You can use the *Dispose* method to release an object's resources. You can also trap for an object's *Disposed* event if you want to execute code when the object's *Dispose* method executes.

If you're going to call the *Dispose* method on any of these objects, it's worth noting that the effect of their *Dispose* method is not recursive. Calling the *Dispose* method of a *DataSet* object does not implicitly call the *Dispose* method of the *DataTable* objects of the *DataSet*.

7

Working with Relational Data

Database tables are rarely independent structures. If you look at the tables in the Microsoft SQL Server 2000 sample Northwind database, shown in Figure 7-1, you'll see that they're all interrelated. Notice that no table stands alone.

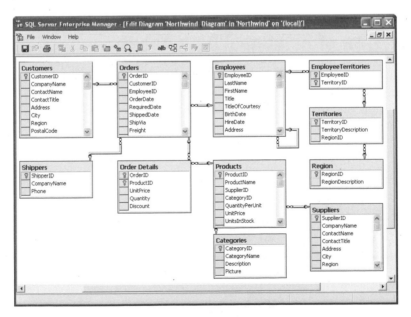

Figure 7-1 Relations between tables in the Northwind database

Not all databases have such a high percentage of related tables, but most contain tables that are related. When you build applications, you'll encounter scenarios in which you want to display or programmatically access data from related tables in your database.

When you're working with data from multiple *DataTable* objects, you're likely to need four types of features—those for navigation, validation, aggregation, and cascadation. OK, cascadation isn't really a word. But even though this is a technical book, I'm still entitled to a little artistic license once in a while.

Users will want to navigate between different tables of information to easily locate related rows, such as the orders for a particular customer. They'll want to validate their data to make sure that they don't create orphaned rows in the database. Applications will often require you to gather aggregate information— for example, to display the number of items in, and total cost of, an order. And when a parent row is modified, you might want the changes to cascade down to child rows—for example, if an order is deleted, you'll probably want the items associated with that order to be deleted as well.

In this chapter, we'll look at how to use the ADO.NET *DataRelation* object to work with data from related *DataTable* objects. I'll also discuss the features of the *ForeignKeyConstraint* object, which I introduced in the previous chapter, in more detail.

A Brief Overview of Relational Data Access

Obviously, ADO.NET did not pioneer relational data access. It was predated by other ways of processing data from related tables. Let's review the most common methods of working with data from related tables and quickly compare them to using the *DataRelation* object.

Join Queries

Join queries predate all Microsoft data access technologies. They're a simple, standard way to retrieve data from multiple tables in a single query. The following query retrieves data from the Customers, Orders, and Order Details tables in the Northwind database:

```
SELECT C.CustomerID, C.CompanyName, C.ContactName, C.Phone,
       O.OrderID, O.EmployeeID, O.OrderDate,
       D.ProductID, D.Quantity, D.UnitPrice
    FROM Customers C, Orders O, [Order Details] D
    WHERE C.CustomerID = O.CustomerID AND O.OrderID = D.OrderID
```

The benefits of join queries include:

- **They're a widely accepted standard**   Every database programmer knows how to use join queries.

- **They return results in a single structure**

- **They're easy to filter**   If you want data only for customers from a particular country, you can simply add a filter to the query and the query will return data for only those customers.

The drawbacks include:

- **They can return redundant data**   If a customer has 100 orders, the same customer information will be returned for each and every order. (See Figure 7-2.)

CustomerID	CompanyName	ContactName	Phone	OrderID	EmployeeID	OrderDate	ProductID	Quantity	UnitPrice
ALFKI	Alfreds Futterkiste	Maria Anders	030-0074321	10643	6	8/25/1997	28	15	45.6
ALFKI	Alfreds Futterkiste	Maria Anders	030-0074321	10643	6	8/25/1997	39	21	18
ALFKI	Alfreds Futterkiste	Maria Anders	030-0074321	10643	6	8/25/1997	46	2	12
ALFKI	Alfreds Futterkiste	Maria Anders	030-0074321	10692	4	10/3/1997	63	20	43.9
ALFKI	Alfreds Futterkiste	Maria Anders	030-0074321	10702	4	10/13/1997	3	6	10
ALFKI	Alfreds Futterkiste	Maria Anders	030-0074321	10702	4	10/13/1997	76	15	18
ALFKI	Alfreds Futterkiste	Maria Anders	030-0074321	10835	1	1/15/1998	59	15	55
ALFKI	Alfreds Futterkiste	Maria Anders	030-0074321	10835	1	1/15/1998	77	2	13
ALFKI	Alfreds Futterkiste	Maria Anders	030-0074321	10952	1	3/16/1998	6	16	25
ALFKI	Alfreds Futterkiste	Maria Anders	030-0074321	10952	1	3/16/1998	28	2	45.6
ALFKI	Alfreds Futterkiste	Maria Anders	030-0074321	11011	3	4/9/1998	58	40	13.25
ALFKI	Alfreds Futterkiste	Maria Anders	030-0074321	11011	3	4/9/1998	71	20	21.5
ANATR	Ana Trujillo Emparedados	Ana Trujillo	(5) 555-4729	10926	4	3/4/1998	11	2	21
ANATR	Ana Trujillo Emparedados	Ana Trujillo	(5) 555-4729	10926	4	3/4/1998	13	10	6
ANATR	Ana Trujillo Emparedados	Ana Trujillo	(5) 555-4729	10926	4	3/4/1998	19	7	9.2
ANATR	Ana Trujillo Emparedados	Ana Trujillo	(5) 555-4729	10926	4	3/4/1998	72	10	34.8
ANATR	Ana Trujillo Emparedados	Ana Trujillo	(5) 555-4729	10759	3	11/28/1997	32	10	32
ANATR	Ana Trujillo Emparedados	Ana Trujillo	(5) 555-4729	10625	3	8/8/1997	14	3	23.25
ANATR	Ana Trujillo Emparedados	Ana Trujillo	(5) 555-4729	10625	3	8/8/1997	42	5	14
ANATR	Ana Trujillo Emparedados	Ana Trujillo	(5) 555-4729	10625	3	8/8/1997	60	10	34
ANATR	Ana Trujillo Emparedados	Ana Trujillo	(5) 555-4729	10308	7	9/18/1996	69	1	28.8
ANATR	Ana Trujillo Emparedados	Ana Trujillo	(5) 555-4729	10308	7	9/18/1996	70	5	12
ANTON	Antonio Moreno Taquería	Antonio Moreno	(5) 555-3932	10365	3	11/27/1996	11	24	16.8
ANTON	Antonio Moreno Taquería	Antonio Moreno	(5) 555-3932	10573	7	6/19/1997	17	18	39
ANTON	Antonio Moreno Taquería	Antonio Moreno	(5) 555-3932	10573	7	6/19/1997	34	40	14
ANTON	Antonio Moreno Taquería	Antonio Moreno	(5) 555-3932	10573	7	6/19/1997	53	25	32.8
ANTON	Antonio Moreno Taquería	Antonio Moreno	(5) 555-3932	10507	7	4/15/1997	43	15	46
ANTON	Antonio Moreno Taquería	Antonio Moreno	(5) 555-3932	10507	7	4/15/1997	48	15	12.75
ANTON	Antonio Moreno Taquería	Antonio Moreno	(5) 555-3932	10535	4	5/13/1997	11	50	21
ANTON	Antonio Moreno Taquería	Antonio Moreno	(5) 555-3932	10535	4	5/13/1997	40	10	18.4
ANTON	Antonio Moreno Taquería	Antonio Moreno	(5) 555-3932	10535	4	5/13/1997	57	5	19.5
ANTON	Antonio Moreno Taquería	Antonio Moreno	(5) 555-3932	10535	4	5/13/1997	59	15	55

Figure 7-2   Data returned by a join query

- **They're difficult to update**   It's hard for a data access model such as ADO.NET to know how to interpret the changes to the results of a join query. For example, if you delete a row, does that mean you want to delete just the corresponding row in the child table or do you want to delete the row in the parent tables as well? If you add a new row, does that mean you want to add a new row to just the child table or do you want to add a new row to the parent tables as well?

- **They're difficult to keep in sync**   If you modify a parent row—by changing the contact name for a customer, for example—you have to submit the change to the database and then reexecute the entire query to see that change in all related rows in the result set.

Separate Queries

Because join queries have always been notoriously difficult to update using data access technologies such as DAO and ADO, many developers use separate queries to retrieve data from each table into separate structures.

The benefits of using separate queries include:

- **They return less total data than join queries do**

- **They're more suitable for updates**   Because you're modifying a structure, such as a *Recordset*, that corresponds to a single table, it's easy for a technology such as ADO to interpret that change and modify the data in your database accordingly.

- **They're suitable for multiple data sources**   You can use this approach if the related tables exist on different database systems.

The drawbacks include:

- **They require synchronization code**   To locate the orders for a particular customer, you must apply a filter to the child *Recordset* and write code to keep the *Recordset* objects in synch with each other.

- **They're difficult to filter**   Constructing queries against child tables that retrieve only the rows that relate to the rows retrieved from the parent table can be challenging. We'll examine this topic further later in the chapter.

Hierarchical ADO *Recordset* Objects

ADO 2.0 introduced the concept of a hierarchical *Recordset*. You can use a special provider and a special query syntax to combine the results of multiple queries into a single structure. The following code snippet retrieves the contents of the Customers, Orders, and Order Details tables into a hierarchical *Recordset*:

```
Dim rsCustomers As ADODB.Recordset, rsOrders As ADODB.Recorders
Dim rsOrderDetails As ADODB.Recordset
Dim strConn As String, strSQL As String
strConn = "Provider=MSDataShape;Data Provider=SQLOLEDB;" & _
          "Data Source=(local)\NetSDK;Initial Catalog=Northwind;" & _
          "Trusted_Connection=Yes;"
```

```
strSQL = "SHAPE {SELECT CustomerID, CompanyName, ContactName, " & _
         "ContactTitle FROM Customers} AS Customers APPEND " & _
         "((SHAPE {SELECT OrderID, CustomerID, EmployeeID, OrderDate " & _
         "FROM Orders} AS Orders APPEND ({SELECT OrderID, ProductID, " & _
         "UnitPrice, Quantity FROM [Order Details]} AS OrderDetails " & _
         "RELATE 'OrderID' TO 'OrderID') AS OrderDetails) AS Orders " & _
         "RELATE 'CustomerID' TO 'CustomerID') AS Orders"
Set rsCustomers = New ADODB.Recordset
rsCustomers.Open strSQL, strConn, adOpenStatic, adLockBatchOptimistic
Set rsOrders = rsCustomers.Fields("Orders").Value
Set rsOrderDetails = rsOrders.Fields("OrderDetails").Value
```

The *Recordset* has three object variables, but they all reference data that's maintained in a single structure. As you navigate through the top-level *Recordset*, only the related data will be visible in the child *Recordset* objects.

The benefits of using hierarchical *Recordset* objects include:

■ **They return less total data than join queries do**

■ **They return data in a single structure**

■ **They don't require complex synchronization code**

■ **They're suitable for simple updates**   However, even though hierarchical *Recordset* objects handle simple updates well, they have limitations. Submitting pending changes against multiple tables can be problematic at best.

The drawbacks include:

■ **The query syntax is hideous**   Look at that query! I like to consider myself an ADO expert, but I never bothered to learn the SHAPE syntax.

■ **They offer limited control**   You have to define the relationship in your query.

■ **You can query only a single data source**

■ **They're difficult to filter**

ADO.NET *DataRelation* Objects

The ADO.NET *DataRelation* is very different in structure from hierarchical *Recordset* objects. *DataRelation* objects do not require an additional provider, and no abominable SHAPE query syntax is required. *DataRelation* objects are considered part of the *DataSet* object's schema.

Quite simply, the *DataRelation* combines the best features of the separate query and hierarchical *Recordset* approaches to managing data from related tables and eliminates nearly all of their drawbacks. The following lists of the pros and cons should whet your appetite for now.

The benefits of using *DataRelation* objects include:

■ **They return less total data than join queries do**

■ **They simplify locating related data**

■ **They don't require complex synchronization code**

■ **They can handle advanced updating scenarios**   For example, you can submit new customers before new orders but also delete existing orders before deleting existing customers. Or, if you have a series of pending orders and order details, you can fetch server-generated autoincrement values for your new orders before submitting their new order details. I'll cover both scenarios in detail in Chapter 11.

■ **They're dynamic**   You can create, modify, and delete *DataRelation* objects programmatically before or after you query the related database tables.

■ **They support cascading changes**   You can control whether changes to a row cascade down to child rows by using properties of the foreign key constraint associated with the *DataRelation*.

■ **They support creating hierarchies from different data sources** Need to relate the results of a customer query against a SQL Server database and an order query against an Oracle database? No problem.

The drawbacks include:

■ **They're difficult to filter**   Unfortunately, *DataRelation* objects do not simplify fetching only child rows that correspond to the desired parent rows. I'll discuss ways of handling such scenarios later in the chapter.

Working with *DataRelation* Objects in Code

You can navigate through multiple tables of data, validate data, aggregate data, and cascade changes using your own code, but you can perform all of these functions quickly and easily with the help of the ADO.NET *DataRelation* object. Let's look at how to create and use *DataRelation* objects in code.

Creating *DataRelation* Objects

The *DataRelation* object has a few important properties, which you can set in its constructors. When you create a *DataRelation*, you should provide a name so that you can locate the object in its collection as well as specify the parent and child columns on which to base the relationship. To simplify creation, the *DataRelation* has separate constructors that accept single *DataColumn* objects and arrays of *DataColumn* objects.

The standard example of creating a relationship relies on *DataTable* objects that contain customer and order information, such as that shown in Figure 7-3. You can use the following code snippet to create that *DataRelation*:

Visual Basic .NET

```
'Create a new DataSet and add DataTable and DataColumn objects.
Dim ds As New DataSet()
  ⋮

'Add a DataRelation between the two tables.
Dim rel As DataRelation
rel = New DataRelation("CustomersOrders", _
                    ds.Tables("Customers").Columns("CustomerID"), _
                    ds.Tables("Orders").Columns("CustomerID"))
ds.Relationships.Add(rel)
```

Visual C# .NET

```
//Create a new DataSet and add DataTable and DataColumn objects.
DataSet ds = new DataSet();
  ⋮

//Add a DataRelation between the two tables.
DataRelation rel;
rel = new DataRelation("CustomersOrders",
                    ds.Tables["Customers"].Columns["CustomerID"],
                    ds.Tables["Orders"].Columns["CustomerID"]);
ds.Relationships.Add(rel);
```

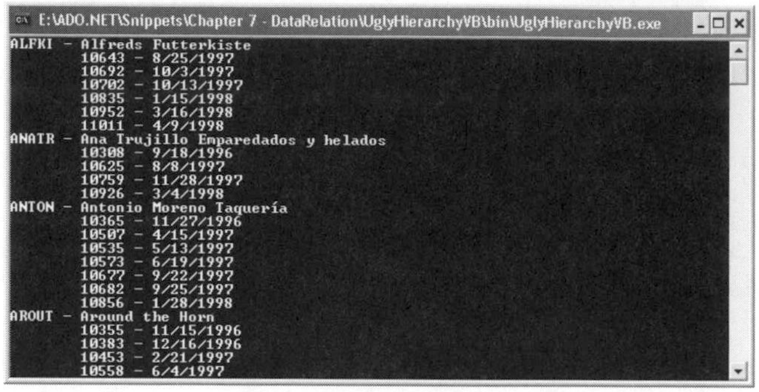

Figure 7-3   Displaying related information

If you want to define a relationship that's based on multiple columns, you can use a constructor of the *DataRelation* that accepts arrays of *DataColumn* objects, as shown in the following code snippet:

Visual Basic .NET

```
'Create a new DataSet and add DataTable and DataColumn objects.
Dim ds As New DataSet()
⋮


'Create arrays that reference the DataColumn objects
'on which we'll base the new DataRelation.
Dim colsParent, colsChild As DataColumn()
With ds.Tables("ParentTable")
    colsParent = New DataColumn() {.Columns("ParentColumn1"), _
                                   .Columns("ParentColumn2")}
End With
With ds.Tables("ChildTable")
    colsChild = New DataColumn() {.Columns("ChildColumn1"), _
                                  .Columns("ChildColumn2")}
End With


'Create the new DataRelation.
Dim rel As DataRelation
rel = New DataRelation("MultipleColumns", colsParent, colsChild)
ds.Relationships.Add(rel)
```

Visual C# .NET

```
//Create a new DataSet and add DataTable and DataColumn objects.
DataSet ds = new DataSet();
⋮


//Create arrays that reference the DataColumn objects
//on which we'll base the new DataRelation.
```

```
DataTable tblParent, tblChild;
DataColumn[] colsParent, colsChild;
tblParent = ds.Tables["ParentTable"];
colsParent = new DataColumn[] {tblParent.Columns["ParentColumn1"],
                              tblParent.Columns["ParentColumn2"]};
tblChild = ds.Tables["ChildTable"];
colsChild = new DataColumn[] {tblChild.Columns["ChildColumn1"],
                             tblChild.Columns["ChildColumn2"]};

//Create the new DataRelation.
DataRelation rel;
rel = new DataRelation("MultipleColumns", colsParent, colsChild);
ds.Relationships.Add(rel);
```

The *DataRelation* also has a pair of constructors whose signatures match the ones we just examined but also expose a fourth parameter to indicate whether to create constraints to enforce referential integrity based on the new relation. By default, creating a new *DataRelation* adds constraints to your *DataTable* objects if such constraints do not already exist. We'll take a closer look at this functionality shortly.

Once you've created a new *DataRelation*, you should append it to the *Relations* collection of your *DataSet*. As with creating new *DataTable* objects and *DataColumn* objects, you can create a new *DataRelation* and append it to a *DataSet* object's *Relations* collection in a single call using code such as the following:

Visual Basic .NET

```
'Create a new DataSet and add DataTable and DataColumn objects.
Dim ds As New DataSet()
    ⋮

'Add a DataRelation between the two tables.
ds.Relationships.Add("CustomersOrders", _
                ds.Tables("Customers").Columns("CustomerID"), _
                ds.Tables("Orders").Columns("CustomerID"))
```

Visual C# .NET

```
//Create a new DataSet and add DataTable and DataColumn objects.
DataSet ds = new DataSet();
    ⋮

//Add a DataRelation between the two tables.
ds.Relationships.Add("CustomersOrders",
                ds.Tables["Customers"].Columns["CustomerID"],
                ds.Tables["Orders"].Columns["CustomerID"]);
```

Locating Related Data

One of the main uses of the *DataRelation* object is to locate related data in different *DataTable* objects. However, the *DataRelation* object does not handle this task, at least not directly. This functionality is actually available through the *DataRow* object's *GetChildRows*, *GetParentRow*, and *GetParentRows* methods. How does the *DataRelation* enter into the equation? When you call any of these methods on the *DataRow* object, you specify a *DataRelation* as a parameter of the method. Let's take a closer look at these methods and how to use them.

The *DataRow* Object's *GetChildRows* Method

Locating a row's related child rows in another *DataTable* is rather straightforward. You simply call the *GetChildRows* method of your *DataRow* and supply the name of the *DataRelation* object that defines the relationship between your *DataTable* objects. You can also supply the actual *DataRelation* object instead of the object's name. The *GetChildRows* method returns the related data as an array of *DataRow* objects.

The following code snippet calls the *GetChildRows* method and loops through the data it returns:

Visual Basic .NET

```
'Loop through the customers.
Dim rowCustomer, rowOrder As DataRow
For Each rowCustomer In ds.Tables("Customers").Rows
    Console.WriteLine(rowCustomer("CustomerID") & " - " & _
                      rowCustomer("CompanyName"))
    'Loop through the related orders.
    For Each rowOrder In rowCustomer.GetChildRows("RelationName")
        Console.WriteLine(vbTab & rowOrder("OrderID") & " - " & _
                          rowOrder("OrderDate"))
    Next rowOrder
Next rowCustomer
```

Visual C# .NET

```
//Loop through the customers.
foreach (DataRow rowCustomer in ds.Tables["Customers"].Rows)
{
    Console.WriteLine(rowCustomer["CustomerID"] + " - " +
                      rowCustomer["CompanyName"]);
    //Loop through the related orders.
    foreach (DataRow rowOrder in rowCustomer.GetChildRows("RelationName"))
        Console.WriteLine("\t" + rowOrder["OrderID"] + " - " +
                          rowOrder["OrderDate"]);
}
```

The *DataRow* Object's *GetParentRow* Method

DataRelation objects let you not only drill down through a hierarchy but also travel upstream. The *DataRow* object exposes a *GetParentRow* method that you can call to locate that row's parent row based on a *DataRelation* within the *DataSet*. Like the *GetChildRows* method, *GetParentRow* accepts a *DataRelation* object or a string that contains the name of the *DataRelation* you want to use, as shown in the following code:

Visual Basic .NET

```
Dim rowCustomer, rowOrder As DataRow
'Loop through the orders.
For Each rowOrder In ds.Tables("Orders").Rows
    Console.Write(rowOrder("OrderID") & vbTab & rowOrder("OrderDate"))
    'Locate the related parent row.
    rowCustomer = rowOrder.GetParentRow("CustomersOrders")
    Console.WriteLine(vbTab & rowCustomer("CompanyName"))
Next rowOrder
```

Visual C# .NET

```
DataRow rowCustomer;
//Loop through the orders.
foreach (DataRow rowOrder in ds.Tables["Orders"].Rows)
{
    Console.Write(rowOrder["OrderID"] + "\t" + rowOrder["OrderDate"]);
    //Locate the related parent row.
    rowCustomer = rowOrder.GetParentRow("CustomersOrders");
    Console.WriteLine("\t" + rowCustomer["CompanyName"]);
}
```

The *DataRow* Object's *GetParentRows* Method

If the relationship that you're working with is a many-to-many relationship and you want to examine all parent rows for a particular *DataRow*, you can use the *DataRow* object's *GetParentRows* method. The signatures for this method are identical to that of the *GetChildRows* method, as shown in the following code:

Visual Basic .NET

```
'Loop through the customers.
Dim rowChild, rowParent As DataRow
For Each rowChild In ds.Tables("ChildTable").Rows
    'Loop through the parent rows.
    Console.WriteLine(rowChild("ChildName"))
    For Each rowParent In rowChild.GetParentRows("RelationName")
        Console.WriteLine(vbTab & rowParent("ParentName"))
    Next rowParent
Next rowChild
```

Visual C# .NET

```
//Loop through the customers.
foreach (DataRow rowChild in ds.Tables["ChildTable"].Rows)
{
    Console.WriteLine(rowChild["ChildName"]);
    //Loop through the related orders.
    foreach (DataRow rowParent in rowChild.GetChildRows("RelationName"))
        Console.WriteLine("\t" + rowParent["ParentName"]);
}
```

> **Note**   Few, if any, relationships in a database are truly many-to-many. You'll see why later in the chapter.

Choosing the Version of Data to View

Imagine that you've already built an application that allows users to retrieve data from your database and modify that data. But the employees who'll use that application aren't terribly reliable; they're prone to making mistakes. So the application uses some functionality exposed by the *DataSet* to store changes in a file rather than submit them to the database. (We'll discuss this feature further in Chapter 12.)

As a result, you must create a second application that allows supervisors to review the pending changes entered by employees using the first application. This auditing application will display both the original and proposed values for the modified rows in your *DataSet*.

In Chapter 6, you learned that you could use the *DataRow* object's *Item* method to examine either the original or the current version of the data in a particular column of that row. The *DataRow* object's *GetChildRows*, *GetParentRow*, and *GetParentRows* methods also let you supply a value from the *DataRowVersion* enumeration to indicate which version of the data you want to access.

So, if you want to loop through the customers and display the original values for each order that the customer has placed, you can use code that looks something like this:

Visual Basic .NET

```
'Loop through the customers.
Dim rowCustomer, rowOrder As DataRow
For Each rowCustomer In ds.Tables("Customers").Rows
    Console.WriteLine(rowCustomer("CustomerID") & " - " & _
                      rowCustomer("CompanyName"))
```

```
'Display the original state of the related child orders.
For Each rowOrder In rowCustomer.GetChildRows("RelationName", _
                                        DataRowVersion.Original)
    Console.WriteLine(vbTab & rowOrder("OrderID") & " - " & _
                        rowOrder("OrderDate"))
    Next rowOrder
Next rowCustomer
```

Visual C# .NET

```csharp
//Loop through the customers.
foreach (DataRow rowCustomer in ds.Tables["Customers"].Rows)
{
    Console.WriteLine(rowCustomer["CustomerID"] + " - " +
                    rowCustomer["CompanyName"]);
    //Display the original state of the related child orders.
    foreach (DataRow rowOrder in rowCustomer.GetChildRows("RelationName",
                                        DataRowVersion.Original))
        Console.WriteLine("\t" + rowOrder["OrderID"] + " - " +
                        rowOrder["OrderDate"]);
}
```

> **Note**   If you use the methods that do not take a value from *DataRow-Version*, you'll view the current version of the data.

Using *DataRelation* Objects to Validate Your Data

Now that you've learned how to use *DataRelation* objects to navigate through data from related *DataTable* objects, let's look at one of the other major functions of the *DataRelation* object—validating data.

When you define a relationship between two *DataTable* objects, you generally want to make sure that you don't allow "orphaned" data in the child *DataTable*—that is, you want to prevent users from entering a row into the Orders table that does not correspond to a row in the Customers table. You can use a *DataRelation* object to enforce constraints on the related *DataTable* objects.

Creating Constraints

By default, when you create a *DataRelation*, you ensure that there is a unique constraint on the parent *DataTable* and a foreign key constraint on the child *DataTable*. The following code snippet creates a unique constraint on the CustomerID column in the Customers *DataTable* and a foreign key constraint on the CustomerID column in the Orders *DataTable*.

Visual Basic .NET

```
Dim strConn, strSQL As String
strConn = "Provider=SQLOLEDB;Data Source=(local)\NetSDK;" & _
          "Initial Catalog=Northwind;Trusted_Connection=Yes;"
Dim cn As New OleDbConnection(strConn)
cn.Open()
strSQL = "SELECT CustomerID, CompanyName, ContactName FROM Customers"
Dim daCustomers As New OleDbDataAdapter(strSQL, cn)
strSQL = "SELECT OrderID, CustomerID, EmployeeID, OrderDate FROM Orders"
Dim daOrders As New OleDbDataAdapter(strSQL, cn)

Dim ds As New DataSet()
daCustomers.Fill(ds, "Customers")
daOrders.Fill(ds, "Orders")
cn.Close()

ds.Relationships.Add("CustomersOrders", _
                    ds.Tables("Customers").Columns("CustomerID"), _
                    ds.Tables("Orders").Columns("CustomerID"))

Console.WriteLine("The parent DataTable now contains " & _
                    ds.Tables("Customers").Constraints.Count & _
                    " constraints")
Console.WriteLine("The child DataTable now contains " & _
                    ds.Tables("Orders").Constraints.Count & _
                    " constraints")
```

Visual C# .NET

```
string strConn, strSQL;
strConn = "Provider=SQLOLEDB;Data Source=(local)\\NetSDK;" +
          "Initial Catalog=Northwind;Trusted_Connection=Yes;";
OleDbConnection cn = new OleDbConnection(strConn);
cn.Open();
strSQL = "SELECT CustomerID, CompanyName, ContactName FROM Customers";
OleDbDataAdapter daCustomers = new OleDbDataAdapter(strSQL, cn);
strSQL = "SELECT OrderID, CustomerID, EmployeeID, OrderDate FROM Orders";
OleDbDataAdapter daOrders = new OleDbDataAdapter(strSQL, cn);

DataSet ds = new DataSet();
daCustomers.Fill(ds, "Customers");
daOrders.Fill(ds, "Orders");
cn.Close();

ds.Relationships.Add("CustomersOrders",
                    ds.Tables["Customers"].Columns["CustomerID"],
                    ds.Tables["Orders"].Columns["CustomerID"]);
```

```
Console.WriteLine("The parent DataTable now contains " +
                ds.Tables["Customers"].Constraints.Count +
                " constraints");
Console.WriteLine("The child DataTable now contains " +
                ds.Tables["Orders"].Constraints.Count +
                " constraints");
```

Using Existing Constraints

We can also define our constraints ahead of time; the new *DataRelation* will use the existing constraints rather than create new ones, as shown in the following code:

Visual Basic .NET

```
⋮
Dim ds As New DataSet()
daCustomers.Fill(ds, "Customers")
daOrders.Fill(ds, "Orders")
cn.Close()

With ds.Tables("Customers")
    .PrimaryKey = New DataColumn() {.Columns("CustomerID")}
End With
With ds.Tables("Orders")
    .Constraints.Add("FK_CustomersOrders", _
                ds.Tables("Customers").Columns("CustomerID"), _
                .Columns("CustomerID"))
End With

ds.Relationships.Add("CustomersOrders", _
                ds.Tables("Customers").Columns("CustomerID"), _
                ds.Tables("Orders").Columns("CustomerID"))

Console.WriteLine("The parent DataTable now contains " & _
                ds.Tables("Customers").Constraints.Count & _
                " constraints")
Console.WriteLine("The child DataTable now contains " & _
                ds.Tables("Orders").Constraints.Count & _
                " constraints")
```

Visual C# .NET

```
⋮
DataSet ds = new DataSet();
daCustomers.Fill(ds, "Customers");
daOrders.Fill(ds, "Orders");
cn.Close();
```

(continued)

```
DataTable tbl = ds.Tables["Customers"];
tbl.PrimaryKey = new DataColumn[] {tbl.Columns["CustomerID"]};

tbl = ds.Tables["Orders"];
tbl.Constraints.Add("FK_CustomersOrders",
                ds.Tables["Customers"].Columns["CustomerID"],
                tbl.Columns["CustomerID"]);

ds.Relationships.Add("CustomersOrders",
                ds.Tables["Customers"].Columns["CustomerID"],
                ds.Tables["Orders"].Columns["CustomerID"]);

Console.WriteLine("The parent DataTable now contains " +
                ds.Tables["Customers"].Constraints.Count +
                " constraints");
Console.WriteLine("The child DataTable now contains " +
                ds.Tables["Orders"].Constraints.Count +
                " constraints");
```

Foreign Key Constraints and Null Values

You might be surprised by what you learn in the course of writing a book. For example, I had no idea that even with a foreign key constraint defined, you can have "orphaned" data both in your database and in your *DataSet*.

You don't believe me? You can run the following query against your favorite Northwind database. (Don't run queries like this against your production database while you're building applications or learning about ADO.NET.)

```
UPDATE Orders SET CustomerID = NULL WHERE CustomerID = 'ALFKI'
```

The query will succeed, and you'll have orders in your Orders table that don't belong to a customer in the Customers table. To set the rows back to the appropriate customer, run the following query:

```
UPDATE Orders SET CustomerID = 'ALFKI' WHERE CustomerID IS NULL
```

To prove that there is a foreign key constraint on the Orders table, run the following query, which will fail if your Customers table has no row with a CustomerID of ZZZZZ:

```
UPDATE Orders SET CustomerID = 'ZZZZZ' WHERE CustomerID = 'ANTON'
```

Rows that contain *Null* values in at least one of the columns defined in the foreign key constraint are exempt from the constraint. Keep this in mind when you define the schema for your database and *DataSet*.

Look, Ma! No Constraints!

You've learned that when you create a *DataRelation*, ADO.NET will by default ensure that your *DataSet* contains a *UniqueConstraint* and a *ForeignKeyConstraint* whose signatures match that of your new *DataRelation*. If such constraints already exist within the *DataSet*, the new *DataRelation* will reference them. Otherwise, ADO.NET will create the new constraints implicitly.

However, there's another option. Earlier, when we discussed the *DataRelation* class's constructors, I mentioned that there are constructors that let you specify that you do not want ADO.NET to create constraints for your *DataRelation*. You can use these constructors when you want to use a *DataRelation* but do not want the corresponding constraints in your *DataSet*.

Self-Referencing *DataRelationship* Objects

Sometimes the parent and child tables in a relationship are one and the same. Take the Employees table in the Northwind database. This table has an EmployeeID column that contains the employee's ID and a ReportsTo column that contains the ID of the employee's manager. The Employees table also has a foreign key constraint defined on the ReportsTo column to ensure that it accepts values from only the EmployeeID column.

The following sample code retrieves data from the Employees table into a *DataSet* and creates a self-referencing *DataRelation*:

Visual Basic .NET

```
Dim strConn, strSQL As String
strConn = "Provider=SQLOLEDB;Data Source=(local)\NetSDK;" & _
          "Initial Catalog=Northwind;Trusted_Connection=Yes;"
strSQL = "SELECT EmployeeID, ReportsTo, " & _
         "LastName + ', ' + FirstName AS EmployeeName FROM Employees"
Dim da As New OleDbDataAdapter(strSQL, strConn)
Dim ds As New DataSet()
da.Fill(ds, "Employees")
Dim tbl As DataTable = ds.Tables("Employees")
ds.Relations.Add("SelfReferencing", tbl.Columns("EmployeeID"), _
                 tblColumns("ReportsTo"), False)
```

Visual C# .NET

```
string strConn, strSQL;
strConn = "Provider=SQLOLEDB;Data Source=(local)\\NetSDK;" +
          "Initial Catalog=Northwind;Trusted_Connection=Yes;";
strSQL = "SELECT EmployeeID, ReportsTo, " +
         "LastName + ', ' + FirstName AS EmployeeName FROM Employees";
OleDbDataAdapter da = new OleDbDataAdapter(strSQL, strConn);
DataSet ds = new DataSet();
```

(continued)

```
da.Fill(ds, "Employees");
DataTable tbl = ds.Tables["Employees"];
ds.Relations.Add("SelfReferencing", tbl.Columns["EmployeeID"],
             tbl.Columns["ReportsTo"], false);
```

Creating the *DataRelation* is only half the battle. The actual goal is to display all employees as a tree, as shown in Figure 7-4. Traversing the hierarchy to display the employees according to their manager is a bit of a challenge, especially if you've never written recursive code. If that's the case, you'd be best served by searching the documentation for your language of choice for information on recursion because that topic is beyond the scope of this book.

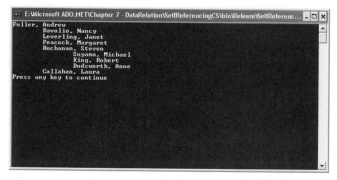

Figure 7-4   Displaying the contents of the Employees table using a self-referencing *DataRelation*

The code snippet that follows loops through the contents of the *DataTable* to locate and display the highest-level employee. In the Employees table, this is the row whose ReportsTo column is set to *Null*. For more information on *Null* values and foreign key constraints, see the sidebar "Foreign Key Constraints and Null Values" earlier in the chapter.

After locating the highest-ranking employee, the code displays that employee's direct reports, printing a tab character before each employee's name. After displaying an employee's name, it displays that employee's direct reports. The process continues until there are no more direct reports to display.

Enough explaining—bring on the code!

Visual Basic .NET

```
Dim row As DataRow
For Each row In tbl.Rows
    If row.IsNull("ReportsTo") Then
        DisplayRow(row, "")
    End If
Next row


Public Sub DisplayRow(DataRow row, string strIndent)
```

```
        Console.WriteLine(strIndent & row("EmployeeName"))
        Dim rowChild As DataRow
        For Each rowChild in row.GetChildRows("SelfReferencing")
            DisplayRow(rowChild, strIndent & vbTab)
        Next rowChild
    End Sub
```

Visual C# .NET

```
foreach (DataRow row in tbl.Rows)
    if (row.IsNull("ReportsTo"))
        DisplayRow(row, "");

static void DisplayRow(DataRow row, string strIndent)
{
    Console.WriteLine(strIndent + row["EmployeeName"]);
    foreach (DataRow rowChild in row.GetChildRows("SelfReferencing"))
        DisplayRow(rowChild, strIndent + "\t");
}
```

> **Note**   The highest-ranking employee in the Employees table has a value of *Null* in the ReportsTo column. Another option is to have the employee report to himself or herself. You would need to change the sample code slightly if you're working with a table that handles self-referencing relationships in that fashion.

Many-to-Many Relationships

Most database relationships are one-to-many. A customer can have multiple orders. An order can have multiple order details. An employee can have multiple direct reports. Many-to-many relationships exist, but they're a little more difficult to define in a database. To understand why, let's take a look at the authors and titles tables in the SQL Server pubs database.

The relationship between the data in these two tables can be considered many-to-many because an author might have written multiple titles and a title might have multiple authors. However, these two tables are not directly related through a foreign key constraint because a foreign key constraint requires a unique key. That prevents a child row from having multiple parent rows in the related table, which means we don't have a direct many-to-many relationship.

The pubs database includes another table called titleauthor (shown in Figure 7-5) that helps create an indirect many-to-many relationship. The titleauthor table has a compound primary key made up of the au_id and title_id columns—the primary key columns of the authors and titles tables, respectively.

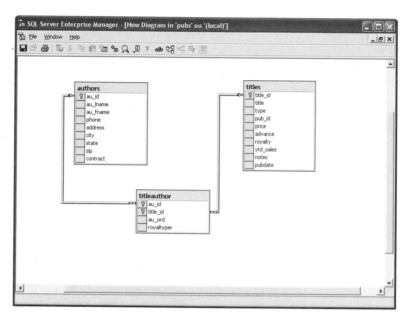

Figure 7-5   The authors, titles, and titleauthor tables in the SQL Server pubs database

Let's say that a title has two coauthors. The titleauthors table will contain two rows for that title, one for each author. So, you can use the titleauthors table to find the primary key values for all the coauthors of a particular title. Similarly, you can also use the table to locate the primary key values for all titles that an author has written or coauthored.

The following code retrieves data from all three tables. It adds *DataRelation* objects between the authors and titleauthor tables and the titles and titleauthor tables. It then loops through the rows in the authors *DataTable*, displaying each author and then using the two *DataRelation* objects to display each author's titles.

Visual Basic .NET

```
Dim strConn, strSQL as string
strConn = "Provider=SQLOLEDB;Data Source=(local)\NetSDK;" & _
          "Initial Catalog=Northwind;Trusted_Connection=Yes;"
Dim cn As New OleDbConnection(strConn)
cn.Open()
```

```
Dim daAuthors, daTitles, daTitleAuthor As OleDbDataAdapter
strSQL = "SELECT au_id, au_lname, au_fname FROM authors"
daAuthors = New OleDbDataAdapter(strSQL, cn)
strSQL = "SELECT title_id, title FROM titles"
daTitles  = New OleDbDataAdapter(strSQL, cn)
strSQL = "SELECT au_id, title_id FROM titleauthor"
daTitleAuthor = New OleDbDataAdapter(strSQL, cn)
Dim ds As New DataSet()
daAuthors.Fill(ds, "authors")
daTitles.Fill(ds, "titles")
daTitleAuthor.Fill(ds, "titleauthor")
cn.Close()

ds.Relations.Add("authors_titleauthor", _
                 ds.Tables("authors").Columns("au_id"), _
                 ds.Tables("titleauthor").Columns("au_id"), _
                 False)

ds.Relations.Add("titles_titleauthor", _
                 ds.Tables("titles").Columns("title_id"), _
                 ds.Tables("titleauthor").Columns("title_id"), _
                 False)

Dim rowAuthor, rowTitle, rowTitleAuthor As DataRow

For Each rowAuthor In ds.Tables("authors").Rows
    Console.WriteLine(rowAuthor("au_lname") & ", " & rowAuthor("au_fname"))
    For Each rowTitleAuthor In _
            rowAuthor.GetChildRows("authors_titleauthor")
        rowTitle = rowTitleAuthor.GetParentRow("titles_titleauthor")
        Console.WriteLine(vbTab & rowTitle("title"))
    Next rowTitleAuthor
Next rowAuthor
```

Visual C# .NET

```
string strConn, strSQL;
strConn = "Provider=SQLOLEDB;Data Source=(local)\\NetSDK;" +
          "Initial Catalog=Northwind;Trusted_Connection=Yes;";
OleDbConnection cn = new OleDbConnection(strConn);
cn.Open();
OleDbDataAdapter dsAuthors, dsTitles, dsTitleAuthor;
strSQL = "SELECT au_id, au_lname, au_fname FROM authors";
daAuthors = new OleDbDataAdapter(strSQL, cn)
strSQL = "SELECT title_id, title FROM titles";
daTitles  = new OleDbDataAdapter(strSQL, cn);
strSQL = "SELECT au_id, title_id FROM titleauthor";
daTitleAuthor = new OleDbDataAdapter(strSQL, cn);
```

(continued)

```
DataSet ds = new DataSet();
daAuthors.Fill(ds, "authors");
daTitles.Fill(ds, "titles");
daTitleAuthor.Fill(ds, "titleauthor");
cn.Close();

ds.Relations.Add("authors_titleauthor",
                ds.Tables["authors"].Columns["au_id"],
                ds.Tables["titleauthor"].Columns["au_id"],
                false);

ds.Relations.Add("titles_titleauthor",
                ds.Tables["titles"].Columns["title_id"],
                ds.Tables["titleauthor"].Columns["title_id"],
                false);

foreach (DataRow rowAuthor in ds.Tables["authors"].Rows)
{
    Console.WriteLine(rowAuthor["au_lname"] + ", " +
                    rowAuthor["au_fname"]);
    foreach (DataRow rowTitleAuthor in
                    rowAuthor.GetChildRows("authors_titleauthor"))
    {
        DataRow rowTitle;
        rowTitle = rowTitleAuthor.GetParentRow("titles_titleauthor");
        Console.WriteLine("\t" + rowTitle["title"]);
    }
}
```

Using *DataRelation* Objects in Expression-Based *DataColumn* Objects

In Chapter 6, you learned how to use the *DataColumn* object's *Expression* property to create *DataColumn* objects that display the results of equations such as *Quantity * UnitPrice*. You can also use expression-based *DataColumn* objects in conjunction with *DataRelation* objects to calculate aggregate information such as the number of child rows and the sums and averages of child data.

The following code snippet includes two examples of using a *DataRelation* in a *DataColumn* object's *Expression* property. The code first creates a *DataRelation* between the Orders and Order Details *DataTable* objects, and then it adds the calculated ItemTotal *DataColumn* to the Order Details *DataTable*, as described earlier. Finally the code adds two expression-based *DataColumn* objects that rely on the new *DataRelation*.

The first of these two *DataColumn* objects returns the number of child rows. In order to gather this information, the code sets the *Expression* property of the *DataColumn* to the following:

```
Count(Child.ProductID)
```

You can use this syntax to refer to child data if the *DataTable* has only one related child *DataTable*. If you have multiple related child *DataTable* objects, you can use the following syntax:

```
Count(Child(RelationName).ProductID)
```

The final expression-based *DataColumn* that the code creates returns the sum of the ItemTotal *DataColumn* in the child *DataTable*. The value of this *DataColumn* object's *Expression* property is similar to the previous *DataColumn*:

```
Sum(Child.ItemTotal)
```

Visual Basic .NET

```vbnet
Dim ds As New DataSet()
    ⋮
ds.Relations.Add("OrdersOrderDetails", _
                ds.Tables("Orders").Columns("OrderID"), _
                ds.Tables("Order Details").Columns("OrderID"))

ds.Tables("Order Details").Columns.Add("ItemTotal", GetType(Decimal), _
                                "Quantity * UnitPrice")
ds.Tables("Orders").Columns.Add("NumItems", GetType(Integer), _
                        "Count(Child.ProductID)")
ds.Tables("Orders").Columns.Add("OrderTotal", GetType(Decimal), _
                        "Sum(Child.ItemTotal)")
```

Visual C# .NET

```csharp
DataSet ds = new DataSet();
    ⋮
ds.Relations.Add("OrdersOrderDetails",
                ds.Tables["Orders"].Columns["OrderID"],
                ds.Tables["Order Details"].Columns["OrderID"]);

ds.Tables["Order Details"].Columns.Add("ItemTotal", typeof(Decimal),
                                "Quantity * UnitPrice");
ds.Tables["Orders"].Columns.Add("NumItems", typeof(int),
                        "Count(Child.ProductID)");
ds.Tables["Orders"].Columns.Add("OrderTotal", typeof(Decimal),
                        "Sum(Child.ItemTotal)");
```

You can also use expression-based *DataColumn* objects to gather information from the parent *DataTable* in a relationship. Earlier in the chapter, we looked at a many-to-many relationship between author and title information in the pubs database. The goal of the code snippet was to list the titles that each author wrote or cowrote.

We can simplify that code slightly by adding an expression-based *Data-Column* to the titleauthor *DataTable* that uses the *DataRelation* to the titles *DataTable* to return the value of the title *DataColumn*. By adding this column to the titleauthor *DataTable*, we no longer need to use the *GetParentRow* method to locate the desired row in the titles *DataTable*.

Visual Basic .NET

```
Dim ds As New DataSet()
  ⋮

ds.Relations.Add("authors_titleauthor", _
                 ds.Tables("authors").Columns("au_id"), _
                 ds.Tables("titleauthor").Columns("au_id"), _
                 False)

ds.Relations.Add("titles_titleauthor", _
                 ds.Tables("titles").Columns("title_id"), _
                 ds.Tables("titleauthor").Columns("title_id"), _
                 False)

ds.Tables("titleauthor").Columns.Add("title", GetType(String), _
                              "Parent(titles_titleauthor).title")
Dim rowAuthor, rowTitleAuthor As DataRow

For Each rowAuthor In ds.Tables("authors").Rows
    Console.WriteLine(rowAuthor("au_lname") & ", " & rowAuthor("au_fname"))
    For Each rowTitleAuthor In _
            rowAuthor.GetChildRows("authors_titleauthor")
        Console.WriteLine(vbTab & rowTitleAuthor("title"))
    Next rowTitleAuthor
Next rowAuthor
```

Visual C# .NET

```
DataSet ds = new DataSet();
  ⋮

ds.Relations.Add("authors_titleauthor",
                 ds.Tables["authors"].Columns["au_id"],
                 ds.Tables["titleauthor"].Columns["au_id"],
                 false);
```

```
ds.Relations.Add("titles_titleauthor",
                ds.Tables["titles"].Columns["title_id"],
                ds.Tables["titleauthor"].Columns["title_id"],
                false);

ds.Tables["titleauthor"].Columns.Add("title", typeof(string),
                                "Parent(titles_titleauthor).title");

foreach (DataRow rowAuthor in ds.Tables["authors"].Rows)
{
    Console.WriteLine(rowAuthor["au_lname"] + ", " +
                    rowAuthor["au_fname"]);
    foreach (DataRow rowTitleAuthor in
                rowAuthor.GetChildRows("authors_titleauthor"))
        Console.WriteLine("\t" + rowTitleAuthor["title"]);
}
```

For an exhaustive list of available aggregate functions in the *Expression* property, see the MSDN documentation.

Cascading Changes

Sometimes the changes you make to one row have, or should have, repercussions on related data. For example, when you delete an order, you probably want to delete the line items associated with the order as well.

Different database systems allow you to handle this situation in various ways. The Order Details table in the SQL Server Northwind database uses a foreign key constraint to prevent users from deleting rows from the Orders table if there are related rows in the Order Details table. SQL Server 2000 introduced support for cascading changes using a foreign key constraint. You can define your foreign key constraints so that when a user updates or deletes a row, the changes automatically cascade to the rows in the related table. Figure 7-6 shows the SQL Server 2000 user interface for setting these properties on a foreign key constraint.

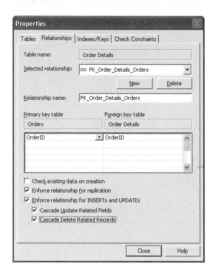

Figure 7-6   Setting a foreign key constraint's cascading update
attributes in SQL Server 2000

The ADO.NET *ForeignKeyConstraint* object has similar features. It
exposes *DeleteRule* and *UpdateRule* properties that you can set to control what
happens when you modify rows of data in the parent table in a foreign key
constraint.

The *ForeignKeyConstraint* Object's *DeleteRule* and *UpdateRule* Properties

The *DeleteRule* and *UpdateRule* properties accept values from the *Rule* enumeration in the *System.Data* namespace. By default, both properties are set to *Cascade*. This means that when you delete a row in a *DataTable*, the child rows in
the related *DataTable* will be deleted as well. If you change the value of the
column in the parent *DataTable* on which the foreign key constraint is
defined—for example, if you change the value of the CustomerID column in
the Customers *DataTable*—the value of that column will also be updated in the
related rows in the child *DataTable*.

You can also set either property to *None*, *SetDefault*, or *SetNull*. Setting the
DeleteRule property to *None* will prevent the deletion from affecting data in the
child *DataTable*. If you want a change to a parent row to set the constraint's
columns in the child table to *Null*, set the *DeleteRule* property and/or the
UpdateRule property to *SetNull*. Similarly, setting the properties to *SetDefault*
will reset the constraint's columns in the child table to the value set in the
Default property.

Moving Away from Join Queries

Many developers have relied on join queries to retrieve data from multiple tables. You can use a *DataTable* to store the results of a query that returns data from multiple tables, but I generally wouldn't recommend it. As you'll see in Chapter 10, the *DataAdapter* object is designed to examine the changes stored in a single *DataTable* and submit them to a specific table in your database. Thus, if you want to modify the contents of your *DataTable* objects, you'll want to separate the data into distinct *DataTable* objects that parallel the tables in your database.

So, what to do with join queries?

The simple answer is to split them up into queries that return data from distinct tables. However, this is often easier said than done. In the snippets of sample code, we've used very simple queries that return all rows from the table in the query. Things get more complex when you're working with a query that uses a filter such as this:

```
SELECT CustomerID, CompanyName, ContactName, Phone
    FROM Customers WHERE Country = 'Canada'
```

If you want to retrieve data from the related Orders table, you'll want to retrieve only the orders that correspond to the customers returned by this query. Because the Orders table does not contain a Country column, you have to use a query that references the Customers table, such as this:

```
SELECT O.OrderID, O.CustomerID, O.EmployeeID, O.OrderDate
    FROM Customers C, Orders O
    WHERE C.CustomerID = O.OrderID AND C.Country = 'Canada'
```

Creating *DataRelation* Objects in Visual Studio .NET

Now that you understand the major features of the *DataRelation* object, let's see how to create *DataRelation* objects in Visual Studio .NET.

Adding a *DataRelation* to a Strongly Typed *DataSet*

After reading Chapter 6, you already know how to create a strongly typed *DataSet* in Visual Studio .NET. You double-click on the DataSet project item (*.xsd) in the Solution Explorer window to view the structure of your *DataSet* in the XML Schema Designer.

Right-click on the *DataTable* you want to use as the parent in the relationship, and choose Add, New Relation from the shortcut menu, as shown in Figure 7-7. You can also access this command from the Schema item on the Visual

Studio .NET menu. You'll see a dialog box that you can use to add your new *DataRelation*, as shown in Figure 7-8.

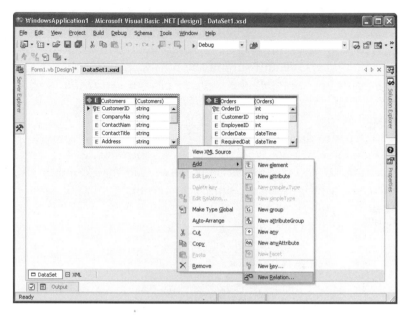

Figure 7-7   Invoking the Edit Relation dialog box

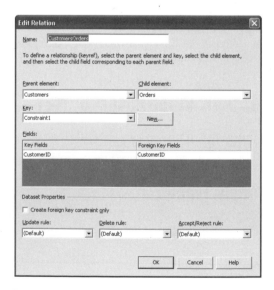

Figure 7-8   Adding a new *DataRelation* in the Edit Relation dialog box

The Edit Relation dialog box lets you specify the parent and child *Data-Table* and *DataColumn* objects for the new *DataRelation*. You can also specify values for the *UpdateRule*, *DeleteRule*, and *AcceptRejectRule* properties of the *ForeignKeyConstraint* that will be associated with the new *DataRelation*. If you want to create a *ForeignKeyConstraint* but not a *DataRelation*, you can select the Create Foreign Key Constraint Only check box.

Click OK, and you'll see a graphical representation of the new *DataRelation* in the XML Schema Designer—a link between the two *DataTable* objects, as shown in Figure 7-9.

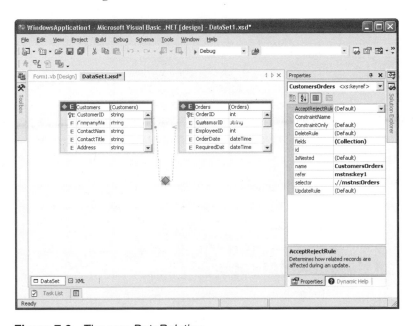

Figure 7-9   The new *DataRelation*

Adding a *DataRelation* to an Untyped *DataSet*

You can also add *DataRelation* objects to untyped *DataSet* objects. In the previous chapter, you learned how to add an untyped *DataSet* to a designer, such as a Windows form, and then add *DataTable* objects and *DataColumn* objects to that new *DataSet*. Adding a new *DataRelation* is just as easy.

Select the *DataSet* in the designer's components tray, and then select the Relations property in the Properties window. You'll see a button to the right of the property that you can click to launch the Relations Collection Editor, as shown in Figure 7-10.

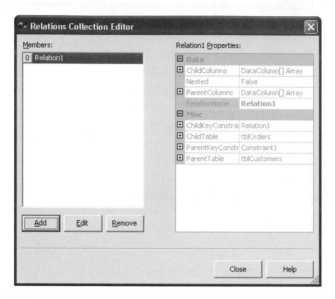

Figure 7-10   Adding a *DataRelation* to an untyped *DataSet* in the Relations Collection Editor

The Relations Collection Editor lets you add, edit, and remove *DataRelation* objects. If you choose to add a new *DataRelation* or edit an existing *DataRelation*, you'll see the Edit Relation dialog box shown earlier in Figure 7-8.

DataRelation Object Reference

The reference information for the *DataRelation* object isn't terribly interesting, to be honest. The object exposes no methods and no events—only properties. However, to leave these out would somehow feel like cheating.

Properties of the *DataRelation* Object

Most of the *DataRelation* object's properties are read-only. You can set their value only using the *DataRelation* object's constructors. The commonly used properties are described in Table 7-1.

Table 7-1   Commonly Used Properties of the *DataRelation* Object

Property	Data Type	Description
ChildColumns	Array of *DataColumn* objects	Indicates the child columns that define the relation. This property is read-only.
ChildKeyConstraint	*ForeignKeyConstraint*	Indicates the foreign key constraint in the child table in the relation. This property is read-only.
ChildTable	*DataTable*	Indicates the child table in the relation. This property is read-only.
DataSet	*DataSet*	Indicates the *DataSet* in which the *DataRelation* resides. This property is read-only.
ExtendedProperties	*PropertyCollection*	Indicates a collection of dynamic properties.
Nested	*Boolean*	Indicates whether the child rows are child elements when the *DataSet* is stored as XML.
ParentColumns	Array of *DataColumn* objects	Indicates the parent columns that define the relation. This property is read-only.
ParentKey-Constraint	*UniqueConstraint*	Indicates the unique constraint in the parent table in the relation. This property is read-only.
ParentTable	*DataTable*	Indicates the parent table in the relation. This property is read-only.
RelationName	*String*	Indicates the name of the relation.

ChildColumns Property

The *ChildColumns* property returns an array that contains the *DataColumn* object or objects from the child *DataTable* in the *DataRelation*. This property is read-only.

ChildKeyConstraint Property

The *ChildKeyConstraint* property returns the *ForeignKeyConstraint* referenced by the *DataRelation*. If you created a *DataRelation* that does not use constraints, this property returns *Nothing* or *null*, depending on your language of choice. The *ChildKeyConstraint* property is read-only.

ChildTable Property

The *ChildTable* property returns the child *DataTable* in the *DataRelation*. This property is read-only.

DataSet Property

The *DataSet* property returns the *DataSet* in which the *DataRelation* resides. This property is read-only.

ExtendedProperties Property

Like the *DataSet*, *DataTable*, and *DataColumn* objects, the *DataRelation* object also exposes an *ExtendedProperties* property in which you can store additional information.

Nested Property

The *Nested* property controls the location of the contents of the child *DataTable* when the *DataSet* is stored in XML format using the *DataSet* object's *WriteXml* method. This is one of the few read-write properties of the *DataRelation* object.

If the *Nested* property is set to *False*, which is the default, the data in the child *DataTable* will be separate from the data in the parent *DataTable*. As you can see here, without looking at the schema information for the *DataSet*, you wouldn't know that there is a *DataRelation* between the *DataTable* objects:

Not Nested

```
<Customers>
    <CustomerID>ALFKI</CustomerID>
    <CompanyName>Alfreds Futterkiste</CompanyName>
</Customers>
<Customers>
    <CustomerID>ANATR</CustomerID>
    <CompanyName>Ana Trujillo Emparedados y helados</CompanyName>
</Customers>
...
<Orders>
    <OrderID>10308</OrderID>
    <CustomerID>ANATR</CustomerID>
</Orders>
<Orders>
    <OrderID>10355</OrderID>
    <CustomerID>AROUT</CustomerID>
</Orders>
...
```

Setting the *Nested* property to *True* causes ADO.NET to embed the data in the child *DataTable* within the data for the parent *DataTable*, as shown here:

Nested

```
<Customers>
    <CustomerID>ALFKI</CustomerID>
    <CompanyName>Alfreds Futterkiste</CompanyName>
```

```
    <Orders>
        <OrderID>10643</OrderID>
        <CustomerID>ALFKI</CustomerID>
    </Orders>
    <Orders>
        <OrderID>10692</OrderID>
        <CustomerID>ALFKI</CustomerID>
    </Orders>
    ...
</Customers>
<Customers>
    <CustomerID>ANATR</CustomerID>
    <CompanyName>Ana Trujillo Emparedados y helados</CompanyName>
    <Orders>
        <OrderID>10308</OrderID>
        <CustomerID>ANATR</CustomerID>
    </Orders>
    <Orders>
        <OrderID>10625</OrderID>
        <CustomerID>ANATR</CustomerID>
    </Orders>
    ...
</Customers>
...
```

ParentColumns Property

The *ParentColumns* property returns an array that contains the *DataColumn* objects from the parent *DataTable* in the *DataRelation*. This property is read-only.

ParentKeyConstraint Property

The *ParentKeyConstraint* property returns the *UniqueConstraint* referenced by the *DataRelation*. If you created a *DataRelation* that does not use constraints, this property returns *Nothing* or *null*, depending on your language of choice. The *ParentKeyConstraint* property is read-only.

ParentTable Property

The *ParentTable* property returns the parent *DataTable* in the *DataRelation*. This property is read-only.

RelationName Property

The *RelationName* property is read-write and can be used to set or retrieve the name of the *DataRelation*.

Questions That Should Be Asked More Frequently

Q.   When should I create my *DataRelation* objects without constraints?

A.   Let's say your application queries your database for customer and order data and displays that information on a simple Windows form. The application allows the user to view the data but not modify it.

   In such an application, a *DataRelation* is useful because it lets you easily display the orders for a particular customer. However, you probably don't want to use constraints within your *DataSet*. Why? Constraints are used to validate your data, and validating data takes time. If the data in the application is read-only and the database has already validated the data through its own set of constraints, there's no need for ADO.NET to revalidate the data.

Q.   I want to work with data from multiple tables, but I'm not going to retrieve all rows from the parent table. The queries you showed that retrieve only the related child rows look complex and inefficient. Wouldn't a single join-based query that returned data from all tables at once be faster?

A.   During the Microsoft .NET Framework beta, a thread in one of the newsgroups focused on this issue. A couple of developers felt that fetching the data from separate queries was inefficient. Their premise made sense and piqued my curiosity, so I set out to see how working with separate queries would affect performance. I built applications in Visual Basic .NET using ADO.NET and Visual Basic 6 using ADO 2.6 to query the SQL Server Northwind database for customer, order, and order detail information for all customers in the United States. I wrote various routines for each application that used a specific type of query to retrieve this information from the database.

   The routine that tested the join query simply retrieved the data into a single *DataTable* that had no validation. The queries I used were as follows:

Join-Based Query

```
SELECT C.CustomerID, C.CompanyName, C.ContactName, C.Phone,
       O.OrderID, O.EmployeeID, O.OrderDate,
       D.ProductID, D.Quantity, D.UnitPrice
    FROM [Order Details] D, Orders O, Customers C
    WHERE D.OrderID = O.OrderID AND O.CustomerID = C.CustomerID
       AND C.Country = N'USA'
```

Separate Queries

```
SELECT CustomerID, CompanyName, ContactName, Phone
       FROM Customers WHERE C.Country = N'USA'

SELECT O.OrderID, O.CustomerID, O.EmployeeID, O.OrderDate
       FROM Orders O, Customers C
       WHERE O.CustomerID = C.CustomerID AND C.Country = N'USA'

SELECT D.OrderID, D.ProductID, D.Quantity, D.UnitPrice
       FROM [Order Details] D, Orders O, Customers C
       WHERE D.OrderID = O.OrderID AND O.CustomerID = C.CustomerID
             AND C.Country = N'USA'
```

Parameterized Queries

```
SELECT CustomerID, CompanyName, ContactName, Phone
       FROM Customers WHERE C.Country = N'USA'

SELECT OrderID, CustomerID, EmployeeID, OrderDate
       FROM Orders WHERE CustomerID = ?

SELECT OrderID, ProductID, Quantity, UnitPrice
       FROM [Order Details] WHERE OrderID = ?
```

Like the others in the newsgroup, I had expected the join-based query and the parameterized queries to be faster than the separate queries. Thankfully, I ran the tests before sharing my opinion on what method of retrieving the data would be fastest. It turned out that retrieving the data using separate queries was fastest. The separate queries were on average 20 percent faster than the join-based query and between six and eight times faster than the parameterized queries.

Why? Well, optimizing queries is not my strong suit, but I believe I can explain the behavior. Retrieving data using separate queries was faster than using the single join query because the single join query returned more data. A join query returns redundant data. There might be 100 entries in the Order Details table that correspond to a single row in the Customers table, but that same customer information appears in each of those 100 rows.

I used the *DataSet* object's *WriteXml* method, which we'll discuss in Chapter 12, to store the contents of the *DataSet* to an XML file. The XML file that corresponded to the *DataSet* I filled with the results of the join-based query was nearly three times as large as the XML file that corresponded to the *DataSet* I filled using the separate queries. The join-based query might look and feel more efficient because it's simpler, but it's actually less efficient because it returns more data.

To test the parameterized queries, I executed the simple query against the Customers table and retrieved the results into a *Data-Table*. I then looped through the results of that query and executed the parameterized query against the Orders table once for each customer. Finally, I looped through each of the combined results of the queries against the Orders table and executed the parameterized query against the Order Details table once for each order. This process required executing a separate query for each customer and for each order. The structure of the parameterized queries is simple, but executing these queries over and over for each customer and order proved inefficient and the performance was lousy.

That's not a knock on parameterized queries in general. They're simply not the best solution for retrieving data from large filtered hierarchies such as the one I tested in this scenario.

Even if you're going to work with read-only data from multiple tables, you should consider breaking up your join queries into separate queries that return data from distinct tables.

> **Note** I also ran two additional routines, one that used IN subqueries and one that bundled the separate queries into a batch. The performance of the IN subqueries was comparable to the routine that used separate queries. Bundling the separate queries into a batch improved performance by about eight percent.

Q. I'm fetching data from stored procedures, but unfortunately I can't change the join queries inside the stored procedures. Is there a simple way to "split" the results into separate *DataTable* objects?

A. There iMs no such method in the ADO.NET object model—at least not yet. However, you can construct code to split the results using a *DataReader* and the *Find* method on the *DataTable* object's *Rows* collection (a feature we'll discuss in the next chapter).

The following code snippet executes a join query against the Customers and Orders tables. It then loops through the data returned in the *DataReader* and appends new rows to separate Customers and Orders *DataTable* objects.

Visual Basic .NET

```
ds.Tables("Customers").BeginLoadData()
ds.Tables("Orders").BeginLoadData()
Dim strConn, strSQL As String
strConn = "Provider=SQLOLEDB;Data Source=(local)\NetSDK;" & _
          "Initial Catalog=Northwind;Trusted_Connection=Yes;"
Dim cn As New OleDbConnection(strConn)
cn.Open()
strSQL = "SELECT C.CustomerID, C.CompanyName, C.ContactName, " & _
         "C.Phone, O.OrderID, O.EmployeeID, O.OrderDate " & _
         "FROM Customers C, Orders O " & _
         "WHERE C.CustomerID = O.CustomerID AND C.Country = 'Canada'"
Dim cmd As New OleDbCommand(strSQL, cn)
Dim rdr As OleDbDataReader = cmd.ExecuteReader
Dim objNewCustomer, objNewOrder As Object()
Do While rdr.Read
    If ds.Tables("Customers").Rows.Find(rdr.GetString(0)) Is Nothing Then
        objNewCustomer = New Object() {rdr.GetString(0), _
                                    rdr.GetString(1), _
                                    rdr.GetString(2), _
                                    rdr.GetString(3)}
        ds.Tables("Customers").LoadDataRow(objNewCustomer, True)
    End If
    objNewOrder = New Object() {rdr.GetInt32(4), _
                                rdr.GetString(0), _
                                rdr.GetInt32(5), _
                                rdr.GetDateTime(6)}
    ds.Tables("Orders").LoadDataRow(objNewOrder, True)
Loop
rdr.Close()
cn.Close()
ds.Tables("Customers").EndLoadData()
ds.Tables("Orders").EndLoadData()
```

Visual C# .NET

```
ds.Tables["Customers"].BeginLoadData();
ds.Tables["Orders"].BeginLoadData();
string strConn, strSQL;
strConn = "Provider=SQLOLEDB;Data Source=(local)\\NetSDK;" +
          "Initial Catalog=Northwind;Trusted_Connection=Yes;";
OleDbConnection cn = new OleDbConnection(strConn);
cn.Open();
strSQL = "SELECT C.CustomerID, C.CompanyName, C.ContactName, " +
         "C.Phone, O.OrderID, O.EmployeeID, O.OrderDate " +
         "FROM Customers C, Orders O " +
         "WHERE C.CustomerID = O.CustomerID AND C.Country = 'Canada'";
```

(continued)

```
OleDbCommand cmd = new OleDbCommand(strSQL, cn);
OleDbDataReader rdr = cmd.ExecuteReader();
object[] objNewCustomer, objNewOrder;
while (rdr.Read())
{
    if (ds.Tables["Customers"].Rows.Find(rdr.GetString(0)) == null)
    {
        objNewCustomer = new object[] {rdr.GetString(0),
                                       rdr.GetString(1),
                                       rdr.GetString(2),
                                       rdr.GetString(3)};
        ds.Tables["Customers"].LoadDataRow(objNewCustomer, true);
    }
    objNewOrder = new object[] {rdr.GetInt32(4),
                                rdr.GetString(0),
                                rdr.GetInt32(5),
                                rdr.GetDateTime(6)};
    ds.Tables["Orders"].LoadDataRow(objNewOrder, true);
}
rdr.Close();
cn.Close();
ds.Tables["Customers"].EndLoadData();
ds.Tables["Orders"].EndLoadData();
```

8

Sorting, Searching, and Filtering

In Chapter 5, you learned how to use a *DataAdapter* object to fetch the results of queries into a *DataSet* object. In Chapter 6, which covered the *DataSet* object and the objects it contains, you learned how to examine the results of such queries by looping through the *DataRow* objects in a *DataTable*.

But how do you locate a specific row in your *DataTable* by a value or set of values? How do you apply a filter so that only rows that satisfy the specified criteria are visible? And how do you control the sort order for the rows you want to access or display?

This chapter will answer these questions and more as it covers the *Find* method of the *DataRowCollection* class and the *Select* method of the *DataTable* class and introduces the *DataView* and *DataRowView* objects.

Using the *DataTable* Object's Searching and Filtering Features

The *DataTable* object exposes two methods that you can use to locate data based on search criteria. One method, *Find*, lets you locate a row based on its primary key values. The other, *Select*, acts as more of a filter, returning multiple rows of data based on more flexible search criteria.

Locating a Row by Its Primary Key Values

When you're querying your database for information, you'll often want to retrieve a specific row of data based on the values of its primary key columns, using a query such as this one:

```
SELECT CustomerID, CompanyName, ContactName, Phone
    FROM Customers WHERE CustomerID = 'ALFKI'
```

You can also locate a *DataRow* in a *DataTable* based on the row's primary key values. You might have noticed that the final code snippet in Chapter 7 looped through the results of a query and had to determine whether a row of data already existed in the *DataTable*. This code used the *Find* method to perform a search of the contents of the *DataTable* based on the primary key value.

Although the *Find* method is designed for *DataTable* objects, it's actually exposed by the *DataRowCollection* class. The *Find* method accepts an object that contains the primary key value for the row you want to locate. Because primary key values are unique, the *Find* method can return at most one *DataRow*. The following code snippet attempts to locate a customer row by its primary key value and then determines whether the search located a row.

Visual Basic .NET

```
Dim strConn, strSQL As String
strConn = "Provider=SQLOLEDB;Data Source=(local)\NetSDK;" & _
          "Initial Catalog=Northwind;Trusted_Connection=Yes;"
strSQL = "SELECT CustomerID, CompanyName, ContactName, Phone " & _
         "FROM Customers"
Dim da As New OleDbDataAdapter(strSQL, strConn)
Dim tbl As New DataTable()
da.Fill(tbl)
tbl.PrimaryKey = New DataColumn() {tbl.Columns("CustomerID")}
Dim row As DataRow = tbl.Rows.Find("ALFKI")
If row Is Nothing Then
    Console.WriteLine("Row not found!")
Else
    Console.WriteLine(row("CompanyName"))
End If
```

Visual C# .NET

```
string strConn, strSQL;
strConn = "Provider=SQLOLEDB;Data Source=(local)\\NetSDK;" +
          "Initial Catalog=Northwind;Trusted_Connection=Yes;";
strSQL = "SELECT CustomerID, CompanyName, ContactName, Phone " +
         "FROM Customers";
OleDbDataAdapter da = new OleDbDataAdapter(strSQL, strConn);
DataTable tbl = new DataTable();
da.Fill(tbl);
tbl.PrimaryKey = new DataColumn[] {tbl.Columns["CustomerID"]};

DataRow row = tbl.Rows.Find("ALFKI");
if (row == null)
    Console.WriteLine("Row not found!");
else
    Console.WriteLine(row["CompanyName"]);
```

> **Note**   Technically, your *DataTable* can contain multiple rows that
> have the same primary key values. If you set the *EnforceConstraints*
> property of the *DataSet* to *False*, the *DataTable* will not throw an
> exception if you violate the primary key constraint. In such a scenario,
> the *Find* method will return the row it finds with the desired primary key
> values.

The *Find* method is overloaded for scenarios in which the primary key for
your *DataTable* consists of multiple *DataColumn* objects. For example, the primary key for the Order Details table is based on the OrderID and ProductID
columns. So, to locate a row in a *DataTable* with a similar schema, you can use
code like the following:

Visual Basic .NET

```
Dim strConn, strSQL As String
strConn = "Provider=SQLOLEDB;Data Source=(local)\NetSDK;" & _
        "Initial Catalog=Northwind;Trusted_Connection=Yes;"
strSQL = "SELECT OrderID, ProductID, Quantity, UnitPrice " & _
        "FROM [Order Details]"
Dim da As New OleDbDataAdapter(strSQL, strConn)
Dim tbl As New DataTable()
da.Fill(tbl)
tbl.PrimaryKey = New DataColumn() {tbl.Columns("OrderID"), _
                                 tbl.Columns("ProductID")}

Dim objCriteria As New Object() {10643, 28}
Dim row As DataRow = tbl.Rows.Find(objCriteria)
If row Is Nothing Then
    Console.WriteLine("Row not found!")
Else
    Console.WriteLine(row("Quantity") & " - " & row("UnitPrice"))
End If
```

Visual C# .NET

```
string strConn, strSQL;
strConn = "Provider=SQLOLEDB;Data Source=(local)\\NetSDK;" +
        "Initial Catalog=Northwind;Trusted_Connection=Yes;";
strSQL = "SELECT OrderID, ProductID, Quantity, UnitPrice " +
        "FROM [Order Details]";
OleDbDataAdapter da = new OleDbDataAdapter(strSQL, strConn);
DataTable tbl = new DataTable();
da.Fill(tbl);
```

(continued)

```
tbl.PrimaryKey = new DataColumn[] {tbl.Columns["OrderID"],
                                   tbl.Columns["ProductID"]};

object[] objCriteria = new object[] {10643, 28};
DataRow row = tbl.Rows.Find(objCriteria);
if (row == null)
    Console.WriteLine("Row not found!");
else
    Console.WriteLine(row["Quantity"] + " - " + row["UnitPrice"]);
```

Conducting More Dynamic Searches

Locating a row based on its primary key values is efficient, but not all searches are that straightforward. What if you want to locate all customers in the United States who are not in the city of Seattle? You can add such criteria to a database query using a WHERE clause, as shown here:

```
SELECT CustomerID, CompanyName, ContactName, Phone, City, Country
    FROM Customers WHERE Country = 'USA' AND City <> 'Seattle'
```

You can use the *DataTable* object's *Select* method to locate rows based on similar criteria. Let's say you retrieve the entire contents of the Customers table into a *DataTable*. You can use the same search criteria as in the WHERE clause in the previous example to locate just the customers from the United States who are not in Seattle:

Visual Basic .NET

```
Dim strConn, strSQL As String
strConn = "Provider=SQLOLEDB;Data Source=(local)\NetSDK;" & _
          "Initial Catalog=Northwind;Trusted_Connection=Yes;"
strSQL = "SELECT CustomerID, CompanyName, ContactName, " & _
         "Phone, City, Country FROM Customers"
Dim da As New OleDbDataAdapter(strSQL, strConn)
Dim tbl As New DataTable()
da.Fill(tbl)

Dim aRows As DataRow()
Dim row As DataRow
aRows = tbl.Select("Country = 'USA' AND City <> 'Seattle'")
For Each row In aRows
    Console.WriteLine(row("CompanyName") & " - " & row("City") & _
                      " - " & row("Country"))
Next row
```

Visual C# .NET

```
string strConn, strSQL;
strConn = "Provider=SQLOLEDB;Data Source=(local)\\NetSDK;" +
          "Initial Catalog=Northwind;Trusted_Connection=Yes;";
strSQL = "SELECT CustomerID, CompanyName, ContactName, " +
          "Phone, City, Country FROM Customers";
OleDbDataAdapter da = new OleDbDataAdapter(strSQL, strConn);
DataTable tbl = new DataTable();
da.Fill(tbl);

DataRow[] aRows = tbl.Select("Country = 'USA' AND City <> 'Seattle'");
foreach (DataRow row in aRows)
    Console.WriteLine(row["CompanyName"] + " - " + row["City"] +
                      " - " + row["Country"]);
```

Conducting Wildcard Searches

ADO.NET allows you to search using wildcards. The following SQL query returns all customers that have a value for the CustomerID column that begins with the letter *A*:

```
SELECT CustomerID, CompanyName, ContactName, Phone
    FROM Customers WHERE CustomerID LIKE 'A%'
```

You can use either % or * as a wildcard at the beginning or the end of the search string. For example, the following filter returns customers in New Hampshire, New Jersey, New Mexico, and New York:

```
strFilter = "State LIKE 'New %'"
```

The following filter returns customers from North and South Dakota:

```
strFilter = "State LIKE '% Dakota'"
```

ADO.NET does not let you use a single-character wildcard such as ? or _.

Working with Delimiters

You might have noticed that in both the database query example and the *DataTable.Select* example, we specified criteria for string-based columns. In each case, we surrounded the value with single quotes. This process appears simple in an example but can pose a bit of a problem for developers.

You can't simply surround a string with single quotes in your search criteria. Well, actually, you can, but you shouldn't. Say your application allows the user to locate an employee based on the employee's last name. When the application prompts the user for the last name, the user enters *O'Malley*. If you simply surround the literal value with single quotes in your search criteria, your string will look like this:

```
LastName = 'O'Malley'
```

If the delimiter appears in the literal string, however, you have to double it. In this situation, the search criteria should look like this:

```
LastName = 'O''Malley'
```

If you build search criteria dynamically, you must be sure to search your strings for delimiters. Use the *Replace* method of the *String* class to handle such situations. The following code snippet builds a string for the *Select* method and uses the *Replace* method of the *String* class to replace single quotes with two single quotes in the string:

Visual Basic .NET

```
strCriteria = "LastName = '" & strLastName.Replace("'", "''") & "'"
```

Visual C# .NET

```
strCriteria = "LastName = '" + strLastName.Replace("'", "''") + "'";
```

How do you delimit dates in search criteria? You surround the date with pound symbols, as shown here. (Thankfully, you don't have to worry about delimiters appearing in your dates.)

```
strCriteria = "OrderDate >= #01/01/2002# AND OrderDate < #02/01/2002#"
```

In some scenarios, you'll need to delimit your column names in your search criteria—perhaps because you have a space or another nonalphanumeric character in your column name or because your column name is a reserved word such as *LIKE* or *SUM*. ADO.NET uses square brackets as column delimiters. So, if your column name is *Space In Name* and you're looking for all rows that have a value of 3 in that column, you can use this string to locate those rows:

```
strCriteria = "[Space In Name] = 3"
```

What if you have a column delimiter in your column name? You can use an escape character (\) before the closing delimiter (]) in your criteria string. For example, if your column name is *Bad]Column[Name* and you're looking for all rows that have a value of 5 in that column, you can construct the following criteria string:

Visual Basic .NET

```
strCriteria = "[Bad\]Column[Name] = 5"
```

Visual C# .NET

```
strCriteria = "[Bad\\]Column[Name] = 5";
```

> **Note**   Remember that in C#, the \ character is an escape character. In the previous code snippet, the actual string assigned to the *strCriteria-Filter* variable is
>
> ```
> "[Bad\]Column[Name] = 5"
> ```

Before (finally) moving on from delimiters, let's take a look at a code snippet that handles a really horrible scenario fairly elegantly. The *DataTable* in the code snippet contains a hideously named column that accepts strings. The code performs a search against that string, successfully delimiting the column name as well as the value to locate.

Visual Basic .NET

```
Dim tbl As New DataTable()
tbl.Columns.Add("ID", GetType(Integer))
tbl.Columns.Add("Why]would[you ever\use.this#column/name?", _
                GetType(String))
tbl.LoadDataRow(New Object() {1, "Thompson"}, True)
tbl.LoadDataRow(New Object() {2, "O'Malley"}, True)

Dim strFilter, strFieldName, strValue As String
Dim row As DataRow
strFieldName = "Why]would[you ever\use.this#column/name?"
strValue = "O'Malley"
strFilter = "[" & strFieldName.Replace("]", "\]") & _
            "] = '" & strValue.Replace("'", "''") & "'"
For Each row In tbl.Select(strFilter)
    Console.WriteLine(row(strFieldName))
Next row
```

Visual C# .NET

```
DataTable tbl = new DataTable();
tbl.Columns.Add("ID", typeof(int));
tbl.Columns.Add("Why]would[you ever\\use.this#column/name?",
                typeof(string));
```

(continued)

```
tbl.LoadDataRow(new object[] {1, "Thompson"}, true);
tbl.LoadDataRow(new object[] {2, "O'Malley"}, true);

string strFilter, strFieldName, strValue;
strFieldName = "Why]would[you ever\\use.this#column/name?";
strValue = "O'Malley";
strFilter = "[" + strFieldName.Replace("]", "\\]") +
            "] = '" + strValue.Replace("'", "''") + "'";
foreach (DataRow row in tbl.Select(strFilter))
    Console.WriteLine(row[strFieldName]);
```

> **Note**   After reading the previous few paragraphs, I hope you've fig-
> ured out the simple and elegant way to avoid problems with delimiters
> and reserved words in column names: Don't use them!!!

Using the Additional *Select* Methods

Like many methods in the ADO.NET object model, the *Select* method is overloaded. You can supply just a search string, but you can also include a sort
order as well as a parameter to control the state of the rows you want to search
(only added rows, for example, or only modified rows). Let's look at these
overloaded methods briefly.

Including a Sort Order

In our initial *Select* method code snippet, we searched a *DataTable* that contained customer information to locate the customers from the United States that
are not located in Seattle. We can control the order of the *DataRow* objects that
the *Select* method returns by using one of the overloaded method signatures.

In a SQL query, you control the sort order of the data returned by the
query using the *ORDER BY* clause. For example, the following query returns
customers sorted by city:

```
SELECT CustomerID, CompanyName, ContactName, Phone, City
    FROM Customers ORDER BY City
```

To sort by city in descending order, you simply change *ORDER BY City* to
ORDER BY City DESC.

The overloaded *Select* method accepts a sort order, just as the SQL *ORDER
BY* clause does. Here, we've modified our initial code snippet so that the
DataRow objects returned by the *Select* method are sorted by the City column
in descending order:

Visual Basic .NET

```
Dim strConn, strSQL As String
strConn = "Provider=SQLOLEDB;Data Source=(local)\NetSDK;" & _
          "Initial Catalog=Northwind;Trusted_Connection=Yes;"
strSQL = "SELECT CustomerID, CompanyName, ContactName, " & _
         "Phone, City, Country FROM Customers"
Dim da As New OleDbDataAdapter(strSQL, strConn)
Dim tbl As New DataTable()
da.Fill(tbl)

Dim strCriteria As String = "Country = 'USA' AND City <> 'Seattle'"
Dim strSortOrder As String = "City DESC"
Dim aRows As DataRow() = tbl.Select(strCriteria, strSortOrder)
Dim row As DataRow
For Each row In aRows
    Console.WriteLine(row("CompanyName") & " - " & row("City") & _
                      " - " & row("Country"))
Next row
```

Visual C# .NET

```
string strConn, strSQL;
strConn = "Provider=SQLOLEDB;Data Source=(local)\\NetSDK;" +
          "Initial Catalog=Northwind;Trusted_Connection=Yes;";
strSQL = "SELECT CustomerID, CompanyName, ContactName, " +
         "Phone, City, Country FROM Customers";
OleDbDataAdapter da = new OleDbDataAdapter(strSQL, strConn);
DataTable tbl = new DataTable();
da.Fill(tbl);

string strCriteria = "Country = 'USA' AND City <> 'Seattle'";
string strSortOrder = "City DESC";
DataRow[] aRows = tbl.Select(strCriteria, strSortOrder);
foreach (DataRow row in aRows)
    Console.WriteLine(row["CompanyName"] + " - " + row["City"] +
                      " - " + row["Country"]);
```

Specifying the *RowState* of the Rows to Search

As you learned in Chapter 6, the *DataSet* supports caching changes. What if you want to perform a search against just the modified rows in a *DataTable?*

You can use an overloaded *Select* method to specify a value from the *DataViewRowState* enumeration. Think of this value as an added filter to your search criteria. Say you want to examine just the modified and deleted rows in a *DataTable.* You can use the *ModifiedOriginal* and *Deleted* values from the *DataViewRowState* enumeration and use empty strings for the filter and sort parameters. The following code snippet does just that.

Visual Basic .NET

```
Dim dvrs As DataViewRowState
dvrs = DataViewRowState.ModifiedOriginal Or DataViewRowState.Deleted
Dim aRows As DataRow() = tbl.Select("", "", dvrs)
Dim row As DataRow
For Each row In aRows
    Console.WriteLine(row("CompanyName", DataRowVersion.Original))
Next row
```

Visual C# .NET

```
DataViewRowState dvrs;
dvrs = DataViewRowState.ModifiedOriginal | DataViewRowState.Deleted;
DataRow[] aRows = tbl.Select("", "", dvrs);
foreach (DataRow row in aRows)
    Console.WriteLine(row["CompanyName", DataRowVersion.Original]);
```

> **Note**   Remember that with deleted rows, you can examine only the original version of the row.

What Is a *DataView* Object?

The *DataTable* object's *Select* method is powerful and flexible, but it's not always the best solution. It has two major limitations. First, because it accepts such dynamic search criteria, it's not terribly efficient. Also, neither Windows nor Web forms support binding to the *Select* method's return value—an array of *DataRow* objects. The ADO.NET solution to both limitations is the *DataView* object.

The ADO.NET *DataTable* object is roughly equivalent to a table in a database, so you might assume that the *DataView* object is similar to a view in a database. While there are some similarities between *DataView* objects and views in a database, they are not as closely related as *DataTable* objects and tables in a database are.

DataView Objects Return Data from a *DataTable*

The *DataView* object does not maintain its own copy of data. When you access data through a *DataView*, the *DataView* returns data stored in the corresponding *DataTable*.

Views in a database behave the same way. When you query a view, the database returns data from the table or tables referenced in the view.

DataView Objects Are Not SQL Queries

A view in a database is really just a query. When you create a view in a database, you supply the query that the database will execute in order to return data for that view:

```
CREATE VIEW ViewCustomersAndOrders AS
    SELECT C.CustomerID, C.CompanyName, C.ContactName, C.Phone,
           O.OrderID, O.EmployeeID, O.OrderDate
    FROM Customers C, Orders O WHERE C.CustomerID = O.CustomerID
```

ADO.NET *DataView* objects let you filter, sort, and search the contents of *DataTable* objects, but they are not SQL queries. You cannot use a *DataView* to join data between two *DataTable* objects, nor can you use a *DataView* to view only certain columns in a *DataTable*. *DataView* objects do support filtering rows based on dynamic criteria, but they can access only a single *DataTable*, and all columns in the *DataTable* are available through the *DataView*.

Simulating joins using a *DataRelation*

You can use a *DataRelation* and an expression-based column to simulate a join. For example, if you have *DataTable* objects for customer and order information, you can create a relationship between the two *DataTable* objects and then add an expression-based *DataColumn* in the orders *DataTable* to display a column from the customers *DataTable*:

Visual Basic .NET

```
ds.Relations.Add("CustomersOrders", _
                ds.Tables("Customers").Columns("CustomerID"), _
                ds.Tables("Orders").Columns("CustomerID"))
ds.Tables("Orders").Columns.Add("CompanyName", GetType(String), _
                    "Parent(CustomersOrders).CompanyName")
```

Visual C# .NET

```
ds.Relations.Add("CustomersOrders",
                ds.Tables["Customers"].Columns["CustomerID"],
                ds.Tables["Orders"].Columns["CustomerID"]);
ds.Tables["Orders"].Columns.Add("CompanyName", typeof(string),
                    "Parent(CustomersOrders).CompanyName");
```

Working with *DataView* Objects in Code

The *DataView* object offers functionality similar to that of the *DataTable* object's *Select* method. Let's take a closer look at this functionality and compare it to the *Select* method as we go.

Creating *DataView* Objects

To use a *DataView* object to view data in a *DataTable*, you must associate it with a *DataTable* object. You can specify the *DataTable* that the *DataView* will use in one of two ways: by using the *DataView* object's *Table* property or by using the *DataView* object's constructor. The following code snippets are equivalent:

Visual Basic .NET

```
Dim tbl As New DataTable("TableName")
Dim vue As DataView

vue = New DataView()
vue.Table = tbl

vue = New DataView(tbl)
```

Visual C# .NET

```
DataTable tbl = new DataTable("TableName");
DataView vue;

vue = new DataView();
vue.Table = tbl;

vue = new DataView(tbl);
```

> **Note**   If you set the *DataView* object's *Table* property to a *DataTable*, the *DataTable* must have its *TableName* property set to something other than an empty string (the default). This restriction is not enforced in the *DataView* object's constructor. I don't claim to know why.

The *DataView* object also has a constructor whose signature more closely matches the *DataTable* object's *Select* method. This more advanced constructor sets the *Table*, *RowFilter*, *Sort*, and *RowStateFilter* properties of the *DataView* in a single line of code. Thus, the following code snippets are equivalent:

Visual Basic .NET

```
Dim tbl As New DataTable("Customers")
Dim dvrs As DataViewRowState
dvrs = DataViewRowState.ModifiedOriginal Or DataViewRowState.Deleted
Dim vue As DataView

vue = New DataView
vue.Table = tbl
vue.RowFilter = "Country = 'USA'"
vue.Sort = "City DESC"
vue.RowStateFilter = dvrs

vue = New DataView(tbl, "Country = 'USA'", "City DESC", dvrs)
```

Visual C# .NET

```
DataTable tbl = new DataTable("Customers");
DataViewRowState dvrs;
dvrs = DataViewRowState.ModifiedOriginal Or DataViewRowState.Deleted;
DataView vue;

vue = new DataView;
vue.Table = tbl;
vue.RowFilter = "Country = 'USA'";
vue.Sort = "City DESC";
vue.RowStateFilter = dvrs;

vue = new DataView(tbl, "Country = 'USA'", "City DESC", dvrs);
```

Using the *RowStateFilter* Property

The *RowStateFilter* property accepts values from the *DataViewRowState* enumeration. (See Table 8-1.) You can think of the enumeration as a combination of the *RowState* property of the *DataRow* object and the *DataRowVersion* enumeration.

The property acts as a dual filter. For example, setting the *DataView* object's *RowStateFilter* property to *ModifiedOriginal* means that only modified rows will be visible through the *DataView* and that you'll see the original values of those rows.

Table 8-1 *DataViewRowState* **Enumerations**

Value	Description
Added	Added rows are included.
CurrentRows	Nondeleted rows are included. (Default)
Deleted	Deleted rows are included.
ModifiedCurrent	Modified rows are included; current values are visible.
ModifiedOriginal	Modified rows are included; original values are visible.
None	No rows are included.
OriginalRows	Deleted, modified, and unmodified rows are included; original values are visible.
Unchanged	Unmodified rows are included.

Using the *DataRowView* Object

If you use the *DataTable* object's *Select* method and specify *ModifiedOriginal*, the method will return only modified rows. However, as you saw in the earlier code snippet illustrating the *Select* method, we still had to specify that we wanted to retrieve original values from the row in calls to the *DataRow* objects returned.

This extra step is not required when you use the *DataView* because the *DataView* returns data using its own specialized object: a *DataRowView*. The *DataRowView* offers much of the same functionality as the *DataRow*. It exposes a default *Item* property that you can use to access the contents of a column by supplying either a column name or the index of a column. You can examine and modify the contents of a row using the *Item* property, but only one version of the row's data is available through the *DataRowView*—the version you specify in the *DataView* object's *DataRowVersion* property.

The following code snippet shows how to use the *DataView* object to return a *DataRowView* object and how to use the *DataRowView* object to examine data from a row:

Visual Basic .NET

```
Dim tbl As New DataTable("Customers")
    ⋮
Dim vue As DataView
vue = New DataView(tbl)
Dim row As DataRowView = vue(0)
Console.WriteLine(vue("CompanyName"))
```

Visual C# .NET

```
DataTable tbl = new DataTable("Customers");
⋮
DataView vue;
vue = new DataView(tbl);
DataRowView row = vue[0];
Console.WriteLine(vue["CompanyName"]);
```

If you find that the *DataRowView* object doesn't give you the power you need, you can use the *DataRowView* object's *Row* property to access the corresponding *DataRow* object.

Examining All Rows of Data Available Through a *DataView*

Using a *DataView* to access data in a *DataTable* is slightly different from accessing the *DataTable* directly. The *DataTable* exposes its rows of data through the *Rows* property, which allows you to scroll through its contents with a For Each loop. The *DataView* object does not expose data via such an easily enumerable collection.

The *DataView* object exposes a *Count* property that returns the number of rows visible through the *DataView*. You can use this property to construct a simple For loop to examine all of the rows.

The *DataView* also exposes a *GetEnumerator* method that returns an *IEnumerator* object. The *IEnumerator* object, which resides in the *System.Collections* namespace, offers navigation functionality similar to what the *DataReader* object offers through its *MoveNext* method.

The following code snippet shows how to examine the contents of a *DataView*—once using the *Count* property and once using the *GetEnumerator* method:

Visual Basic .NET

```
Dim tbl As New DataTable("Customers")
'Retrieve data into the DataTable, and modify some rows.
⋮
'Create a DataView that contains only modified rows
'and returns the original contents of those rows.
Dim vue As DataView
vue = New DataView(tbl, "", "", DataViewRowState.ModifiedOriginal)
Dim row As DataRowView

'Use a simple For loop to examine the contents of the DataView.
Dim intCounter As Integer
For intCounter = 0 To vue.Count - 1
```

(continued)

```
    row = vue(intCounter)
    Console.WriteLine(row("CompanyName"))
Next intCounter

'Use an enumerator to loop through the contents of the DataView.
Dim objEnum As IEnumerator = vue.GetEnumerator
Do While objEnum.MoveNext()
    row = CType(objEnum.Current, DataRowView)
    Console.WriteLine(row("CompanyName"))
Loop
```

Visual C# .NET

```
DataTable tbl = new DataTable("Customers");
//Retrieve data into the DataTable, and modify some rows.
⋮
//Create a DataView that contains only modified rows
//and returns the original contents of those rows.
DataView vue;
vue = new DataView(tbl, "", "", DataViewRowState.ModifiedOriginal);
DataRowView row;

//Use a simple for loop to examine the contents of the DataView.
for (int intCounter = 0; intCounter < vue.Count; intCounter++)
{
    row = vue[intCounter];
    Console.WriteLine(row["CompanyName"]);
}

//Use an enumerator to loop through the contents of the DataView.
IEnumerator objEnum = vue.GetEnumerator();
while (objEnum.MoveNext())
{
    row = (DataRowView) objEnum.Current;
    Console.WriteLine(row["CompanyName"]);
}
```

Searching for Data in a *DataView*

You've already seen how the *DataView* object supports filtering using the *RowFilter* and *RowStateFilter* properties. It also supports searching using the *Find* and *FindRows* methods. These methods are similar to the *Find* method of the *DataTable* object's *Rows* collection.

The *Find* Method

Once you've set the *Sort* property on a *DataView* object, you can call its *Find* method to locate a row based on the columns specified in the *Sort* property. As with the *Find* method of the *DataRowCollection* object, you can supply a single value or an array of values.

The *DataView* object's *Find* method does not, however, return a *DataRow* or a *DataRowView* object. Instead, it returns an integer value that corresponds to the index of the desired row in the *DataView*. If the *DataView* cannot locate the desired row, the *Find* method returns a value of −1.

The following code snippet shows how to use the *DataView* object's *Find* method to locate a customer based on the value of the ContactName column. It also uses the return value of the *Find* method to determine whether the *Find* method located the desired row.

Visual Basic .NET

```
Dim strConn As String = "Provider=SQLOLEDB;Data Source=(local)\NetSDK;" & _
                        "Initial Catalog=Northwind;Trusted_Connection=Yes;"
Dim strSQL As String = "SELECT CustomerID, CompanyName, ContactName, " & _
                       "Phone, City, Country FROM Customers"
Dim da As New OleDbDataAdapter(strSQL, strConn)
Dim tbl As New DataTable("Customers")
da.Fill(tbl)
Dim vue As New DataView(tbl)

vue.Sort = "ContactName"
Dim intIndex As Integer = vue.Find("Fran Wilson")
If intIndex = -1 Then
    Console.WriteLine("Row not found!")
Else
    Console.WriteLine(vue(intIndex)("CompanyName"))
End If
```

Visual C# .NET

```
string strConn = "Provider=SQLOLEDB;Data Source=(local)\\NetSDK;" +
                 "Initial Catalog=Northwind;Trusted_Connection=Yes;";
string strSQL = "SELECT CustomerID, CompanyName, ContactName, " +
                "Phone, City, Country FROM Customers";
OleDbDataAdapter da = new OleDbDataAdapter(strSQL, strConn);
DataTable tbl = new DataTable("Customers");
da.Fill(tbl);
DataView vue = new DataView(tbl);

vue.Sort = "ContactName";
int intIndex = vue.Find("Fran Wilson");
if (intIndex == -1)
    Console.WriteLine("Row not found!");
else
    Console.WriteLine(vue[intIndex]["CompanyName"]);
```

The *FindRows* Method

The *DataRowCollection* object's *Find* method performs a search based on the column(s) specified in the *DataTable* object's *PrimaryKey* property. Because a primary key is also associated with a unique key constraint, one row at most will satisfy the criteria specified in the *DataRowCollection* object's *Find* method.

The *DataView* object's *Find* method performs searches based on the column(s) specified in the *DataView* object's *Sort* property. Multiple rows of data might have the same values for the columns used to sort the data in the *DataView*. For example, you can sort customers based on the Country column, and multiple rows have a value of *Spain* in the Country column. But you can't use the *DataView* object's *Find* method to locate all customers in Spain because the *Find* method returns only an integer.

Thankfully, the *DataView* object also exposes a *FindRows* method. You call the *FindRows* method just as you call the *DataView* object's *Find* method, but the *FindRows* method returns an array of *DataRowView* objects that contains the rows that satisfied the criteria you specified.

The following code snippet shows how to use the *FindRows* method and checks whether the method found any rows:

Visual Basic .NET

```
...
Dim vue As New DataView(tbl)

vue.Sort = "Country"
Dim aRows As DataRowView() = vue.FindRows("Spain")
If aRows.Length = 0 Then
    Console.WriteLine("No rows found!")
Else
    Dim row As DataRowView
    For Each row In aRows
        Console.WriteLine(row("City"))
    Next row
End If
```

Visual C# .NET

```
...
DataView vue = new DataView(tbl);

vue.Sort = "Country";
DataRowView[] aRows = vue.FindRows("Spain");
if (aRows.Length == 0)
    Console.WriteLine("No rows found!");
else
    foreach (DataRowView row in aRows)
        Console.WriteLine(row["City"]);
```

Modifying *DataRowView* Objects

Modifying a row of data using a *DataRowView* object is similar to modifying the contents of a *DataRow* object. The *DataRowView* object exposes *BeginEdit*, *EndEdit*, *CancelEdit*, and *Delete* methods, just as the *DataRow* object does.

Creating a new row of data using a *DataRowView* object is slightly different from creating a new *DataRow*. The *DataView* has an *AddNew* method that returns a new *DataRowView* object. The new row is not actually added to the underlying *DataTable* until you call the *EndEdit* method of the *DataRowView* object.

The following code snippet shows how to create, modify, and delete a row of data using the *DataRowView* object:

Visual Basic .NET

```
Dim tbl As New DataTable("Customers")
 :
Dim vue As New DataView(tbl)

'Add a new row.
Dim row As DataRowView = vue.AddNew()
row("CustomerID") = "ABCDE"
row("CompanyName") = "New Company"
row("ContactName") = "New Contact"
row("Phone") = "(617) 555-1212"
row.EndEdit()

'Modify a row.
row.BeginEdit()
row("CompanyName") = "Modified"
row.EndEdit()

'Delete a row.
row.Delete()
```

Visual C# .NET

```
DataTable tbl = new DataTable("Customers");
 :
DataView vue = new DataView(tbl);

//Add a new row.
DataRowView row = vue.AddNew();
row["CustomerID"] = "ABCDE";
row["CompanyName"] = "New Company";
row["ContactName"] = "New Contact";
row["Phone"] = "(617) 555-1212";
row.EndEdit();

//Modify a row.
row.BeginEdit();
row["CompanyName"] = "Modified";
```

(continued)

```
row.EndEdit();

//Delete a row.
row.Delete();
```

Creating *DataView* Objects in Visual Studio .NET

Creating a *DataView* object is much simpler than creating a *DataTable*. You don't have to add columns and data types. You simply point the *DataView* at a *DataTable* and set the desired properties (*RowFilter*, *RowStateFilter*, *Sort*, and so on).

Adding a New *DataView* Object to Your Designer

You can add a new *DataView* object to your designer by dragging the DataView item from the Data tab of the Visual Studio .NET Toolbox and dropping the item onto the designer or the component tray. You can also simply double-click the DataView item in the Toolbox.

Setting Properties of Your *DataView* Object

Once you've created your new *DataView* object, you'll want to set a few of its properties. Visual Studio .NET simplifies this process. As you can see in Figure 8-1, you can use the Properties window to select an available *DataTable*. You can also set other available properties of the *DataView* object, such as *RowFilter*, *RowStateFilter*, and *Sort*.

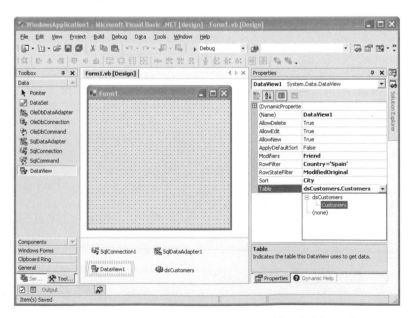

Figure 8-1 Setting properties of the *DataView* object in Visual Studio .NET

That's really all there is to it.

DataView Object Reference

Properties of the *DataView* Object

In Table 8-2 you'll find all the properties of the *DataView* object.

Table 8-2   Properties of the *DataView* Object

Property	Data Type	Description
AllowDelete	*Boolean*	Specifies whether rows in the *DataView* can be deleted.
AllowEdit	*Boolean*	Specifies whether rows in the *DataView* can be edited.
AllowNew	*Boolean*	Specifies whether rows can be added to the *DataView*.
ApplyDefaultSort	*Boolean*	Specifies whether the default sort (primary key) is used.
Count	*Integer*	Returns the number of rows visible in the *DataView*. (Read-only.)
DataViewManager	*DataViewManager*	Returns a reference to the *DataView* object's *DataViewManager*. (Read-only.)
Item	*DataRowView*	Returns a *DataRowView* that encapsulates a row of data visible through the *DataView*. (Read-only.)
RowFilter	*String*	Contains a filter that specifies which rows in the *DataTable* are visible through the *DataView*. Similar to the WHERE clause in a SQL query.
RowStateFilter	*DataViewRowState*	Specifies what rows can be visible through the *DataView* as well as the version of the rows.
Sort	*String*	Specifies the sort order of the rows visible through the *DataView*.
Table	*DataTable*	Returns the corresponding *DataTable* to which the *DataView* is bound.

AllowDelete, *AllowEdit*, and *AllowNew* Properties

DataView objects are often used in conjunction with bound controls. The *AllowDelete*, *AllowEdit*, and *AllowNew* properties simplify the process of restricting the types of changes that the user can make using the bound controls. Rather than setting properties on each of the bound controls, you can set these properties on just the *DataView*.

By default, each of these properties is set to *True* on the *DataView* object.

ApplyDefaultSort Property

The *ApplyDefaultSort* property is set to *False* by default. Setting it to *True* will sort the contents of the *DataView* according to the primary key of the *DataView* object's *DataTable*. If you set *ApplyDefaultSort* to *True*, the *DataView* object's *Sort* property will be set to the columns in the *DataTable* object's primary key. For example, if a *DataView* is bound to a *DataTable* that contains order detail information and whose primary key is the combination of the OrderID and ProductID columns, setting *ApplyDefaultSort* to *True* will implicitly set the *Sort* property of the *DataView* to *OrderID, ProductID*.

Count and *Item* Properties

The *Item* property returns a *DataRowView* object and is parameterized. When you call the *Item* property, you supply an integer that represents the row you want to retrieve. You can use the *Count* property to specify the number of rows visible through the *DataView*. The following code snippet loops through the contents of the *DataView* by using the *Count* and *Item* properties:

Visual Basic .NET

```
Dim tbl As New DataTable("Customers")
'Retrieve data into the DataTable, and modify some rows.
⋮
'Create a DataView that contains only modified rows
'and returns the original contents of those rows.
Dim vue As DataView
vue = New DataView(tbl)
Dim row As DataRowView

'Use a simple For loop to examine the contents of the DataView.
Dim intCounter As Integer
For intCounter = 0 To vue.Count - 1
    row = vue(intCounter)
    Console.WriteLine(row("CompanyName"))
Next intCounter
```

Visual C# .NET

```
DataTable tbl = new DataTable("Customers");
//Retrieve data into the DataTable, and modify some rows.
  ⋮
//Create a DataView that contains only modified rows
//and returns the original contents of those rows.
DataView vue;
vue = new DataView(tbl);
DataRowView row;

//Use a simple for loop to examine the contents of the DataView.
for (int intCounter = 0; intCounter < vue.Count; intCounter++)
{
    row = vue[intCounter];
    Console.WriteLine(row["CompanyName"]);
}
```

DataViewManager Property

If you created your *DataView* using the *CreateDataView* method of an instance of a *DataViewManager* object, the *DataViewManager* property will return the *DataViewManager* object that created the *DataView*. Otherwise, the property will return an uninitialized *DataViewManager*.

For more information on the *DataViewManager* object, see the section titled "Questions That Should Be Asked More Frequently" later in the chapter.

RowFilter Property

The *RowFilter* property is similar to a WHERE clause in a SQL query. Only rows that satisfy the criteria in the property are visible through the view. The default for the *RowFilter* property is an empty string.

Simple filter that uses a column containing strings:
```
vue.RowFilter = "Country = 'Spain'"
```

Filter that uses a wildcard (displaying only rows whose CustomerID starts with *A*):
```
vue.RowFilter = "CustomerID LIKE 'A%'"
```

Delimiting dates:
```
vue.RowFilter = "OrderDate >= #01/01/2002# AND OrderDate < #02/01/2002#"
```

Delimiting the column name and handling the delimiter in the column value:
```
vue.RowFilter = "[Spaces In Column Name] = 'O''Malley'"
```

RowStateFilter Property

The *RowStateFilter* property affects the data visible through a *DataView* in two ways. It filters rows based on their *RowState*, and it controls the version of the row that's visible through the *DataView*. The *RowStateFilter* property accepts values and combinations of values from the *DataViewRowState* enumeration, as described earlier in the chapter.

You can set the *RowStateFilter* property using the *DataView* object's constructor. The default value for the *RowStateFilter* property is *CurrentRows*, which causes the view to display the current version of all rows in the *DataTable* that satisfy the criteria specified in the *DataView* object's *Sort* property and are not marked as deleted.

Sort Property

The *Sort* property controls the sort order of data visible in the *DataView*; it works much like the ORDER BY clause in a SQL query. You can create a sort order based on a single column or a combination of columns. By default, the rows are sorted in ascending order. To sort columns in descending order, you add the keyword *DESC* after the column name. Remember to delimit your column name if it contains a nonalphanumeric character (such as a space) or if the column name is a reserved word.

Simple sort by two columns (Country and then City):
```
vue.Sort = "Country, City"
```

Sorting in descending order:
```
vue.Sort = "OrderDate DESC"
```

Delimiting the column name:
```
vue.Sort = "[Space In ColumnName]"
```

By default, the *Sort* property is set to an empty string, which will display the contents of the *DataView* in the same order that they appear in the underlying *DataTable*. You can set this property using the *DataView* object's constructor.

Table Property

You use the *DataView* object's *Table* property to set or access the *DataTable* to which the *DataView* is bound. Changing the value of the *Table* property resets the *RowFilter* and *RowStateFilter* properties of the *DataView* to their respective default values.

You can also set the *Table* property using the *DataView* object's constructors.

As of this writing, setting the *Table* property to a *DataTable* whose *Table-Name* property is an empty string generates an exception.

Methods of the *DataView* Object

Table 8-3 lists the methods of the *DataView* object.

Table 8-3   Methods of the *DataView* Object

Method	Description
AddNew	Creates a new *DataRowView* object
BeginInit	Temporarily caches changes to the *DataView* object
CopyTo	Copies *DataRowView* objects to an array
Delete	Marks a *DataRowView* as deleted
EndInit	Commits cached changes to the *DataView* object
Find	Searches the *DataView* for a row of data
FindRows	Searches the *DataView* for multiple rows of data
GetEnumerator	Returns an *IEnumerator* object to enumerate through the rows visible through the *DataView*

AddNew and *Delete* Methods

You can use the *AddNew* and *Delete* methods to add rows of data to and remove rows of data from the underlying *DataTable*. The *AddNew* method returns a new *DataRowView* object. Once you've set the values of the desired columns, you can call the *DataRowView* object's *EndEdit* method to add the row of data to the underlying *DataTable*.

You can use the *Delete* method to delete a row if you know the index of the row within the *DataView*. If you have a reference to the *DataRow* or the *DataRowView*, you can call the *Delete* method of the *DataRow* or *DataRowView* object instead. Remember that using the *Delete* method of any of these objects simply marks the row as deleted. To remove the row from the *DataTable*, you call the *AcceptChanges* method (of the *DataRow* or of the *DataTable* or *DataSet* that contains the row) or submit the change to your database using a *DataAdapter*.

BeginInit and *EndInit* Methods

If you want to change multiple properties of the *DataView* object but don't want the changes to affect the data visible through the *DataView* until you've changed all of the desired properties, you can use the *BeginInit* and *EndInit* methods.

For example, say you have a *DataView* bound to a particular *DataTable* and you've also set the *DataView* object's *RowFilter* property so that only a small fraction of the rows are visible through the *DataView*. You're displaying the contents of the *DataView* on a Windows form using a *DataGrid*, and based on input from the user you want to change the settings of the *DataView* object's *Table* and *RowFilter* properties. In this situation, you should enclose the code that changes the *DataView* object's properties within calls to the *DataView* object's *BeginInit* and *EndInit* property to prevent the *DataGrid* from momentarily displaying all rows from the new *DataTable*.

CopyTo Method

The *DataView* object exposes a *CopyTo* method that behaves like the *CopyTo* method of the *Array* object. You can copy the *DataRowView* objects available through the *DataView* to an array using the *CopyTo* method.

> **Note**   Developers who have experience using DAO, RDO, and ADO might assume that the *CopyTo* method behaves like *GetRows*, which returns the contents of the data structure as a two-dimensional array. Alas, this is not the case.

To be honest, I'm not sure how having an array of *DataRowView* objects helps. However, let's look at a code snippet that demonstrates using this method, on the off chance that someone will find a groundbreaking use for the feature. That person might remember how helpful this code snippet was and thank me profusely. I also accept cash.

Visual Basic .NET

```
Dim tbl As New DataTable("Customers")
  ⋮
Dim vue As DataView
vue = New DataView(tbl)
Dim aRows As DataRowView()
aRows = Array.CreateInstance(GetType(DataRowView), vue.Count)
vue.CopyTo(aRows, 0)
```

Visual C# .NET

```
DataTable tbl = new DataTable("Customers");
  ⋮
DataView vue;
vue = new DataView(tbl);
DataRowView[] aRows;
aRows = Array.CreateInstance(typeof(DataRowView), vue.Count);
vue.CopyTo(aRows, 0);
```

Find and *FindRows* Methods

The *DataView* allows you to locate one or more rows of data using its *Find* and *FindRows* methods. Both methods are overloaded to accept a single value or an array of values. The *DataView* uses the values specified to search its contents based on the columns specified in the *Sort* property, as shown here:

Visual Basic .NET

```
Dim strConn As String = "Provider=SQLOLEDB;Data Source=(local)\NetSDK;" & _
                        "Initial Catalog=Northwind;Trusted_Connection=Yes;"
Dim strSQL As String = "SELECT CustomerID, CompanyName, ContactName, " & _
                       "Phone, City, Country FROM Customers"
Dim da As New OleDbDataAdapter(strSQL, strConn)
Dim tbl As New DataTable("Customers")
da.Fill(tbl)
Dim vue As New DataView(tbl)

Console.WriteLine("Use the Find method to locate a row " & _
                  "based on the ContactName column")
vue.Sort = "ContactName"
Dim intIndex As Integer = vue.Find("Fran Wilson")
If intIndex = -1 Then
    Console.WriteLine(vbTab & "Row not found!")
Else
    Console.WriteLine(vbTab & vue(intIndex)("CompanyName"))
End If
Console.WriteLine()

Console.WriteLine("Use the FindRows method to locate rows " & _
                  "based on the Country column")
vue.Sort = "Country"
Dim aRows As DataRowView() = vue.FindRows("Spain")
If aRows.Length = 0 Then
    Console.WriteLine(vbTab & "No rows found!")
Else
    Dim row As DataRowView
    For Each row In aRows
        Console.WriteLine(vbTab & row("City"))
    Next row
End If
```

Visual C# .NET

```
string strConn = "Provider=SQLOLEDB;Data Source=(local)\\NetSDK;" +
                "Initial Catalog=Northwind;Trusted_Connection=Yes;";
string strSQL = "SELECT CustomerID, CompanyName, ContactName, " +
                "Phone, City, Country FROM Customers";
OleDbDataAdapter da = new OleDbDataAdapter(strSQL, strConn);
DataTable tbl = new DataTable("Customers");
da.Fill(tbl);
DataView vue = new DataView(tbl);

Console.WriteLine("Use the Find method to locate a row " +
                  "based on the ContactName column");
vue.Sort = "ContactName";
int intIndex = vue.Find("Fran Wilson");
if (intIndex == -1)
    Console.WriteLine("\t" + "Row not found!");
else
    Console.WriteLine("\t" + vue[intIndex]["CompanyName"]);
Console.WriteLine();

Console.WriteLine("Use the FindRows method to locate rows " +
                  "based on the Country column");
vue.Sort = "Country";
DataRowView[] aRows = vue.FindRows("Spain");
if (aRows.Length == 0)
    Console.WriteLine("\t" + "No rows found!");
else
    foreach (DataRowView row in aRows)
        Console.WriteLine("\t" + row["City"]);
```

GetEnumerator Method

The *GetEnumerator* method offers another way to view the contents of a *Data-View*. It returns an instance of an *IEnumerator* object, which resides in the *System.Collections* namespace.

You use the *IEnumerator* object's *MoveNext* method the same way that you use the *DataReader* object's *Read* method. *MoveNext* returns a Boolean value that indicates whether another object in the collection is available. The *Current* property returns the currently available object using the generic *Object* data type. The following code snippet converts the output to a *DataRowView* object:

Visual Basic .NET

```
Dim tbl As New DataTable("Customers")
    ⋮
Dim vue As DataView(tbl)
Dim row As DataRowView
Dim objEnum As IEnumerator = vue.GetEnumerator
```

```
Do While objEnum.MoveNext()
    row = CType(objEnum.Current, DataRowView)
    Console.WriteLine(row("CompanyName"))
Loop
```

Visual C# .NET

```
DataTable tbl = new DataTable("Customers");
⋮
DataView vue = new DataView(tbl);
DataRowView row;
IEnumerator objEnum = vue.GetEnumerator();
while (objEnum.MoveNext())
{
    row = (DataRowView) objEnum.Current;
    Console.WriteLine(row["CompanyName"]);
}
```

The *ListChanged* Event of the *DataView* Object

The *DataView* object has one event, *ListEvent*, which fires when the contents of the *DataView* change—such as when a row visible through the *DataView* is added, deleted, or modified; when a *DataAdapter* fills the underlying *Data-Table*; or when the *DataView* object's *RowFilter*, *RowStateFilter*, *Sort*, or *Table* property changes. Here's one example:

Visual Basic .NET

```
Dim vue As New DataView()
AddHandler vue.ListChanged, vue_ListChanged

Private Sub vue_ListChanged(ByVal sender As Object, _
                            ByVal e As ListChangedEventArgs)
    Console.WriteLine("ListChanged - " & _
                    e.ListChangedType.ToString())
End Sub
```

Visual C# .NET

```
//Assumes using System.ComponentModel

DataView vue = new DataView;
vue.ListChanged += new ListChangedEventHandler(vue_ListChanged);

private void vue_ListChanged(object sender, ListChangedEventArgs e)
{
    Console.WriteLine("ListChanged - " +
                    e.ListChangedType.ToString());
}
```

Properties of the *DataRowView* Object

Most of the properties of the *DataRowView* object are read-only. Table 8-4 summarizes the properties.

Table 8-4 Properties of the *DataRowView* Object

Property	Data Type	Description
DataView	*DataView*	Returns the *DataView* to which the *DataRowView* belongs (read-only)
IsEdit	*Boolean*	Indicates whether the row is currently being modified (read-only)
IsNew	*Boolean*	Indicates whether the row is a new pending row (read-only)
Item	*Object*	Sets or returns the contents of a column
Row	*DataRow*	Returns the corresponding *DataRow* object for the *DataRowView* (read-only)
RowVersion	*DataRowVersion*	Returns the *RowVersion* of the corresponding *DataRow* that is visible via the *DataViewRow* (read-only)

DataView Property

The *DataView* property returns the *DataView* to which the *DataRowView* object belongs.

IsEdit and *IsNew* Properties

You can use the *IsEdit* and *IsNew* properties to determine whether the *DataRowView* object is currently being edited and what type of edit is being made.

If you're in the process of editing a new row (you've created the new *DataRowView* using *DataView.AddNew* but haven't called *EndEdit* to add the row to the underlying *DataTable*), *IsNew* will return *True* and *IsEdit* will return *False*. If you're editing a row that already exists in the table, *IsEdit* will return *True* and *IsNew* will return *False*.

Item Property

The *DataRowView* object's *Item* property offers much of the same functionality as the *DataRow* object's *Item* property. You can use the *DataRowView* object's *Item* property to modify or examine the contents of a column of data for that row. You can access the column by using its name or its ordinal value in the *Item* property.

Row Property

The *DataRowView* object doesn't offer all of the functionality available through the *DataRow* object. For example, the *DataRowView* object doesn't expose methods such as *AcceptChanges* and *GetChanges*. If you need to work with features of the *DataRow* interface, you can use the *DataRowView* object's *Row* property. This property returns the *DataRow* object that corresponds to the *DataRowView* object.

RowVersion Property

If you're working with a row of data using the *DataRowView* interface and you want to determine which version of the data you're seeing through the *Item* property, you can check the *RowVersion* property of the *DataRowView*.

The *RowVersion* property is read-only and returns a value from the *DataRowVersion* enumeration.

Methods of the *DataRowView* Object

Table 8-5 summarizes the methods that the *DataRowView* object exposes.

Table 8-5   Methods of the *DataRowView* Object

Method	Description
BeginEdit	Begins the process of editing the row
CancelEdit	Cancels pending changes for the row
CreateChildView	Creates a new *DataView* containing only the child rows for the current row
Delete	Marks the row as deleted
EndEdit	Saves pending changes for the row

BeginEdit, *CancelEdit*, and *EndEdit* Methods

The *BeginEdit*, *CancelEdit*, and *EndEdit* methods of the *DataRowView* object work the same way as the corresponding methods of the *DataRow* object. If you call the *BeginEdit* method before modifying the row, your changes will not be committed to the row until you call *EndEdit*. If you want to discard the changes instead, you can call *CancelEdit*.

CreateChildView Method

Let's say you want to create a *DataView* object that displays only the related child rows for a particular row. If you're working with the customers and orders relation we've used throughout this book, setting up the new *DataView* is simple. You set the *Table* property to the orders *DataTable* and then set the *RowFilter* property to a string such as *CustomerID = 'ALFKI'*.

That sounds very straightforward. But what if you also need to check the column value (CustomerID) for delimiters? Or what if you're working with a relationship that's based on a combination of columns?

The *DataRowView* object offers a simpler and more elegant solution—using the *CreateChildView* method. You can call this method and supply either a relation name or a *DataRelation* object (just as the *GetChildRows* method on the *DataRow* object). The *CreateChildView* method will return a new *DataView* object that uses that relation as its filter.

The following code snippet shows how to use the *CreateChildView* method:

Visual Basic .NET

```
Dim ds As New DataSet()
Dim tblCustomers, tblOrders As DataTable
⋮
tblCustomers = ds.Tables("Customers")
tblOrders = ds.Tables("Orders")
ds.Relations.Add("CustomersOrders", tblCustomers.Columns("CustomerID"), _
                 tblOrders.Columns("CustomerID"))

Dim vueCustomers, vueOrders As DataView
vueCustomers = New DataView(tblCustomers)
vueOrders = vueCustomers(0).CreateChildView("CustomersOrders")
```

Visual C# .NET

```
DataSet ds = new DataSet();
DataTable tblCustomers, tblOrders;
⋮
tblCustomers = ds.Tables["Customers"];
tblOrders = ds.Tables["Orders"];
ds.Relations.Add("CustomersOrders", tblCustomers.Columns["CustomerID"],
                 tblOrders.Columns["CustomerID"]);

DataView vueCustomers, vueOrders;
vueCustomers = new DataView(tblCustomers);
vueOrders = vueCustomers[0].CreateChildView("CustomersOrders");
```

> **Note** When you use the *CreateChildView* method to create a new *DataView*, the *RowFilter* property will return an empty string. However, only the expected child rows will be visible. How is this possible? Well, the new *DataView* object uses a feature that technical people like to refer to as "magic."

Delete Method

You can use the *DataRowView* object's *Delete* method to delete a row. Remember that the row will still exist in the *DataTable* and will be marked as deleted. The row will not actually be removed from the *DataTable* until you call *AcceptChanges* or submit the pending deletion to your database using a *DataAdapter*.

Questions That Should Be Asked More Frequently

Q. How do I determine which method to use to search for data in my *DataTable?*

A. That depends on what type of search you want to perform and what you want to do with the results of the search. Here's a simple set of guidelines:

- ❑ If you need to locate a row based on its primary key value(s), use *DataTable.Rows.Find.*

- ❑ If you need to bind controls to the rows that satisfy your search criteria, use a *DataView.*

- ❑ If you're going to perform repeated searches against a nonkey column or combination of columns, use *DataView.Find.*

- ❑ In all other situations, use the *DataTable.Select* method.

Q. Setting up a *DataView* in code is relatively simple, so is there really any benefit to setting it up at design time using Visual Studio .NET?

A. I'm so glad you asked. Creating *DataView* objects using Visual Studio .NET offers two major benefits over creating them in code. First, if you're creating the *DataView* for use with bound controls, you can bind the controls to the *DataView* at design time if you also create the *DataView* at design time. Personally, I'd rather set these properties at design time with mouse clicks than write code.

Visual Studio .NET actually creates a *DataView* for you behind the scenes, which leads us to the second major benefit. As you set properties using the Properties window, Visual Studio .NET applies your input to the *DataView* object you created. If you set a property incorrectly by making a typo in the column name or by forgetting to include that column in the *DataTable*, Visual Studio .NET will alert you to this at design time. Believe it or not, the information in the alert, shown in Figure 8-2, is actually helpful. If you make a similar mistake in straight code, the code will compile successfully and you won't realize your error until you run your application.

Figure 8-2   An alert generated by an invalid column name entered in a *DataView* at design time in Visual Studio .NET

Q.   What is the purpose of the *DataViewManager* object?

A.   The *DataViewManager* object is a container that contains *DataView-Setting* objects, which are somewhat similar to *DataView* objects but have less functionality. I've yet to see a significant scenario in which you can use the *DataViewManager* but not the *DataView*. For that reason, I'm not covering the *DataViewManager* object in this book.

Q.   How do I locate a row in a *DataView* if I need to perform a search on a column other than the one that's referenced in the *DataView* object's *Sort* property?

A.   This is a fairly common scenario when you're using bound controls on a Windows form. Unfortunately, neither the *DataView* nor the Windows form's data binding objects offer functionality to handle this scenario elegantly.

Let's say you have a grid bound to a *DataView* that shows customer information sorted by the Country column. You want to let the user locate a customer based on another column such as *Contact-Name*. Figure 8-3 shows such a form.

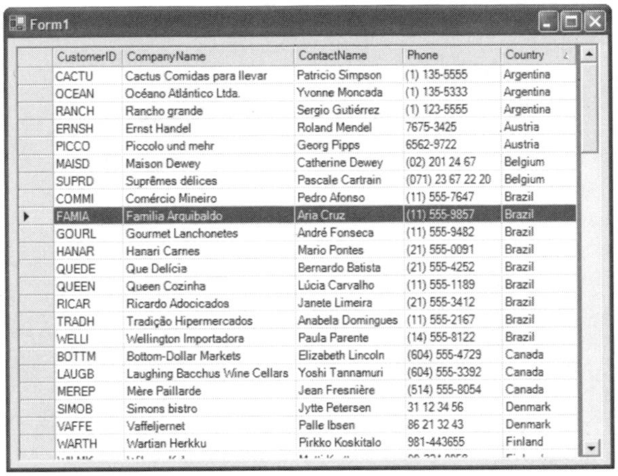

Figure 8-3   Customer information sorted by country

The goal is to select the appropriate row in the grid. In the figure, the currently selected row has a value of *Aria Cruz* for the ContactName column and a value of *Brazil* for the Country column.

We first need to determine the index of the desired row in the *DataView*, which means we have to locate the desired row in the *DataTable*. You can do this in two ways: using the *Select* method of the *DataTable* or using the *Find* method of a *DataView*. Let's opt for the latter.

We'll need a new *DataView* whose *Sort* property is set to the *ContactName* column. Then we can use the *Find* method to determine the index of the desired row within the *DataView*. With that information, we can access the desired *DataRow* and determine the country for that customer as well. The following code snippet does all of this:

Visual Basic .NET

```
Dim tbl As New DataTable("Customers")
⋮
Dim vueByCountry As New DataView(tbl)
vueByCountry.Sort = "Country"
Dim vueByContactName As New DataView(tbl)
vueByContactName.Sort = "ContactName"
Dim intIndexCountry, intIndexContactName As Integer
intIndexCountry = -1
intIndexContactName = vueByContactName.Find("Aria Cruz")
```

(continued)

```
Dim row As DataRow = vueByContactName(intIndexContactName).Row
Dim strCountry As String = row("Country")
```

Visual C# .NET

```
DataTable tbl = new DataTable("Customers");
    ⋮
DataView vueByCountry = new DataView(tbl);
vueByCountry.Sort = "Country";
DataView vueByContactName = new DataView(tbl);
vueByContactName.Sort = "ContactName";
int intIndexCountry, intIndexContactName;
intIndexCountry = -1;
intIndexContactName = vueByContactName.Find("Aria Cruz");
DataRow row = vueByContactName[intIndexContactName].Row;
string strCountry = row["Country"];
```

Believe it or not, that was the simple part. It gets uglier from here.

The next step is to call the *Find* method of the *DataView* that has the customers sorted by Country. But multiple rows could have the same value for the Country column, so that won't be the end of our journey.

Because the values in the Country column are not necessarily unique, it makes sense to call the *FindRows* method of the *DataView*. The *GetRows* method returns an array of *DataRowView* objects. One of the entries in that array represents the desired row, but there is no way to determine the index of a *DataRowView* object, so unfortunately the *FindRows* method cannot help us.

Another option is to simply scan the entire *DataView* until we find the desired row. We could write very simple code to do this, but the code would be inefficient.

In Figure 8-3, you can see multiple rows with the same value for the Country column as our desired row. There's one other major drawback to using the *DataView* object's *Find* method in this scenario: The index value returned is not guaranteed to correspond to the first row in the *DataView* that satisfies the search criteria.

So, once we have the index for a customer that has the same country as the customer we're looking for, we might still have to look at other customers. The following code uses the return value of *Find* as a starting point, moving forward through the *DataView* until it finds the desired row or either moves beyond the bounds of the *DataView* or moves to a row that does not have the expected value for the Country column. If this process does not locate the desired row, the code will check rows that precede the row that served as the starting point. The code is inelegant, but it is as efficient as possible given that the *DataView* was not designed to handle such scenarios.

Visual Basic .NET

```
Dim intStartingPoint As Integer = vueByCountry.Find(row("Country"))
Dim intCounter As Integer = intIndexStartingPoint
Do
    If vueByCountry(intCounter).Row Is row Then
        intIndexCountry = intCounter
        blnFound = True
        Exit Do
    End If
    intCounter += 1
Loop While intCounter < vueByCountry.Count And _
        vueByCountry(intCounter)("Country") = strCountry

If Not blnFound Then
    intCounter = intIndexStartingPoint - 1
    Do While intCounter >= 0 And _
            vueByCountry(intCounter)("Country") = strCountry
        If vueByCountry(intCounter).Row Is row Then
            intIndexCountry = intCounter
            blnFound = True
            Exit Do
        End If
        intCounter -= 1
    Loop
End If

If blnFound Then
    Console.WriteLine(vueByCountry(intIndexCountry)("CompanyName"))
Else
    Console.WriteLine("Not found!")
End If
```

Visual C# .NET

```
int intStartingPoint = vueByCountry.Find(row["Country"]);
while (intCounter < vueByCountry.Count &&
        vueByCountry[intCounter]["Country"].Equals(strCountry))
{
    if (vueByCountry[intCounter].Row == row)
    {
        intIndexCountry = intCounter;
        blnFound = true;
        break;
    }
    intCounter++;
}

if (!blnFound)
{
    intCounter = intStartingPoint - 1;
    while (intCounter >= 0 &&
            vueByCountry[intCounter]["Country"].Equals(strCountry))
```

(continued)

```
        {
            if (vueByCountry[intCounter].Row == row)
            {
                intIndexCountry = intCounter;
                blnFound = true;
                break;
            }
            intCounter--;
        }
    }

    if (blnFound)
        Console.WriteLine(vueByCountry[intIndexCountry]["CompanyName"]);
    else
        Console.WriteLine("Not found!");
```

9

Working with Strongly Typed *DataSet* Objects

Over the past three chapters, you've learned how to create and use *DataSet* objects. The code used to access the contents of a *DataSet* is programmatically similar to code for accessing earlier objects such as the ADO and DAO *Recordset* objects, as you can see by comparing the following examples:

ADO.NET and Visual Basic .NET

```
txtCompanyName.Text = ds.Tables("Customers").Rows(0)("CompanyName")
```

ADO.NET and Visual C# .NET

```
txtCompanyName.Text = ds.Tables["Customers"].Rows[0]["CompanyName"];
```

ADO, DAO, and Visual Basic "Classic"

```
txtCompanyName.Text = rs.Fields("CompanyName").Value
```

Developers have been writing this kind of code since the early days of Visual Basic. Technically, there's nothing wrong with this code; it works. But that doesn't mean we can't improve on the old coding techniques.

To help you write data access code more easily, Microsoft Visual Studio .NET has introduced strongly typed *DataSet* objects. You can now write code that looks like this instead:

Visual Basic .NET

```
txtCompanyName.Text = ds.Customers(0).CompanyName
```

Visual C# .NET

```
txtCompanyName.Text = ds.Customers[0].CompanyName;
```

You can think of a strongly typed *DataSet* as a *DataSet* with class. More specifically, a strongly typed *DataSet* is a class that inherits from the *DataSet* class and also includes properties and methods based on the schema you specify. This class also contains other classes for your *DataTable* objects and *DataRow* objects. These are the classes that enable you to write data access code more efficiently.

Creating Strongly Typed *DataSet* Objects

So how do you create a strongly typed *DataSet* class? You can choose one of two basic approaches. One involves writing code and using a command-line tool that's part of the .NET Framework SDK. The other approach, which is much simpler, relies on the Visual Studio .NET development environment and doesn't require you to open a Command window.

The Hard Way

The .NET Framework SDK includes a command-line utility called the XML Schema Definition Tool, which helps you generate class files based on XML schema (.xsd) files. You can use this utility in conjunction with the *DataSet* object's *WriteXmlSchema* method to translate your *DataSet* into a strongly typed *DataSet* class.

Using the *DataSet* Object's *WriteXmlSchema* Method

In Chapter 6, when we looked at how to create *DataSet* objects in the Visual Studio .NET development environment, you saw that Visual Studio .NET added a file to your project with an .xsd extension. This file contains schema information (tables, columns, constraints, and relationships) for your *DataSet*. You can create this file programmatically using the *DataSet* object's *WriteXmlSchema* method.

The *WriteXmlSchema* method is overloaded to accept a *Stream* object, a *TextWriter* object, an *XmlWriter* object, or a filename as a string. The following code snippet builds a *DataSet* using columns from the Customers and Orders tables in the sample Northwind database. It also adds a *DataRelation* between the two *DataTable* objects before writing the schema for the *DataSet* to a file.

Visual Basic .NET

```
Dim strConn, strSQL As String
strConn = "Provider=SQLOLEDB;Data Source=(local)\NetSDK;" & _
          "Initial Catalog=Northwind;Trusted_Connection=Yes;"
Dim cn As New OleDbConnection(strConn)
```

```
strSQL = "SELECT CustomerID, CompanyName, ContactName, Phone " & _
         "FROM Customers"
Dim daCustomers As New OleDbDataAdapter(strSQL, cn)
strSQL = "SELECT OrderID, CustomerID, EmployeeID, OrderDate " & _
         "FROM Orders"
Dim daOrders As New OleDbDataAdapter(strSQL, cn)
Dim ds As New DataSet()
ds.DataSetName = "Chapter9"
cn.Open()
daCustomers.FillSchema(ds, SchemaType.Source, "Customers")
daOrders.FillSchema(ds, SchemaType.Source, "Orders")
cn.Close()
ds.Relations.Add("CustomersOrders", _
                 ds.Tables("Customers").Columns("CustomerID"), _
                 ds.Tables("Orders").Columns("CustomerID"))
ds.WriteXmlSchema("C:\Chapter9.XSD")
```

Visual C# .NET

```
string strConn, strSQL;
strConn = "Provider=SQLOLEDB;Data Source=(local)\\NetSDK;" +
          "Initial Catalog=Northwind;Trusted_Connection=Yes;";
strSQL = "SELECT CustomerID, CompanyName, ContactName, Phone " +
         "FROM Customers";
OleDbDataAdapter daCustomers = new OleDbDataAdapter(strSQL, strConn);
strSQL = "SELECT OrderID, CustomerID, EmployeeID, OrderDate " + _
         "FROM Orders";
OleDbDataAdapter daOrders = new OleDbDataAdapter(strSQL, strConn);
DataSet ds = new DataSet();
ds.DataSetName = "Chapter9";
cn.Open();
daCustomers.FillSchema(ds, SchemaType.Source, "Customers");
daOrders.FillSchema(ds, SchemaType.Source, "Orders");
cn.Close();
ds.Relations.Add("CustomersOrders",
                 ds.Tables["Customers"].Columns["CustomerID"],
                 ds.Tables["Orders"].Columns["CustomerID"]);
ds.WriteXmlSchema("C:\\Chapter9.XSD");
```

> **Note** The preceding code snippet uses the *FillSchema* method of the *DataAdapter* object. I generally advise developers to avoid using this method in their applications whenever possible. The purpose of the code snippet is to generate an .xsd file that contains *DataSet* schema information, so I consider it to be "design-time" code, which is exactly the type of scenario for which the method was created.

Using the XML Schema Definition Tool

The XML Schema Definition Tool is simply a file in the bin directory called XSD.exe. The tool can generate class files based on XML schema (.xsd or .xdr) files. It can also create XML schema files from libraries (.dll) and executables (.exe).

In the previous code snippet, we saved the schema for a *DataSet* to an .xsd file. Now let's use the XML Schema Definition Tool to generate a class file based on this file. Open a Command window and type the following:

> **Note**   To create a Command window, choose Programs, Accessories, Command Prompt from the Start menu. Or, you can choose Run from the Start menu and then type **cmd.exe**.

Visual Basic .NET

```
C:\>XSD Chapter9.XSD /d /l:VB
```

Visual C# .NET

```
C:\>XSD Chapter9.XSD /d
```

> **Note**   You can either enter the full path to the XSD.exe file or add the .NET Framework SDK's bin directory to your system's *Path* environment variable. You'll also need to supply the path to your XML schema file.

The first parameter is the path to the XML schema file. The second parameter indicates that the class we want to create is derived from the *DataSet* class. The Visual Basic .NET example uses a third parameter to specify the language for the output file. By default, the tool generates Visual C# .NET class files.

The XML Schema Definition Tool also offers other options that are documented in the .NET Framework SDK. You can type **XSD /?** to list the available options in the Command window.

Now you can simply add your new class file to your project, and you can create an instance of your new strongly typed *DataSet* class, as shown in the following code snippet:

Visual Basic .NET

```
Dim ds As New Chapter9()
```

Visual C# .NET

```
Chapter9 ds = new Chapter9();
```

> **Note**   The name of your class is based on the *DataSetName* property of the *DataSet* used to generate your .xsd file. In the code snippet that generated the .xsd file, the *DataSetName* property is set to *Chapter9*, which is also the name of our new strongly typed *DataSet* class.

The Easy Way

Creating a strongly typed *DataSet* class in Visual Studio .NET is much simpler than the approach you saw in the previous example. There's no code to write and, best of all, no Command window.

To demonstrate how much easier it is to create a strongly typed *DataSet* class in Visual Studio .NET, let's build the same strongly typed *DataSet* class that we built in the previous section using code and the Command window. Like the previous *DataSet*, the new *DataSet* will include two *DataTable* objects and a *DataRelation*.

First, create a new Microsoft Windows application in your language of choice. Then, using the Data tab of the Toolbox, add two *OleDbDataAdapter* objects to your Windows form. In the Data Adapter Configuration Wizard, point both *OleDbDataAdapter* objects to your favorite Northwind database. Enter the following SQL statements on the Generate SQL Statement page of the wizard for your *DataAdapter* objects:

```
SELECT CustomerID, CompanyName, ContactName, Phone FROM Customers

SELECT OrderID, CustomerID, EmployeeID, OrderDate FROM Orders
```

Right-click on the designer and choose Generate Dataset from the shortcut menu. In the dialog box that appears, shown in Figure 9-1, type **Chapter9** as the *DataSet* name and choose OK.

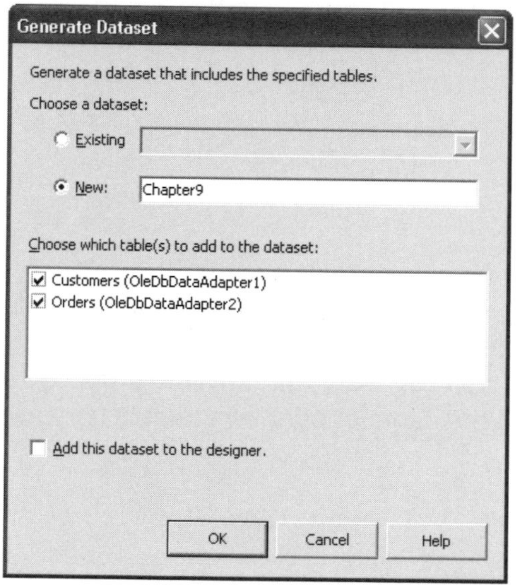

Figure 9-1 Generating a new strongly typed *DataSet*

In one swift step, you've created both the *DataSet* schema file and the strongly typed *DataSet* class. The only difference between this *DataSet* and the one we created earlier is that this one does not have a *DataRelation* defined. Yet.

In the Solution Explorer window, double-click on the schema file. Right-click on the Orders table in the XML Schema Designer and choose Add, New Relation from the shortcut menu. The Edit Relation dialog box will open, as shown in Figure 9-2. Accept the defaults, and then click OK.

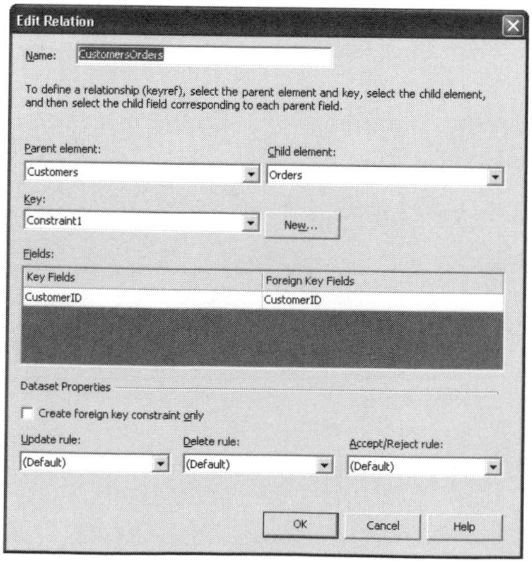

Figure 9-2 Adding a *DataRelation* to your *DataSet*

That's it. No muss, no fuss. No oily residue. You can now create instances of your new strongly typed *DataSet* class in code, as you saw earlier, or at design time using the *DataSet* item on the Data tab of the Toolbox.

When you generated your *DataSet*, Visual Studio .NET went through the following steps to create your new strongly typed *DataSet* class:

1. Created a new instance of the *DataSet* class.

2. Called the *FillSchema* method of all of the *DataAdapter* objects selected in the Generate Dataset dialog box to add schema information to the new *DataSet*.

3. Called the *WriteXmlSchema* method of the *DataSet*.

4. Added the .xsd file to the project.

5. Used the XML Schema Definition Tool to generate the strongly typed *DataSet* class based on the .xsd file.

6. Added the new class file to the project.

Where Is the Class File?

But where is the class file for the strongly typed *DataSet*? If you look closely, you'll see a toolbar at the top of the Solution Explorer window. One of the toolbar buttons has an icon showing multiple files. If you move your mouse over the button, the ToolTip will say "Show All Files." Click this toolbar button to see all of the hidden files in your project in a tree view.

The schema file for your *DataSet* (Chapter9.xsd) will have two files associated with it. The first will be the class file for your strongly typed *DataSet*—either Chapter9.vb or Chapter9.cs, depending on your language of choice. The second associated file will have an .xsx extension; this is just a text file that contains settings for the layout of your *DataSet* in the XML Schema Designer.

The class file actually contains many classes. There's the main class, which is derived from *DataSet*. This class exposes the two *DataTable* objects—*Customers* and *Orders*, each of which returns a class derived from *DataTable*. Each of these classes (*CustomersDataTable* and *OrdersDataTable*) exposes a default *Item* property that returns a table-specific class derived from *DataRow*, as shown here:

Visual Basic .NET

```
Dim ds As New Chapter9()
OleDbDataAdapter1.Fill(ds)
Dim tblCustomers As Chapter9.CustomersDataTable = ds.Customers
Dim rowCustomer As Chapter9.CustomersRow = tblCustomers(0)
```

Visual C# .NET

```
Chapter9 ds = new Chapter9();
OleDbDataAdapter1.Fill(ds);
Chapter9.CustomersDataTable tblCustomers = ds.Customers;
Chapter9.CustomersRow rowCustomer = tblCustomers[0];
```

Using Strongly Typed *DataSet* Objects

Strongly typed *DataSet* objects simplify the development process, making it easier to write code to access and modify the contents of your *DataSet*. Let's look at a few examples that compare working with data in a standard untyped *DataSet* vs. working with a strongly typed *DataSet*.

Adding a Row

Each class for the *DataTable* objects in your *DataSet* offers two ways to add a new row to the *DataTable*. Calling *New\<TableName\>Row* returns a new strongly typed *DataRow* for your *DataTable*. You can then set values for columns in the row using properties of the strongly typed *DataRow*, as shown in the following code snippet.

Visual Basic .NET

```
Dim ds As New Chapter9()
Dim tblCustomers As Chapter9.CustomersDataTable = ds.Customers
Dim rowCustomer As Chapter9.CustomersRow
                  rowCustomer = tblCustomers.NewCustomersRow()
rowCustomer.CustomerID = "ABCDE"
rowCustomer.CompanyName = "New Company"
rowCustomer.ContactName = "New Contact"
rowCustomer.Phone = "(800) 555-1212"
tblCustomers.AddCustomersRow(rowCustomer)


'Instead of
Dim rowCustomer As DataRow = tblCustomers.NewRow()
rowCustomer("CustomerID") = "ABCDE"
rowCustomer("CompanyName") = "New Company"
rowCustomer("ContactName") = "New Contact"
rowCustomer("Phone") = "(800) 555-1212"
tblCustomers.Rows.Add(rowCustomer)
```

Visual C# .NET

```
Chapter9 ds = new Chapter9();
Chapter9.CustomersDataTable tblCustomers = ds.Customers;
Chapter9.CustomersRow rowCustomer = tblCustomers.NewCustomersRow();
```

```
rowCustomer.CustomerID = "ABCDE";
rowCustomer.CompanyName = "New Company";
rowCustomer.ContactName = "New Contact";
rowCustomer.Phone = "(800) 555-1212";
tblCustomers.AddCustomersRow(rowCustomer);

//Instead of
DataRow rowCustomer = tblCustomers.NewRow();
rowCustomer["CustomerID"] = "ABCDE";
rowCustomer["CompanyName"] = "New Company";
rowCustomer["ContactName"] = "New Contact";
rowCustomer["Phone"] = "(800) 555-1212";
tblCustomers.Rows.Add(rowCustomer);
```

The benefits of using the strongly typed *DataRow* in this example are not clear when you see the code in print. Seeing this code in the Visual Studio .NET development environment will provide a better demonstration.

Figure 9-3 is a snapshot of the development environment. It shows that the columns of the strongly typed *DataRow* are easily accessible through statement completion. I was thrilled when Visual Basic introduced statement completion in version 5. However, if I made a mistake typing the name of a column in my Visual Basic 6 and ADO 2.*x* code, I would not discover that mistake until I ran my application. Strongly typed *DataSet* objects and statement completion can all but eliminate such problems in the development cycle.

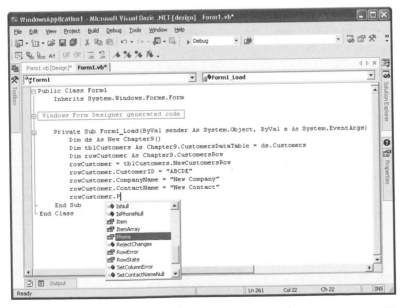

Figure 9-3   Using a strongly typed *DataSet* in code in Visual Studio .NET

Like the *Add* method of the *DataRowCollection*, the *Add<TableName>Row* method of the strongly typed *DataTable* is overloaded. The following code snippet uses the Customers *DataTable* in the strongly typed *DataSet* we created earlier in the chapter.

Visual Basic .NET

```
Dim ds As New Chapter9()
Dim tblCustomers As Chapter9.CustomersDataTable = ds.Customers
tblCustomers.AddCustomersRow("ABCDE", "New Company", _
                            "New Contact", "(800) 555-1212")


'Instead of
tblCustomers.Rows.Add(New Object() {"ABCDE", "New Company", _
                            "New Contact", "(800) 555-1212"})
```

Visual C# .NET

```
Chapter9 ds = new Chapter9();
Chapter9.CustomersDataTable tblCustomers = ds.Customers;
tblCustomers.AddCustomersRow("ABCDE", "New Company",
                            "New Contact", "(800) 555-1212");


//Instead of
tblCustomers.Rows.Add(new object[] {"ABCDE", "New Company",
                            "New Contact", "(800) 555-1212"});
```

Again, thanks to IntelliSense and statement completion, this is one of those features that looks more impressive as you write code. In the Visual Studio .NET development environment, the names of the parameters of the method appear as you type, so you don't have to jump back to other parts of your code to figure out the names and order of your columns.

Finding a Row

With a standard untyped *DataSet*, you can use the *Find* method of the *Data-Table* object's *Rows* collection to locate a particular row based on its primary key value(s). Using that *Find* method can be confusing, especially if the *Data-Table* has a multi-column primary key. For example, the Order Details table in the Northwind database uses the OrderID and ProductID columns as its primary key. Code that uses the *Find* method for a corresponding *DataTable* would therefore look like this:

Visual Basic .NET

```
Dim tblDetails As DataTable
⋮
Dim rowDetail As DataRow
rowDetail = tblDetails.Find(New Object() {10245, 7})
```

Visual C# .NET

```
DataTable tblDetails;
⋮
DataRow rowDetail;
rowDetail = tblDetails.Find(new object[] {10245, 7});
```

This code works, but it can be confusing to write. More important, it is difficult to read, which makes it challenging to maintain.

Each *DataTable* class in a strongly typed *DataSet* exposes its own *Find* method if the *DataTable* has a primary key defined. If we add a *DataTable* for the Order Details table to our strongly typed *DataSet*, we can replace the previous code snippet with this one, which is much easier to write and maintain.

Visual Basic .NET

```
Dim ds As New Chapter9()
...
Dim tblDetails As Chapter9.Order_DetailsDataTable = ds.Order_Details
Dim rowDetail As Chapter9.Order_DetailsRow
rowDetail = tblDetails.FindByOrderIDProductID(10245, 7)
If rowCustomer Is Nothing Then
    Console.WriteLine("Row not found!")
Else
    Console.WriteLine("Found " & rowDetail.OrderID & " - " & _
                        rowDetail.ProductID)
End If
```

Visual C# .NET

```
Chapter9 ds = new Chapter9();
...
Chapter9.Order_DetailsDataTable tblDetails = ds.Order_Details;
Chapter9.Order_DetailsRow rowDetail;
rowDetail = tblDetails.FindByOrderIDProductID(10245, 7);
if (rowDetail == null)
    Console.WriteLine("Row not found!");
else
    Console.WriteLine("Found " + rowDetail.OrderID.ToString() +
                        " - " + rowDetail.ProductID.ToString());
```

Editing a Row

Editing rows in a strongly typed *DataSet* is similar to editing rows in a standard *DataSet*. You still have the option of using the *BeginEdit*, *EndEdit*, and *CancelEdit* methods. However, you can access the values of columns of the *DataRow* using properties of the strongly typed *DataRow*, as shown here.

Visual Basic .NET

```
Dim ds As New Chapter9()
OleDbDataAdapter1.Fill(ds)
Dim rowCustomer As Chapter9.CustomersRow = ds.Customers(0)
rowCustomer.CompanyName = "Modified"

'Instead of
rowCustomer("CompanyName") = "Modified"
```

Visual C# .NET

```
Chapter9 ds = new Chapter9();
OleDbDataAdapter1.Fill(ds);
Chapter9.CustomersRow rowCustomer = ds.Customers[0];
rowCustomer.CompanyName = "Modified";

//Instead of
rowCustomer["CompanyName"] = "Modified";
```

Working with Null Data

During the Visual Studio .NET beta, several newsgroup threads were concerned with null values. Many developers were confused about how to set the value in a column to null or how to determine whether a column contains a null value. In Chapter 6, you saw that you can use the *DataRow* object's *IsNull* function to check for null values and use *System.Convert.DBNull* to assign null values to columns.

Strongly typed *DataSet* objects also make working with null values easier. Each strongly typed *DataRow* also includes two methods per column—one to check whether the column contains a null value and one to set the column's value to null. The following code snippet works with the ContactName column for a row, so these methods are named *IsContactNameNull* and *SetContactNameNull*.

Visual Basic .NET

```
Dim ds As New Chapter9()
OleDbDataAdapter1.Fill(ds)
Dim rowCustomer As Chapter9.CustomersRow = ds.Customers(0)
'Check to see whether the ContactName property is Null.
If rowCustomer.IsContactNameNull() Then
    Console.WriteLine("Contact name is Null")
Else
    Console.WriteLine("Contact name: " & rowCustomer.ContactName)
End If
```

```
'Set the ContactName property to Null.
rowCustomer.SetContactNameNull()

'Instead of
If rowCustomer.IsNull("ContactName") Then
...
'And
rowCustomer("ContactName") = Convert.DBNull
```

Visual C# .NET

```
Chapter9 ds = new Chapter9();
OleDbDataAdapter1.Fill(ds);
Chapter9.CustomersRow rowCustomer = ds.Customers[0];
//Check to see whether the ContactName property is Null.
if (rowCustomer.IsContactNameNull()) then
    Console.WriteLine("Contact name is Null");
else
    Console.WriteLine("Contact name: " + rowCustomer.ContactName);

//Set the ContactName property to Null.
rowCustomer.SetContactNameNull();

//Instead of
if (rowCustomer.IsNull("ContactName"))
...
//And
rowCustomer["ContactName"] = Convert.DBNull;
```

Working with Hierarchical Data

The *DataRow* object exposes two methods that let you navigate through your hierarchical data—*GetChildRows* and *GetParentRow*. These methods require you to supply either the name of the *DataRelation* you want to reference or the object itself.

If your strongly typed *DataSet* contains *DataRelation* objects, the XML Schema Definition Tool will add methods that let you navigate through your hierarchical data without having to specify the *DataRelation* or its name. In the strongly typed *DataSet* we built, we added a *DataRelation* to relate the Customers and Orders *DataTable* objects. When we saved the changes to the *DataSet* object's .xsd file, the XML Schema Definition Tool added a *GetOrdersRows* method to the strongly typed *DataRow* class for the Customers *DataTable* and a *GetCustomersRow* method to the strongly typed *DataRow* class for the Orders *DataTable*.

The following code snippet uses the *GetOrdersRows* method to display all customers as well as the orders for each customer.

Visual Basic .NET

```
Dim ds As New Chapter9()
OleDbDataAdapter1.Fill(ds)
OleDbDataAdapter2.Fill(ds)
Dim rowCustomer As Chapter9.CustomersRow
Dim rowOrder As Chapter9.OrdersRow
For Each rowCustomer In ds.Customers
    Console.WriteLine("Orders for " & rowCustomer.CompanyName)
    For Each rowOrder In rowCustomer.GetOrdersRows()
        Console.WriteLine(vbTab & rowOrder.OrderID & _
                        " - " & rowOrder.OrderDate)
    Next rowOrder
Next rowCustomer

'Instead of
Dim rowCustomer, rowOrder As DataRow
For Each rowCustomer In ds.Tables("Customers").Rows
    Console.WriteLine("Orders for " & rowCustomer("CompanyName"))
    For Each rowOrder In rowCustomer.GetChildRows("CustomersOrders")
        ...
```

Visual C# .NET

```
Chapter9 ds = new Chapter9();
OleDbDataAdapter1.Fill(ds);
OleDbDataAdapter2.Fill(ds);
CustomersDataTable tblCustomers = ds.Customers;
CustomersRow rowCustomer = tblCustomers[0];
foreach (Chapter9.CustomersRow rowOrder
        in ds.Tables["Customers"].Rows)
{
    Console.WriteLine("Orders for " + rowCustomer.CompanyName);
    foreach (Chapter9.OrdersRow rowOrder
            in rowCustomer.GetOrdersRows())
        Console.WriteLine("\t" + rowOrder.OrderID.ToString() + _
                        " - " + rowOrder.OrderDate.ToString());
}

//Instead of
foreach (DataRow rowCustomer in ds.Tables["Customers"].Rows)
{
    Console.WriteLine("Orders for " + rowCustomer["CompanyName"]);
    foreach (DataRow rowOrder in
            rowCustomer.GetChildRows("CustomersOrders"))
        ...
}
```

Other *DataSet*, *DataTable*, and *DataRow* Features

The classes that the XML Schema Definition Tool generates are derived from the *DataSet*, *DataTable*, and *DataRow* classes. This means you can also treat the classes as their untyped counterparts.

For example, the strongly typed *DataSet* classes do not have their own methods for reading and writing XML data and schema information. But because the classes are derived from the *DataSet* class, they still expose methods such as *ReadXml* and *WriteXml*. So for all other tasks, such as using a *DataAdapter* to retrieve data or submit changes, you can treat the strongly typed *DataSet* just like any other *DataSet*.

When to Use Strongly Typed *DataSet* Objects

Every developer I've spoken with, both inside and outside of Microsoft, has been impressed by how strongly typed *DataSet* objects simplify the development process. However, many developers still have reservations about using strongly typed *DataSet* objects in their applications.

Most of these developers have not looked at the code that the XML Schema Definition Tool generates, nor have they compared the performance of untyped and strongly typed *DataSet* objects. And you know what? I was one of those skeptical developers until I started doing research for this chapter. (What did I find? I'll get to that shortly.)

Software Components and Swiss Army Knives

A decade or two ago, I was a Boy Scout. There's an unwritten rule that every Boy Scout must own a Swiss Army knife. Swiss Army knives came in handy on our camping trips. Most of the food we ate came out of cans, so the can opener blade got a lot of use. And you'd always find Scouts whittling wood around the campfire.

Some Swiss Army knives have more gadgets than others. Thankfully, at least one Scout always had a knife that came with a pair of tweezers, because when you combine young boys and wood, you're bound to get splinters. At one point, I owned a Swiss Army knife that had 20-some gadgets. It had everything but a squeegee to wash a car's windshield. I probably used two or three gadgets regularly, but the rest got little use because I had no need for them or they didn't work well.

Another unwritten rule says that children will lose small items and that the chances of the child losing an item are proportional to the cost of the item. At the end of any camping trip, at least one Scout would have lost a knife. When I lost my super-sized knife, I bought a nice but much more basic model. In fact,

I still have it. I don't use it often, but all of the gadgets have come in handy at one time or another. The bottle opener and corkscrew get more use now than when I was 12 years old.

Why didn't I buy another knife with a plethora of gadgets? Simple. The larger one was more expensive and heavier. I didn't buy the very simplest knife, however, because I did occasionally need a couple gadgets. So, I bought a mid-size knife with just the gadgets I thought I would find useful.

The same premise holds true with software components. Simpler components are generally faster than the ones that offer a long list of features.

Strongly typed *DataSet* objects definitely expose more functionality than untyped *DataSet* objects do. However, as with Swiss Army knives, you won't always need the advanced features. If you're not going to use the additional gadgets, you're better off sticking with a more basic model.

Design-Time Benefits

I've already covered the most obvious design-time benefit of strongly typed *DataSet* objects: writing code to access data in a strongly typed *DataSet* is much easier than with a standard untyped *DataSet*, thanks to statement completion and IntelliSense in Visual Studio .NET.

There's also less code to write because the strongly typed *DataSet* class contains code to build the schema and to create the necessary *DataTable*, *Data-Column*, *DataRelation*, and *Constraint* objects in the class's initialization code. If you're using an untyped *DataSet*, you have three options for adding schema information to your *DataSet*: writing the code yourself, loading the schema from an .xsd file using the *DataSet* object's *ReadXmlSchema* method, or using the *DataAdapter* object's *FillSchema* method. Of these three options, using *FillSchema* requires the least amount of work at design time (because *ReadXmlSchema* requires that you build your .xsd file). However, in Chapter 5 we discussed why you should avoid using this feature in your code whenever possible.

If you're building a Windows or Web application that uses data binding, it will be much easier to bind your controls at design time if you're using a strongly typed *DataSet*. Why? Because the strongly typed *DataSet* contains its own schema information, Visual Studio .NET can provide you with a list of tables and columns to which you can bind your control.

Figure 9-4 shows an example. We can specify that we want to view just the orders for the current customer by selecting the *DataRelation* called *Customers-Orders*. Notice that the grid displays the structure of the Orders *DataTable*. No code was written (or harmed) in the building of this sample.

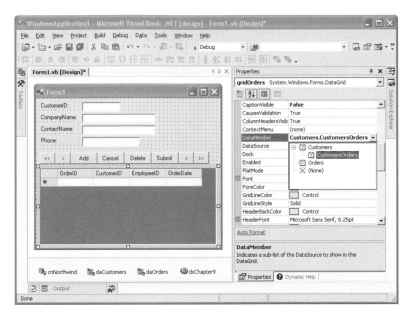

Figure 9-4   Data binding using a strongly typed *DataSet*

Developers who build multi-tiered applications can gain design-time benefits by using strongly typed *DataSet* objects. When you add a reference to a class library or a Web service that returns a strongly typed *DataSet*, your project will have its own copy of the .xsd file and the class file for the strongly typed *DataSet*. Thus, the client application can still take advantage of the design-time benefits of strongly typed *DataSet* objects.

Run-Time Benefits

What are the run-time implications of using strongly typed *DataSet* objects? How do they affect the performance of your applications? Not only is it easier to write code to access the contents of a strongly typed *DataSet*, but that code can also improve the performance of your application. The following code snippet shows the standard way to assign the contents of a column to a text box, using both an untyped and a strongly typed *DataSet*:

Visual Basic .NET

```
'Untyped
Dim dsUntyped As New DataSet()
'Create and fill the DataSet.
⋮
```

(continued)

```
txtCompanyName.Text =
  dsUntyped.Tables("Customers").Rows(0)("CompanyName")

'Strongly typed
Dim dsTyped As New Chapter9()
'Fill the DataSet.
⋮
txtCompanyName.Text = dsTyped.Customers(0).CompanyName
```

Visual C# .NET

```
//Untyped
DataSet dsUntyped = new DataSet();
//Create and fill the DataSet.
⋮
txtCompanyName.Text =
  (string) dsUntyped.Tables["Customers"].Rows[0]["CompanyName"];

//Strongly typed
Chapter9 dsTyped = new Chapter9();
//Fill the DataSet.
⋮
txtCompanyName.Text = dsTyped.Customers[0].CompanyName;
```

The strongly typed code yields better performance. How much better? Well, as of this writing, Visual Studio .NET is still in beta, and it's always tricky to gauge the performance of beta products. However, the tests I've run have shown that the strongly typed code runs nearly twice as fast as the untyped code in the preceding code snippet.

How does the strongly typed *DataSet* provide improved performance? In Chapter 6, you learned that the *DataRow* object allows you to access the contents of a column by supplying the name of the column, the ordinal for the column, or the *DataColumn* object itself. Code that uses the actual *DataColumn* object yields the best performance, but it's the most difficult to write and maintain. Supplying the column name as a string results in code that's easy to write and maintain, but it also results in the worst performance.

The code generated by the XML Schema Definition Tool gives you the best of both worlds. The code you write is easy to maintain, and the code that the tool generates uses the *DataColumn* object. Figure 9-5 shows the code that the XML Schema Definition Tool generates to return the value of the CompanyName column in a Customers row. Through the miracles of cut and paste, the figure shows the code generated in both Visual Basic .NET and Visual C# .NET.

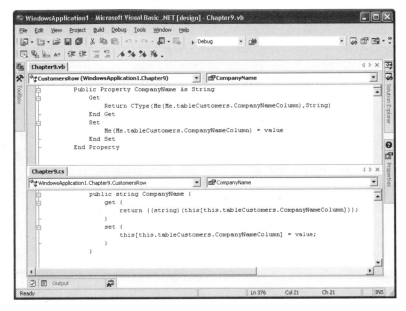

Figure 9-5   Code from the strongly typed *DataSet* class that accesses the CompanyName column from a Customers row

You can achieve comparable performance by accessing the contents of a column using a *DataColumn* object, as shown in the following code:

Visual Basic .NET

```
Dim dsUntyped As New DataSet()
'Initialize and fill DataSet.
Dim tblCustomers As DataTable = dsUntyped.Tables(0)
'Get a reference to the desired column.
Dim colCompanyName As DataColumn
colCompanyName = tblCustomers.Columns("CompanyName")
⋮
Dim row As DataRow = tblCustomers.Rows(0)
txtCompanyName.Text = CType(row(colCompanyName), String)
```

Visual C# .NET

```
DataSet dsUntyped = new DataSet();
//Initialize and fill DataSet.
DataTable tblCustomers = dsUntyped.Tables[0];
//Get a reference to the desired column.
DataColumn colCompanyName;
colCompanyName = tblCustomers.Columns["CompanyName"];
⋮
DataRow row = tblCustomers.Rows[0];
txtCompanyName.Text = (string) row[colCompanyName];
```

This brings up an important point. There's nothing in the code for the strongly typed *DataSet* object's class that you can't write yourself. In fact, anything a strongly typed *DataSet* can do, you can do just as well. But writing your own code can take time. To access the contents of an untyped *DataSet* with the same performance as a strongly typed *DataSet*, you must avoid performing string-based lookups in your collections. Instead, use index-based lookups or maintain references to the columns in your untyped *DataSet*.

In the test I described earlier in this section, code that used the strongly typed *DataSet* was nearly twice as fast as code that used the untyped *DataSet*. I modified my code slightly to use code that accessed the contents of the row using the appropriate *DataColumn* object and also used the appropriate type conversion code. The results? The new and improved code that accessed the untyped *DataSet* was 5 to 10 percent faster than the code that accessed the strongly typed *DataSet*.

Because of the added overhead that comes with a strongly typed *DataSet*, creating, filling, and accessing strongly typed *DataSet* objects takes more time. In tests I've run, untyped *DataSet* objects provided slightly better performance (usually between 8 and 10 percent) than strongly typed *DataSet* objects.

Additional Considerations

Strongly typed *DataSet* objects can simplify your coding and help save a modicum of sanity. Here are a few more matters for you to consider if you decide to use strongly typed *DataSet* objects.

Making Structural Changes

If you need to change the structure of your strongly typed *DataSet* by adding or changing some of the *DataColumn* objects, you have to regenerate your strongly typed *DataSet*. Keep this in mind if you build a multi-tiered application in which the middle tier returns strongly typed *DataSet* objects. If you regenerate the strongly typed *DataSet* that the middle tier returns, you'll also need to rebuild the client application after refreshing the reference to the middle-tier object. However, if you're going to change the structure of the data returned by your server, you'll probably need to change the client code that accesses that structure anyway, regardless of whether you're using strongly typed *DataSet* objects.

Converting *DataSet* Objects

Because strongly typed *DataSet* objects inherit from the standard *DataSet* class, the following code that accesses a strongly typed *DataSet* through an untyped *DataSet* interface is valid:

Visual Basic .NET

```
Dim dsStrong As New Chapter9()
Dim dsUntyped As DataSet
dsUntyped = CType(dsStrong, DataSet)
```

Visual C# .NET

```
Chapter9 dsStrong = new Chapter9();
DataSet dsUntyped;
dsUntyped = (DataSet) dsStrong;
```

However, you can "promote" an untyped *DataSet* to a strongly typed *DataSet* class only if the untyped *DataSet* was originally created as an instance of that same strongly typed *DataSet* class. The following code snippet should help clarify this behavior:

Visual Basic .NET

```
Dim dsStrong1, dsStrong2 As Chapter9
Dim dsUntyped As DataSet

'This code will succeed.
dsStrong1 = New Chapter9()
dsUntyped = CType(dsStrong1, DataSet)
dsStrong2 = CType(dsUntyped, Chapter9)

'This code will throw an exception.
dsUntyped = New DataSet()
dsStrong2 = CType(dsUntyped, Chapter9)
```

Visual C# .NET

```
Chapter9 dsStrong1, dsStrong2;
DataSet dsUntyped;

//This code will succeed.
dsStrong1 = new Chapter9();
dsUntyped = (DataSet) dsStrong1;
dsStrong2 = (Chapter9) dsUntyped;

//This code will throw an exception.
dsUntyped = new DataSet();
dsStrong2 = (Chapter9) dsUntyped;
```

What if you have an untyped *DataSet* and you want to access its contents using a strongly typed *DataSet* class? If the untyped *DataSet* object was created as an untyped *DataSet*, you cannot cast the object to a strongly typed *DataSet*.

However, you can use the *Merge* method of the strongly typed *DataSet* to import the data from the untyped *DataSet*, as the following code snippet illustrates:

Visual Basic .NET

```
Dim dsStrong As New Chapter9()
Dim dsUntyped As New DataSet()
dsStrong.Merge(dsUntyped)
```

Visual C# .NET

```
Chapter9 dsStrong = new Chapter9();
DataSet dsUntyped = new DataSet();
dsStrong.Merge(dsUntyped);
```

The *Merge* method is also useful if you need to move data back and forth between instances of two different strongly typed *DataSet* classes. You can also use the *WriteXml* and *ReadXml* methods to move data back and forth between different strongly typed *DataSet* classes if you include the XML schema in the calls to *WriteXml* and *ReadXml*.

Untyped Features of Strongly Typed *DataSet* Objects

Let's say your application uses strongly typed *DataSet* objects and you want to send a *DataSet* back to your middle-tier server to submit changes to your database. You can use the strongly typed *DataSet* object's *GetChanges* method to create a new *DataSet* that contains only modified rows. However, the *GetChanges* method returns an untyped *DataSet*. Can you cast the untyped *DataSet* returned by the *GetChanges* method to a strongly typed *DataSet*? Absolutely. The following code snippet demonstrates this functionality:

Visual Basic .NET

```
Dim dsStrongAllRows As New Chapter9()
'Fill the strongly typed DataSet and modify some of its rows.
Dim dsUntyped As DataSet
dsUntyped = dsStrongAllRows.GetChanges()
Dim dsStrongModifiedRows As Chapter9
dsStrongModifiedRows = CType(dsUntyped, Chapter9)
```

Visual C# .NET

```
Chapter9 dsStrongAllRows = new Chapter9();
//Fill the strongly typed DataSet and modify some of its rows.
DataSet dsUntyped;
dsUntyped = dsStrongAllRows.GetChanges();
Chapter9 dsStrongModifiedRows;
dsStrongModifiedRows = (Chapter9) dsUntyped;
```

The strongly typed *DataSet* has other methods that return untyped data. For example, the *Select* method returns an array of *DataRow* objects. You can't cast the array to an array of strongly typed *DataRow* objects, but you can cast the individual *DataRow* objects to their strongly typed counterparts.

Similar rules apply to the *DataView*. You can't access its contents directly through the strongly typed classes, but you can convert the *DataRow* returned by the *DataRowView* object's *Row* property to a strongly typed class using the code in the following code snippet:

Visual Basic .NET

```
Dim dsStrong As New Chapter9()
'Fill the strongly typed DataSet and modify some of its rows.
Dim vueCustomers As New DataView(dsStrong.Customers)
Dim rowCustomer As Chapter9.CustomersRow
rowCustomer = CType(vueCustomers(0).Row, Chapter9.CustomersRow)
```

Visual C# .NET

```
Chapter9 dsStrong = new Chapter9();
//Fill the strongly typed DataSet and modify some of its rows.
DataView vueCustomers = new DataView(dsStrong.Customers);
Chapter9.CustomersRow rowCustomer;
rowCustomer = (Chapter9.CustomersRow) vueCustomers(0).Row;
```

Choosing Your Path

So, what's the right choice for you? Strongly typed *DataSet* objects can help you build your application more quickly. They can also help you to write efficient code more easily. But they don't offer the best possible performance. You can build an application that will run faster if you use untyped *DataSet* objects along with intelligent code.

It all depends on the needs of your application. If the performance of your application is the absolute highest priority, you should use only untyped *DataSet* objects. However, if saving a few hours of development time is worth a small performance hit, you should consider using strongly typed *DataSet* objects.

Questions That Should Be Asked More Frequently

Q.   I need to get the best possible performance out of my middle-tier components, so I'm using untyped *DataSet* objects on the server. But strongly typed *DataSet* objects are so handy when I build the client portion of the application. Is there a way to get the best of both worlds?

A. Yes. Have your middle tier return and accept untyped *DataSet* objects. Use instances of strongly typed *DataSet* objects in the client application, and use the *Merge* method to import the contents of the untyped *DataSet* objects returned by the middle tier.

Q. *DataSet* objects offer limited validation features. I can't set properties on either an untyped or a strongly typed *DataSet* to ensure that the value of a column falls between certain limits. Can I add my own code to the class file for added validation?

A. Of course. You can add validation code to the desired properties of your strongly typed classes, but this was not an intended use of the strongly typed *DataSet*. Your validation code will not be stored in the .xsd file for the strongly typed *DataSet* class. If you modify the contents of the .xsd file, Visual Studio .NET will regenerate the class for the strongly typed *DataSet* and you'll lose the code that you've written.

You have another option: create a new class that inherits from the strongly typed *DataSet* class and add your validation code there.

Q. What other options do I have when I use the XML Schema Definition Tool to generate a class?

A. If you check the "Using Annotations with a Typed DataSet" topic in the .NET Framework SDK, you'll find various options for controlling the names of some of the strongly typed classes generated by the tool. You'll also discover how to control how the properties on your strongly typed *DataRow* classes react when they contain null values. The XML Schema Definition Tool checks your .xsd file for the annotations listed in the documentation.

The XML Schema designer does not let you add annotations to your *DataSet* object's .xsd file through the designer's user interface. You can switch to XML view and add the annotations by hand. Or you can add annotations to your *DataSet* class in code and then save the *DataSet* object's schema to an .xsd file using the *DataSet* object's *WriteXmlSchema* method.

Adding annotations to your *DataSet* in code is actually fairly simple if you use the *ExtendedProperties* collection of the *DataTable* and *DataColumn* objects. The following code snippet is an example:

Visual Basic .NET

```
Dim ds As New DataSet()
ds.DataSetName = "NameForYourNewClass"
```

```
Dim tbl As DataTable = ds.Tables.Add("Table1")
Dim col As DataColumn

'Set the name of the strongly typed DataRow for the DataTable.
tbl.ExtendedProperties.Add("typedName", "MyTable1Row")

'Set the name of the DataTable property of the DataSet.
tbl.ExtendedProperties.Add("typedPlural", "MyTable1Rows")

col = tbl.Columns.Add("StringColumn", GetType(String))
'Have the class return "<Null>" if the column contains null.
col.ExtendedProperties.Add("nullValue", "<Null>")

col = tbl.Columns.Add("StringColumn2", GetType(String))
'Have the class return String.Empty if the column contains null.
col.ExtendedProperties.Add("nullValue", String.Empty)

col = tbl.Columns.Add("IntegerColumn", GetType(Integer))
'Have the class return 0 if the column contains null.
col.ExtendedProperties.Add("nullValue", "0")

ds.WriteXmlSchema("C:\Desired\Path\To\YourNew.XSD")
```

Visual C# .NET

```
DataSet ds = new DataSet();
ds.DataSetName = "NameForYourNewClass";
DataTable tbl = ds.Tables.Add("Table1");
DataColumn col;

//Set the name of the strongly typed DataRow for the DataTable.
tbl.ExtendedProperties.Add("typedName", "MyTable1Row");

//Set the name of the DataTable property of the DataSet.
tbl.ExtendedProperties.Add("typedPlural", "MyTable1Rows");

col = tbl.Columns.Add("StringColumn", typeof(string));
//Have the class return "<Null>" if the column contains null.
col.ExtendedProperties.Add("nullValue", "<Null>");

col = tbl.Columns.Add("StringColumn2", typeof(string));
//Have the class return String.Empty if the column contains null.
col.ExtendedProperties.Add("nullValue", String.Empty);

col = tbl.Columns.Add("IntegerColumn", typeof(int));
//Have the class return 0 if the column contains null.
col.ExtendedProperties.Add("nullValue", "0");

ds.WriteXmlSchema("C:\\Desired\\Path\\To\\YourNew.XSD");
```

10

Submitting Updates to Your Database

"When you believe in things that you don't understand, then you suffer. Superstition ain't the way."

—*Stevie Wonder*

Although Stevie Wonder probably wasn't talking about submitting updates, the quote is still relevant to the topic. ADO.NET gives database programmers unprecedented power and control over submitting updates. However, based on the questions I've handled personally on internal and external newsgroups and at conferences during the .NET beta, I'd say that few developers really understand how to effectively wield this control and power.

So many of the ADO.NET code snippets I've seen rely on the *Command-Builder* object to generate updating logic. Sometimes the code snippet comes with a warning that says you should generate your own updating logic instead, but those comments rarely explain why or how this is done.

How many times have you asked someone how they got their code to work only to have them shrug, smile, and say, "It just works"? That's the sort of superstition I want to dispel in this chapter and the following chapter.

> **Note** I've actually seen a technical support organization adopt "It just works" as their slogan. Sad but true.

The more you understand how you can use ADO.NET to submit updates, the more comfortable you'll become generating your own updating logic and/ or submitting updates via stored procedures. This chapter will help you understand how to use a *DataAdapter* to submit the pending changes from your *DataSet* to your database. Along the way, you'll also learn how and when to use tools to save time without sacrificing performance or control.

If you've been reading the chapters of this book in sequence, you should already be comfortable creating untyped and strongly typed *DataSet* objects to store the data returned by *DataAdapter* objects. You should also be comfortable modifying the contents of a *DataSet*. This chapter will help you understand the basics of using *DataAdapter* objects to submit the changes stored in your *DataSet* to your database.

Let's look at an order from the sample Northwind database. Figure 10-1 shows the query issued in SQL Server Query Analyzer to retrieve information for the order. For the sake of argument, let's say the customer calls and wants to change the order. Tofu isn't selling, but bottles of hot sauce are flying off the shelves and people keep asking for chai tea.

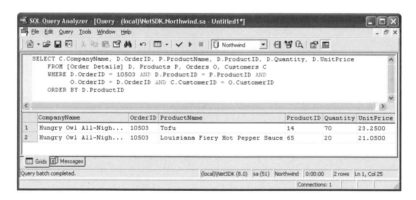

Figure 10-1   Contents of an order in the Northwind database.

Thanks to the knowledge you gained in Chapter 5, you know how to fetch the results of a query into a *DataSet*. You can use that knowledge to build an application that allows the user to fetch the customer's order into a *DataSet*. Based on what you learned in Chapter 6, you can enable your application to modify the data in the *DataSet* per the customer's instructions. However, as I've noted, changing the contents of a *DataSet* doesn't change the corresponding rows in the database.

In Chapter 5, you also learned that the *DataAdapter* exposes an *Update* method that you can use to submit pending changes to your database. So, you can build an application that uses code such as this to submit the changes to the order:

Visual Basic .NET

```
'Retrieve the contents of the order into a DataTable.
Dim strConn, strSQL As String
strConn = "Provider=SQLOLEDB;Data Source=(local)\NetSDK;" & _
          "Initial Catalog=Northwind;Trusted_Connection=Yes;"
strSQL = "SELECT OrderID, ProductID, Quantity, UnitPrice " & _
         "FROM [Order Details] WHERE OrderID = 10503 " & _
         "ORDER BY ProductID"
Dim da As New OleDbDataAdapter(strSQL, strConn)
Dim tbl As New DataTable("Order Details")
da.Fill(tbl)

'Modify the contents of the order.
tbl.Rows(0).Delete()
tbl.Rows(1)("Quantity") = CShort(tbl.Rows(1)("Quantity")) * 2
tbl.Rows.Add(New Object() {10503, 1, 24, 18})

'Submit the pending changes.
Try
    da.Update(tbl)
    Console.WriteLine("Successfully submitted new changes")
Catch ex As Exception
    Console.WriteLine("Call to DataAdapter.Update " & _
                      "threw exception:" & vbCrLf & ex.Message)
End Try
```

Visual C# .NET

```
//Retrieve the contents of the order into a DataTable.
string strConn, strSQL;
strConn = "Provider=SQLOLEDB;Data Source=(local)\\NetSDK;" +
          "Initial Catalog=Northwind;Trusted_Connection=Yes;";
strSQL = "SELECT OrderID, ProductID, Quantity, UnitPrice " +
         "FROM [Order Details] WHERE OrderID = 10503 " +
         "ORDER BY ProductID";
OleDbDataAdapter da = new OleDbDataAdapter(strSQL, strConn);
DataTable tbl = new DataTable("Order Details");
da.Fill(tbl);

//Modify the contents of the order.
tbl.Rows[0].Delete();
tbl.Rows[1]["Quantity"] = (short) (tbl.Rows[1]["Quantity"]) * 2;
tbl.Rows.Add(new object[] {10503, 1, 24, 18});

//Submit the pending changes.
try
```

(continued)

```
{
    da.Update(tbl);
    Console.WriteLine("Successfully submitted new changes");
}
catch (Exception ex)
{
    Console.WriteLine("Call to DataAdapter.Update threw exception:\n"
                      + ex.Message);
}
```

This code will successfully compile, but it will not successfully submit the changes to the order to your database. Instead, you'll receive an exception that says, "Update requires a valid DeleteCommand when passed DataRow collection with deleted rows."

Exceptions such as these confused many developers during the Microsoft .NET Framework beta. Previous data access technologies such as ADO include features that let you submit changes automatically. With ADO.NET, you can submit changes using the *DataAdapter* object, but the *DataAdapter* does not automatically include the logic required to submit updates.

So how do you add the necessary updating logic to your ADO.NET *DataAdapter*? You have three basic options: you can write your own code, ask ADO.NET to generate the updating logic for you, or rely on a code generation tool such as the Visual Studio .NET Data Adapter Configuration Wizard.

This chapter will cover all three of these options and explain the pros and cons of each.

A History Lesson

Before we look at how to submit pending changes using ADO.NET, let's take a look at how the process works in ADO.NET's predecessor, ADO. ADO.NET will not automatically generate updating logic for you, but ADO does. By taking a cursory look at how the ADO cursor engine submits updates "automagically," we'll gain insight into how and why the ADO.NET development team chose to go a different route by pushing developers towards writing their own updating logic. Understanding how the ADO cursor engine submits your changes will also make it easier to understand how to generate your own updating logic in ADO.NET.

The ADO cursor engine supports functionality similar to the ADO.NET *DataSet*. You can use a client-side ADO *Recordset* object as an offline data cache. The *Recordset* object is also ADO's mechanism for submitting updates to the database.

The following code snippet retrieves the contents of the order we discussed earlier, modifies the contents of the order, and then submits those pending changes to the database:

Visual Basic "Classic" and ADO 2.*x*

```
Dim strConn As String, strSQL As String
strConn = "Provider=SQLOLEDB;Data Source=(local)\NetSDK;" & _
          "Initial Catalog=Northwind;Trusted_Connection=Yes;"
strSQL = "SELECT OrderID, ProductID, Quantity, UnitPrice " & _
          "FROM [Order Details] WHERE OrderID = 10503 " & _
          "ORDER BY ProductID"

Dim rs As ADODB.Recordset
Set rs = New ADODB.Recordset
rs.CursorLocation = adUseClient
rs.Open strSQL, strConn, adOpenStatic, adLockBatchOptimistic, _
        adCmdText

rs.Delete
rs.MoveNext

rs.Fields("Quantity") = 2 * rs.Fields("Quantity")
rs.Update

rs.AddNew
rs.Fields("OrderID") = 10503
rs.Fields("ProductID") = 1
rs.Fields("Quantity") = 24
rs.Fields("UnitPrice") = 18
rs.Update

rs.UpdateBatch

rs.Close
cn.Close
```

This code snippet demonstrates many of the benefits and drawbacks of submitting updates using a *Recordset* in the ADO object model, as I'll explain in the upcoming sections.

Benefits of Submitting Updates Using ADO *Recordset* Objects

The first major benefit of this approach is that it requires minimal code. You open the *Recordset*, modify its contents, and then submit the changes to your database. You can accomplish a lot of work in just a few lines of code.

The code has no updating logic because ADO generates this logic automatically at run time. That's the other major benefit. ADO does not require you to supply updating logic programmatically. In fact, someone with minimal knowledge of the SQL language can write this code: you can use the ADO cursor engine's updating features without any understanding of concurrency, locking, or how to generate a SQL UPDATE query. The fact that developers can build working data access applications without this knowledge is a testament to the technology's design. It continually amazes me—in a good way—that so many developers use the ADO cursor engine to submit updates but have no idea how the ADO cursor engine accomplishes this task.

Drawbacks of Submitting Updates Using ADO *Recordset* Objects

Unfortunately, the ADO cursor engine's updating features also have their drawbacks—less than stellar performance and a lack of control. Countless developers have relied on the ADO cursor engine to submit changes to their databases since the release of ADO 1.5, so these problems aren't monumental. However, they are significant. To better understand these drawbacks, let's take a quick look at how the ADO cursor engine submits the changes to the database.

When you call the *UpdateBatch* method of the *Recordset* object, the ADO cursor engine scans the *Recordset* for modified rows and translates the changes to each modified row into a SQL query that will modify the corresponding row in the database. Earlier, I made reference to developers generating their own SQL UPDATE, INSERT, and DELETE queries to modify the contents of a database. The ADO cursor engine builds similar statements.

You can use SQL Profiler to watch the SQL calls to your database. If you watch the queries that the ADO cursor engine generates to submit your changes, you'll actually see a call to the SQL Server *sp_executesql* stored procedure with a batch of parameterized queries. That stored procedure call is equivalent to the following queries:

```
DELETE FROM [Order Details] WHERE OrderID = 10503 AND ProductID = 14

UPDATE [Order Details] SET Quantity = 40
    WHERE OrderID = 10503 AND ProductID = 65 AND Quantity = 20

INSERT INTO [Order Details] (OrderID, ProductID, Quantity, UnitPrice)
    VALUES (10503, 1, 24, 18)
```

After you reexamine the initial query and the changes made to the *Recordset* in code, these queries should look relatively straightforward to you—that is, you can look at the queries and understand their purpose even if you're really not comfortable constructing such queries yourself. Translating the changes in the *Recordset* into SQL queries is pretty simple if you know where the data came from.

It's pretty obvious to us where the data came from, but how did the ADO cursor engine discover this information? When the ADO cursor engine fetched the results of your query, it also asked the database for additional metadata. To construct the UPDATE query shown earlier, the cursor engine needed to know the base table and column names for each of the columns in the result set, along with primary key information for the tables referenced by the query.

You can examine this metadata yourself by using the ADO *Field* object's *Properties* collection in code such as this:

```
With rs.Fields("Quantity")
    Debug.Print "BaseTableName = " & .Properties("BaseTableName")
    Debug.Print "BaseColumnName = " & .Properties("BaseColumnName")
    Debug.Print "KeyColumn = " & .Properties("KeyColumn")
End With
```

This brings us to the first major drawback of the ADO cursor engine's updating features: performance. The queries that the ADO cursor engine issues in order to gather table, column, and primary key data from the database constitute a significant performance hit. Most developers who write data access code know where the data comes from. Unfortunately, ADO offers no way to provide this metadata in code to save you from having to query the database for this information every time you open your *Recordset*.

The ADO cursor engine is a "black box" technology. It does not let you define your own updating logic. This is the second major drawback of the ADO cursor engine's updating features. Even though the ADO cursor engine's updating logic is impressive, it offers you little or no control over your updating logic. You cannot choose to submit the updates cached in your *Recordset* via stored procedure calls. If you don't like the updating logic that the ADO cursor engine generates, you're on your own.

Using ADO.NET *Command* Objects to Submit Updates

As you now know, the ADO cursor engine builds parameterized queries to submit updates. You can use what you learned in Chapter 4 to build equivalent parameterized queries in ADO.NET. Later in the chapter, you'll learn how to use these parameterized *Command* objects to submit the changes stored in an ADO.NET *DataSet* to your database.

Our ADO.NET *Command* objects will not be quite as dynamic as their ADO counterparts. To simplify the process, we'll build one *Command* to handle updates, one to handle insertions, and one to handle deletions. They'll be based on the following parameterized queries:

```
UPDATE [Order Details]
    SET OrderID = ?, ProductID = ?, Quantity = ?, UnitPrice = ?
    WHERE OrderID = ? AND ProductID = ? AND
        Quantity = ? AND UnitPrice = ?

INSERT INTO [Order Details] (OrderID, ProductID, Quantity, UnitPrice)
    VALUES (?, ?, ?, ?)

DELETE FROM [Order Details]
    WHERE OrderID = ? AND ProductID = ? AND
        Quantity = ? AND UnitPrice = ?
```

> **Note**   The UPDATE and INSERT queries submit new values to the database for each column in the original query. These queries reference each column in the original query in their WHERE clauses. This approach has its benefits and drawbacks, which I'll discuss later in the chapter.

The following code snippet builds our three parameterized *Command* objects. In each case, the code assumes that there is an externally defined *Ole-DbConnection* object called *cn*.

Visual Basic .NET

```
Private Function CreateUpdateCommand() As OleDbCommand
    Dim strSQL As String
    strSQL = "UPDATE [Order Details] " & _
          "    SET OrderID = ?, ProductID = ?, " & _
          "        Quantity = ?, UnitPrice = ? " & _
          "    WHERE OrderID = ? AND ProductID = ? AND " & _
          "        Quantity = ? AND UnitPrice = ?"
    Dim cmd As New OleDbCommand(strSQL, cn)

    Dim pc As OleDbParameterCollection = cmd.Parameters
    pc.Add("OrderID_New", OleDbType.Integer)
    pc.Add("ProductID_New", OleDbType.Integer)
    pc.Add("Quantity_New", OleDbType.SmallInt)
    pc.Add("UnitPrice_New", OleDbType.Currency)

    pc.Add("OrderID_Orig", OleDbType.Integer)
    pc.Add("ProductID_Orig", OleDbType.Integer)
```

```vbnet
            pc.Add("Quantity_Orig", OleDbType.SmallInt)
            pc.Add("UnitPrice_Orig", OleDbType.Currency)

        Return cmd
    End Function

    Private Function CreateInsertCommand() As OleDbCommand
        Dim strSQL As String
        strSQL = "INSERT INTO [Order Details] " & _
                 "    (OrderID, ProductID, Quantity, UnitPrice) " & _
                 "    VALUES (?, ?, ?, ?)"
        Dim cmd As New OleDbCommand(strSQL, cn)

            Dim pc As OleDbParameterCollection = cmd.Parameters
            pc.Add("OrderID", OleDbType.Integer)
            pc.Add("ProductID", OleDbType.Integer)
            pc.Add("Quantity", OleDbType.SmallInt)
            pc.Add("UnitPrice", OleDbType.Currency)

        Return cmd
    End Function

    Private Function CreateDeleteCommand() As OleDbCommand
        Dim strSQL As String
        strSQL = "DELETE FROM [Order Details] " & _
                 "    WHERE OrderID = ? AND ProductID = ? AND " & _
                 "        Quantity = ? AND UnitPrice = ?"
        Dim cmd As New OleDbCommand(strSQL, cn)

            Dim pc As OleDbParameterCollection = cmd.Parameters
            pc.Add("OrderID", OleDbType.Integer)
            pc.Add("ProductID", OleDbType.Integer)
            pc.Add("Quantity", OleDbType.SmallInt)
            pc.Add("UnitPrice", OleDbType.Currency)

        Return cmd
    End Function
```

Visual C# .NET

```csharp
static OleDbCommand CreateUpdateCommand()
{
    string strSQL;
    strSQL = "UPDATE [Order Details] " & _
             "    SET OrderID = ?, ProductID = ?, " +
             "        Quantity = ?, UnitPrice = ? " +
             "    WHERE OrderID = ? AND ProductID = ? AND " +
             "        Quantity = ? AND UnitPrice = ?";
    OleDbCommand cmd = new OleDbCommand(strSQL, cn);
```

(continued)

```
        OleDbParameterCollection pc = cmd.Parameters;
        pc.Add("OrderID_New", OleDbType.Integer);
        pc.Add("ProductID_New", OleDbType.Integer);
        pc.Add("Quantity_New", OleDbType.SmallInt);
        pc.Add("UnitPrice_New", OleDbType.Currency);

        pc.Add("OrderID_Orig", OleDbType.Integer);
        pc.Add("ProductID_Orig", OleDbType.Integer);
        pc.Add("Quantity_Orig", OleDbType.SmallInt);
        pc.Add("UnitPrice_Orig", OleDbType.Currency);

        return cmd;
    }

    static OleDbCommand CreateInsertCommand()
    {
        string strSQL;
        strSQL = "INSERT INTO [Order Details] " +
                 "    (OrderID, ProductID, Quantity, UnitPrice) " +
                 "    VALUES (?, ?, ?, ?)";
        OleDbCommand cmd = new OleDbCommand(strSQL, cn);

        OleDbParameterCollection pc = cmd.Parameters;
        pc.Add("OrderID", OleDbType.Integer);
        pc.Add("ProductID", OleDbType.Integer);
        pc.Add("Quantity", OleDbType.SmallInt);
        pc.Add("UnitPrice", OleDbType.Currency);

        return cmd;
    }

    static OleDbCommand CreateDeleteCommand()
    {
        string strSQL;
        strSQL = "DELETE FROM [Order Details] " +
                 "    WHERE OrderID = ? AND ProductID = ? AND " +
                 "        Quantity = ? AND UnitPrice = ?";
        OleDbCommand cmd = new OleDbCommand(strSQL, cn);

        OleDbParameterCollection pc = cmd.Parameters;
        pc.Add("OrderID", OleDbType.Integer);
        pc.Add("ProductID", OleDbType.Integer);
        pc.Add("Quantity", OleDbType.SmallInt);
        pc.Add("UnitPrice", OleDbType.Currency);

        return cmd;
    }
```

Using our parameterized *Command* objects to submit updates is fairly straightforward. We need to examine the modified rows in our *DataTable* and determine the type of change stored in each of these rows (update, insert, or delete). Then we can use the contents of the row to populate the values of the parameters of the appropriate command.

After we call the *ExecuteNonQuery* method to execute the query stored in the *Command*, we can use the method's return value to determine whether the update attempt succeeded. If we successfully submit the pending change, we can call the *AcceptChanges* method of the *DataRow*. Otherwise, we can set the *DataRow* object's *RowError* property to indicate that the attempt to submit the pending change failed.

Visual Basic .NET

```vb
Private Sub SubmitChangesByHand()
    Dim cmdUpdate As OleDbCommand = CreateUpdateCommand()
    Dim cmdInsert As OleDbCommand = CreateInsertCommand()
    Dim cmdDelete As OleDbCommand = CreateDeleteCommand()
    Dim row As DataRow
    Dim intRowsAffected As Integer
    Dim dvrs As DataViewRowState
    dvrs = DataViewRowState.ModifiedCurrent _
            Or DataViewRowState.Deleted Or DataViewRowState.Added
    For Each row In tbl.Select("", "", dvrs)
        Select Case row.RowState
            Case DataRowState.Modified
                intRowsAffected = SubmitUpdate(row, cmdUpdate)
            Case DataRowState.Added
                intRowsAffected = SubmitInsert(row, cmdInsert)
            Case DataRowState.Deleted
                intRowsAffected = SubmitDelete(row, cmdDelete)
        End Select
        If intRowsAffected = 1 Then
            row.AcceptChanges()
        Else
            row.RowError = "Update attempt failed"
        End If
    Next row
End Sub

Private Function SubmitUpdate(ByVal row As DataRow, _
                              ByVal cmd As OleDbCommand) As Integer
    Dim pc As OleDbParameterCollection = cmd.Parameters
    pc("OrderID_New").Value = row("OrderID")
    pc("ProductID_New").Value = row("ProductID")
    pc("Quantity_New").Value = row("Quantity")
    pc("UnitPrice_New").Value = row("UnitPrice")
```

(continued)

```vb
            pc("OrderID_Orig").Value = row("OrderID", _
                                        DataRowVersion.Original)
            pc("Quantity_Orig").Value = row("Quantity", _
                                        DataRowVersion.Original)
            pc("ProductID_Orig").Value = row("ProductID", _
                                        DataRowVersion.Original)
            pc("UnitPrice_Orig").Value = row("UnitPrice", _
                                        DataRowVersion.Original)
        Return cmd.ExecuteNonQuery
End Function

    Private Function SubmitInsert(ByVal row As DataRow, _
                            ByVal cmd As OleDbCommand) As Integer
        Dim pc As OleDbParameterCollection = cmd.Parameters
        pc("OrderID").Value = row("OrderID")
        pc("ProductID").Value = row("ProductID")
        pc("Quantity").Value = row("Quantity")
        pc("UnitPrice").Value = row("UnitPrice")
        Return cmd.ExecuteNonQuery
End Function

    Private Function SubmitDelete(ByVal row As DataRow, _
                            ByVal cmd As OleDbCommand) As Integer
        Dim pc As OleDbParameterCollection = cmd.Parameters
        pc("OrderID").Value = row("OrderID", DataRowVersion.Original)
        pc("ProductID").Value = row("ProductID", DataRowVersion.Original)
        pc("Quantity").Value = row("Quantity", DataRowVersion.Original)
        pc("UnitPrice").Value = row("UnitPrice", DataRowVersion.Original)
        Return cmd.ExecuteNonQuery
End Function
```

Visual C# .NET

```csharp
static void SubmitChangesByHand()
{
    OleDbCommand cmdUpdate = CreateUpdateCommand();
    OleDbCommand cmdInsert = CreateInsertCommand();
    OleDbCommand cmdDelete = CreateDeleteCommand();
    DataViewRowState dvrs;
    dvrs = DataViewRowState.ModifiedCurrent |
            DataViewRowState.Deleted | DataViewRowState.Added;
    int intRowsAffected = 0;
    foreach (DataRow row in tbl.Select("", "", dvrs))
    {
        switch (row.RowState)
        {
            case DataRowState.Modified:
                intRowsAffected = SubmitUpdate(row, cmdUpdate);
                break;
```

```
                    case DataRowState.Added:
                        intRowsAffected = SubmitInsert(row, cmdInsert);
                        break;
                    case DataRowState.Deleted:
                        intRowsAffected = SubmitDelete(row, cmdDelete);
                        break;
            }
            if (intRowsAffected == 1)
                row.AcceptChanges();
            else
                row.RowError = "Update attempt failed";
        }
}

static int SubmitUpdate(DataRow row, OleDbCommand cmd)
{
    OleDbParameterCollection pc = cmd.Parameters;
    pc["OrderID_New"].Value = row["OrderID"];
    pc["ProductID_New"].Value = row["ProductID"];
    pc["Quantity_New"].Value = row["Quantity"];
    pc["UnitPrice_New"].Value = row["UnitPrice"];
    pc["OrderID_Orig"].Value = row["OrderID",
                                      DataRowVersion.Original];
    pc["ProductID_Orig"].Value = row["ProductID",
                                        DataRowVersion.Original];
    pc["Quantity_Orig"].Value = row["Quantity",
                                      DataRowVersion.Original];
    pc["UnitPrice_Orig"].Value = row["UnitPrice",
                                        DataRowVersion.Original];
    return cmd.ExecuteNonQuery();
}

static int SubmitInsert(DataRow row, OleDbCommand cmd)
{
    OleDbParameterCollection pc = cmd.Parameters;
    pc["OrderID"].Value = row["OrderID"];
    pc["ProductID"].Value = row["ProductID"];
    pc[Quantity"].Value = row["Quantity"];
    pc["UnitPrice"].Value = row["UnitPrice"];
    return cmd.ExecuteNonQuery();
}

static int SubmitDelete(DataRow row, OleDbCommand cmd)
{
    OleDbParameterCollection pc = cmd.Parameters;
    pc["OrderID"].Value = row["OrderID", DataRowVersion.Original];
    pc["ProductID"].Value = row["ProductID",
                                 DataRowVersion.Original];
    pc["Quantity"].Value = row["Quantity", DataRowVersion.Original];
```

(continued)

```
    pc["UnitPrice"].Value = row["UnitPrice",
                                DataRowVersion.Original];
    return cmd.ExecuteNonQuery();
}
```

Note The preceding code snippet used the *DataTable* object's *Select* method to loop through the modified rows. I had a good reason to not use a *For* or *For Each* loop to examine each item in the *DataTable* object's *Rows* collection. When you successfully submit a pending deletion and call the *AcceptChanges* method of that *DataRow*, the item is removed from its parent collection. The *Select* method returns an array of *DataRow* objects. The array essentially contains pointers to the modified rows. If we remove items from the *DataTable* object's collection of *DataRow* objects, the code will still succeed.

Now it's time to put all this code to good use.

The following code snippet fetches the details for the order into a *DataTable*, modifies the contents of the order, and submits the changes to the database. The code will demonstrate that the code from the previous snippets will successfully submit pending changes. It relies on the procedures we defined earlier in the chapter. The code also includes a procedure to display the current contents of the *DataTable*, which is used to verify that we've successfully updated the contents of the order. To ensure that you can run this code snippet more than once, the code also includes a *ResetOrder* procedure, which re-creates the original contents of the order.

Visual Basic .NET

```
Dim cn As OleDbConnection
Dim da As OleDbDataAdapter
Dim tbl As DataTable = GenTable()

Sub Main()
    Dim strConn, strSQL As String
    strConn = "Provider=SQLOLEDB;Data Source=(local)\NetSDK;" & _
              "Initial Catalog=Northwind;Trusted_Connection=Yes;"
    strSQL = "SELECT OrderID, ProductID, Quantity, UnitPrice " & _
             "FROM [Order Details] WHERE OrderID = 10503 " & _
             "ORDER BY ProductID"
    cn = New OleDbConnection(strConn)
    da = New OleDbDataAdapter(strSQL, cn)
```

```
        cn.Open()
        ResetOrder()
        da.Fill(tbl)
        DisplayOrder("Initial contents of database")
        ModifyOrder()
        DisplayOrder("Modified data in DataSet")
        SubmitChangesByHand()
        tbl.Clear()
        da.Fill(tbl)
        DisplayOrder("New contents of database")
        cn.Close()
End Sub

Private Sub ModifyOrder()
        Dim row As DataRow

        row = tbl.Rows(0)
        row.Delete()

        row = tbl.Rows(1)
        row("Quantity") = CType(row("Quantity"), Int16) * 2

        row = tbl.NewRow
        row("OrderID") = 10503
        row("ProductID") = 1
        row("Quantity") = 24
        row("UnitPrice") = 18.0
        tbl.Rows.Add(row)
End Sub

Public Sub DisplayOrder(ByVal strStatus As String)
        Dim row As DataRow
        Dim col As DataColumn
        Console.WriteLine(strStatus)
        Console.WriteLine("      OrderID      ProductID      " & _
                    "Quantity      UnitPrice")
        For Each row In tbl.Select("", "ProductID")
            For Each col In tbl.Columns
                Console.Write(vbTab & row(col) & vbTab)
            Next
            Console.WriteLine()
        Next
        Console.WriteLine()
End Sub

Private Sub ResetOrder()
        Dim strSQL As String
        Dim cmd As OleDbCommand = cn.CreateCommand()
        strSQL = "DELETE FROM [Order Details] WHERE OrderID = 10503"
```

(continued)

```vb
    cmd.CommandText = strSQL
    cmd.ExecuteNonQuery()
    strSQL = "INSERT INTO [Order Details] " & _
            "    (OrderID, ProductID, Quantity, UnitPrice) " & _
            "    VALUES (10503, 14, 70, 23.25) "
    cmd.CommandText = strSQL
    cmd.ExecuteNonQuery()
    strSQL = "INSERT INTO [Order Details] " & _
            "    (OrderID, ProductID, Quantity, UnitPrice) " & _
            "    VALUES (10503, 65, 20, 21.05)"
    cmd.CommandText = strSQL
    cmd.ExecuteNonQuery()
End Sub

Public Function GenTable() As DataTable
    Dim tbl As New DataTable("Order Details")
    Dim col As DataColumn
    With tbl.Columns
        col = .Add("OrderID", GetType(Integer))
        col.AllowDBNull = False
        col = .Add("ProductID", GetType(Integer))
        col.AllowDBNull = False
        col = .Add("Quantity", GetType(Int16))
        col.AllowDBNull = False
        col = .Add("UnitPrice", GetType(Decimal))
        col.AllowDBNull = False
    End With
    tbl.PrimaryKey = New DataColumn() {tbl.Columns("OrderID"), _
                                        tbl.Columns("ProductID")}
    Return tbl
End Function
```

Visual C# .NET

```csharp
static OleDbConnection cn;
static OleDbDataAdapter da;
static DataTable tbl;

static void Main(string[] args)
{
    string strConn, strSQL;
    strConn = "Provider=SQLOLEDB;Data Source=(local)\\NetSDK;" +
            "Initial Catalog=Northwind;Trusted_Connection=Yes;";
    strSQL = "SELECT OrderID, ProductID, Quantity, UnitPrice " +
            "FROM [Order Details] WHERE OrderID = 10503 " +
            "ORDER BY ProductID";
    cn = new OleDbConnection(strConn);
    da = new OleDbDataAdapter(strSQL, cn);
    tbl = GenTable();
```

```
        cn.Open();
        ResetOrder();
        da.Fill(tbl);
        DisplayOrder("Initial contents of database");
        ModifyOrder();
        DisplayOrder("Modified contents of DataSet");
        SubmitChangesByHand();
        tbl.Clear();
        da.Fill(tbl);
        DisplayOrder("New contents of database");
        cn.Close();
    }

    static void ModifyOrder()
    {
        DataRow row;

        row = tbl.Rows[0];
        row.Delete();

        row = tbl.Rows[1];
        row["Quantity"] = (Int16) row["Quantity"] * 2;

        row = tbl.NewRow();
        row["OrderID"] = 10503;
        row["ProductID"] = 1;
        row["Quantity"] = 24;
        row["UnitPrice"] = 18.0;
        tbl.Rows.Add(row);
    }

    static void DisplayOrder(string strStatus)
    {
        Console.WriteLine(strStatus);
        Console.WriteLine("        OrderID      ProductID      " +
                        "Quantity      UnitPrice");
        foreach(DataRow row in tbl.Select("", "ProductID"))
        {
            foreach(DataColumn col in tbl.Columns)
                Console.Write("\t" + row[col] + "\t");
            Console.WriteLine();
        }
        Console.WriteLine();
    }

    static void ResetOrder()
    {
        string strSQL;
        OleDbCommand cmd = cn.CreateCommand();
```

(continued)

```
    strSQL = "DELETE FROM [Order Details] WHERE OrderID = 10503"
    cmd.CommandText = strSQL;
    cmd.ExecuteNonQuery();
    strSQL = "INSERT INTO [Order Details] " +
             "    (OrderID, ProductID, Quantity, UnitPrice) " +
             "    VALUES (10503, 14, 70, 23.25) "
    cmd.CommandText = strSQL;
    cmd.ExecuteNonQuery();
    strSQL = "INSERT INTO [Order Details] " +
             "    (OrderID, ProductID, Quantity, UnitPrice) " +
             "    VALUES (10503, 65, 20, 21.05)";
    cmd.CommandText = strSQL;
    cmd.ExecuteNonQuery();
}


static DataTable GenTable()
{
    DataTable tbl = new DataTable("Order Details");
    DataColumn col;
    col = tbl.Columns.Add("OrderID", typeof(int));
    col.AllowDBNull = false;
    col = tbl.Columns.Add("ProductID", typeof(int));
    col.AllowDBNull = false;
    col = tbl.Columns.Add("Quantity", typeof(Int16));
    col.AllowDBNull = false;
    col = tbl.Columns.Add("UnitPrice", typeof(Decimal));
    col.AllowDBNull = false;
    tbl.PrimaryKey = new DataColumn[] {tbl.Columns["OrderID"],
                                       tbl.Columns["ProductID"]};
    return tbl;
}
```

We just wrote a huge amount of code in order to submit pending updates. The code that we used to generate the parameterized *Command* objects is specific to the initial query. The code in the *SubmitChangesByHand* procedure, however, is generic. It examines the cached changes in our *DataTable*, determines the type of change stored in each modified *DataRow*, calls a function to execute the query to submit the pending change, and then marks the *DataRow* appropriately, depending on the function's return value.

Essentially, we just re-created the updating functionality available through the *DataAdapter* object, which I'll cover next.

Using ADO.NET *DataAdapter* Objects to Submit Updates

Chapter 5 focused on using the DataAdapter to store the results of queries into DataTables, but that's really only half the functionality of the DataAdapter. The object is also designed to submit pending changes to your DataSet.

You have the following three choices when it comes to generating the updating logic that your *DataAdapter* objects use to submit changes to your database:

- Use code to manually configure your *DataAdapter* objects.

- Use a *CommandBuilder* at run time.

- Use the Data Adapter Configuration Wizard at design time.

Each of these methods has benefits and drawbacks. In the following sections, I will explain both in great detail.

Manually Configuring Your *DataAdapter* Objects

The *DataAdapter* object exposes four properties that contain *Command* objects. You've already learned that the *SelectCommand* property contains the *Command* that the *DataAdapter* uses to fill your *DataTable*. The other three properties—*UpdateCommand*, *InsertCommand*, and *DeleteCommand*—contain the *Command* objects that the *DataAdapter* uses to submit pending changes.

This architecture represents a major change from the ADO object model. There is no magical "black box" technology involved. You control how the *DataAdapter* submits pending changes because you supply the *Command* objects that the *DataAdapter* uses.

The *DataAdapter* object's *Update* method is very flexible. You can supply a *DataSet*, a *DataSet* and a table name, a *DataTable*, or an array of *DataRow* objects. Regardless of how you call the *DataAdapter* object's *Update* method, the *DataAdapter* will attempt to submit the pending changes through the appropriate *Command*. All the work we performed earlier in the *SubmitChangesByHand* procedure can be accomplished using a single call to the *DataAdapter* object's *Update* method.

Introducing Bound Parameters

The *SubmitChangesByHand* procedure that we created was not terribly complex. The procedure also didn't do much work. Instead, it delegated the nasty work to one of three functions: *SubmitUpdate*, *SubmitInsert*, or *SubmitDelete*.

These functions populate the values for the parameters in the appropriate query based on the contents of the modified row.

We'll use the same parameterized queries to submit pending changes using a *DataAdapter*.

```
UPDATE [Order Details]
    SET OrderID = ?, ProductID = ?, Quantity = ?, UnitPrice = ?
    WHERE OrderID = ?  AND ProductID = ? AND
        Quantity = ? AND UnitPrice = ?

INSERT INTO [Order Details] (OrderID, ProductID, Quantity, UnitPrice)
    VALUES (?, ?, ?, ?)

DELETE FROM [Order Details]
    WHERE OrderID = ? AND ProductID = ? AND
        Quantity = ? AND UnitPrice = ?
```

However, when we add *Parameter* objects to the *DataAdapter* object's *Command* objects, we'll use two properties of the ADO.NET *Parameter* object that are designed specifically for updates using the *DataAdapter*: *SourceColumn* and *SourceVersion*.

These properties basically bind a *Parameter* to a *DataColumn* in your *DataTable*. The *DataAdapter* uses these properties to determine how to populate the *Parameter* object's *Value* property before executing the query, similar to how we accomplished this task in the *SubmitUpdate*, *SubmitInsert*, and *SubmitDelete* functions. Figure 10-2 better illustrates this behavior.

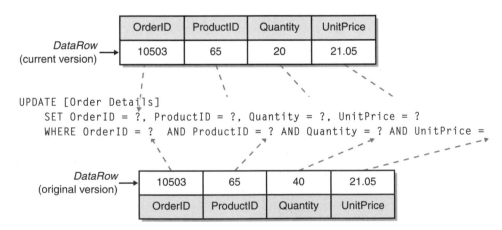

Figure 10-2   Binding *Parameter* objects to *DataColumn* objects.

The following code snippet creates our parameterized *Command* objects but sets the *SourceColumn* and *SourceVersion* properties of the *Parameter* objects. The default value for the *SourceVersion* property is *DataRowVersion.Current*,

so we need to set the property only if we want to bind the *Parameter* objects
to the original values in the desired column.

Visual Basic .NET

```
Private Function CreateDataAdapterUpdateCommand() As OleDbCommand
    Dim strSQL As String
    strSQL = "UPDATE [Order Details] " & _
            "    SET OrderID = ?, ProductID = ?, " & _
            "        Quantity = ?, UnitPrice = ? " & _
            "    WHERE OrderID = ?  AND ProductID = ? AND " & _
            "        Quantity = ? AND UnitPrice = ?"
    Dim cmd As New OleDbCommand(strSQL, cn)

    Dim pc As OleDbParameterCollection = cmd.Parameters
    pc.Add("OrderID_New", OleDbType.Integer, 0, "OrderID")
    pc.Add("ProductID_New", OleDbType.Integer, 0, "ProductID")
    pc.Add("Quantity_New", OleDbType.SmallInt, 0, "Quantity")
    pc.Add("UnitPrice_New", OleDbType.Currency, 0, "UnitPrice")

    Dim param As OleDbParameter
    param = pc.Add("OrderID_Orig", OleDbType.Integer, 0, "OrderID")
    param.SourceVersion = DataRowVersion.Original
    param = pc.Add("ProductID_Orig", OleDbType.Integer, 0, _
                "ProductID")
    param.SourceVersion = DataRowVersion.Original
    param = pc.Add("Quantity_Orig", OleDbType.SmallInt, 0, _
                "Quantity")
    param.SourceVersion = DataRowVersion.Original
    param = pc.Add("UnitPrice_Orig", OleDbType.Currency, 0, _
                "UnitPrice")
    param.SourceVersion = DataRowVersion.Original

    Return cmd
End Function

Private Function CreateDataAdapterInsertCommand() As OleDbCommand
    Dim strSQL As String
    strSQL = "INSERT INTO [Order Details] " & _
            "    (OrderID, ProductID, Quantity, UnitPrice) " & _
            "    VALUES (?, ?, ?, ?)"
    Dim cmd As New OleDbCommand(strSQL, cn)

    Dim pc As OleDbParameterCollection = cmd.Parameters
    pc.Add("OrderID", OleDbType.Integer, 0, "OrderID")
    pc.Add("ProductID", OleDbType.Integer, 0, "ProductID")
    pc.Add("Quantity", OleDbType.SmallInt, 0, "Quantity")
    pc.Add("UnitPrice", OleDbType.Currency, 0, "UnitPrice")
```

(continued)

```
        Return cmd
End Function


Private Function CreateDataAdapterDeleteCommand() As OleDbCommand
    Dim strSQL As String
    strSQL = "DELETE FROM [Order Details] " & _
            "   WHERE OrderID = ? AND ProductID = ? AND " & _
            "         Quantity = ? AND UnitPrice = ?"
    Dim cmd As New OleDbCommand(strSQL, cn)

    Dim pc As OleDbParameterCollection = cmd.Parameters
    Dim param As OleDbParameter
    pc.Add("OrderID", OleDbType.Integer, 0, "OrderID")
    param.SourceVersion = DataRowVersion.Original
    pc.Add("ProductID", OleDbType.Integer, 0, "ProductID")
    param.SourceVersion = DataRowVersion.Original
    pc.Add("Quantity", OleDbType.SmallInt, 0, "Quantity")
    param.SourceVersion = DataRowVersion.Original
    pc.Add("UnitPrice", OleDbType.Currency, 0, "UnitPrice")
    param.SourceVersion = DataRowVersion.Original

    Return cmd
End Function
```

Visual C# .NET

```
static OleDbCommand CreateDataAdapterUpdateCommand()
{
    string strSQL;
    strSQL = "UPDATE [Order Details] " & _
            "   SET OrderID = ?, ProductID = ?, " +
            "       Quantity = ?, UnitPrice = ? " +
            "   WHERE OrderID = ? AND ProductID = ? AND " +
            "         Quantity = ? AND UnitPrice = ?";
    OleDbCommand cmd = new OleDbCommand(strSQL, cn);

    OleDbParameterCollection pc = cmd.Parameters;
    pc.Add("OrderID_New", OleDbType.Integer, 0, "OrderID");
    pc.Add("ProductID_New", OleDbType.Integer, 0, "ProductID");
    pc.Add("Quantity_New", OleDbType.SmallInt, 0, "Quantity");
    pc.Add("UnitPrice_New", OleDbType.Currency, 0, "UnitPrice");

    OleDbParameter param;
    param = pc.Add("OrderID_Orig", OleDbType.Integer, 0, "OrderID");
    param.SourceVersion = DataRowVersion.Original;
    param = pc.Add("ProductID_Orig", OleDbType.Integer, 0,
                "ProductID");
    param.SourceVersion = DataRowVersion.Original;
    param = pc.Add("Quantity_Orig", OleDbType.SmallInt, 0,
                "Quantity");
```

```
        param.SourceVersion = DataRowVersion.Original;
        param = pc.Add("UnitPrice_Orig", OleDbType.Currency, 0,
                        "UnitPrice");
        param.SourceVersion = DataRowVersion.Original;

        return cmd;
    }


    static OleDbCommand CreateDataAdapterInsertCommand()
    {
        string strSQL;
        strSQL = "INSERT INTO [Order Details] " +
                    "    (OrderID, ProductID, Quantity, UnitPrice) " +
                    "    VALUES (?, ?, ?, ?)";
        OleDbCommand cmd = new OleDbCommand(strSQL, cn);

        OleDbParameterCollection pc = cmd.Parameters;
        pc.Add("OrderID", OleDbType.Integer, 0, "OrderID");
        pc.Add("ProductID", OleDbType.Integer, 0, "ProductID");
        pc.Add("Quantity", OleDbType.SmallInt, 0, "Quantity");
        pc.Add("UnitPrice", OleDbType.Currency, 0, "UnitPrice");

        return cmd;
    }


    static OleDbCommand CreateDataAdapterDeleteCommand()
    {
        string strSQL;
        strSQL = "DELETE FROM [Order Details] " +
                    "    WHERE OrderID = ? AND ProductID = ? AND " +
                    "        Quantity = ? AND UnitPrice = ?";
        OleDbCommand cmd = new OleDbCommand(strSQL, cn);

        OleDbParameter param;
        OleDbParameterCollection pc = cmd.Parameters;
        param = pc.Add("OrderID", OleDbType.Integer, 0, "OrderID");
        param.SourceVersion = DataRowVersion.Original;
        param = pc.Add("ProductID", OleDbType.Integer, 0, "ProductID");
        param.SourceVersion = DataRowVersion.Original;
        param = pc.Add("Quantity", OleDbType.SmallInt, 0, "Quantity");
        param.SourceVersion = DataRowVersion.Original;
        param = pc.Add("UnitPrice", OleDbType.Currency, 0, "UnitPrice");
        param.SourceVersion = DataRowVersion.Original;

        return cmd;
    }
```

We can now replace the *SubmitChangesByHand*, *SubmitUpdate*, *Submit-Insert*, and *SubmitDelete* procedures with the following code:

Visual Basic .NET

```
Private Sub SubmitChangesViaDataAdapter()
    da.UpdateCommand = CreateDataAdapterUpdateCommand()
    da.InsertCommand = CreateDataAdapterInsertCommand()
    da.DeleteCommand = CreateDataAdapterDeleteCommand()
    da.Update(tbl)
End Sub
```

Visual C# .NET

```
static void SubmitChangesViaDataAdapter()
{
    da.UpdateCommand = CreateDataAdapterUpdateCommand();
    da.InsertCommand = CreateDataAdapterInsertCommand();
    da.DeleteCommand = CreateDataAdapterDeleteCommand();
    da.Update(tbl);
}
```

Using Stored Procedures to Submit Updates

A common complaint of developers who used ADO to retrieve data from their databases was that they couldn't use the *Recordset* object's *UpdateBatch* method to submit updates using stored procedures.

Earlier, I mentioned that the *DataAdapter* lets you define your own updating logic. The previous code snippets showed how you can build your own *Command* objects that the *DataAdapter* can then use to submit pending changes. We can use similar code to submit updates using stored procedures.

First we need to define stored procedures in the Northwind database that can modify, insert, and delete rows from the Order Details table. You can paste and then execute the following code in SQL Query Analyzer to create the stored procedures that we're going to call in our code. If you don't have access to SQL Query Analyzer because you have only MSDE installed, you can call a procedure named *CreateSprocs* (which appears in a later code snippet) to create the desired stored procedures.

```
USE Northwind

GO

CREATE PROCEDURE spUpdateDetail
    (@OrderID_New int, @ProductID_New int,
     @Quantity_New smallint, @UnitPrice_New money,
```

```
    @OrderID_Orig int, @ProductID_Orig int,
    @Quantity_Orig smallint, @UnitPrice_Orig money)
AS
UPDATE [Order Details]
    SET OrderID = @OrderID_New, ProductID = @ProductID_New,
        Quantity = @Quantity_New, UnitPrice = @UnitPrice_New
    WHERE OrderID = @OrderID_Orig AND ProductID = @ProductID_Orig AND
        Quantity = @Quantity_Orig AND UnitPrice = @UnitPrice_Orig

GO

CREATE PROCEDURE spInsertDetail
    (@OrderID int, @ProductID int,
    @Quantity smallint, @UnitPrice money)
AS
INSERT INTO [Order Details]
    (OrderID, ProductID, Quantity, UnitPrice)
    VALUES (@OrderID, @ProductID, @Quantity, @UnitPrice)

GO

CREATE PROCEDURE spDeleteDetail
    (@OrderID int, @ProductID int,
    @Quantity smallint, @UnitPrice money)
AS
DELETE FROM [Order Details]
    WHERE OrderID = @OrderID AND ProductID = @ProductID AND
        Quantity = @Quantity AND UnitPrice = @UnitPrice
```

Now that we have stored procedures that we can call to submit changes to the Order Details table, we can write *Command* objects to call those stored procedures automatically when we call the *DataAdapter* object's *Update* method.

The following code snippet contains functions that create *Command* objects that contain calls to the stored procedures I just described. It also contains a procedure you can call to create those stored procedures in your database. All that's left to do to submit updates using stored procedures is to wire up our new *Command* objects to the *DataAdapter*, which we can do in the *SubmitChangesViaStoredProcedures* procedure.

Visual Basic .NET

```
Private Sub SubmitChangesViaStoredProcedures()
    da.UpdateCommand = CreateUpdateViaSPCommand()
    da.InsertCommand = CreateInsertViaSPCommand()
    da.DeleteCommand = CreateDeleteViaSPCommand()
    da.Update(tbl)
End Sub
```

(continued)

```vb
Private Function CreateUpdateViaSPCommand() As OleDbCommand
    Dim cmd As New OleDbCommand("spUpdateDetail", cn)
    cmd.CommandType = CommandType.StoredProcedure

    Dim pc As OleDbParameterCollection = cmd.Parameters
    pc.Add("OrderID_New", OleDbType.Integer, 0, "OrderID")
    pc.Add("ProductID_New", OleDbType.Integer, 0, "ProductID")
    pc.Add("Quantity_New", OleDbType.SmallInt, 0, "Quantity")
    pc.Add("UnitPrice_New", OleDbType.Currency, 0, "UnitPrice")

    Dim param As OleDbParameter
    param = pc.Add("OrderID_Orig", OleDbType.Integer, 0, "OrderID")
    param.SourceVersion = DataRowVersion.Original
    param = pc.Add("ProductID_Orig", OleDbType.Integer, 0, _
                "ProductID")
    param.SourceVersion = DataRowVersion.Original
    param = pc.Add("Quantity_Orig", OleDbType.SmallInt, 0, _
                "Quantity")
    param.SourceVersion = DataRowVersion.Original
    param = pc.Add("UnitPrice_Orig", OleDbType.Currency, 0, _
                "UnitPrice")
    param.SourceVersion = DataRowVersion.Original

    Return cmd
End Function

Private Function CreateInsertViaSPCommand() As OleDbCommand
    Dim cmd As New OleDbCommand("spInsertDetail", cn)
    cmd.CommandType = CommandType.StoredProcedure

    Dim pc As OleDbParameterCollection = cmd.Parameters
    pc.Add("OrderID", OleDbType.Integer, 0, "OrderID")
    pc.Add("ProductID", OleDbType.Integer, 0, "ProductID")
    pc.Add("Quantity", OleDbType.SmallInt, 0, "Quantity")
    pc.Add("UnitPrice", OleDbType.Currency, 0, "UnitPrice")

    Return cmd
End Function

Private Function CreateDeleteViaSPCommand() As OleDbCommand
    Dim cmd As New OleDbCommand("spDeleteDetail", cn)
    cmd.CommandType = CommandType.StoredProcedure

    Dim pc As OleDbParameterCollection = cmd.Parameters
    Dim param As OleDbParameter
    param = pc.Add("OrderID", OleDbType.Integer, 0, "OrderID")
    param.SourceVersion = DataRowVersion.Original
    param = pc.Add("ProductID", OleDbType.Integer, 0, "ProductID")
    param.SourceVersion = DataRowVersion.Original
```

```
        param = pc.Add("Quantity", OleDbType.SmallInt, 0, "Quantity")
        param.SourceVersion = DataRowVersion.Original
        param = pc.Add("UnitPrice", OleDbType.Currency, 0, "UnitPrice")
        param.SourceVersion = DataRowVersion.Original


        Return cmd
    End Function

    Private Sub CreateSprocs()
        Dim cmd As OleDbCommand = cn.CreateCommand
        Dim strSQL As String

        strSQL = "CREATE PROCEDURE spUpdateDetail " & vbCrLf & _
                "    (@OrderID_New int, @ProductID_New int, " & vbCrLf & _
                "     @Quantity_New smallint, " & vbCrLf & _
                "     @UnitPrice_New money, " & vbCrLf & _
                "     @OrderID_Orig int, " & vbCrLf & _
                "     @ProductID_Orig int, " & vbCrLf & _
                "     @Quantity_Orig smallint, " & vbCrLf & _
                "     @UnitPrice_Orig money) " & vbCrLf & _
                "AS " & vbCrLf & _
                "UPDATE [Order Details] " & vbCrLf & _
                "    SET OrderID = @OrderID_New, " & vbCrLf & _
                "        ProductID = @ProductID_New, " & vbCrLf & _
                "        Quantity = @Quantity_New, " & vbCrLf & _
                "        UnitPrice = @UnitPrice_New " & vbCrLf & _
                "    WHERE OrderID = @OrderID_Orig AND " & vbCrLf &_
                "        ProductID = @ProductID_Orig AND " & vbCrLf & _
                "        Quantity = @Quantity_Orig AND " & vbCrLf & _
                "        UnitPrice = @UnitPrice_Orig"
        cmd.CommandText = strSQL
        cmd.ExecuteNonQuery()

        strSQL = "CREATE PROCEDURE spInsertDetail " & vbCrLf & _
                "    (@OrderID int, @ProductID int, " & vbCrLf & _
                "     @Quantity smallint, @UnitPrice money) " & vbCrLf & _
                "AS " & vbCrLf & _
                "INSERT INTO [Order Details] " & vbCrLf & _
                "    (OrderID, ProductID, Quantity, UnitPrice) " & vbCrLf & _
                "    VALUES (@OrderID, @ProductID, @Quantity, @UnitPrice)"
        cmd.CommandText = strSQL
        cmd.ExecuteNonQuery()

        strSQL = "CREATE PROCEDURE spDeleteDetail " & vbCrLf & _
                "    (@OrderID int, @ProductID int, " & vbCrLf & _
                "     @Quantity smallint, @UnitPrice money) " & vbCrLf & _
                "AS " & vbCrLf & _
                "DELETE FROM [Order Details] " & vbCrLf & _
                "    WHERE OrderID = @OrderID AND " & vbCrLf & _
```

(continued)

```
"                  ProductID = @ProductID AND " & vbCrLf & _
"                  Quantity = @Quantity AND UnitPrice = @UnitPrice"
        cmd.CommandText = strSQL
        cmd.ExecuteNonQuery()
End Sub
```

Visual C# .NET

```
static void SubmitChangesViaStoredProcedures()
{
    da.UpdateCommand = CreateUpdateViaSPCommand();
    da.InsertCommand = CreateInsertViaSPCommand();
    da.DeleteCommand = CreateDeleteViaSPCommand();
    da.Update(tbl);
}


static OleDbCommand CreateUpdateViaSPCommand()
{
    OleDbCommand cmd = new OleDbCommand("spUpdateDetail", cn);
    cmd.CommandType = CommandType.StoredProcedure;

    OleDbParameterCollection pc = cmd.Parameters;
    pc.Add("OrderID_New", OleDbType.Integer, 0, "OrderID");
    pc.Add("ProductID_New", OleDbType.Integer, 0, "ProductID");
    pc.Add("Quantity_New", OleDbType.SmallInt, 0, "Quantity");
    pc.Add("UnitPrice_New", OleDbType.Currency, 0, "UnitPrice");

    OleDbParameter param;
    param = pc.Add("OrderID_Orig", OleDbType.Integer, 0, "OrderID");
    param.SourceVersion = DataRowVersion.Original;
    param = pc.Add("ProductID_Orig", OleDbType.Integer, 0, "ProductID");
    param.SourceVersion = DataRowVersion.Original;
    param = pc.Add("Quantity_Orig", OleDbType.SmallInt, 0, "Quantity");
    param.SourceVersion = DataRowVersion.Original;
    param = pc.Add("UnitPrice_Orig", OleDbType.Currency, 0, "UnitPrice");
    param.SourceVersion = DataRowVersion.Original;

    return cmd;
}


static OleDbCommand CreateInsertViaSPCommand()
{
    OleDbCommand cmd = new OleDbCommand("spInsertDetail", cn);
    cmd.CommandType = CommandType.StoredProcedure;

    OleDbParameterCollection pc = cmd.Parameters;
    pc.Add("OrderID", OleDbType.Integer, 0, "OrderID");
    pc.Add("ProductID", OleDbType.Integer, 0, "ProductID");
    pc.Add("Quantity", OleDbType.SmallInt, 0, "Quantity");
```

```
        pc.Add("UnitPrice", OleDbType.Currency, 0, "UnitPrice");

        return cmd;
}


static OleDbCommand CreateDeleteViaSPCommand()
{
        OleDbCommand cmd = new OleDbCommand("spDeleteDetail", cn);
        cmd.CommandType = CommandType.StoredProcedure;

        OleDbParameterCollection pc = cmd.Parameters;
        OleDbParameter param;
        param = pc.Add("OrderID", OleDbType.Integer, 0, "OrderID");
        param.SourceVersion = DataRowVersion.Original;
        param = pc.Add("ProductID", OleDbType.Integer, 0, "ProductID");
        param.SourceVersion = DataRowVersion.Original;
        param = pc.Add("Quantity", OleDbType.SmallInt, 0, "Quantity");
        param.SourceVersion = DataRowVersion.Original;
        param = pc.Add("UnitPrice", OleDbType.Currency, 0, "UnitPrice");
        param.SourceVersion = DataRowVersion.Original;

        return cmd;
}


static void CreateSprocs()
{
        OleDbCommand cmd = cn.CreateCommand();
        string strSQL;

        strSQL = "CREATE PROCEDURE spUpdateDetail \n\r" +
                 "   (@OrderID_New int, @ProductID_New int, \n\r" +
                 "    @Quantity_New smallint, @UnitPrice_New money, \n\r" +
                 "    @OrderID_Orig int, @ProductID_Orig int, \n\r" +
                 "    @Quantity_Orig smallint, @UnitPrice_Orig money) \n\r" +
                 "AS \n\r" +
                 "UPDATE [Order Details] \n\r" +
                 "   SET OrderID = @OrderID_New, \n\r" +
                 "       ProductID = @ProductID_New, \n\r" +
                 "       Quantity = @Quantity_New, \n\r" +
                 "       UnitPrice = @UnitPrice_New \n\r" +
                 "   WHERE OrderID = @OrderID_Orig AND \n\r" +
                 "         ProductID = @ProductID_Orig AND \n\r" +
                 "         Quantity = @Quantity_Orig AND \n\r" +
                 "         UnitPrice = @UnitPrice_Orig";
        cmd.CommandText = strSQL;
        cmd.ExecuteNonQuery();

        strSQL = "CREATE PROCEDURE spInsertDetail \n\r" +
                 "   (@OrderID int, @ProductID int, \n\r" +
```

(continued)

```
"        @Quantity smallint, @UnitPrice money) \n\r" +
"AS \n\r" +
"INSERT INTO [Order Details] \n\r" +
"        (OrderID, ProductID, Quantity, UnitPrice) \n\r" +
"        VALUES (@OrderID, @ProductID, @Quantity, @UnitPrice)";
    cmd.CommandText = strSQL;
    cmd.ExecuteNonQuery();

    strSQL = "CREATE PROCEDURE spDeleteDetail \n\r" +
"        (@OrderID int, @ProductID int, \n\r" +
"        @Quantity smallint, @UnitPrice money) \n\r" +
"AS \n\r" +
"DELETE FROM [Order Details] \n\r" +
"        WHERE OrderID = @OrderID AND \n\r" +
"                ProductID = @ProductID AND \n\r" +
"                Quantity = @Quantity AND UnitPrice = @UnitPrice";
    cmd.CommandText = strSQL;
    cmd.ExecuteNonQuery();
}
```

Supplying Your Own Updating Logic

Now let's look at the benefits and drawbacks of supplying your own updating logic in code.

Benefits

The two biggest benefits of supplying your own updating logic are control and performance. The ADO.NET *DataAdapter* offers you more control over your updating logic than any previous Microsoft data access technology. You're no longer restricted to submitting updates directly against tables; you can finally leverage your stored procedures in a RAD way.

Plus, because you're not relying on the data access technology to determine the origin of your data, you can treat any result set as updateable. With the ADO cursor engine, if the cursor engine cannot gather the metadata necessary to submit changes back to your database, there is no way for you to supply that information programmatically. With ADO.NET, you can fill your *DataSet* with the results of a stored procedure call, a query against a temporary table, or the union of multiple queries—or fill it in any other way you see fit—and still be able to submit changes to your database.

Supplying updating logic in your code improves the performance of your application. The code snippet that used the ADO cursor engine to submit updates contained fewer lines of code, but it required the ADO cursor engine to query the database for the source table name, source column names, and primary key information for the source table. Querying database system tables for metadata and then using that metadata to generate updating logic takes more time than simply loading it from local code.

Drawbacks

The drawbacks of supplying your own updating logic mirror the benefits of the ADO cursor engine's approach. First, it takes a lot more code to supply your own updating logic. Take a quick peek back, and compare how much code it took to submit updates using an ADO.NET *DataAdapter* with the ADO cursor engine's approach. Writing that code is time consuming and rather tedious.

The other drawback is that many developers are not comfortable writing their own updating logic. They would rather not have to ponder such questions as: Do I need to delimit the table name in the query? What type of parameter markers should I use? Which columns should appear in the WHERE clause of the *CommandText* for the *UpdateCommand* and *DeleteCommand*? What is the appropriate setting for the *OleDbType* property for a parameter that contains a date/time value?

Thankfully, there are more RAD ways to generate your updating logic, as I'll explain in the upcoming sections.

Using the *CommandBuilder* Object to Generate Updating Logic

The ADO.NET object model not only allows you to define your own updating logic, but it also provides dynamic updating logic generation similar to that of the ADO cursor engine, using the *CommandBuilder* object. If you instantiate a *CommandBuilder* object and associate it with a *DataAdapter* object, the *CommandBuilder* will attempt to generate updating logic based on the query contained in the *DataAdapter* object's *SelectCommand*.

To demonstrate how the *CommandBuilder* works, I'll use it to generate updating logic for our sample code that queries the Order Details table. The following code snippet instantiates an *OleDbCommandBuilder*, supplying an *OleDbDataAdapter* in the constructor. It then writes the text of the *Command* that the *CommandBuilder* generated to submit new rows.

Visual Basic .NET

```
Dim strConn, strSQL As String
strConn = "Provider=SQLOLEDB;Data Source=(local)\NetSDK;" & _
          "Initial Catalog=Northwind;Trusted_Connection=Yes;"
strSQL = "SELECT OrderID, ProductID, Quantity, UnitPrice " & _
         "FROM [Order Details] WHERE OrderID = 10503 " & _
         "ORDER BY ProductID"
Dim da As New OleDbDataAdapter(strSQL, strConn)
Dim cb As New OleDbCommandBuilder(da)
Console.WriteLine(cb.GetInsertCommand.CommandText)
```

Visual C# .NET

```
string strConn, strSQL;
strConn = "Provider=SQLOLEDB;Data Source=(local)\\NetSDK;" +
          "Initial Catalog=Northwind;Trusted_Connection=Yes;";
strSQL = "SELECT OrderID, ProductID, Quantity, UnitPrice " +
         "FROM [Order Details] WHERE OrderID = 10503 " +
         "ORDER BY ProductID";
OleDbDataAdapter da = new OleDbDataAdapter(strSQL, strConn);
OleDbCommandBuilder cb = new OleDbCommandBuilder(da);
Console.WriteLine(cb.GetInsertCommand().CommandText);
```

You'll notice that the text of this query looks remarkably similar to the queries we built earlier in the chapter to submit new rows, as shown here:

```
INSERT INTO Order Details( OrderID , ProductID , Quantity , UnitPrice )
VALUES ( ? , ? , ? , ? )
```

How the *CommandBuilder* Generates Updating Logic

The logic that the *CommandBuilder* uses to generate UPDATE, INSERT, and DELETE queries isn't terribly complex. Like the ADO cursor engine, the *CommandBuilder* queries the database to determine base table and column names as well as key information for the results of your query. The *CommandBuilder* can generate updating logic if all of the following are true:

■   Your query returns data from only one table.

■   That table has a primary key.

■   The primary key is included in the results of your query.

As we discussed earlier, the primary key ensures that the query-based updates that the *CommandBuilder* generates can update one row at most. Why does the *CommandBuilder* place a restriction on the number of tables referenced in the results of your query? We'll discuss this later in the chapter.

The *CommandBuilder* object uses the *DataAdapter* object's *SelectCommand* to fetch the metadata necessary for the updating logic. Actually, we discussed this feature briefly in Chapter 4. The *Command* object's *ExecuteReader* allows you to request this type of metadata with the results of your query. The following code snippet demonstrates this feature:

Visual Basic .NET

```
Dim strConn, strSQL As String
strConn = "Provider=SQLOLEDB;Data Source=(local)\NetSDK;" & _
          "Initial Catalog=Northwind;Trusted_Connection=Yes;"
strSQL = "SELECT OrderID, ProductID, Quantity, UnitPrice " & _
         "FROM [Order Details] WHERE OrderID = 10503 " & _
```

```
                "ORDER BY ProductID"
Dim cn As New OleDbConnection(strConn)
Dim cmd As New OleDbCommand(strSQL, cn)
cn.Open()
Dim rdr As OleDbDataReader
rdr = cmd.ExecuteReader(CommandBehavior.SchemaOnly Or _
                        CommandBehavior.KeyInfo)
Dim tbl As DataTable = rdr.GetSchemaTable
rdr.Close()
cn.Close()

Dim row As DataRow
Dim col As DataColumn
For Each row In tbl.Rows
    For Each col In tbl.Columns
        Console.WriteLine(col.ColumnName & ": " & row(col).ToString)
    Next col
    Console.WriteLine()
Next row
```

Visual C# .NET

```
string strConn, strSQL;
strConn = "Provider=SQLOLEDB;Data Source=(local)\\NetSDK;" +
          "Initial Catalog=Northwind;Trusted_Connection=Yes;";
strSQL = "SELECT OrderID, ProductID, Quantity, UnitPrice " +
         "FROM [Order Details] WHERE OrderID = 10503 " +
         "ORDER BY ProductID";
OleDbConnection cn = new OleDbConnection(strConn);
OleDbCommand cmd = new OleDbCommand(strSQL, cn);
cn.Open();
OleDbDataReader rdr;
rdr = cmd.ExecuteReader(CommandBehavior.SchemaOnly |
                        CommandBehavior.KeyInfo);
DataTable tbl = rdr.GetSchemaTable();
rdr.Close();
cn.Close();

foreach (DataRow row in tbl.Rows)
{
    foreach (DataColumn col in tbl.Columns)
        Console.WriteLine(col.ColumnName + ": " +
                          row[col].ToString());
    Console.WriteLine();
}
```

If you run this code, you'll see all the data that the *CommandBuilder* needs for each column in order to generate updating logic. What's the name of the column? What are the base table and base column names for the column? Is the column part of the base table's primary key? Does the column contain a long data type (large text or binary)? What is the scale and precision of that floating point column? And so on.

Benefits and Drawbacks of Using the *CommandBuilder*

You can see the two major benefits of using the *CommandBuilder* object if you compare the code snippet that created the *CommandBuilder* with the code that we used to generate our own updating logic. Using the *CommandBuilder* object requires less code. It also allows you to generate updating logic without requiring in-depth knowledge of the SQL syntax for UPDATE, INSERT, and DELETE queries.

The *CommandBuilder* can also be helpful if you're having problems generating your own updating logic. If the *CommandBuilder* can generate the updating logic successfully, you can check the value of the *CommandText* property of the *Command* objects it generated or the various properties on the *Parameter* objects it constructed.

The *CommandBuilder* is also extremely handy in any application where you need to support updating but you won't know the structure of your queries at design time.

Like the ADO cursor engine, the *CommandBuilder* generates updating logic for you automatically at run time. As a result, the *CommandBuilder* is also subject to the same problems and limitations as the ADO cursor engine.

The *CommandBuilder* does not offer the best possible run-time performance. You can supply your own updating logic in code in less time than it takes the *CommandBuilder* to request and process the metadata required to generate similar updating logic. The *CommandBuilder* doesn't offer options to let you control the updating logic that they generate. You can't specify the type of optimistic concurrency you want to use. A *CommandBuilder* will not help you submit updates using stored procedures.

If only there were a way to generate updating logic quickly and easily at design time....

Using the Data Adapter Configuration Wizard to Generate Updating Logic

In Chapter 5, you saw that you could use the Data Adapter Configuration Wizard to create *DataAdapter* objects using the OLE DB and SQL Client .NET Data Providers. The wizard also generates updating logic and stores that logic in your code.

One purpose of the Data Adapter Configuration Wizard is to generate updating logic for you at design time to let you build efficient updating code quickly and easily. Obviously, that's an ambitious goal. Although the wizard is not foolproof (what wizard is?), it actually achieves this goal in the vast majority of situations.

Open a project in Visual Studio .NET that contains a project item that exposes a designer (such as a Windows form, a Web form, a Web service, or a component), and add an *OleDbDataAdapter* to your designer. Specify a connection to your favorite Northwind database, and then enter the following query in the SQL statement page of the wizard:

```
SELECT OrderID, ProductID, UnitPrice, Quantity
    FROM [Order Details]
    WHERE OrderID = ? ORDER BY ProductID
```

Click Next. On the View Wizard Results screen, you'll see the output shown in Figure 10-3.

Figure 10-3   The View Wizard Results screen of the Data Adapter Configuration Wizard.

Examining the Structure of the *DataAdapter*

As you can see in Figure 10-3, the wizard generated UPDATE, INSERT, and DELETE queries for the new *DataAdapter*. Click the wizard's Finish button. Select the new *DataAdapter* in the Component Tray, and then go to the Properties window and drill down into the *DataAdapter* object's *DeleteCommand*. Select the *CommandText* property, and then click the button to the right of the property's value. This will bring up the Query Builder and display the *CommandText* for the *DataAdapter* object's *DeleteCommand*, as shown in Figure 10-4.

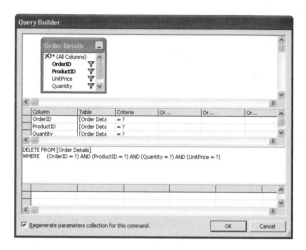

Figure 10-4   The wizard-generated *DeleteCommand*.

As you can see, the query that the Data Adapter Configuration Wizard generated to submit pending deletions is identical to the one we created by hand earlier in the chapter. You can also drill down into the *DataAdapter* object's *InsertCommand* and *UpdateCommand* to view the rest of the updating logic that the wizard generated.

Options for Building Updating Logic

The SQL Statement screen of the wizard has an Advanced Options button that you can click to display a dialog box that offers a series of options, as shown in Figure 10-5. These options offer you a small level of control over the updating logic that the Data Adapter Configuration Wizard generates.

If you're using your *DataAdapter* only to fetch data from your database, you can save some time, both at design time and at run time, by deselecting the Generate Insert, Update And Delete Statements option.

By default, the Data Adapter Configuration Wizard will add all non-BLOB columns to the WHERE clause of the queries for submitting pending updates and deletes. If you deselect the Use Optimistic Concurrency option, the wizard will include only primary key columns in the WHERE clauses for these queries.

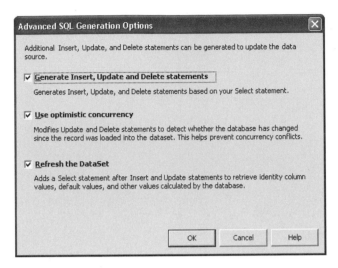

Figure 10-5 Advanced options offered by the Data Adapter Configuration Wizard.

Some databases, such as SQL Server, support batched queries that can return rows of data. If you're using the Data Adapter Configuration Wizard to build a *DataAdapter* that talks to such a database, the Refresh The DataSet option will be enabled and selected. When this option is selected, the wizard will generate queries to refetch the contents of your modified row immediately after submitting that change. This means that new server-generated values such as timestamp and auto-increment values will be available in your *DataSet* after you call *DataAdapter.Update*.

We'll discuss this feature in more depth in the next chapter, and we'll also look at how to implement similar functionality against databases that don't support batched queries that return results.

Using Stored Procedures to Submit Updates

The Data Adapter Configuration Wizard can also help you build *DataAdapter* objects that submit updates to your SQL Server database using stored procedures. On the Choose A Query Type screen of the wizard, you'll see a Use Existing Stored Procedures option, as shown in Figure 10-6. Select this option, and then click Next.

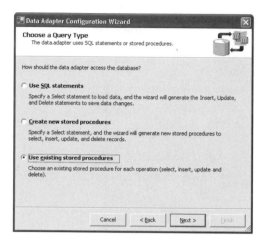

Figure 10-6   The Choose A Query Type screen of the Data Adapter Configuration Wizard.

The next screen allows you to select the stored procedures for each of the *Command* objects of your *DataAdapter*. The first step is to select the stored procedure for your *DataAdapter* object's *SelectCommand*. The drop-down list will contain the available stored procedures, as shown in Figure 10-7. When you select a stored procedure, the columns that the stored procedure returns will appear in the list to the right.

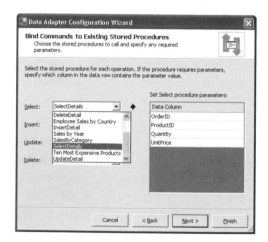

Figure 10-7   Selecting a stored procedure for the *DataAdapter* object's *SelectCommand*.

Once you've set the *DataAdapter* object's *SelectCommand*, you can specify the stored procedures for the updating *Command* objects. To set the *Source-Column* property for the parameters of your updating stored procedures, use the drop-down lists on the right side of the wizard screen, as shown in Figure 10-8.

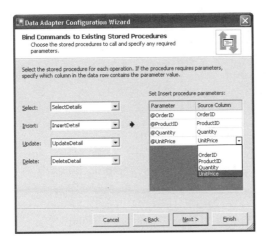

Figure 10-8   Setting the *SourceColumn* property for the parameters of the *InsertCommand*.

> **Note**   The Data Adapter Configuration Wizard does not give you the option to set the *SourceVersion* property for the *Parameter* objects. Because the default value for this property is *Current*, you must change the value of this property using the Properties window for all parameters you want to bind to the original value of your modified columns.

If you have the Enterprise edition of Visual Studio .NET installed, you can also supply a SQL query and the Data Adapter Configuration Wizard will generate new SQL Server stored procedures for your *DataAdapter* object's *Select-Command*, *UpdateCommand*, *InsertCommand*, and *DeleteCommand*. Select the Create New Stored Procedures option on the Choose A Query Type screen of the Data Adapter Configuration Wizard, and the wizard will prompt you for the SQL query that returns data from your database, as shown in Figure 10-9.

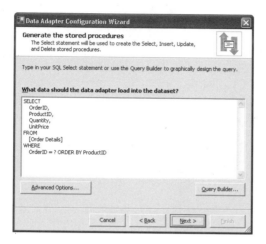

Figure 10-9 Specifying a SQL query for your new stored procedures.

The next wizard screen lets you supply names for the stored procedures that the wizard generates. This screen also includes a Preview SQL Script button, which you can click to bring up a dialog box showing the SQL script that the wizard generated to create your stored procedures (as shown in Figure 10-10). If you're building your application against a sample database, you can use the dialog box to save the SQL script to a file so that you can run the script later against your production database.

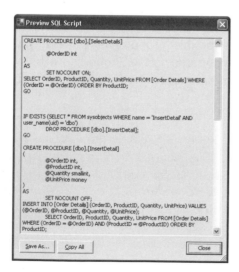

Figure 10-10 Viewing the SQL script for creating your new stored procedures.

Once you've completed the wizard, you'll have new stored procedures in your database and your new *DataAdapter* will be set to use those stored procedures.

Benefits and Drawbacks of Using the Wizard

I mentioned that one of the Data Adapter Configuration Wizard's goals is to generate updating logic to let you build efficient updating code quickly and easily. The wizard offers more options than the *CommandBuilder* object. It also generates the tedious code that most developers would rather not write.

Although the wizard requests the same schema information from your database to generate updating logic that the *CommandBuilder* object does, it requests this information once at design time and then stores the newly generated logic in your code. Thus, your application avoids the run-time performance penalty that goes with using the *CommandBuilder* object.

But alas, the Data Adapter Configuration Wizard is not perfect. In the initial release of Visual Studio .NET, the wizard works only with the *DataAdapter* objects in the OLE DB and SQL Client .NET Data Providers. The wizard also offers limited concurrency options. You can modify the updating *Command* objects that the wizard generates, but you'll lose those changes if you reconfigure the *DataAdapter*. However, even though the wizard is not perfect, it is still a powerful and helpful tool.

Other Updating Concerns

You now know the basics of updating a database with the changes stored in a *DataSet*. If you're generating your own updating logic—whether in the form of INSERT, UPDATE, and DELETE queries or stored procedure calls—you'll need to know more than just the basics.

For example, how do you handle concurrency so that you don't accidentally overwrite another user's changes? How do you handle null values in your concurrency checks? How do you submit updates in a transaction? What part does the *TableMappings* collection for a *DataAdapter* play when submitting updates?

Would you like to know how to accomplish these tasks? Read on.

Optimistic Concurrency Options

When you build a multi-user database application that relies on optimistic concurrency to submit updates to your database, it is important to perform the appropriate optimistic concurrency checks in your update queries. Let's say you've built your application and two users request the same row of data and then they both attempt to update the same row of data. What happens next? That depends on how you construct your update queries.

You have four basic optimistic concurrency options in SQL update queries.

Include Only the Primary Key Columns

You can include only the primary columns in the SQL UPDATE and DELETE queries, which creates a "last in wins" updating scenario. Both update attempts will succeed. Obviously, the database won't maintain both sets of changes. There can be only one. The changes made by the last update will override the previous changes.

Here's a quick breakdown of the scenario:

■   User A fetches the row.

■   User B fetches the row.

■   User B modifies the row and successfully submits the changes.

■   User A modifies the row and successfully submits the changes, over-writing the changes that User B just submitted.

User A is not even aware that the contents of the row in the database have changed between the time of the initial query and the time the user submits the changes.

If the "last in wins" scenario is what you're looking for, this is the option for you. However, this option is not appropriate if you want to prevent users from unwittingly overwriting other users' changes.

The *CommandBuilder* object does not offer this optimistic concurrency option; the Data Adapter Configuration Wizard does. On the Advanced Options tab, deselect the Use Optimistic Concurrency check box.

Include All Columns in the WHERE Clause

What if you don't want to go with "last in wins" updating? Maybe you don't want User A's changes to overwrite changes made to the database between the time the user queries the database and submits the modified row.

The default behavior of both the *CommandBuilder* and the Data Adapter Configuration Wizard is to include all columns in the WHERE clause. Using this logic prevents your code from overwriting changes made by other users between the time your code retrieves the row and the time your code attempts to submit the pending change in the row.

Let's look at an example. Say that Users A and B retrieve the same row of customer data. User B makes a change to the ContactName column and submits the change. The application includes all columns in the WHERE clause of the query-based updates, so the UPDATE query looks like this:

```
UPDATE Customers
    SET CustomerID = 'ABCDE', CompanyName = 'Original Company Name',
        ContactName = 'New Contact', Phone = '800-555-1212'
    WHERE CustomerID = 'ABCDE' AND
          CompanyName = 'Original Company Name' AND
          ContactName = 'Original Contact' AND
          Phone = '800-555-1212'
```

Meanwhile, User A modifies the same row of customer data, changing the value of the CompanyName column. Because User A retrieved the row before User B submitted the change to the ContactName column, User A's UPDATE query will look like this:

```
UPDATE Customers
    SET CustomerID = 'ABCDE', CompanyName = 'New Company Name',
        ContactName = 'Original Contact', Phone = '800-555-1212'
    WHERE CustomerID = 'ABCDE' AND
          CompanyName = 'Original Company Name' AND
          ContactName = 'Original Contact' AND
          Phone = '800-555-1212'
```

Because the value of the ContactName column for this row of data has changed in the database, no row in the table satisfies all the criteria in the query's WHERE clause. Thus, the database does not modify the customer row. The *DataAdapter* queries the database to determine how many rows the query modified, discovers that the query did not successfully update the desired row, and marks the *DataRow* accordingly. We'll discuss identifying and resolving such conflicts in Chapter 11.

This is the concurrency option that the *CommandBuilder* object uses. The Data Adapter Configuration Wizard uses this concurrency option by default.

Note Generally speaking, databases do not let you perform comparisons of two BLOB values. Because you can store many megabytes of data in a BLOB column, comparing them would be extremely inefficient—if it were even possible. Code-generation tools such as the *CommandBuilder* and the Data Adapter Configuration Wizard should not include BLOB columns in the WHERE clause of the query-based updates. Keep this in mind if you're generating your own updating logic.

Include the Primary Key and Timestamp Columns

You can simplify the WHERE clause of your query-based updates by relying on timestamp columns. The SQL Server timestamp column does not actually contain date and time information. Instead, it contains binary data that's unique within the database.

You can define a timestamp column on your SQL Server table, and any time the contents of a row changes, SQL Server will modify the value of the timestamp column for that row. We can add a timestamp column to the Customers table and change the query in the previous example to look like this:

```
UPDATE Customers
    SET CustomerID = 'ABCDE', CompanyName = 'Original Company Name',
       ContactName = 'New Contact', Phone = '800-555-1212'
    WHERE CustomerID = 'ABCDE' AND
         TimestampColumn = 0x00000000000000CC
```

Because the server will generate a new value for the timestamp column each time it updates a row, you can use a combination of the primary key and timestamp columns in the WHERE clause of your query-based updates to ensure that you don't overwrite another user's changes.

Most database systems support a similar data type. Some use a unique binary value, and others use a date/time value. Check your database system's documentation to determine the back end's data type and learn how you can force the database to update the value each time you modify the contents of a row.

Currently, neither the *CommandBuilder* nor the Data Adapter Configuration Wizard supports generating updating logic using this optimistic concurrency strategy.

> **Note**   As of SQL Server 2000, *rowversion* is synonymous with the *timestamp* data type. The SQL Server documentation recommends using the *rowversion* keyword instead of *timestamp*. I've used the term *timestamp* in this book because, as of this writing, it is more widely recognized.

I prefer using the primary key and timestamp columns in my concurrency checks because this option yields much simpler updating logic and the database has fewer columns to examine per update attempt.

Include the Primary Key Columns and Modified Columns

By default, the ADO cursor engine includes only the primary key columns and the original values of modified columns in the WHERE clause of its query-based updates. The cursor engine also includes only the modified columns in the SET clause of UPDATE queries.

Let's look at our multi-user example using this updating strategy. Let's say that User A and User B retrieve the same row of customer data at the same time. They each modify a different column of data—User A changes the Company-Name column, and User B changes the ContactName column. User B submits the pending change to the ContactName column first. User B's UPDATE query looks like this:

```
UPDATE Customers
    SET ContactName = 'New Contact'
    WHERE CustomerID = 'ABCDE' AND
        ContactName = 'Original Contact'
```

User A then submits the pending change to the CompanyName column using the following UPDATE query:

```
UPDATE Customers
    SET CompanyName = 'New Company Name'
    WHERE CustomerID = 'ABCDE' AND
        CompanyName = 'Original Company Name'
```

The contents of the row will change from

CustomerID	CompanyName	ContactName
ABCDE	Original Company Name	Original Contact

to

CustomerID	CompanyName	ContactName
ABCDE	Original Company Name	New Contact

and finally to

CustomerID	CompanyName	ContactName
ABCDE	New Company Name	New Contact

Both updates will succeed, and the change made by User A will not overwrite changes made by User B.

The structure of the ADO.NET *DataAdapter* does not lend itself to this updating strategy because it requires that you change the structure of the query based on the columns that have been modified in the row that contains the pending change. The *DataAdapter* supplies values for the parameters in its query-based updates on a row-by-row basis, but it does not modify the actual structure of the parameterized query.

Theoretically, you could write code to dynamically change the structure of the appropriate *Command* object and use that code while handling the *DataAdapter* object's *RowUpdating* event. I think that this updating strategy has benefits, but the costs outweigh them.

Working with Null Values

The Customers table in the Northwind database contains a Region column that accepts strings of up to 15 characters and also accepts Null values. A number of rows in the Region column have a Null value. Many developers will try to use a query such as the following to retrieve those rows:

```
SELECT CustomerID, CompanyName, ContactName, Phone
    FROM Customers WHERE Region = NULL
```

If you use this query in ADO.NET or run this query in SQL Query Analyzer, you'll find that it returns zero rows.

Null values are a special case in the database world, especially when it comes to comparing Null values in a query. According to ANSI standards, you can't compare Null values using the = operator. Instead, you must use *IS NULL* in your query. The following query returns the rows in the Customers table that have Null values for the Region column:

```
SELECT CustomerID, CompanyName, ContactName, Phone
    FROM Customers WHERE Region IS NULL
```

What do Null values have to do with submitting changes to your database using a *DataAdapter*? Let's take a quick look at the *CommandText* for the *Command* we created earlier to submit modified rows in the Order Details table:

```
UPDATE [Order Details]
    SET OrderID = ?, ProductID = ?, Quantity = ?, UnitPrice = ?
    WHERE OrderID = ? AND ProductID = ? AND
        Quantity = ? AND UnitPrice = ?
```

None of the columns referenced in this query accepts Null values. As a result, the WHERE clause for this query is relatively simple. But what if the Quantity and UnitPrice columns were to allow Null values? Let's say you have a row that currently has a Null value in the Quantity column and you want to change that value to *20*. If we replace the parameters with actual values, we get a query that looks like this:

```
UPDATE [Order Details]
    SET OrderID = 12345, ProductID = 1, Quantity = 20, UnitPrice = 18
    WHERE OrderID = 12345 AND ProductID = 1 AND
        Quantity = Null AND UnitPrice = 18
```

In this scenario, the query will modify zero rows because of the *Quantity = Null* portion of the WHERE clause. The Quantity column for the desired row in the database is Null, but *Null = Null* evaluates to *false*, so the database does not modify the row.

So how do we change the WHERE clause of our queries to accommodate Null values in our concurrency check? If a particular column accepts Null values, we can replace the following portion of a query

```
ColumnName = ?
```

with

```
(ColumnName = ? OR ((ColumnName IS NULL) AND (? IS NULL)))
```

We want the clause to evaluate to *true* if the column and the parameter equate to the same non-Null value or if both the column and the parameter are Null.

Let's say your *DataAdapter* will query the Customers table for the CustomerID, CompanyName, ContactName, and Phone columns. Neither the CustomerID nor CompanyName columns accepts Null, but the ContactName and Phone columns do. As a result, you must perform Null checks in the WHERE clauses of your query-based updates. If you build your updating logic using the Data Adapter Configuration Wizard, you'll find that the wizard generates the following query to submit modified rows, complete with the appropriate Null checks:

```
UPDATE Customers
    SET CustomerID = ?, CompanyName = ?, ContactName = ?, Phone = ?
    WHERE (CustomerID = ?) AND (CompanyName = ?) AND
        (ContactName = ? OR ((? IS NULL) AND (ContactName IS NULL)))
        AND (Phone = ? OR ((? IS NULL) AND (Phone IS NULL)))
```

As I mentioned earlier, the Data Adapter Configuration Wizard does a very good job of generating updating logic. Even if you're going to generate your own logic, you might want to look at the code that the wizard generates in order to double-check your work.

Submitting Updates in Transactions

What if you want to submit all of your updates as a single unit of work so that either all of the updates succeed or none of them does? The simple answer is to wrap your updates in a transaction. However, the *DataAdapter* does not expose a *Transaction* property.

The *DataAdapter* does not actually submit the updates. It simply hands the work off to the *Command* objects in its *UpdateCommand*, *InsertCommand*, and *DeleteCommand* properties. The *Command* object exposes a *Transaction* property, so in order to submit the changes using the *DataAdapter*, you must set the *Transaction* property of the *Command* objects that the *DataAdapter* will use.

The following code snippet shows one way to accomplish this task:

Visual Basic .NET

```
Dim strConn, strSQL As String
strConn = "Provider=SQLOLEDB;Data Source=(local)\NetSDK;" & _
          "Initial Catalog=Northwind;Trusted_Connection=Yes;"
strSQL = "SELECT OrderID, ProductID, Quantity, UnitPrice " & _
          "FROM [Order Details] WHERE OrderID = 10503 " & _
          "ORDER BY ProductID"
Dim tbl As New DataTable()
Dim cn As New OleDbConnection(strConn)
Dim da As New OleDbDataAdapter(strSQL, cn)
'Define updating logic for the DataAdapter.

'Open the connection and fetch the results of the query.
cn.Open()
da.Fill(tbl)

'Modify the contents of the DataTable.

'Create a new transaction.
Dim txn As OleDbTransaction = cn.BeginTransaction()
'Set the Transaction property of the DataAdapter's Commands.
da.UpdateCommand.Transaction = txn
da.InsertCommand.Transaction = txn
da.DeleteCommand.Transaction = txn

'Submit the changes.
da.Update(tbl)

'Commit the changes and close the connection.
txn.Commit()
cn.Close()
```

Visual C# .NET

```
string strConn, strSQL;
strConn = "Provider=SQLOLEDB;Data Source=(local)\\NetSDK;" +
          "Initial Catalog=Northwind;Trusted_Connection=Yes;";
strSQL = "SELECT OrderID, ProductID, Quantity, UnitPrice " +
          "FROM [Order Details] WHERE OrderID = 10503 " +
          "ORDER BY ProductID";
DataTable tbl = new DataTable();
OleDbConnection cn = new OleDbConnection(strConn);
OleDbDataAdapter da = new OleDbDataAdapter(strSQL, cn);
//Define updating logic for the DataAdapter.

//Open the connection and fetch the results of the query.
```

```
cn.Open();
da.Fill(tbl);

//Modify the contents of the DataTable.

//Create a new transaction.
OleDbTransaction txn = cn.BeginTransaction();
//Set the Transaction property of the DataAdapter's Commands.
da.UpdateCommand.Transaction = txn;
da.InsertCommand.Transaction = txn;
da.DeleteCommand.Transaction = txn;

//Submit the changes.
da.Update(tbl);

//Commit the changes and close the connection.
txn.Commit();
cn.Close();
```

It's slightly more challenging to submit changes in a transaction if you're relying on the *CommandBuilder* object to generate your updating logic. The *CommandBuilder* does not actually generate the updating logic when you instantiate it. If you instantiate a *CommandBuilder* object and later call *DataAdapter.Update*, the *CommandBuilder* will not actually build the updating logic until you call the *DataAdapter* object's *Update* method. This behavior poses a slight problem if you want to use the *CommandBuilder* to submit changes in a transaction.

If you use code that looks like the following, ADO.NET will throw an exception when you try to submit the pending changes:

Visual Basic .NET

```
Dim strConn, strSQL As String
  :
Dim tbl As New DataTable()
Dim cn As New OleDbConnection(strConn)
Dim da As New OleDbDataAdapter(strSQL, cn)
Dim cb As New OleDbCommandBuilder(da)
cn.Open()
da.Fill(tbl)
Dim txn As OleDbTransaction = cn.BeginTransaction()
da.Update(tbl)
txn.Commit()
cn.Close()
```

Visual C# .NET

```
string strConn, strSQL;
    ⋮
DataTable tbl = new DataTable();
OleDbConnection cn = new OleDbConnection(strConn);
OleDbDataAdapter da = new OleDbDataAdapter(strSQL, cn);
OleDbCommandBuilder cb = new OleDbCommandBuilder(da);
cn.Open();
da.Fill(tbl);
OleDbTransaction txn = cn.BeginTransaction();
da.Update(tbl);
txn.Commit();
cn.Close();
```

When you call *DataAdapter.Update*, the *CommandBuilder* will fetch the required metadata from the database using the *DataAdapter* object's *SelectCommand*. We have not associated the *Command* object in the *SelectCommand* property with the newly created transaction. As a result, the *CommandBuilder* cannot use the *SelectCommand* and the *CommandBuilder* throws an exception.

If we add the following line of code just before the call to the *Data-Adapter* object's *Update* method, our code will succeed:

```
da.SelectCommand.Transaction = txn
```

However, this means that the *CommandBuilder* fetches schema information from your database within a transaction. Generally speaking, you want to touch as little data as possible in your database during a transaction. A more palatable option is to force the *CommandBuilder* to generate updating logic before starting the transaction. We can accomplish this by calling the *CommandBuilder* object's *GetUpdateCommand* (or *GetInsertCommand* or *Get-DeleteCommand*) method.

We can then associate the *Command* objects that the *CommandBuilder* generated with our new *Transaction* object using the following code, and the *DataAdapter* will submit updates within the transaction:

Visual Basic .NET

```
Dim strConn, strSQL As String
    ⋮
Dim tbl As New DataTable()
Dim cn As New OleDbConnection(strConn)
Dim da As New OleDbDataAdapter(strSQL, cn)
Dim cb As New OleDbCommandBuilder(da)
cn.Open()
cb.GetUpdateCommand()
da.Fill(tbl)
Dim txn As OleDbTransaction = cn.BeginTransaction()
cb.GetUpdateCommand.Transaction = txn
```

```
cb.GetInsertCommand.Transaction = txn
cb.GetDeleteCommand.Transaction = txn
da.Update(tbl)
txn.Commit()
cn.Close()
```

Visual C# .NET

```
string strConn, strSQL;
⋮
DataTable tbl = new DataTable();
OleDbConnection cn = new OleDbConnection(strConn);
OleDbDataAdapter da = new OleDbDataAdapter(strSQL, cn);
OleDbCommandBuilder cb = new OleDbCommandBuilder(da);
cn.Open();
cb.GetUpdateCommand();
da.Fill(tbl);
OleDbTransaction txn = cn.BeginTransaction();
cb.GetUpdateCommand().Transaction = txn;
cb.GetInsertCommand().Transaction = txn;
cb.GetDeleteCommand().Transaction = txn;
da.Update(tbl);
txn.Commit();
cn.Close();
```

Using the *TableMappings* Collection

In Chapter 5, you learned how the *DataAdapter* object's *TableMappings* collection affects how the *DataAdapter* populates a *DataSet* via the *Fill* method. In the following code, calling the *Fill* method of the *DataAdapter* creates a new *DataTable* whose *TableName* property is set to *Table*:

Visual Basic .NET

```
Dim strConn, strSQL As String
strConn = "Provider=SQLOLEDB;Data Source=(local)\NetSDK;" & _
          "Initial Catalog=Northwind;Trusted_Connection=Yes;"
strSQL = "SELECT OrderID, ProductID, Quantity, UnitPrice " & _
         "FROM [Order Details] WHERE OrderID = 10503 " & _
         "ORDER BY ProductID"
Dim da As New OleDbDataAdapter(strSQL, strConn)
Dim ds As New DataSet()
da.Fill(ds)
```

Visual C# .NET

```
string strConn, strSQL;
strConn = "Provider=SQLOLEDB;Data Source=(local)\\NetSDK;" +
          "Initial Catalog=Northwind;Trusted_Connection=Yes;";
strSQL = "SELECT OrderID, ProductID, Quantity, UnitPrice " +
```

(continued)

```
        "FROM [Order Details] WHERE OrderID = 10503 " +
        "ORDER BY ProductID";
OleDbDataAdapter da = new OleDbDataAdapter(strSQL, strConn);
DataSet ds = new DataSet();
da.Fill(ds);
```

If we want our new *DataTable* to have a *TableName* of *Order Details,* we can change our code in one of two ways. The first option is to use the overloaded *Fill* method to supply the desired *TableName*:

Visual Basic .NET

```
⋮
Dim da As New OleDbDataAdapter(strSQL, strConn)
Dim ds As New DataSet()
da.Fill(ds, "Order Details")
```

Visual C# .NET

```
⋮
OleDbDataAdapter da = new OleDbDataAdapter(strSQL, strConn);
DataSet ds = new DataSet();
da.Fill(ds, "Order Details");
```

The other option is to add an entry to the *DataAdapter* object's *TableMappings* collection so that the *DataAdapter* knows that it's associated with the *Order Details DataTable*:

Visual Basic .NET

```
⋮
Dim da As New OleDbDataAdapter(strSQL, strConn)
da.TableMappings.Add("Table", "Order Details")
Dim ds As New DataSet()
da.Fill(ds)
```

Visual C# .NET

```
⋮
OleDbDataAdapter da = new OleDbDataAdapter(strSQL, strConn);
da.TableMappings.Add("Table", "Order Details");
DataSet ds = new DataSet();
da.Fill(ds);
```

The *TableMappings* collection has a similar effect when you submit updates. If you supply just a *DataSet* object in the *DataAdapter* object's *Update* method, the *DataAdapter* will rely on its *TableMappings* collection to determine which *DataTable* in the *DataSet* to examine:

Visual Basic .NET

```
:
Dim da As New OleDbDataAdapter(strSQL, strConn)
da.TableMappings.Add("Table", "Order Details")
'Define updating logic.
Dim ds As New DataSet()
da.Fill(ds)
'Modify a series of rows.
da.Update(ds)
```

Visual C# .NET

```
:
OleDbDataAdapter da = new OleDbDataAdapter(strSQL, strConn);
//Define updating logic.
da.TableMappings.Add("Table", "Order Details");
DataSet ds = new DataSet();
da.Fill(ds);
//Modify a series of rows.
da.Update(ds);
```

If you have not populated the *DataAdapter* object's *TableMappings* collection, you must either use the *Update* method that accepts a *DataSet* and a table name or use the *Update* method that accepts a *DataTable* object:

Visual Basic .NET

```
:
Dim da As New OleDbDataAdapter(strSQL, strConn)
'Define updating logic.
Dim ds As New DataSet()
da.Fill(ds, "Order Details")
'Modify a series of rows.
da.Update(ds, "Order Details")

'or

:
Dim da As New OleDbDataAdapter(strSQL, strConn)
'Define updating logic.
Dim tbl As New DataTable()
da.Fill(tbl)
'Modify a series of rows.
da.Update(tbl)
```

Visual C# .NET

```
  ⋮
OleDbDataAdapter da = new OleDbDataAdapter(strSQL, strConn);
//Define updating logic.
DataSet ds = new DataSet();
da.Fill(ds, "Order Details");
//Modify a series of rows.
da.Update(ds, "Order Details");

//or

  ⋮
OleDbDataAdapter da = new OleDbDataAdapter(strSQL, strConn);
//Define updating logic.
DataTable tbl = new DataTable();
da.Fill(tbl);
//Modify a series of rows.
da.Update(tbl);
```

As a basic rule, you should use the same logic to control the *DataTable* you're referencing in both *DataAdapter.Fill* and *DataAdapter.Update*.

The Best Way to Update

ADO.NET gives you many options for submitting changes. You can generate updating logic at run time using *CommandBuilder* objects. You can supply your own updating logic in code, submitting changes via INSERT, UPDATE, or DELETE queries or via stored procedure calls. You can also use the Data Adapter Configuration Wizard to generate such code easily at design time. Which of these options is right for you?

The answer really depends on the parameters of your application. You could get the best performance by configuring your *DataAdapter* objects to submit updates via stored procedure calls. However, if your application must work with databases, such as Microsoft Access, that don't support stored procedures, that solution is not appropriate. You'd be better off using INSERT, UPDATE, and DELETE queries. You'll need to consider such factors when deciding what's appropriate for your application.

From a general standpoint, I strongly recommend submitting changes via stored procedures whenever possible. If the ability to work with multiple back ends is a greater priority, use query-based updates (INSERT, UPDATE, DELETE) instead. Regardless of which option you choose, generate your own updating logic. Use the Data Adapter Configuration Wizard or a similar code-generation tool to save development time, but avoid generating updating logic at run time whenever possible. If you remember only one thing from this chapter, remember this: Don't rely on *CommandBuilder* objects in your applications unless absolutely necessary.

There are a number of more advanced updating scenarios that we've yet to discuss. How do I fetch newly generated autoincrement values? How do I submit changes from a *DataSet* that contains new and deleted rows to multiple related tables? How do I detect and handle failed update attempts? How can I use ADO.NET with distributed transactions? We'll cover these and other more advanced updating scenarios in the next chapter.

OleDbCommandBuilder Object Reference

Because this chapter introduces the ADO.NET *CommandBuilder* object, I think it will be helpful to review the properties and methods of the *OleDbCommandBuilder* object.

One aspect of the *CommandBuilder* object is particularly worth noting. The *OleDbCommandBuilder* and *SqlCommandBuilder* objects are not derived from the same base class. In fact, there is no base *CommandBuilder* class in the initial release of the ADO.NET object model.

Writing code to fetch the necessary metadata from the back end and convert this data into updating logic is not a simple task. If it were, the *CommandBuilder* object would be unnecessary. Because the code required to create a *CommandBuilder* class for a .NET data provider is far from trivial and because of the performance penalty associated with using *CommandBuilder* objects at run time, I wouldn't be surprised to see third-party .NET data providers that do not include a *CommandBuilder* class.

Properties of the *OleDbCommandBuilder* Object

Table 10-1 lists the properties of the *OleDbCommandBuilder* object.

Table 10-1   Properties of the *OleDbCommandBuilder* Object

Property	Data Type	Description
DataAdapter	*DataAdapter*	Returns the *DataAdapter* for which the *CommandBuilder* is generating updating logic
QuotePrefix	*String*	Contains the prefix the *CommandBuilder* will use when delimiting column and table names
QuoteSuffix	*String*	Contains the suffix the *CommandBuilder* will use when delimiting column and table names

DataAdapter

The *CommandBuilder* object's *DataAdapter* property allows you to examine or change the *DataAdapter* with which the *CommandBuilder* object is associated. You can also set this property in the *CommandBuilder* object's constructor.

QuotePrefix and QuoteSuffix

The *CommandBuilder* object's *QuotePrefix* and *QuoteSuffix* properties contain the strings that the *CommandBuilder* object will use to delimit the table and column names in the queries that it generates. By default, these properties contain empty strings.

Methods of the *OleDbCommandBuilder* Object

Table 10-2 lists the methods of the *OleDbCommandBuilder* object.

Table 10-2   Methods of the *OleDbCommandBuilder* Object

Method	Description
DeriveParameters	Retrieves parameter information for a *Command* that calls a stored procedure
GetDeleteCommand	Returns the *Command* that contains the logic for the *DataAdapter* object's *DeleteCommand*
GetInsertCommand	Returns the *Command* that contains the logic for the *DataAdapter* object's *InsertCommand*
GetUpdateCommand	Returns the *Command* that contains the logic for the *DataAdapter* object's *UpdateCommand*
RefreshSchema	Tells the *CommandBuilder* that it will need to regenerate its updating logic

DeriveParameters

The *CommandBuilder* object can do more than just generate updating logic for *DataAdapter* objects. You can also use a *CommandBuilder* to fetch parameter information for stored procedures. The following code snippet uses the *Command-Builder* object's *DeriveParameters* method to retrieve and display parameter information for a stored procedure call:

Visual Basic .NET

```
Dim strConn As String
strConn = "Provider=SQLOLEDB;Data Source=(local)\NetSDK;" & _
          "Initial Catalog=Northwind;Trusted_Connection=Yes;"
Dim cn As New OleDbConnection(strConn)
Dim cmd As New OleDbCommand("CustOrdersOrders", cn)
cmd.CommandType = CommandType.StoredProcedure
```

```
Dim cb As New OleDbCommandBuilder()
cn.Open()
cb.DeriveParameters(cmd)
cn.Close()
Dim param As OleDbParameter
For Each param In cmd.Parameters
    Console.WriteLine(param.ParameterName)
    Console.WriteLine(vbTab & param.Direction.ToString)
    Console.WriteLine(vbTab & param.OleDbType.ToString)
    Console.WriteLine()
Next param
```

Visual C# .NET

```
string strConn;
strConn = "Provider=SQLOLEDB;Data Source=(local)\\NetSDK;" +
        "Initial Catalog=Northwind;Trusted_Connection=Yes;";
OleDbConnection cn = new OleDbConnection(strConn);
OleDbCommand cmd = new OleDbCommand("CustOrdersOrders", cn);
cmd.CommandType = CommandType.StoredProcedure;
OleDbCommandBuilder cb = new OleDbCommandBuilder();
cn.Open();
cb.DeriveParameters(cmd);
cn.Close();
foreach (OleDbParameter param in cmd.Parameters)
{
    Console.WriteLine(param.ParameterName);
    Console.WriteLine("\t" + param.Direction.ToString());
    Console.WriteLine("\t" + param.OleDbType.ToString());
    Console.WriteLine();
}
```

If you're trying to build the parameters collection for a command that calls a stored procedure but you're unsure of what value to set for the *Size, Precision*, and *Size* properties, you might want to use this type of code once at design time.

> **Note**   In order for you to use the *DeriveParameters* method, the *Connection* for the supplied *Command* object must be open and available.

GetDeleteCommand, GetInsertCommand, and *GetUpdateCommand*

The *CommandBuilder* object's *GetUpdateCommand, GetInsertCommand*, and *GetDeleteCommand* methods let you examine the logic that the *Command-Builder* generated.

These methods can also prove helpful at design time. You can create a *CommandBuilder* in code in a small sample application and then use these methods to display the *CommandText* and parameter information that the *CommandBuilder* generated. You can then use that same updating logic using the same query and parameter information in your code.

RefreshSchema

If you're changing the structure of your *DataAdapter* object's query in your application, you'll probably need to use the *CommandBuilder* object's *RefreshSchema* method.

The *DataAdapter* object does not fire an event when the *CommandText* property of its *SelectCommand* changes. Once the *CommandBuilder* object has generated your updating logic, as far as it knows, its work is done. If you've changed the structure of the *DataAdapter* object's query so that the *CommandBuilder* needs to regenerate the updating logic, you can call the *RefreshSchema* method of the *CommandBuilder* object.

Calling the *RefreshSchema* method does not force the *CommandBuilder* to regenerate its updating logic immediately. It simply sets a flag within the *CommandBuilder* to indicate that the current logic is no longer accurate. The *CommandBuilder* will regenerate the updating logic when you call the *DataAdapter* object's *Update* method or when you call one of the *CommandBuilder* object's *Get<Update/Insert/Delete>Command* methods.

Questions That Should Be Asked More Frequently

Q.   So the *DataAdapter* can fill a *DataSet* with the results of a query and submit changes stored in a *DataSet* to my database. Do I have to use the same object to accomplish both tasks? I'm working with multi-tiered applications, and it sounds like I need to keep my *DataAdapter* objects alive in the middle tier between calls from the client application. Is that the case?

A.   You *can* use the same *DataAdapter* to fill your *DataSet* and submit changes to your database, but that's not a requirement.

Say your middle-tier object has two simple methods—one to return a new *DataSet* and one to submit the pending changes in your *DataSet* to your database. You could use separate *DataAdapter* objects for each of the methods. When you're simply filling a *DataSet*, the *DataAdapter* does not need updating logic. Conversely, if you're using a *DataAdapter* only to submit updates, the *DataAdapter* does not require you to define a *SelectCommand*.

The *DataAdapter* really needs *Command* objects defined for only the *Command* objects it will need to execute. For example, if you know that your *DataAdapter* will submit only new rows (rather than modify or delete existing rows), you will need only an *InsertCommand*. Because the *DataAdapter* will not execute the *Command* objects stored in its *SelectCommand*, *UpdateCommand*, and *DeleteCommand* properties, you won't need to set those properties.

The one caveat to this rule is if you use a *CommandBuilder* object to define the updating logic in your *DataAdapter*. The *CommandBuilder* cannot generate your updating logic if you do not have a *SelectCommand* defined for the *DataAdapter*.

Q. I want to fill a *DataTable* based on the results of a join query, modify the data in the *DataTable*, and then submit the changes back to the database using a *DataAdapter*. Neither the Data Adapter Configuration Wizard nor the *CommandBuilder* object will build this logic for me. What should I do?

A. My first recommendation is to reread the section on join queries in Chapter 7.

The reason that neither component generates updating logic is that it's not clear what modifying the data returned by a join query truly means. Let's say that we take the query we've been using to retrieve order detail information and change it slightly so that the query also returns the name of the product in the line item:

```
SELECT D.OrderID, P.ProductName, D.ProductID,
      D.Quantity, D.UnitPrice
   FROM [Order Details] D, Products P
   WHERE D.OrderID = 10503 AND D.ProductID = P.ProductID
   ORDER BY P.ProductID
```

When we fetch the results of this query into a *DataTable* and modify a row, how do we want to change the contents of the database? The answer is clear to us. We want to modify the corresponding row in the Order Details table in the database. But that's not clear to the Data Adapter Configuration Wizard or the *CommandBuilder* object.

The ADO cursor engine generates updating logic for you automatically, even with join queries, but this logic has frustrated most developers. If you generate an ADO *Recordset* using this query and modify only columns that correspond to the Order Details table, the ADO cursor engine will try to modify only the corresponding row in the Order Details table.

But if you want to change the product that the line item references and you change both the ProductID column (Order Details table) and the ProductName column (Products table) so that the row of data looks correct on your screen, the ADO cursor engine will try to modify the ProductID column in the Order Details table and the ProductName in the Products table. Chances are that isn't what you want the ADO cursor engine to do.

Thankfully, ADO.NET is not a black box technology like ADO. You can supply your own updating logic. In this scenario, you want to submit changes only to the Order Details table, so you can define your updating logic to ignore changes stored in the ProductName column.

How can you generate that updating logic? Neither the *CommandBuilder* nor the Data Adapter Configuration Wizard will be of much help with the actual join query. But you can temporarily leave off the ProductName column, use either tool to generate the desired updating logic, and then re-add the ProductName column to your query. Devious, yet effective.

Let's get back to my first recommendation. The section inChapter 7 titled "Using *DataRelation* Objects in Expression-Based *DataColumn* Objects" includes a code snippet that shows how you can use multiple *DataTable* objects and a *DataRelation* to simulate the results of a join query. The other major benefit to this approach is that you've greatly simplified your updating logic. The data in each *DataTable* corresponds to a single table in your database. The *CommandBuilder* and Data Adapter Configuration Wizard can generate the appropriate updating logic for you.

Q. You talked about optimistic concurrency only. How do I handle pessimistic concurrency in ADO.NET?

A. With pessimistic concurrency, you lock the row before you start making your changes. Because the contents of the *DataSet* are disconnected from the database, there is no simple way to lock the data in the database before you modify a row in a *DataSet*. However, you can achieve similar functionality using transactions.

Let's say you want to lock data in your database before the user modifies data on the screen to ensure that the user's changes will succeed. You could open a transaction and lock those rows in the database so that other users cannot modify those rows by issuing the following query within the transaction:

```
SELECT * FROM [Order Details] HOLDLOCK WHERE OrderID = 10503
```

> **Note**   This query was written specifically for SQL Server 2000. Not all databases support this query syntax. If you're working with another database, see your database's documentation for information on how to lock data in a query.

This approach has some major drawbacks. What if your user forgets to click the Submit Changes button in your application and strolls off to the kitchen to grab a donut and some caffeine? Those rows in the database are locked. The more data you lock and the longer you maintain those locks, the less scalable your application becomes.

It's time for me to confess. I've made some mistakes in my life. I used a similar approach in an application years ago, but not because I was young or needed the money. It was because the users requested this "feature." They didn't want to run into a situation where the changes they made on the screen could not be committed to the database and they would have to reenter those changes later.

One employee, whom I'll call Steve (half the people in the company were named Steve) would repeatedly forget to commit his changes. When other users could not modify data in the database, they'd find me and then I'd have to find Steve, which sometimes took a while. Trying to explain that this was the functionality they asked for didn't make anyone any happier.

Hey, I was in college. That's when kids are supposed to experiment with things like pessimistic locking. I learned my lesson, and no one got hurt. Not even Steve.

Q.   What if I want to submit updates when my *DataSet* contains BLOB columns?

A.   The short answer is that you should take the initial query and break it out into separate queries—one that retrieves your non-BLOB columns and one that retrieves just the primary key columns and your BLOB column.

Because the structure of the queries that the *DataAdapter* uses to submit changes is static, the values from all columns are used in the SET clause of the *UpdateCommand* object's *CommandText*, even if only one column contains changed data. This is a small nuisance for most queries (and a necessary evil when you submit changes using a stored procedure), but it can be a major pain if you're working with BLOB columns. Why?

Let's say we're working with employee information and the database contains an Employees table with columns for the employee's name, identification number, title, and photo. The photo column holds large amounts of binary information—the contents of a JPEG file.

If you have a *DataTable* that contains all of these columns and you modify just the title column for a row, the *DataAdapter* will include the current values for all columns in the query to update the row in the database. This means that even though you've only modified a small string-based column, you'll still pass the binary contents of the employee photo across the wire to your database.

Another approach is to split the data into separate tables, as shown in Figure 10-11. The figure shows two *DataTable* objects linked by a *DataRelation*. The parent *DataTable* includes the main columns for the Employees table—EmployeeID, LastName, and First-Name. The child *DataTable* contains the BLOB column Photo as well as the EmployeeID column in order to maintain the relationship to the parent *DataTable*.

Employees		
EmployeeID	**LastName**	**FirstName**
1	Davolio	Nancy
2	Fuller	Andrew
3	Leverling	Janet
4	Peacock	Margaret

EmployeesPhotos	
EmployeeID	**Photo**
1	\<Binary contents of Photo column\>
2	\<Binary contents of Photo column\>
3	\<Binary contents of Photo column\>
4	\<Binary contents of Photo column\>

Figure 10-11 Splitting a *DataTable* based on a BLOB column.

If you use a *DataSet* with this architecture with separate *Data-Adapter* objects for each *DataTable*, a change to the Title column will result in a query-based update that does not include the Photo column. The only time the contents of the Photo column will be sent back to the database in this architecture is when the contents of the Photo column change.

   Of course, this entire discussion would be moot if you were to store the binary data in a file and use the database to maintain the location of the file.

Q.   I tried using the code earlier in the chapter that showed how to submit changes to the Order Details table using the *CommandBuilder*, but my code failed with an error about "Incorrect syntax near the keyword 'Order.'" Did I do something wrong?

A.   I hate to answer a question with a question, but why did you want to put a space in your table name? I've yet to hear a developer say, "Boy, I sure am glad we put spaces in our table and column names. That made my life so much easier." But I digress.

   As of this writing, the *CommandBuilder* object does not query the database to determine the characters that the database uses to delimit table and column names that are reserved words or that contain spaces and other bad characters. If you use the *Command-Builder* to generate updating logic for a query that includes such table or column names, your update attempts will fail unless you specify values for the *CommandBuilder* object's *QuotePrefix* and *QuoteSuffix* properties.

   What if you're not comfortable supplying values for those properties because you're writing code that must run successfully against various back ends? If you're working with the OLE DB .NET Data Provider, you might be able to use the *OleDbConnection* object's *GetOleDbSchemaTable* method to fetch the proper delimiters from the database. I've tested the following code, and it's worked successfully using the Microsoft OLE DB providers that communicate with SQL Server, Oracle, and Access:

Visual Basic .NET

```
Dim strConn, strSQL As String
strConn = "Provider=SQLOLEDB;Data Source=(local)\NetSDK;" & _
          "Initial Catalog=Northwind;Trusted_Connection=Yes;"
strSQL = "SELECT OrderID, ProductID, Quantity, UnitPrice " & _
          "FROM [Order Details] WHERE OrderID = 10503 " & _
          "ORDER BY ProductID"
Dim cn As New OleDbConnection(strConn)
Dim da As New OleDbDataAdapter(strSQL, cn)
cn.Open()
Dim cb As New OleDbCommandBuilder(da)
```

(continued)

```
Dim tblSchema As DataTable
tblSchema = cn.GetOleDbSchemaTable(OleDbSchemaGuid.DbInfoLiterals, _
                                   New Object() {})
cn.Close()
tblSchema.PrimaryKey = New DataColumn() _
                       {tblSchema.Columns("LiteralName")}
Dim row As DataRow
row = tblSchema.Rows.Find("Quote_Prefix")
If Not row Is Nothing Then
    cb.QuotePrefix = row("LiteralValue")
End If
row = tblSchema.Rows.Find("Quote_Suffix")
If Not row Is Nothing Then
    cb.QuoteSuffix = row("LiteralValue")
End If
```

Visual C# .NET

```
string strConn, strSQL;
strConn = "Provider=SQLOLEDB;Data Source=(local)\\NetSDK;" +
          "Initial Catalog=Northwind;Trusted_Connection=Yes;";
strSQL = "SELECT OrderID, ProductID, Quantity, UnitPrice " +
         "FROM [Order Details] WHERE OrderID = 10503 " +
         "ORDER BY ProductID";
OleDbConnection cn = new OleDbConnection(strConn);
OleDbDataAdapter da = new OleDbDataAdapter(strSQL, cn);
cn.Open();
OleDbCommandBuilder cb = new OleDbCommandBuilder(da);
DataTable tblSchema;
tblSchema = cn.GetOleDbSchemaTable(OleDbSchemaGuid.DbInfoLiterals,
                                   new object[] {});
cn.Close();
tblSchema.PrimaryKey = new DataColumn[]
                       {tblSchema.Columns["LiteralName"]};
DataRow row;
row = tblSchema.Rows.Find("Quote_Prefix");
if (row != null)
    cb.QuotePrefix = row["LiteralValue"];
row = tblSchema.Rows.Find("Quote_Suffix");
if (row != null)
    cb.QuoteSuffix = row["LiteralValue"];
```

Of course, you can avoid such problems by making sure your table and column names do not require delimiters.

Q. When I submit new rows using an ADO.NET *DataAdapter*, I see null values in the new row in my database rather than the default values I defined for those columns in my database. When I submitted changes via ADO, I got default values. What gives?

A.   SQL Server, and other databases, lets you define default values for columns in your database. As we saw in Chapter 6, the *DefaultValue* property of the ADO.NET *DataColumn* object is not an exact match for this functionality. So ADO.NET will not generate your database's default values for you automatically. There's also another factor involved.

Databases generate default values for columns in your new rows if you use an INSERT query that omits the column or specifies the keyword DEFAULT rather than a value for the column. ADO.NET will not omit the column from its updating logic, nor will it use the keyword DEFAULT.

ADO.NET's predecessor, ADO, generates dynamic updates on a per-row basis. When submitting updates, it omitted unmodified columns from the INSERT statements that it generated. Thus, the new rows in your database that you create with ADO might automatically contain the default values, whereas the ones you create with ADO.NET will not.

The simplest solution in ADO.NET is to add code to your application so that when you create a new row, you automatically supply the desired default values for your columns.

11

Advanced Updating Scenarios

In Chapter 10, you learned how to use the updating features of the *Data-Adapter* object to submit changes to your database. At this point, you should be comfortable generating updating logic using either the Visual Studio .NET Data Adapter Configuration Wizard or the *CommandBuilder* object. You should also feel comfortable with the UPDATE, INSERT, and DELETE SQL queries that these tools generate to translate the pending changes stored in your *DataSet* into changes in your database.

All the examples in Chapter 10 involve simple updating scenarios. All of the updates succeed. After you submit the changes, there is no need to requery the database for any information. The tables used in the code snippets do not have columns of server-generated data such as autoincrement values or time-stamps, and changes are submitted to only a single table. You will likely face more challenging updating scenarios in your applications, however.

For example, if you're working with tables that have autoincrement columns, you'll want to retrieve the autoincrement values that your database generates for new rows. In other situations, you'll want to refetch the contents of your row after you submit an update, such as when you're relying on time-stamp columns to enforce optimistic concurrency.

The more complex your application is, the more complex the updating scenarios you'll likely face. Submitting changes to hierarchical data can prove challenging. Multi-tiered applications pose their own special set of problems—such as transmitting *DataSet* objects that contain only the data required to submit updates to your database and reintegrating newly fetched values such as timestamps and autoincrement values into a preexisting *DataSet*.

Optimistic update attempts don't always succeed. For example, your update attempts might fail if another user has modified the rows you wanted to update. You're probably better off learning to handle such failures elegantly rather than going to extreme lengths to try to prevent the failures in the first place.

This chapter will take a closer look at these and other advanced updating scenarios. However, I'll be taking a slightly different approach. Previous chapters are peppered with code snippets that you can copy and paste into console applications and run successfully without having to change the code. Creating fully functional code snippets for advanced updating scenarios in this chapter would be unrealistic. So this chapter will instead use small snippets of code from sample applications on the companion CD.

Refreshing a Row After Submitting an Update

In Chapter 10, you learned how to construct and use INSERT, UPDATE, and DELETE queries to submit changes to your database. These queries are basically one-way streets. The database modifies the contents of the row based on the information you supply in the query. Although the database reports how many rows the query affected, it does not return the new contents of the modified rows.

Sometimes submitting an update to your database needs to be a two-way street. In Chapter 10, I discussed using the Microsoft SQL Server timestamp data type to ensure that you don't unintentionally overwrite another user's changes to the database. When the contents of the row change, the database generates a new value for the timestamp column for that row. Consider the following scenario.

Your application displays the contents of an order. The user adds a new a line item to the order, which corresponds to a row in your table, which is similar to the Northwind database's Order Details table. However, in your table you have a timestamp column and you're using the value of this timestamp column in your updating logic. When the user submits the new line item to the database, the database generates the value for the timestamp column of the new row. No problem there.

For the sake of discussion, let's say the application has a Microsoft Windows front end instead of using Web forms. After the user submits the new line item, the contents of the order are still visible in the application. What if the user needs to modify that same line item and submit that change to the database?

Remember that the *DataAdapter* object's updating logic uses the value of the timestamp column in the *UpdateCommand*. The database generates a value for the timestamp column for the row when you submit the new row. If that timestamp value does not appear in your *DataRow* object, the update attempt will fail.

You can run into the same problem when you modify a row, submit that change to the database, and then attempt to modify that row again. The database will generate a new value for the timestamp column when you submit the first change. If you don't have the new value for the timestamp column in your *DataRow* object, the subsequent update attempt will fail.

Retrieving the Newly Generated Value for the Timestamp Column After You Submit an Update

Let's say the initial query to retrieve data from the Order Details table looks like this:

```
SELECT OrderID, ProductID, Quantity, UnitPrice, TimestampColumn
    FROM [Order Details] WHERE OrderID = ?
```

You learned in the previous chapter that you can submit updates to the table using the following parameterized query:

```
UPDATE [Order Details]
    SET OrderID = ?, ProductID = ?, Quantity = ?, UnitPrice = ?
    WHERE OrderID = ? AND ProductID = ? AND TSCol = ?
```

We can issue the following query to retrieve the new value that the database generates for the timestamp column:

```
SELECT TSCol FROM [Order Details] WHERE OrderID = ? AND ProductID = ?
```

Sure, you could manually execute this query after submitting an update. But what if you have a series of changes to submit?

Let's see how we can use this query in conjunction with the ADO.NET object model to retrieve these values automatically after submitting updates.

Using Batch Queries to Retrieve Data After You Submit an Update

In Chapter 5, you learned how to use a *DataAdapter* to fetch the results of a batch query such as this one:

```
SELECT CustomerID, CompanyName, ContactName, Phone FROM Customers;
SELECT OrderID, CustomerID, EmployeeID, OrderDate FROM Orders
```

You can also use batched queries to retrieve data after you submit an update. You can combine the update query and the query to retrieve the new timestamp value by using a batched query. Set the *CommandText* of the *Data-Adapter* object's *UpdateCommand* to the following parameterized query:

```
UPDATE [Order Details]
    SET OrderID = ?, ProductID = ?, Quantity = ?, UnitPrice = ?
    WHERE OrderID = ? AND ProductID = ? AND TSCol = ?;
SELECT TSCol FROM [Order Details] WHERE OrderID = ? AND ProductID = ?
```

> **Note**   Not all databases support row-returning batch queries.
> Microsoft SQL Server supports this functionality. Oracle and Microsoft
> Access databases do not. Check your database's documentation to
> determine whether it supports this functionality.

When the *DataAdapter* submits the pending change, it will also execute the subsequent SELECT query and store the results in the modified *DataRow*. The *DataRow* object will have the newly generated value for the timestamp column, which means you can modify the row again and successfully submit those new changes.

The *Command* Object's *UpdatedDataSource* Property

The *DataAdapter* uses the *Command* objects stored in its *InsertCommand*, *UpdateCommand*, and *DeleteCommand* properties to submit updates to your database. But how does the *DataAdapter* know to look for results from *InsertCommand* and *UpdateCommand*? The answer lies in the *Command* object's *UpdatedRowSource* property.

The *UpdatedRowSource* property accepts a value from the *UpdateRowSource* enumeration. (The available values are listed in Table 11-1.) By default, the *Command* will fetch new data for the modified row by checking for output parameters and the first row returned by the query.

Table 11-1   Members of the *UpdateRowSource* Enumeration

Constant	Value	Description
Both	3	Tells *Command* to fetch new data for the row using both the first returned record and output parameters. This is the default.
FirstReturnedRecord	2	Tells *Command* to fetch new data for the row through the first returned record
None	0	Tells *Command* not to fetch new data for the row upon execution.
OutputParameters	1	Tells *Command* to fetch new data for the row using output parameters

You can improve the performance of your update by setting the value of the *UpdatedDataSource* property to the appropriate value. I performed a small, informal test using this property. I used a *DataAdapter* to retrieve the contents of the

Order Details table and insert all the rows in a new table with the same structure. Initially, I left the *UpdatedDataSource* property at its default value, *Both*.

In my test, the *InsertCommand* simply submitted the new row. It does not include a batch query to refetch the contents of the row after the update is submitted, so there's no need to have the *InsertCommand* property's *UpdatedData-Source* property set to anything other than *None*. When I set the property to *None* and reran the test, the test ran between 1 and 2 percent faster.

When the *UpdatedDataSource* property is set to *Both*, the default, the *Command* will check for output parameters and for the first row returned by the *Command*, even if the *Command* does not return data. You should set the *UpdatedDataSource* property of your *Command* objects to the appropriate value, or else you'll pay a small but unnecessary performance penalty.

Retrieving New Data Using Output Parameters

The *UpdatedDataSource* property also lets you specify that you will retrieve new data using output parameters.

We can build a stored procedure that uses a similar UPDATE query to modify a row in the Order Details table and returns the new timestamp value using an output parameter, as shown here:

```
CREATE PROCEDURE spUpdateDetail
(@OrderIDNew int, @ProductIDNew int, @QuantityNew smallint,
 @UnitPriceNew money, @OrderIDOrig int, @ProductIDOrig int,
 @TSCol timestamp OUTPUT)
AS
UPDATE [Order Details]
    SET OrderID = @OrderIDNew, ProductID = @ProductIDNew,
        Quantity = @QuantityNew, UnitPrice = @UnitPriceNew
    WHERE OrderID = @OrderIDOrig AND ProductID = @ProductIDOrig
        AND TSCol = @TSCol;
IF @@ROWCOUNT = 1
    SELECT @TSCol = TSCol FROM [Order Details]
        WHERE OrderID = @OrderIDNew AND ProductID = @OrderIDNew
```

All that's left to do is to set the *UpdateCommand* property's *CommandText* to the stored procedure, build the *Command* object's *Parameters* collection, and set the *Command* object's *UpdatedRowSource* property to *OutputParameters* or *Both*. It's really that easy.

This process is more efficient than returning data in a SELECT query. It's much faster to check the value of a parameter than to fetch the results of a query. Plus, databases such as Oracle support output parameters but not batch queries that return rows.

Using the *DataAdapter* Object's *RowUpdated* Event to Retrieve Data After You Submit an Update

Some databases, such as Microsoft Access, don't support batch queries and don't support output parameters on stored procedures. If you're using such a database, the two previous methods of retrieving data after performing an update aren't available. However, you do have one option, apart from moving to a database that supports more functionality.

The *DataAdapter* object exposes two events that it throws when it submits the changes cached in a *DataRow*: *RowUpdating* and *RowUpdated*. As their names imply, the former occurs just before you submit the change and the latter occurs immediately after you submit the change.

If you submit the changes in multiple rows, the *RowUpdating* and *Row-Updated* events will fire for each row. You won't get all of the *RowUpdating* events and then all of the *RowUpdated* events. If you add logging code to the events, you'll see entries like the following in your log file:

```
RowUpdating event fired for row #1
RowUpdated event fired for row #1
RowUpdating event fired for row #2
RowUpdated event fired for row #2
RowUpdating event fired for row #3
RowUpdated event fired for row #3
```

We can use the *RowUpdated* event to fetch the new value that the database generates for the updated row. The following code snippet includes such an example. The code demonstrates how to handle the *RowUpdated* event. For the sake of brevity, it references imaginary functions that create the *DataTable*, the *DataAdapter*, and the *Command* used to fetch the new timestamp value.

Note that in the *RowUpdated* event handler, the code tests to make sure the update succeeded and that the change stored in the row constituted an insert or an update. Obviously, if we've just deleted a row from the database, there's no need to query for a timestamp value. Also, because the *Command* to fetch the new timestamp value fetches only a single value, the code snippet uses the *ExecuteScalar* method to retrieve that value.

Visual Basic .NET

```
Dim da As OleDbDataAdapter = CreateMyDataAdapter()
Dim cmdGetNewTS As OleDbCommand = CreateGetNewTSCommand()
AddHandler da.RowUpdated, AddressOf HandleRowUpdated
Dim tbl As DataTable = CreateMyDataTable()
da.Fill(tbl)
⋮
da.Update(tbl)
```

```
Private Sub HandleRowUpdated(ByVal sender As Object, _
                              ByVal e As OleDbRowUpdatedEventArgs)
    If e.Status = UpdateStatus.Continue AndAlso _
      (e.StatementType = StatementType.Insert OrElse _
       e.StatementType = StatementType.Update) Then
          cmdGetNewTS.Parameters("@OrderID").Value = e.Row("OrderID")
          cmdGetNewTS.Parameters("@ProductID").Value = e.Row("ProductID")
          e.Row("TSCol") = CType(cmdGetNewTS.ExecuteScalar, Byte())
          e.Row.AcceptChanges()
    End If
End Sub
```

Visual C# .NET

```
OleDbDataAdapter da = CreateMyDataAdapter();
OleDbCommand cmdGetNewTS = CreateGetNewTSCommand();
da.RowUpdated += new OleDbRowUpdatedEventHandler(HandleRowUpdated);
DataTable tbl = CreateMyDataTable();
da.Fill(tbl);
⋮
da.Update(tbl);

private void HandleRowUpdated(object sender, OleDbRowUpdatedEventArgs e)
{
    if ((e.Status == UpdateStatus.Continue) &&
       ((e.StatementType == StatementType.Insert) ||
        (e.StatementType == StatementType.Update)))
    {
        cmdGetNewTS.Parameters["@OrderID"].Value = e.Row["OrderID"];
        cmdGetNewTS.Parameters["@ProductID"].Value = e.Row["ProductID"];
        e.Row["TSCol"] = (byte[]) cmdGetNewTS.ExecuteScalar();
        e.Row.AcceptChanges();
    }
}
```

After retrieving the new timestamp value and assigning it to the appropriate column in the *DataRow* object, the code calls the *AcceptChanges* method of the *DataRow* object to commit this change to the *DataRow*. Without the call to the *AcceptChanges* method, the *DataRow* object would cache this change so that it can submit the change to the database later. That's not what we want to accomplish by retrieving the new timestamp value. The call to the *Accept-Changes* method tells ADO.NET to simply accept the change stored in the *DataRow*.

This approach is very flexible because it will work with any database, but you pay a price in performance. In the tests I've run, using events to retrieve timestamp values proved to be about 35 percent slower than the batch query approach and about 50 percent slower than using output parameters on stored procedures.

The Timestamp Sample Application

On the companion CD, you'll find a sample application written in Visual Basic .NET and in Visual C# .NET that demonstrates all three methods of retrieving data after you submit an update. (See Figure 11-1.)

The application demonstrates the initial problem: unless you fetch new timestamp values after you submit changes to your database, subsequent attempts to update those same rows will fail.

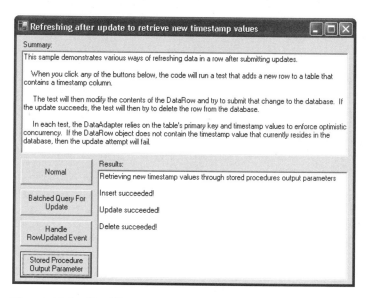

Figure 11-1   The Timestamp sample application

Retrieving Newly Generated Autoincrement Values

SQL Server, Access, Sybase, and other databases use autoincrement columns (also referred to as *identity columns*). You can insert a new row into a table, and the database will generate a new value for the autoincrement column for that row. Many tables in the Northwind database—such as Employees, Orders, and Products—use autoincrement columns for their primary keys.

Why does working with autoincrement columns constitute an advanced updating scenario? You can submit the new row to your table, but the database will generate the value for that row's autoincrement column. This means you won't know the value of the autoincrement column for your new row once you've submitted the new row to your table. Generally speaking, you want to know the primary key value for your rows.

So how do you use the ADO.NET object model to retrieve the newly generated autoincrement value for your row?

Working with SQL Server

For the moment, imagine that you're not submitting changes to your database using a *DataAdapter*. Let's say you're building your own queries to submit changes.

If you're working with order information from the Northwind database, you might use the following query to retrieve data from your table:

```
SELECT OrderID, CustomerID, EmployeeID, OrderDate FROM Orders
```

To insert a new row into your table, you might issue a query like this:

```
INSERT INTO Orders (CustomerID, EmployeeID, OrderDate) VALUES (?, ?, ?)
```

To retrieve the autoincrement value that the database generated for your new row, you might use the following query:

```
SELECT @@IDENTITY
```

> **Note** Why "might use" rather than "should use"? See the discussion on @ @IDENTITY vs. SCOPE_IDENTITY later in the chapter.

This query is the key to retrieving the new autoincrement value. We can use this query in the ADO.NET object model the same way we used the query to retrieve the timestamp value in the previous example.

We can modify the *CommandText* of the *DataAdapter* object's *InsertCommand* to execute the SELECT @@IDENTITY query after each insert:

```
INSERT INTO Orders (CustomerID, EmployeeID, OrderDate) VALUES (?, ?, ?);
SELECT @@IDENTITY AS OrderID
```

Note that the SELECT @@IDENTITY query includes an alias so that the *Command* knows the column in which it should store the results of the query.

As with fetching new timestamp values, we can also return the new autoincrement value by using a stored procedure output parameter, as shown here:

```
CREATE PROCEDURE spOrdersInsert
(@OrderID int OUTPUT, @CustomerID nchar(5),
 @EmployeeID int, @OrderDate datetime)
AS
INSERT INTO Orders (CustomerID, EmployeeID, OrderDate)
    VALUES (@CustomerID, @EmployeeID, @OrderDate)
SELECT @OrderID = @@IDENTITY
```

Finally, we can use the *DataAdapter* object's *RowUpdated* event to execute a query to fetch the new autoincrement value, as shown in the following code samples:

Visual Basic .NET

```
Dim da As OleDbDataAdapter = CreateMyDataAdapter()
Dim cn As OleDbConnection = da.SelectCommand.Connection
Dim cmdGetIdentity As New OleDbCommand("SELECT @@IDENTITY", cn)
AddHandler da.RowUpdated, AddressOf HandleRowUpdated
Dim tbl As DataTable = CreateMyDataTable()
da.Fill(tbl)
⋮
da.Update(tbl)


Private Sub HandleRowUpdated(ByVal sender As Object, _
                             ByVal e As OleDbRowUpdatedEventArgs)
    If e.Status = UpdateStatus.Continue AndAlso _
       e.StatementType = StatementType.Insert Then
        e.Row("OrderID") = CType(cmdGetIdentity.ExecuteScalar, Integer)
        e.Row.AcceptChanges()
    End If
End Sub
```

Visual C# .NET

```
OleDbDataAdapter da = CreateMyDataAdapter();
OleDbConnection cn = da.SelectCommand.Connection;
OleDbCommand cmdGetIdentity = new OleDbCommand("SELECT @@IDENTITY", cn);
da.RowUpdated += new OleDbRowUpdatedEventHandler(HandleRowUpdated);
DataTable tbl = CreateMyDataTable();
da.Fill(tbl);
⋮
da.Update(tbl);


private void HandleRowUpdated(object sender, OleDbRowUpdatedEventArgs e)
{
    if ((e.Status == UpdateStatus.Continue) &&
        ((e.StatementType == StatementType.Insert))
    {
        e.Row["OrderID"] = (int) cmdGetIdentity.ExecuteScalar();
        e.Row.AcceptChanges();
    }
}
```

This code snippet differs slightly from the code that fetched new timestamp values in the *RowUpdated* event in two ways. First, and most obviously, the query we're executing to fetch data is different.

The second difference is in performance. What's the fastest way to fetch your new autoincrement values? The performance numbers I generated in simple tests mirrored those from the timestamp tests. Stored procedure output parameters provided the best performance, with batched queries second and using the *RowUpdated* event a distant third.

@@IDENTITY vs. SCOPE_IDENTITY( )

The SELECT @@IDENTITY query returns the last identity value generated on your connection. This means that work done by other users on other connections will not affect the results of your query. However, that does not mean you'll receive the value you expected.

Database administrators often use their own audit tables to track changes made to the database. To track those changes, they generally rely on triggers or stored procedures. Figure 11-2 shows an example.

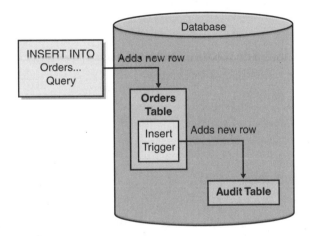

Figure 11-2   Tracking changes using audit tables

Why have I drifted into a discussion of audit logs and triggers in the middle of a discussion of retrieving autoincrement values? Let's assume that the audit table that the trigger shown in Figure 11-2 references has an autoincrement column. If you insert a new row into the Orders table and then issue the SELECT @@IDENTITY query, you'll receive the autoincrement value that the trigger generated for the new row in the audit table.

Remember that SELECT @@IDENTITY returns the last autoincrement value generated for your connection.

To address this type of scenario, SQL Server 2000 introduced a new way to retrieve autoincrement values: SCOPE_IDENTITY(). If you issue a SELECT SCOPE_IDENTITY() query in this situation, you'll receive the autoincrement value generated for the new row in the Orders table.

If you're working with SQL Server 2000 or later or Microsoft Desktop Engine (MSDE) 2000 or later, you should consider using SCOPE_IDENTITY instead of @@IDENTITY. There's one minor exception to this rule. If you insert the new row using a stored procedure but you want to retrieve that value after calling the stored procedure, SCOPE_IDENTITY() will return *Null*. As I said, this is a minor exception. If you're going to insert new rows using stored procedures and you want to retrieve the newly generated autoincrement value, you should return this information using an output parameter.

For more information on the differences between @@IDENTITY and SCOPE_IDENTITY(), see *SQL Server Books Online*.

Working with Access 2000

If you're working with an Access database, you can also use the SELECT @@IDENTITY query to retrieve new autoincrement values. This feature was added in version 4.0 of the Jet OLE DB provider and works only with databases formatted for Access databases version 2000 or later. Like its SQL Server counterpart, the SELECT @@IDENTITY query returns the last autoincrement value generated on your connection.

Access databases do not support output parameters on QueryDefs— stored queries that are similar to views and stored procedures. The Jet OLE DB provider does not support batch queries. So the only way to fetch newly generated autoincrement values is to use the *DataAdapter* object's *RowUpdated* event, as shown earlier in the chapter.

Working with Oracle Sequences

Oracle databases do not support autoincrement columns, but they do support a similar construct—a sequence. With SQL Server, you mark a column as an auto-increment column and SQL Server will automatically generate new values for the column when you insert a new row. An Oracle sequence is slightly different. You generally create a sequence to generate new values for a column in your table, but there is no direct link between the sequence and the table or column. An Oracle sequence is an object, like a table or a stored procedure.

The following query creates a new Oracle sequence:

```
CREATE SEQUENCE MySequence
```

You can set a number of options when you create an Oracle sequence, such as the minimum and maximum values for the sequence.

> **Note** I don't claim to be an expert on Oracle sequences. I have managed to create and use them in simple INSERT and SELECT queries, but that's about the extent of my knowledge on the topic. For more information on Oracle sequences, see your Oracle documentation.

You can use the sequence in two ways. You can reference the sequence in your INSERT query, as shown here:

```
INSERT INTO MyTable (ID, OtherColumn)
    VALUES (MySequence.NEXTVAL, 'New Row')
```

The sequence returns a new value each time you issue this query.

Once you've inserted the new row, you can query the sequence to determine the last value you used, as shown here:

```
SELECT MySequence.CURRVAL FROM DUAL
```

As with using the SELECT @@IDENTITY query with SQL Server and Access databases, the results of this query are not affected by other users referencing the sequence to insert new rows.

How do you retrieve the new sequence values into your *DataRow* objects? Oracle does not support batch queries that return data, so you can't use the Sequence.CURRVAL query in the *CommandText* of the *InsertCommand*. However, you can issue this query when you handle the *DataAdapter* object's *RowUpdated* event, much like how we used the *RowUpdated* event in previous examples:

Visual Basic .NET

```
Dim da As OleDbDataAdapter = CreateMyDataAdapter()
Dim cn As OleDbConnection = da.SelectCommand.Connection
Dim strSQL As String = "SELECT MySequence.CURRVAL FROM DUAL"


Dim cmdGetSequence As New OleDbCommand(strSQL, cn)
AddHandler da.RowUpdated, AddressOf HandleRowUpdated
Dim tbl As DataTable = CreateMyDataTable()
da.Fill(tbl)
⋮
da.Update(tbl)

Private Sub HandleRowUpdated(ByVal sender As Object, _
                             ByVal e As OleDbRowUpdatedEventArgs)
    If e.Status = UpdateStatus.Continue AndAlso _
       e.StatementType = StatementType.Insert Then
        e.Row("OrderID") = CType(cmdGetSequence.ExecuteScalar, Integer)
        e.Row.AcceptChanges()
    End If
End Sub
```

Visual C# .NET

```
OleDbDataAdapter da = CreateMyDataAdapter();
OleDbConnection cn = da.SelectCommand.Connection;
```

(continued)

```
string strSQL = "SELECT MySequence.CURRVAL FROM DUAL";
OleDbCommand cmdGetSequence = new OleDbCommand(strSQL, cn);
da.RowUpdated += new OleDbRowUpdatedEventHandler(HandleRowUpdated);
DataTable tbl = CreateMyDataTable();
da.Fill(tbl);
⋮
da.Update(tbl);

private void HandleRowUpdated(object sender, OleDbRowUpdatedEventArgs e)
{
    if ((e.Status == UpdateStatus.Continue) &&
        ((e.StatementType == StatementType.Insert))
    {
        e.Row["OrderID"] = (int) cmdGetSequence.ExecuteScalar();
        e.Row.AcceptChanges();
    }
}
```

You don't have to use Sequence.NEXTVAL in your INSERT INTO query. You can query the sequence before issuing the INSERT INTO query. The following code snippet creates a new procedure that queries a sequence for a new value and stores the new value in a variable. The procedure uses that value to insert the new row using an INSERT INTO query.

```
CREATE PROCEDURE MyStoredProc
    (pOtherCol IN VARCHAR2, pID OUT NUMBER) IS
BEGIN
    SELECT MySequence.NEXTVAL INTO pID FROM DUAL;
    INSERT INTO MyTable (ID, OtherCol)
        VALUES (pID, pOtherCol);
END;
```

The stored procedure returns the new sequence value using an output parameter. You can use this type of stored procedure in your *DataAdapter* object's *InsertCommand* to insert new rows. If you bind the output parameter to the corresponding column in your *DataRow* object, the *DataRow* will contain the new value immediately after you've submitted the new row to your database.

> **Note**   Remember that there is no direct link between the sequence and the column in the table. You don't have to use the sequence when you insert a new row into the table. If users insert new rows without referencing the sequence, the sequence might generate new values that already exist in your database. To avoid the problem, make sure that the only way to insert new rows into your table is to call a stored procedure that references the sequence.

Generating Dummy Values for Your Sequence *DataColumn* Objects

Sequences are not autoincrement columns, but you can have ADO.NET generate dummy values for new rows by setting the *AutoIncrement* property of the corresponding *DataColumn* objects to *True*. However, you must do this manually. There is no direct link between the sequence and the table. If you use the *DataAdapter* object's *FillSchema* method or the Visual Studio .NET Data Adapter Configuration Wizard to retrieve database schema information, ADO.NET won't know that the column in your table is associated with a sequence.

You'll face similar problems when you use tools to generate updating logic for your *DataAdapter* objects. The *CommandBuilder* object and the Data Adapter Configuration Wizard won't know to omit the column from the logic in the *InsertCommand*. If you're going to rely on such tools to generate your updating logic, you must make some minor changes to the logic they generate.

It might sound like I'm knocking these tools. I'm not. There is no schema information that links the column in the table to the sequence, so the tools are doing the best they can to generate the appropriate code.

The fact that you can treat a column that's indirectly linked to an Oracle sequence as an autoincrement column and control how and when you retrieve new sequence values into your *DataSet* is a testament to the power and control that the ADO.NET object model gives to developers. Such functionality was not an option in previous Microsoft data access object models.

Sample Applications That Retrieve Autoincrement Values

I've covered a number of scenarios that deal with retrieving new autoincrement and sequence values into your *DataSet*. To retrieve new SQL Server autoincrement values, we can use batch queries, stored procedure output parameters, or the *DataAdapter* object's *RowUpdated* event. To retrieve new Access autoincrement values, we can use the *DataAdapter* object's *RowUpdated* event. And to retrieve new Oracle sequence values, we can use stored procedure output parameters and the *DataAdapter* object's *RowUpdated* event. That's a lot of choices.

To help you sort through all of this, the companion CD contains sample applications (in both Visual Basic .NET and Visual C# .NET) that cover each of these scenarios and options. Figure 11-3 shows one sample application, AutoIncrementSql. The CD also includes similar samples that cover retrieving autoincrement values from Access databases as well as sequence values from Oracle databases.

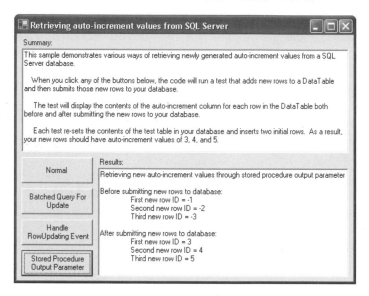

Figure 11-3 The AutoIncrementSql sample application

Using SQL Server's NOCOUNT Setting

Many database administrators add logic to triggers and/or stored procedures to track the queries that applications run. A stored procedure that inserts a new row might look like this:

```
CREATE PROCEDURE spOrderInsert
(@OrderID int OUTPUT, @CustomerID nchar(5),
 @EmployeeID int, @OrderDate datetime)
AS
INSERT INTO Orders (CustomerID, EmployeeID, OrderDate)
    VALUES (@CustomerID, @EmployeeID, @OrderDate)
SELECT @OrderID = SCOPE_IDENTITY()
INSERT INTO OrdersLog (TypeOfChange, DateOfChange)
    VALUES (@OrderID + ' added', GetDate())
RETURN
```

You can use this stored procedure as your *DataAdapter* object's *InsertCommand* to submit your changes successfully. Using a similar stored procedure to submit updates, however, will cause problems. Even worse, it might cause problems that you won't even discover until you've deployed your application.

To understand why, first look at the following update procedure that includes similar logging code:

```
CREATE PROCEDURE spOrderUpdate
(@CustomerID_New nchar(5), @EmployeeID_New int,
 @OrderDate_New datetime, @OrderID_Orig int,
```

```
@CustomerID_Orig nchar(5), @EmployeeID_Orig int,
@OrderDate_Orig datetime)
AS
UPDATE Orders
    SET CustomerID = @CustomerID_New, EmployeeID = @EmployeeID_New,
        OrderDate = @OrderDate_New
    WHERE OrderID = @OrderID_Orig AND CustomerID = @CustomerID_Orig
     AND EmployeeID = @EmployeeID_Orig AND OrderDate = @OrderDate_Orig
IF @@ROWCOUNT = 1
    INSERT INTO OrdersLog (TypeOfChange, DateOfChange)
        VALUES ('Modified order ' + @OrderID_Orig, GetDate())
ELSE
    INSERT INTO OrdersLog (TypeOfChange, DateOfChange)
        VALUES ('Failed to modify order ' + @OrderID_Orig, GetDate())
RETURN
```

If you call this stored procedure to update an order from SQL Server's Query Analyzer, you'll see the following output in the Results window:

```
(1 row(s) affected)
```

```
(1 row(s) affected)
```

Two rows affected? The stored procedure updated only one order. Including the primary key in the WHERE clause of the UPDATE query ensures that the query can modify at most one row. The second row that the stored procedure affected is the one that it inserted into the logging table.

You would see similar results if you built an ADO.NET *Command* object to call the stored procedure and update an order. The *ExecuteNonQuery* method would return 2.

This stored procedure adds an entry to the log table whether the update succeeds or fails. So, if the update attempt fails because the optimistic concurrency check failed, the stored procedure will still report that it affected one row.

You might understand that if the stored procedure affects one row it translates to a failed update attempt, but ADO.NET does not. The *DataAdapter* checks the number of rows that the query affected, and if it finds that the query affected zero rows, it interprets this result as a failed update attempt. Otherwise, it assumes that the update succeeded.

So, if you use this stored procedure as the *UpdateCommand* for your *DataAdapter*, the *DataAdapter* will always assume that the update attempt succeeded.

SQL Server lets you control whether queries report their results using the NOCOUNT setting. If we modify the update stored procedure by adding SET NOCOUNT ON before the UPDATE query and then call the stored procedure from Query Analyzer, we'll get the following result:

```
The command(s) completed successfully.
```

This doesn't necessarily mean that the update succeeded. It simply means that the query did not generate an error. The database does not consider a query that affects no rows a failure, even though you might.

Suppressing all the messages about the number of rows affected by the queries that the stored procedure executes will not solve the problem. If you use the stored procedure in its new state as a *DataAdapter* object's *Update-Command*, the *DataAdapter* will again assume that all updates succeed.

What we need to do is suppress the "row(s) affected" messages for all queries except the one that will attempt to update the desired row in the database. To do this, we can move the call to SET NOCOUNT ON so that it appears just after the UPDATE query in the stored procedure, as shown here:

```
CREATE PROCEDURE spOrderUpdate
(@CustomerID_New nchar(5), @EmployeeID_New int,
 @OrderDate_New datetime, @OrderID_Orig int,
 @CustomerID_Orig nchar(5), @EmployeeID_Orig int,
 @OrderDate_Orig datetime)
AS
UPDATE Orders
    SET CustomerID = @CustomerID_New, EmployeeID = @EmployeeID_New,
        OrderDate = @OrderDate_New
    WHERE OrderID = @OrderID_Orig AND CustomerID = @CustomerID_Orig
      AND EmployeeID = @EmployeeID_Orig AND OrderDate = @OrderDate_Orig

SET NOCOUNT ON
IF @@ROWCOUNT = 1
    INSERT INTO OrdersLog (TypeOfChange, DateOfChange)
        VALUES ('Modified order ' + @OrderID_Orig, GetDate())
ELSE
    INSERT INTO OrdersLog (TypeOfChange, DateOfChange)
        VALUES ('Failed to modify order ' + @OrderID_Orig, GetDate())
RETURN
```

If the stored procedure adds an entry to the log table before running our UPDATE query, we can use code that looks like this:

```
CREATE PROCEDURE MyUpdateProcedure
(...) AS

SET NOCOUNT ON
INSERT INTO MyLogTable ...

SET NOCOUNT OFF
UPDATE MyTable SET ...

RETURN
```

If you're unsure how the *DataAdapter* will interpret the results of the query you've specified in the *InsertCommand*, *UpdateCommand*, or *Delete-Command*, call the *ExecuteNonQuery* method of the *Command* and check its return value. What is the return value when you supply parameters that cause the *Command* to succeed? What is the return value when you supply parameters that cause the *Command* to fail?

Submitting Hierarchical Changes

When you modify data in multiple levels of a hierarchical *DataSet*, you will face two challenges when you submit those changes to your database. Let's take a look at these scenarios.

Submitting Pending Insertions and Deletions

Say you're dealing with a hierarchy that contains customers and orders. The application you've built is an order entry system. The user has made a number of changes to the data and now wants to submit those changes to your database. The modified data in the *DataSet* contains new customers and new orders. The *DataSet* also contains customers and orders that are marked for deletion.

The challenge is to submit these changes in the proper order to comply with the referential integrity constraints in your database. The Northwind database contains referential integrity constraints that require all orders to refer back to customers in the database.

If the *DataSet* contains new customers and new orders for those customers, we must submit those new customers before submitting the new orders for them. As a general rule, you should submit new rows in a top-down approach.

The opposite is true for deleted rows, however. You can't delete customers in the Northwind database that have orders. You must delete the customers' orders first.

> **Note**   This example is a simplification of a general problem. The Northwind database will not let you delete an order that has corresponding rows in the Order Details table.

The following code will not work because it will attempt to delete customers that still have pending orders.

Visual Basic .NET

```
CustomersAdapter.Update(MyDataSet.Tables("Customers"))
OrdersAdapter.Update(MyDataSet.Tables("Orders"))
```

Visual C# .NET

```
CustomersAdapter.Update(MyDataSet.Tables["Customers"]);
OrdersAdapter.Update(MyDataSet.Tables["Orders"]);
```

But if we reverse the order of the updates, the first update attempt will fail because the *DataAdapter* for the Orders table will attempt to submit new orders for customers that do not yet exist in the database.

Visual Basic .NET

```
OrdersAdapter.Update(MyDataSet.Tables("Orders"))
CustomersAdapter.Update(MyDataSet.Tables("Customers"))
```

Visual C# .NET

```
OrdersAdapter.Update(MyDataSet.Tables["Orders"]);
CustomersAdapter.Update(MyDataSet.Tables["Customers"]);
```

What's a poor programmer to do? We need a way to control the order of updates in a hierarchical *DataSet* to submit the changes in the following order:

1. Submit new customers.
2. Submit new orders.
3. Submit modified customers.
4. Submit modified orders.
5. Submit deleted orders.
6. Submit deleted customers.

Using the *DataTable* Object's *Select* Method to Submit Hierarchical Changes

In Chapter 7, I discussed the *Select* method of the *DataTable* object as a way to locate *DataRow* objects that satisfy the desired criteria. For example, the following line of code returns an array of the pending new *DataRow* objects whose City column contains *Seattle*. The *DataRow* objects are sorted based on the value of the *ContactName* column.

```
tbl.Select("City = 'Seattle'", "ContactName", DataViewRowState.Added)
```

The *Select* method returns an array of *DataRow* objects. And one of the overloaded *DataAdapter Update* methods accepts an array of *DataRow* objects. What a pleasant coincidence.

The following code snippet uses the *Select* method to isolate just the desired changes and submit them to the database in the desired order:

Visual Basic .NET

```
Dim ds As DataSet = CreateDataSet()
Dim tblCustomers As DataTable = ds.Tables("Customers")
Dim tblOrders As DataTable = ds.Tables("Orders")
Dim daCustomers As OleDbDataAdapter = CreateCustomersAdapter()
Dim daOrders As OleDbDataAdapter = CreateOrdersAdapter()

FillDataSetAndModifyItsContents(ds)

'Submit the new customers and then the new orders.
daCustomers.Update(tblCustomers.Select("", "", DataViewRowState.Added))
daOrders.Update(tblOrders.Select("", "", DataViewRowState.Added))

'Submit the modified customers and then the modified orders.
daCustomers.Update(tblCustomers.Select("", "", _
                                        DataViewRowState.ModifiedCurrent))
daOrders.Update(tblOrders.Select("", "", DataViewRowState.ModifiedCurrent))

'Submit the deleted orders and then the deleted customers.
daOrders.Update(tblOrders.Select("", "", DataViewRowState.Deleted))
daCustomers.Update(tblCustomers.Select("", "", DataViewRowState.Deleted))
```

Visual C# .NET

```
DataSet ds = CreateDataSet();
DataTable tblCustomers = ds.Tables["Customers"];
DataTable tblOrders = ds.Tables["Orders"];
OleDbDataAdapter daCustomers = CreateCustomersAdapter();
OleDbDataAdapter daOrders = CreateOrdersAdapter();

FillDataSetAndModifyItsContents(ds);

//Submit the new customers and then the new orders.
daCustomers.Update(tblCustomers.Select("", "", DataViewRowState.Added));
daOrders.Update(tblOrders.Select("", "", DataViewRowState.Added));

//Submit the modified customers and then the modified orders.
daCustomers.Update(tblCustomers.Select("", "",
                                        DataViewRowState.ModifiedCurrent));
daOrders.Update(tblOrders.Select("", "",
                                 DataViewRowState.ModifiedCurrent));

//Submit the deleted orders and then the deleted customers.
daOrders.Update(tblOrders.Select("", "", DataViewRowState.Deleted));
daCustomers.Update(tblCustomers.Select("", "", DataViewRowState.Deleted));
```

Using the *GetChanges* Method to Submit Hierarchical Changes

You can also use the *GetChanges* method of the *DataSet* or *DataTable* to control the order of updates. The following code snippet creates a new *DataTable* that contains just the pending new rows in the initial *DataTable*:

```
tblNewCustomers = tblCustomers.GetChanges(DataRowState.Added)
daCustomers.Update(tblNewCustomers)
tblNewOrders = tblOrders.GetChanges(DataRowState.Added)
daOrders.Update(tblNewOrders)
```

I find this code easier to read and write than the approach that uses the *Select* method. However, I don't recommend using this approach.

When you use the *GetChanges* method of the *DataSet* or *DataTable* object, you're creating a new and separate object. The previous code snippet submits new rows to the Customers and Orders tables in the database. In the Northwind database, the Orders table has an autoincrement column: OrderID. If the *DataAdapter* that submits the changes to the Orders table includes logic to fetch the newly generated values for the OrderID column, the values will be inserted into the *DataTable* used in the *Update* method—tblNewOrders. However, this *DataTable* object is separate from the main tblOrders DataTable, so those new OrderID values will not appear in the main *DataTable*.

This scenario will make more sense when we discuss isolating and reintegrating changes later in the chapter.

If you use the *Select* method to submit modified rows, the changes returned by the *DataAdapter* will be applied to your main *DataTable* because the *Select* method returns an array of *DataRow* objects. The *DataRow* objects in the array are actually pointers to the *DataRow* objects in the *DataTable*. Changes you make to the contents of the array will be visible in the main *DataTable*.

Working with Autoincrement Values and Relational Data

Let's shift the focus of our hierarchical *DataSet* slightly. We'll use a *DataSet* that contains data from the Northwind Orders and Order Details tables. The application that uses the *DataSet* will still be an order entry application. In this example, the user will enter two new orders for a customer as well as details for each order.

In Chapter 6, I recommended that you set the *AutoIncrementSeed* and *AutoIncrementStep* properties of the *DataColumn* object to − 1 when you work with autoincrement columns. If you follow that recommendation and add new orders and details to your hierarchy, your *DataSet* will look something like the depiction in Figure 11-4 before you submit the new orders to your database.

In order to successfully submit the new orders and the line items for each new order, we need to submit the new orders, retrieve the new autoincrement values for the new orders, apply those values to the appropriate line items, and then submit the new line items to the database. This process sounds complicated, but it's actually fairly simple.

Orders			
OrderID	CustomerID	EmployeeID	OrderDate
10268	GROSR	8	7/30/1996
10785	GROSR	1	12/18/1997
-1	GROSR	7	1/14/2002
-2	GROSR	7	1/14/2002

Order Details			
OrderID	ProductID	Quantity	UnitPrice
10268	29	10	99.00
10268	72	4	27.80
10785	10	10	31.00
10785	75	10	7.75
-1	1	12	18.00
-1	67	24	14.00
-2	4	6	22.00
-2	65	8	21.05

Figure 11-4   A *DataSet* with pending new orders and details

You already know how to submit the new orders. If you need to submit only new orders, you use the *Select* method of the *DataTable* that contains order information, as we discussed earlier in the chapter. You can also fetch your new autoincrement values using any of the options we discussed earlier in the chapter.

But how do you apply the new autoincrement values to the pending new line items? Actually, you don't. You let ADO.NET do the work for you through the *DataRelation*. By default, the *DataRelation* object will cascade changes through your *DataSet*. If you've set up a *DataRelation* between the orders and order details *DataTable* objects in your *DataSet*, as soon as you've submitted the new orders, the *DataRelation* will cascade the new value to the order details *DataTable*, as shown in Figure 11-5.

Orders			
OrderID	CustomerID	EmployeeID	OrderDate
10268	GROSR	8	7/30/1996
10785	GROSR	1	12/18/1997
12000	GROSR	7	1/14/2002
12001	GROSR	7	1/14/2002

Order Details			
OrderID	ProductID	Quantity	UnitPrice
10268	29	10	99.00
10268	72	4	27.80
10785	10	10	31.00
10785	75	10	7.75
12000	1	12	18.00
12000	67	24	14.00
12001	4	6	22.00
12001	65	8	21.05

Figure 11-5   Cascading the autoincrement values into the child table in your hierarchy

Once the new rows in the order details *DataTable* contain the appropriate values for the OrderID column, you can successfully submit the pending new rows to your database. Thanks to the functionality in the *DataRelation* object, cascading the new autoincrement values throughout your hierarchy is the simplest part of the process.

Isolating and Reintegrating Changes

Say you're building a multi-tiered application with a Windows client user interface that accesses your database via a Web service. The Web service returns *DataSet* objects that contain the requested information to clients. The client application allows the user to modify the contents of the *DataSet*. After modifying the data, the user can click a button and the client will submit the changes to the database via the Web service. The simplest way to submit these changes is to send the *DataSet* back to the Web service and have the Web service use *DataAdapter* objects to submit the changes.

To get the best possible performance out of your application, you'll want to make the best possible use of your bandwidth. The less data you pass back and forth between the client application and the Web service, the faster your application will run.

Limiting the amount of data that the Web service returns is fairly simple and intuitive. Don't design your Web service to return the entire contents of your tables if they might contain thousands or millions or rows; if you do, the performance of your application will suffer. Also make sure that the Web service returns only the data that the client application needs.

What about limiting the amount of data that the client application passes back to the Web service? You can pass a *DataSet* back to the Web service to have the Web service submit changes to your database. But if that's the goal of calling to the Web service, you probably don't want to pass the entire *DataSet*. If the *DataSet* contains a few hundred rows and the user has modified only a handful of those rows, passing the entire *DataSet* back to the Web service will be extremely inefficient. How can we improve upon this process?

Saving Bandwidth Using the *GetChanges* Method

The *DataSet* and *DataTable* objects each expose an overloaded *GetChanges* method. When you call a *DataSet* object's *GetChanges* method, you receive a new *DataSet* object that has the same structure as the original *DataSet* but contains only the modified rows from the original *DataSet*.

If you're calling your Web service to submit changes to your database, you might gain a significant improvement in performance by first calling the *GetChanges* method on your *DataSet* and sending the results to your Web service.

> **Note**   When I said that the *DataSet* object's *GetChanges* method returns a new *DataSet* object that contains only the modified rows, I bent the truth a tiny bit. The new *DataSet* that the *GetChanges* method returns has the same structure as the original *DataSet* and contains the modified rows that you requested, but it might also contain other rows needed to maintain referential integrity. For example, say you have a *DataSet* that contains *DataTable* objects for customer and order information with a *DataRelation* defined between the two *DataTable* objects. If you add some new orders and then call the *DataSet* object's *GetChanges* method, the *DataSet* that the method returns will contain those new rows as well as the corresponding rows from the customers *DataTable*. Otherwise, the new *DataSet* would violate the constraint associated with the *DataRelation*.

Earlier in the chapter, I talked about enforcing optimistic concurrency by using timestamp columns in your updates. This process gets a little more complicated in a multi-tiered application. Let's say you're using timestamp concurrency checks in the *DataAdapter* object's updating logic in your Web service. You're also retrieving the new timestamp values using one of the options we discussed earlier in the chapter. But what happened to those new timestamp values?

You retrieved the new values and stored them in the *DataSet* in the Web service. But that *DataSet* is separate from the one in your client application. How can you get the new timestamp values into the *DataSet* in your client application?

You could simply have the Web service return a new *DataSet* that contains all the same data as the client application. But even though this approach will ensure that the client application has more up-to-date data, it might not be the best use of your bandwidth.

A more economical solution, shown in Figure 11-6, is to have the Web service return the *DataSet* it received, with the new timestamp values included.

Main *DataSet* with original data			
CustomerID	CompanyName	ContactName	TSCol
ALFKI	Alfreds Futterkiste	Maria Anders	\<Original Value\>
ANATR	Ana Trujillo	Ana Trujillo	\<Original Value\>
ANTON	Antonio Moreno	Antonio Moreno	\<Original Value\>
AROUT	Around the Horn	Thomas Hardy	\<Original Value\>

Main *DataSet* with modified rows			
CustomerID	CompanyName	ContactName	TSCol
ALFKI	Alfreds Futterkiste	New Contact #1	\<Original Value\>
ANATR	Ana Trujillo	Ana Trujillo	\<Original Value\>
ANTON	Antonio Moreno	Antonio Moreno	\<Original Value\>
AROUT	Around the Horn	New Contact #2	\<Original Value\>

DataSet returned by *GetChanges* and sent to Web service			
CustomerID	CompanyName	ContactName	TSCol
ALFKI	Alfreds Futterkiste	New Contact #1	\<Original Value\>
AROUT	Around the Horn	New Contact #2	\<Original Value\>

Figure 11-6   Returning new server-generated values via a Web service

But that solves only part of the problem. The client application now has the new timestamp values, but how can you integrate the *DataSet* that the Web service returns into the client application's *DataSet?*

The *Merge* Method of the *DataSet* Object

The simple answer is to use the *Merge* method of the *DataSet* object. The *DataSet* object's *Merge* method lets you merge the contents of a *DataSet*, a *DataTable*, or an array of *DataRow* objects into an existing *DataSet*. Figure 11-7 shows a basic example of this functionality.

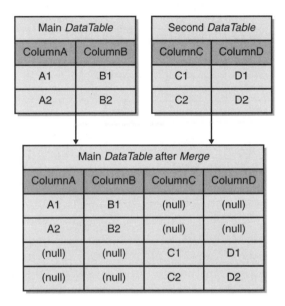

Figure 11-7   Basic example of the results of the *DataSet* object's *Merge* method

Each *DataSet* initially contains a single *DataTable* with the same name. After you call the *Merge* method on the main *DataSet* and supply the second *DataSet*, the main *DataSet* will contain all its original columns plus those from the second *DataSet*. The main *DataSet* will also contain the rows from the second *DataSet*.

This example is not terribly useful, however. Few developers will combine two *DataSet* objects that contain *DataTable* objects with the same name but that have completely different structures. Figure 11-8 shows a more typical example. The two *DataSet* objects contain *DataTable* objects with similar structures. In each *DataTable*, the ID column is the primary key.

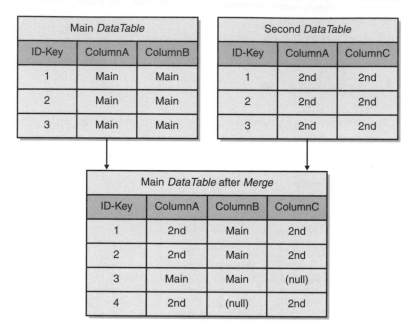

Figure 11-8   A more typical example of the results of the *DataSet* object's *Merge* method

After the call to the *Merge* method, the main *DataSet* will contain an additional column from the second *DataSet*. The contents of the main *DataSet* will also have changed as a result of the call to the *Merge* method. In the previous example, the *Merge* method simply appended existing rows to the main *DataSet*. In this example, the *Merge* method combines the contents of the two *DataSet* objects.

The difference in this example is the primary key. If ADO.NET encounters rows that have the same primary key values while it is merging data, it combines the contents into a single row. In this example, both *DataSet* objects have rows that have primary key values of 1 and 2. Each *DataSet* also has an additional row that has no counterpart in the other *DataSet*.

Notice that in the results of the *Merge* method, the data from the *DataSet* that's being merged in takes precedence. The values for Column A in the second *DataSet* replace the corresponding values from the main *DataSet* when ADO.NET combines rows. In the diagram, these are rows whose ID value is 1 or 2.

Now that you're armed with a better understanding of how the *Merge* method works, let's recap the scenario.

Our client application retrieves customer information from a Web service. The user modifies the contents of that *DataSet*. The client application uses the *GetChanges* method to create a new *DataSet* that contains only the modified rows and sends this smaller *DataSet* back to the Web service.

The Web service submits the changes to the database using timestamp values in the updating logic to enforce optimistic concurrency. The Web service also retrieves the new timestamp values for the modified rows (using one of the techniques we discussed earlier in the chapter) and stores that information in its *DataSet*. After the Web service completes this operation, it returns the *DataSet* with those new timestamp values included. The client application receives this *DataSet* and merges it into the main *DataSet*, as shown in the following code snippet, to integrate the new timestamp values in the main *DataSet*, as shown in Figure 11-9.

Main *DataSet* with modified rows			
CustomerID	CompanyName	ContactName	TSCol
ALFKI	Alfreds Futterkiste	New Contact #1	<Original Value>
ANATR	Ana Trujillo	Ana Trujillo	<Original Value>
ANTON	Antonio Moreno	Antonio Moreno	<Original Value>
AROUT	Around the Horn	New Contact #2	<Original Value>

DataSet returned by Web service with new timestamp values			
CustomerID	CompanyName	ContactName	TSCol
ALFKI	Alfreds Futterkiste	New Contact #1	<New Value>
AROUT	Around the Horn	New Contact #2	<New Value>

Main *DataSet* after merging *DataSet* returned by Web service			
CustomerID	CompanyName	ContactName	TSCol
ALFKI	Alfreds Futterkiste	New Contact #1	<New Value>
ANATR	Ana Trujillo	Ana Trujillo	<Original Value>
ANTON	Antonio Moreno	Antonio Moreno	<Original Value>
AROUT	Around the Horn	New Contact #2	<New Value>

Figure 11-9   Merging newly fetched data into an existing *DataSet*

Visual Basic .NET

```
Dim objWebService As New WebServiceClass()
Dim dsMain As DataSet = objWebService.GetDataSet()
ModifyDataSetContents(dsMain)
Dim dsChanges As DataSet = dsMain.GetChanges()
dsChanges = objWebService.SubmitChanges(dsChanges)
dsMain.Merge(dsChanges)
```

Visual C# .NET

```
WebServiceClass objWebService = new WebServiceClass();
DataSet dsMain = objWebService.GetDataSet();
ModifyDataSetContents(dsMain);
DataSet dsChanges = dsMain.GetChanges();
dsChanges = objWebService.SubmitChanges(dsChanges);
dsMain.Merge(dsChanges);
```

The *Merge* Method and the *RowState* Property

We're almost done, but not quite. If you check the contents of the rows that we originally modified in the main *DataSet*, you'll see that they do have the new timestamp values. However, those rows still have a *RowState* of *Modified*.

If the user clicks a button in the application to submit changes to the database, the *DataSet* that the *GetChanges* method returns will still contain the rows that the user previously modified. When the Web service receives this *DataSet* and tries to submit the changes, the update attempt will generate an exception because the database already contains those changes.

We know that we've submitted those changes to the database, but ADO.NET doesn't understand this. When the Web service submits the changes, ADO.NET changes the *RowState* of the modified rows from *Modified* to *Unmodified*. But that change occurs in the Web service's *DataSet*. ADO.NET does not change the *RowState* of the modified rows in the client application's main *DataSet* because there is no link between these two *DataSet* objects.

Merging the *DataSet* that the Web service returns will not change the *RowState* property of the modified rows in the main *DataSet*. That's definitely what we want to have happen, but ADO.NET will not do this for us automatically. However, because we know that we successfully submitted the changes that currently reside in the main *DataSet*, we can change the *RowState* of the modified rows back to *Unmodified* by calling the *AcceptChanges* method on the main *DataSet* after we call *Merge*, as shown in the following code:

Visual Basic .NET

```
Dim objWebService As New WebServiceClass()
Dim dsMain As DataSet = objWebService.GetDataSet()
ModifyDataSetContents(dsMain)
Dim dsChanges As DataSet = dsMain.GetChanges()
dsChanges = objWebService.SubmitChanges(dsChanges)
dsMain.Merge(dsChanges)
dsMain.AcceptChanges()
```

Visual C# .NET

```
WebServiceClass objWebService = new WebServiceClass();
DataSet dsMain = objWebService.GetDataSet();
ModifyDataSetContents(dsMain);
```

```
DataSet dsChanges = dsMain.GetChanges();
dsChanges = objWebService.SubmitChanges(dsChanges);
dsMain.Merge(dsChanges);
dsMain.AcceptChanges();
```

The *Merge* Method and Autoincrement Values

Let's change the example slightly. Instead of working with customer information, let's work with order information. In this example, the database table that contains the order information will use an autoincrement column as its primary key, like the Orders table in the Northwind database does.

As in the previous example, the client application will communicate with the database through a Web service. Let's say the user retrieves two orders for an existing customer, adds two new orders for the customer, and then submits those new orders to the database. You already know how to use the *GetChanges* method to pass just the modified rows to the Web service, as shown in Figure 11-10.

Main *DataSet* with original data			
OrderID	CustomerID	EmployeeID	OrderDate
10643	ALFKI	6	09/22/1997
10692	ALFKI	4	10/31/1997

Main *DataSet* with new rows			
OrderID	CustomerID	EmployeeID	OrderDate
10643	ALFKI	6	09/22/1997
10692	ALFKI	4	10/31/1997
-1	ALFKI	7	02/24/2002
-2	ALFKI	7	02/24/2002

DataSet returned by *GetChanges* and sent to Web service			
OrderID	CustomerID	EmployeeID	OrderDate
-1	ALFKI	7	02/24/2002
-2	ALFKI	7	02/24/2002

Figure 11-10   Using the *GetChanges* method to submit just the pending new orders to a Web service

You also know how to retrieve new autoincrement values into the *DataSet* that the Web service uses to submit new orders to the database. These values are included in the *DataSet* that the Web service returns after you submit the modified orders to the database. However, if we merge this *DataSet* into our main *DataSet*, we won't get the desired behavior.

Instead, we'll get the results shown in Figure 11-11. The main *DataSet* will contain the original pending orders with the "dummy" values for the OrderID column as well as the orders returned by the Web service with the actual values for the OrderID column. What's going wrong?

Main *DataSet* with new rows			
OrderID	CustomerID	EmployeeID	OrderDate
10643	ALFKI	6	09/22/1997
10692	ALFKI	4	10/31/1997
-1	ALFKI	7	02/24/2002
-2	ALFKI	7	02/24/2002

DataSet returned by Web service with new values			
OrderID	CustomerID	EmployeeID	OrderDate
12000	ALFKI	7	02/24/2002
12001	ALFKI	7	02/24/2002

Main *DataSet* after merging *DataSet* returned by Web service			
OrderID	CustomerID	EmployeeID	OrderDate
10643	ALFKI	6	09/22/1997
10692	ALFKI	4	10/31/1997
-1	ALFKI	7	02/24/2002
-2	ALFKI	7	02/24/2002
12000	ALFKI	7	02/24/2002
12001	ALFKI	7	02/24/2002

Figure 11-11   The results of merging the *DataSet* returned by the Web service into the main *DataSet*

This *Merge* method relies on the *DataTable* object's primary key in order to match up the rows from the different *DataSet* objects. The rows that we want the *Merge* method to combine do not have the same values for their primary key columns. The *Merge* method does not realize that the orders in the *DataSet* that the Web service returns match existing pending orders in the main *DataSet*.

As a result, the *Merge* method simply adds the rows from the Web service's *DataSet* to the main *DataSet*.

Obviously, this is not the behavior we want, but a couple of solutions are available to us.

Purge before *Merge*   Look again at the results of the call to the *Merge* method in Figure 11-11. Our goal was to combine the contents of the two *DataSet* objects and pull the new OrderID values into the existing *DataSet*. The results really aren't that far off. We have the new OrderID values, but we also have copies of those new orders with the "dummy" OrderID values.

We can achieve the desired results by removing the new orders from the main *DataSet* just before we merge in the *DataSet* returned by the Web service. The following code snippet uses the *Select* method of the *DataTable* object to loop through the rows whose *RowState* property is *Added* and removes those rows from the *DataSet* before merging in the *DataSet* that the Web service returns.

Visual Basic .NET

```
Dim objWebService As New WebServiceClass()
Dim dsMain As DataSet = objWebService.GetDataSet()
ModifyDataSetContents(dsMain)
Dim dsChanges As DataSet = dsMain.GetChanges()
dsChanges = objWebService.SubmitChanges(dsChanges)

'Remove the pending new orders from the main DataSet
'before merging the orders returned by the Web service.
Dim tbl As DataTable = dsMain.Tables("Orders")
Dim row As DataRow
For Each row in tbl.Select("", "", DataRowViewState.Added)
    tbl.Rows.Remove(row)
Next row
dsMain.Merge(dsChanges)
dsMain.AcceptChanges()
```

Visual C# .NET

```
WebServiceClass objWebService = new WebServiceClass();
DataSet dsMain = objWebService.GetDataSet();
ModifyDataSetContents(dsMain);
DataSet dsChanges = dsMain.GetChanges();
dsChanges = objWebService.SubmitChanges(dsChanges);

//Remove the pending new orders from the main DataSet
//before merging the orders returned by the Web service.
DataTable tbl = dsMain.Tables["Orders"];
foreach(DataRow row in tbl.Select("", "", DataRowViewState.Added))
    tbl.Rows.Remove(row);
dsMain.Merge(dsChanges);
dsMain.AcceptChanges();
```

Looping through the main *DataSet* and removing the pending inserts isn't terribly elegant, but it definitely solves the problems.

Changing the primary keys in your *DataSet* objects Another solution is available, but it's not for the weak of code. You now understand how the *Merge* method works and why it doesn't combine the *DataSet* objects from our example in the way we want. The rows that we want to combine do not have the same primary key values.

What if we change the primary key? Just before merging the two *DataSet* objects, we can change the primary key of each *DataTable* to a different column. If the corresponding rows in the *DataSet* have the same values in this column, we'll get the desired results when we merge the *DataSet* objects. After merging, we can reset the primary keys to their original values.

Let's add a new column to the original *DataTable* and call it PseudoKey. It's just an arbitrary column. It does not map back to an actual column in the database. It's just there to help force the results of the *Merge* method to suit our needs. Figure 11-12 shows an example.

Main *DataSet* with new rows				
OrderID	CustomerID	EmployeeID	OrderDate	PseudoKey
10643	ALFKI	6	09/22/1997	1
10692	ALFKI	4	10/31/1997	2
-1	ALFKI	7	02/24/2002	3
-2	ALFKI	7	02/24/2002	4

DataSet returned by Web service with new values				
OrderID	CustomerID	EmployeeID	OrderDate	PseudoKey
12000	ALFKI	7	02/24/2002	3
12001	ALFKI	7	02/24/2002	4

Main *DataSet* after merging *DataSet* returned by Web service				
OrderID	CustomerID	EmployeeID	OrderDate	PseudoKey
10643	ALFKI	6	09/22/1997	1
10692	ALFKI	4	10/31/1997	2
12000	ALFKI	7	02/24/2002	3
12001	ALFKI	7	02/24/2002	4

Figure 11-12 Adding a pseudokey to the *DataSet* to merge in new auto-increment values

How can we programmatically change the primary key on each table just before merging and reset the primary key afterwards? The solution isn't terribly elegant, but it's not terribly complex, either. The following sample code accomplishes the task nicely:

Visual Basic .NET

```
Dim objWebService As New WebServiceClass()
Dim dsMain As DataSet = objWebService.GetDataSet()
ModifyDataSetContents(dsMain)
Dim dsChanges As DataSet = dsMain.GetChanges()
dsChanges = objWebService.SubmitChanges(dsChanges)

'Change the primary key in each table to be the pseudokey.
Dim tblMain As DataTable = ds.Tables("Orders")
Dim pkOriginal As DataColumn() = tblMain.PrimaryKey
tblMain.PrimaryKey = New DataColumn() {tblMain.Columns("PseudoKey")}
Dim tblChanges As DataTable = dsChanges.Tables("Orders")
tblChanges.PrimaryKey = New DataColumn() {tblChanges.Columns("PseudoKey")}

dsMain.Merge(dsChanges)

'Set the primary key in the main table back to its original value.
tblMain.PrimaryKey = pkOriginal

dsMain.AcceptChanges()
```

Visual C# .NET

```
WebServiceClass objWebService = new WebServiceClass();
DataSet dsMain = objWebService.GetDataSet();
ModifyDataSetContents(dsMain);
DataSet dsChanges = dsMain.GetChanges();
dsChanges = objWebService.SubmitChanges(dsChanges);

//Change the primary key in each table to be the pseudokey.
DataTable tblMain = ds.Tables["Orders"];
DataColumn[] pkOriginal = tblMain.PrimaryKey;
tblMain.PrimaryKey = new DataColumn[] {tblMain.Columns["PseudoKey"]};
DataTable tblChanges = dsChanges.Tables["Orders"];
tblChanges.PrimaryKey = new DataColumn[] {tblChanges.Columns["PseudoKey"]};

dsMain.Merge(dsChanges);

//Set the primary key in the main table back to its original value.
tblMain.PrimaryKey = pkOriginal;

dsMain.AcceptChanges();
```

But what about the contents of the PseudoKey column? How can we generate unique values for this column when it does not correspond to a column in the database? We can use...another autoincrement column.

Reviewing your options   Personally, I don't like either solution I've presented. They're inelegant at best. The solution that involves changing the primary key can become overly complex, especially if the table in question has related child *DataTable* objects in the *DataSet*. If I had to pick one solution, I'd choose the one that removes the pending inserts from the original *DataSet* before calling *Merge*. However, I will say this: even having these inelegant solutions is a major step forward from ADO, in which there were no solutions to this scenario.

You'll find a sample application called ComplexHierarchy on the companion CD that demonstrates the problem and various solutions. The sample modifies the contents of a hierarchy that contains orders and order details. Like the Northwind database, the table that contains order information uses an autoincrement column as its primary key.

The sample lets you submit the changes from the *DataSet* to the database using *DataAdapter* objects and the *DataTable* object's *Select* method (as shown in Figure 11-13). To ensure that the update attempts succeed, the code submits new orders before new order details and deletes existing order details before deleting existing orders. You can submit the updates from the *DataSet* directly to the database, or you can isolate the changes into a new *DataSet* by calling *GetChanges* and then merging in the submitted changes afterwards. Alternatively, you can include a pseudokey in each *DataTable* and use this pseudokey to merge the two *DataSet* objects, as described earlier.

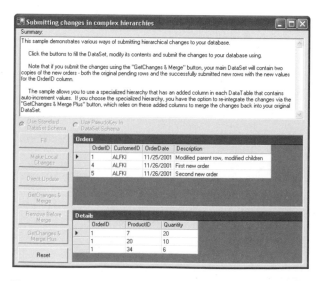

Figure 11-13   The ComplexHierarchy sample application

One final option is to avoid the problem altogether by structuring your data so that you know the primary key values for your new rows before you submit them to the database. A growing number of developers are using globally unique identifiers (GUIDs) in their databases. Although you might not want to use a GUID column as the primary key for your database table, you can use it as the primary key for your *DataTable* and avoid the problem altogether.

Handling Failed Update Attempts Elegantly

ADO.NET is designed to work with disconnected data. When a user modifies the contents of a *DataSet*, he or she does not directly modify the contents of the database. Instead, ADO.NET caches the change in the modified *DataRow* object or objects. You can submit the changes to the database later using a *Data-Adapter* object.

However, there are no guarantees that the data in the database won't be changed after the user runs the initial query. The updating logic that *Data-Adapter* objects use to submit changes uses optimistic concurrency. As with being an optimist in life, things don't always turn out the way you'd like.

Consider the following scenario. User A retrieves customer information from your database into a *DataSet*. That user modifies information for a particular customer. Between the time that User A queries the database and attempts to submit the new customer data, User B modifies that same row of data in your database. As a result, User A's update attempt fails.

Many developers see this behavior as a major headache, but consider the alternative. What if User A's update attempt were to succeed? User A would overwrite the changes that User B made without even realizing that the data had been changed.

Planning Ahead for Conflicts

If you're building a multi-user application that works with disconnected data and relies on optimistic concurrency to submit changes, there's a chance that update attempts will fail. You should plan ahead and determine how your application should respond to such situations.

Say you modify the contents of 10 rows and attempt to submit those changes. The *DataAdapter* successfully submits the changes in the first three rows, but the attempt to submit the change stored in the fourth row fails. How should your application respond? Should the *DataAdapter* attempt to submit the remaining pending changes?

The *DataAdapter* Object's *ContinueUpdateOnError* Property

You can control how the *DataAdapter* responds to a failed update attempt by using the *ContinueUpdateOnError* property. By default, this property is set to *False*, which means that the *DataAdapter* will throw a *DBConcurrencyException* when it encounters a failed update attempt. If you want the *DataAdapter* to attempt to submit the remaining changes, set its *ContinueUpdateOnError* property to *True*.

If you set this property to *True* and one or more of the update attempts fail, the *DataAdapter* will not throw an exception. When the *DataAdapter* encounters a failed update attempt, it will set the *HasErrors* property of the corresponding *DataRow* object to *True* and set the *RowError* property of the *DataRow* to the concurrency error message. You can check the *HasErrors* property of your *DataSet* or *DataTable* after calling *DataAdapter.Update* to determine whether any of the update attempts failed. Of course, this will not be a valid test if your *DataSet* or *DataTable* has errors before you call *DataAdapter.Update*.

Some developers will want to submit changes in a transaction and commit the changes only if all update attempts succeed. In such scenarios, you'll probably want to leave the *ContinueUpdateOnError* property set to its default value of *False* and roll back the transaction if the *Update* method throws an exception.

Informing the User of Failures

It's important to inform the user if an update attempt fails. Some components will help you show the user which rows did not update successfully. For example, if you modify a number of rows in a Windows DataGrid control and the attempt to submit those modified rows fails, the rows that did not update successfully will be marked with a warning icon in the row header. If you move the mouse over the icon, the grid will display a tooltip that shows the contents of the error.

If you're not using a bound Windows DataGrid, you can use code like the following to provide information about the rows whose updates failed:

Visual Basic .NET

```
Try
    MyDataAdapter.ContinueUpdateOnError = True
    MyDataAdapter.Update(MyDataTable)
    If MyDataTable.HasErrors
        Dim strMessage As String
        strMessage = "The following row(s) were not updated " & _
                    "successfully:"
```

```
        Dim row As DataRow
        For Each row In MyDataTable.Rows
            If row.HasErrors Then
                strMessage &= vbCrLf & row("ID") & " - " & _
                                 row.RowError
            End If
        Next row
        MessageBox.Show(strMessage)
    Else
        MessageBox.Show("All updates succeeded")
    End If
Catch ex As Exception
    MessageBox.Show("The following exception occurred:" & vbCrLf & _
                        ex.Message)
End Try
```

Visual C# .NET

```
try
{
    MyDataAdapter.ContinueUpdateOnError = true;
    MyDataAdapter.Update(MyDataTable);
    if (MyDataTable.HasErrors)
    {
        string strMessage;
        strMessage = "The following row(s) were not updated " +
                        "successfully:";
        foreach (DataRow row in MyDataTable.Rows)
            if (row.HasErrors)
                strMessage += "\n\r" + (string) row["ID"] +
                                row.RowError;
        MessageBox.Show(strMessage);
    }
    else
        MessageBox.Show("All updates succeeded");
}
catch (Exception ex)
{
    MessageBox.Show("The following exception occurred: \n\r" +
                        ex.Message);
}
```

Users can be demanding. If an update attempt fails, they don't just want to know that it failed. They generally want to know why the update attempt failed and how to make the update successful. First, let's focus on determining why an update attempt failed.

What if we could extract the information shown in Figure 11-14 for each failed update attempt?

	CustomerID	CompanyName	BalanceDue
You tried to submit the following data:	ABCDE	ABCDE Inc.	$200.00
The original data for the row was:	ABCDE	ABCDE Inc.	$100.00
The row in the database now contains:	ABCDE	ABCDE Inc.	$125.00

Figure 11-14   Displaying information about failed update attempts

You already know how to use the *DataRow* object to access the current and original contents of a row.

Visual Basic .NET

```
Dim tbl As DataTable = CreateFillAndModifyTable()
Dim row As DataRow = tbl.Rows(0)
Console.WriteLine("Current  Balance Due: " & row("BalanceDue"))
Console.WriteLine("Original Balance Due: " & _
                row("BalanceDue", DataRowVersion.Original))
```

Visual C# .NET

```
DataTable tbl = CreateFillAndModifyTable();
DataRow row = tbl.Rows[0];
Console.WriteLine("Current  Balance Due: " + row["BalanceDue"]);
Console.WriteLine("Original Balance Due: " +
                row["BalanceDue", DataRowVersion.Original]);
```

But how can we fetch the current contents of the desired rows in the database?

Fetching the Current Contents of Conflicting Rows

To fetch the current contents of the desired rows, we can use the *DataAdapter* object's *RowUpdated* event. The following code snippet determines whether the *DataAdapter* encountered an error on the update attempt. If the error is a concurrency exception, the code will use a parameterized query to fetch the current contents of the corresponding row in the database.

To make the code snippet concise and readable, I've omitted the definition of the *DataAdapter* objects and *DataSet* objects. The *ConflictAdapter* is a *DataAdapter* that contains a parameterized query that retrieves the contents of a row in the database. The parameter for this query is the primary key column for the database. That column in the *DataTable* is ID. The code uses the value of the ID column for the row whose update failed as the value for the parameter, executes the query using that parameter, and stores the results into a separate *DataSet*.

There's also the chance that the row you tried to update no longer exists in the database. The code determines whether the query retrieved a row and sets the *DataRow* object's *RowUpdate* property appropriately.

Visual Basic .NET

```vb
Private Sub HandleRowUpdated(ByVal sender As Object, _
                             ByVal e As OleDbRowUpdatedEventArgs)
    If e.Status = UpdateStatus.ErrorsOccurred AndAlso _
        TypeOf(e.Errors) Is DBConcurrencyException Then
        ConflictAdapter.SelectCommand.Parameters(0).Value = e.Row("ID")
        Dim intRowsReturned As Integer
        intRowsReturned = ConflictAdapter.Fill(ConflictDataSet)
        If intRowsReturned = 1 Then
            e.Row.RowError = "The row has been modified by another user."
        Else
            e.Row.RowError = "The row no longer exists in the database."
        End If
        e.Status = UpdateStatus.Continue
    End If
End Sub
```

Visual C# .NET

```csharp
private void HandleRowUpdated(object sender, OleDbRowUpdatedEventArgs e)
{
    if ((e.Status == UpdateStatus.ErrorsOccurred) &&
        (e.Errors.GetType == typeof(DBConcurrencyException)))
    {
        ConflictAdapter.SelectCommand.Parameters[0].Value = e.Row["ID"];
        int intRowsReturned = ConflictAdapter.Fill(ConflictDataSet);
        if (intRowsReturned == 1)
            e.Row.RowError = "The row has been modified by another user.";
        else
            e.Row.RowError = "The row no longer exists in the database.";
        e.Status = UpdateStatus.Continue;
    }
}
```

> **Note**   The *DataAdapter* will automatically append text to the *Row-Error* property on a failed update attempt if you do not change *Status* to *Continue* or *SkipCurrentRow*.

This code snippet fetches the current contents of the corresponding rows in the database into a separate *DataSet* so that you can examine the data after the update attempt. You now have all the data you need to construct a dialog box similar to Figure 11-14.

If at First You Don't Succeed...

Telling the user why an update attempt failed is helpful, but your users probably don't want to requery your database and reapply the same set of changes to the new data in order to try to resubmit their changes. How can we use the ADO.NET object model to simplify the process?

Let's think back to why the update attempt failed in the first place. The data that the *DataAdapter* used in its concurrency checks no longer matches the current contents of the row in the database. The *DataAdapter* uses the original content of the *DataRow* object in the updating logic's concurrency checks. Until we refresh the original values in the *DataRow* object, we will not be able to submit the changes stored in that *DataRow* to the database no matter how many times we call the *DataAdapter* object's *Update* method.

If we can change the original content of a *DataRow* object without losing the current content of the *DataRow*, we can successfully submit the changes stored in that *DataRow*, assuming that the contents of the corresponding row in the database don't change again.

Using the *DataSet* Object's *Merge* Method to Import "New Original" Values

Earlier in the chapter, you learned how to use the *DataSet* object's *Merge* method to combine the contents of two *DataSet* objects. If the *Merge* method detects that two rows have the same primary key values, it will combine the contents of the two rows into one. The *Merge* method also lets you specify that you want to preserve the changes stored in your *DataSet*.

In the previous code snippet, we trapped for the *DataAdapter* object's *RowUpdated* event. If the current row did not update successfully, the code retrieved the current contents of the corresponding row in the database into a new *DataSet* called *ConflictDataSet*. Assuming that the main *DataSet* is called *MainDataSet*, we can use the following line of code to merge the contents of *ConflictDataSet* into *MainDataSet*:

Visual Basic .NET

```
MainDataSet.Merge(ConflictDataSet, True)
```

Visual C# .NET

```
MainDataSet.Merge(ConflictDataSet, true);
```

The code does not change the current contents of the *DataRow* objects in the main *DataSet*. It overwrites only the original values of the *DataRow* objects with the data in the conflict *DataSet*.

With this "new original" data in the main *DataSet*, we can attempt to submit the remaining pending changes to the database. If the contents of the corresponding rows have not changed since we retrieved them in the *RowUpdated* event, our updates will succeed.

Keep in mind that you can't get "more up-to-date" information about a row that no longer exists in the database. If an update attempt fails because the row no longer exists in the database, you can't use this approach to refresh the original values in the row. If you want to re-add the current contents of the *DataRow* object to the database, you can remove the *DataRow* from the *Data-Table* object's *Rows* collection and then re-add it. This will change the *DataRow* object's *RowState* to *Added*. When you use the *DataAdapter* to submit the change, it will try to insert the row into the database.

The Conflicts Sample Application

The companion CD includes a sample application called Conflicts (shown in Figure 11-15) that's an example of how you can detect, analyze, and resolve failed update attempts. The sample retrieves data from the database into a *DataSet* and modifies that data. I've designed the sample to modify some of the rows in the database directly to simulate another user submitting changes. When you click the button to submit the changes cached in the *DataSet* to your database, some of the update attempts will fail as a result of the "other user's" changes.

The sample application handles these failed update attempts and fetches the current contents of those rows from the database into a second *DataSet*. As you navigate through the main *DataSet*, the sample displays the status for the row, its current contents, and its original contents. If the row contains a failed update attempt, you'll also see the current contents of the corresponding row in the database. The sample application forces you to resolve the conflicts before attempting to update the database.

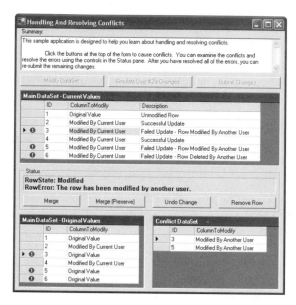

Figure 11-15   The Conflicts sample application

Working with Distributed Transactions

In Chapter 4, I talked about the ADO.NET *Transaction* object. You can use a *Transaction* object to group the results of multiple queries on a connection as a single unit of work.

Let's say your database contains banking information. You can transfer money from a savings account to a checking account by executing the following two queries:

```
UPDATE Savings
    SET BalanceDue = BalanceDue - 100
    WHERE AccountID = 17
UPDATE Checking
    SET BalanceDue = BalanceDue + 100
    WHERE AccountID = 17
```

To make sure you can group the two changes into a single unit of work that you can commit or roll back, you can create a new *Transaction* object before executing the queries. If an error occurs or one of the queries doesn't have the desired row, you can roll back the transaction. Otherwise, you can commit the changes you made in the transaction. Figure 11-16 shows how to wrap both changes in a single transaction. (You know all this already.)

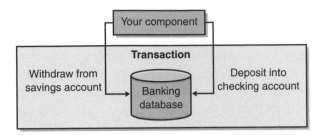

Figure 11-16 Wrapping multiple changes to a database in a transaction

But what do you do if the checking and savings accounts aren't in the same database?

You can start a transaction on each connection. Then, if you determine that the withdrawal from the savings account or the deposit into the checking account failed, you can roll back both transactions. Otherwise, you can commit them both. That sounds simple enough. Figure 11-17 depicts such an application.

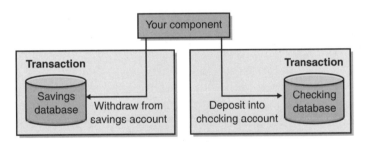

Figure 11-17 Wrapping changes to separate databases in separate transactions

Let's say you commit the withdrawal from the savings account, but just before you commit the deposit into the checking account, you lose your network connection. The database will detect the lost connection and roll back the transaction automatically. You will have withdrawn the money from the savings account but not deposited that money into the checking account.

Oops. Maybe using a transaction on each connection isn't a completely reliable solution to the problem. In order to make the system more reliable, your application needs to work more closely with both databases to coordinate the transactions and resolve problems like the one I've just described. You need to use a transaction that enlists multiple database connections. A transaction that can span multiple resources is generally known as a *distributed transaction*.

> **Note** Entire books are dedicated to transaction processing or to COM+. Obviously, I can't cover either topic nearly as thoroughly over the next few pages. I will simply provide an introduction to the basics of transaction processing and working with COM+ components. For more information on transaction processing, I strongly recommend *Principles of Transaction Processing* by Philip A. Bernstein and Eric Newcomer (Morgan Kaufmann, 1997).

Transaction Coordinators and Resource Managers

Two main components are involved in a distributed transaction: the resource manager and the transaction coordinator. A resource manager performs the desired work, whether it's modifying the contents of a database or reading a message from a queue. It then reports whether it was able to complete the work.

The transaction coordinator communicates with the resource managers participating in the transaction and manages the current state of the transaction. If one resource manager indicates that an error occurred, the transaction coordinator will receive this message and inform the other resource managers to cancel the work performed in the transaction. If all resource managers indicate that they successfully completed their tasks, the transaction coordinator will tell all the resource managers to commit the results of those tasks.

Two-Phase Commits

Each resource manager implements what's known as a "two-phase commit." The transaction coordinator tells each resource manager to prepare the changes performed during the lifetime of the transaction. This is just the first phase of the process. The resource managers have not actually committed the changes yet. They're simply preparing to commit the changes.

Once all the resource managers indicate that they are ready to commit the changes, the transaction coordinator will tell each resource manager to do so. If, however, one or more resource managers indicate that they could not prepare the changes, the transaction coordinator will tell each resource manager to cancel the work performed in the transaction.

Let's apply this to the problem scenario. When the transaction coordinator asks the resource managers to prepare to commit the changes, they both indicate that they are ready, willing, and able to commit the changes. The transaction coordinator sends a message to the resource manager for the savings account to commit the changes, but a fatal error (such as a power outage) occurs before it can communicate with the resource manager for the checking account. What happens now?

It's up to the transaction coordinator and the resource manager for the checking account to resolve the transaction. Each component is responsible for maintaining information about the status of the transaction. The transaction coordinator must be able to recover from the failure, determine that the transaction is still pending, and contact the appropriate resource managers to resolve the transaction.

The resource manager must be able to commit all changes that it prepared in the first phase of the commit process. Let's say the power outage that threw the resolution of the transaction into doubt occurred on the machine where the database that maintains the checking account is located. The database system needs to recover from the failure, determine that the transaction is still pending, provide the ability to commit those changes, and resolve the transaction with the coordinator.

As you can already tell, it takes a lot of work to develop a transaction coordinator or a resource manager.

Distributed Transactions in the .NET Framework

Microsoft initially introduced its transaction coordinator and supporting technologies for the Windows operating system as an add-on to Windows NT 4. This functionality is now integrated into the Windows operating system as part of Component Services.

The beauty of this architecture is that you have to write only a small amount of code to take advantage of the transactional features in Component Services. You write your code just like you would normally. You then tell Component Services whether to commit or abort the transaction, and it will take care of the grunt work necessary to manage a distributed transaction. Figure 11-18 shows an example of working with multiple databases in a distributed transaction using Component Services.

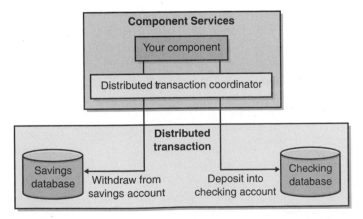

Figure 11-18   Using Component Services to wrap changes to multiple databases in a distributed transaction

Database Support for Distributed Transactions

In order to use distributed transactions with your database, your database system needs to have a resource manager that can communicate with the transaction coordinator that's built into Component Services.

Some database systems (such as SQL Server and Oracle) have resource managers that support such functionality, but many others (such as Access and dBASE) do not. Before you start planning an application that relies on distributed transactions, make sure you're using a database that has a resource manager that implements two-phase commits and can communicate with Component Services.

Actually, distributed transactions aren't just for databases. Microsoft Message Queuing services, for example, lets you send and receive messages as part of a distributed transaction.

Building Your Components

Building support for distributed transactions into your .NET component is relatively simple. First, be sure your project is a class library. Component Services is designed to run without any user interface. You wouldn't want your transactions to time out because they're displaying modal dialog boxes on a server that your users won't see. Second, be sure your project contains a reference to the *System.EnterpriseServices* namespace and that your class inherits from the *ServicedComponent* class. Now you're ready to write some transactional code.

To register your libraries in Component Services, you must use two command-line tools, Sn.exe and RegSvcs.exe. You use Sn.exe, which is located in the Framework SDK's Bin directory, to generate a strong name for your library. You then use RegSvcs.exe, which is located in the Framework's directory, to register your library with Component Services. In your code, you use the application name for your library and reference the strong name file, as shown in the following code snippet:

Visual Basic .NET

```
Imports System.Reflection

' Supply the COM+ application name.
<assembly: ApplicationName("MyServiceComponent")>
' Supply a strongly named assembly.
<assembly: AssemblyKeyFileAttribute("MyServiceComponent.snk")>
```

Visual C# .NET

```
using System.Reflection;

// Supply the COM+ application name.
[assembly: ApplicationName("MyServiceComponent")]
// Supply a strongly named assembly.
[assembly: AssemblyKeyFileAttribute("MyServiceComponent.snk")]
```

For more information on these settings and using the command-line tools, see the MSDN documentation.

The *TransactionOption* Attribute

Not all objects that run in Component Services are designed to use distributed transactions. You can move business objects for your application into Component Services for other reasons, such as to better leverage connection pooling.

The *TransactionOption* attribute of the class controls whether instances of your class will participate in a transaction. In the following code snippet, instances of the class will always run in a transaction. If an instance of the class is created within the context of a transaction, the instance will participate in that transaction. Otherwise, the instance will receive its own transaction.

Visual Basic .NET

```
<Transaction(TransactionOption.Required)> _
Public Class clsDistributedTransaction
    Inherits ServicedComponent
    ⋮
```

Visual C# .NET

```
[Transaction(TransactionOption.Required)]
public class TxDemoSvr : ServicedComponent
{
    ⋮
```

You can set the *TransactionOption* attribute to any value in the *TransactionOption* enumeration, as shown in Table 11-2.

Table 11-2   Members of the *TransactionOption* Enumeration

Constant	Value	Description
Disabled	0	The component will not participate in a transaction. This is the default.
NotSupported	1	The component will run outside of the context of the transaction, if one exists.

(continued)

Table 11-2   Members of the *TransactionOption* Enumeration   *(continued)*

Constant	Value	Description
Supported	2	The component will participate in a transaction if one exists, but it does not require a transaction.
Required	3	The component will participate in the current transaction if one exists. If no transaction exists, the component will be created in a new transaction.
RequiresNew	4	The component will always be created in a new transaction.

Enlisting Your ADO.NET Connection in the Transaction

Part of the beauty of the Component Services model is that you don't have to write code to enlist your ADO.NET connection in the Component Services transaction. You don't even have to use ADO.NET transactions. You simply let Component Services do the work for you. If your code is running in the context of a transaction, Component Services will automatically enlist your connection in the transaction.

Committing or Canceling Your Work

All that's left to do is add logic to your component to decide whether to commit or roll back the work you perform. If you find that your queries do not return the desired results or your code catches an unexpected exception from which you can't recover, you only need to execute a single line of code to roll back the work you've done on your connections. You simply call the *SetAbort* method of the *ContextUtil* object that's available to your class, as shown in the following code snippet. To commit the work performed in the transaction, you call the *ContextUtil* object's *SetComplete* method.

Visual Basic .NET

```
Public Sub MyTransactionalMethod()
    Try
        'Connect.
        'Run queries.
        'Disconnect.
        If blnSuccess Then
            ContextUtil.SetComplete()
        Else
            ContextUtil.SetAbort()
        End If
    Catch ex As Exception
        ContextUtil.SetAbort()
```

```
        Throw New Exception("Unexpected exception: " & ex.Message)
    End Try
End Sub
```

Visual C# .NET

```
public void MyTransactionalMethod()
    try
    {
        //Connect.
        //Run queries.
        //Disconnect.
        if (blnSuccess)
            ContextUtil.SetComplete();
        else
            ContextUtil.SetAbort();
    }
    catch (Exception ex)
    {.SetAbort();
        throw
        ContextUtil new Exception("Unexpected exception: " + ex.Message);
    }
}
```

> **Note**   The *ContextUtil* object contains information about the COM+ context information. For more information on this object's features, see the MSDN documentation.

Remember that calling *SetComplete* at the end of your procedure does not necessarily mean that Component Services will commit the work performed on your transaction. This is simply the first phase of the two-phase commit. If any component that participates in the same transaction calls *SetAbort*, the transaction coordinator will tell the resource managers for all components to roll back the work performed in the transaction.

This behavior is analogous to a wedding ceremony. The marriage isn't official just because you say "I do." If the other person backs out at the last second, you're not married.

Distributed Transactions Made Simpler

Developers who have built components in previous incarnations of the Component Services technology (such as Microsoft Transaction Server) will remember the *SetComplete* and *SetAbort* methods. There's also a new way to tell the transaction coordinator whether you want to commit the changes made during the transaction.

Determining whether to commit or abort the changes made in the transaction is often very simple: you commit the changes unless an unexpected error occurs. To simplify the process, you can set the *AutoComplete* attribute on a procedure. When you set the *AutoComplete* attribute on a method, *Component-Services* will assume that you want to commit the transaction unless the method throws an unhandled exception.

Just keep in mind that if you use the *AutoComplete* attribute and you trap for an exception in your code, you'll need to throw a new exception or rethrow the current one in order to indicate that you want to abort the transaction.

You can set the *AutoComplete* attribute on methods in your class, as shown in the following code snippet:

Visual Basic .NET

```
<AutoComplete()> _
Public Sub MyTransactionalMethod()
    ⋮
```

Visual C# .NET

```
[AutoComplete()]
public void MyTransactionalMethod()
{
    ⋮
```

> **Note**   If you're executing action queries or calling stored procedures to modify the contents of your database, be sure to check that the desired change or changes occurred. Remember that a query that modifies zero rows does not throw an error.

The DistributedTransaction Sample Application

The companion CD contains a working sample application (in Visual Basic .NET and in Visual C# .NET) that demonstrates the power of distributed transaction. The server component moves money between a checking account and a savings account, each of which is associated with a separate ADO.NET *Connection* object.

In fact, the server component uses separate child classes to change the balance due of each account. The server component also includes methods to let you abort the transaction even after both of the child classes have completed their work. The client application, shown in Figure 11-19, retrieves the current balance due for both accounts after each attempted transfer. You can use this client application to verify that the changes made in an aborted transaction were not committed to the database.

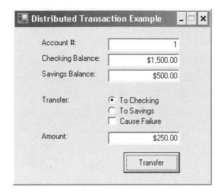

Figure 11-19   The client application in the DistributedTransaction sample

Other Benefits of Using Component Services

Other benefits go along with running your business objects in Component Services, such as connection pooling, object pooling, and having a central location for controlling your business logic. For more information on these features, see the MSDN and online documentation for Component Services. You'll also find samples in the Component Services subdirectory of the Framework SDK.

When Handling Advanced Updating Scenarios, Use ADO.NET

The *CommandBuilder* object and code-generation tools such as the Data Adapter Configuration Wizard make handling basic updating scenarios simple. Unfortunately, these tools do not generate the logic required to handle more advanced updating scenarios, such as detecting and resolving failed update attempts.

However, you can use various ADO.NET features to handle the more advanced updating scenarios. Armed with the knowledge you've gained from reading this chapter, you now have the ability to handle such scenarios using the ADO.NET features described in the chapter.

Questions That Should Be Asked More Frequently

Q.   How do the Data Adapter Configuration Wizard and *Command-Builder* objects handle a scenario in which I want to refresh the contents of my row after submitting an update? Some things seem to work automatically, but others don't.

A.   The wizard will include queries to refresh your data immediately after you submit a new row or modify an existing row if your database supports such features. You will get these queries if you're using SQL Server or MSDE, but not if you're using databases such as Oracle or Access that don't support batched queries that return rows. If you do not want the Data Adapter Configuration Wizard to generate these refresh queries, click the Advanced Options button in the wizard and turn this feature off.

The *CommandBuilder* object does not generate refresh queries no matter what back end you're using.

Q.   I have cascading referential integrity constraints in my database. If I delete an existing customer, the database automatically deletes the remaining orders for that customer. If I have deleted customers and orders in my *DataSet*, I get errors when I try to submit those changes, even though it looks like all the changes succeeded when I look at the contents of my database. What's going on?

A.   If you have a *DataRelation* defined between orders and details *DataTable* objects in your *DataSet* and you delete an order, ADO.NET will automatically mark the related child rows as deleted. Some databases allow you to define cascading referential integrity constraints in a similar fashion. So, when you submit the pending delete on the order, the database will delete the order and the related child rows from your database.

However, ADO.NET will not know that the database has cascaded the change. The child rows will still be marked as pending deletions in the ADO.NET *DataSet*. If you submit the pending changes stored in the child *DataTable* to your database, the *Data-Adapter* will attempt to delete the rows you've already deleted because of the database's cascading rules.

The simplest solution is to use the techniques for submitting pending changes from a hierarchical *DataSet* that I described earlier in the chapter. Use the *Select* method of the *DataTable* to submit new rows, starting at the top level of the hierarchy and working your way down. Submit pending deletions starting at the bottom level or levels of the hierarchy, working your way up to the top.

Q.   The ADO *Recordset* object has a *Resync* method that you can use to fetch information on rows that did not update successfully. What is the equivalent method in the ADO.NET object model?

A.   The ADO.NET object model has no direct equivalent of this feature. However, you can achieve similar functionality by filling a new *DataSet* and merging the contents into your existing *DataSet* using the *Merge* method, as described earlier in the chapter.

12

Working with XML Data

In this chapter, I'll explain how to use ADO.NET's XML features, most notably those that allow you to read and write data in XML format. But before I do so, I need to offer a disclaimer: this chapter is not intended to teach you all about XML. Entire books are dedicated to that task.

Although this chapter won't offer an in-depth guide to XML and related technologies such as XSLT and XPath, it will demonstrate some of the power of these technologies. I'll assume that you know the basics of working with XML, XSLT, and XPath, but this knowledge is not required. Even if you can't spell XML, this chapter can help you develop an appreciation for XML and whet your appetite for learning more.

While discussing using ADO.NET with XML data, I'll also show off some of the XML features of Microsoft SQL Server 2000. Again, entire books are dedicated to explaining these features in depth, such as Graeme Malcolm's *Programming Microsoft SQL Server 2000 with XML* (Microsoft Press, 2001). This chapter will assume that you understand the basics of SQL Server 2000's XML features and want to access them via ADO.NET, but even if you're not familiar with them, you can use the code snippets and appreciate the power of these features.

Bridging the Gap Between XML and Data Access

XML is one of the hot technologies in the development world right now. I was at a major local bookstore today and was amazed at the number of XML books on the shelves. If it wasn't the largest category in the computer section, it was a close second.

You can use an XML document to store data such as information about a series of customers and each customer's order history. In some ways, an XML document is similar to an ADO.NET *DataSet* or an ADO *Recordset*. Each object can store multiple pieces of data in a well-defined structure.

With previous development technologies such as Microsoft Visual Basic or Microsoft Active Server Pages (ASP), developers traditionally used either XML or a data access technology such as ADO, but rarely both. Why? The technologies don't really work together. You can't easily move between an XML document and an ADO *Recordset*.

Technically, ADO 2.1 introduced features that allow you to save the contents of a *Recordset* as XML and later reload that XML data into a *Recordset*. However, if you examine the contents of the XML file that ADO creates, you'll find that it includes a series of schema tags. There is no way to control the schema for the XML document that ADO creates. Also, ADO cannot read generic XML documents. Unless you generate your XML document using the (undocumented) schema that ADO expects, you can't load the data into a *Recordset* using the *Recordset* object's *Open* method.

One major goal of the ADO.NET development team was to bridge the gap between XML and data access so that you can easily integrate the two technologies. Loading data from an XML document into an ADO.NET *DataSet* and vice versa is simple. If you're working with SQL Server 2000, you can retrieve data from your database as XML and store the results in an ADO.NET *DataSet* or an XML document. You can also synchronize an ADO.NET *DataSet* and an XML document so that the changes made in one are visible in the other.

Let's take a closer look at these features.

Reading and Writing XML Data

First let's look at the different ways we can read and write XML data using the *DataSet* object.

The *DataSet* Object's XML Methods

The *DataSet* object has a series of methods that let you examine its contents as XML as well as load XML data into the *DataSet*. Let's take a look at these methods.

GetXml Method

The simplest of these XML methods is the *GetXml* method, which you can use to extract the contents of your *DataSet* into a string. The *GetXml* method is simple almost to a fault. It is not overloaded and accepts no parameters.

Figure 12-1 shows the contents of a *DataSet* in the Console window. The code that generates and displays this *DataSet* follows.

Figure 12-1   Using the *GetXml* method to view the contents of a *DataSet* as XML

Visual Basic .NET

```
Dim ds As New DataSet()
FillMyDataSet(ds)
Console.WriteLine(ds.GetXml)

Public Sub FillMyDataSet(ByVal ds As DataSet)
    Dim strConn, strSQL As String
    strConn = "Provider=SQLOLEDB;Data Source=(local)\NetSDK;" & _
              "Initial Catalog=Northwind;Trusted_Connection=Yes;"
    strSQL = "SELECT OrderID, CustomerID, OrderDate FROM Orders " & _
             "WHERE CustomerID = 'GROSR'"
    Dim daOrders, daDetails As OleDbDataAdapter
    daOrders = New OleDbDataAdapter(strSQL, strConn)
    strSQL = "SELECT OrderID, ProductID, Quantity, UnitPrice " & _
             "FROM [Order Details] WHERE OrderID IN (SELECT " & _
             "OrderID FROM Orders WHERE CustomerID = 'GROSR')"
    daDetails = New OleDbDataAdapter(strSQL, strConn)
    daOrders.Fill(ds, "Orders")
    daDetails.Fill(ds, "Order Details")
End Sub
```

Visual C# .NET

```
DataSet ds = new DataSet();
FillMyDataSet(ds);
Console.WriteLine(ds.GetXml());

static void FillMyDataSet(DataSet ds)
{
    string strConn, strSQL;
    strConn = "Provider=SQLOLEDB;Data Source=(local)\\NetSDK;" +
            "Initial Catalog=Northwind;Trusted_Connection=Yes;";
    strSQL = "SELECT OrderID, CustomerID, OrderDate FROM Orders " +
            "WHERE CustomerID = 'GROSR'";
    OleDbDataAdapter daOrders, daDetails;
    daOrders = new OleDbDataAdapter(strSQL, strConn);
    strSQL = "SELECT OrderID, ProductID, Quantity, UnitPrice " +
            "FROM [Order Details] WHERE OrderID IN (SELECT " +
            "OrderID FROM Orders WHERE CustomerID = 'GROSR')";
    daDetails = new OleDbDataAdapter(strSQL, strConn);
    daOrders.Fill(ds, "Orders");
    daDetails.Fill(ds, "Order Details");
}
```

WriteXml and *ReadXml* Methods

As I noted earlier, the *GetXml* method is rather limited. The *DataSet* object's *WriteXml* method is more robust. It is overloaded so that you can write the contents of your *DataSet* to a file or to an object that implements the *Stream, TextWriter*, or *XmlWriter* interfaces.

The *WriteXml* method also lets you specify values from the *XmlWriteMode* enumeration for added control over the output. You can use this enumeration to choose whether to include the schema information for the *DataSet* and whether to write the contents of the *DataSet* in diffgram format.

I'd rather examine the contents of an XML document in Microsoft Internet Explorer than in the Console window because Internet Explorer will format the data nicely. The code snippet that follows shows how to use the *WriteXml* method to write the contents of a *DataSet* (including its schema) to a file and display that file in Internet Explorer, as shown in Figure 12-2. The code snippet relies on the *FillMyDataSet* procedure from the previous code snippet. It also requires a reference to the Microsoft Internet Controls library, which is available on the COM tab of the Add Reference dialog box.

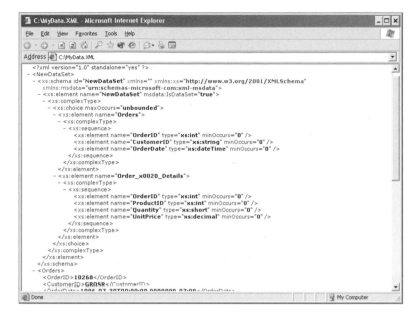

Figure 12-2   Viewing the *DataSet* and its schema in Internet Explorer

Visual Basic .NET

```
Dim ds As New DataSet()
FillMyDataSet(ds)
Dim strPathToXml As String = "C:\MyData.XML"
ds.WriteXml(strPathToXml, XmlWriteMode.WriteSchema)
ShowXmlInIE(strPathToXml)

Public Sub ShowXmlInIE(ByVal strPathToXml As String)
    Dim ie As New SHDocVw.InternetExplorer()
    ie.Navigate(strPathToXml)
    ie.Visible = True
End Sub
```

Visual C# .NET

```
DataSet ds = new DataSet();
FillMyDataSet(ds);
string strPathToXml = "C:\\MyData.XML";
ds.WriteXml(strPathToXml, XmlWriteMode.WriteSchema);
ShowXmlInIE(strPathToXml);

static void ShowXmlInIE(string strPathToXml)
```

(continued)

```
{
    SHDocVw.InternetExplorer ie = new SHDocVw.InternetExplorerClass();
    object objEmpty = Type.Missing;
    ie.Navigate(strPathToXml, ref objEmpty, ref objEmpty,
            ref objEmpty, ref objEmpty);
    ie.Visible = true;
}
```

> **Note** The *InternetExplorer* class's *Navigate* method has many optional parameters. The C# language does not support optional parameters with COM interop calls. You can supply *Type.Missing* for the parameters that you want to omit.

The *DataSet* object has an overloaded *ReadXml* method that you can use to load data into your *DataSet*. The *ReadXml* method is basically the inverse of the *WriteXml* method. It can read XML data from a file or from an object that implements the *Stream*, *TextReader*, or *XmlReader* interfaces. You can also control how the method reads the contents of the XML data by supplying values from the *XmlReadMode* enumeration.

WriteXmlSchema, *ReadXmlSchema*, and *InferXmlSchema* Methods

The *DataSet* object also exposes *ReadXmlSchema* and *WriteXmlSchema* methods that allow you to read and write just the schema information for your *DataSet*. Each method supports working with files and objects that implement the *Stream*, *TextReader*, or *XmlReader* interface.

The *ReadXmlSchema* method can load schema information from an XML schema document using the XML Schema Definition (XSD) or XML Data Reduced (XDR) standard. It can also read an inline schema from an XML document.

The *DataSet* object also exposes an *InferXmlSchema* method, which works just like the *ReadXmlSchema* method except that *InferXmlSchema* has a second parameter. You can supply an array of strings in the second parameter to tell ADO.NET which namespaces you want to ignore in the XML document.

Inferring Schemas

In previous chapters, I've supplied metadata or schema information in code to provide better performance than when you generate this information programmatically at run time. The same holds true for inferring XML schemas, and the *ReadXml* method is a prime example.

Say that you use the *ReadXml* method to load data into a *DataSet* and that neither the XML document nor the *DataSet* has any schema information. You can't add rows of data to the *DataSet* if it has no schema information. The *ReadXml* method must first scan the entire XML document to add the appropriate schema information to the *DataSet* before it adds the contents of the document to the *DataSet*. The larger the XML document, the greater the performance penalty incurred by inferring the schema from the document.

This approach can lead to another problem: You might not get the schema you want. ADO.NET will assume that all data types are strings and won't create any constraints. Why? Imagine that your XML document contains a list of contacts and addresses (XML tags omitted) in the following format:

```
<MailingLabel>
  <First_Name>Randal</First_Name>
  <Last_Name>Stephens</Last_Name>
  <Address>123 Main St.</Address>
  <City>Sometown</City>
  <Region>MA</Region>
  <PostalCode>01234</PostalCode>
</MailingLabel>
```

Let's say that the contents of the document represent a small sampling of the actual data in your database. In other entries in your database, the contact might have a second address line or an address outside of the United States with a postal code in a different format. You must remember that if you ask ADO.NET to infer a schema from the contents of an XML document that contains no schema information, it will do its best to build an appropriate schema. You should therefore supply a schema whenever possible, either by using straight code or by supplying an XML document that contains the desired schema information. In this way, you can improve the performance of your application and avoid headaches.

ADO.NET Properties That Affect the Schema of Your XML Document

You can format an XML document in more than one way. As the saying goes, the devil is in the details. Look at the XML documents in Figures 12-3 and 12-4. They contain the same information, but they differ in their schema.

If you try to load data into a *DataSet* that already contains schema information, ADO.NET will ignore data that does not match up with the *DataSet* object's schema. It's therefore important that you match your *DataSet* object's schema to that of the data you want to load.

```
<?xml version="1.0" standalone="yes" ?>
- <NewDataSet>
  - <Orders>
      <OrderID>10268</OrderID>
      <CustomerID>GROSR</CustomerID>
      <OrderDate>1996-07-30T00:00:00.0000000-07:00</OrderDate>
    </Orders>
  - <Orders>
      <OrderID>10785</OrderID>
      <CustomerID>GROSR</CustomerID>
      <OrderDate>1997-12-18T00:00:00.0000000-08:00</OrderDate>
    </Orders>
  - <Order_x0020_Details>
      <OrderID>10268</OrderID>
      <ProductID>29</ProductID>
      <Quantity>10</Quantity>
      <UnitPrice>99</UnitPrice>
    </Order_x0020_Details>
  - <Order_x0020_Details>
      <OrderID>10268</OrderID>
      <ProductID>72</ProductID>
      <Quantity>4</Quantity>
      <UnitPrice>27.8</UnitPrice>
    </Order_x0020_Details>
  - <Order_x0020_Details>
      <OrderID>10785</OrderID>
      <ProductID>10</ProductID>
      <Quantity>10</Quantity>
      <UnitPrice>31</UnitPrice>
    </Order_x0020_Details>
  - <Order_x0020_Details>
      <OrderID>10785</OrderID>
      <ProductID>75</ProductID>
      <Quantity>10</Quantity>
      <UnitPrice>7.75</UnitPrice>
    </Order_x0020_Details>
  </NewDataSet>
```

Figure 12-3   An XML document that contains the order history for a customer

```
<?xml version="1.0" standalone="yes" ?>
- <MyNs:OrderHistory xmlns:MyNs="http://www.microsoft.com/MyNamespace">
  - <MyNs:Order MyNs:OrderID="10268" MyNs:CustomerID="GROSR" MyNs:OrderDate="1996-07-30T00:00:00.0000000-07:00">
      <MyNs:LineItem MyNs:OrderID="10268" MyNs:ProductID="29" MyNs:Quantity="10" MyNs:UnitPrice="99" />
      <MyNs:LineItem MyNs:OrderID="10268" MyNs:ProductID="72" MyNs:Quantity="4" MyNs:UnitPrice="27.8" />
    </MyNs:Order>
  - <MyNs:Order MyNs:OrderID="10785" MyNs:CustomerID="GROSR" MyNs:OrderDate="1997-12-18T00:00:00.0000000-08:00">
      <MyNs:LineItem MyNs:OrderID="10785" MyNs:ProductID="10" MyNs:Quantity="10" MyNs:UnitPrice="31" />
      <MyNs:LineItem MyNs:OrderID="10785" MyNs:ProductID="75" MyNs:Quantity="10" MyNs:UnitPrice="7.75" />
    </MyNs:Order>
  </MyNs:OrderHistory>
```

Figure 12-4   An XML document that contains the same order history in a different format

You can use properties of the objects within your *DataSet* to control the format that ADO.NET uses to read and write XML documents for your *DataSet*. In fact, I used the same *DataSet* object to generate both Figure 12-3 and Figure 12-4. I simply changed the values of these properties.

Names of Elements and Attributes

Notice that the names of the elements in the two documents are different. ADO.NET uses the name property for each object as the name of the corresponding element or attribute. The *DataSet* object's *DataSetName* property controls the name of the root element. Similarly, the *DataTable* object's *Table-Name* property and the *DataColumn* object's *ColumnName* property control the names that ADO.NET will use for the elements and attributes that correspond to those tables and columns.

Choosing Elements or Attributes

The two documents also differ in how they represent the order and detail data. Figure 12-3 uses elements to store this information, and Figure 12-4 uses attributes.

You can use the *DataColumn* object's *ColumnMapping* property to control this behavior. By default, the *ColumnMapping* property is set to *Element*. You can set the property to *Attribute* if you want to store the column's data in an attribute rather than an element. You can also set the *ColumnMapping* property to *Hidden* if you don't want the contents of the column to appear in your XML document.

Nesting Relational Data

In Figure 12-3, all of the line items for the orders appear at the end of the document, whereas in Figure 12-4, the line items appear within the order. You can control whether the relational data is nested by setting the *Nested* property of the *DataRelation* object. By default, the property is set to *False*, which results in the format shown in Figure 12-3. Setting the *Nested* property to *True* will cause ADO.NET to nest the relational data as shown in Figure 12-4.

Namespaces and Prefixes

The *DataSet*, *DataTable*, and *DataColumn* objects all expose *Namespace* and *Prefix* properties. Both properties contain strings and are empty by default. The *DataSet* used in Figure 12-4 has each object's *Namespace* property set to *http://www.microsoft.com/MyNamespace* and the *Prefix* property set to *MyNs*.

Caching Changes and XML Documents

Shortly after ADO 2.1 added the ability to read and write *Recordset* objects in XML format, I spoke to a number of developers who used the *Recordset* object as a middleman, pulling data from the database and storing the data as XML. They would then modify the contents of the XML document and expect that they could just read the data back into an ADO *Recordset*, which would somehow be able to submit the changes back to the database. It didn't work. Here's why.

In Chapter 6 and Chapter 10, I discussed how the ADO.NET *DataRow* object stores the current and original contents of the row so that you can submit the changes back to the database. If you change the contents of an element or an attribute in an XML document, the document will not retain the original value for that object. If you then read that modified document into an ADO.NET *DataSet*, ADO.NET will not be able to tell whether any of the rows have been modified, let alone how they've been modified.

In fact, if you modify the contents of a *DataSet* and use the *WriteXml* method to save that data in an XML document using the code shown earlier in the chapter, you'll lose the changes. By default, the *WriteXml* method writes just the current contents of the rows to the document.

ADO.NET Diffgrams

As I discussed earlier, you can supply values from the *XmlWriteMode* enumeration when calling the *WriteXml* method. One of the entries in the enumeration is *DiffGram*. If you supply this value in the call to the *XmlWriteMode* method, ADO.NET will write both the current and original contents of the *DataSet* to the document in a diffgram. Figure 12-5 shows an example of this format. You can later read this document back into your *DataSet* and submit the pending changes to your database using your *DataAdapter* objects.

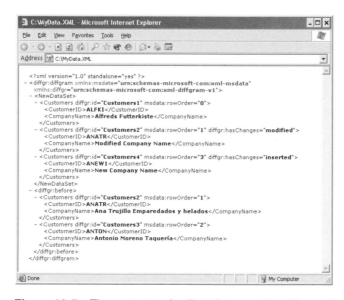

Figure 12-5   The contents of a *DataSet* stored in diffgram format

The following code snippet generates the XML document shown in Figure 12-5. The code modifies the *DataSet*—modifying one row, deleting another, and adding a third—and then displays the contents of the *DataSet* as an XML diffgram. By looking at the document in the figure, you can see how the changes that the code makes to the *DataSet* correspond to the entries in the diffgram. The code uses the *ShowXmlInIE* procedure defined in an earlier code snippet and thus requires a reference to the Microsoft Internet Controls library.

Visual Basic .NET

```
Dim strConn, strSQL As String
strConn = "Provider=SQLOLEDB;Data Source=(local)\NetSDK;" & _
          "Initial Catalog=Northwind;Trusted_Connection=Yes;"
```

```
strSQL = "SELECT TOP 3 CustomerID, CompanyName FROM Customers"
Dim da As New OleDbDataAdapter(strSQL, strConn)
Dim ds As New DataSet()
da.Fill(ds, "Customers")
Dim tbl As DataTable = ds.Tables("Customers")

'Leave the first customer unchanged.
'Modify the second customer.
tbl.Rows(1)("CompanyName") = "Modified Company Name"

'Delete the third customer.
tbl.Rows(2).Delete()

'Add a new customer.
tbl.Rows.Add(New Object() {"ANEW1", "New Company Name"})

'Write the contents to an XML document in diffgram format
'and display the document in Internet Explorer.
Dim strPathToXml As String = "C:\MyData.XML"
ds.WriteXml(strPathToXml, XmlWriteMode.DiffGram)
ShowXmlInIE(strPathToXml)
```

Visual C# .NET

```
string strConn, strSQL;
strConn = "Provider=SQLOLEDB;Data Source=(local)\\NetSDK;" +
          "Initial Catalog=Northwind;Trusted_Connection=Yes;";
strSQL = "SELECT TOP 3 CustomerID, CompanyName FROM Customers";
OleDbDataAdapter da = new OleDbDataAdapter(strSQL, strConn);
DataSet ds = new DataSet();
da.Fill(ds, "Customers");
DataTable tbl = ds.Tables["Customers"];

//Leave the first customer unchanged.
//Modify the second customer.
tbl.Rows[1]["CompanyName"] = "Modified Company Name";

//Delete the third customer.
tbl.Rows[2].Delete();

//Add a new customer.
tbl.Rows.Add(new object[] {"ANEW1", "New Company Name"});

//Write the contents to an XML document in diffgram format
//and display the document in Internet Explorer.
string strPathToXml = "C:\\MyData.XML";
ds.WriteXml(strPathToXml, XmlWriteMode.DiffGram);
ShowXmlInIE(strPathToXml);
```

DataSet + XmlDocument = XmlDataDocument

The previous code snippets used some of the *DataSet* object's XML features, but they weren't terribly exciting. If you're using these features simply to store the contents of a *DataSet* to a file and later read that data back into your *DataSet*, the fact that ADO.NET is storing the data as XML is irrelevant.

If you're really interested in working with the contents of a *DataSet* in XML format, you'll probably want to load the data into an *XmlDocument* object. This object has a *Load* method that you can use to load the contents of an XML file, so you could use the *DataSet* object's *WriteXml* method to create your XML file and then call the *XmlDocument* object's *Load* method to load the file. That might sound fine at first, but you'll have two objects storing the same data and you'll have no simple way to synchronize them. If you want to keep the objects synchronized and you change the contents of one object, you'll need to locate and modify the corresponding data in the other object. What a hassle!

Using the *XmlDataDocument* Object

The simple solution to this problem is to use an *XmlDataDocument* object. You can think of an *XmlDataDocument* as an *XmlDocument* that knows how to communicate with a *DataSet* object. The *XmlDataDocument* class is derived from the *XmlDocument* class, so an *XmlDataDocument* object exposes all the same features as an *XmlDocument*.

The *XmlDataDocument* object provides two key features. It lets you easily load the contents of a *DataSet* into an *XmlDocument*, and vice versa. The *Xml-DataDocument* also synchronizes itself with the *DataSet*. If the *DataSet* object contains data, that same data will be available through the *XmlDataDocument* object. Also, when you change the contents of one object, that change will affect the other.

Accessing Your *DataSet* as an XML Document

If you're an XML programmer who's used to working with XML documents to access data, you'll find it easy to use the *XmlDataDocument* object to access the contents of a *DataSet* through XML interfaces.

For example, you can create an *XmlDataDocument* synchronized with your *DataSet* to use XPath queries to examine the contents of the *DataSet*. The following code snippet creates an *XmlDataDocument* synchronized with a *DataSet* that contains order and line item information for a customer. The code then uses XPath queries to extract the contents of an order from the *XmlData-Document* object. It uses the *FillMyDataSet* procedure from previous code snippets and requires you to use the appropriate construct for the language to reference the *System.Xml* namespace.

Visual Basic .NET

```
'Add this line of code at the beginning of the code module.
Imports System.Xml

Dim ds As New DataSet()
FillMyDataSet(ds)
Dim xmlDataDoc As New XmlDataDocument(ds)
Dim nodOrder, nodDetail As XmlNode
Dim strXPathQuery As String
strXPathQuery = "/NewDataSet/Orders[OrderID=10268]"
nodOrder = xmlDataDoc.SelectSingleNode(strXPathQuery)
Console.WriteLine("OrderID = " & nodOrder.ChildNodes(0).InnerText)
Console.WriteLine("CustomerID = " & nodOrder.ChildNodes(0).InnerText)
Console.WriteLine("OrderDate = " & nodOrder.ChildNodes(0).InnerText)
Console.WriteLine("Line Items:")
strXPathQuery = "/NewDataSet/Order_x0020_Details[OrderID=10268]"
For Each nodDetail In xmlDataDoc.SelectNodes(strXPathQuery)
    Console.WriteLine(vbTab & "ProductID = " & _
                       nodDetail.ChildNodes(1).InnerText)
    Console.WriteLine(vbTab & "Quantity = " & _
                       nodDetail.ChildNodes(2).InnerText)
    Console.WriteLine(vbTab & "UnitPrice = " & _
                       nodDetail.ChildNodes(3).InnerText)
    Console.WriteLine()
Next nodDetail
```

Visual C# .NET

```
//Add this line of code at the beginning of the code module.
using System.Xml;

DataSet ds = new DataSet();
FillMyDataSet(ds);
XmlDataDocument xmlDataDoc = new XmlDataDocument(ds);
XmlNode nodOrder;
string strXPathQuery;
strXPathQuery = "/NewDataSet/Orders[OrderID=10268]";
nodOrder = xmlDataDoc.SelectSingleNode(strXPathQuery);
Console.WriteLine("OrderID = " + nodOrder.ChildNodes[0].InnerText);
Console.WriteLine("CustomerID = " +
                    nodOrder.ChildNodes[1].InnerText);
Console.WriteLine("OrderDate = " + nodOrder.ChildNodes[2].InnerText);
Console.WriteLine("Line Items:");
strXPathQuery = "/NewDataSet/Order_x0020_Details[OrderID=10268]";
foreach (XmlNode nodDetail in xmlDataDoc.SelectNodes(strXPathQuery))
```

(continued)

```
    {
        Console.WriteLine("\tProductID = " +
                            nodDetail.ChildNodes[1].InnerText);
        Console.WriteLine("\tQuantity = " +
                            nodDetail.ChildNodes[2].InnerText);
        Console.WriteLine("\tUnitPrice = " +
                            nodDetail.ChildNodes[3].InnerText);
        Console.WriteLine();
    }
```

Caching Updates to the XML Document

Earlier in the chapter, I pointed out that XML documents don't maintain state in a way that lets you later submit changes to your database. The *XmlDataDocument* object actually provides this functionality by synchronizing the XML document and the *DataSet*. As you modify the contents of the XML document, the *Xml-DataDocument* object modifies the corresponding data in the *DataSet* object. The *DataSet* object then has all the information it needs to submit the change to the database.

The following code snippet demonstrates this functionality. The code uses an XPath query to locate an order and modifies the contents of the child node that corresponds to the CustomerID for the order. The code then examines the contents of the corresponding *DataRow* to show that both the current and original values for the order's CustomerID are available in the *DataRow*. You can use a *DataAdapter* with the necessary updating logic to submit this change to your database.

Just before modifying the contents of the XML document, the code sets the *EnforceConstraints* property of the *DataSet* object to *False*. Without this line of code, the snippet would generate an exception. You will receive an error if you modify the contents of an XML document using the *XmlDataDocument* object if the *DataSet* associated with the *XmlDataDocument* has its *EnforceConstraints* property set to *True*.

Visual Basic .NET

```
'Add this line of code at the beginning of the code module.
Imports System.Xml

Dim ds As New DataSet()
FillMyDataSet(ds)
Dim tblOrders As DataTable = ds.Tables("Orders")
tblOrders.PrimaryKey = New DataColumn() _
                    {tblOrders.Columns("OrderID")}
Dim xmlDataDoc As New XmlDataDocument(ds)
Dim nodOrder, nodDetail As XmlNode
```

```
Dim strXPathQuery As String = "/NewDataSet/Orders[OrderID=10268]"
nodOrder = xmlDataDoc.SelectSingleNode(strXPathQuery)
ds.EnforceConstraints = False
nodOrder.ChildNodes(1).InnerText = "ALFKI"
ds.EnforceConstraints = True
Dim row As DataRow = tblOrders.Rows.Find(10268)
Console.WriteLine("OrderID = " & row("OrderID"))
Console.WriteLine(vbTab & "Current  CustomerID = " & _
                  row("CustomerID"))
Console.WriteLine(vbTab & "Original CustomerID = " & _
                  row("CustomerID", DataRowVersion.Original))
```

Visual C# .NET

```
//Add this line of code at the beginning of the code module.
using System.Xml;

DataSet ds = new DataSet();
FillMyDataSet(ds);
DataTable tblOrders = ds.Tables["Orders"];
tblOrders.PrimaryKey = new DataColumn[]
                        {tblOrders.Columns["OrderID"]};
XmlDataDocument xmlDataDoc = new XmlDataDocument(ds);
XmlNode nodOrder, nodDetail;
string strXPathQuery = "/NewDataSet/Orders[OrderID=10268]";
nodOrder = xmlDataDoc.SelectSingleNode(strXPathQuery);
ds.EnforceConstraints = false;
nodOrder.ChildNodes[1].InnerText = "ALFKI";
ds.EnforceConstraints = true;
DataRow row = tblOrders.Rows.Find(10268);
Console.WriteLine("OrderID = " + row["OrderID"]);
Console.WriteLine("\tCurrent  CustomerID = " + row["CustomerID"]);
Console.WriteLine("\tOriginal CustomerID = " +
                  row["CustomerID", DataRowVersion.Original]);
```

As you can see, the changes are now cached in the *DataSet*. We could then use a *DataAdapter* to submit those cached changes back to the database.

Retrieving XML Data from SQL Server 2000

More and more developers want to work with the results of their database queries as XML documents. To address this need, SQL Server 2000 added support for queries that return data in XML format. You could pull data into an ADO.NET *DataSet* and then use an *XmlDataDocument* object to access the data as an XML document, but this process involves more overhead than simply retrieving the data as XML.

Working with SELECT... FOR XML Queries

SQL Server 2000 added an optional FOR XML clause to queries, which lets you indicate that you want to retrieve the results of your query as XML. Let's look at a couple of examples that use this clause and discuss how you can retrieve the results of your query into an ADO.NET *DataSet* or an *XmlDocument* object.

Executing a SELECT...FOR XML Query in SQL Server Query Analyzer

The simplest way to execute such a query and examine the results is to execute the query in SQL Server Query Analyzer. Let's take a simple query that retrieves the values of the CustomerID and CompanyName columns for the first two rows in the Customers table

```
SELECT TOP 2 CustomerID, CompanyName FROM Customers
```

and append

```
" FOR XML AUTO, ELEMENTS"
```

to the query.

The FOR XML portion tells SQL Server to return the results of the query in XML format. AUTO tells SQL Server to name the element for each row in the result set after the table that is referenced in the query. ELEMENTS tells SQL Server to store the value of each column in an element. By default, SQL Server will return this information in attributes rather than elements.

Choose Results In Text from the Query menu, and then execute the query. The results will look like those shown in Figure 12-6, except that in the figure I've manually formatted the data to make it easier to read.

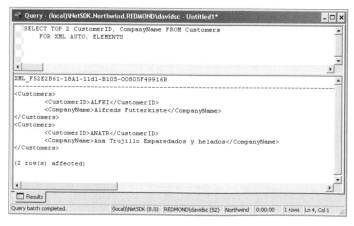

Figure 12-6 Executing a FOR XML query in SQL Server Query Analyzer

Of course, fetching XML data into SQL Server Query Analyzer isn't terribly helpful. Let's look at how to retrieve this data into more accessible objects using ADO.NET.

The *OleDbCommand* object is not designed to retrieve the results of FOR XML queries, but the *SqlCommand* object is. The *SqlCommand* object, which is part of the SQL Server Client .NET Data Provider, exposes an *ExecuteXml-Reader* method that returns an *XmlReader* object, which you can use to access the results of the query.

Loading the Results of Your Query into a *DataSet*

The ADO.NET object model makes it simple to load the results of your query into a *DataSet* object. You can use the *DataSet* object's *ReadXml* method to read the data from the *XmlReader* object into your *DataSet*. The following code snippet demonstrates this functionality:

Visual Basic .NET

```
'Add the following lines of code at the beginning of the code module.
Imports System.Data.SqlClient
Imports System.Xml


Dim strConn, strSQL As String
strConn = "Data Source=(local)\NetSDK;" & _
          "Initial Catalog=Northwind;Trusted_Connection=Yes;"
strSQL = "SELECT TOP 2 CustomerID, CompanyName FROM Customers " & _
          "FOR XML AUTO, ELEMENTS"
Dim cn As New SqlConnection(strConn)
cn.Open()
Dim cmd As New SqlCommand(strSQL, cn)
Dim rdr As XmlReader = cmd.ExecuteXmlReader
Dim ds As New DataSet()
ds.ReadXml(rdr, XmlReadMode.Fragment)
rdr.Close()
cn.Close()
Dim strPathToXml As String = "C:\MyData.XML"
ds.WriteXml(strPathToXml)
ShowXmlInIE(strPathToXml)
```

Visual C# .NET

```
//Add the following lines of code at the beginning of the code module.
using System.Data.SqlClient;
using System.Xml;


string strConn, strSQL;
strConn = "Data Source=(local)\\NetSDK;" +
          "Initial Catalog=Northwind;Trusted_Connection=Yes;";
```

(continued)

```
strSQL = "SELECT TOP 2 CustomerID, CompanyName FROM Customers " +
         "FOR XML AUTO, ELEMENTS";
SqlConnection cn = new SqlConnection(strConn);
cn.Open();
SqlCommand cmd = new SqlCommand(strSQL, cn);
XmlReader rdr = cmd.ExecuteXmlReader();
DataSet ds = new DataSet();
ds.ReadXml(rdr, XmlReadMode.Fragment);
rdr.Close();
cn.Close();
string strPathToXml = "C:\\MyData.XML";
ds.WriteXml(strPathToXml);
ShowXmlInIE(strPathToXml);
```

You might have noticed that the call to the *DataSet* object's *ReadXml* method uses the constant *Fragment* in the second parameter. The results of the query are in XML format, but the results don't compose a well-formed XML document. Take another look at Figure 12-6, and you'll see that there is no single top-level node for the results. One requirement for an XML document to be well formed is that it have a single top-level node. The results of this query are considered an XML fragment. Thus, in the call to the *ReadXml* method, we specified that the information in the *XmlReader* object is a fragment.

Loading the Results of Your Query into an *XmlDocument* Object

If the results of the query were to represent a well-formed XML document, loading the data into an *XmlDocument* object would be simple. You'd only need to call the *XmlDocument* object's *Load* method and supply the *XmlReader* object.

Instead, we need to add a top-level node to the *XmlDocument* object and then append the results of the query to that top-level node, one node at a time. The following code snippet demonstrates this technique:

Visual Basic .NET

```
'Add the following lines of code at the beginning of the code module.
Imports System.Data.SqlClient
Imports System.Xml

Dim xmlDoc As New XmlDocument()
Dim nodRoot As XmlElement
nodRoot = xmlDoc.AppendChild(xmlDoc.CreateElement("ROOT"))
Dim strConn, strSQL As String
strConn = "Data Source=(local)\NetSDK;" & _
          "Initial Catalog=Northwind;Trusted_Connection=Yes;"
strSQL = "SELECT TOP 2 CustomerID, CompanyName FROM Customers " & _
          "FOR XML AUTO, ELEMENTS"
Dim cn As New SqlConnection(strConn)
cn.Open()
```

```vb
Dim cmd As New SqlCommand(strSQL, cn)
Dim rdr As XmlReader = cmd.ExecuteXmlReader
Do Until rdr.EOF
    nodRoot.AppendChild(xmlDoc.ReadNode(rdr))
Loop
rdr.Close()
cn.Close()
Dim strPathToXml As String = "C:\MyData.XML"
xmlDoc.Save(strPathToXml)
ShowXmlInIE(strPathToXml)
```

Visual C# .NET

```csharp
//Add the following lines of code at the beginning of the code module.
using System.Data.SqlClient;
using System.Xml;

XmlDocument xmlDoc = new XmlDocument();
XmlElement nodRoot;
nodRoot = xmlDoc.AppendChild(xmlDoc.CreateElement("ROOT"));
string strConn, strSQL;
strConn = "Data Source=(local)\\NetSDK;" +
        "Initial Catalog=Northwind;Trusted_Connection=Yes;";
strSQL = "SELECT TOP 2 CustomerID, CompanyName FROM Customers " +
        "FOR XML AUTO, ELEMENTS";
SqlConnection cn = new SqlConnection(strConn);
cn.Open();
SqlCommand cmd = new SqlCommand(strSQL, cn);
XmlReader rdr = cmd.ExecuteXmlReader();

rdr.Close();
cn.Close();
string strPathToXml = "C:\\MyData.XML";
xmlDoc.Save(strPathToXml);
ShowXmlInIE(strPathToXml);
```

The SQL XML .NET Data Provider

There's an easier way to fetch XML data from SQL Server: using the SQL XML .NET Data Provider. This .NET Data Provider is not included in the .NET Framework, but you should be able to find it on the MSDN or SQL Server Web site by the time this book becomes available. Once you've installed the .NET Data Provider, you can use it in your applications by adding a reference to the *Microsoft.Data.SqlXml* namespace.

The SQL XML .NET Data Provider is designed to help .NET developers access SQL Server's XML features. This provider is very different from the other providers because SQL Server's XML features aren't traditional data access features. The initial release of the SQL XML .NET Data Provider consists of only three objects from the "traditional" .NET Data Provider (if you can refer to anything as traditional this close to the initial release of a set of technologies): the *SqlXmlCommand*, the *SqlXmlAdapter*, and the *SqlXmlParameter*.

If you want to access the results of a SQL Server XML query, you should consider using the SQL XML .NET Data Provider. Let's see why.

Using a *SqlXmlCommand* to Load Data into an *XmlDocument*

Storing the results of a SQL Server XML query into an *XmlDocument* object is simpler than using a *SqlXmlCommand*. The *SqlXmlCommand* object offers a single constructor that requires a connection string to your SQL Server database. The SQL XML .NET Data Provider doesn't talk directly to your database, but it can communicate using OLE DB. You can therefore use the same connection string that you use for an *OleDbConnection* object.

As with the *OleDbCommand* object, you use the *CommandText* property to specify the query you want to execute. You can then use the *ExecuteXml-Reader* object to execute the query and fetch the results in an *XmlReader* object.

In the previous code snippet, the XML data that the query returned was a fragment rather than a well-formed document because the results did not have a top-level node. The *SqlXmlCommand* object has a *RootTag* property that you can use to add a top-level node to the results of a query, which means that the results will constitute a well-formed document. You can thus use the *XmlDocument* object's *Load* method rather than programmatically add a top-level node to the *XmlDocument* and then add the results of the query one node at a time, as shown here:

Visual Basic .NET

```
'Add the following lines of code at the beginning of the code module.
Imports Microsoft.Data.SqlXml
Imports System.Xml

Dim strConn, strSQL As String
strConn = "Provider=SQLOLEDB;Data Source=(local)\NetSDK;" & _
          "Initial Catalog=Northwind;Trusted_Connection=Yes;"
strSQL = "SELECT TOP 2 CustomerID, CompanyName FROM Customers " & _
          "FOR XML AUTO, ELEMENTS"
Dim cmd As New SqlXmlCommand(strConn)
cmd.CommandText = strSQL
cmd.RootTag = "ROOT"
Dim xmlDoc As New XmlDocument()
Dim rdr As XmlReader = cmd.ExecuteXmlReader
xmlDoc.Load(rdr)
```

```
rdr.Close()
Dim strPathToXml As String = "C:\MyData.XML"
xmlDoc.Save(strPathToXml)
ShowXmlInIE(strPathToXml)
```

Visual C# .NET

```
//Add the following lines of code at the beginning of the code module.
using Microsoft.Data.SqlXml;
using System.Xml;

string strConn, strSQL;
strConn = "Provider=SQLOLEDB;Data Source=(local)\\NetSDK;" +
        "Initial Catalog=Northwind;Trusted_Connection=Yes;";
strSQL = "SELECT TOP 2 CustomerID, CompanyName FROM Customers " +
        "FOR XML AUTO, ELEMENTS";
SqlXmlCommand cmd = new SqlXmlCommand(strConn);
cmd.CommandText = strSQL;
cmd.RootTag - "ROOT";
XmlDocument xmlDoc = new XmlDocument();
XmlReader rdr = cmd.ExecuteXmlReader();
xmlDoc.Load(rdr);
rdr.Close();
string strPathToXml = "C:\\MyData.XML";
xmlDoc.Save(strPathToXml);
ShowXmlInIE(strPathToXml);
```

Using a *SqlXmlAdapter* to Load Data into a *DataSet*

You could use the same process to load the contents of the *XmlReader* object into a *DataSet*, but the SQL XML .NET Data Provider offers a simpler way—using the *SqlXmlAdapter*. Just as you can easily store the results of a standard SQL query in a *DataSet* using an *OleDbDataAdapter*, you can store the results of a FOR XML query in a *DataSet* using a *SqlXmlAdapter*.

You use the same code to create your *SqlXmlCommand*, and then you create a *SqlXmlAdapter*, specifying your *SqlXmlCommand* in the constructor. You can then fill your *DataSet* with the results of your query by calling the *SqlXmlAdapter* object's *Fill* method, as shown in the following code snippet:

Visual Basic .NET

```
'Add the following lines of code at the beginning of the code module.
Imports Microsoft.Data.SqlXml

Dim strConn, strSQL As String
strConn = "Provider=SQLOLEDB;Data Source=(local)\NetSDK;" & _
        "Initial Catalog=Northwind;Trusted_Connection=Yes;"
```

(continued)

```
strSQL = "SELECT TOP 2 CustomerID, CompanyName FROM Customers " & _
         "FOR XML AUTO, ELEMENTS"
Dim cmd As New SqlXmlCommand(strConn)
cmd.CommandText = strSQL
cmd.RootTag = "ROOT"
Dim da As New SqlXmlAdapter(cmd)
Dim ds As New DataSet()
da.Fill(ds)
Dim strPathToXml As String = "C:\MyData.XML"
ds.WriteXml(strPathToXml)
ShowXmlInIE(strPathToXml)
```

Visual C# .NET

```
//Add the following lines of code at the beginning of the code module.
using Microsoft.Data.SqlXml;

string strConn, strSQL;
strConn = "Provider=SQLOLEDB;Data Source=(local)\\NetSDK;" +
          "Initial Catalog=Northwind;Trusted_Connection=Yes;";
strSQL = "SELECT TOP 2 CustomerID, CompanyName FROM Customers " +
         "FOR XML AUTO, ELEMENTS";
SqlXmlCommand cmd = new SqlXmlCommand(strConn);
cmd.CommandText = strSQL;
cmd.RootTag = "ROOT";
Dim da As New SqlXmlAdapter(cmd)
Dim ds As New DataSet()
da.Fill(ds)
string strPathToXml = "C:\\MyData.XML";
ds.WriteXml(strPathToXml);
ShowXmlInIE(strPathToXml);
```

Working with Template Queries

To give you greater control over the format of the results of your queries, the SQL XML .NET Data Provider supports XML template queries. Basically, a template query is an XML document that contains queries. When you execute such a query, the SQL XML .NET Data Provider combines the XML in the query along with the results of your query.

Let's look at an example of a template query. The template query that follows contains two SELECT...FOR XML queries that retrieve order and line item information for a particular customer:

```
<?xml version="1.0" encoding="utf-8" ?>
<ROOT xmlns:sql='urn:schemas-microsoft-com:xml-sql'>
  <sql:query>
    SELECT OrderID, CustomerID, OrderDate FROM Orders
        WHERE CustomerID = 'GROSR'
```

```
        FOR XML AUTO, ELEMENTS
  </sql:query>
  <sql:query>
    SELECT OrderID, ProductID, Quantity, UnitPrice
        FROM [Order Details] WHERE OrderID IN
        (SELECT OrderID FROM Orders WHERE CustomerID = 'GROSR')
        FOR XML AUTO, ELEMENTS
  </sql:query>
</ROOT>
```

The query itself is an XML document. The SQL XML .NET Data Provider examines the elements that reside in the *sql* namespace and executes the text in the query elements. The rest of the elements are treated simply as XML and appear in the results as such.

You can execute this query using the SQL XML .NET Data Provider, and you'll receive the XML document shown in Figure 12-7. As you can see in the figure, the root element in the template query appears in the results.

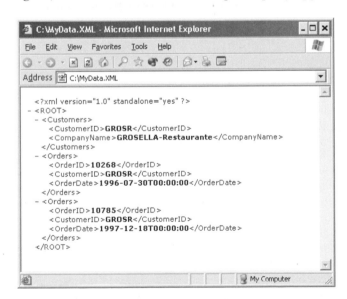

Figure 12-7   The results of an XML template query

Executing a Template Query Using a *SqlXmlCommand*

To tell the *SqlXmlCommand* object that you're working with a template query using the *SqlXmlCommand* object, you set the *SqlXmlCommand* object's *CommandType* property to the appropriate value in the *SqlXmlCommandType* enumeration. If you supply the path to the file that contains your query, set the *CommandType* property to *TemplateFile*. If, instead, you supply the actual text of the query, you should set the *CommandType* property to *Template*.

You can then execute the query to store the results in an XML document or a *DataSet*, as shown in the previous examples. The following code snippet stores the results in a *DataSet*:

Visual Basic .NET

```
'Add the following lines of code at the beginning of the code module.
Imports Microsoft.Data.SqlXml

Dim strPathToResults As String = "C:\MyResults.XML"
Dim strPathToQuery As String = "C:\MyTemplateQuery.XML"
Dim strConn As String = "Provider=SQLOLEDB;" & _
                        "Data Source=(local)\NetSDK;" & _
                        "Initial Catalog=Northwind;" & _
                        "Trusted_Connection=Yes;"
Dim cmd As New SqlXmlCommand(strConn)
cmd.CommandText = strPathToQuery
cmd.CommandType = SqlXmlCommandType.TemplateFile
Dim ds As New DataSet()
Dim da As New SqlXmlAdapter(cmd)
da.Fill(ds)
ds.WriteXml(strPathToResults)
ShowXmlInIE(strPathToResults)
```

Visual C# .NET

```
//Add the following lines of code at the beginning of the code module.
using Microsoft.Data.SqlXml;

string strPathToResults = "C:\\MyResults.XML";
string strPathToQuery = "C:\\MyTemplateQuery.XML";
string strConn = "Provider=SQLOLEDB;Data Source=(local)\\NetSDK;" +
                 "Initial Catalog=Northwind;Trusted_Connection=Yes;";
SqlXmlCommand cmd = new SqlXmlCommand(strConn);
cmd.CommandText = strPathToQuery;
cmd.CommandType = SqlXmlCommandType.TemplateFile;
DataSet ds = new DataSet();
SqlXmlAdapter da = new SqlXmlAdapter(cmd);
da.Fill(ds);
ds.WriteXml(strPathToResults);
ShowXmlInIE(strPathToResults);
```

Parameterized Template Queries

You can also add parameters to template queries. The following template query retrieves the same information—orders and line item information for a customer—except the query contains a parameter marker for the value of the CustomerID column rather than specifies that value explicitly:

```xml
<?xml version="1.0" encoding="utf-8" ?>
<ROOT xmlns:sql='urn:schemas-microsoft-com:xml-sql'>
  <sql:header>
    <sql:param name="CustomerID"/>
  </sql:header>
  <sql:query>
    SELECT OrderID, CustomerID, OrderDate FROM Orders
        WHERE CustomerID = @CustomerID
        FOR XML AUTO, ELEMENTS
  </sql:query>
  <sql:query>
    SELECT OrderID, ProductID, Quantity, UnitPrice
        FROM [Order Details] WHERE OrderID IN
        (SELECT OrderID FROM Orders WHERE CustomerID = @CustomerID)
        FOR XML AUTO, ELEMENTS
  </sql:query>
</ROOT>
```

To set the value of this parameter programmatically, you use the *SqlXml-Parameter* object. You can't create a *SqlXmlParameter* using the *New* keyword. The only way to create one is to use the *CreateParameter* method of the *Sql-Command* object. Once you have your *SqlXmlParameter* object, you set its *Name* and *Value* properties accordingly before executing your query, as shown in the following code snippet:

Visual Basic .NET

```vbnet
Dim cmd As SqlXmlCommand
⋮
Dim param As SqlXmlParameter = cmd.CreateParameter()
param.Name = "@CustomerID"
param.Value = "GROSR"
```

Visual C# .NET

```csharp
SqlXmlCommand cmd;
⋮
SqlXmlParameter param = cmd.CreateParameter();
param.Name = "@CustomerID";
param.Value = "GROSR";
```

Working with XPath Queries

If we had an XML document that contained all the orders in the Northwind database, we could use the following XPath query to examine just the orders for the customer whose CustomerID is GROSR:

```
Orders[CustomerID='GROSR']
```

If you look at the *SqlXmlCommandType* enumeration, you'll find an *XPath* entry. You could set the *CommandType* property of a *SqlXmlCommand* to *XPath*, supply the XPath query in the *CommandText*, and then execute the query, but doing so would throw an exception stating that the query is invalid.

The SQL Server database engine doesn't really know what to do with an XPath query. The SQL XML .NET Data Provider supports XPath queries, but what it actually does is translate XPath queries into SELECT...FOR XML queries. Although you can interpret the query and perform this translation, the SQL XML .NET Data Provider needs a little help.

Adding Schema Information

You can help the SQL XML .NET Data Provider translate this XPath query by supplying an XML schema that defines the tables and columns in your database to include in the query as well as the structure for the results, as shown here:

```xml
<?xml version="1.0" ?>
<xsd:schema xmlns:xsd="http://www.w3.org/2001/XMLSchema"
            xmlns:sql="urn:schemas-microsoft-com:mapping-schema">
  <xsd:annotation>
    <xsd:appinfo>
      <sql:relationship name="relOrdersDetails"
                        parent="Orders"
                        parent-key="OrderID"
                        child="[Order Details]"
                        child-key="OrderID" />
    </xsd:appinfo>
  </xsd:annotation>
  <xsd:element name="Orders">
    <xsd:complexType>
      <xsd:sequence>
        <xsd:element name="OrderID" type="xsd:int" />
        <xsd:element name="CustomerID" type="xsd:string" />
        <xsd:element name="OrderDate" type="xsd:dateTime"
                    sql:datatype="datetime" />
        <xsd:element name="Order_x0020_Details"
                    sql:relation="[Order Details]"
                    sql:relationship="relOrdersDetails">
          <xsd:complexType>
            <xsd:sequence>
              <xsd:element name="ProductID" type="xsd:int" />
              <xsd:element name="Quantity" type="xsd:int" />
              <xsd:element name="UnitPrice" type="xsd:decimal" />
            </xsd:sequence>
          </xsd:complexType>
        </xsd:element>
      </xsd:sequence>
    </xsd:complexType>
  </xsd:element>
</xsd:schema>
```

The schema has entries that reference tables and columns, that relate data from two tables (*sql:relationship*), and that help the SQL XML .NET Data Provider understand the SQL data type for a column (*sql:datatype*). However, this schema demonstrates just a fraction of the features that you can use in an XML schema file with the SQL XML .NET Data Provider. For more information on all of the features, see the "Using Annotations in XSD Schemas" topic in the documentation for SQL XML 3.

Once you've created your schema file, you set the *SchemaPath* property of your *SqlXmlCommand* object to the file that contains this schema information. The following code snippet executes the XPath query described earlier to retrieve the orders and line items for a particular customer using this schema. The code then stores the results of the query in an *XmlDocument* object.

Visual Basic .NET

```
'Add the following lines of code at the beginning of the code module.
Imports Microsoft.Data.SqlXml
Imports System.Xml

Dim strPathToResults As String = "C:\MyResults.XML"
Dim strPathToSchema As String = "C:\MySchema.XSD"
Dim strConn As String = "Provider=SQLOLEDB;" & _
                        "Data Source=(local)\NetSDK;" & _
                        "Initial Catalog=Northwind;" & _
                        "Trusted_Connection=Yes;"
Dim cmd As New SqlXmlCommand(strConn)
cmd.SchemaPath = strPathToSchema
cmd.CommandText = "Orders[CustomerID='GROSR']"
cmd.CommandType = SqlXmlCommandType.XPath
Dim rdr As XmlReader = cmd.ExecuteXmlReader()
Dim xmlDoc As New XmlDocument()
xmlDoc.Load(rdr)
rdr.Close()
xmlDoc.Save(strPathToResults)
ShowXmlInIE(strPathToResults)
```

Visual C# .NET

```
//Add the following lines of code at the beginning of the code module.
using Microsoft.Data.SqlXml;
using System.Xml;

string strPathToResults = "C:\\MyResults.XML";
string strPathToSchema = "C:\\MySchema.XSD";
string strConn = "Provider=SQLOLEDB;Data Source=(local)\\NetSDK;" +
                "Initial Catalog=Northwind;Trusted_Connection=Yes;";
SqlXmlCommand cmd = new SqlXmlCommand(strConn);
```

(continued)

```
cmd.SchemaPath = strPathToSchema;
cmd.CommandText = "Orders[CustomerID='GROSR']";
cmd.CommandType = SqlXmlCommandType.XPath;
XmlReader rdr = cmd.ExecuteXmlReader();
XmlDocument xmlDoc = new XmlDocument();
xmlDoc.Load(rdr);
rdr.Close();
xmlDoc.Save(strPathToResults);
ShowXmlInIE(strPathToResults);
```

Applying an XSLT Transform

Earlier in the chapter, I said that you could format an XML document in more than one way and that it's possible for two XML documents to contain the same data but differ only in their schema. You can use a companion technology called XSLT to transform the structure of your XML documents.

XSLT stands for Extensible Stylesheet Language Transformations. You can think of an XSLT transform as an XML document that contains a set of instructions describing how to transform the contents of another XML document. XLST transforms are handy if you want to change the structure of your document. You can also use an XSLT transform to translate XML into HTML.

If you have an XSLT transform and you want to apply it to the results of your SQL XML query, you can set the *XslPath* property of the *SqlXmlCommand* object to a string that contains the path to your XSLT transform.

We'll touch on this feature again shortly.

Submitting Updates

The SQL XML .NET Data Provider lets you submit updates to your database. The *SqlXmlAdapter* object has an *Update* method that you can use to submit the changes stored in your *DataSet* to your database. If you've read Chapter 10, you're probably not surprised to see an *Update* method on a *DataAdapter*.

However, the *SqlXmlAdapter* doesn't handle updating in the same way that other *DataAdapter* objects do. Most *DataAdapter* objects (such as the *OleDbDataAdapter*, the *SqlDataAdapter*, and the *OdbcDataAdapter*) expose properties that contain *Command* objects that contain the logic necessary to submit changes to your database. These *Command* objects generally contain a number of parameters that are bound to columns in the *DataTable*. When you call the *Update* method on most *DataAdapter* objects, the *DataAdapter* looks at the rows in a particular *DataTable*. Each time the *DataAdapter* discovers a modified row, it uses the appropriate *Command* object to submit the pending change before calling the *DataRow* object's *AcceptChanges* method.

The *SqlXmlAdapter* takes a different approach. Earlier in the chapter, you learned a little about diffgrams. Figure 12-5 shows the contents of a diffgram. Rather than locating pending changes in a *DataSet* by looping through *DataRow* objects one row at a time, the *SqlXmlAdapter* processes the pending changes in a *DataSet* by generating a diffgram for the *DataSet*. The SQL XML .NET Data Provider then processes the entire diffgram, creating a complex batch query to submit all the changes to your database at once.

If you look at the contents of the diffgram in Figure 12-5, you can probably figure out how to generate a series of INSERT, UPDATE, and DELETE queries to submit the pending changes to your database. The SQL XML .NET Data Provider cannot generate those queries without a little help.

Remember the annotated XML schema file that we used to help the SQL XML .NET Data Provider translate an XPath query into a SQL query? Different challenge, same solution. When we were working with the XPath query, we set the *SchemaPath* property of the *SqlXmlCommand* to the path to our schema file. You can use the *SqlXmlAdapter* to submit changes to your database by making sure that the *SqlXmlAdapter* object's *SqlXmlCommand* object has a schema file that contains all the necessary table and column information for the data in the diffgram.

In fact, you can submit the update by using a *SqlXmlCommand* whose *CommandText* property is set to *DiffGram*. You simply use the *DataSet* object's *WriteXml* method to create your diffgram. Then you set up a *SqlXmlCommand* to use that diffgram and a schema file and...*voilà*! The following code snippet demonstrates this functionality:

Visual Basic .NET

```
'Add the following lines of code at the beginning of the code module.
Imports Microsoft.Data.SqlXml
Imports System.Xml
Imports System.IO

Dim strConn As String = "Provider=SQLOLEDB;" & _
                        "Data Source=(local)\NetSDK;" & _
                        "Initial Catalog=Northwind;" & _
                        "Trusted_Connection=Yes;"
Dim cmd As New SqlXmlCommand(strConn)
Dim strPathToSchema As String = "C:\MySchema.XSD"
cmd.SchemaPath = strPathToSchema
cmd.CommandText = "Orders[CustomerID='GROSR']"
cmd.CommandType = SqlXmlCommandType.XPath
cmd.RootTag = "ROOT"
Dim da As New SqlXmlAdapter(cmd)
Dim ds As New DataSet()
da.Fill(ds)
```

(continued)

```
ds.Tables("Orders").Rows(0)("CustomerID") = "ALFKI"
ds.Tables("Orders").Rows(1)("CustomerID") = "ALFKI"

Dim strPathToDiffGram As String = "C:\MyDiffGram.XML"
ds.WriteXml(strPathToDiffGram, XmlWriteMode.DiffGram)
cmd = New SqlXmlCommand(strConn)
cmd.SchemaPath = strPathToSchema
cmd.CommandType = SqlXmlCommandType.DiffGram
cmd.CommandStream = New FileStream(strPathToDiffGram, _
                                   FileMode.Open, FileAccess.Read)
cmd.ExecuteNonQuery()

'Undo the changes.
Dim strSQL As String = "UPDATE Orders SET CustomerID = 'GROSR' " & _
                       "WHERE OrderID = 10268 OR OrderID = 10785"
cmd = New SqlXmlCommand(strConn)
cmd.CommandText = strSQL
cmd.CommandType = SqlXmlCommandType.Sql
cmd.ExecuteNonQuery()
```

Visual C# .NET

```
//Add the following lines of code at the beginning of the code module.
using Microsoft.Data.SqlXml;
using System.Xml;
using System.IO;

string strConn = "Provider=SQLOLEDB;Data Source=(local)\\NetSDK;" +
                 "Initial Catalog=Northwind;Trusted_Connection=Yes;";
SqlXmlCommand cmd = new SqlXmlCommand(strConn);
string strPathToSchema = "C:\\MySchema.XSD";
cmd.SchemaPath = strPathToSchema;
cmd.CommandText = "Orders[CustomerID='GROSR']";
cmd.CommandType = SqlXmlCommandType.XPath;
cmd.RootTag = "ROOT";
SqlXmlAdapter da = new SqlXmlAdapter(cmd);
DataSet ds = new DataSet();
da.Fill(ds);

ds.Tables["Orders"].Rows[0]["CustomerID"] = "ALFKI";
ds.Tables["Orders"].Rows[1]["CustomerID"] = "ALFKI";

string strPathToDiffGram = "C:\\MyDiffGram.XML";
ds.WriteXml(strPathToDiffGram, XmlWriteMode.DiffGram);
cmd = new SqlXmlCommand(strConn);
cmd.SchemaPath = strPathToSchema;
cmd.CommandType = SqlXmlCommandType.DiffGram;
cmd.CommandStream = new FileStream(strPathToDiffGram, FileMode.Open,
                                   FileAccess.Read);
```

```
cmd.ExecuteNonQuery();

//Undo the changes.
string strSQL  = "UPDATE Orders SET CustomerID = 'GROSR' " +
                 "WHERE OrderID = 10268 OR OrderID = 10785";
cmd = new SqlXmlCommand(strConn);
cmd.CommandText = strSQL;
cmd.CommandType = SqlXmlCommandType.Sql;
cmd.ExecuteNonQuery();
```

> **Note**   The code also executes an action query to undo the changes
> to the database. This ensures that you can run the code snippet multi-
> ple times. To verify that the *SqlXmlCommand* submitted the changes
> stored in the diffgram, you can set a breakpoint so that you can pause
> the execution of the code before the execution of this last query.

The *SqlXmlCommand* Object's Updating Logic

Before we move on, I'd like to show you some of the logic that the *SqlXml-
Command* object generates to submit changes to your database. This informa-
tion might help you better understand the benefits and drawbacks of using the
SQL XML .NET Data Provider to submit changes.

When the previous code snippet called the *SqlXmlCommand* object's *Exe-
cuteNonQuery* method to submit the changes stored in the diffgram, the SQL
XML .NET Data Provider generated and submitted the following batch query to
SQL Server:

```
SET XACT_ABORT ON
BEGIN TRAN
DECLARE @eip INT, @r__ int, @e__ int
SET @eip = 0

UPDATE Orders SET CustomerID=N'ALFKI' WHERE ( OrderID-10268 )  AND
( CustomerID=N'GROSR' )  AND  ( OrderDate=N'1996-07-30 00:00:00' ) ;
SELECT @e__ = @@ERROR, @r__ = @@ROWCOUNT
 IF (@e__ != 0 OR @r__ != 1) SET @eip = 1
 IF (@r__ > 1) RAISERROR ( N'SQLOLEDB Error Description: Ambiguous update,
               unique identifier required  Transaction aborted ', 16, 1)
 ELSE IF (@r__ < 1) RAISERROR ( N'SQLOLEDB Error Description: Empty update,
               no updatable rows found  Transaction aborted ', 16, 1)

UPDATE Orders SET CustomerID=N'ALFKI' WHERE ( OrderID=10785 )  AND
( CustomerID=N'GROSR' )  AND  ( OrderDate=N'1997-12-18 00:00:00' ) ;
SELECT @e__ = @@ERROR, @r__ = @@ROWCOUNT
```

(continued)

```
IF (@e__ != 0 OR @r__ != 1) SET @eip = 1
IF (@r__ > 1) RAISERROR ( N'SQLOLEDB Error Description: Ambiguous update,
                unique identifier required  Transaction aborted ', 16, 1)
ELSE IF (@r__ < 1) RAISERROR ( N'SQLOLEDB Error Description: Empty update,
                no updatable rows found  Transaction aborted ', 16, 1)

IF (@eip != 0) ROLLBACK ELSE COMMIT
SET XACT_ABORT OFF
```

The batch query starts off by telling SQL Server to abort the current transaction if it raises an error, starts a transaction, and defines some variables to store data. Once this preparation work is done, the code executes the first UPDATE query and then pulls data into variables to determine whether an error occurred and how many rows the query affected. If the query affected one row and did not generate an error, the code continues, issuing action queries and determining whether the updates succeeded. After issuing all the action queries, the code commits the work in the transaction if all the updates succeeded and turns off the setting that tells SQL Server to abort transactions in case of an error.

This is impressive and well-designed code. It's a large and complex batch of queries, but this query minimizes the number of round-trips required to submit changes and determine the success or failure of those changes. If you're looking to provide similar functionality in your application by generating your own queries, this is a great example to reference.

Although it's not important that you understand the individual queries in this batch, you must understand the following points if you're going to rely on this provider to submit changes:

- The SQL XML .NET Data Provider wraps this batch of updates in a transaction and will roll back the transaction if it detects that an error occurred or if any individual query reports that it did not update only one row. This means that you'll submit either all of the updates or none of them.

- The SQL XML .NET Data Provider does not retrieve data from your database while submitting changes. You will not see any new auto-increment or timestamp values after you submit your updates.

- If you submit changes to your database using the *SqlXmlAdapter* object's *Update* method, the *SqlXmlAdapter* will call your *DataSet* object's *AcceptChanges* method after successfully submitting your changes. The *SqlXmlAdapter* does not call the *AcceptChanges* method on only the *DataTable* objects that appear in the schema file.

A Simple ADO.NET and XML Sample

We've looked at snippets of code that demonstrate isolated features. Now it's time to put some of these features into a small sample application that shows off the power of XML and of ADO.NET's XML features. To do this, I'll pull together functionality from many of the previous code snippets.

The sample will use parameterized queries to retrieve an order history for a particular customer. Before you roll your eyes, note that we're going to collect more information in this set of queries. The queries will retrieve data from four related tables: Customers, Orders, Order Details, and Products. In this way, our order history will be more robust. We'll see company names as well as the names of the products ordered.

The sample turns the results of the queries into XML, uses an XSLT transformation to turn that XML data into HTML, and then displays this HTML data in Internet Explorer, as shown in Figure 12-8.

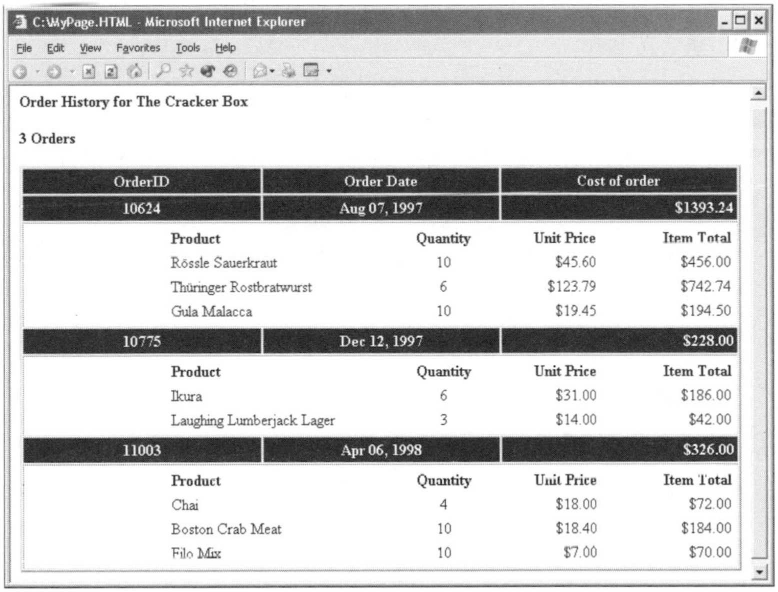

Figure 12-8   The Web page generated by the XML sample application

The sample is a console application that launches an instance of Internet Explorer. Using a console application as a starting point makes the sample less flashy but easier to use as a resource. You can apply the same logic in two scenarios in which turning the results of queries into HTML can be extremely helpful: building Web applications and generating reports. I think that these are the most compelling uses of ADO.NET's XML features.

Keep in mind that I'm still a relative novice when it comes to HTML and XSLT. I built a very simple Web page using Microsoft FrontPage, and then I compared the structure of that page's HTML to the structure of the XML document I created using ADO.NET, which contained my date. I then relied on a book on XSLT to figure out how to build a transform to get from point X to point H.

I point out my lack of expertise for two reasons:

- To show that even a database programmer who doesn't have a strong XML background can learn enough XSLT to transform XML into HTML

- To apologize for the lack of style in the Web page

Two Paths, One Destination

Actually, I lied. I didn't create a sample. I created two of them. Both samples rely on the same XSLT transform and produce the same HTML, but they differ in how they generate an XML document that contains data from the standard Northwind database.

The first sample, called DataSetToHTML, connects to the local .NET SDK MSDE Northwind database using the OLE DB .NET Data Provider. The sample uses standard SQL queries and stores the results in a *DataSet*. In order to access this data as an XML document to perform the XSLT transform and generate HTML, the sample creates an *XmlDataDocument* object linked to the *DataSet*.

The second sample, called SqlXmlToHTML, relies on the SQL XML .NET Data Provider and an XML template query that uses the same Northwind tables but uses the FOR XML syntax. The *SqlXmlCommand* object that this sample uses has its *XslPath* property set to the location of the XSLT transform.

ADO.NET and XML: A Happy Couple

ADO.NET offers robust support for XML. ADO.NET's XML features allow programmers to easily move back and forth between traditional data access objects and XML objects. You can use the features of the *DataSet* object to read and write data and/or schema information as XML. The *XmlDataSet* object allows you to easily access the contents of a *DataSet* as XML. The SQL XML .NET Data Provider helps you use SQL Server 2000's XML features to retrieve the results of queries in XML format to files, XML documents, and *DataSet* objects.

Questions That Should Be Asked More Frequently

Q. The *DataSet*, *DataTable*, and *DataColumn* objects give me some flexibility in the structure of the XML document I create in the *WriteXml* method, but I need even more control. I want to add a processing instruction to my XML that references my XSLT transformation. How do I do this?

A. You can use the *XmlDataDocument* object to access the contents of the *DataSet* as an *XmlDocument*. You set the *EnforceConstraints* property of the *DataSet* to *False* and then use the *XmlDataDocument* object to customize the structure of your XML document as you see fit. In this case, you can use the *CreateProcessingInstruction* method of the *XmlDataDocument* object, as shown in the following code snippet. Once you're done, you call the *XmlDataDocument* object's *Save* method to create your file.

Visual Basic .NET

```
Dim ds As New DataSet()
⋮
ds.EnforceConstraints = False
Dim xmlDoc As New XmlDataDocument(ds)
Dim strPI as String = "type='text/xsl' href='MyTransform.XSLT'"
Dim xmlPI as XmlProcessingInstruction
xmlPI = xmlDoc.CreateProcessingInstruction("xml-stylesheet", strPI)
xmlDoc.InsertBefore(xmlPI, xmlDoc.DocumentElement)
Dim strPathToXmlFile As String = "C:\MyData.XML"
xmlDoc.Save(strPathToXmlFile)
```

Visual C# .NET

```
DataSet ds = new DataSet();
⋮
ds.EnforceConstraints = false;
XmlDataDocument xmlDoc = new XmlDataDocument(ds);
string strPI = "type='text/xsl' href='MyTransform.XSLT'";
XmlProcessingInstruction xmlPI;
xmlPI = xmlDoc.CreateProcessingInstruction("xml-stylesheet", strPI);
xmlDoc.InsertBefore(xmlPI, xmlDoc.DocumentElement);
string strPathToXmlFile = "C:\\MyData.XML";
xmlDoc.Save(strPathToXmlFile);
```

Q. I want to retrieve the results of my queries as XML, but I'm calling stored procedures that already exist. Is there anything I can do to fetch the results as XML?

A. You can ask the SQL XML .NET Data Provider to format the results of the query as XML by setting the *SqlXmlCommand* object's *Client-SideXml* property to *True*. The following code snippet demonstrates this functionality:

Visual Basic .NET

```
Dim strConn, strSQL As String
strConn = "Provider=SQLOLEDB;Data Source=(local)\NetSDK;" & _
          "Initial Catalog=Northwind;Trusted_Connection=Yes;"
strSQL = "EXEC CustOrdersOrders 'ALFKI' FOR XML NESTED"
Dim cmd As New SqlXmlCommand(strConn)
cmd.CommandText = strSQL
cmd.ClientSideXml = True
cmd.RootTag = "ROOT"

Dim xmlDoc As New XmlDocument()
Dim xmlRdr As XmlReader = cmd.ExecuteXmlReader
xmlDoc.Load(xmlRdr)
xmlRdr.Close
Console.WriteLine(xmlDoc.InnerXml)
```

Visual C# .NET

```
string strConn, strSQL;
strConn = "Provider=SQLOLEDB;Data Source=(local)\\NetSDK;" +
          "Initial Catalog=Northwind;Trusted_Connection=Yes;";
strSQL = "EXEC CustOrdersOrders 'ALFKI' FOR XML NESTED";
SqlXmlCommand cmd = new SqlXmlCommand(strConn);
cmd.CommandText = strSQL;
cmd.ClientSideXml = true;
cmd.RootTag = "ROOT";

XmlDocument xmlDoc = new XmlDocument();
XmlReader xmlRdr = cmd.ExecuteXmlReader();
xmlDoc.Load(xmlRdr);
xmlRdr.Close();
Console.WriteLine(xmlDoc.InnerXml);
```

For more information on using client-side XML formatting with the SQL XML .NET Data Provider, see the "Comparing Client-Side XML Formatting to Server-Side XML Formatting" topic in the SQL XML 3 help file.

Part IV

Building Effective Applications with ADO.NET

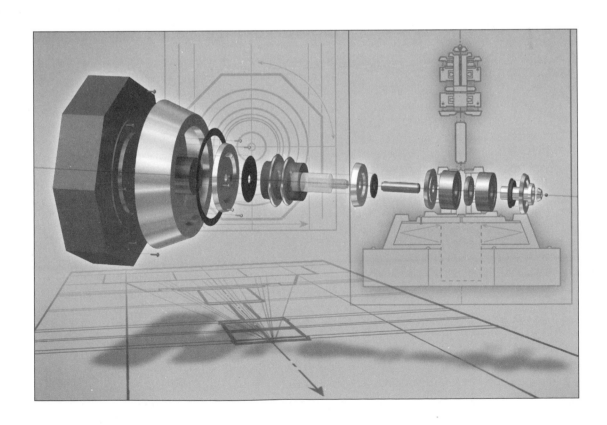

13

Building Effective Windows-Based Applications

You should now feel comfortable working with the various objects in the ADO.NET object model. Need to create a *DataSet* and store the results of a query in a *DataTable* using a *DataAdapter*? No problem. Need to add a *DataRelation* so that you can navigate between parent and child data in two related *DataTable* objects? Child's play. Need to create the logic required to submit changes back to the database? Piece of cake.

Although these skills are important, they're still not enough to build an application that allows a user to view and modify the contents of a database. You also need to build a user interface.

In this chapter, we'll use the knowledge you gained from previous chapters to discuss building effective Windows-based applications. In the first part of the chapter, we'll look at the stages of building a sample application that is similar to the one we created in Chapter 2 using the Data Form Wizard. Along the way, I'll talk about how you can use data binding to save time while you're developing the user interface for your application. We'll also examine different strategies for updating and connection strategies. Finally I'll discuss different ways to work with binary large object (BLOB) data in a Windows-based application.

Building a User Interface Quickly Using Data Binding

So you want to build a user interface. You can write code that retrieves data from your database and submits changes, but you need to display data on a form and allow users to interact with that data by adding, modifying, and deleting rows of data. You also want to develop this user interface quickly.

Obviously, you can write code to read the contents of a *DataRow* and display that data in TextBox controls on a form. You can also write code that gives the user the ability to navigate through different rows of data, as well as the ability to add, modify, and delete rows in your *DataSet*. If you wrote a series of applications that all shared these same basic goals but really only differed in the type of data they handled, you'd find yourself writing the same basic routines in each application.

The Windows Forms package that's part of the Microsoft .NET Framework includes support for data binding. Data binding offers functionality similar to the routines I described in earlier chapters for displaying the contents of a *DataSet* in various controls and includes features that allow users to modify that data. In short, data binding allows you to build data access applications more quickly and easily by reducing the amount of code required to develop the user interface.

> **Note**   Data binding actually supports more than just *DataSet* objects. You can bind controls to ADO.NET structures such as *DataSet* objects and *DataTable* objects, to arrays, or to any object that implements the IList interface. Because this book is dedicated to ADO.NET, I'll focus on using data binding with ADO.NET structures. For more information on using data binding with other structures, see the corresponding documentation in the .NET Framework SDK.

Enough preliminary talk about data binding. Let's use data binding to develop a fairly simple order entry application. The application, shown in Figure 13-1, allows users to view and modify orders for a customer. We'll build the application in phases to demonstrate the various data binding features needed to develop an application.

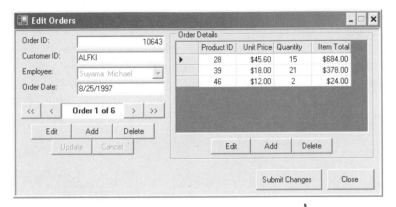

Figure 13-1   A sample order entry application

On this book's companion CD, you'll find the completed version of the sample application as well as a version corresponding to each step described in this chapter. You'll find versions of the application built in Microsoft Visual Basic .NET as well as Microsoft Visual C# .NET.

> **Note**   The sample application is designed to work with the sample Northwind database. In Chapter 3, you'll find instructions on how to install the version of the Microsoft Desktop Engine (MSDE) that's included with the .NET Framework SDK. The instructions also explain how to install the sample databases that accompany the .NET Framework SDK. The Northwind database is one of the sample databases installed.

Step 1: Creating Your *DataAdapter* and *DataSet*

Because this is a Windows-based application, you start by creating a new Windows project in your language of choice. Name the application *Chapter13*. Rename the default form *frmEditOrders*, and change the caption to *Edit Orders*. In the sample application, I've set the *MaximizeBox* property on the form to *False* and set the *FormBorderStyle* property to *Fixed3D*. These settings prevent the user from resizing the form. Setting these properties isn't really necessary, but I don't like having users resize a form that wasn't designed to be resized.

The application will display order information for a particular customer, so we'll need a *DataAdapter* to fetch order information from the Northwind database. On the Data tab of the Toolbox, select an *OleDbDataAdapter* and drag it onto the form. This will launch the Data Adapter Configuration Wizard, which is described in detail in Chapter 5.

On the Connection screen of the wizard, select an existing connection to the Northwind database. If one does not exist, use the New Connection button to create one. On the Query Type screen, stick with the Use SQL Statements default option. Then, on the SQL Statement screen, enter the following SQL statement:

```
SELECT OrderID, CustomerID, EmployeeID, OrderDate
    FROM Orders WHERE CustomerID = ?
```

I chose this query for two reasons. First, we're creating a very basic application, so I want to limit the number of columns we retrieve. Second, rather than retrieve all orders from the database, I want to retrieve only the orders for a particular customer. Remember that your applications will run faster if you limit the amount of data your queries return.

When you exit the wizard, you'll see an *OleDbDataAdapter* and an *OleDb-Connection* object in the components tray for your form. Rename them *daOrders* and *cnNorthwind*, respectively. Right-click in the components tray, and choose Generate Dataset from the shortcut menu. In the resulting dialog box, change the name of the new *DataSet* class to *xsdChapter13* and then click OK. You'll see a new item in Solution Explorer—xsdChapter13.xsd—and an instance of the *DataSet* class in the components tray. Rename this instance *dsChapter13*.

The OrderID column in the Orders table is an autoincrement column. In Chapter 6, I recommended setting both the *AutoIncrementSeed* and *AutoIncrementStep* properties to −1 on autoincrement columns in a *DataSet*. Let's set these properties on the OrderID column in the strongly typed *DataSet* class that we just created. Double-click on the strongly typed *DataSet* schema file in Solution Explorer (xsdChapter13.xsd). Select the OrderID column. Set the *AutoIncrementSeed* and *AutoIncrementStep* properties to −1. Then close the window and save the changes.

Step 2: Adding Bound Textboxes

You now have a *DataAdapter* and a *DataSet* for your form. Let's add some TextBox controls to the form that we'll use to display data for a particular order. To make the user interface more intuitive, we'll also add a label for each TextBox to indicate what type of data the TextBox contains.

First let's add a label and the TextBox for the OrderID column. From the Toolbox, drag a Label onto the form. Set the Label's name to *lblOrderID* and its *Text* property to *Order ID:*. Now click the TextBox on the Toolbox and drag it onto the form. Change its name to *txtOrderID*, and clear its *Text* property.

At this point, we still have a simple TextBox. To bind the TextBox to the OrderID column in the *DataSet*, go to the Properties window. Look for the section marked *(DataBindings)*. This section appears in the Data category if you have the properties arranged by category, the default setting. I prefer sorting the properties alphabetically, in which case the section will appear close to the top of the list. We want the contents of the OrderID column bound to the *Text* property for the control. Expand the section, select the entry marked *Text*, and click the down arrow to show the list of available columns. You'll see the *DataSet* in the list. Expand the *DataSet*, and you'll see the list of *DataTable* objects in the *DataSet*. In this case, there's only the Orders *DataTable*. Expand the *DataTable*, and you'll see the *DataColumn* objects available in that *DataTable*. Select the OrderID column, as shown in Figure 13-2.

Figure 13-2   Binding the *Text* property of a TextBox to a *DataColumn* in a *DataSet*

Follow the same steps to create Label and TextBox controls for the CustomerID, EmployeeID, and OrderDate columns. Use the same prefixes for the control names and the same format for the *Text* property of each control. Bind the TextBox controls to the appropriate columns in the *DataSet*. Arrange the controls so that they look similar to those shown in Figure 13-3.

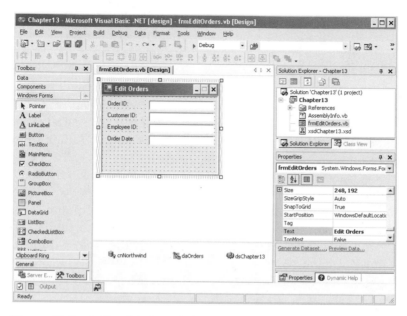

Figure 13-3 Adding labels and TextBoxes to your form

As you can see, binding a TextBox to a column in a *DataSet* at design time in Visual Studio .NET is easy. You can also accomplish this same task using code, as shown here:

Visual Basic .NET

```
txtOrderID.DataBindings.Add("Text", dsChapter13, "Orders.OrderID")
```

Visual C# .NET

```
txtOrderID.DataBindings.Add("Text", dsChapter13, "Orders.OrderID");
```

The code binds the *Text* property on the control to the OrderID column of the Orders table in the dsChapter13 *DataSet*.

Note In the sample application, I set the *ReadOnly* property for the OrderID TextBox to *True* so that the user can't edit the contents of the OrderID column. By default, text in a read-only TextBox is gray rather than black. Personally, I don't like that default, so I set the *ForeColor* property for the control to *Black*. Out of habit, I also set the *TextAlignment* property of the OrderID and EmployeeID TextBoxes to *Right* because the corresponding columns contain numerical data.

Step 3: Retrieving Data

You now have a *DataSet* and some TextBox controls bound to columns in that *DataSet*, but you don't yet have any data to display. If you run your project, you'll see your form with its Label and TextBox controls, but the TextBox controls will be empty. You've done nothing wrong. The *DataSet* simply doesn't contain any orders.

If you used previous versions of Visual Basic, you might recall that displaying a bound control automatically forced the application to execute the associated query and retrieve its results. This behavior does not occur with .NET.

You'll have to add some code so that the application will fetch some orders from the database when it starts up. Double-click on the form to bring up the code window for the form. You'll see the procedure that will handle the *Load* event for the form. Just before the procedure for the *Load* event, add the following line of code:

Visual Basic .NET

```
Dim strCustomerID As String = "ALFKI"
```

Visual C# .NET

```
string strCustomerID = "ALFKI";
```

Then add the following code in the procedure for the *Load* event:

Visual Basic .NET

```
daOrders.SelectCommand.Parameters(0).Value = strCustomerID
daOrders.Fill(dsChapter13.Orders)
```

Visual C# .NET

```
daOrders.SelectCommand.Parameters[0].Value = strCustomerID;
daOrders.Fill(dsChapter13.Orders);
```

We need the first line of code because the query we specified for the *DataAdapter* is parameterized. Once you've added this code, you can run your project and you'll see the contents of an order on your form.

In the sample application, I also added a Close button to the lower right of the form. In the *Click* event of the button, I call the form's *Close* method to end the application. To do the same in your application, drag the button from the Toolbox, set its *Name* property to *btnClose*, and set its *Text* property to *Close*. Double-click on the button to access a procedure for its *Click* event, and then add the following code:

Visual Basic .NET

```
Me.Close()
```

Visual C# .NET

```
this.Close();
```

Step 4: Adding Navigation Buttons

Right now, our application can display only the contents of a single order. You could add code to check the *Count* property of the Orders *DataTable* in our *DataSet* and find that we retrieved multiple orders. The sample application isn't terribly useful if it can show only a single order. Let's add functionality to the application so that the user can see how many orders are available and can move from one order to the next.

In the sample application, I've added four buttons and a label just below the order information on the form, as shown in Figure 13-4. The buttons let the user navigate through the available orders. The Label control displays the current position and the number of available orders.

Figure 13-4   Adding navigation controls to the form

The controls use an instance of the *CurrencyManager* class to provide this functionality. Although the class's name implies that the class acts as a financial consultant, it's really the class that makes data binding work. A Windows Form exposes a *BindingContext* property that you can use to access the *Currency-Manager* objects that manage the bound controls on the form.

The TextBox controls are bound to a single row in the Orders *DataTable*. To change which row those controls display, you can change the *Position* property on an instance of the *CurrencyManager* class. To move to the next row, you can add 1 to the value of the *Position* property. To move to the previous row, you subtract 1.

Rather than try to explain each line of code and where to place it, I've clipped code from the sample and pasted it here. The code includes a form-level *CurrencyManager* variable. The code in the procedure that handles the form's *Load* event initializes this variable and adds handlers for the *Currency-Manager* object's *ItemChanged* and *PositionChanged* events. The procedures that handle these events set the text for the label that displays the position of the current order. You'll also find procedures that handle the click events for the various buttons and set the *CurrencyManager* object's *Position* property accordingly.

Visual Basic .NET

```
'Form-level variable
Dim cmOrders As CurrencyManager

Private Sub frmEditOrders_Load...
    cmOrders = CType(BindingContext(dsChapter13, "Orders"), _
                    CurrencyManager)
    AddHandler cmOrders.ItemChanged, AddressOf cmOrders_ItemChanged
    AddHandler cmOrders.PositionChanged, AddressOf cmOrders_PositionChanged

    DisplayOrdersPosition()
End Sub

Private Sub DisplayOrdersPosition()
    lblOrdersPosition.Text = "Order " & cmOrders.Position + 1 & _
                        " of " & cmOrders.Count
End Sub

Private Sub cmOrders_ItemChanged(ByVal sender As Object, _
                            ByVal e As ItemChangedEventArgs)
    DisplayOrdersPosition()
End Sub

Private Sub cmOrders_PositionChanged(ByVal sender As Object, _
                            ByVal e As System.EventArgs)
    DisplayOrdersPosition()
End Sub

Private Sub btnOrdersMoveFirst_Click...
    cmOrders.Position = 0
End Sub

Private Sub btnOrdersMovePrevious_Click...
    cmOrders.Position -= 1
End Sub
```

(continued)

```
Private Sub btnOrdersMoveNext_Click...
    cmOrders.Position += 1
End Sub

Private Sub btnOrdersMoveLast_Click...
    cmOrders.Position = cmOrders.Count - 1
End Sub
```

Visual C# .NET

```csharp
//Form-level variable
CurrencyManager cmOrders;

private void frmEditOrders_Load...
{
    cmOrders = (CurrencyManager) BindingContext[dsChapter13, "Orders"];
    cmOrders.ItemChanged +=
                       new ItemChangedEventHandler(cmOrders_ItemChanged);
    cmOrders.PositionChanged += new EventHandler(cmOrders_PositionChanged);
    DisplayOrdersPosition();
}

private void DisplayOrdersPosition()
{
    lblOrdersPosition.Text = "Order " + (cmOrders.Position + 1) +
                        " of " + cmOrders.Count;
}

private void cmOrders_ItemChanged(object sender, ItemChangedEventArgs e)
{
    DisplayOrdersPosition();
}

private void cmOrders_PositionChanged(object sender, EventArgs e)
{
    DisplayOrdersPosition();
}

private void btnOrdersMoveFirst_Click(object sender, System.EventArgs e)
{
    cmOrders.Position = 0;
}

private void btnOrdersMovePrevious_Click(object sender, System.EventArgs e)
{
    cmOrders.Position--;
}

private void btnOrdersMoveNext_Click(object sender, System.EventArgs e)
```

```
{
    cmOrders.Position++;
}

private void btnOrdersMoveLast_Click(object sender, System.EventArgs e)
{
    cmOrders.Position = cmOrders.Count - 1;
}
```

Step 5: Adding Add and Delete Buttons

The user now has the ability to view all the orders that the *DataAdapter* retrieved. The user can also change the contents of an order by editing the contents of the bound TextBox controls.

Run the form, and change the EmployeeID for the first order. Remember the original and new EmployeeID values? Once you've changed the EmployeeID for the first order, click the button to move to the next row and then click the back button to move back to the first order. You'll see that the value you specified for the EmployeeID is still there. I'm fighting the urge to use a vaudeville magician voice and ask, "Is this your EmployeeID?"

Although you can modify the contents of an order with the form, you can't add or delete orders…yet. The *CurrencyManager* object exposes methods that you can use to add or remove items from the structure to which your controls are bound. The *AddNew* method adds a new item, and the *RemoveAt* method removes an existing item. When you call either of these methods, the controls bound to the *CurrencyManager* object react accordingly. If you remove add an item using the *AddNew* method, the controls show the contents of the new item. Calling the *RemoveAt* method causes the controls to display the contents of the next available item.

Visual Basic .NET

```
Private Sub btnOrdersAdd_Click...
    cmOrders.AddNew()
End Sub

Private Sub btnOrdersDelete_Click...
    If cmOrders.Count > 0 Then
        cmOrders.RemoveAt(cmOrders.Position)
    Else
        MessageBox.Show("No Order to Delete!", "Delete Order", _
                        MessageBoxButtons.OK, MessageBoxIcon.Error)
    End If
End Sub
```

Visual C# .NET

```csharp
private void btnOrdersAdd_Click(object sender, System.EventArgs e)
{
    cmOrders.AddNew();
    SetOrdersEditMode(true);
}


private void btnOrdersDelete_Click(object sender, System.EventArgs e)
{
    if (cmOrders.Count > 0)
        cmOrders.RemoveAt(cmOrders.Position);
    else
        MessageBox.Show("No Order to Delete!", "Delete Order",
                    MessageBoxButtons.OK, MessageBoxIcon.Error);
}
```

Step 6: Submitting Changes

Our sample application can now modify, add, and delete orders. However, you might have noticed that the application does not submit these changes to the database. I hope you remember enough information from Chapter 5 and Chapter 10 to realize why. The bound controls modify the contents of the *DataSet*, but we do not have code that calls the *DataAdapter* object's *Update* method.

Because we built the *DataAdapter* using the Data Adapter Configuration Wizard, we do not need to define updating logic. The wizard created the updating logic for us. All we need to do is add a Submit Changes button to the form and then call the *DataAdapter* object's *Update* method in the procedure that handles the button's *Click* event in order to submit the changes. The code traps for the return value on the call to the *DataAdapter* object's *Update* method, which indicates the number of updates submitted to the database.

I've added a couple lines of code to display the number of modified orders, trap the exception if the update attempt fails, and throw a dialog box if the *DataSet* contains no changes. The meat of the code is still the call to the *DataAdapter* object's *Update* method, as shown here:

Visual Basic .NET

```vbnet
If dsChapter13.HasChanges Then
    Try
        Dim intOrdersModified As Integer
        intOrdersModified = daOrders.Update(dsChapter13.Orders)
        Dim strOutput As String
        strOutput = "Modified " & intOrdersModified & " order(s)"
        MessageBox.Show(strOutput, "Update succeeded!", _
                    MessageBoxButtons.OK, MessageBoxIcon.Information)
```

```
        Catch ex As Exception
            MessageBox.Show(ex.Message, "Update failed!", _
                            MessageBoxButtons.OK, MessageBoxIcon.Error)
        End Try
    Else
        MessageBox.Show("No changes to submit!", "SubmitChanges", _
                        MessageBoxButtons.OK, MessageBoxIcon.Information)
    End If
```

Visual C# .NET

```csharp
if (dsChapter13.HasChanges())
{
    try
    {
        int intOrdersModified;
        intOrdersModified = daOrders.Update(dsChapter13.Orders);
        string strOutput;
        strOutput = "Modified " + intOrdersModified + " order(s)";
            MessageBox.Show(strOutput, "Update succeeded!",
                        MessageBoxButtons.OK, MessageBoxIcon.Information);
    }
    catch (Exception ex)
    {
        MessageBox.Show(ex.Message, "Update failed!",
                        MessageBoxButtons.OK, MessageBoxIcon.Error);
    }
}
else
    MessageBox.Show("No changes to submit!", "SubmitChanges",
                    MessageBoxButtons.OK, MessageBoxIcon.Information);
```

Step 7: Adding Edit, Update, and Cancel Buttons

The application we've built is simple. The form has only a few controls on it. However, the application is not as intuitive as you might think.

Start the application, and modify the value of the EmployeeID for the first order. Then click the Submit Changes button. You'll see a dialog box stating that there are no changes to submit. What happened?

According to our code, the *DataSet* object does not contain any changes. So what happened to the change you just made? The *CurrencyManager* object is still managing that change and has not yet written it to the *DataSet*. If you navigate to the next order and then click the Submit Changes button, you'll successfully submit the change.

The *CurrencyManager* object will not commit the pending changes to the *DataSet* until one of two events occurs—the *CurrencyManager* moves to another row or the *CurrencyManager* object's *EndCurrentEdit* method is called. In some ways, this behavior is similar to the *BeginEdit* method of the *DataRow* object. The changes aren't really written to the *DataRow* object until you call the *EndEdit* method.

We could include a call to the *CurrencyManager* object's *EndCurrentEdit* method just before calling the *DataAdapter* object's *Update* method to submit our changes. Adding that line of code would definitely handle this particular scenario. But I prefer a different approach.

In step 7 of creating the sample application, I've added buttons marked Edit, Cancel, and Update. When the application starts up, the data in the TextBox controls are all read-only. You have to click the Edit button to edit the contents of an order. Once you click the Edit button, you can edit the TextBox contents (except for the OrderID column). However, the navigation buttons as well as the Add, Edit, Delete, and Submit Changes buttons are all disabled. You must click either the Update or Cancel button to continue, as shown in Figure 13-5. Clicking the Update button commits the change to the current order; clicking the Cancel button cancels the changes to the current order.

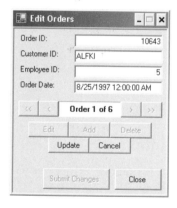

Figure 13-5   Forcing users to commit or cancel changes to the current order

Adding this functionality requires just a few minutes of coding, but I think it's time well spent. As a result of these changes, the application's behavior is much more intuitive. Users won't encounter problems submitting changes due to uncommitted changes. Plus, you won't be left scratching your head trying to figure out how and when the *CurrencyManager* object commits changes to the *DataSet*.

I've added a procedure to the form called *SetOrdersEditMode* that accepts a Boolean value to indicate whether the user can edit the current order. The procedure then sets the *ReadOnly* property of the TextBox controls and the *Enabled* property of the buttons as appropriate. I call this procedure from the click events of the Add, Edit, Update, and Cancel buttons.

Visual Basic .NET

```
Private Sub SetOrdersEditMode(ByVal blnEdit As Boolean)
    txtCustomerID.ReadOnly = Not blnEdit
    txtEmployeeID.ReadOnly = Not blnEdit
    txtOrderDate.ReadOnly = Not blnEdit

    btnOrdersMoveFirst.Enabled = Not blnEdit
    btnOrdersMovePrevious.Enabled = Not blnEdit
    btnOrdersMoveNext.Enabled = Not blnEdit
    btnOrdersMoveLast.Enabled = Not blnEdit

    btnOrdersCancel.Enabled = blnEdit
    btnOrdersUpdate.Enabled = blnEdit
    btnOrdersEdit.Enabled = Not blnEdit
    btnOrdersAdd.Enabled = Not blnEdit
    btnOrdersDelete.Enabled = Not blnEdit
    btnSubmitChanges.Enabled = Not blnEdit
End Sub
```

Visual C# .NET

```
private void SetOrdersEditMode(bool blnEdit)
{
    txtCustomerID.ReadOnly = !blnEdit;
    txtEmployeeID.ReadOnly = !blnEdit;
    txtOrderDate.ReadOnly = !blnEdit;

    btnOrdersMoveFirst.Enabled = !blnEdit;
    btnOrdersMovePrevious.Enabled = !blnEdit;
    btnOrdersMoveNext.Enabled = !blnEdit;
    btnOrdersMoveLast.Enabled = !blnEdit;

    btnOrdersCancel.Enabled = blnEdit;
    btnOrdersUpdate.Enabled = blnEdit;
    btnOrdersEdit.Enabled = !blnEdit;
    btnOrdersAdd.Enabled = !blnEdit;
    btnOrdersDelete.Enabled = !blnEdit;
    btnSubmitChanges.Enabled = !blnEdit;
}
```

Step 8: Viewing Child Data

Our application now allows users to view and modify data from the Orders table. However, that functionality isn't terribly helpful unless we also allow the user to view and modify the line items for those orders.

Figure 13-6 shows the user interface for the next phase of the sample application. As you can see, I've added a grid that displays data from the Order Details table. As you move from one order to the next, the grid displays just the related rows.

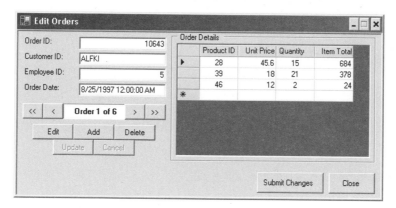

Figure 13-6   Displaying an order and its line items

To add this functionality to the application, do the following:

1. Add a *DataAdapter* that fetches all rows from the Order Details table that correspond to a customer's orders.

2. Regenerate the strongly typed *DataSet* to add a *DataTable* for this new data, and then add a *DataRelation* to the *DataSet* to easily locate just the line items for a particular order.

3. Add to the form a DataGrid control that's bound to the *DataSet* in such a way that the grid shows only the line items for the current order.

4. Add logic to the procedure for the Submit Changes button to submit changes from both *DataTable* objects.

Retrieving Just the Order Details for a Customer

It was easy to create a *DataAdapter* that retrieves just the orders for a particular customer because the Orders table has a CustomerID column. The Order Details table does not. So, to retrieve just the order details for a particular customer, we need to reference both the Order Details and Orders tables in our query.

You can structure such a query in a number of ways. Here are three examples:

```
SELECT D.OrderID, D.ProductID, D.UnitPrice, D.Quantity
    FROM Orders O INNER JOIN [Order Details] D
        ON O.OrderID = D.OrderID
    WHERE O.CustomerID = ?

SELECT OrderID, ProductID, UnitPrice, Quantity FROM [Order Details]
    WHERE OrderID IN (SELECT OrderID FROM Orders WHERE CustomerID = ?)

SELECT D.OrderID, D.ProductID, D.UnitPrice, D.Quantity
    FROM [Order Details] D, Orders O
    WHERE D.OrderID = O.OrderID AND O.CustomerID = ?
```

According to SQL Query Analyzer, which displays estimated execution plans, SQL Server creates the same execution plan for each query. I prefer the syntax in the third query for two reasons. First, it seems like the most intuitive syntax. And second, the Data Adapter Configuration Wizard is unable to handle the second query syntax because of the parameter in the subquery. The wizard seems to prefer the INNER JOIN syntax. Even though I used the syntax for the first query when I built the sample application, the wizard changed the query to the first syntax. To each his, her, or its own.

After you create a new *OleDbDataAdapter* using this query, rename the new *DataAdapter daDetails*.

Adding an Order Details *DataTable* to the Strongly Typed *DataSet* Class

Once you've added the *DataAdapter* to fetch rows from the Order Details table, you can use the Generate Dataset dialog box to add a new *DataTable* to the strongly typed *DataSet* class. Figure 13-7 shows how. Select the existing *DataSet* from the list of available *DataSet* objects. Then make sure the table that corresponds to the new *DataAdapter* is the only one that's checked in the list of tables in the middle of the dialog box.

When you click OK, Visual Studio .NET will add the new *DataTable* to the existing strongly typed *DataSet* class. If you leave both items in the list of available tables checked, Visual Studio .NET will overwrite the existing Orders *DataTable* in the strongly typed *DataSet*, which means you'll lose the settings for the *AutoIncrementSeed* and *AutoIncrementStep* properties. Resetting those properties isn't difficult, just annoying.

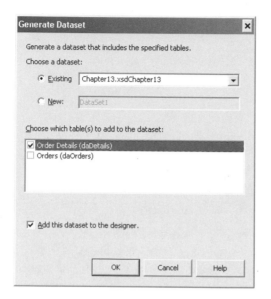

Figure 13-7   Adding a new *DataTable* to an existing strongly typed
DataSet

Now that the strongly typed *DataSet* class has *DataTable* objects for the
Orders and Order Details tables, you can add a *DataRelation* between the two
DataTable objects based on the OrderID *DataColumn*. Double-click on the
class's .xsd file in Solution Explorer to launch the XML Schema Designer. Drag
the CustomerID column from the Orders *DataTable* to the Order Details *Data-
Table*. Accept the defaults in the dialog box that the designer displays.

The sample application also adds a calculated column to show the total
cost of a line item. You can do the same by adding a new column to the Order
Details *DataTable*. Set its data type to *Decimal*, and then set the *Expression*
property to *UnitPrice * Quantity*.

Close the designer and save the changes.

Adding a DataGrid That Displays Child Data

Binding a DataGrid is simple. You need to set two properties—*DataSource* and
DataMember.

Add a DataGrid to your form, and set its *Name* property to *gridDetails*.
Select the *DataSource* property in the Properties window. Open the drop-down
list on the right to see the list of available data sources. You'll see the *DataSet*
as well as the individual *DataTable* objects. Select the *DataMember* property.
You'll find a list of possible values for this property as well, as shown in
Figure 13-8. Expand the Orders *DataTable* in the list, and you'll see the *Data-
Relation* you created earlier. Setting the *DataMember* property to the *DataRela-
tion* will make the DataGrid show just the child rows using the *DataRelation*.

Figure 13-8   Setting the *DataMember* property for a DataGrid that will
display child rows

If you wanted to bind the DataGrid at run time, you could use the following code:

Visual Basic .NET

```
gridDetails.DataSource = dsChapter13
gridDetails.DataMember = "Orders.Order_x0020_Details"
```

Visual C# .NET

```
gridDetails.DataSource = dsChapter13;
gridDetails.DataMember = "Orders.Order_x0020_Details";
```

In the sample application, you'll find a line of code toward the end of the procedure for the form's *Load* event that calls a procedure named *Format-DetailsGrid*. This procedure adds a new *DataGridTableStyle* to the DataGrid to control the DataGrid's display. Supplying a *DataGridTableStyle* allows you to select which columns to display as well as control the size, format, and alignment of each column.

Submitting Changes to Both Tables

Chapter 11 discusses the complexities involved in submitting hierarchical changes to a database. Basically, you need to submit new rows starting at the top of the hierarchy (orders before order details) but deleted rows starting at the bottom (order details before orders). As a result, you can't simply supply the entire *DataTable* when you call the *DataAdapter* objects' *Update* methods.

First you submit the new and modified orders. Then you can submit all the changes to the Order Details table. After that, you can submit the deleted orders. If you look at the code in the procedure for the Submit Changes button's *Click* event, you'll see that it uses that same logic. I've included that code here, though I've omitted the *Try/Catch* block to make the code a little more readable:

Visual Basic .NET

```
Dim intOrdersModified, intDetailsModified As Integer
Dim aRowsToUpdate As DataRow()
Dim dvrs As DataViewRowState
'Submit new or modified orders.
dvrs = DataViewRowState.Added Or DataViewRowState.ModifiedCurrent
aRowsToUpdate = dsChapter13.Orders.Select("", "", dvrs)
intOrdersModified = daOrders.Update(aRowsToUpdate)
'Submit all changes to the Order Details DataTable.
intDetailsModified = daDetails.Update(dsChapter13.Order_Details)
'Submit deleted orders.
dvrs = DataViewRowState.Deleted
aRowsToUpdate = dsChapter13.Orders.Select("", "", dvrs)
intOrdersModified += daOrders.Update(aRowsToUpdate)
Dim strOutput As String
strOutput = "Modified " & intOrdersModified & " order(s)" & vbCrLf & _
            "Modified " & intDetailsModified & " detail(s)"
MessageBox.Show(strOutput, "Update succeeded!", _
                MessageBoxButtons.OK, MessageBoxIcon.Information)
```

Visual C# .NET

```
int intOrdersModified, intDetailsModified;
DataRow[] aRowsToUpdate;
DataViewRowState dvrs;
//Submit new or modified orders.
dvrs = DataViewRowState.Added | DataViewRowState.ModifiedCurrent;
aRowsToUpdate = dsChapter13.Orders.Select("", "", dvrs);
intOrdersModified = daOrders.Update(aRowsToUpdate);
//Submit all changes to the Order Details DataTable.
intDetailsModified = daDetails.Update(dsChapter13.Order_Details);
//Submit deleted orders.
dvrs = DataViewRowState.Deleted;
aRowsToUpdate = dsChapter13.Orders.Select("", "", dvrs);
intOrdersModified += daOrders.Update(aRowsToUpdate);
string strOutput;
strOutput = "Modified " + intOrdersModified + " order(s)\n\r" +
            "Modified " + intDetailsModified + " detail(s)";
MessageBox.Show(strOutput, "Update succeeded!",
                MessageBoxButtons.OK, MessageBoxIcon.Information);
```

Step 9: Binding a Second Form to the Same Data Source

Trying to bind controls on multiple forms to the same data source is challenging but possible. Before I explain how to accomplish this, I want to make a quick detour to show you how to improve the user interface to help even novice users edit data easily.

The DataGrid is a helpful and powerful tool. I regularly use DataGrid controls to display the contents of multiple rows. However, I'm not a big fan of having users modify data in a DataGrid. You might be aware that you can undo a change in the DataGrid by pressing the Escape key or by pressing Ctrl+Z, but few novice users will realize this.

Rather than hoping that users will discover and remember such functionality, I prefer making the process more intuitive even if it forces the user to go through an extra step or two. So, in step 9 of the sample application, I made the DataGrid that shows the line items for a particular order read-only. To add, modify, or delete a line item, the user must click a button—the same requirement for editing an order. If the user chooses to add or modify a line item, the sample application will launch a modal form that lets the user edit the desired row, as shown in Figure 13-9.

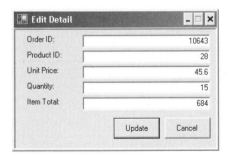

Figure 13-9   Editing a line item in a new form

The user can modify the information for the line item using this form. Just as when he or she edits an order, the user must click Update or Cancel to exit edit mode.

Now let's get back to binding controls on multiple forms to the same data source. The TextBox controls on the new form are bound to the same row of data that's currently shown in the DataGrid for the main form. Although you can't do this at design time, you can do it at run time. Here's how.

If you look at the code that's executed when you click the Edit button below the details DataGrid, you'll see that the code creates an instance of the details form and then calls the *EditDetail* method on the form. The *EditDetail* method accepts a *CurrencyManager* object as a parameter.

The code for the *EditDetail* method follows. As you can see, the code uses the *CurrencyManager* object to bind the TextBox controls on the new form to the same row of data. The *Current* property of the *CurrencyManager* object returns a *DataRowView* object cast as an object. You can bind the TextBox controls to a *DataView* object, so the code uses the *DataView* property of the *DataRow-View* object to access the *DataView* to which the *DataRowView* belongs.

Visual Basic .NET

```
Dim drvDetail As DataRowView
Dim vueDetail As DataView

Public Sub EditDetail(ByVal cm As CurrencyManager)
    drvDetail = CType(cm.Current, DataRowView)
    vueDetail = drvDetail.DataView

    Me.BindingContext(vueDetail).Position = cm.Position

    txtOrderID.DataBindings.Add("Text", vueDetail, "OrderID")
    txtProductID.DataBindings.Add("Text", vueDetail, "ProductID")
    txtUnitPrice.DataBindings.Add("Text", vueDetail, "UnitPrice")
    txtQuantity.DataBindings.Add("Text", vueDetail, "Quantity")
    txtItemTotal.DataBindings.Add("Text", vueDetail, "ItemTotal")

    If Me.ShowDialog = DialogResult.OK Then
        cm.EndCurrentEdit()
    Else
        cm.CancelCurrentEdit()
    End If
End Sub
```

Visual C# .NET

```
DataRowView drvDetail;
DataView vueDetail;

public void EditDetail(CurrencyManager cm)
{
    drvDetail = (DataRowView) cm.Current;
    vueDetail = drvDetail.DataView;

    this.BindingContext[vueDetail].Position = cm.Position;

    txtOrderID.DataBindings.Add("Text", vueDetail, "OrderID");
    txtProductID.DataBindings.Add("Text", vueDetail, "ProductID");
    txtUnitPrice.DataBindings.Add("Text", vueDetail, "UnitPrice");
    txtQuantity.DataBindings.Add("Text", vueDetail, "Quantity");
    txtItemTotal.DataBindings.Add("Text", vueDetail, "ItemTotal");
```

```
    if (this.ShowDialog() == DialogResult.OK)
        cm.EndCurrentEdit();
    else
        cm.CancelCurrentEdit();
}
```

Step 10: Improving the User Interface

We now have an application that lets users view and edit order information for a customer, but we can do a couple more things to improve the overall user experience.

Given the choice, most users would rather see descriptive information than cryptic key information on a form. For example, the child form that allows the user to modify a line item forces the user to know the key value rather than the name of the product. Also, the formatting for the unit price and item total for each line item looks unprofessional.

Let's see how we can present the data in a more user-friendly format, as shown in Figure 13-10.

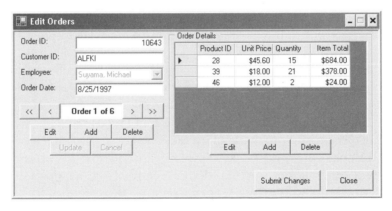

Figure 13-10   Presenting data in a more user-friendly format

Adding Lookup Functionality Using a ComboBox Control

If you look at Figure 13-10, you'll see that I replaced the TextBox that listed the EmployeeID for the current order with a ComboBox control that shows the employee's name. Adding this functionality is really quite simple. In fact, you need to set only four properties on the ComboBox.

Before you add a ComboBox to your form to try to use this functionality, you need to add a *DataAdapter* to retrieve information from the Employees table. I created one with the following query:

```
SELECT EmployeeID, LastName + ', ' + FirstName AS EmployeeName
    FROM Employees
```

Once you've added a *DataAdapter* to fetch employee information, you regenerate the *DataSet* to add an Employees *DataTable* to the strongly typed *DataSet*.

> **Note**   The application will not modify data in the Employees table, so there's no need to generate updating logic for the *DataAdapter* that queries the Employees table. You can click the Advanced Options button on the SQL Statement screen of the wizard and tell the wizard to not generate updating logic.

We want the ComboBox to display values from the EmployeeName column in the Employees *DataTable*. When the user selects an employee name from the list, we want the ComboBox to take the value from the EmployeeID column for that employee and store it in the EmployeeID column for the current order. We'll actually bind the ComboBox to two separate data sources at once—the Employees *DataTable* and the current row of order information.

First let's look at how to bind the ComboBox to the Employees *DataTable*. The ComboBox has a *DataSource* property that you set just like you set the *DataSource* property of the DataGrid. Select the *DataSet* object from the list of available data sources. To control which column the ComboBox will use to populate its list, you set the *DisplayMember* property—in this case, we want to display the EmployeeName column in the Employees *DataTable*. Then set the *ValueMember* property to the EmployeeID column in the Employees *DataTable*.

All that's left to do is associate the ComboBox with the EmployeeID property for the current row of order information. This last part of the process is similar to binding the *Text* property of a TextBox control to a column in a *DataSet*. Locate the (DataBindings) area in the Properties window. Expand the area, locate the *SelectedValue* property, and bind it to the EmployeeID column in the Orders *DataTable*.

You can accomplish these same steps at run time by executing the following code:

Visual Basic .NET

```
cboEmployee.DataSource = dsChapter13
cboEmployee.DisplayMember = "Employees.EmployeeName"
cboEmployee.ValueMember = "Employees.EmployeeID"
cboEmployee.DataBindings.Add("SelectedValue", dsChapter13, _
                        "Orders.EmployeeID")
```

Visual C# .NET

```
cboEmployee.DataSource = dsChapter13;
cboEmployee.DisplayMember = "Employees.EmployeeName";
cboEmployee.ValueMember = "Employees.EmployeeID";
cboEmployee.DataBindings.Add("SelectedValue", dsChapter13,
                            "Orders.EmployeeID");
```

Now, as you navigate through the orders, you'll see the EmployeeName rather than the value of the EmployeeID column. You can also edit an order and change the value of the EmployeeID column by changing the employee listed in the ComboBox control.

Controlling the Format of Bound Data

The data type of the UnitPrice column in the *DataSet* is *Decimal*. As a result, the TextBox on the details form that's bound to the UnitPrice column will display the contents of that column using the standard numerical formatting. If the unit price for an item is $4.50, the TextBox will display *4.5*.

We can write code to manually change the display of this data to a format that's more appropriate.

Earlier in the chapter, I showed an example of code that binds the *Text* property of a TextBox to a column in a *DataView*.

Visual Basic .NET

```
txtOrderID.DataBindings.Add("Text", dsChapter13, "Orders.OrderID")
```

Visual C# .NET

```
txtOrderID.DataBindings.Add("Text", dsChapter13, "Orders.OrderID");
```

The *Add* method returns a *Binding* object, which responds to the *Currency-Manager* object's events and moves data back and forth between the TextBox and the column to which the TextBox is bound.

The *Binding* object exposes two events—*Format* and *Parse*. The *Format* event fires when the *Binding* object loads data from the data source into the property to which it's bound. The *Parse* event fires when the *Binding* object reads data from the bound property and assigns this data to the data source. We can use these two events to change the format of the data displayed in the bound TextBox controls.

The following code snippet from the sample shows how it formats the data in the TextBox for the UnitPrice column as currency. The code uses an overloaded *ToString* method of the *Decimal* class to format the decimal as currency.

Visual Basic .NET

```vbnet
Public Sub EditDetail(ByVal cm As CurrencyManager)
    ⋮
    Dim b As Binding
    b = txtUnitPrice.DataBindings.Add("Text", vueDetail, "UnitPrice")
    AddHandler b.Format, AddressOf DecimalToCurrencyString
    AddHandler b.Parse, AddressOf CurrencyStringToDecimal
    ⋮
End Sub


Private Sub DecimalToCurrencyString(ByVal sender As Object, _
                                    ByVal cevent As ConvertEventArgs)
    If Not cevent.DesiredType Is GetType(String) Then
        Exit Sub
    End If

    If cevent.Value Is DBNull.Value Then
        cevent.Value = CDec(0).ToString("c")
    Else
        cevent.Value = CDec(cevent.Value).ToString("c")
    End If
End Sub


Private Sub CurrencyStringToDecimal(ByVal sender As Object, _
                                    ByVal cevent As ConvertEventArgs)
    If Not cevent.DesiredType Is GetType(Decimal) Then
        Exit Sub
    End If

    cevent.Value = Decimal.Parse(cevent.Value.ToString, _
                                 Globalization.NumberStyles.Currency, _
                                 Nothing)
End Sub
```

Visual C# .NET

```csharp
public void EditDetail(CurrencyManager cm)
{
    ⋮
    Binding b;
    b = txtUnitPrice.DataBindings.Add("Text", vueDetail, "UnitPrice");
    b.Format += new ConvertEventHandler(DecimalToCurrencyString);
    b.Parse += new ConvertEventHandler(CurrencyStringToDecimal);
    ⋮
}


private void DecimalToCurrencyString(object sender,
                                     ConvertEventArgs cevent)
```

```
{
    if (!cevent.DesiredType.Equals(typeof(string)))
        return;

    if (cevent.Value == DBNull.Value)
        cevent.Value = ((Decimal) 0).ToString("c");
    else
        cevent.Value = ((Decimal) cevent.Value).ToString("c");
}

private void CurrencyStringToDecimal(object sender,
                              ConvertEventArgs cevent)
{
    if (!cevent.DesiredType.Equals(typeof(Decimal)))
        return;

    cevent.Value = Decimal.Parse(cevent.Value.ToString(),
                          System.Globalization.NumberStyles.Currency,
                          null);
}
```

Step 11: If You Want Something Done (Just) Right...

Let's take a short break and look at the sample application we've built. Thanks to data binding features, it took very little code to let users view and edit data from two related *DataTable* objects through bound controls. That's the whole point of the data binding features—providing basic functionality so that you can build user interfaces with minimal code.

When we initially bound the controls, we had little control over how the controls interacted with the data in our *DataSet*. In step 10, we added code to control the format of data in bound TextBox controls. Step 10 of the sample application on the CD also includes code to format and accept *Null* values. You can add more code to gain more control over the bound controls, but remember that the more code you write, the less benefit you'll really get from using data binding in the first place.

Here's an example. I finished step 10 and started using the sample application, looking for ways to improve the application. I discovered that on the Edit Detail form, changing the contents of the Quantity and UnitPrice TextBox controls did not update the contents of the ItemTotal TextBox. I therefore started looking for a way to automatically update the ItemTotal TextBox when the contents of the Quantity or UnitPrice TextBox controls changed. I tried setting the *Text* property for the ItemTotal TextBox in the *Leave* event of the Quantity and UnitPrice TextBox controls. I tried calling the *Refresh* method of the *Currency-Manager* object. I tried relying on the *SuspendBinding* and *ResumeBinding* methods of the *CurrencyManager* object. No matter what I tried, I couldn't get the functionality I was looking for. Although I think it's possible to accomplish this task with data binding, this isn't the type of scenario that data binding was designed to address.

The more functionality we add to this application through code, the more we relegate the data binding features to three simple tasks—navigation through the available rows, displaying the contents of the current row in a series of controls, and saving user input to the current row. That's not terribly complex code to write.

If you rely on your own code to display data in controls and write changes back to the data structure, you take control and responsibility for the interaction between the user interface and your data structures. Step 11 of the sample application no longer relies on data binding to display data in TextBox controls. If you look at the code for the Edit Orders form, you'll find a *ShowCurrent-Order* procedure as well as code to determine which order and which line items to display using *DataView* objects. The forms also include code to validate input into the various TextBox controls. If the user enters invalid data, such as entering *Thursday* as the unit price for a line item, the user receives a descriptive error message.

Data Binding Summary

As you've seen in the various steps in the sample application, the data binding features in the Windows forms package allow you to create a powerful and robust user interface with minimal code. However, as you try to take more control of the user interface and add more and more code to your application, you might find that your code is battling data binding rather than complementing it. In such cases, you might be better off writing your own code to manage the interaction between your data and the user interface.

Application Design Considerations

Creating a helpful and intuitive user interface is just one of many facets of building an effective Windows-based application. Let's discuss some important application design considerations.

Fetching Only the Data You Need

As you develop your application, it's important that you consider how your database will grow. Executing a SELECT ... FROM MyTable query when your application starts up might seem fine while you're developing the application, but as the table grows in size, fetching the results of the query will take more time. The more data you retrieve, the more time your application will take to retrieve that data.

Take our sample order entry application. As the application starts, it issues queries to retrieve information for all the orders that a customer has placed. Is that the right call? Perhaps retrieving all orders for a customer is overkill. Maybe the users of the application are primarily interested in viewing the orders that have not yet shipped. Maybe the application should fetch only orders that a particular customer has placed in the past three months.

The application's environment can also be a factor in determining which data to fetch. Perhaps the user needs to be able to download data onto a laptop using a 28-Kbps modem, access and modify that data off line while at a remote site, and then reconnect using the same modem at the end of the day to transmit changes back to the database. You won't want to waste any bandwidth because the pipeline is so thin, but because of the environment, the application will require you to download all the necessary data from the database.

Updating Strategies

The sample application caches changes and relies on optimistic locking to submit updates. Let's discuss some other updating strategies.

Immediate Updates vs. Cached Updates

Whether you decide to submit changes immediately or cache those changes and submit them later should depend on what's appropriate for your application.

When the user modifies an order in the sample application, the application does not immediately submit the change to the database. The application relies on ADO.NET to cache the update until the user clicks the Submit Changes button.

We could easily change the application so that it submits the change to an order when the user clicks the Update button. When the user clicks the Edit button, the application will allow the user to modify the order and its line items. If the user clicks the Cancel button, the application will discard the changes. If the user clicks the Update button instead, the application will save the changes and then use the *DataAdapter* to submit the changes to the database.

One benefit of working with data off line and caching changes is that the application does not need to communicate with the database as frequently. However, the longer the user waits to submit cached changes, the greater the chances that another user will have modified the same data in the database, which can cause the update attempt to fail.

You should weigh the pros and cons of each approach to determine what's appropriate for your application. If the users of our sample application will handle incoming phone orders from customers with slow-moving inventory, caching the changes will probably suffice. But that approach isn't appropriate for an airline ticket reservation system. You wouldn't want a user to try to save a traveler's itinerary only to discover that the last seat on the return flight was sold while the traveler was trying to find his or her frequent flyer number.

Refetching Before Allowing Changes

When you retrieve data into a disconnected structure such as a *DataSet*, the data can become stale. But unlike a carton of milk, your *DataSet* does not come with an expiration date. The *DataSet* does not fire an event when the corresponding rows in your database change. By the time the user modifies data in your application and attempts to submit the changes to your database, another user might have modified that same row of data and the update attempt will fail.

Take our sample application. It fetches data when the application starts. The user might click the Edit button within seconds of starting the application. The longer the application is open, the more stale the data becomes. In fact, the user might wait minutes or hours before modifying the contents of a row.

By the time the user clicks the Edit button, another user might have modified the corresponding row in the database. If you're developing an application that might face this scenario, you might want to refetch the contents of the corresponding row from the database when the user clicks the Edit button.

To refetch the contents of the row, you can create a *DataAdapter* that executes a parameterized query that looks like this:

```
SELECT ... FROM MyTable WHERE KeyCol = ?
```

If you've set the *PrimaryKey* property of your *DataTable*, the *DataAdapter* will update the contents of the *DataRow* with data from your database. Remember that this query will not generate an exception if another user has deleted the corresponding row in the database. In that case, the query will just return no rows. The *DataAdapter* object's *Fill* method returns an integer that contains the number of rows that the database fetched. If the *Fill* method returns 0, you know that the row no longer exists in the database. You can trap for that scenario and elegantly inform the user that the row that he or she wanted to edit no longer exists.

ADO.NET and Pessimistic Locking

Even if you submit changes to the database as soon as they're made, rather than cache them, and you refetch the contents of a row before allowing the user to modify the contents, the user's update attempt might fail because the data on the server is not locked. You can use pessimistic locking to make sure the update attempt will succeed.

> **Warning**   Pessimistic locking is a powerful and somewhat dangerous feature. Be afraid. Be very afraid.
>
> This is an advanced topic, intended for developers who really understand the impact of locking data on their servers. Only a small number of applications require pessimistic locking, such as airline reservation systems.
>
> I don't recommend using pessimistic locking as a general way of avoiding failed update attempts. For most applications, it's better to have optimistic update attempts occasionally fail than to have queries fail because data on the server is locked.

Updating data using pessimistic locking involves locking the row in the database before editing its contents, which ensures that the update attempt will not fail as a result of changes made by another user. The ADO.NET object model is designed to submit changes through optimistic updates. As you learned in Chapter 10 and Chapter 11, the *DataAdapter* object lets you submit pending changes stored in a *DataSet*. The *DataSet* object does not lock data on the database when you modify the contents of a *DataRow* object. There are no properties you can set on ADO.NET objects to achieve pessimistic locking, at least not in the initial release of ADO.NET.

You can still achieve pessimistic locking through the use of *Transaction* objects. However, you'll probably need to do more than issue a simple SELECT query from within a transaction. Whether issuing a SELECT query from within a transaction locks the rows returned by the query depends on the database, the type of query, and the isolation level for the transaction.

A transaction's isolation level controls how, or if, the work performed on a transaction will affect work performed on other transactions. SQL Server uses "read committed" as its default transaction isolation level. With this isolation level, rows are locked once they're modified in the transaction. Simply retrieving the contents of a row in a SELECT query will not lock the row. If, however, you use an isolation level of "repeatable read" or "serializable," you lock the rows you retrieve in a SELECT query.

Some databases support the use of locking hints in a query. With SQL Server, you can issue the following query to lock a row of data in a transaction, regardless of the transaction's isolation level:

```
SELECT CustomerID, CompanyName, ContactName, Phone FROM Customers
    WITH (UPDLOCK) WHERE CustomerID = 'ALFKI'
```

See your database's documentation to find out what types of transaction isolation levels and locking hints it supports.

The following code snippet pessimistically locks a row in an MSDE database through the use of an *OleDbTransaction* object and the use of locking hints in the SELECT query. As soon as the code retrieves the results of the query, the row of data is locked on the server. You can set a breakpoint after the call to the *DataAdapter* object's *Fill* method to verify that the data is locked. At this point, you can examine the contents of the row in an ad hoc query tool such as SQL Server's Query Analyzer, but attempts to modify the contents of the row will fail.

Visual Basic .NET

```
Dim strConn, strSQL As String
strConn = "Provider=SQLOLEDB;Data Source=(local)\NetSDK;" & _
          "Initial Catalog=Northwind;Trusted_Connection=Yes;"
strSQL = "SELECT CustomerID, CompanyName FROM Customers " & _
          "WITH (UPDLOCK) WHERE CustomerID = 'ALFKI'"
Dim cn As New OleDbConnection(strConn)
cn.Open()
Dim txn As OleDbTransaction = cn.BeginTransaction
Dim cmd As New OleDbCommand(strSQL, cn, txn)
Dim da As New OleDbDataAdapter(cmd)
Dim cb As New OleDbCommandBuilder(da)
Dim tbl As New DataTable()
da.Fill(tbl)
Dim row As DataRow = tbl.Rows(0)
row("CompanyName") = "Modified"
da.Update(tbl)
txn.Rollback()
cn.Close()
```

Visual C# .NET

```
string strConn, strSQL;
strConn = "Provider=SQLOLEDB;Data Source=(local)\\NetSDK;" +
          "Initial Catalog=Northwind;Trusted_Connection=Yes;";
strSQL = "SELECT CustomerID, CompanyName FROM Customers " +
          "WITH (UPDLOCK) WHERE CustomerID = 'ALFKI'";
OleDbConnection cn = new OleDbConnection(strConn);
cn.Open();
OleDbTransaction txn = cn.BeginTransaction();
OleDbCommand cmd = new OleDbCommand(strSQL, cn, txn);
OleDbDataAdapter da = new OleDbDataAdapter(cmd);
OleDbCommandBuilder cb = new OleDbCommandBuilder(da);
```

```
DataTable tbl = new DataTable();
da.Fill(tbl);
DataRow row = tbl.Rows[0];
row["CompanyName"] = "Modified";
da.Update(tbl);
txn.Rollback();
cn.Close();
```

> **Note**   I use a *CommandBuilder* in the sample code solely for the sake of brevity. Chapter 11 discusses why you're better off supplying your own updating logic.

Connection Strategies

You can choose between two connection strategies. The appropriate approach will depend on the parameters of your application.

Connecting and Disconnecting

The simplest approach to connecting to your database is to let *DataAdapter* objects open the connection implicitly. The sample application uses this approach. The *DataAdapter* objects implicitly open the connection on calls to the *DataAdapter* object's *Fill* and *Update* methods and close the *Connection* object at the end of the calls. This approach is simple, but it's not always the best approach.

Depending on the responsiveness of your network and database, opening a connection to your database can be time consuming. You might be able to improve the performance of your application by opening a connection to your database when the application starts and keeping the connection open for the lifetime of the application, but this approach also has its drawbacks. It works well for small numbers of users but might not be appropriate for large numbers of simultaneous users. Also, this approach is really applicable only in two-tier applications in which the application can connect to the database directly. If your application relies on middle-tier components to communicate with your database, this approach isn't feasible.

The best approach is a kind of hybrid of these two approaches. You explicitly open a connection to your database but only when you need it. This approach is similar to the one in which you let the *DataAdapter* objects manage the state of your connection. The application executes the following code when it starts up:

Visual Basic .NET

```
daProducts.Fill(dsChapter13.Products)
daEmployees.Fill(dsChapter13.Employees)
daOrders.SelectCommand.Parameters(0).Value = strCustomerID
daOrders.Fill(dsChapter13.Orders)
daDetails.SelectCommand.Parameters(0).Value = strCustomerID
daDetails.Fill(dsChapter13.Order_Details)
```

Visual C# .NET

```
daProducts.Fill(dsChapter13.Products);
daEmployees.Fill(dsChapter13.Employees);
daOrders.SelectCommand.Parameters[0].Value = strCustomerID;
daOrders.Fill(dsChapter13.Orders);
daDetails.SelectCommand.Parameters[0].Value = strCustomerID;
daDetails.Fill(dsChapter13.Order_Details)
```

Each call to the *Fill* method of a *DataAdapter* object implicitly opens and closes the *Connection* object associated with the *DataAdapter*. This means that the code opens and closes the *Connection* object four times. Calling the *Connection* object's *Open* method before the calls to the *DataAdapter* objects' *Fill* methods will improve the performance slightly. Explicitly opening the *Connection* object before calls to the *DataAdapter* objects' methods also allows you to group the changes you submit to the database in a single transaction.

If I were pressed to recommend a single, general approach to managing connection state, this is the one I'd recommend.

Connection Pooling

Connection pooling can greatly improve the performance of your multi-tiered applications. In fact, because connection pooling is enabled by default, you might be taking advantage of connection pooling without even realizing it. The only connections that are reused are the ones with the same connection string and credentials, so you're not really using connection pooling unless the middle-tier components use the same connection string and credentials.

Some developers rely on their database to enforce security in their multi-tiered applications. Because the middle-tier components use the users' credentials to connect to the database, applications that use this approach will not benefit from connection pooling. To get the full benefit of connection pooling, you should have your middle-tier components rely on their own specific credentials. Use network security to make sure that only users who have the appropriate credentials can access the middle-tier components.

Although connection pooling is primarily geared toward multi-tiered applications, it can also improve the performance of your simple two-tiered application. When the sample application closes its *Connection* object, implicitly or explicitly, the actual connection to the database is cached in the connection pool. If the application reopens the *Connection* object before the actual connection times out in the pool, the connection will be reused.

If you're working with the OLE DB .NET Data Provider and you don't want to use connection pooling in your application, add the following attribute to your connection string:

```
OLE DB Services=-4;
```

Developers working with the SQL Client .NET Data Provider can use the following attribute to ensure that their connections are not pooled when the *Connection* object is closed:

```
Pooling=False;
```

Working with BLOB Data

You'll get better performance by storing BLOB data in files on your server and storing the location of those files in your database. Operating systems are better suited to working with files. Storing that same data in a database is less efficient. SQL Server 2000, for example, breaks up BLOB data that's greater than 8 KB in size into multiple pages in the database. That means that storing the contents of a 40-KB file involves separating the contents of that file into five separate pieces.

While I'm not a big fan of storing BLOB data in databases, I can definitely see the appeal. Storing some data in a database and other data in files increases the number of technologies involved. Keeping the data secure and backing up your data becomes more complex.

In case you do decide to store BLOB data in your database, here are some tips for working with BLOB data in ADO.NET.

Delaying BLOB Fetching

If your query fetches a hundred rows and the query includes BLOB columns, do you really want to retrieve all that data along with the results of your query? SQL Server BLOB columns can contain up to 2 GB of data. Do you know how much BLOB data your query will return?

One way to improve the performance of your application is to avoid fetching BLOB data from your database until you need it. Fetch the non-BLOB data ahead of time, and then fetch the BLOB data as necessary. This technique is especially helpful when the user will access the BLOB data only for the currently visible row.

Handling BLOBs in *DataSet* Objects

Accessing and modifying the contents of a BLOB column in a *DataSet* is actually very straightforward. ADO.NET stores BLOBs of text as strings and binary BLOBs as byte arrays. The *DataRow* object does not expose *GetChunk* or *AppendChunk* methods as in previous data access models. You must retrieve or modify the entire contents of the column.

You treat a BLOB of text just as you would any other text-based column.

Visual Basic .NET

```
Dim row As DataRow
Dim strBlob As String
    :
'Accessing the contents of a BLOB of text
strBlob = CStr(row("TextBlob"))
'Modifying the contents of a BLOB of text
row("TextBlob") = strBlob
```

Visual C# .NET

```
DataRow row;
string strBlob;
    :
//Accessing the contents of a BLOB of text
strBlob = (string) row["TextBlob"];
//Modifying the contents of a BLOB of text
row["TextBlob"] = strBlob;
```

Similarly, you treat binary BLOB columns just as you would smaller binary columns.

Visual Basic .NET

```
Dim row As DataRow
Dim aBinaryBlob As Byte()
    :
'Accessing the contents of a BLOB of text
aBinaryBlob = CType(row("BinaryBlob"), Byte())
'Modifying the contents of a BLOB of text
row("BinaryBlob") = aBinaryBlob
```

Visual C# .NET

```
DataRow row;
Byte[] aBinaryBlob;
    :
//Accessing the contents of a BLOB of text
aBinaryBlob = (Byte[]) row["BinaryBlob"];
//Modifying the contents of a BLOB of text
row["BinaryBlob"] = aBinaryBlob;
```

Handling BLOBs Using *DataReader* Objects

The *DataReader* object offers you a choice: you can access the contents of a BLOB column all at once, or you can fetch data from the column in chunks.

The following code snippet uses a single call to the *DataReader* to retrieve the contents of a BLOB column:

Visual Basic .NET

```
Dim cmd As OleDbCommand
Dim rdr As OleDbDataReader
Dim intTextBlobColumnNo, intBinaryBlobColumnNo As Integer
Dim strTextBlob As String
Dim aBinaryBlob As Byte()
    :
rdr = cmd.ExecuteReader(CommandBehavior.SequentialAccess)
Do While rdr.Read
    strTextBlob = rdr.GetString(intTextBlobColumnNo)
    aBinaryBlob = CType(rdr(intBinaryBlobColumnNo), Byte())
Loop
rdr.Close
```

Visual C# .NET

```
OleDbCommand cmd;
OleDbDataReader rdr;
int intTextBlobColumnNo, intBinaryBlobColumnNo;
string strTextBlob;
Byte[] aBinaryBlob;
    :
rdr = cmd.ExecuteReader(CommandBehavior.SequentialAccess);
while (rdr.Read())
{
    strTextBlob = rdr.GetString(intTextBlobColumnNo);
    aBinaryBlob = (Byte[]) rdr[intBinaryBlobColumnNo];
}
rdr.Close()
```

> **Note**   The preceding code snippet retrieves the contents of the text BLOB column using the strongly typed *GetString* method but retrieves binary BLOB data by implicitly calling the untyped *Item* property and then converting the return value to a byte array. The *DataReader* object does expose a *GetBytes* method, but it returns data in chunks rather than in a single call.

BLOB columns can be rather large. Storing the entire contents of a BLOB column in a single string or byte array might not be the best idea if the column contains a couple hundred megabytes of data. In such cases, your best bet is to fetch the BLOB data a chunk at a time, write the contents to the hard drive, and access the contents when appropriate.

The *DataReader* object exposes two methods—*GetBytes* and *GetChars*—that let you retrieve binary data in chunks. The following code snippet demonstrates how you can use the *GetBytes* method to retrieve the contents of a binary BLOB column from a *DataReader* in 8-KB chunks and write that data to a file. You can follow the same logic to retrieve text BLOB data using the *GetChars* method instead.

Visual Basic .NET

```
'Add the following line of code at the beginning of the code module.
Imports System.IO

Dim cmd As OleDbCommand
Dim rdr As OleDbDataReader
Dim intBlobColumnNo As Integer = 1
Dim intChunkSize As Integer = 8192
Dim intOffset As Integer = 0
Dim intBytesReturned As Integer
Dim aBinaryBlob(intChunkSize) As Byte
Dim strPathToFile As String = "C:\GetBytes.jpg"
Dim filOutput As New FileStream(strPathToFile, FileMode.Create)
rdr = cmd.ExecuteReader(CommandBehavior.SequentialAccess)
rdr.Read()
Do
    intBytesReturned = CInt(rdr.GetBytes(intBlobColumnNo, intOffset, _
                                    aBinaryBlob, 0, intChunkSize))
    If (intBytesReturned > 0) Then
        filOutput.Write(aBinaryBlob, 0, intBytesReturned)
    End If
    intOffset += intBytesReturned
Loop Until intBytesReturned <> intChunkSize
filOutput.Close()
rdr.Close()
```

Visual C# .NET

```
//Add the following line of code at the beginning of the code module.
using System.IO;

OleDbCommand cmd;
OleDbDataReader rdr;
int intBinaryBlobCol = 1;
```

```
int intChunkSize = 8192;
int intOffset = 0;
int intBytesReturned;
Byte[] aBinaryBlob = new Byte[intChunkSize];
string strPathToFile = "C:\\GetBytes.jpg";
FileStream filOutput = new FileStream(strPathToFile, FileMode.Create);
rdr = cmd.ExecuteReader(CommandBehavior.SequentialAccess);
rdr.Read();
do
{
    intBytesReturned = (int) rdr.GetBytes(intBinaryBlobCol, intOffset,
                                  aBinaryBlob, 0, intChunkSize);
    if (intBytesReturned > 0)
        filOutput.Write(aBinaryBlob, 0, intBytesReturned);
    intOffset += intBytesReturned;
} while (intBytesReturned == intChunkSize);
filOutput.Close();
rdr.Close();
```

Binary BLOBs in the Northwind Database

You might have noticed that the Northwind database includes BLOB columns. For example, the Employees table includes a column called Photo, which contains a picture of the employee.

Unfortunately, the Photo column also contains some extra bytes in the form of an Access OLE header. This header allows Microsoft Access to know what type of data the BLOB column contains—such as a .jpg file, a Word document, or an Excel spreadsheet. As a result, if you try to fetch the contents of the Photo column using ADO.NET (or ADO, or RDO, or...) you won't be able to load that data into a PictureBox control or view the contents of the file in an imaging program such as Paint.

How can you discard the Access OLE header so that you're left with just the desired data? In short, you can't. The format of the Access OLE header is proprietary and is not documented.

However, the companion CD includes a sample application called Load-EmployeePhotos that can help you replace the default contents of the Photo column in the Employees table with pure .jpg images. In the application's directory, you'll find .jpg files that contain pictures of the employees. The application loads this data into the Northwind database by executing a series of parameterized queries.

You can also look to this application as an example of how to load the contents of files into a database using parameterized queries.

A Sample BLOB Application

Now that you have actual pictures in the Employees table, let's take a brief look at a sample application that retrieves this data and displays it on a Windows form. This application, ShowEmployeesPhotos, which is on the companion CD, retrieves employee information from the Northwind database into a *DataSet*. Figure 13-11 shows the user interface for the sample application.

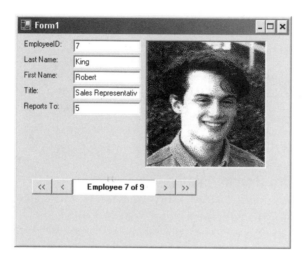

Figure 13-11 Displaying binary BLOB data and displaying it in a PictureBox control

To build the application more quickly, I relied on the *CurrencyManager* and bound controls to manage the current position and simplify the process of displaying employee information.

The *DataSet* that the sample application uses has two separate *DataTable* objects—one for the non-BLOB data and one for the BLOB data. The child *DataTable* also includes the primary key column (EmployeeID) to simplify the process of moving from a row in the parent *DataTable* to the corresponding row in the child *DataTable*. I added a column called FetchedPhoto to the parent *DataTable* to keep track of whether I've fetched the photo for that employee.

When the application starts up, it retrieves non-BLOB employee information (EmployeeID, LastName, FirstName, and so on) from the Employees table. The application then retrieves the contents of the Photo column the first time the user navigates to a particular employee. (The photos are small in size—only 22 KB—so the application wouldn't incur a large performance hit if it had loaded this data on startup, especially if the size of the table remains small.)

This approach can greatly improve the performance of applications in which the user can view only a fraction of the rows that the application retrieves.

User Interfaces Built with ADO.NET Power

You've seen how the data binding features that are intrinsic to Windows forms can help you build user interfaces quickly and easily. You've also learned that you can achieve greater control over your user interface by relying on your own code rather than on bound controls. You now also know the pros and cons of different strategies for connecting to your database, querying your database, submitting updates, and working with BLOB data.

Questions That Should Be Asked More Frequently

Q. Should I rely on data binding in an application that I plan to distribute?

A. I rely on data binding when I build the user interface for an application. It lets me develop the basic user interface quickly with a small amount of code. Once I'm comfortable with the layout of the user interface and the schema of the data that the application uses, I consider whether to continue relying on data binding. If I need more control than I can achieve using data binding, or if I decide that relying on data binding will not save time in completing the application, I replace the data binding functionality with my own code.

You'll notice that step 11 in the chapter's main sample application still relies on a bound DataGrid control to display the contents of an order. I disabled the DataGrid's updating features, but I felt that trying to replace the DataGrid's functionality would require a great deal of time without providing enough value to make that effort worthwhile.

Q. Can I bind controls with an untyped *DataSet*?

A. Absolutely. You can still bind controls at design time with untyped *DataSet* objects whose schemas you define at design time through the Property pages. You can also bind controls at run time with both typed and untyped *DataSet* objects using the code I showed you earlier in the chapter.

Visual Basic .NET

```
'Binding a TextBox to a DataColumn
TextBox.DataBindings.Add("Text", DataSet, "TableName.ColumnName")

'Binding a DataGrid to a DataTable
DataGrid.DataSource = DataSet
DataGrid.DataMember = "TableName"
```

Visual C# .NET

```
//Binding a TextBox to a DataColumn
TextBox.DataBindings.Add("Text", DataSet, "TableName.ColumnName");

//Binding a DataGrid to a DataTable
DataGrid.DataSource = DataSet;
DataGrid.DataMember = "TableName";
```

Q.   I have to load a lot of data when my application starts up. Any recommendations?

A.   Make sure you really need all that data. Obviously, if you can retrieve fewer rows and/or columns, it will take less time to fetch the results of your queries. Another option is to rely on the threading support in the .NET Framework to load data on another thread as the application starts up. For more information, see the documentation for the *System.Threading* namespace in the .NET Framework SDK. The .NET Framework simplifies threading, especially for Visual Basic users, but threading is still an advanced topic and beyond the scope of this book.

Q.   Why does the code in step 11 use a *DataView* rather than the *DataTable* to determine the position of the current order?

A.   If you mark a *DataRow* as deleted, it will still reside in the *DataTable* object's *Rows* collection. The application allows the user to mark an order as deleted. If the application were to rely solely on the *DataTable* object, it would require a great deal more code to skip orders that are marked as deleted while navigating through the remaining orders.

   Instead, the application uses the *DataView* object. With the default setting for the *DataView* object's *RowStateFilter* property, rows marked as deleted are not visible through the *DataView*, which simplifies the process of navigating through the remaining orders. The *CurrencyManager* object behaves in the same way.

Q.   How can I achieve pessimistic locking in a multi-tiered application that relies on a stateless middle tier?

A.   As I stated earlier in the chapter, only a small percentage of applications truly require pessimistic locking. Pessimistically locking data in a multi-tiered application with a stateless middle tier is definitely an advanced scenario. Airline reservation systems require this functionality. The user requests a seat on a flight, and the application locks that seat so that no one else can purchase it.

   Consider the architecture for a moment. Because the application accesses the database through a stateless middle tier, this means the application must allow the user to maintain locks on data without a live connection. Offhand, I don't know of any database that lets you persist a lock on data so that you can disconnect and later reconnect while the lock remains.

   However, you could devise your own locking scheme to achieve this functionality. To be honest, I haven't deployed large multi-user applications that rely on this type of architecture. But if my livelihood depended on developing such applications using SQL Server as the back end, here's what I'd do:

1.   Set the database's security so that users can modify the contents of the table only through calls to stored procedures.

2.   Add two columns to the table—one to contain a unique lock key and one to indicate the date and time the user successfully locked the row.

3.   Create a stored procedure that allows the user to request a lock on a row. The stored procedure will take the row's primary key and a GUID as input parameters. The stored procedure marks the row of data as locked if it is not already locked. Here's an example of such a stored procedure:

```
CREATE PROCEDURE spPessimisticLockAcquireLock
(@ID int, @LockID uniqueidentifier)
AS
UPDATE tblPessimisticLock
    SET LockAcquired = GetDate(), LockID = @LockID
    WHERE ID = @ID AND LockAcquired IS NULL
```

4. Create a stored procedure that lets the user modify the contents of the row. The stored procedure takes parameters for the row's primary key columns, the new data for the column, and the lock key. The stored procedure updates the row only if the lock key supplied matches the one in the database. If the stored procedure successfully updates the row, it will mark the row as available.

    ```
    CREATE PROCEDURE spPessimisticLockUpdateRow
    (@ID int, @DescCol varchar(32), @LockID uniqueidentifier)
    AS
    UPDATE tblPessimisticLock
        SET DescCol = @DescCol
        WHERE ID = @ID AND LockID = @LockID
    IF @@ROWCOUNT = 1
    BEGIN
        SET NOCOUNT ON
        UPDATE tblPessimisticLock
            SET LockAcquired = NULL, LockID = NULL
            WHERE ID = @ID AND LockID = @LockID
    END
    ```

5. Create a stored procedure that the user can call to mark the row as available again.

    ```
    CREATE PROCEDURE spPessimisticLockReleaseLock
    (@ID int, @LockID uniqueidentifier)
    AS
    UPDATE tblPessimisticLock
        SET LockAcquired = NULL, LockID = NULL
        WHERE ID = @ID AND LockID = @LockID
    ```

6. Create a job that will clean up all the locks that have not been released in a timely fashion. The following query locates rows marked as locked that have been locked for more than five minutes and marks those rows as available:

    ```
    UPDATE tblPessimisticLock
        SET LockAcquired = NULL, LockID = NULL
        WHERE DateAdd(mi, 5, LockAcquired) <= GetDate()
    ```

14

Building Effective Web Applications

Now that you've learned about building Windows data applications, let's look at their Internet counterparts—Web applications.

Brief Introduction to Web Applications

This chapter will serve as an introduction to Web applications. Many books are dedicated to the ASP.NET technology, including some specifically geared toward ASP.NET data access programming, such as *Building Web Solutions with ASP.NET and ADO.NET* by Dino Esposito (Microsoft Press, 2002). This chapter will provide some basic background to building Web applications that use ADO.NET to communicate with your database. Along the way we'll learn a little about data binding, the pros and cons of various ASP.NET caching options, paging, and submitting updates. Most of the examples will focus on the most powerful and flexible of the ASP.NET data bound controls: the DataGrid.

ASP.NET Makes Building Web Applications Easier

In order to build a Web application, you write code that runs in a Web server that generates HTML that the browser will translate into a Web page. You also need to include functionality in the Web page that allows the user to click buttons or links to post data back to the server. Finally, you need to write code to allow your Web server to respond to those post-back events and interpret the information that the user posted.

ASP.NET greatly simplifies the process of building Web applications. You can write ASP.NET code in your language of choice—Visual Basic .NET or Visual C# .NET. Simply set properties on ASP.NET Web controls like you would with standard Windows controls, and the controls automatically translate those settings into HTML. If you place an ASP.NET Button on your Web Form and add code to the Button control's *Click* event, ASP.NET will automatically add HTML to the corresponding Web page so that the Web server will run the code for the *Click* event when the user clicks the button. Thanks to the metadata that ASP.NET adds to the page, your code can access settings on your controls to collect the information that the user posted.

Many developers who have built ASP.NET applications aren't aware of the ASP.NET features that make building Web applications so simple. That's part of the power of ASP.NET. For example, some developers might not truly understand that the ASP.NET code and the HTML user interface are running on separate machines. Many more developers are not aware that most ASP.NET applications use a stateless middle tier; some might not even know what a stateless middle tier is.

The Good and Bad of Statelessness

When a user directs his or her browser to an ASP.NET page (*.aspx), IIS hands off the request to ASP.NET, which loads the compiled library for that page if it's not already in memory. Once ASP.NET responds to the request, it releases the resources for the page. When the user posts information back to that page, ASP.NET re-creates the page and responds to the post-back event. By default, ASP.NET does not maintain any information about the user's session between requests.

This statelessness makes your ASP.NET applications more scalable, but it can also prove challenging to developers who might not have experience building applications that rely on a stateless middle tier.

Forgetful Server, Dumb Client

In some ways, Web applications are similar to traditional mainframe applications. The Web server performs the majority of the actual processing. The Web browser might offer helpful features such as allowing you to bookmark sites, but its primary job is to transform the data that the Web server returns into a simple user interface.

For example, say you write ASP.NET code that uses a *DataAdapter* to fetch product information from your database into a *DataTable*. You then bind a Web DataGrid to the *DataTable* to display the product information on your

Web page. Let's also assume that you've added a button or a link for each product to the Web page so that the user can add that particular product to a shopping cart.

ASP.NET helped you convert the results of the query into HTML that the Web browser then displayed. But once ASP.NET finished responding to the page request it released the page's resources, including the *DataTable* of product information. The Web browser displays a visual representation of the results, but it didn't actually receive the *DataTable* object. In fact, even if the browser did receive the *DataTable* object, it wouldn't know what to do with it; it's not .NET aware, so to speak.

Connecting to Your Database

Connecting to your database in a Web application is similar to connecting to your database in Windows applications. You still use a *Connection* object to manage the connection to your database. However, there are some slight differences to keep in mind when connecting in a Web application.

Working with Trusted Connections

Throughout this text, we've used trusted connections to connect to the local .NET Framework SDK MSDE installation on your development machine:

```
Provider=SQLOLEDB;Data Source=(local)\NetSDK;
Initial Catalog=Northwind;Trusted_Connection=Yes;
```

You can use this same connection string at design time in a Web application, but you might encounter problems using this connection string at run time. Say you create a new Web application and add the following code to your Web Form's *Load* event:

Visual Basic .NET

```
Dim strConn As String
strConn = "Provider=SQLOLEDB;Data Source=(local)\NetSDK;" & _
        "Initial Catalog=Northwind;Trusted_Connection=Yes;"
Dim cn As New OleDbConnection(strConn)
cn.Open()
```

Visual C# .NET

```
string strConn;
strConn = "Provider=SQLOLEDB;Data Source=(local)\\NetSDK;" +
        "Initial Catalog=Northwind;Trusted_Connection=Yes;";
OleDbConnection cn = new OleDbConnection(strConn);
cn.Open();
```

Depending on the version of Windows that you're using to build your Web application, you might generate an exception when you try to run this application with the following message:

```
Login failed for user 'MyMachineName\ASPNET'
```

This same connection string worked just fine in Windows and Console applications. Why would it fail in a Web application? Remember that when you connect to SQL Server using a trusted connection, SQL Server uses your network credentials to determine whether you can connect to the database. The exception's message indicates why the connection is failing. The connection attempt is made using the ASP.NET account's credentials, not yours, because the code is running in the ASP.NET process. The result of the connection attempt depends on whether the ASP.NET account has privileges to the SQL Server database.

SQL Server Enterprise Manager makes granting database access to an account simple. Expand the Security folder for the server, right-click Logins, and select New Login. If you're working with an MSDE database and don't have access to Enterprise Manager, you can also execute the following query to grant account access to SQL Server:

```
exec sp_grantlogin 'DomainOrMachineName\AccountName'
```

Impersonating Users

What if you want to use the actual user's credentials to log in to your database?

ASP.NET makes impersonating users relatively straightforward. When you create a new Web application using Visual Studio .NET, you'll see a file called Web.config in Solution Explorer. This file is an XML document that contains settings for your application. In this document, you'll find an authorization section that looks like this:

```
<authorization>
    <allow users="*" />
</authorization>
```

These settings allow all users to connect to the application. You can have the application impersonate the current user and deny anonymous logins by changing these settings to the following:

```
<authorization>
    <deny users="?" />
</authorization>
<identity impersonate="true" />
```

Once you've made these changes, attempts to connect to your database using trusted connections rely on the actual user's network credentials. However, I'm not a big fan of using trusted connections in this fashion for Web applications for a number of reasons.

This architecture does not benefit from connection pooling. If three different users connect to a Web application that relies on impersonation and trusted connections, each of these connections has a different security context. As a result, ADO.NET can't pool User A's connection and then reuse it for User B. In fact, connection pooling can adversely affect the performance of this type of application. Each user's connection will remain open until it's removed from the pool, but it can be reused only by that particular user.

I don't like the idea of relying on the database to enforce security in an application. If you're familiar with trusted connections to your database, it's tempting to rely on this feature rather than learn about different ASP.NET authentication options. There's no need to incur a network round-trip to your database in order to authenticate the current user. ASP.NET offers plenty of options for enforcing security in your application—Windows authentication, Passport authentication, and Forms authentication.

Working with Access Databases

Many developers are used to communicating with Access databases and plan on relying on them in their ASP.NET applications. I don't want to encourage that. Access databases are not designed for large numbers of simultaneous users. They're not scalable like SQL Server and Oracle databases. However, I can understand their appeal. They're extremely simple to create and manage.

So, I'd be performing a disservice if I didn't talk briefly about working with Access databases in ASP.NET applications. Late in the development of .NET, Microsoft made some changes to the network permissions associated with the ASP.NET account. These changes can affect developers working with Access databases in their ASP.NET applications.

When you open an Access database, the Jet database engine uses a locking file associated with the database to keep track of the various locks (both read and write) that users have placed on various rows and pages. As a result, the user who is accessing the database needs read/write permissions on the directory in which the Access database resides. If you receive either of the following exceptions,

```
The Microsoft Jet database engine cannot open the file
'C:\Path\To\MyDatabase.mdb'. It is already opened exclusively by another
user, or you need permission to view its data.
```

or

```
Operation must use an updateable query.
```

the likely cause of the problem is the fact that the ASP.NET account cannot write to the lock file. Make sure that the ASP.NET account has read/write access to the directory in which your Access database resides.

Displaying Data on Your Web Page

Of course, connecting to a database is just the first step. Once you've done that, you generally want to execute a query, retrieve the results, and display the data you've retrieved onto the Web page.

As with Windows Forms, you can write ASP.NET code to set properties of controls by hand using code such as the following:

Visual Basic .NET

```
TextBox1.Text = MyDataSet.Tables("MyTable").Rows(0)("MyColumn")
```

Visual C# .NET

```
TextBox1.Text = (string) MyDataSet.Tables["MyTable"].Rows[0]["MyColumn"];
```

You can also take advantage of data binding features in ASP.NET controls to simplify this process. Let's say you've added code to your Web application to execute a query and fetch the results in a *DataSet*. Now you want to display the contents of the *DataSet* in an HTML table on your Web page. You could generate the HTML for the table by writing a lot of code, or by using XML and XSLT, but you'll save yourself a lot of headaches by using ASP.NET's data binding features.

Bound ASP.NET controls convert the data into HTML for your Web page. ASP.NET data binding is a one-way street. If you bind a text box to a column in a *DataTable*, display the page, and edit the contents of the text box, the new contents of the text box aren't assigned to that column of data in the *DataTable*. The DataGrid control does offer features that let you build updating functionality into your Web pages, but for the most part bound ASP.NET controls are used for read-only data.

Just as with Windows data binding, you can bind single-value controls such as text boxes or multivalue controls such as grids to data sources. You can bind multivalue controls using the standard *DataSource* and *DataMember* properties. You can bind both single-value and multivalue controls using the *DataBinder* object that's static to the page.

Using *DataBinder.Eval*

Let's start working with ASP.NET data binding by binding a TextBox control using the *DataBinder* object's *Eval* method. The *DataBinder* object uses reflection to extract data from an object. For example, you could use the following code to return the value of the CompanyName column in the first row in a *DataTable*:

```
DataBinder.Eval(DataTable, "Rows[0].[CompanyName]")
```

This *Eval* method returns data using the generic *Object* data type, which you can then cast to the appropriate data type.

The *Eval* method is overloaded. There's another *Eval* method that lets you supply a format string. Say you're retrieving information for a particular product and you want to display the product's unit price in a text box. You could use the following call to the *Eval* method to format the contents of the UnitPrice column as currency:

```
DataBinder.Eval(DataTable, "Rows[0].[UnitPrice]", "{0:c}")
```

This *Eval* method returns data in a string, using the format you've supplied. For more information on expressions for formatting strings, see the documentation for the *String* object's *Format* method.

The *DataBinder* object isn't just for data access objects. You can use the *DataBinder* object to extract data from properties of other objects as well. For example, the following code returns the value of a TextBox control's *Visible* property:

```
DataBinder.Eval(TextBox1, "Visible")
```

This syntax is roughly equivalent to directly calling the TextBox control's *Visible* property, except that the *DataBinder* code is late bound. If you made a typo and accidentally wrote the following code:

```
DataBinder.Eval(TextBox1, "Visibile")
```

you would receive an error at run time rather than at compile time.

The fact that the *DataBinder* object uses late binding to return data makes the object more flexible but represents a small performance hit because there's more work to do at run time.

Binding a TextBox to a *DataSet*

Now that we've learned a little about the *DataBinder* object, let's use it to bind a TextBox to a column of data returned by a *DataAdapter*. The following code retrieves information from the Customers table into a *DataSet*, and then uses the *DataBinder* object to set the TextBox control's *Text* property to the CompanyName column for the first row returned by the query:

Visual Basic .NET

```
Dim strConn, strSQL, strExpression As String
strConn = "Provider=SQLOLEDB;Data Source=(local)\NetSDK;" & _
        "Initial Catalog=Northwind;Trusted_Connection=Yes;"
strSQL = "SELECT CustomerID, CompanyName FROM Customers " & _
        "WHERE CustomerID = 'WOLZA'"
Dim da As New OleDbDataAdapter(strSQL, strConn)
Dim ds As New DataSet()
da.Fill(ds, "Customers")
strExpression = "Tables[Customers].Rows[0].[CompanyName]"
TextBox1.Text = CStr(DataBinder.Eval(ds, strExpression))
```

Visual C# .NET

```
string strConn, strSQL, strExpression;
strConn = "Provider=SQLOLEDB;Data Source=(local)\\NetSDK;" +
        "Initial Catalog=Northwind;Trusted_Connection=Yes;";
strSQL = "SELECT CustomerID, CompanyName FROM Customers " +
        "WHERE CustomerID = 'WOLZA'";
OleDbDataAdapter da = new OleDbDataAdapter(strSQL, strConn);
DataSet ds = new DataSet();
da.Fill(ds, "Customers");
strExpression = "Tables[Customers].Rows[0].[CompanyName]";
TextBox1.Text = (string) DataBinder.Eval(ds, strExpression);
```

Binding a TextBox to a *DataReader*

You can also use the *DataBinder* object to extract data from a *DataReader* object. The following code snippet uses a *DataReader* object to retrieve the results of a query. Because we're going to use only the first row returned by the query, the code uses the *SingleRow* constant in the *CommandBehavior* enumeration.

Visual Basic .NET

```
Dim strConn, strSQL As String
strConn = "Provider=SQLOLEDB;Data Source=(local)\NetSDK;" & _
        "Initial Catalog=Northwind;Trusted_Connection=Yes;"
Dim cn As New OleDbConnection(strConn)
cn.Open()
strSQL = "SELECT CustomerID, CompanyName FROM Customers " & _
        "WHERE CustomerID = 'WOLZA'"
Dim cmd As New OleDbCommand(strSQL, cn)
Dim rdr As OleDbDataReader
rdr = cmd.ExecuteReader(CommandBehavior.SingleRow)
rdr.Read()
TextBox1.Text = CStr(DataBinder.Eval(rdr, "[CompanyName]"))
rdr.Close()
cn.Close()
```

Visual C# .NET

```
string strConn, strSQL;
strConn = "Provider=SQLOLEDB;Data Source=(local)\\NetSDK;" +
        "Initial Catalog=Northwind;Trusted_Connection=Yes;";
OleDbConnection cn = new OleDbConnection(strConn);
cn.Open();
strSQL = "SELECT CustomerID, CompanyName FROM Customers " +
        "WHERE CustomerID = 'WOLZA'";
OleDbCommand cmd = new OleDbCommand(strSQL, cn);
OleDbDataReader rdr;
rdr = cmd.ExecuteReader(CommandBehavior.SingleRow);
rdr.Read();
TextBox1.Text = (string) DataBinder.Eval(rdr, "[CompanyName]");
rdr.Close();
cn.Close();
```

Binding DataGrid Controls to the Results of Queries

ASP.NET includes a built-in DataGrid control that can transform the results of a query into an HTML table. The DataGrid control offers a number of powerful features such as paging, sorting, and updating. For now, let's just focus on using the DataGrid to display the results of a query.

Binding a DataGrid to a *DataSet*

The following code creates an *OleDbDataAdapter* and a *DataSet*, fetches the results of a query into the *DataSet*, and binds a Web Forms DataGrid control to the desired *DataTable* in the *DataSet*.

Visual Basic .NET

```
Dim strConn, strSQL As String
strConn = "Provider=SQLOLEDB;Data Source=(local)\NetSDK;" & _
        "Initial Catalog=Northwind;Trusted_Connection=Yes;"
strSQL = "SELECT CustomerID, CompanyName, ContactName, Phone " & _
        "FROM Customers"
Dim da As New OleDbDataAdapter(strSQL, strConn)
Dim ds As New DataSet()
da.Fill(ds, "Customers")
gridCustomers.DataSource = ds
gridCustomers.DataMember = "Customers"
gridCustomers.DataBind()
```

Visual C# .NET

```
string strConn, strSQL;
strConn = "Provider=SQLOLEDB;Data Source=(local)\\NetSDK;" +
        "Initial Catalog=Northwind;Trusted_Connection=Yes;";
```

(continued)

```
strSQL = "SELECT CustomerID, CompanyName, ContactName, Phone " +
        "FROM Customers";
OleDbDataAdapter da = new OleDbDataAdapter(strSQL, strConn);
DataSet ds = new DataSet();
da.Fill(ds, "Customers");
gridCustomers.DataSource = ds;
gridCustomers.DataMember = "Customers";
gridCustomers.DataBind();
```

The code is identical to the code required to bind a Windows Forms Data-Grid to a *DataSet*, except for one small but important difference. After setting the *DataSource* and *DataMember* properties, the code calls the *DataBind* method on the DataGrid. With the Windows Forms *DataGrid*, the grid is bound to the data source as soon as you set the *DataSource* and *DataMember* properties. The same is not true with Web Forms data binding. The control will not display data from its data source unless you call its *DataBind* method. You can also call the page's *DataBind* method, which implicitly calls the *DataBind* method on the page's controls.

Binding a DataGrid to a *DataReader*

As I noted earlier, data on a Web page is generally read-only. *DataSet* objects offer a great deal more functionality (caching updates, simplifying navigating between related tables, and so on) that you might not need if you want to simply execute a query and display the results on a Web page. To provide better performance, ASP.NET controls also support binding to *DataReader* objects.

The following code snippet executes the same query but retrieves the results via an *OleDbDataReader* and binds a Web Forms DataGrid to that *DataReader*.

Visual Basic .NET

```
Dim strConn, strSQL As String
strConn = "Provider=SQLOLEDB;Data Source=(local)\NetSDK;" & _
        "Initial Catalog=Northwind;Trusted_Connection=Yes;"
strSQL = "SELECT CustomerID, CompanyName, ContactName, Phone " & _
        "FROM Customers"
Dim cn As New OleDbConnection(strConn)
cn.Open()
Dim cmd As New OleDbCommand(strSQL, cn)
Dim rdr As OleDbDataReader = cmd.ExecuteReader()
gridCustomers.DataSource = rdr
gridCustomers.DataBind()
rdr.Close()
cn.Close()
```

Visual C# .NET

```
string strConn, strSQL;
strConn = "Provider=SQLOLEDB;Data Source=(local)\\NetSDK;" +
         "Initial Catalog=Northwind;Trusted_Connection=Yes;";
strSQL = "SELECT CustomerID, CompanyName, ContactName, Phone " +
         "FROM Customers";
OleDbConnection cn = new OleDbConnection(strConn);
cn.Open()
OleDbCommand cmd = new OleDbCommand(strSQL, strConn);
OleDbDataReader rdr = cmd.ExecuteReader();
gridCustomers.DataSource = rdr;
gridCustomers.DataBind();
rdr.Close();
cn.Close();
```

Caching Data Between Round-Trips

All right. So you know how to display data on a Web page. You know how to execute queries and use bound controls to convert that data to HTML. What if you don't want to execute the same queries every time someone hits your Web server? Maybe you want to cache the results of a process-intensive query. Maybe you want to store the contents of the user's shopping cart.

ASP.NET offers many caching features that let you control how you maintain data for your application or for each separate session. The features themselves are very straightforward. However, there's no single universal "right" or "wrong" way to cache data. Relying on a particular caching feature in one application might improve performance, while using the same feature in another application might hinder performance.

To understand which, if any, caching feature you should use in your application, you need to understand the architecture of the application you're building, as well as how each caching feature works, its pros and its cons. Rather than make sweeping statements like "Caching data in the *Application* object is a lousy idea," this text will quickly cover the basics of the various ASP.NET caching features as well as some of the pros and cons for each feature.

The Stateless Approach—Maintaining No State

There's no programming law saying that you must cache data. You can have your Web application's ASP.NET code be completely stateless.

You can have your ASP.NET code execute queries and convert the results to HTML using bound controls. If you're working with an order-entry application in which the user stores items in a shopping cart, you can store the contents of the current user's shopping cart in your database, relying on the session ID as a way to locate which rows in the database belong to the current user.

Benefits to Statelessness

This approach has obvious merits. By not caching data in your ASP.NET code, the application requires a minimum of memory per user. Purely from a memory standpoint, this approach is the most scalable.

Drawbacks to Statelessness

However, that's a very simplistic view of building scalable applications. Say application is an online catalog and you're displaying a list of product categories on all pages. Do you really want to query your database for the list of product categories each and every time a user accesses a page?

Caching Data at the Client

If you want to cache data but don't want to maintain that data on your servers, you can use various options to cache data at the client.

Cookies

Many Web sites use cookies to store user information at the client. The ASP.NET *Request* and *Response* objects each expose a *Cookies* collection that you can use to store and retrieve information between round-trips. For example, you could use the following code in your ASP.NET code to track the date and time of the user's last visit in a cookie:

Visual Basic .NET

```
If Request.Cookies("LastVisit") Is Nothing Then
    lblLastVisit.Text = "This is your first visit!  Welcome!"
    Response.AppendCookie(New HttpCookie("LastVisit", Now.ToString))
Else
    lblLastVisit.Text = "Welcome back.  Your last visit was: " & _
                        Request.Cookies("LastVisit").Value
    Response.Cookies("LastVisit").Value = Now.ToString
End If
```

Visual C# .NET

```
if (Request.Cookies["LastVisit"] == null)
{
    lblLastVisit.Text = "This is your first visit!  Welcome!";
    Response.AppendCookie(new HttpCookie("LastVisit",
                                DateTime.Now.ToString()));
}
```

```
else
{
    lblLastVisit.Text = "Welcome back.  Your last visit was: " +
                        Request.Cookies["LastVisit"].Value;
    Response.Cookies["LastVisit"].Value = DateTime.Now.ToString();
}
```

Benefits to maintaining state using cookies   ASP.NET makes working with cookies simple. Storing data at the client allows your ASP.NET code to be stateless, which improves your scalability. Cookies are also configurable. You can control when the cookie expires by setting the *HttpCookie* object's *Expires* property.

Drawbacks to maintaining state using cookies   Cookies are designed to store small pieces of information. Most browsers will not let you store more than a couple kilobytes of data in a cookie, so they're not terribly handy for caching the results of a query that returns more than a couple rows.

Also, Internet developers are becoming less reliant on cookies. Depending on the browser's settings, the browser might reject the cookie. Keep that in mind before deciding to use cookies to store user settings.

Cookies aren't completely secure. The user can modify the contents of the cookie.

Hidden Fields

You can store information in a hidden field on your Web page. This process is somewhat analogous to a hidden control on a Windows Form. However, hidden fields aren't easily accessible through ASP.NET code. So, rather than examine the benefits and drawbacks to hidden fields in any depth, let's move along to a similar feature that's more developer-friendly—*ViewState*.

ViewState

The *Page* class in the *System.Web.UI* namespace exposes a *ViewState* property, which contains a *StateBag* object. Essentially, a *StateBag* object is similar to a collection of name/value pairs. You use it to store information, similar to the *Cookies* collections on the *Request* and *Response* objects.

You can store data in a page's *ViewState* and then retrieve that data in the next post-back event for the page. Working with the page's *ViewState* is as simple as working with cookies, as shown in the following code sample:

Visual Basic .NET

```
If ViewState("LastVisit") Is Nothing Then
    lblLastVisit.Text = "This is your first visit!  Welcome!"
    ViewState("LastVisit") = Now.ToString
```

(continued)

```
Else
    lblLastVisit.Text = "Welcome back.  Your last visit was: " & _
                        ViewState("LastVisit")
    ViewState("LastVisit") = Now.ToString
End If
```

Visual C# .NET

```
if (ViewState["LastVisit"] == null)
{
    lblLastVisit.Text = "This is your first visit!  Welcome!";
    ViewState["LastVisit"] = DateTime.Now.ToString();
}
else
{
    lblLastVisit.Text = "Welcome back.  Your last visit was: " +
                        ViewState["LastVisit"];
    ViewState["LastVisit"] = DateTime.Now.ToString();
}
```

Figure 14-1 shows the source for a page that uses the preceding code snippet to maintain the data and time of the user's last visit in the page's *View-State*. If you look closely at the page's HTML, you'll see that the *ViewState* is maintained in a hidden field. Because all browsers support hidden fields regardless of their configuration, you can use the *ViewState* to store data for many scenarios in which using cookies would cause problems.

Figure 14-1 Examining a page's *ViewState*

Benefits to maintaining state in *ViewState*   As with cookies, storing data in a page's *ViewState* allows the ASP.NET code to remain stateless, which improves your code's scalability. Because *ViewState* is implemented as a hidden field, you can store and retrieve data from a page's *ViewState* regardless of the browser's security settings. And unlike cookies, the page can hold much larger items in its *ViewState*.

Drawbacks to maintaining state in *ViewState* The data you store in a page's *ViewState* is sent down to the browser, so the more data you store the longer it takes to load pages and post back to the server. Also, while the data stored in *ViewState* is hashed, it's still possible for the user to decrypt the data stored there. Thus, it's not completely secure.

You can't store just any data in *ViewState*. You can store only data that your ASP.NET code knows how to serialize. You can store simple data types such as strings and integers. However, you can't store generic objects in *ViewState* because ASP.NET doesn't know how to store and re-create generic objects. Classes that support the *ISerializable* interface, such as *DataSet* objects and *DataTable* objects, can be written to *ViewState*.

Maintaining State in Your Web Server

ASP.NET also gives you various options for maintaining state on the server.

Session

The *Page* class exposes a *Session* property, which returns an instance of an *HttpSessionState* class. You can store data in the page's *Session*, just as you can in the page's *ViewState*. However, the data that you store in the page's *Session* is kept on the server rather than sent down to the browser along with the HTML for the page.

ASP.NET maintains the settings stored in *Session* until the user's session ends. Also, these settings are kept separate from those of other sessions. So the information stored in the page's *Session* is specific to that session.

Benefits to maintaining state in *Session* Because the data is maintained by the Web server rather than by the browser, the data is secure. The user cannot access or modify the contents of the *Session* object through the browser. Also, because the data is maintained on the server, you can rely on the *Session* object regardless of the user's browser settings.

Drawbacks to maintaining state in *Session* Storing data in the page's *Session* means your ASP.NET code might be less scalable as a result. Maintaining state in *Session* requires resources for each session of your application.

Say the user searches your product catalog and you maintain the results of that search in *Session* so that the user can page back and forth through the results without having to re-execute the query with each change of a page. Estimate how much memory is required to store the results of that query. 5 KB? 50 KB? 500 KB? Now multiply that by the number of people accessing this feature of your Web application. 10? 100? 1000? More? Think about the total server resources you'll likely use if you decide to maintain state in *Session* scope.

Application

The *Application* object is similar to the *Session* object except that the data available through the page's *Application* property is shared across all sessions. Thus, data you store in *Application* is available to all users.

Benefits to maintaining state in *Application*   As with data that you store in *Session*, the data you store in *Application* is secure because it's maintained on the server and the functionality is available regardless of the user's browser settings.

Because the data stored in *Application* is global to all sessions of the application, it's an ideal place to store non-volatile data that's used in all sessions, such as a list of product categories.

Drawbacks to maintaining state in *Application*   Data that you store in *Application* uses resources on your server. Storing too much data in *Application* can adversely affect the performance of your application.

Cache

The *Page* object exposes a *Cache* property, which returns an instance of the *Cache* object. You can think of the *Cache* object as a more robust *Application* object. The data stored in *Cache* is available in all sessions of the application. You can access and modify the contents of the *Cache* object just like the *Application* object, but the *Cache* object gives you the following additional functionality when you add an item to the *Cache* via the *Add* or *Insert* method:

- You can specify when that item will be removed from the cache by supplying either a specific (*DateTime*) value or a relative (*TimeSpan*) value.

- You can specify a *CacheDependancy*, which will force the item to be removed from the cache when the dependent item changes. For example, you can supply a *CacheDependancy* that will force the item in the cache to be removed when the contents of a specific XML file change.

- You can specify a callback function that ASP.NET will call when the item is removed from the cache.

- The benefits and drawbacks to using the *Cache* object are the same as those for the *Application* object, except that the *Cache* object offers additional cache removal features.

Output Caching

Imagine that all pages in your Web application will show a list of site options along the left margin of the page. This list might contain the available product categories or it might simply list the various areas of your Web site. In either case, let's say that the data that you use to construct this list is stored in your database somewhere and rarely changes.

You might decide to retrieve this data into a *DataSet* and store this *DataSet* in the *Application* object. This way your ASP.NET code does not need to fetch that data from the database each time it serves up a page. That would probably save a lot of network traffic, but you still wind up converting the contents of the *DataSet* to HTML each time you serve up a page of data.

ASP.NET offers another option: output caching. You can cache the output for a page or a portion of a page. You can also cache full or partial pages based on parameters. If you're looking to cache data to HTML for a page or a portion of the page, you should take a look at this powerful feature.

Benefits to using output caching   If you need to repeatedly generate the same HTML based on the contents of the *DataSet*, output caching is more efficient because it requires less processing at the server. Like the *Cache* object, you can control how long the output remains cached.

Drawbacks to using output caching   As with other server-side caching features, output caching still consumes resources on your server.

Maintaining State in Your Database

No one says you must maintain state in your Web server. Database servers are designed to maintain and serve up data. You can use your database to store global and session-specific data for your Web application, such as the contents of each user's shopping cart.

Your application might execute a query that's so complex or time consuming that you'd rather store the results of the query in a separate table than execute the query each time the user requests the next page worth of results. For example, the user might supply input to query your inventory database to find CD burners under $200, capable of writing at 20x or greater, that support USB and FireWire, and that are available at stores within a 30-mile radius of the user's home. The query might look something like this:

```
SELECT ProductID, ProductName, Description, UnitPrice, ... FROM Products
    WHERE UnitPrice < 200 AND Description LIKE '%USB%' AND
        Description LIKE '%FireWire%' AND ...
```

Suppose that query returns 50 records and the user will see 10 items per page. You can execute the query each time the user requests another page of results, or you can store the results in a table in your database. You could create a table to store the results of queries against this table using an INSERT INTO query and include the user's session ID so that you can keep track of which results belong to which session:

```
INSERT INTO ProductsQueryCache
SELECT ? AS SessionID, ProductID, ProductName, Description, UnitPrice, ...
    FROM Products
    WHERE UnitPrice < 200 AND Description LIKE '%USB%' AND
          Description LIKE '%FireWire%' AND ...
```

Then you could simply retrieve the next page's rows from this results table rather than executing the original query against your main catalog table. This particular example might not do the technique justice, but it can prove helpful when working with queries that you'd rather not execute repeatedly.

> **Note**   If you use this technique, be sure you remove the cached rows from the database in the *Session* object's *End* event, or wherever is appropriate.

Benefits to Maintaining State in Your Database

By storing state in your database, your ASP.NET code can remain stateless. Data that you store in your database is durable. If your Web server crashes for whatever reason, the data that you've stored in your database will still be available once you get the Web server back on line. The data that you store in the database is secure because it is not readily available to the user except through your ASP.NET code. Databases are designed to handle large result sets. If you absolutely must maintain large result sets between page requests, storing that data in your database is probably your best bet.

Drawbacks to Maintaining State in Your Database

Maintaining state in your database is more complex than simply storing data in simple objects and collections such as *Session*, *Application*, *Cache*, *ViewState*, or a cookie.

Guidelines for Maintaining State

How and where you maintain your state can have an enormous impact on the performance, scalability, and security of your Web applications. There are no absolute guidelines to determining if, how, and where you should maintain state for your Web application. However, here are some general guidelines.

Storing Data in *ViewState*

Store data in *ViewState* if you're working with small result sets and you're OK with the user being able to view this data. If you're concerned about security and don't want to take any chances on the user modifying this data, store it in the *Session* object or in your database. Remember that the data you store in *ViewState* is passed back and forth between the server and the client on each round-trip. The more data you store in *ViewState*, the longer each round-trip will take.

Storing Data in the *Application* Object

Store in the *Application* object small amounts of data that's global to all sessions for the application. Remember that the more data you store in the *Application* object, the more you'll adversely affect performance.

Storing Data in the *Session* Object

Store in the *Session* object small amounts of data that's critical to that particular session and that you're not comfortable storing in *ViewState* for security reasons. Remember that the more data you store in the *Session* object, the more you'll adversely affect performance, and at a more accelerated rate than with the *Application* object. For example, storing 100 KB of data in a *Session* doesn't sound like much until you multiply that by the number of sessions that ASP.NET will maintain at any given time. Store large amounts of session-specific data in your database instead.

Storing Data in the Database

Store large amounts of session-specific data in your database. Accessing data from memory is obviously faster than retrieving the same information from your database. But, if you need to store large amounts of session-specific data, maintaining that data in your database lowers the total amount of memory in use on your server at any given time.

Using Output Caching

If you want to generate the same static HTML over and over again, use ASP.NET output caching rather than caching the data required to generate that HTML.

Paging

Few companies' catalogs can fit on a single Web page. Say you set up a search engine for your product catalog and a hundred items fit the search criteria that the user specified. Rather than provide links to all of those products on the resulting Web page, you'll probably want to break up the results into a series of pages and display the contents of only the first page.

Displaying just the first page is generally simple. But how do you supply functionality to allow the user to move to the next page of the result set, or to move to a specific page?

ASP.NET and ADO.NET offer features that can help you serve up the results of your queries a page at a time. Let's look at those features now.

Paging Features of the Web DataGrid

The Web DataGrid includes features that make it extremely easy to display the results of a query a page at a time. The DataGrid control includes properties such as *AllowPaging* and *PagerStyle* that you can set programmatically to control how and where you display paging information for the data to which the DataGrid is bound. Figure 14-2 shows an example of a Web page that was built using a bound DataGrid and its paging features.

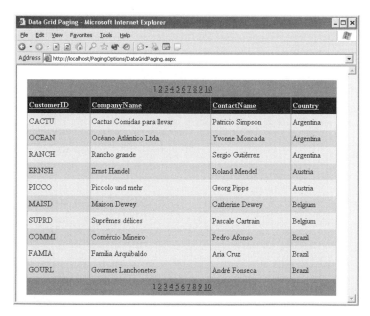

Figure 14-2   A sample Web page that uses the DataGrid's paging features

For developers building Web applications with Visual Studio .NET, the simplest way to set these properties is to use the Property Builder for the Web DataGrid. To invoke this builder, right-click a DataGrid on a Web Form and select Property Builder from the resulting context menu. Then select the Paging option on the left side of the builder, and you'll see the options displayed in Figure 14-3.

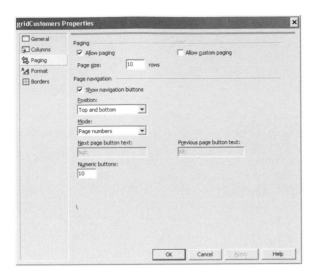

Figure 14-3   Setting paging properties of the DataGrid using the Property Builder

The *AllowPaging* Property

Setting the *AllowPaging* property to *True* tells the DataGrid to build links that will allow the user to jump from one page of the result set to the next. Once you've set this property, the DataGrid will automatically create page links along with the results when you bind the control to your data source. You can choose to display Next and Previous buttons or numeric links that allow the user to jump to a specific page.

When the user moves to a new page, the DataGrid control's *PageIndex-Changed* event will fire. You can use this event to determine which page of data the user has selected and set the DataGrid control's *CurrentPageIndex* property accordingly.

The *AllowCustomPaging* and *VirtualItemCount* Properties

Let's say that you know how to retrieve just the contents of the desired page, but you still want to use the DataGrid control's paging features to build the links to other pages in the result set. If you set the DataGrid control's *AllowCustomPaging* property to *True*, you can then set the DataGrid control's *VirtualItemCount* property to the total number of rows in the result set. The DataGrid will then build the page links based on the *VirtualItemCount* property rather than on the number of rows in the data source.

The following code snippet retrieves just the first 10 rows of a query into a *DataReader* but sets other properties of the DataGrid to create the links to the other pages of results.

Visual Basic .NET

```
gridResults.AllowPaging = True
gridResults.AllowCustomPaging = True
gridResults.CurrentPageIndex = 0
gridResults.PageSize = 10
gridResults.PagerStyle.Mode = PagerMode.NumericPages
gridResults.PagerStyle.Position = PagerPosition.TopAndBottom

Dim strConn, strSQL As String
strConn = "Provider=SQLOLEDB;Data Source=(local)\NetSDK;" & _
          "Initial Catalog=Northwind;Trusted_Connection=Yes;"
Dim cnNorthwind As New OleDbConnection(strConn)
strSQL = "SELECT COUNT(CustomerID) FROM Customers"
Dim cmdFetchRowCount As New OleDbCommand(strSQL, cnNorthwind)
strSQL = "SELECT TOP 10 CustomerID, CompanyName, ContactName, Country " & _
         "FROM Customers"
Dim cmdFetchOnePage As New OleDbCommand(strSQL, cnNorthwind)

cnNorthwind.Open()
gridResults.VirtualItemCount = cmdFetchRowCount.ExecuteScalar()
Dim rdrOnePage As OleDbDataReader = cmdFetchOnePage.ExecuteReader()
gridResults.DataSource = rdrOnePage
gridResults.DataBind()
rdrOnePage.Close()
cnNorthwind.Close()
```

Visual C# .NET

```
gridResults.AllowPaging = true;
gridResults.AllowCustomPaging = true;
gridResults.CurrentPageIndex = 0;
gridResults.PageSize = 10;
gridResults.PagerStyle.Mode = PagerMode.NumericPages;
gridResults.PagerStyle.Position = PagerPosition.TopAndBottom;

string strConn, strSQL;
strConn = "Provider=SQLOLEDB;Data Source=(local)\\NetSDK;" +
          "Initial Catalog=Northwind;Trusted_Connection=Yes;";
OleDbConnection cnNorthwind = new OleDbConnection(strConn);
strSQL = "SELECT COUNT(CustomerID) FROM Customers";
OleDbCommand cmdFetchRowCount = new OleDbCommand(strSQL, cnNorthwind);
strSQL = "SELECT TOP 10 CustomerID, CompanyName, ContactName, Country " +
         "FROM Customers";
OleDbCommand cmdFetchOnePage = new OleDbCommand(strSQL, cnNorthwind);

cnNorthwind.Open();
gridResults.VirtualItemCount =
                    Convert.ToInt32(cmdFetchRowCount.ExecuteScalar());
```

```
OleDbDataReader rdrOnePage = cmdFetchOnePage.ExecuteReader();
gridResults.DataSource = rdrOnePage;
gridResults.DataBind();
rdrOnePage.Close();
cnNorthwind.Close();
```

The query that we used in this code snippet is simple. It uses the TOP clause to fetch just the first 10 rows for the query. That syntax is great if you want to retrieve the first page of data, but how do you retrieve the contents of other pages in the result set?

Paging Features of the *DataAdapter Fill* Method

In Chapter 5, you learned about the features of the *DataAdapter* object. You might remember that the *DataAdapter* object's *Fill* method is overloaded and that one of the signatures lets you retrieve a subset of the results returned by the *DataAdapter*. In this particular method, the second parameter controls how many rows you skip before you start fetching data and the third parameter controls the maximum number of rows to retrieve.

Let's say you want to display only 10 rows per page. So, to fetch just the rows for the fifth page, you would skip the first 40 rows and fetch the next 10. The following code would retrieve that fifth page of rows into a *DataSet*:

Visual Basic .NET

```
Dim strConn, strSQL As String
strConn = "Provider=SQLOLEDB;Data Source=(local)\NetSDK;" & _
        "Initial Catalog=Northwind;Trusted_Connection=Yes;"
strSQL = "SELECT CustomerID, CompanyName, ContactName, Country " & _
        "FROM Customers"
Dim da As New OleDbDataAdapter(strSQL, strConn)
Dim ds As New DataSet()
da.Fill(ds, 40, 10, "Customers")
```

Visual C# .NET

```
string strConn, strSQL;
strConn = "Provider=SQLOLEDB;Data Source=(local)\\NetSDK;" +
        "Initial Catalog=Northwind;Trusted_Connection=Yes;";
strSQL = "SELECT CustomerID, CompanyName, ContactName, Country " +
        "FROM Customers";
OleDbDataAdapter da = new OleDbDataAdapter(strSQL, strConn);
DataSet ds = new DataSet();
da.Fill(ds, 40, 10, "Customers");
```

While this code is very simple, there's a major drawback to the approach. In this example, you're still asking the database to return data for all rows in the table. You're still paying the performance penalty of fetching those 40 rows even though the *DataAdapter* isn't adding those rows to the *DataSet*.

Building Queries That Return a Page of Data

SQL Server and Access databases support the TOP clause in a query. You can use the TOP clause to return just the first *n* rows from a query. So, you could use the following query to return just the first 10 rows from the Customers table, ordered by the Country and CustomerID columns:

```
SELECT TOP 10 CustomerID, CompanyName, ContactName, Country
    FROM Customers
    ORDER BY Country, CustomerID
```

If you want to break the results into pages, you can use this syntax to return just the rows for that particular page. For example, if you want to return the rows for the fifth page, you would want to retrieve rows 41–50 from the Customers table.

```
SELECT TOP 10 CustomerID, CompanyName, ContactName, Country
    FROM Customers WHERE CustomerID NOT IN
    (SELECT TOP 40 CustomerID FROM Customers ORDER BY Country, CustomerID)
    ORDER BY Country, CustomerID
```

This query includes a subquery that locates the first 40 rows ordered by the Country and CustomerID columns and then looks for the first 10 rows that do not appear in that subquery, again ordered by the Country and CustomerID columns. Here's a more generic way to write the query:

```
SELECT TOP PageSize Column1, Column2, ... FROM MyTable
    WHERE KeyColumn NOT IN
    (SELECT TOP RowsToSkip KeyColumn FROM MyTable ORDER BY SortOrder)
    ORDER BY SortOrder
```

Both SQL Server and Access support both the TOP and NOT IN clauses. However, these clauses aren't supported by all databases, so this isn't a completely universal solution. Oracle, for example, does not support the TOP clause.

While Oracle does not support the TOP clause, it does support a somewhat analogous feature: *rownum*. Oracle numbers the rows that the query returns and you can use *rownum* to retrieve just the first *n* rows that the query returns. However, Oracle generates the row numbers before applying the sort order for the query, so it's a little tricky to use *rownum* to return a page of data for a query where you want to use a sort order. With a little cajoling and a couple subqueries, you can use the *rownum* feature to return a specific page of data for a query that uses a sort order. The following Oracle query returns the same page (rows 41–50) of the Customers table:

```
SELECT CustomerID, CompanyName, ContactName, Country FROM
    (SELECT CustomerID, CompanyName, ContactName, Country,
            rownum AS Row_Num FROM
        (SELECT CustomerID, CompanyName, ContactName, Country
            FROM Customers ORDER BY Country, CustomerID)
        WHERE rownum <= 10)
WHERE ROW_NUM > 40
```

> **Note**   I don't claim to be an Oracle guru. There's probably an easier way to build such queries for Oracle.

The PagingOptions Sample

On the companion CD, you'll find a sample Web application called PagingOptions. This Web application uses various techniques to allow the user to page through the results of the query. Each example displays data and page links using the DataGrid. One page in the sample application relies on the DataGrid to control paging. There are other pages that cache data in *ViewState*, *Session*, and the database. There's a page that relies on subqueries to retrieve a single page worth of data from the database, one that stores the results of the initial query in the database, and one that retrieves.

Editing Data on a Web Page

So far we've focused on simply displaying data on a Web page. How do you build Web pages that allow users to edit data?

Editing data on a Web page is more complex than editing data on a Windows Form. Remember that when you use bound controls on a Web page, the bound controls use the data source to generate HTML. If you display data using a bound TextBox control and the user modifies the contents of the TextBox, that change does not automatically occur in the data source. To build a Web page that allows the user to edit data, you have to display data, give the user the ability to edit that data, and then have your ASP.NET code respond to those changes and act accordingly.

The stateless nature of Web applications also complicates building Web pages that let the user modify data. Say you display the contents of a row of data in a series of TextBox controls. Once the user modifies the contents of the row and clicks an Update button on the page, how do you locate the row you want to modify and apply those changes? Did you cache the data in the *DataSet* somewhere, such as in *ViewState* or the *Session* object? Do you have to query your database to re-fetch that row of data? What about optimistic concurrency? How can you tell if the data has changed since the user first requested it?

Using the DataGrid to Simplify Editing Data

Let's start slowly. First we'll focus on using the DataGrid to add features to the Web page that let the user select and edit rows. The goal is to build a Web page like the one shown in Figure 14-4.

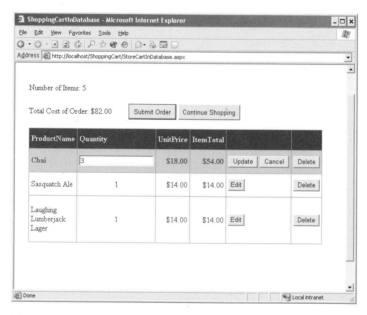

Figure 14-4   A sample Web page that allows you to edit data

Just as the DataGrid simplifies the process of building a user interface that supports paging, it also simplifies the process of building the user interface to let users select and edit rows. You can right-click a DataGrid in Visual Studio .NET and select Property Builder from the context menu to launch the Data-Grid's Property Builder, shown in Figure 14-5. From this Property Builder, you can control which columns of data appear in the grid and whether the DataGrid will allow the user to edit their contents, and you can add buttons to the grid for editing, updating, and deleting rows.

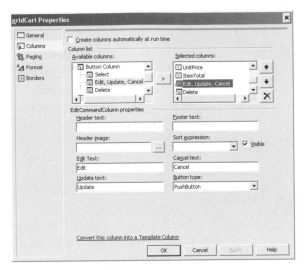

Figure 14-5   Adding editing options using the DataGrid's Property Builder

Handling the DataGrid's Editing Events

However, setting properties on the DataGrid using the Property Builder doesn't actually give the user the ability to change the contents of the data to which the DataGrid object is bound.

The DataGrid shown in Figure 14-5 has an Edit, Update, Cancel column and a Delete column. If you bind this DataGrid to a data source, your Web page will look like the one shown in Figure 14-6.

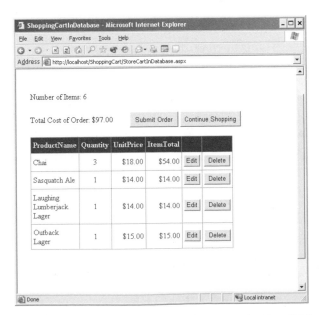

Figure 14-6   A sample Web page that uses the DataGrid's editing features

Let's say the user clicks the Edit button for the first item in the shopping cart. The DataGrid doesn't let the user edit the contents of the row directly. Instead, the button forces the page to post back to the server where the Data-Grid fires its *EditCommand* event. It's up to you to add code to this event to set the DataGrid's *EditItemIndex* property to the appropriate value.

Then, when you call the DataGrid control's *DataBind* method, the Data-Grid will include TextBox controls in the HTML table so that the user can modify the contents of the row. The DataGrid also adds Update and Cancel buttons for that particular row.

Submitting Changes to Your Database

When the user is satisfied that he or she has made the appropriate changes to the desired row and clicks the Update button, the DataGrid's *UpdateCommand* event fires. You can use the event's arguments to determine which row the user modified, as well as the current contents of the row, but it's up to you to supply the logic to submit the modified contents of the row to your database.

Applying Changes to a *DataSet*

If you want to apply the changes to a *DataSet*, you can use the *UpdateCommand* event's arguments to locate the corresponding *DataRow*, apply the changes, and submit the changes using the *DataAdapter*. The following code snippet uses the event's arguments to extract the name of the product in the shopping cart that's been modified as well as the new quantity. The code then submits this change using a *DataAdapter*.

Visual Basic .NET

```
Private Sub gridCart_UpdateCommand(ByVal source As Object, _
                                   ByVal e As DataGridCommandEventArgs)
    Dim daCart As New OleDbDataAdapter()
    Dim tblCart As New DataTable()
    ⋮
    Dim vueCart As New DataView(tblCart)
    vueCart.Sort = "ProductName"
    Dim strNewQuantity As String
    strNewQuantity = CType(e.Item.Cells(2).Controls(0), TextBox).Text
    Dim intIndexToEdit As Integer
    intIndexToEdit = vueCart.Find(e.Item.Cells(1).Text)
    vueCart(intIndexToEdit)("Quantity") = CInt(strNewQuantity)
    daCart.Update(tblCart)
End Sub
```

Visual C# .NET

```
private void gridCart_UpdateCommand(object source,
                                    DataGridCommandEventArgs e)
{
    OleDbDataAdapter daCart = new OleDbDataAdapter();
    DataTable tblCart = new DataTable();
    ⋮
    DataView vueCart = new DataView(tblCart);
    vueCart.Sort = "ProductName";
    string strNewQuantity;
    strNewQuantity = ((TextBox) e.Item.Cells[2].Controls[0]).Text;
    int intIndexToEdit;
    intIndexToEdit = vueCart.Find(e.Item.Cells(1).Text);
    vueCart[intIndexToEdit]["Quantity"] = Convert.ToInt32(strNewQuantity);
    daCart.Update(tblCart);
}
```

Building Your Own Update Queries

The previous code snippet used the event's arguments to extract the name of the product in the shopping cart that's been modified as well as the new quantity. Rather than use that data to modify the contents of a *DataSet* and then submit those changes via a *DataAdapter*, you could use that same information to build your own UPDATE query. In the previous example, you could easily build a query like

```
UPDATE ShoppingCarts SET Quantity = <NewQuantity>
    WHERE ProductName = <ProductName> AND ShoppingCartID = <SessionID>
```

The ShoppingCart Sample

On the companion CD, you'll find a sample Web application called Shopping-Cart. This Web application lets the user browse through the Northwind catalog and fill a shopping cart. The user can add items to the cart from the catalog. The user can also modify the contents of the cart by removing items from the cart or changing the quantity for a particular item. The application also allows the user to submit the order, which is then stored in the Northwind database's Order Details table.

There are two Web pages in the application: StoreCartInDatabase and StoreCartInViewState. Each page offers the user the same functionality. They simply differ in where they store the contents of the user's shopping cart. As their names imply, StoreCartInDatabase stores the contents of the user's shopping cart in the database and StoreCartInViewState stores the cart in *ViewState*.

If I had to choose one of the two approaches for a Web ordering system, I'd store the contents of the shopping cart in the database, but I thought I'd include the *ViewState* solution as well.

Questions That Should Be Asked More Frequently

Q.   How can I determine whether my query returned data before I bind my *DataReader* to the bound control?

A.   This is a very common question for Web developers. Unfortunately, there's no simple answer. If you call the *DataReader* object's *Read* method to determine whether the query returned rows and then bind controls to your *DataReader*, the controls will not bind to that first row of data.

If you're simply binding the *DataReader* to a DataGrid, you could check the *Count* property of the DataGrid's *Items* collection to determine how many rows the query returned. However, there are times when you want to know whether the query returned rows before you bind controls to the *DataReader*.

Let's say you want to retrieve the orders for a particular customer using the following query:

```
SELECT OrderID, CustomerID, OrderDate FROM Orders
    WHERE CustomerID = ?
```

If you're working with a database that supports batch queries, you could execute a batch query that first returns the number of rows that satisfy the criteria for the query and then returns the actual rows. The following query is such an example:

```
SELECT COUNT(OrderID) FROM Orders WHERE CustomerID = ?;
SELECT OrderID, CustomerID, OrderDate FROM Orders
    WHERE CustomerID = ?
```

Visual Basic .NET

```
Dim strConn, strSQL As String
strConn = "Provider=SQLOLEDB;Data Source=(local)\NetSDK;" & _
          "Initial Catalog=Northwind;Trusted_Connection=Yes;"
Dim cn As New OleDbConnection(strConn)
strSQL = "SELECT COUNT(OrderID) FROM Orders WHERE CustomerID = ?;" & _
         "SELECT OrderID, CustomerID, OrderDate FROM Orders " & _
         "WHERE CustomerID = ?"
Dim cmd As New OleDbCommand(strSQL, cn)
cmd.Parameters.Add("@CustomerID", OleDbType.WChar, 5)
```

```
cmd.Parameters.Add("@CustomerID2", OleDbType.WChar, 5)
cmd.Parameters("@CustomerID").Value = "ALFKI"
cmd.Parameters("@CustomerID2").Value = "ALFKI"
cn.Open()
Dim rdr As OleDbDataReader = cmd.ExecuteReader()
rdr.Read()
If rdr(0) > 0 Then
    'Query returned rows
    rdr.NextResult()
    gridOrders.DataSource = rdr
    gridOrders.DataBind()
Else
    'Query did not return rows
End If
rdr.Close()
cn.Close()
```

Visual C# .NET

```
string strConn, strSQL;
strConn = "Provider=SQLOLEDB;Data Source=(local)\\NetSDK;" +
          "Initial Catalog=Northwind;Trusted_Connection=Yes;";
OleDbConnection cn = new OleDbConnection(strConn);
strSQL = "SELECT COUNT(OrderID) FROM Orders WHERE CustomerID = ?;" +
         "SELECT OrderID, CustomerID, OrderDate FROM Orders " +
         "WHERE CustomerID = ?";
OleDbCommand cmd = new OleDbCommand(strSQL, cn);
cmd.Parameters.Add("@CustomerID", OleDbType.WChar, 5);
cmd.Parameters.Add("@CustomerID2", OleDbType.WChar, 5);
cmd.Parameters["@CustomerID"].Value = "ALFKI";
cmd.Parameters["@CustomerID2"].Value = "ALFKI";
cn.Open();
OleDbDataReader rdr = cmd.ExecuteReader();
rdr.Read();
if (Convert.ToInt32(rdr[0]) > 0)
{
    //Query returned rows
    rdr.NextResult();
    gridOrders.DataSource = rdr;
    gridOrders.DataBind();
}
else
{
    //Query did not return rows
}
rdr.Close();
cn.Close();
```

If you're working with a database that does not support row-returning batch queries, you can use the same approach but use separate queries instead of a batch.

Q. How do I handle optimistic concurrency when submitting changes to my database in a Web application?

A. The answer really depends on the needs of your application. The ShoppingCart sample relies on just the primary key columns when submitting changes to the cart. This logic works because the application maintains a separate shopping cart for each session. So there's no chance that multiple users will attempt to edit the contents of the same shopping cart.

If you need more restrictive concurrency checking, you could cache the contents of the row that the user is editing just before the user edits it. You would then have the original values for the row and could use those values in the WHERE clause for your update attempt to ensure that the update does not succeed if another user has modified the same row of data.

A more elegant solution is to include a timestamp value in your database table and then rely on the primary key and timestamp values in the WHERE clause. This solution is more elegant because it requires you to cache less data in *ViewState*, hidden fields, or *Session*.

Q. I'm working with a *DataSet* that contains two *DataTable* objects related by a *DataRelation* object. How do I display just the child rows for a particular parent row in a bound DataGrid?

A. The *DataRow* object has a *GetChildRows* method that returns an array of *DataRow* objects with only the child rows in the array. However, you can't bind controls such as the DataGrid to an array of *DataRow* objects. You could create a *DataView* object, initialize it to the child *DataTable* and then set the *RowFilter* property on the *DataView* so that only the desired child rows are visible through the *DataView*. Thankfully, there's an easier way.

Create a *DataView* object that's initialized to the parent *DataTable*. Then locate the desired parent row in the *DataView* and call the *CreateChildView* method to create a *DataView* that contains just the child rows.

Visual Basic .NET

```
Dim dsCustomersOrders As New DataSet()
    ⋮
Dim vueCustomers, vueOrders As DataView
vueCustomers = New DataView(dsCustomersOrders.Tables("Customers"))
vueCustomers.Sort = "CustomerID"
Dim intCustomerIndex As Integer = vueCustomers.Find("ALFKI")
If intCustomerIndex >= 0 Then
    'Located the desired parent row
    Dim drvCustomer As DataRowView = vueCustomers(intCustomerIndex)
    vueOrders = drvCustomer.CreateChildView("CustomersOrders")
    gridOrders.DataSource = vueOrders
    gridOrders.DataBind()
Else
    'Couldn't locate the desired parent row
End If
```

Visual C# .NET

```
DataSet dsCustomersOrders = new DataSet();
    ⋮
DataView vueCustomers, vueOrders;
vueCustomers = new DataView(dsCustomersOrders.Tables["Customers"]);
vueCustomers.Sort = "CustomerID";
int intCustomerIndex = vueCustomers.Find("ALFKI");
if (intCustomerIndex >= 0)
{
    //Located the desired parent row
    DataRowView drvCustomer = vueCustomers[intCustomerIndex];
    vueOrders = drvCustomer.CreateChildView("CustomersOrders");
    gridOrders.DataSource = vueOrders;
    gridOrders.DataBind();
}
else
{
    //Couldn't locate the desired parent row
}
```

Part V

Appendixes

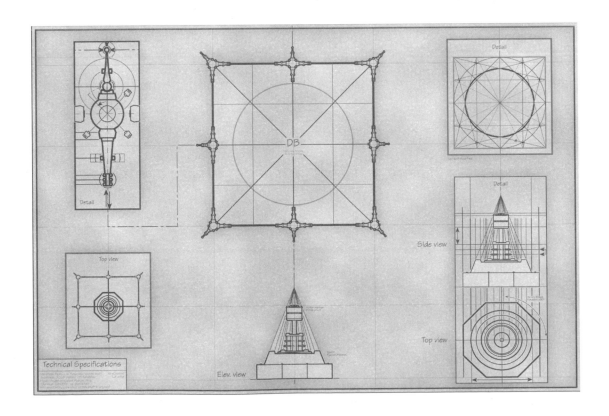

Appendix A

Using Other .NET Data Providers

This appendix takes a close look at working with .NET data providers other than the OLE DB .NET Data Provider. In most of the code snippets and documentation in this book, we communicated with a database using the OLE DB .NET Data Provider. Of course, there are other .NET data providers. The initial release of the Microsoft .NET Framework included the SQL Client .NET Data Provider. Shortly thereafter, Microsoft released the ODBC .NET Data Provider. As of this writing, Microsoft is developing an Oracle Client .NET Data Provider.

Let's look at how to use these .NET data providers and how they differ from the OLE DB .NET Data Provider.

The SQL Client .NET Data Provider

The SQL Client .NET Data Provider is designed to provide the fastest possible access to Microsoft SQL Server and Microsoft Desktop Engine (MSDE) databases.

Named Parameters vs. Parameter Markers

The SQL Client .NET Data Provider supports named parameters rather than the ? parameter marker used by OLE DB and ODBC drivers. To build a parameterized query for the SQL Client .NET Data Provider that returns just the orders for a particular customer, you would use the following query:

```
SELECT OrderID, CustomerID, EmployeeID, OrderDate
    FROM Orders WHERE CustomerID = @CustomerID
```

The OLE DB .NET Data Provider relies on positional parameter markers (?). You would use the following query to return the same data using the OLE DB .NET Data Provider:

```
SELECT OrderID, CustomerID, EmployeeID, OrderDate
    FROM Orders WHERE CustomerID = ?
```

Why the difference in syntax? The OLE DB .NET Data Provider supports the generic parameter markers that have been used to construct parameterized queries in previous data access technologies (OLE DB and ODBC) to help developers who have experience working with those technologies. OLE DB and ODBC were designed as universal data access technologies. The goal was to write back-end independent code and have the underlying components translate the generic syntax into the database-specific code.

So why does the SQL Client .NET Data Provider rely on named parameters? Because that's what SQL Server actually requires. If you try to run a parameterized query in SQL Server Query Analyzer, you'll run into problems if you try to use ? parameter markers in your query.

When you use a parameterized query to access SQL Server data using the OLE DB .NET Data Provider, the SQL Server OLE DB provider will parse the query and replace the parameter markers with named parameters. The SQL Server OLE DB provider supports the generic standard and converts the query into the format that SQL Server expects. The SQL Client .NET Data Provider is designed to more closely map its features to that of SQL Server in order to get the best possible performance when you're working with a SQL Server database. As a result, the SQL Client .NET Data Provider does not parse your queries to convert the parameter markers to named parameters.

The back-end-specific .NET data providers are designed to deliver the best possible performance when communicating with that database. As a result, you sacrifice some level of portability to gain those performance benefits.

Connecting to a SQL Server Database Using a *SqlConnection*

The SQL Client .NET Data Provider's connection object is the *SqlConnection* object. You can use this object to connect to SQL Server and MSDE databases. You set the *SqlConnection* object's *ConnectionString* property explicitly or through the object's constructor, and then you call its *Open* method, as shown in the following code snippet:

Visual Basic .NET

```
Dim strConn As String
strConn = "Data Source=(local)\NetSDK;Initial Catalog=Northwind;" & _
        "Trusted_Connection=Yes;"
Dim cn As New SqlConnection(strConn)
cn.Open()
cn.Close()
```

Visual C# .NET

```
string strConn;
strConn = "Data Source=(local)\\NetSDK;Initial Catalog=Northwind;" +
        "Trusted_Connection=Yes;";
SqlConnection cn = new SqlConnection(strConn);
cn.Open();
cn.Close();
```

You might have noticed that the connection string in the previous code snippet looks nearly identical to those we've used when connecting to SQL Server and MSDE databases using the *OleDbConnection* object. The only difference is that you omit the *Provider=...* connection string attribute. For more information on the connection string attributes that are available when you use the *SqlConnection* object, see the MSDN documentation for the object's *ConnectionString* property.

The *SqlConnection* object also exposes two properties not available on the *OleDbConnection* object: the *PacketSize* and *WorkstationId* properties. These properties are read-only, but you can set values for each property via the *SqlConnection* object's *ConnectionString* property.

Retrieving the Results of a Query Using a *SqlDataAdapter*

You can retrieve the results of a query and store them in a *DataSet* or a *DataTable* by using the *SqlDataAdapter* object. You use the *SqlDataAdapter* object just like you use the *OleDbDataAdapter* object, with one notable exception. If you want to execute a parameterized query, you need to use named parameters, as described earlier in this appendix.

Visual Basic .NET

```
Dim strConn, strSQL As String
strConn = "Data Source=(local)\NetSDK;Initial Catalog=Northwind;" & _
          "Trusted_Connection=Yes;"
strSQL = "SELECT OrderID, CustomerID, OrderDate FROM Orders " & _
         "WHERE CustomerID = @CustomerID"
Dim da As New SqlDataAdapter(strSQL, strConn)
Dim param As SqlParameter
param = da.SelectCommand.Parameters.Add("@CustomerID", SqlDbType.NChar, 5)
param.Value = "ALFKI"
Dim tbl As New DataTable("Orders")
da.Fill(tbl)
```

Visual C# .NET

```
string strConn, strSQL;
strConn = "Data Source=(local)\\NetSDK;Initial Catalog=Northwind;" +
          "Trusted_Connection=Yes;";
strSQL = "SELECT OrderID, CustomerID, OrderDate FROM Orders " +
         "WHERE CustomerID = @CustomerID";
SqlDataAdapter da = new SqlDataAdapter(strSQL, strConn);
SqlParameter param;
param = da.SelectCommand.Parameters.Add("@CustomerID", SqlDbType.NChar, 5);
param.Value = "ALFKI";
DataTable tbl = new DataTable("Orders");
da.Fill(tbl);
```

(continued)

Using the *SqlCommand* and *SqlDataReader* Objects

You can use the *SqlCommand* object to execute action queries or to retrieve the results of a query using a *SqlDataReader* object. The following code snippet demonstrates this functionality:

Visual Basic .NET

```
Dim strConn, strSQL As String
strConn = "Data Source=(local)\NetSDK;Initial Catalog=Northwind;" & _
        "Trusted_Connection=Yes;"
strSQL = "SELECT OrderID, CustomerID, OrderDate FROM Orders " & _
        "WHERE CustomerID = @CustomerID"
Dim cn As New SqlConnection(strConn)
Dim cmd As New SqlCommand(strSQL, cn)
Dim param As SqlParameter
param = cmd.Parameters.Add("@CustomerID", SqlDbType.NChar, 5)
param.Value = "ALFKI"
cn.Open()
Dim rdr As SqlDataReader = cmd.ExecuteReader()
Do While rdr.Read()
    Console.WriteLine("OrderID = " & rdr.GetInt32(0))
    Console.WriteLine("CustomerID = " & rdr.GetString(1))
    Console.WriteLine("OrderDate = " & rdr.GetDateTime(2))
    Console.WriteLine()
Loop
rdr.Close()
cn.Close()
```

Visual C# .NET

```
string strConn, strSQL;
strConn = "Data Source=(local)\\NetSDK;Initial Catalog=Northwind;" +
        "Trusted_Connection=Yes;";
strSQL = "SELECT OrderID, CustomerID, OrderDate FROM Orders " +
        "WHERE CustomerID = @CustomerID";
SqlConnection cn = new SqlConnection(strConn);
SqlCommand cmd = new SqlCommand(strSQL, cn);
SqlParameter param;
param = cmd.Parameters.Add("@CustomerID", SqlDbType.NChar, 5);
param.Value = "ALFKI";
cn.Open();
SqlDataReader rdr = cmd.ExecuteReader();
while (rdr.Read())
{
    Console.WriteLine("OrderID = " + rdr.GetInt32(0));
    Console.WriteLine("CustomerID = " + rdr.GetString(1));
    Console.WriteLine("OrderDate = " + rdr.GetDateTime(2));
    Console.WriteLine();
}
rdr.Close();
cn.Close();
```

> **Note**   The *SqlCommand* object does not support the *Table* value from the *CommandType* enumeration.

As noted in Chapter 12, the *SqlCommand* object also exposes an *Execute-XmlReader* object. You can use this method to retrieve the results of a *...FOR XML* query via an *XmlReader* object.

The *GetSql<DataType>* Methods and the *SqlTypes* Namespace

The *SqlDataReader* object exposes various *Get<DataType>* methods to return data into the different .NET data types, just as the *OleDbDataReader* does. But the *SqlDataReader* object also exposes additional *Get<DataType>* methods. These methods correspond to the various data types in the *System.Data.SqlTypes* namespace.

The following snippet of code retrieves data from a row in the Orders table and stores the contents of that row in data types that are part of the *SqlTypes* namespace: *SqlInt32*, *SqlString*, and *SqlDateTime*.

Visual Basic .NET

```
'Imports System.Data.SqlTypes
Dim strConn, strSQL As String
strConn = "Data Source=(local)\NetSDK;Initial Catalog=Northwind;" & _
          "Trusted_Connection=Yes;"
strSQL = "SELECT OrderID, CustomerID, OrderDate FROM Orders " & _
          "WHERE OrderID = 10643"
Dim cn As New SqlConnection(strConn)
Dim cmd As New SqlCommand(strSQL, cn)
Dim rdr As SqlDataReader
Dim intOrderID As SqlInt32
Dim strCustomerID As SqlString
Dim datOrderDate As SqlDateTime
cn.Open()
rdr = cmd.ExecuteReader(CommandBehavior.SingleRow)
If rdr.Read Then
    intOrderID = rdr.GetSqlInt32(0)
    strCustomerID = rdr.GetSqlString(1)
    datOrderDate = rdr.GetSqlDateTime(2)
End If
rdr.Close()
cn.Close()
```

Visual C# .NET

```
//using System.Data.SqlTypes;
string strConn, strSQL;
strConn = "Data Source=(local)\\NetSDK;Initial Catalog=Northwind;" +
          "Trusted_Connection=Yes;";
```

(continued)

```
strSQL = "SELECT OrderID, CustomerID, OrderDate FROM Orders " +
         "WHERE OrderID = 10643";
SqlConnection cn = new SqlConnection(strConn);
SqlCommand cmd = new SqlCommand(strSQL, cn);
SqlDataReader rdr;
SqlInt32 intOrderID;
SqlString strCustomerID;
SqlDateTime datOrderDate;
cn.Open();
rdr = cmd.ExecuteReader(CommandBehavior.SingleRow);
if (rdr.Read())
{
    intOrderID = rdr.GetSqlInt32(0);
    strCustomerID = rdr.GetSqlString(1);
    datOrderDate = rdr.GetSqlDateTime(2);
}
rdr.Close();
cn.Close();
```

Why use these provider-specific data types? There are two main reasons:

■ **Performance** The data types in the *SqlTypes* namespace help your code run faster because the SQL Client .NET Data Provider uses these data types internally. If you retrieve data into .NET data types using calls such as *GetInt32* or *GetString*, the SQL Client .NET Data Provider must convert the data. Using the provider-specific data types avoids this conversion. I've found that code that uses the *Sql-Types* namespace generally runs between 10 and 15 percent faster than code that uses the standard .NET data types.

■ **Simplified code** Few developers like dealing with null values. The code snippet that used the standard .NET data types did not include null checks. If the rows contained null values in any of the columns referenced, the code would generate an exception. You can't store a null value in the .NET data types. You can use the *IsDBNull* method of the *DataReader* to make sure the column does not contain null values before retrieving that data.

The provider-specific data types, however, can handle null values. Each class in the *SqlTypes* namespace exposes an *IsNull* method. So, you can store the results of your query into these data types without having to check for null data ahead of time. While you should still check for null values in your code, you can perform those checks later. Using the *SqlTypes* data types simplifies your *SqlData-Reader* call, which means you can retrieve the results of your queries more quickly. This also allows you to close the *SqlDataReader* and free up your connection again more quickly.

Calling Stored Procedures

You can use the *SqlCommand* objects to call SQL Server and MSDE stored procedures. The *SqlCommand* object exposes a *CommandType* property that you can use to help simplify the code you use to call your stored procedures. You can set the *SqlCommand* object's *CommandText* property to the stored procedure name, set the *CommandType* property to *StoredProcedure*, and then call the stored procedure, as shown in the following code snippet:

Visual Basic .NET

```
Dim strConn As String
strConn = "Data Source=(local)\NetSDK;Initial Catalog=Northwind;" & _
          "Trusted_Connection=Yes;"
Dim cn As New SqlConnection(strConn)
Dim cmd As New SqlCommand("CustOrdersOrders", cn)
cmd.CommandType = CommandType.StoredProcedure
Dim param As SqlParameter
param = cmd.Parameters.Add("@CustomerID", SqlDbType.NChar, 5)
param.Value = "ALFKI"
cn.Open()
Dim rdr As SqlDataReader = cmd.ExecuteReader()
Do While rdr.Read()
    Console.WriteLine(rdr("OrderID"))
Loop
rdr.Close()
cn.Close()
```

Visual C# .NET

```
string strConn;
strConn = "Data Source=(local)\\NetSDK;Initial Catalog=Northwind;" +
          "Trusted_Connection=Yes;";
SqlConnection cn = new SqlConnection(strConn);
SqlCommand cmd = new SqlCommand("CustOrdersOrders", cn);
cmd.CommandType = CommandType.StoredProcedure;
SqlParameter param;
param = cmd.Parameters.Add("@CustomerID", SqlDbType.NChar, 5);
param.Value = "ALFKI";
cn.Open();
SqlDataReader rdr = cmd.ExecuteReader();
while (rdr.Read())
    Console.WriteLine(rdr["OrderID"]);
rdr.Close();
cn.Close();
```

If you use SQL Server's tracing tools, you'll discover that the SQL Client .NET Data Provider transforms this information into the following syntax:

```
EXEC CustOrdersOrders @CustomerID
```

If you want to get the best possible performance out of your code, you can use this same syntax and leave the *CommandType* property set to its default value of *Text*. To retrieve data using this syntax with output parameters, simply add the keyword *OUT* after the parameter name, as shown here:

```
EXEC MyStoredProcedure @InputParameter, @OutputParameter OUT
```

Retrieving Database Schema Information

The *OleDbConnection* object exposes a *GetOleDbSchemaTable* method that you can use to retrieve schema information for your database, such as a list of tables or columns. There is no direct equivalent to this feature in the SQL Client .NET Data Provider.

However, SQL Server does allow you to retrieve this data via the Information Schema views. You can execute the following query to retrieve information regarding the various tables on your SQL Server database:

```
SELECT * FROM INFORMATION_SCHEMA.TABLES
```

There are various views for retrieving information about tables, columns, stored procedures, constraints, and so forth. I've included some of the more common queries to help you get started.

To retrieve a list of table names:

```
SELECT TABLE_NAME FROM INFORMATION_SCHEMA.TABLES
    WHERE TABLE_TYPE = 'BASE TABLE'
```

To retrieve a list of view names:

```
SELECT TABLE_NAME FROM INFORMATION_SCHEMA.TABLES
    WHERE TABLE_TYPE = 'VIEW'
```

To retrieve a list of columns for the tables:

```
SELECT TABLE_NAME, COLUMN_NAME, DATA_TYPE, CHARACTER_MAXIMUM_LENGTH,
        NUMERIC_PRECISION, NUMERIC_SCALE
    FROM INFORMATION_SCHEMA.COLUMNS
    WHERE TABLE_NAME IN (SELECT TABLE_NAME FROM INFORMATION_SCHEMA.TABLES
                        WHERE TABLE_TYPE = 'BASE TABLE')
    ORDER BY TABLE_NAME
```

To retrieve a list of procedure names:

```
SELECT SPECIFIC_NAME FROM INFORMATION_SCHEMA.ROUTINES
    WHERE ROUTINE_TYPE = 'PROCEDURE'
```

To retrieve a list of the parameters for those stored procedures:

```
SELECT SPECIFIC_NAME, PARAMETER_NAME, PARAMETER_MODE, DATA_TYPE,
        CHARACTER_MAXIMUM_LENGTH, NUMERIC_PRECISION, NUMERIC_SCALE
    FROM INFORMATION_SCHEMA.PARAMETERS
```

```
WHERE SPECIFIC_NAME IN (SELECT SPECIFIC_NAME
                        FROM INFORMATION_SCHEMA.ROUTINES
                        WHERE ROUTINE_TYPE = 'PROCEDURE')
ORDER BY SPECIFIC_NAME
```

For more information on using Information Schema views, see SQL Server Books Online.

The ODBC .NET Data Provider

Shortly after the release of the .NET Framework, Microsoft released a third .NET data provider: the ODBC .NET Data Provider. This provider is designed to communicate with databases using ODBC drivers.

Because the initial release of the ODBC .NET Data Provider is not part of the .NET Framework, you can't simply create a new project in Visual Studio .NET and start using this new data provider. Once you've downloaded and installed the ODBC .NET Data Provider from the MSDN Web site, you must add a reference to the component in your project in the Add Reference dialog box, as shown in Figure A-1.

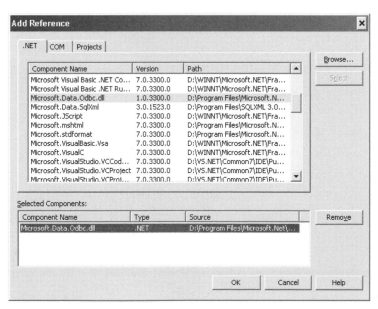

Figure A-1   Adding a reference to the ODBC .NET Data Provider

You might have noticed in Figure A-1 that the ODBC .NET Data Provider's namespace differs from that of the OLE DB and SQL Client .NET Data Providers. The objects in the ODBC .NET Data Provider reside in the *Microsoft.Data.Odbc* namespace, at least as of the initial release of the provider. Future releases of the .NET Framework will likely include this provider. As a result, the namespace might change to *System.Data.Odbc* in subsequent releases.

The code snippets in this section assume that you've added a reference to the ODBC .NET Data Provider in your project as well as your code module, using the construct for your language of choice (the *Imports* command for Visual Basic .NET developers and the *using* command for Visual C# .NET developers).

Connecting to Your Database Using an *OdbcConnection*

To connect to your database using the ODBC .NET Data Provider, you use the *OdbcConnection* class. You instantiate an *OdbcConnection* object, set its *ConnectionString* property (either explicitly or via the object's constructor), and call the object's *Open* method.

Here are a few examples of connection strings that you can use to connect to your database using the *OdbcConnection* object. For more information on how to connect to your database, see the documentation for the *OdbcConnection* object's *ConnectionString* property and the documentation for your ODBC driver of choice.

Connecting to a SQL Server database with a username and password:

```
Driver={SQL Server};Server=(local)\NetSDK;
    Database=Northwind;UID=MyUserName;PWD=MyPassword;
```

Connecting to a SQL Server database using a trusted connection:

```
Driver={SQL Server};Server=(local)\NetSDK;
    Database=Northwind;Trusted_Connection=Yes;
```

Connecting to a database using an ODBC data source name (DSN):

```
DSN=MyDataSource;
```

Connecting to a database using an ODBC file DSN:

```
FileDSN=MyFileDataSource;
```

The following code snippet connects to the .NET Framework SDK installation of the MSDE database on the local machine:

Visual Basic .NET

```
Dim strConn As String
strConn = "Driver={SQL Server};Server=(local)\NetSDK;" & _
        "Database=Northwind;Trusted_Connection=Yes;"
Dim cn As New OdbcConnection(strConn)
cn.Open()
cn.Close()
```

Visual C# .NET

```
string strConn;
strConn = "Driver={SQL Server};Server=(local)\\NetSDK;" +
        "Database=Northwind;Trusted_Connection=Yes;";
```

```
OdbcConnection cn = new OdbcConnection(strConn);
cn.Open();
cn.Close();
```

Working with Parameterized Queries

The ODBC .NET Data Provider supports parameterized queries in the same way that the OLE DB .NET Data Provider does. In your query string, you use the ? parameter marker to denote a parameter, and then you add a corresponding *OdbcParameter* object to the *OdbcCommand* object's *Parameters* collection. The ODBC .NET Data Provider does not support named parameters.

Retrieving the Results of a Query Using an *OdbcDataAdapter*

If you want to retrieve the results of a query and store them in a *DataSet* or *DataTable* object, you use the *OdbcDataAdapter* object:

Visual Basic .NET

```
Dim strConn, strSQL As String
strConn = "Driver={SQL Server};Server=(local)\NetSDK;" & _
          "Database=Northwind;Trusted_Connection=Yes;"
strSQL = "SELECT OrderID, CustomerID, OrderDate FROM Orders " & _
          "WHERE CustomerID = ?"
Dim da As New OdbcDataAdapter(strSQL, strConn)
Dim param As OdbcParameter
param = da.SelectCommand.Parameters.Add("@CustomerID", OdbcType.NChar, 5)
param.Value = "ALFKI"
Dim tbl As New DataTable("Orders")
da.Fill(tbl)
```

Visual C# .NET

```
string strConn, strSQL;
strConn = "Driver={SQL Server};Server=(local)\\NetSDK;" +
          "Database=Northwind;Trusted_Connection=Yes;";
strSQL = "SELECT OrderID, CustomerID, OrderDate FROM Orders " +
          "WHERE CustomerID = ?";
OdbcDataAdapter da = new OdbcDataAdapter(strSQL, strConn);
OdbcParameter param;
param = da.SelectCommand.Parameters.Add("@CustomerID", OdbcType.NChar, 5);
param.Value = "ALFKI";
DataTable tbl = new DataTable("Orders");
da.Fill(tbl);
```

Examining the Results of a Query Using an *OdbcDataReader*

The following code uses the same query, but it uses an *OdbcCommand* and an *OdbcDataReader* object to retrieve and display the results.

Visual Basic .NET

```
Dim strConn, strSQL As String
strConn = "Driver={SQL Server};Server=(local)\NetSDK;" & _
          "Database=Northwind;Trusted_Connection=Yes;"
strSQL = "SELECT OrderID, CustomerID, OrderDate FROM Orders " & _
          "WHERE CustomerID = ?"
Dim cn As New OdbcConnection(strConn)
Dim cmd As New OdbcCommand(strSQL, cn)
Dim param As OdbcParameter
param = cmd.Parameters.Add("@CustomerID", OdbcType.NChar, 5)
param.Value = "ALFKI"
cn.Open()
Dim rdr As OdbcDataReader = cmd.ExecuteReader()
Do While rdr.Read()
    Console.WriteLine("OrderID = " & rdr.GetInt32(0))
    Console.WriteLine("CustomerID = " & rdr.GetString(1))
    Console.WriteLine("OrderDate = " & rdr.GetDateTime(2))
    Console.WriteLine()
Loop
rdr.Close()
cn.Close()
```

Visual C# .NET

```
string strConn, strSQL;
strConn = "Driver={SQL Server};Server=(local)\\NetSDK;" +
          "Database=Northwind;Trusted_Connection=Yes;";
strSQL = "SELECT OrderID, CustomerID, OrderDate FROM Orders " +
          "WHERE CustomerID = ?";
OdbcConnection cn = new OdbcConnection(strConn);
OdbcCommand cmd = new OdbcCommand(strSQL, cn);
OdbcParameter param;
param = cmd.Parameters.Add("@CustomerID", OdbcType.NChar, 5);
param.Value = "ALFKI";
cn.Open();
OdbcDataReader rdr = cmd.ExecuteReader();
while (rdr.Read())
{
    Console.WriteLine("OrderID = " + rdr.GetInt32(0));
    Console.WriteLine("CustomerID = " + rdr.GetString(1));
    Console.WriteLine("OrderDate = " + rdr.GetDateTime(2));
    Console.WriteLine();
}
rdr.Close();
cn.Close();
```

Calling a Stored Procedure

In the initial release of the ODBC .NET Data Provider, the *OdbcCommand* object does not support the *Table* or *StoredProcedure* values from the *CommandType* enumeration. If you want to call a stored procedure using the ODBC .NET Data Provider, you have to learn the ODBC *CALL* syntax. Thankfully, the syntax is simple. Here's an example:

```
{? = CALL MyStoredProc(?, ?, ?)}
```

You use the keyword *CALL* before the name of the stored procedure. If you want to supply parameters for the stored procedure call—regardless of whether they're input, output, or both—you use the ? parameter marker. You separate the parameter markers with commas and enclose the list of parameter markers in parentheses. If you want to trap for the return value, preface the *CALL* keyword with *? =*, just as you would to retrieve the return value of a function call in your code. Finally, surround the entire query in curly braces.

The following code snippet demonstrates how to call a parameterized stored procedure using the ODBC .NET Data Provider.

Visual Basic .NET

```
Dim strConn, strSQL As String
strConn = "Driver={SQL Server};Server=(local)\NetSDK;" & _
        "Database=Northwind;Trusted_Connection=Yes;"
strSQL = "{CALL CustOrdersOrders(?)}"
Dim cn As New OdbcConnection(strConn)
Dim cmd As New OdbcCommand(strSQL, cn)
Dim param As OdbcParameter
param = cmd.Parameters.Add("@CustomerID", OdbcType.NChar, 5)
param.Value = "ALFKI"
cn.Open()
Dim rdr As OdbcDataReader = cmd.ExecuteReader()
Do While rdr.Read()
    Console.WriteLine("OrderID = " & rdr.GetInt32(0))
    Console.WriteLine("OrderDate = " & rdr.GetDateTime(1))
    Console.WriteLine()
Loop
rdr.Close()
cn.Close()
```

Visual C# .NET

```
string strConn, strSQL;
strConn = "Driver={SQL Server};Server=(local)\\NetSDK;" +
        "Database=Northwind;Trusted_Connection=Yes;";
strSQL = "{CALL CustOrdersOrders(?)}";
```

(continued)

```
OdbcConnection cn = new OdbcConnection(strConn);
OdbcCommand cmd = new OdbcCommand(strSQL, cn);
OdbcParameter param;
param = cmd.Parameters.Add("@CustomerID", OdbcType.NChar, 5);
param.Value = "ALFKI";
cn.Open();
OdbcDataReader rdr = cmd.ExecuteReader();
while (rdr.Read())
{
    Console.WriteLine("OrderID = " + rdr.GetInt32(0));
    Console.WriteLine("OrderDate = " + rdr.GetDateTime(1));
    Console.WriteLine();
}
rdr.Close();
cn.Close();
```

Retrieving Database Schema Information

Unfortunately, there is no singular way to retrieve schema information from your database using the ODBC .NET Data Provider, at least not in its initial release. The ODBC .NET Data Provider does not support an equivalent of the *OleDbConnection* object's *GetOleDbSchema* method. You can still query the Information Schema views mentioned in the discussion of the SQL Client .NET Data Provider to retrieve schema information from SQL Server and MSDE databases, but these queries are not supported by all database systems. These limitations might be addressed in a future release of the provider.

The Oracle Client .NET Data Provider

As of this writing, Microsoft is developing a .NET data provider for Oracle databases. This provider will communicate with Oracle databases version 8i and later and will allow you to access the newer Oracle data types, such as LOBs and BFILEs. The provider will also allow you to fetch the contents of multiple REF cursors from a stored procedure.

Microsoft has not indicated how or when the Oracle Client .NET Data Provider will be released or whether it will be a separate component or part of a subsequent release of the .NET Framework. If the provider is not released as part of the .NET Framework, you'll need to add a reference to the component in your projects, as described earlier for the ODBC .NET Data Provider. At the time of this writing, the provider's namespace is *Microsoft.Data.OracleClient*.

The Oracle Client .NET Data Provider will communicate with your Oracle database using Oracle's client libraries. In order to connect to your Oracle database using the Oracle Client .NET Data Provider, you'll have to have the Oracle client components (version 8.1.7 or later) installed. You'll also have to create a database alias for each database to which you want to connect using the Oracle's client configuration utility.

The code snippets in this section assume that you've added a reference to the Oracle Client .NET Data Provider in your project as well as your code module, using the construct for your language of choice (the *Imports* command for Visual Basic .NET developers and the *using* command for Visual C# .NET developers).

Connecting to Your Oracle Database Using an *OracleConnection*

You'll use the *OracleConnection* object to connect to your Oracle database. As with the other .NET data providers, to connect to your Oracle database you'll simply need to create an *OracleConnection* object, set its *ConnectString* property (either explicitly or via the object's constructor), and call its *Open* method, as shown in the following code snippet.

Visual Basic .NET

```
Dim strConn As String
strConn = "Data Source=MyOracleDatabaseAlias;" & _
          "User ID=MyUserID;Password=MyPassword;"
Dim cn As New OracleConnection(strConn)
cn.Open()
cn.Close()
```

Visual C# .NET

```
string strConn;
strConn = "Data Source=MyOracleDatabaseAlias;" +
          "User ID=MyUserID;Password=MyPassword;";
OracleConnection cn = new OracleConnection(strConn);
cn.Open();
cn.Close();
```

Working with Parameterized Queries

The Oracle Client .NET Data Provider will support only named parameters, much like the SQL Client .NET Data Provider does. The one difference is that you'll have to preface your parameter names with a colon. A parameterized query would look like this:

```
SELECT EMPNO, ENAME FROM EMP WHERE JOB = :JOB
```

Retrieving the Results of a Query Using an *OracleDataAdapter*

Let's look at an example of code that uses an *OracleDataAdapter* to fill a *DataTable* based on the results of this parameterized query.

Visual Basic .NET

```
Dim strConn, strSQL As String
strConn = "Data Source=MyOracleDatabaseAlias;" & _
          "User ID=MyUserID;Password=MyPassword;"
strSQL = "SELECT EMPNO, ENAME FROM EMP WHERE JOB = :JOB"
Dim da As New OracleDataAdapter(strSQL, strConn)
Dim param As OracleParameter
param = da.SelectCommand.Parameters.Add(":JOB", OracleType.VarChar, 9)
param.Value = "CLERK"
Dim tbl As New DataTable()
da.Fill(tbl)
Console.WriteLine("Retrieved " & tbl.Rows.Count & " row(s)")
```

Visual C# .NET

```
string strConn, strSQL;
strConn = "Data Source=MyOracleDatabaseAlias;" +
          "User ID=MyUserID;Password=MyPassword;";
strSQL = "SELECT EMPNO, ENAME FROM EMP WHERE JOB = :JOB";
OracleDataAdapter da = new OracleDataAdapter(strSQL, strConn);
OracleParameter param;
param = da.SelectCommand.Parameters.Add(":JOB", OracleType.VarChar, 9);
param.Value = "CLERK";
DataTable tbl = new DataTable();
da.Fill(tbl);
Console.WriteLine("Retrieved " + tbl.Rows.Count + " row(s)");
```

Examining the Results of a Query Using an *OracleDataReader*

Now let's see how to retrieve that same data using an *OracleDataReader*.

Visual Basic .NET

```
Dim strConn, strSQL As String
strConn = "Data Source=MyOracleDatabaseAlias;" & _
          "User ID=MyUserID;Password=MyPassword;"
strSQL = "SELECT EMPNO, ENAME FROM EMP WHERE JOB = :JOB"
Dim cn As New OracleConnection(strConn)
Dim cmd As New OracleCommand(strSQL, cn)
Dim param As OracleParameter
param = cmd.Parameters.Add(":JOB", OracleType.VarChar, 9)
param.Value = "CLERK"
cn.Open()
Dim rdr As OracleDataReader = cmd.ExecuteReader()
Do While rdr.Read()
    Console.WriteLine("EmpNo = " & rdr.GetDecimal(0))
```

```
        Console.WriteLine("EName = " & rdr.GetString(1))
        Console.WriteLine()
Loop
rdr.Close()
cn.Close()
```

Visual C# .NET

```
string strConn, strSQL;
strConn = "Data Source=MyOracleDatabaseAlias;" +
        "User ID=MyUserID;Password=MyPassword;";
strSQL = "SELECT EMPNO, ENAME FROM EMP WHERE JOB = :JOB";
OracleConnection cn = new OracleConnection(strConn);
OracleCommand cmd = new OracleCommand(strSQL, cn);
OracleParameter param;
param = cmd.Parameters.Add(":JOB", OracleType.VarChar, 9);
param.Value = "CLERK";
cn.Open();
OracleDataReader rdr = cmd.ExecuteReader();
while (rdr.Read())
{
    Console.WriteLine("EmpNo = " + rdr.GetDecimal(0));
    Console.WriteLine("EName = " + rdr.GetString(1));
    Console.WriteLine();
}
rdr.Close();
cn.Close();
```

Oracle-Specific Data Types

The Oracle Client .NET Data Provider will include Oracle-specific data types, much like the SQL Client .NET Data Provider does for SQL Server data types. Using these Oracle-specific data types will improve the performance of your code and allow you to retrieve data from your *DataReader* more quickly because you'll be able to store data in these data types without having to perform checks for Null values ahead of time. Plus, many of these data types will offer additional functionality not available on the corresponding .NET data type.

The following code snippet uses the Oracle-specific data types to retrieve and display the results of a query:

Visual Basic .NET

```
Dim strConn, strSQL As String
strConn = "Data Source=MyOracleDatabaseAlias;" & _
        "User ID=MyUserID;Password=MyPassword;"
strSQL = "SELECT EMPNO, ENAME FROM EMP WHERE JOB = :JOB"
Dim cn As New OracleConnection(strConn)
Dim cmd As New OracleCommand(strSQL, cn)
```

(continued)

```
Dim param As OracleParameter
param = cmd.Parameters.Add(":JOB", OracleType.VarChar, 9)
param.Value = "CLERK"
Dim numEmpNo As OracleNumber
Dim strEName As OracleString
cn.Open()
Dim rdr As OracleDataReader = cmd.ExecuteReader()
Do While rdr.Read()
    numEmpNo = rdr.GetOracleNumber(0)
    strEName = rdr.GetOracleString(1)
    Console.WriteLine("EmpNo = " & numEmpNo.ToString())
    Console.WriteLine("EName = " & strEName.ToString())
    Console.WriteLine()
Loop
rdr.Close()
cn.Close()
```

Visual C# .NET

```
string strConn, strSQL;
strConn = "Data Source=MyOracleDatabaseAlias;" +
          "User ID=MyUserID;Password=MyPassword;";
strSQL = "SELECT EMPNO, ENAME FROM EMP WHERE JOB = :JOB";
OracleConnection cn = new OracleConnection(strConn);
OracleCommand cmd = new OracleCommand(strSQL, cn);
OracleParameter param;
param = cmd.Parameters.Add(":JOB", OracleType.VarChar, 9);
param.Value = "CLERK";
OracleNumber numEmpNo;
OracleString strEName;
cn.Open();
OracleDataReader rdr = cmd.ExecuteReader();
while (rdr.Read())
{
    numEmpNo = rdr.GetOracleNumber(0);
    strEName = rdr.GetOracleString(1);
    Console.WriteLine("EmpNo = " + numEmpNo.ToString());
    Console.WriteLine("EName = " + strEName.ToString());
    Console.WriteLine();
}
rdr.Close();
cn.Close();
```

Calling a Stored Procedure

You can set an *OracleCommand* object's *CommandText* property to your stored procedure name and then add parameters to the *Command* object's *Parameters* collection. When you add stored procedure parameters in this fashion, you need not preface the parameter name with a colon when you're populating the *Parameters* collection. You then simply call the *ExecuteNonQuery* method, as shown in the following code snippet.

Visual Basic .NET

```
Dim strConn As String
strConn = "Data Source=MyOracleDatabaseAlias;" & _
          "User ID=MyUserID;Password=MyPassword;"
Dim cn As New OracleConnection(strConn)
Dim cmd As New OracleCommand("GetNumOrders", cn)
cmd.CommandType = CommandType.StoredProcedure
Dim param As OracleParameter
param = cmd.Parameters.Add("pCustomerID", OracleType.Char, 5)
param.Value = "ALFKI"
param = cmd.Parameters.Add("pNumOrders", OracleType.Int32)
param.Direction = ParameterDirection.Output
cn.Open()
cmd.ExecuteNonQuery()
Console.WriteLine(param.Value)
cn.Close()
```

Visual C# .NET

```
string strConn;
strConn = "Data Source=MyOracleDatabaseAlias;" +
          "User ID=MyUserID;Password=MyPassword;";
OracleConnection cn = new OracleConnection(strConn);
OracleCommand cmd = new OracleCommand("GetNumOrders", cn);
cmd.CommandType = CommandType.StoredProcedure;
OracleParameter param;
param = cmd.Parameters.Add("pCustomerID", OracleType.Char, 5);
param.Value = "ALFKI";
param = cmd.Parameters.Add("pNumOrders", OracleType.Int32);
param.Direction = ParameterDirection.Output;
cn.Open();
cmd.ExecuteNonQuery();
Console.WriteLine(param.Value);
cn.Close();
```

You can avoid the overhead of having the provider translate this information into the appropriate Oracle syntax by leaving the *CommandType* property as *Text* and setting the *CommandText* property to a query in the following format:

```
BEGIN GetNumOrders(:pCustomerID, :pNumOrders); END;
```

Fetching Data from Oracle REF Cursors

The Oracle Client .NET Data Provider will let you retrieve data from multiple REF cursors from a stored procedure call. Say you have the following definition for your Oracle package:

```
CREATE PACKAGE PackCursorTest AS
  TYPE curOrders IS REF CURSOR RETURN Orders%ROWTYPE;
  TYPE curDetails IS REF CURSOR RETURN Order_Details%ROWTYPE;
  PROCEDURE OrdersAndDetailsForCustomer
    (pCustomerID IN CHAR, pOrders OUT curOrders, pDetails OUT curDetails);
END;

CREATE PACKAGE BODY PackCursorTest AS
  PROCEDURE OrdersAndDetailsForCustomer
  (
    pCustomerID IN CHAR,
    pOrders OUT curOrders,
    pDetails OUT curDetails
  )
  AS
  BEGIN
    OPEN pOrders FOR SELECT * FROM Orders WHERE CustomerID = pCustomerID;
    OPEN pDetails FOR SELECT * FROM Order_Details WHERE OrderID IN
      (SELECT OrderID FROM Orders WHERE CustomerID = pCustomerID);
  END;
END;
```

You could use the following code to call the stored procedure and fetch the contents of both REF cursors into a single *DataSet*:

Visual Basic .NET

```
Dim strConn, strSQL As String
strConn = "Data Source=MyOracleDatabaseAlias;" & _
          "User ID=MyUserID;Password=MyPassword;"
Dim cn As New OracleConnection(strConn)
strSQL = "PackCursorTest.OrdersAndDetailsForCustomer"
Dim cmd As New OracleCommand(strSQL, cn)
cmd.CommandType = CommandType.StoredProcedure
Dim param As OracleParameter
param = cmd.Parameters.Add("pCustomerID", OracleType.Char, 5)
param.Value = "ALFKI"
param = cmd.Parameters.Add("pOrders", OracleType.Cursor)
param.Direction = ParameterDirection.Output
param = cmd.Parameters.Add("pDetails", OracleType.Cursor)
param.Direction = ParameterDirection.Output
Dim da As New OracleDataAdapter(cmd)
da.TableMappings.Add("Table", "Orders")
da.TableMappings.Add("Table1", "Order_Details")
```

```
Dim ds As New DataSet()
Dim tbl As DataTable
da.Fill(ds)
For Each tbl In ds.Tables
    Console.WriteLine(tbl.TableName & " now has " & _
                        tbl.Rows.Count & " row(s)")
Next tbl
```

Visual C# .NET

```
string strConn, strSQL;
strConn = "Data Source=MyOracleDatabaseAlias;" +
        "User ID=MyUserID;Password=MyPassword;";
OracleConnection cn = new OracleConnection(strConn);
strSQL = "PackCursorTest.OrdersAndDetailsForCustomer";
OracleCommand cmd = new OracleCommand(strSQL, cn);
cmd.CommandType = CommandType.StoredProcedure;
OracleParameter param;
param = cmd.Parameters.Add("pCustomerID", OracleType.Char, 5);
param.Value = "ALFKI";
param = cmd.Parameters.Add("pOrders", OracleType.Cursor);
param.Direction = ParameterDirection.Output;
param = cmd.Parameters.Add("pDetails", OracleType.Cursor);
param.Direction = ParameterDirection.Output;
OracleDataAdapter da = new OracleDataAdapter(cmd);
da.TableMappings.Add("Table", "Orders");
da.TableMappings.Add("Table1", "Order_Details");
DataSet ds = new DataSet();
da.Fill(ds);
foreach (DataTable tbl in ds.Tables)
    Console.WriteLine(tbl.TableName + " now has " +
                        tbl.Rows.Count + " row(s)");
```

Retrieving Database Schema Information

The Oracle Client .NET Data Provider will not directly provide schema discovery features to allow you to fetch information such as table and column names from your Oracle database. However, you'll be able to query the Oracle data dictionary to retrieve this information. For example, the following two queries retrieve a list of tables and a list of columns from the database:

```
SELECT TABLE_NAME FROM USER_TABLES
```

```
SELECT TABLE_NAME, COLUMN_NAME FROM USER_TAB_COLUMNS
    ORDER BY TABLE_NAME
```

For more information on using the Oracle data dictionary, see your Oracle documentation.

Common Cross-Provider Concerns

Microsoft .NET data providers offer better control and performance because each provider can be tuned for the specific back-end with which it's designed to communicate. However, the move to separate .NET data providers has caused some confusion in the developer community.

Writing Provider-Portable Code

Let's say you've built an application that uses the SQL Client .NET Data Provider. Time goes by and, due to customer demand, you decide to modify your application so it can communicate with either SQL Server or Oracle databases. The more code you have in your application that relies on the objects in the SQL Client .NET Data Provider, the more code you'll have to change in your application.

However, if you've separated your code into components and you've made sure that the components interact through generic interfaces, such as *DataSet*, *DataTable*, *IDataReader*, and *DbDataAdapter*, you'll have to change code in only specific components.

Let's look at two examples using this approach. In the first example, we'll create a function that uses the SQL Client .NET Data Provider internally but returns data through the generic *DataTable* interface. We'll then show how we can convert the function to use a different provider without having to change the code that calls the function. The second example uses a similar approach but relies on a function that returns a *DataAdapter* using the generic *IDbDataAdapter*.

The following code snippet calls a function called *GetOrdersForCustomer* that accepts a string that contains a value for the CustomerID column and returns a *DataTable* that contains the orders for that particular customer. The function uses a parameterized *SqlDataAdapter* internally.

Visual Basic .NET

```
Dim strCustomerID As String = "ALFKI"
Dim tblOrders As DataTable
tblOrders = GetOrdersForCustomer(strCustomerID)

Private Function GetOrdersForCustomer(CustomerID As String) As DataTable
    Dim strSQL, strConn As String
    strSQL = "SELECT OrderID, CustomerID, EmployeeID, OrderDate " & _
            "FROM Orders WHERE CustomerID = @CustomerID"
    strConn = "Data Source=(local)\NetSDK;" & _
            "Initial Catalog=Northwind;Trusted_Connection=Yes;"
    Dim da As New SqlDataAdapter(strSQL, strConn)
    Dim param As SqlParameter
    param = da.SelectCommand.Parameters.Add("@CustomerID", SqlDbType.NChar, 5)
    param.Value = CustomerID
```

```
      Dim tbl As New DataTable("Orders")
      da.Fill(tbl)
      Return tbl
End Function
```

Visual C# .NET

```
string strCustomerID = "ALFKI";
DataTable tblOrders;
tblOrders = GetOrdersForCustomer(strCustomerID);

private DataTable GetOrdersForCustomer(string CustomerID)
{
    string strSQL, strConn;
    strSQL = "SELECT OrderID, CustomerID, EmployeeID, OrderDate " +
            "FROM Orders WHERE CustomerID = @CustomerID";
    strConn = "Data Source=(local)\\NetSDK;" +
            "Initial Catalog=Northwind;Trusted_Connection=Yes;";
    SqlDataAdapter da = new SqlDataAdapter(strSQL, strConn);
    SqlParameter param;
    param = da.SelectCommand.Parameters.Add("@CustomerID", SqlDbType.NChar, 5);
    param.Value = CustomerID;
    DataTable tbl = new DataTable("Orders");
    da.Fill(tbl);
    return tbl;
}
```

As we described in the scenario earlier in the chapter, you might need to modify your application to support other back-end databases. The *GetOrders-ForCustomer* function uses the SQL Client .NET Data Provider internally but uses generic data types—*string* and *DataTable*—for its parameter and return value. So we can rewrite the function to use a different .NET data provider without having to change the code that consumes the *DataTable*. In the following code snippet, we've changed the code inside the *GetOrdersForCustomer* function but we have not changed the function's signature.

Visual Basic .NET

```
Private Function GetOrdersForCustomer(CustomerID As String) As DataTable
    Dim strSQL, strConn As String
    strSQL = "SELECT OrderID, CustomerID, EmployeeID, OrderDate " & _
            "FROM Orders WHERE CustomerID = :CustomerID"
    strConn = "Data Source=MyOracleDatabaseAlias;" & _
            "User ID=MyUserID;Password=MyPassword;"
    Dim da As New OracleDataAdapter(strSQL, strConn)
    Dim param As OracleParameter
    param = da.SelectCommand.Parameters.Add(":CustomerID", OracleType.Char, 5)
    param.Value = CustomerID
    Dim tbl As New DataTable("Orders")
```

(continued)

```
        da.Fill(tbl)
        Return tbl
End Function
```

Visual C# .NET

```csharp
private DataTable GetOrdersForCustomer(string CustomerID)
{
    string strSQL, strConn;
    strSQL = "SELECT OrderID, CustomerID, EmployeeID, OrderDate " +
             "FROM Orders WHERE CustomerID = :CustomerID";
    strConn = "Data Source=MyOracleDatabaseAlias;" +
              "User ID=MyUserID;Password=MyPassword;";
    OracleDataAdapter da = new OracleDataAdapter(strSQL, strConn);
    OracleParameter param;
    param = da.SelectCommand.Parameters.Add(":CustomerID", OracleType.Char, 5);
    param.Value = CustomerID;
    DataTable tbl = new DataTable("Orders");
    da.Fill(tbl);
    return tbl;
}
```

Another approach is to have your data access code return objects via the generic interfaces that the various .NET data providers support. For example, we could have created a function that instantiates a *SqlDataAdapter* and returns the *DataAdapter* via the generic *IDbDataAdapter* interface.

Visual Basic .NET

```vbnet
Dim daOrders As IDbDataAdapter = GetOrdersAdapter()
Dim strCustomerID As String = "ALFKI"
Dim param As IDbDataParameter
param = CType(daOrders.SelectCommand.Parameters(0), IDbDataParameter)
param.Value = strCustomerID
Dim ds As New DataSet()
Dim tblOrders As DataTable = ds.Tables.Add("Orders")
daOrders.Fill(ds)

Private Function GetOrdersAdapter() As IDbDataAdapter
    Dim strSQL, strConn As String
    strSQL = "SELECT OrderID, CustomerID, EmployeeID, OrderDate " & _
             "FROM Orders WHERE CustomerID = @CustomerID"
    strConn = "Data Source=(local)\NetSDK;" & _
              "Initial Catalog=Northwind;Trusted_Connection=Yes;"
    Dim da As New SqlDataAdapter(strSQL, strConn)
    da.TableMappings.Add("Table", "Orders")
    da.SelectCommand.Parameters.Add("@CustomerID", SqlDbType.NChar, 5)
    Return da
End Function
```

Visual C# .NET

```csharp
IDbDataAdapter daOrders = GetOrdersAdapter();
string strCustomerID = "ALFKI";
IDbDataParameter param;
param = (IDbDataParameter) daOrders.SelectCommand.Parameters[0];
param.Value = strCustomerID;
DataSet ds = new DataSet();
DataTable tblOrders = ds.Tables.Add("Orders");
daOrders.Fill(ds);

private IDbDataAdapter GetOrdersAdapter()
{
    string strSQL, strConn;
    strSQL = "SELECT OrderID, CustomerID, EmployeeID, OrderDate " +
            "FROM Orders WHERE CustomerID = @CustomerID";
    strConn = "Data Source=(local)\\NetSDK;" +
            "Initial Catalog=Northwind;Trusted_Connection=Yes;";
    SqlDataAdapter da = new SqlDataAdapter(strSQL, strConn);
    da.TableMappings.Add("Table", "Orders");
    da.SelectCommand.Parameters.Add("@CustomerID", SqlDbType.NChar, 5);
    return da;
}
```

We could later change the *GetOrdersAdapter* function as shown here to create and return an *OracleDataAdapter* through the *IDbDataAdapter* interface without having to change the code that uses the *IDbDataAdapter* interface.

Visual Basic .NET

```vbnet
Private Function GetOrdersAdapter() As IDbDataAdapter
    Dim strSQL, strConn As String
    strSQL = "SELECT OrderID, CustomerID, EmployeeID, OrderDate " & _
            "FROM Orders WHERE CustomerID = :CustomerID"
    strConn = "Data Source=MyOracleDatabaseAlias;" & _
            "User ID=MyUserID;Password=MyPassword;"
    Dim da As New OracleDataAdapter(strSQL, strConn)
    da.TableMappings.Add("Table", "Orders")
    da.SelectCommand.Parameters.Add(":CustomerID", OracleType.Char, 5)
    Return da
End Function
```

Visual C# .NET

```csharp
private IDbDataAdapter GetOrdersAdapter()
{
    string strSQL, strConn;
    strSQL = "SELECT OrderID, CustomerID, EmployeeID, OrderDate " +
            "FROM Orders WHERE CustomerID = :CustomerID";
```

(continued)

```
strConn = "Data Source=MyOracleDatabaseAlias;" +
          "User ID=MyUserID;Password=MyPassword;";
OracleDataAdapter da = new OracleDataAdapter(strSQL, strConn);
da.TableMappings.Add("Table", "Orders");
da.SelectCommand.Parameters.Add(":CustomerID", OracleType.Char, 5);
return da;
}
```

Determining the Correct .NET Provider Data Type

If you understand the basic object model for .NET data providers, writing code for one provider or another is fairly simple. As I jump from one .NET data provider to another, I sometimes forget the appropriate format for that provider's connection strings or how to create parameterized queries for that provider, but that's still rather basic stuff.

On the public ADO.NET newsgroups, one question that has surfaced repeatedly for the ODBC .NET Data Provider is "How do I determine the correct 'provider' data type for my parameters?" Developers most often face this question when they generate their own updating logic code for their *DataAdapter* objects. For example, say you're using the following query in your *DataAdapter* object's *UpdateCommand*:

```
UPDATE Orders SET CustomerID = ?, OrderDate = ?
    WHERE OrderID = ?
```

What is the correct provider type for the *OrderDate* parameter? Hopefully, you'll be able to determine the correct type based on the data type for the column in your database. But even then, things aren't entirely clear. If you're working with a SQL Server Northwind database and the ODBC .NET Data Provider, you would set the *OdbcParameter* object's *OdbcType* property to *OdbcType.DateTime*. But if you're using the OLE DB .NET Data Provider with the same data, you would set the *OleDbParameter* object's *OleDbType* property to *OleDbType.DBTimeStamp*. What's a poor developer to do?

The best answer that I can provide is to use the *DataReader* object's *GetSchemaTable* method. If the parameter corresponds to a column in your database, create a query that retrieves data from that column. Then use a *Command* object to execute that query using the *ExecuteReader* method. Call the *GetSchemaTable* method on the resulting *DataReader* object. Each row in the *DataTable* returned by *GetSchemaTable* corresponds to a column in the original query. Find the row in the *DataTable* returned by *GetSchemaTable* that corresponds to the column for your parameter. Examine the contents of the ProviderType column for that row and translate the integer to the appropriate enumeration.

Here's an example that determines the appropriate *OdbcType* for the OrderDate column in the Northwind database.

Visual Basic .NET

```
Dim strConn, strSQL As String
strConn = "Driver={SQL Server};Server=(local)\NetSDK;" & _
          "Database=Northwind;Trusted_Connection=Yes;"
Dim cn As New OdbcConnection(strConn)
cn.Open()
strSQL = "SELECT OrderDate FROM Orders"
Dim cmd As New OdbcCommand(strSQL, cn)
Dim rdr As OdbcDataReader
rdr = cmd.ExecuteReader(CommandBehavior.SchemaOnly)
Dim tbl As DataTable = rdr.GetSchemaTable()
rdr.Close()
cn.Close()
Dim intOrderDateType As Integer
intOrderDateType = CType(tbl.Rows(0)("ProviderType"), Integer)
Dim odbcOrderDateType As OdbcType
odbcOrderDateType = CType(intOrderDateType, OdbcType)
Console.WriteLine("OrderDate")
Console.WriteLine(vbTab & "ProviderType = " & intOrderDateType)
Console.WriteLine(vbTab & "OdbcType = " & odbcOrderDateType.ToString())
```

Visual C# .NET

```
string strConn, strSQL;
strConn = "Driver={SQL Server};Server=(local)\\NetSDK;" +
          "Database=Northwind;Trusted_Connection=Yes;";
OdbcConnection cn = new OdbcConnection(strConn);
cn.Open();
strSQL = "SELECT OrderDate FROM Orders";
OdbcCommand cmd = new OdbcCommand(strSQL, cn);
OdbcDataReader rdr = cmd.ExecuteReader(CommandBehavior.SchemaOnly);
DataTable tbl = rdr.GetSchemaTable();
rdr.Close();
cn.Close();
int intOrderDateType = (int) tbl.Rows[0]["ProviderType"];
OdbcType odbcOrderDateType = (OdbcType) intOrderDateType;
Console.WriteLine("OrderDate");
Console.WriteLine("\tProviderType = " + intOrderDateType);
Console.WriteLine("\tOdbcType = " + odbcOrderDateType.ToString());
```

If you don't feel like writing all this code, you can simply use the Ad Hoc Query Tool that's included on the book's companion CD and is discussed in Appendix B. Figure A-2 shows the Ad Hoc Query Tool displaying schema information for the results of a query, including a column that contains the .NET data provider–specific provider type. As you can see in the figure, the OrderDate column in the database corresponds to the *DateTime* value in the *OdbcType* enumeration.

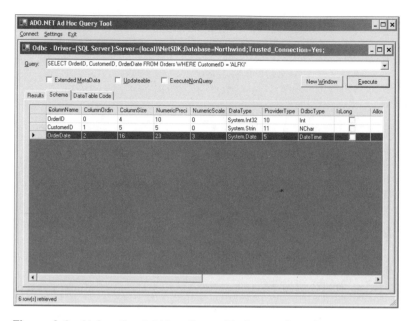

Figure A-2 Using the Ad Hoc Query Tool to retrieve "provider" type information

Appendix B

Tools

This appendix describes the three tools included on the book's companion CD that I created to help developers build data access applications: the ADO.NET Ad Hoc Query Tool, the ADO.NET DataAdapter Builder, and the ADO.NET Navigation Control.

Each tool is a work in progress. In the coming months, I'll post periodic updates to add features and fix bugs I might have missed. You can download these updates at the URL listed in the Readme file on the companion CD.

As the saying goes, you can't please all of the people all of the time. With that in mind, I've included the source code for each tool on the companion CD. The Ad Hoc Query Tool and the DataAdapter Builder are both written in Microsoft Visual Basic .NET. The CD includes source code for the Navigation Control in both Visual Basic .NET and Visual C# .NET.

Please note that these tools are not supported, nor are they intended for distribution. (See the Microsoft License Agreement at the end of this book for more gory legal details.) Use these tools at your own risk.

ADO.NET Ad Hoc Query Tool

When I'm building data access applications, I often find myself wanting to check the contents of tables in my database. There are ways to examine the contents of your database in Visual Studio .NET, but there isn't a way to execute ad hoc queries against your database using the .NET data provider of your choice. So, I decided to create a tool to do just this.

The ADO.NET Ad Hoc Query Tool, shown in Figure B-1, lets you execute ad hoc queries against the .NET data provider of your choice. It also lets you modify the results of your queries and submit those changes back to your database. You can use the tool to view schema information for the results of your query and to generate the ADO.NET code required to build a *DataTable* to store the results of your query.

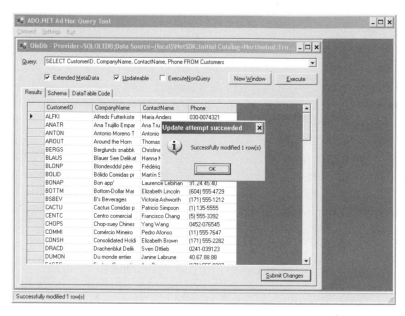

Figure B-1   The ADO.NET Ad Hoc Query Tool

Let's take a quick tour of the tool.

Connecting to Your Database

To connect to your database, choose Connect from the application's main menu. You'll see the dialog box shown in Figure B-2, where you can specify the connection string and .NET data provider you want to use.

Figure B-2   Creating a connection using the Ad Hoc Query Tool

Adding .NET Data Providers

By default, the Ad Hoc Query Tool lists the two .NET data providers included with the Microsoft .NET Framework: the OLE DB .NET Data Provider and the SQL Client .NET Data Provider. However, I've designed the tool to work with other .NET data providers as well.

If you want to use a different .NET data provider that's installed on your machine, select <Add Provider> from the list of available providers in the Connect dialog box. This will open a dialog box that lets you add a .NET data provider, as shown in Figure B-3.

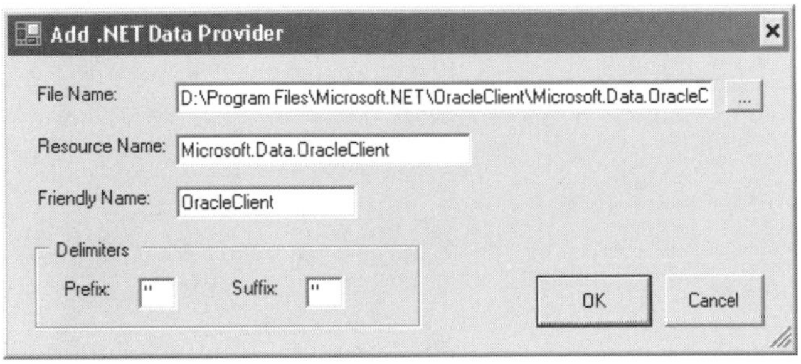

Figure B-3   Adding a .NET data provider in the Ad Hoc Query Tool

There is no generic way in the ADO.NET object model to determine what delimiters to use for table and column names for a particular connection, so the Add .NET Data Provider dialog box lets you specify delimiters for the provider. The Ad Hoc Query Tool uses these settings when it generates updating logic.

The OLE DB and ODBC .NET Data Providers are designed to talk to various back ends. When you use these .NET data providers, the Ad Hoc Query Tool determines the appropriate delimiters when you establish a new connection to your database.

Executing Queries

Once you've connected to your database, the Ad Hoc Query Tool displays a window in which you can enter and execute your queries. Simply enter the text for the query and click the Execute button. The tool executes the queries and displays the results in a grid on the Results tab of the window, as shown in Figure B-4.

You can also view the ADO.NET code required to build the resulting *DataTable* by selecting the DataTable Code tab.

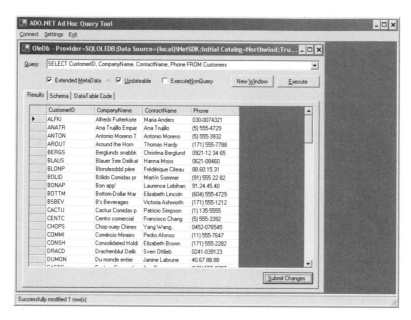

Figure B-4   Querying your database using the Ad Hoc Query Tool

Viewing Query Schema Information

You can view the schema information returned by the query by clicking on the Schema tab (shown in Figure B-5). The Ad Hoc Query Tool uses the *GetSchema-Table* method of the *DataReader* object to generate this schema information. The Extended MetaData option controls whether the Ad Hoc Query Tool will use *CommandBehavior.KeyInfo* in its call to the *Command* object's *Execute-Reader* method. If you select this option, you're asking the database to supply the names of the tables and columns referenced in your query, as well as indicating which columns are considered key columns for the query results.

Many developers have had problems using the *CommandBuilder* object or the Visual Studio .NET Data Adapter Configuration Wizard to generate updating logic for their queries. These problems often happen because the OLE DB providers and ODBC drivers don't return the schema information that these tools require to generate updating logic—table names, column names, and key column information. You can use the Ad Hoc Query Tool to easily see the schema information that's returned with your queries.

One more column in the schema information is worth mentioning. Most of the column names that you see in Figure B-5 are rather intuitive—Column-Name, ColumnSize, DataType, and so forth. However, what's arguably the most helpful column in the schema table is also the least discoverable: ProviderType. This column contains an integer, which on its own isn't terribly helpful.

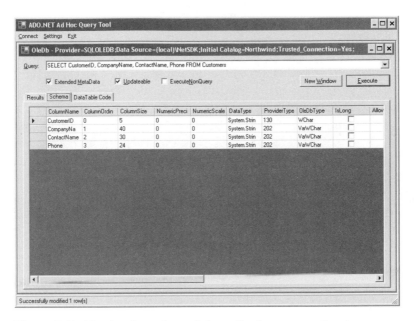

Figure B-5   Viewing the schema information for your result set

Looking at the figure, the numbers 130 and 202 won't mean much to you, but the contents of the column are quite meaningful to the .NET data provider. This example uses the OLE DB .NET Data Provider. If you execute the following code, you'll find that, in that data provider, CustomerID is a *WChar* column and CompanyName is a *VarWChar* column:

Visual Basic .NET

```
Dim typCustomerID, typCompanyName As OleDbType
typCustomerID = CType(130, OleDbType)
typCompanyName = CType(202, OleDbType)
Console.WriteLine("CustomerID is " & typCustomerID.ToString())
Console.WriteLine("CompanyName is " & typCompanyName.ToString())
```

Visual C# .NET

```
OleDbType typCustomerID, typCompanyName;
typCustomerID = (OleDbType) 130;
typCompanyName = (OleDbType) 202;
Console.WriteLine("CustomerID is " + typCustomerID.ToString());
Console.WriteLine("CompanyName is " + typCompanyName.ToString());
```

Based on this information, I'm sure you'll agree that the data available in the ProviderType column can be very helpful.

The Ad Hoc Query Tool uses the *DataReader* object's *GetSchemaTable* method to retrieve the schema information that you see in Figure B-5. You might have noticed that the column to the right of ProviderType is OleDbType, which displays the corresponding value from the *OleDbType* enumeration. The OleDbType column is not actually part of the *DataTable* returned by the *GetSchemaTable* method. The Ad Hoc Query Tool inserts a column into that schema table using the appropriate enumeration for the .NET data provider that you're using. It then uses the data available in the ProviderType column to supply values to this new column.

Disclaimer: There really isn't a well-defined set of requirements for .NET data providers. The SQL XML .NET Data Provider is a prime example. It doesn't implement all of the same objects or constructors as the OLE DB and SQL Client .NET data providers.

Thankfully, Microsoft's OLE DB, SQL Client, ODBC, and Oracle Client .NET Data Providers all work much the same way. As a result, I've been able to build the Ad Hoc Query Tool and DataAdapter Builder in such a way that the tools work quite well with each of these .NET data providers.

The tools use reflection and make assumptions about class names. For example, if you use the Ad Hoc Query Tool with the ODBC .NET Data Provider, the tool searches through the classes available in the provider to find one whose name ends in *CommandBuilder* in order to provide support for submitting updates. Similarly, the DataAdapter Builder looks for classes whose names end in *DataAdapter*. The DataAdapter Builder also looks for specific columns in the *DataTable* returned by the *DataReader* object's *GetSchemaTable* method to determine how to generate its updating logic.

Because there is no well-defined set of requirements for .NET data providers (yet), building tools such as the ones included on the companion CD is an inexact science and I can't guarantee they'll work with other .NET data providers.

Submitting Changes

The Query window has an Updateable check box. When you execute a query, the Ad Hoc Query Tool will create a *CommandBuilder* to generate updating logic for your query if this check box is selected. If the *CommandBuilder* successfully generates that updating logic, you'll see a Submit Changes button at the bottom of the window as shown in Figure B-4. Click this button to have the Ad Hoc Query Tool use the *CommandBuilder* to submit the changes you've made to your database and let you know whether the update attempt succeeded.

Application Settings

The Ad Hoc Query Tool uses a strongly typed *DataSet* to maintain application settings, including the list of .NET data providers, past connections, and past queries. You can modify these settings through the Settings command on the tool's main menu. When the tool shuts down, it stores this information in an XML file in

\Documents and Settings*username*\Application Data\Microsoft ADO.NET\Ad Hoc Query Tool\. The tool then loads this information the next time it is launched.

ADO.NET DataAdapter Builder

The *CommandBuilder* object and the Visual Studio .NET Data Adapter Configuration Wizard each do a wonderful job of generating *DataAdapter* updating logic, but they each have limitations. The *CommandBuilder* object is a very helpful run-time tool, but it doesn't generate code. The Data Adapter Configuration Wizard generates code, but only for the .NET data providers that are included in the .NET Framework. Neither component generates updating logic if your query doesn't include primary key columns.

I created the ADO.NET DataAdapter Builder to address these scenarios. You want to generate updating logic but your OLE DB provider or ODBC driver doesn't return table names, column names, or key column information? No problem. You want to generate updating logic for a *DataAdapter* that's not part of the .NET Framework? No problem.

The user interface for the DataAdapter Builder is similar to that of the Ad Hoc Query Tool. The Connect dialog box works in the same way. You enter the connection string and select the .NET data provider you want to use. The DataAdapter Builder will display a form, shown in Figure B-6, where you can enter and execute queries. Like the Ad Hoc Query Tool, the DataAdapter Builder executes queries and displays their results, along with the schema information for the result set.

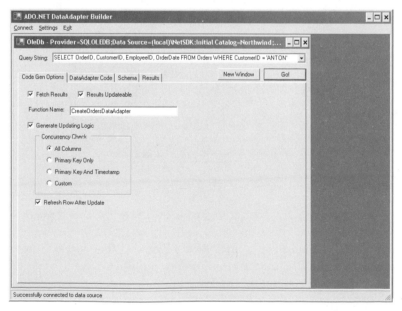

Figure B-6   Generating updating logic using the ADO.NET DataAdapter Builder

The major difference between the tools is that the DataAdapter Builder lets you specify the updating logic for your *DataAdapter*, and it displays the ADO.NET code used to generate that *DataAdapter*.

Specifying Your Updating Logic

The DataAdapter Builder generates updating logic for the *DataAdapter* by creating parameterized INSERT, UPDATE, and DELETE queries based on the results of the query you've supplied.

You can control the logic that the tool generates for the UPDATE and DELETE queries by selecting the desired Concurrency Check option, as shown in Figure B-6. By default, the DataAdapter Builder will use the original values of all columns in the WHERE clause for these queries. You can specify that you want to use just the primary key columns or the primary key and timestamp columns instead.

If you select the Custom option and execute your query, you'll see the dialog box shown in Figure B-7. This dialog box displays column and table information from the query schema as well as delimiter information for your connection.

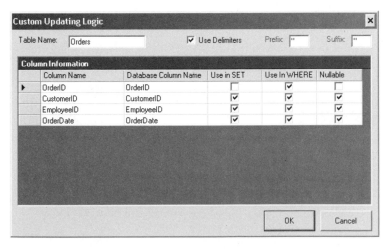

Figure B-7   Specifying custom updating logic

You control which columns are used in the SET and WHERE clauses of your *DataAdapter* object's updating logic by selecting or deselecting the various columns in the dialog box's grid. Be forewarned that this feature can generate UPDATE and DELETE queries that update multiple rows in your database. You can also specify the name of the base table to update in this dialog box.

I designed this custom concurrency check feature with three scenarios in mind. First, you can use it if you're working with OLE DB providers and ODBC drivers that do not report the key column information. The Microsoft Visual FoxPro OLE DB Provider and Oracle's OLE DB Provider fall into this group. Tools such as the *CommandBuilder* and the Visual Studio .NET Data Adapter Configuration Wizard require key column information to guarantee that the UPDATE and DELETE queries that they generate will update a single row at most. Without that key column information, those tools are unable to generate updating logic. If you're working with an OLE DB provider that does not return this information, you can still use the DataAdapter Builder's custom concurrency check feature to generate updating logic for your *DataAdapter*.

The custom concurrency check feature is also handy if you want to use more customized concurrency checks than All Columns, Primary Key Only, or Primary Key And Timestamp. For example, if you're querying the Customers table in the sample Northwind database, you might want to use just a subset of those columns in the WHERE clause for your INSERT and UPDATE queries. The custom concurrency check feature lets you do this.

Finally, the custom concurrency check feature can be handy if your query returns data from multiple tables. For example, you might want to use the following query to retrieve information from the Order Details table but also include the product name from the Products table:

```
SELECT O.OrderID, O.ProductID, P.ProductName, O.Quantity, O.UnitPrice
    FROM [Order Details] O, Products P
    WHERE P.ProductID = O.ProductID AND O.OrderID = 10643
```

In Chapter 10, you learned that the *DataAdapter* is designed to submit updates against a single table. You can use the DataAdapter Builder's custom concurrency checks to submit changes to just the Order Details table. In the Custom Updating Logic dialog box, specify that you want to submit changes to the Order Details table and that you want to exclude the ProductName column from both the SET and WHERE clauses for your updating queries.

ADO.NET Navigation Control

Chapter 13 showed you the steps required to build a fairly standard Microsoft Windows–based data access application. You might have noticed that creating buttons to allow the user to navigate through the contents of your DataSet is actually more time-consuming than creating DataAdapter objects and strongly typed DataSet objects or creating bound controls. However, the code and the buttons required to add those navigation features to your code are very basic.

To address this basic scenario, I created the ADO.NET Navigation Control. This control includes buttons that let you navigate through the contents of your *DataSet*. You can also use the control to add and delete rows in your *DataSet*, as well as submit the pending changes to your database. Figure B-8 shows a simple form that employs the ADO.NET Navigation Control.

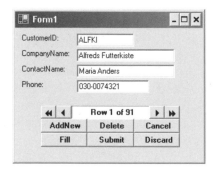

Figure B-8   Using the ADO.NET Navigation Control on a Windows Form

Using the ADO.NET Navigation Control in a Windows-based application is simple. Once you've added the control to the Visual Studio .NET Toolbox, you need only to add an instance of the control to your form and set a few properties in order to use it in your application.

Adding the ADO.NET Navigation Control to the Visual Studio .NET Toolbox

If you're working with a Visual Studio .NET solution and you add the ADO.NET Navigation Control project to your solution, the control will be automatically available on the Windows Forms tab of the Visual Studio .NET Toolbox.

You can also add the Navigation Control to the Toolbox by right-clicking on a tab and choosing Customize Toolbox from the shortcut menu. In the dialog box that appears, select the .NET Framework Components tab, click the Browse button, and then select the Navigation Control's library. Click OK, and the control will be available in the Toolbox.

Setting the Data Properties of the ADO.NET Navigation Control

When you add the Navigation Control to a Windows Form, you'll see that it exposes four basic data properties: *DataSource*, *DataMember*, *DataAdapter*, and *DataTable*.

You set the *DataSource* and *DataMember* properties of the Navigation Control just as you would for a *DataGrid* object. The Navigation Control works much like bound controls such as the *TextBox* and *DataGrid* controls. The Navigation Control uses the values you specify for the *DataSource* and

DataMember properties to reference the appropriate *CurrencyManager* for the Windows Form. It uses this *CurrencyManager* object internally to navigate through the underlying data structure.

The Navigation Control also includes Fill and Update buttons. To make these features work, you must set the *DataAdapter* and *DataTable* properties of the Navigation Control.

Setting the Remaining Properties of the ADO.NET Navigation Control

Three other properties are available for the Navigation Control: *FillOnLoad*, *ConfirmDeletes*, and *ShowTips*.

The Navigation Control has a *FillOnLoad* property that's set to *True* by default. This setting controls whether the Navigation Control will implicitly call the *DataAdapter* object's *Fill* method when the form starts up.

The Navigation Control exposes a *ConfirmDeletes* property, which is set to *True* by default. When you click the Navigation Control's Delete button, if the *ConfirmDeletes* property is set to *True*, the control will prompt the user to confirm the deletion.

By default, the Navigation Control displays a ToolTip when you move the mouse over one of the control's buttons. You can turn this behavior off by setting the Navigation Control's *ShowTips* property to *False*.

Index

Send feedback about this index to *mspindex@microsoft.com*.

Symbols

A

classes (listed by name). *See also* classes
  clsSlowQuery, 152
  Command, 6
  Connection, 6, 65
  CurrencyManager, 568
  CustomersDataTable, 381
  DataAdapter, 39
  DataColumn, 15–16
  DataColumnMappingCollection, 163
  DataReader, 6
  DataRowCollection, 241, 338
  DataSet, 21–23, 202, 209, 394–96, 398, 564, 577–78
  DataTable, 211
  DBNull, 240
  Decimal, 585
  ForeignKeyConstraint, 216
  HttpSessionState, 619
  InternetExplorer, 528
  MarshalByValueComponent, 297
  OleDbConnection, 64, 90
  OrdersDataTable, 381
  Page, 617, 619
  Parameter, 6
  PrimaryKey, 216
  ServicedComponent, 514
  String, 342
  Transaction, 6
  UniqueConstraint, 216–17
  xsdChapter13, 564
Clear method, 263, 265, 272, 274
ClearErrors method, 287, 289
Click event, 37, 39
  Web applications and, 606
  Windows-based applications and, 567, 572–73, 580
clients. *See also* client/server systems
  caching and, 616–19
  SQL and, 558
  XML and, 558
client/server systems, 50, 206, 606–7. *See also* clients; Web servers
ClientSideXml property, 558
Clone method, 220, 263, 265, 273, 274
Close method, 64, 84, 86, 90, 135, 138–39
  DataAdapter objects and, 170
  Windows-based applications and, 567–68
CloseConnection constant, 132
Closed constant, 83
clsSlowQuery class, 152
cmd.exe, 378
Collection Editor, 254–57
Collection method, 64
ColumnChanged event, 238, 277
ColumnChanging event, 238, 277
ColumnMapping property, 187, 278, 280–81, 531

ColumnMappings collection, 13
ColumnName property, 252, 269, 278, 280–81, 530
columns
  adding, to DataTable objects, 220
  defining default values for, 464–65
  expression-based, 230–32
  including all, in the WHERE clause, 442–46
  primary key, 442, 444–46
  searches based on, 352–53, 354
  selecting, 33–34, 184
  setting the value of, 237
Columns collection, 14
Columns property, 14, 210, 267, 269, 293–95
COM (Component Object Model). *See also* COM+
  Connection object and, 51, 54, 58
  interoperability, 58, 528
  libraries, 51
COM+
  Data Form Wizard and, 42
  context information, 517
  transaction processing and, 512
COM tab, 58, 526
ComboBox controls, 583–85
Command class, 6
Command object, 10–11, 65–66
  asynchronous queries and, 151–52
  Cancel method and, 130
  creating, 97–120, 124–25
  DataAdapter object and, 12–13, 158–59, 161–62, 164, 176, 459
  database queries and, 110–14, 117–20, 124–25, 129–32, 151–52
  disconnected data and, 158–59
  ExecuteNonQuery method and, 131–32
  extensibility and, 9
  NOCOUNT setting and, 483, 485
  null values and, 446
  parameterized, 12
  retrieving rows and, 176
  run time usage of, 122–23
  submitting updates and, 407–18, 425, 438–39, 446–47, 470–72, 483, 485
  transactions and, 129, 447
  Visual Studio .NET and, 118–20
  XML and, 550
Command windows, creating, 378
CommandBehavior enumeration, 131–32, 612
CommandBuilder object, 481, 593
  benefits and drawbacks of, 434
  Refresh method and, 150–51
  reliance upon, avoiding, 455
  submitting updates and, 401, 431–34, 441, 443, 449, 455, 463–64
  transactions and, 449

About the Author

This is David Sceppa's second book for Microsoft Press. In 2000, he wrote *Programming ADO*. There are rumors that he'll write a third book and then take time off before writing the first three books in the saga.

David currently works as a tester on the Visual Basic .NET team, working with the data access features in the product. He's a Microsoft Certified Solution Developer, a speaker at technical conferences, and a frequent contributor to the public ADO.NET newsgroup at *microsoft.public.dotnet.framework.adonet*.

After speaking at a recent SQL Server conference in Sydney, Australia, David finally got the chance to see a couple Australian Rules Football matches at the prestigious Melbourne Cricket Grounds.

Shortly before Mario Lemieux and Michael Jordan returned to their respective sports, there was a less heralded return in the sporting world. After a long hiatus, David Sceppa returned to the indoor soccer hotbed of Redmond, Washington. While he may have lost a step from his heyday, David proved to be a crafty veteran defender. Surprisingly, the layoff did not affect David's skills on offense where he was still described as a "liability" on most scouting reports. Under the tutelage of player/coach Psycho Steve DuMosch, the team went deep into the playoffs.

David is still amazed that the New England Patriots completed their miracle season with a Super Bowl win and admits to getting a little misty-eyed upon seeing Ray Bourque finally raise the Stanley Cup over his head.

Putty Knife

A putty knife lets you spread putty or spackling paste evenly across a surface in woodworking or wall painting. Artists also use putty knives to spread paint across a canvas.

At Microsoft Press, we use tools to illustrate our books for software developers and IT professionals. Tools are an elegant symbol of human inventiveness and a powerful metaphor for how people can extend their capabilities, precision, and reach. From basic calipers and pliers to digital micrometers and lasers, our stylized illustrations of tools give each book a visual identity and each book series a personality. With tools and knowledge, there are no limits to creativity and innovation. Our tag line says it all: *The tools you need to put technology to work.*

The manuscript for this book was prepared and galleyed using Microsoft Word. Pages were composed by Microsoft Press using Adobe FrameMaker+SGML for Windows, with text in Garamond and display type in Helvetica Condensed. Composed pages were delivered to the printer as electronic prepress files.

Cover Designer:	Methodologie, Inc.
Interior Graphic Designer:	James D. Kramer
Principal Compositor:	Elizabeth Hansford
Interior Artist:	Michael Kloepfer
Principal Copy Editors:	Cheryl Penner and Holly M. Viola
Indexer:	Liz Cunningham

Work in ADO.NET right away

with this accessible, modular primer.

U.S.A. **$39.99**
Canada $57.99
ISBN: 0-7356-1236-6

ADO.NET—the data-access component of the Microsoft® .NET Framework—works with any component on any platform that understands XML. Get a solid handle on ADO.NET and learn how to exploit the database functionality of Microsoft Visual Basic® .NET and Microsoft Visual C#™ with this step-by-step primer. You'll be working in ADO.NET right away with easy-to-grasp examples drawn from the real-world challenges developers face every day. Learn about the ADO.NET object model and how to use it to develop data-bound Windows Forms and Web Forms. See how ADO.NET interacts with XML, and how to access older versions of ADO from the .NET environment. Throughout, you'll find insightful tips and expert explanations for rapid acceleration of development productivity, faster applications, and more powerful results.

Microsoft Press® products are available worldwide wherever quality computer books are sold. For more information, contact your book or computer retailer, software reseller, or local Microsoft® Sales Office, or visit our Web site at microsoft.com/mspress. To locate your nearest source for Microsoft Press products, or to order directly, call 1-800-MSPRESS in the United States (in Canada, call 1-800-268-2222).

Prices and availability dates are subject to change.

Microsoft®
microsoft.com/mspress

Learn the latest *Web database technologies* for the *.NET Framework—* complete with line-by-line explanations and code samples.

U.S.A. **$39.99**
Canada $57.99
ISBN: 0-7356-1637-X

The Microsoft® .NET Framework is all about simplifying the exchange of data among applications across the Internet, regardless of operating system or back-end software. The step-by-step lessons in this easy-to-grasp tutorial detail the major .NET database technologies to demonstrate how to create powerful, flexible Web databases that can serve your needs today and scale for the future. You'll discover the background behind the latest Web database technologies—and see them in action with complete code samples. If you know how to use HTML, know something about databases, and want to integrate the two in the .NET era with Microsoft Visual Basic® .NET, this book is for you.

Microsoft Press® products are available worldwide wherever quality computer books are sold. For more information, contact your book or computer retailer, software reseller, or local Microsoft® Sales Office, or visit our Web site at microsoft.com/mspress. To locate your nearest source for Microsoft Press products, or to order directly, call 1-800-MSPRESS in the United States (in Canada, call 1-800-268-2222).

Prices and availability dates are subject to change.

microsoft.com/mspress

Learn how to *turn data into solutions* with SQL Server 2000, Visual Basic .NET, and XML Web services.

Programming Microsoft® SQL Server™ 2000 with Microsoft Visual Basic® .NET

U.S.A.   **$59.99**
Canada $86.99
ISBN: 0-7356-1535-7

Discover the fastest ways to transform data into potent business solutions with this definitive guide for professional developers. You'll get complete details about the programmatic features of SQL Server 2000, the language enhancements in Visual Basic .NET, the development advances in the Microsoft Visual Studio® .NET integrated development environment, and the state-of-the-art technologies of the .NET Framework, including ADO.NET, ASP.NET, and XML Web services. You'll also get in-depth coverage of SQL Server programming topics, including details about using T-SQL, and tips on creating user-defined objects such as tables, views, and stored procedures. If you're looking for expert insights on how to build powerful, secure solutions with SQL Server 2000 and Visual Basic .NET, this is the book for you.

Microsoft Press® products are available worldwide wherever quality computer books are sold. For more information, contact your book or computer retailer, software reseller, or local Microsoft® Sales Office, or visit our Web site at microsoft.com/mspress. To locate your nearest source for Microsoft Press products, or to order directly, call 1-800-MSPRESS in the United States (in Canada, call 1-800-268-2222).

Prices and availability dates are subject to change.

microsoft.com/mspress

Get a **Free**
e-mail newsletter, updates,
special offers, links to related books,
and more when you

register on line!

Register your Microsoft Press® title on our Web site and you'll get
a FREE subscription to our e-mail newsletter, *Microsoft Press
Book Connections.* You'll find out about newly released and upcoming
books and learning tools, online events, software downloads, special
offers and coupons for Microsoft Press customers, and information
about major Microsoft® product releases. You can also read useful
additional information about all the titles we publish, such as de-
tailed book descriptions, tables of contents and indexes, sample
chapters, links to related books and book series, author biographies,
and reviews by other customers.

Registration is easy. Just visit this Web page and fill in your information:

http://www.microsoft.com/mspress/register

Microsoft®

Proof of Purchase

Use this page as proof of purchase if participating in a promotion or rebate offer on
this title. Proof of purchase must be used in conjunction with other proof(s) of
payment such as your dated sales receipt—see offer details.

Microsoft® ADO.NET (Core Reference)
0-7356-1423-7

CUSTOMER NAME

Microsoft Press, PO Box 97017, Redmond, WA 98073-9830

MICROSOFT LICENSE AGREEMENT

Book Companion CD

IMPORTANT—READ CAREFULLY: This Microsoft End-User License Agreement ("EULA") is a legal agreement between you (either an individual or an entity) and Microsoft Corporation for the Microsoft product identified above, which includes computer software and may include associated media, printed materials, and "online" or electronic documentation ("SOFTWARE PRODUCT"). Any component included within the SOFTWARE PRODUCT that is accompanied by a separate End-User License Agreement shall be governed by such agreement and not the terms set forth below. By installing, copying, or otherwise using the SOFTWARE PRODUCT, you agree to be bound by the terms of this EULA. If you do not agree to the terms of this EULA, you are not authorized to install, copy, or otherwise use the SOFTWARE PRODUCT; you may, however, return the SOFTWARE PRODUCT, along with all printed materials and other items that form a part of the Microsoft product that includes the SOFTWARE PRODUCT, to the place you obtained them for a full refund.

SOFTWARE PRODUCT LICENSE

The SOFTWARE PRODUCT is protected by United States copyright laws and international copyright treaties, as well as other intellectual property laws and treaties. The SOFTWARE PRODUCT is licensed, not sold.

1. **GRANT OF LICENSE.** This EULA grants you the following rights:

   a. **Software Product.** You may install and use one copy of the SOFTWARE PRODUCT on a single computer. The primary user of the computer on which the SOFTWARE PRODUCT is installed may make a second copy for his or her exclusive use on a portable computer.

   b. **Storage/Network Use.** You may also store or install a copy of the SOFTWARE PRODUCT on a storage device, such as a network server, used only to install or run the SOFTWARE PRODUCT on your other computers over an internal network; however, you must acquire and dedicate a license for each separate computer on which the SOFTWARE PRODUCT is installed or run from the storage device. A license for the SOFTWARE PRODUCT may not be shared or used concurrently on different computers.

   c. **License Pak.** If you have acquired this EULA in a Microsoft License Pak, you may make the number of additional copies of the computer software portion of the SOFTWARE PRODUCT authorized on the printed copy of this EULA, and you may use each copy in the manner specified above. You are also entitled to make a corresponding number of secondary copies for portable computer use as specified above.

   d. **Sample Code.** Solely with respect to portions, if any, of the SOFTWARE PRODUCT that are identified within the SOFTWARE PRODUCT as sample code (the "SAMPLE CODE"):

      i. **Use and Modification.** Microsoft grants you the right to use and modify the source code version of the SAMPLE CODE, *provided* you comply with subsection (d)(iii) below. You may not distribute the SAMPLE CODE, or any modified version of the SAMPLE CODE, in source code form.

      ii. **Redistributable Files.** Provided you comply with subsection (d)(iii) below, Microsoft grants you a nonexclusive, royalty-free right to reproduce and distribute the object code version of the SAMPLE CODE and of any modified SAMPLE CODE, other than SAMPLE CODE, or any modified version thereof, designated as not redistributable in the Readme file that forms a part of the SOFTWARE PRODUCT (the "Non-Redistributable Sample Code"). All SAMPLE CODE other than the Non-Redistributable Sample Code is collectively referred to as the "REDISTRIBUTABLES."

      iii. **Redistribution Requirements.** If you redistribute the REDISTRIBUTABLES, you agree to: (i) distribute the REDISTRIBUTABLES in object code form only in conjunction with and as a part of your software application product; (ii) not use Microsoft's name, logo, or trademarks to market your software application product; (iii) include a valid copyright notice on your software application product; (iv) indemnify, hold harmless, and defend Microsoft from and against any claims or lawsuits, including attorney's fees, that arise or result from the use or distribution of your software application product; and (v) not permit further distribution of the REDISTRIBUTABLES by your end user. Contact Microsoft for the applicable royalties due and other licensing terms for all other uses and/or distribution of the REDISTRIBUTABLES.

2. **DESCRIPTION OF OTHER RIGHTS AND LIMITATIONS.**

   - **Limitations on Reverse Engineering, Decompilation, and Disassembly.** You may not reverse engineer, decompile, or disassemble the SOFTWARE PRODUCT, except and only to the extent that such activity is expressly permitted by applicable law notwithstanding this limitation.

   - **Separation of Components.** The SOFTWARE PRODUCT is licensed as a single product. Its component parts may not be separated for use on more than one computer.

   - **Rental.** You may not rent, lease, or lend the SOFTWARE PRODUCT.

   - **Support Services.** Microsoft may, but is not obligated to, provide you with support services related to the SOFTWARE PRODUCT ("Support Services"). Use of Support Services is governed by the Microsoft policies and programs described in the user manual, in "online" documentation, and/or in other Microsoft-provided materials. Any supplemental software code provided to you as part of the Support Services shall be considered part of the SOFTWARE PRODUCT and subject to the terms and conditions of this EULA. With respect to technical information you provide to Microsoft as part of the Support Services, Microsoft may use such information for its business purposes, including for product support and development. Microsoft will not utilize such technical information in a form that personally identifies you.

- **Software Transfer.** You may permanently transfer all of your rights under this EULA, provided you retain no copies, you transfer all of the SOFTWARE PRODUCT (including all component parts, the media and printed materials, any upgrades, this EULA, and, if applicable, the Certificate of Authenticity), **and** the recipient agrees to the terms of this EULA.

- **Termination.** Without prejudice to any other rights, Microsoft may terminate this EULA if you fail to comply with the terms and conditions of this EULA. In such event, you must destroy all copies of the SOFTWARE PRODUCT and all of its component parts.

3. **COPYRIGHT.** All title and copyrights in and to the SOFTWARE PRODUCT (including but not limited to any images, photographs, animations, video, audio, music, text, SAMPLE CODE, REDISTRIBUTABLES, and "applets" incorporated into the SOFTWARE PRODUCT) and any copies of the SOFTWARE PRODUCT are owned by Microsoft or its suppliers. The SOFTWARE PRODUCT is protected by copyright laws and international treaty provisions. Therefore, you must treat the SOFTWARE PRODUCT like any other copyrighted material **except** that you may install the SOFTWARE PRODUCT on a single computer provided you keep the original solely for backup or archival purposes. You may not copy the printed materials accompanying the SOFTWARE PRODUCT.

4. **U.S. GOVERNMENT RESTRICTED RIGHTS.** The SOFTWARE PRODUCT and documentation are provided with RESTRICTED RIGHTS. Use, duplication, or disclosure by the Government is subject to restrictions as set forth in subparagraph (c)(1)(ii) of the Rights in Technical Data and Computer Software clause at DFARS 252.227-7013 or subparagraphs (c)(1) and (2) of the Commercial Computer Software—Restricted Rights at 48 CFR 52.227-19, as applicable. Manufacturer is Microsoft Corporation/One Microsoft Way/Redmond, WA 98052-6399.

5. **EXPORT RESTRICTIONS.** You agree that you will not export or re-export the SOFTWARE PRODUCT, any part thereof, or any process or service that is the direct product of the SOFTWARE PRODUCT (the foregoing collectively referred to as the "Restricted Components"), to any country, person, entity, or end user subject to U.S. export restrictions. You specifically agree not to export or re-export any of the Restricted Components (i) to any country to which the U.S. has embargoed or restricted the export of goods or services, which currently include, but are not necessarily limited to, Cuba, Iran, Iraq, Libya, North Korea, Sudan, and Syria, or to any national of any such country, wherever located, who intends to transmit or transport the Restricted Components back to such country; (ii) to any end user who you know or have reason to know will utilize the Restricted Components in the design, development, or production of nuclear, chemical, or biological weapons; or (iii) to any end user who has been prohibited from participating in U.S. export transactions by any federal agency of the U.S. government. You warrant and represent that neither the BXA nor any other U.S. federal agency has suspended, revoked, or denied your export privileges.

DISCLAIMER OF WARRANTY

NO WARRANTIES OR CONDITIONS. MICROSOFT EXPRESSLY DISCLAIMS ANY WARRANTY OR CONDITION FOR THE SOFTWARE PRODUCT. THE SOFTWARE PRODUCT AND ANY RELATED DOCUMENTATION ARE PROVIDED "AS IS" WITHOUT WARRANTY OR CONDITION OF ANY KIND, EITHER EXPRESS OR IMPLIED, INCLUDING, WITHOUT LIMITATION, THE IMPLIED WARRANTIES OF MERCHANTABILITY, FITNESS FOR A PARTICULAR PURPOSE, OR NONINFRINGEMENT. THE ENTIRE RISK ARISING OUT OF USE OR PERFORMANCE OF THE SOFTWARE PRODUCT REMAINS WITH YOU.

LIMITATION OF LIABILITY. TO THE MAXIMUM EXTENT PERMITTED BY APPLICABLE LAW, IN NO EVENT SHALL MICROSOFT OR ITS SUPPLIERS BE LIABLE FOR ANY SPECIAL, INCIDENTAL, INDIRECT, OR CONSEQUENTIAL DAMAGES WHATSOEVER (INCLUDING, WITHOUT LIMITATION, DAMAGES FOR LOSS OF BUSINESS PROFITS, BUSINESS INTERRUPTION, LOSS OF BUSINESS INFORMATION, OR ANY OTHER PECUNIARY LOSS) ARISING OUT OF THE USE OF OR INABILITY TO USE THE SOFTWARE PRODUCT OR THE PROVISION OF OR FAILURE TO PROVIDE SUPPORT SERVICES, EVEN IF MICROSOFT HAS BEEN ADVISED OF THE POSSIBILITY OF SUCH DAMAGES. IN ANY CASE, MICROSOFT'S ENTIRE LIABILITY UNDER ANY PROVISION OF THIS EULA SHALL BE LIMITED TO THE GREATER OF THE AMOUNT ACTUALLY PAID BY YOU FOR THE SOFTWARE PRODUCT OR US$5.00; PROVIDED, HOWEVER, IF YOU HAVE ENTERED INTO A MICROSOFT SUPPORT SERVICES AGREEMENT, MICROSOFT'S ENTIRE LIABILITY REGARDING SUPPORT SERVICES SHALL BE GOVERNED BY THE TERMS OF THAT AGREEMENT. BECAUSE SOME STATES AND JURISDICTIONS DO NOT ALLOW THE EXCLUSION OR LIMITATION OF LIABILITY, THE ABOVE LIMITATION MAY NOT APPLY TO YOU.

MISCELLANEOUS

This EULA is governed by the laws of the State of Washington USA, except and only to the extent that applicable law mandates governing law of a different jurisdiction.

Should you have any questions concerning this EULA, or if you desire to contact Microsoft for any reason, please contact the Microsoft subsidiary serving your country, or write: Microsoft Sales Information Center/One Microsoft Way/Redmond, WA 98052-6399.